SCHEHERAZADE'S CHILDREN

Scheherazade's Children

Global Encounters with the Arabian Nights

Edited by Philip F. Kennedy and Marina Warner

NEW YORK UNIVERSITY PRESS

New York and London

Copublished with the
New York University
Abu Dhabi Institute

NEW YORK UNIVERSITY PRESS
New York and London
www.nyupress.org

References to Internet websites (URLs) were accurate at the time of writing.
Neither the author nor New York University Press is responsible for URLs
that may have expired or changed since the manuscript was prepared.

Library of Congress Cataloging-in-Publication Data
Scheherazade's children : global encounters with The Arabian Nights /
edited by Philip F. Kennedy and Marina Warner.
pages   cm
Includes bibliographical references and index.
ISBN 978-1-4798-4031-1 (cl : acid-free paper)
ISBN 978-1-4798-5709-8 (pb : acid-free paper)
1. Arabian nights. 2. Scheherazade (Legendary character)   I. Kennedy, Philip F.,
editor of compilation. II. Warner, Marina, 1946– editor of compilation.
PJ7737.S44 2013
398.22—dc23   2013007849

New York University Press books are printed on acid-free paper,
and their binding materials are chosen for strength and durability.
We strive to use environmentally responsible suppliers and materials
to the greatest extent possible in publishing our books.

Manufactured in the United States of America

10 9 8 7 6 5 4 3 2 1

Also available as an ebook

CONTENTS

The illustrations appear in two groups, following pages 176 and 224. For information about the illustrations, see the list of illustrations on page ix.

Color Figures

1. M. M. Samarkandi and M. Sharif, *A Reader in the World of Stories*, miniature, Iran, seventeenth century (© RMN-Grand Palais / Art Resource, NY)

2. François de Troy, *The duchesse du Maine*, circa 1700, Musée des Beaux-Arts d'Orléans. During the last days of the reign of Louis XIV Louise-Bénédicte de Bourbon, the duchesse du Maine (1676–1753) presided over a rival court at the Château de Sceaux, where, in the summers of 1714 and 1715, she threw a celebrated series of all-night parties known as the *nuits blanches*, or "white nights." At one of these parties, Voltaire entertained the duchesse and her guests by telling them the story "The One-Eyed Porter," a wittily allusive and innuendo-rich spoof of Antoine Galland's newly popular *Mille et une nuit*. (© Musée des Beaux-Arts d'Orléans)

3. Catherine Lusurier, after Nicolas de Largillière, portrait of Voltaire (François-Marie Arouet; 1694–1778), at age thirty. Voltaire's earliest recorded prose tale was prompted by the *Arabian Nights*, and Galland's Oriental tales were one of his principal models in the 1740s when he began to publish a series of philosophical stories, beginning with *Zadig* and including *The Princess of Babylon* and *The White and the Black*. *Candide* concludes on a note of Islamic wisdom in Constantinople, where East meets West. Like Scheherazade herself, Voltaire found storytelling a powerful weapon against tyranny and prejudice. (© RMN-Grand Palais / Art Resource, NY)

4. Sir Joshua Reynolds, portrait of William Beckford, 1782. That year, Beckford wrote, "Arabian Tales spring up like mushrooms on the fresh green downs of Fonthill" (MS Beckford e.1, fol. 100, Beckford Papers, Bodleian Library, University of Oxford). (© National Portrait Gallery, London)

5. Ozias Humphry, portrait of Elizabeth Berkeley, also known as Lady Craven, later Margravine of Anspach. Beckford nicknamed Lady Craven his "charmante, gentille Arabe" (MS Beckford e.1, fol. 103–4, Beckford Papers); she encouraged every one of his Oriental compositions: "Etrange Arabe," she wrote in French on May 29, 1782, "you made me slip into a strange Lethargy—yes, I did fall asleep—and I dreamt the life of Vathek—what a dream—good God, through and through it is just Beckfordism—but seriously 'tis very fine, horribly fine" (Lady Craven to Beckford, 29 May 1782, MS Beckford c.29, Beckford Papers). (© Tate 2013, on loan to the National Portrait Gallery, London)

6. Edmund Dulac, "Princess Badoura," from Laurence Housman, *Princess Badoura; A Tale of the Arabian Nights*, 1913. (© Arcadian Library 18401, London)

7. Hōsai, *Fūsennori uwasa no takadono* (The sensational balloonist), woodblock print, 1891. (© The Tsubouchi Memorial Theatre Museum)

8. Persian (*right*) and Turkish (*left*) depicted in *Bankoku jinbutsu emaki*, or "A Picture Scroll of People of the World," early nineteenth century. (© National Museum of Ethnology, Osaka)

9. A scene from the revue of *Sabaku no kurobara*, or "A Black Rose in the Desert" (2000). (© Takarazuka)

10. Film cover for *Gul Bakawali*, 1932. *Gul-e-Bakavali* (The Bakavali flower), a *qissa-dastan* tale of Persian origin, was a popular subject for India's *Arabian Nights* fantasy films. A 1924 silent version was Bombay's first all-India superhit. This song-booklet cover for the 1932 film shows Prince Taj-ul-Mulk on his quest for the magical flower that will cure his father's blindness, entranced by the fairy princess Bakavali, in whose gardens it grows. (© Virchand Dharamsey)

11. Program cover for *Aladdin* at the Theatre Royal Drury Lane, 1885. (© City of Westminster Archives Centre)

12. Alfred Jacobsen, *Aladdin* Toy Theatre characters, 1889. (© Sven-Erik Olsen, Oldfux)

13. *Umanusubito* performed at the Nissay Theatre, July 2008. (© Shochiku)

14. Still of Ian McKellen as Widow Twankey in British pantomime, 2006. (© Manuel Harlan)

15. Helen Stratton, "Next morning he followed the bird as it flew from tree to tree," illustration for the 1899 edition of *The Arabian Nights' Entertainments, or The Thousand and One Nights*, ed. Andrew Lang (1898; repr., New York: Longmans, Green, 1899), 209. Budur's talisman, which Qamar al-Zaman took from his wife while she was sleeping, is taken from him in turn by a bird that keeps flying out of reach. Budur follows to recover it until he is thoroughly lost, and the loving couple is separated for years.

16. Paul Klee, *Sindbad the Sailor / The Seafarer*, 1923. Tests and trials fill the many adventures of Sinbad and have inspired further works in every medium, including Paul Klee's rendition in painting, *The Seafarer* (1923). (© Arcadian Library, London; photo © Erich Lessing / Art Resource, NY. © 2013 Artists Rights Society, New York)

Black-and-White Figures

17. Engraving of Jullanar, the frontispiece of the seventh volume of Antoine Galland's *Les mille et une nuit: Contes arabes* (Paris: A. Barbin, 1706). Both stories in this volume, that of "Noureddin" and that of "Beder," open with the introduction of a beautiful female slave by a merchant to a powerful man, the scene represented in the larger, superior engraving. Below: Jullanar (Gulnare) in the "Histoire de Beder" greets her brother, mother, and members of their sea court from her window in her Persian palace as they approach across the waves. (© Arcadian Library, London)

18. Pages from the Jewish Physician's tale in the fourteenth-century Antoine Galland manuscript. (© Bibliothèque Nationale)

19. A 1668 illustration of a contemporary London coffeehouse. The *Arabian Nights' Entertainments* was serialized in the periodicals and newspapers available in the new social spaces of eighteenth-century England, which serviced the enthusiasm for another Oriental import, coffee. By 1675, there were more than three thousand coffeehouses in England; a number, such as the Chapter Coffee House in Paternoster Row, came to keep their own libraries

by the Dalziel brothers, was published in 1864–65. Hugo von Hofmannsthal owned it as a child. (Scanned image and text by George P. Landow; Victorian Web, http://www.victorianweb.org/)

26. Hubert-François Bourguignon Gravelot (French, 1699–1773), "Soliman II" with Justine Favart née Duronceray as Roxane, 1762, from Charles-Simon Favart, *Soliman second* (1762). For the frontispiece of Favart's *Soliman second*, the illustrator, Gravelot, engraved the scene in which Roxelane, played by the playwright's wife, Justine Favart, bewitches Soliman by singing. The singer-actress was accompanied onstage by three Turkish instruments shown in the background: the *zil* (handheld cymbals), the *zurna* (an oboelike woodwind), and probably the *tanbur* (a lute-like instrument). (© The Bodleian Library, University of Oxford, Taylorian Vet.Fr.II.B.321)

27. F. Le Rousseau (French, n.d.), "Türkish Dance Perform'd by Mr Desnoyer & Mrs Younger," c. 1725, from Anthony L'Abbé, *A New Collection of Dances, Containing . . . the Best Ball and Stage Dances* (c. 1725). Anthony L'Abbé's choreography for a male and female dancer was performed around 1721 by Philip Desnoyer and Elizabeth Young at a London theater. L'Abbé notated the dance in Beauchamp-Feuillet notation, using music from André Campra's French court ballet *L'Europe galante* (1697), which had originally featured a Turkish scene. For London audiences, L'Abbé used extreme virtuosity and defiance of convention to represent the Turkish "character." (© The Bodleian Library, University of Oxford, G.Pamph, 1818)

28. Joshua Reynolds (English, 1723–1792), *Roxelana* (Frances Abington), 1791. Joshua Reynolds's oil portrait of Frances Abington, later engraved, represents her in the character of Roxelana in Isaac Bickerstaff's *The Sultan* after Charles-Simon Favart's *Soliman second*. At Abington's request, David Garrick in 1774 adapted Bickerstaff's translation to showcase her. She appears coyly from behind a curtain, which she pushes aside. (© Trustees of the British Museum)

29. William Harvey, "Camaralzaman Disguised as an Astrologer," from Edward Lane, *The Thousand and One Nights*, 3 vols. (London: Charles Knight, 1838–40), 1:313.

ACKNOWLEDGMENTS

This book could not have come into being without the collaboration of a number of colleagues and friends; several of these have not appeared in the collection for different reasons (chiefly prior commitments and the scope of this volume).

The first conference from which articles have been selected, "The Compass of Story: The Oriental Tale and Western Imagination," was convened by Marina Warner and took place at the British Academy on March 28–29, 2008. The focus was on retellings, particularly in fiction, and short papers were given. The liveliness, insights, and fruitfulness of the event inspired Philip Kennedy, as Faculty Director of the NYU Abu Dhabi Institute, to convene a larger conference; with the generous support of Professor Hilary Ballon and Professor Mariët Westermann, then Provost of NYU Abu Dhabi, and in collaboration with Marina Warner, the inquiry was broadened, in order to look at the *Nights'* metamorphoses beyond Europe and beyond the printed page. In December 2009, most of the original speakers from "The Compass of Story" were joined by several additional scholars who illuminated the *Nights* in the performing arts—theater, pantomime, puppetry, and cinema; we also decided to represent the living tradition in the work of contemporary writers and filmmakers, and we would like to thank Gamal Al-Ghitani, Aboubakr Chraïbi, Githa Hariharan, Amira al-Zein, and Nacer Khemir for their inspiring participation.

The following year, a third conference was convened to explore more deeply the theater history of the *Nights'* efflorescence: "Staging the East: Oriental Masking in the British Theatre, 1660–1830" was instigated by the research of the playwright and drama historian Elizabeth Kuti (University of Essex), who convened it with Marina Warner, with further funding from the British Academy, for which we are most grateful. It was held on June 10–11, 2010, in the Theatre Royal, Bury St. Edmunds, a unique working Regency stage. The editors would like to thank Wen-chin Ouyang, Peter Chelkowski, Donna Landry, Gerald Maclean, Anne Deneys, Ulrich Marzolph, Sinan Antoon, Peter Heath, Tim Supple, Nasser Al-Taee, Shareah Talehgani, Srinivas Aravamudan, Samer Ali, Muhsin Al-Mussawi, Abdulla Al-Dabbagh, Jeannie Miller, Clémence Boulouque, and Rebecca Johnson for their engaged participation at the London and Abu Dhabi meetings. They are grateful also to the late Jane Moody, who was an inspiring presence and support at "Staging the East." The tireless professionalism and grace of the staff of the British Academy, London, of Gila Waels at the NYU Abu Dhabi Institute, and of Gemma Juan-Simó at NYU Press on different stages of this book's creation have been invaluable—engaged and courteous under pressure, as well as prompt and meticulous.

For permissions to reproduce artwork and photographic images we acknowledge gratefully RMN-Grand Palais; Art Resource, NY; Erich Lessing; Artists Rights Society, New York; Musée des Beaux-Arts d'Orléans; The National Portrait Gallery, London; The Bodleian Library, Oxford; Virchand Dharamsey and Juzer Mohammedhusain; Sven-Erik Olsen; Royal Geographical Society; The Tsubouchi Memorial Theatre Museum; The Arcadian Library, London; The National Museum of Ethnology, Osaka; The Takarazuka Revue; Shochiku and The Nissay Theatre, Japan; Tate, London; The Bibliothèque Nationale, Paris; The Lordprice Collection; Alnwick: W. Davison; The Victoria and Albert Museum; The Trustees of the British Museum; George P. Landow and *Victorian Web*, http://www.victorianweb.org/; Wadia Movietone / Roy Wadia; The British Library Board; Manuel Harlan; Farnsworth Museum; City of Westminster Archives Centre; The Lilly Library; Travelers in the Middle East Archive; National Diet Library.

Introduction

PHILIP F. KENNEDY AND MARINA WARNER

The year 2009 in Paris was *l'année de la Turquie*, the Year of Turkey, and many events were held to explore the history and culture of the country. Among them, an exhibition at the Grand Palais, called "De Byzance à Istanbul—*Un port pour deux continents*" (From Byzantium to Istanbul: A port for two continents), brought many artifacts from the city's multilayered past and displayed them on two floors. Christianity —Roman and Byzantine Orthodox—occupied the ground floor, Islam the first floor. The imposing staircase symbolized the fateful year of 1453, when the city was taken by the Ottoman Sultan Mehmet I, and the Byzantine Empire, the last representative of the Romans in the East, drew formally to a close.

The year 2009 was also the sixth year of the second Gulf war within eighteen years, the one which began in 2003 with the invasion of Baghdad. The exhibition about the magnificent maritime capital on the Bosphorus was taking place at a particular historical moment. Visiting it could not but be colored by the present context: the French had not joined forces with the Americans, the British, and their many allies in the operations, first called "Shock and Awe" and characterized by the then US president and his policymakers as "the war on terror." Very controversially, Jacques Chirac, the president of France at the time, had refused his support, and so the French looked on the ongoing fighting from a different angle. Yet even so, the exhibition at the Grand Palais was structured around a total split at the date of 1453. The tangled story of West-East interactions was set out from a narrowly military angle of view, and the multiply interwoven strands that have long connected and continue to connect the East and the West of Europe were neatly severed by the outcome of a battle.

This is one way to tell the story of the past, and it has long been a favorite historiographical angle of view. Yet attending to evidence of another sort yields another narrative. The artifacts selected on both floors unfolded a differently nuanced vision of the conflicts and interactions, of the results of rivalry and ambition. Emulation and clashes led to intermingling; consequent exchanges and borrowings generated likenesses and complicity, developing a common understanding which moved at a different rhythm from political and religious antagonisms. The language of things speaks differently from the language of statecraft and religious oppositions, although political encounters themselves do not corroborate an idea of fundamental difference, of ringing and insurmountable clashes. (They sometimes take an unexpectedly contrary direction: the traditional keeper of the keys of the Church of the Holy Sepulchre is the Muslim family of Nusseibeh, since the Christian sects present in the sacred place quarreled so badly among themselves that they could not be trusted.) Customs and manufactures traveled regardless of politics: the taste and smell of coffee, still one of the strongest features of Istanbul, wafted over boundaries of belief, though the process of adoption was rather slow, and cafés and coffeehouses, where the delicious drink was served, opened in Western cities in the eighteenth century; in Britain, after that first burst of enthusiastic Orientalism, cafés followed the milk bars of the sixties and were not common until the second half of the twentieth century. In the era of bitter conflict, during the Crusades and afterward, through to 1453 and continuing after that, culture goes on telling an alternative story: glass, mirrors, velvet, brocade, metallurgy, fashions, furnishings (carpets, sofas), gardens, fountains, even garden swings reveal a process of reverse colonization. In some branches of arts and crafts, Eastern methods were imported and their originators eclipsed: Venetians began to excel at the manufacture of cut silk velvets and damask, gold-flecked and luminously colored glassware. At a deeper level as well, the conversation with Islamic culture continued, regardless of differences in faith. (There is work to be done, for example, on the affinities between the iconoclasm of the Reformers and Islamic doctrine.)

Literature is one of the most speaking of cultural artifacts since, unlike coffee, glass, brass, or velvet, it has a voice—or rather many voices. The book called *Alf layla wa-layla* in Arabic, and known in the Anglophone world as the *Arabian Nights*, is the prime example of such a polyphonic, traveling text, which leaped over borders of creed, nation, allegiance, its stories spreading irrepressibly, immediately after they were first translated into French and English at the beginning of the eighteenth century. It was read in public and in private, in bedrooms and in coffeehouses (fig. 19); it was passed on in different print versions, and its characteristic features entered European culture and operated profound cultural transformations. Just as the young man reading tales in a Persian illumination of the beginning of the seventeenth century (fig. 1) is figured and patterned all over by the characters whom he is meeting in the book he holds, so the society that encountered the *Nights* was imprinted and colored by the stories' particular character.

Scholars in the humanities, especially those who study literature and culture, can illuminate the dense growth—from the roots through the bedrock to the canopy above—in which political and ideological attitudes are entangled. This collection of essays arose during the long and intense afterlife of Edward Said's famous polemical book of 1978, and it expresses a response to his urgent call for ending ignorance and prejudice. *Orientalism* is not the focus of the discussion of our contributors, but it was the catalyst to rethinking relations with the multifaceted world of Islamic culture. Desire to know and to comprehend is singled out for praise by Said, in contrast to the drive to possess and dominate. The *Arabian Nights* seemed a place to start to look at this long entanglement from a different perspective.

In the introduction to *The Arabian Nights in Historical Context: Between East and West* (2008), Saree Makdisi and Felicity Nussbaum lay stress on the cultural politics of accretions to the *Nights*, across their various media, after the publication of Antoine Galland's translation of the *Nights* (fig. 18). The *Arabian Nights* evolved in an "uneven and discontinuous process . . . according to the shifts in relations between Europe and Arabs."[1] And "the gap between Galland's edition in the early eighteenth century and . . . [Richard] Burton's in the late nineteenth century—and between those texts and the various editions circulating to this day in Arabic itself—offers a kind of measure of the shifting nature of political and cultural relationships between Europe and the Arab world."[2] The contours evoked here mark out in general an expansive terrain for study that is bound—some of it—to be inflected by Edward Said, and some of it not. Makdisi and Nussbaum continue, Said's *Orientalism* "remains essentially coherent and continues to provide the dominant theoretical explanation of the relationship between East and West to this day"; they propose that "any discussion of the East, and especially the literature of the East, still begins with *Orientalism*'s influential claims, whether to refute them or to elaborate upon them."[3] One must also bear in mind, however, when focusing on a given area of imagined influence that the devil (or angel) may lie in the details, that the fierce denunciations of *Orientalism* and the vision of the reader and scholar's role in *The World, the Text and the Critic*, which followed soon after, set the stakes very high and demanded a response—in the forms of attention given to the world and its texts. If, at the microlevel of scrutiny, the relevance (and often broad sweeps) of *Orientalism* fail to convince, the larger provocation has reshaped the field.

Our title here deliberately echoes the concluding chapter of Robert Irwin's landmark study *The Arabian Nights: A Companion* (1994, repr. 2004);[4] in "Children of the Nights," Irwin strikes out on the terrain we have set out to explore. *Scheherazade's Children: Global Encounters with the Arabian Nights* follows the threefold principal areas opened for discussion by the various contributors at a number of stimulating scholarly gatherings over the course of the past four years; the selection of essays here is clustered under three rubrics: "Translating," "Engaging," and "Staging."

The Eye in the Story: A Figure for Reading

Elliott Colla's essay opens part 2 of *Scheherazade's Children*, "Engaging," and it provides the reader with a key metaphor of this book's approach:

exploring the figure of the eye in the cycle of "The Porter and the Three Ladies of Baghdad," Colla draws attention to the shifting optics at stake in revisiting the *Nights* today. His is the only study in the volume not to concern itself with the contact of the tales with other cultures; the principal argument is indeed to salvage, in a perceptive reading of the original story, the subtexts of a figure the resonances of which may in fact be lost in the disruptive and variously transformative processes of translation. Concentrating on the figure of the eye, Colla posits a suggestive triple layering of meaning enfolded into one of the recurring images of the story cycle. The eye in the "Porter" cycle is invested with three ideas, offering a matrix of the tension between desire (for love, sex, and especially narrative) and dark menace, between envy and curiosity. The three wandering dervishes who enter the "Porter" cycle tell how they each came to lose an eye—after a transgression that took them beyond a licit boundary. The eye is also, by analogy, a door to the forbidden chambers of story and to the *terrae incognitae* of history. The reader's eye changes focus in keeping with the words on the page; the *Kulturbrillen*, the cultural spectacles each reader brings, will be modified—perhaps corrected even—and the light of a new understanding will flood through the lens. Colla explores those aspects of the *Arabian Nights* that are relinquished unthinkingly when its narrative forms migrate into other literatures beyond the Arabic sphere. It is the ambiguities and polyvalence—the multiple resonances and richness—of the complex metaphor of the eye that remain untranslated when cultural borders are crossed. Perhaps. Yet it must be the ambiguity of stories— their open-endedness and porousness of meaning—that attracts and wields a magic grip on other, foreign, imaginations that rework them. So while Colla's essay states a fascinating proposition, it is significant that in the studies that ensue we encounter again the lurking, transformed eye in the *Nights*: Roger Pearson's study of Voltaire reminds us that his earliest *conte oriental* of 1717, *Le crocheteur borgne*, prefigures Zadig, who almost loses an eye. This image of the one-eyed hero is cardinal to Pearson's reading and to reading in general as promoted by Voltaire in his *contes orientaux*. Seeing with one eye is to see with reduced perspective; in a narrative context it is to observe the significance of only half the story and to recognize only half the message. Tales and fables, as against (official) history, are open-ended, disposed to be interpreted: the reader complements the vision; that is the essential humanism of writing. "History teaches us what human beings are, Fable what human beings should be."[5] Elliott Colla stresses "ambiguation" in the *Nights* (more precisely, in the very imagery of the *Nights*); Pearson evinces the same in Voltaire: "the humanizing effect of storytelling, . . . how it breeds broad-mindedness and tolerance by presenting the perplexing details and contradictions of human experience." He traces that to Voltaire's own reception of the original corpus.

In this collection, the writers are looking outside the range of their *Kulturbrillen*; they are attempting a realignment of vision.

The Literary and Scholarly Context

An extraordinary and vigorous surge of renewed interest in the *Nights* began in the 1980s and early '90s with the work of scholars such as Ferial Ghazoul (*Nocturnal Poetics*), Sandra Naddaf (*Arabesque*), Peter Caracciolo (*The Arabian Nights in English Literature*), a collection of essays by Abdelfattah Kilito (*L'œil et l'aiguille*, 1992), and Robert Irwin's indispensable *The Arabian Nights: A Companion*; these studies have revealed the exuberant variety of the *Arabian Nights'* metamorphoses in literature and the arts across cultures since 1704 and Galland's translation, and they have stimulated the appetite for more inquiry, for more listening to the resonances of the stories in their global travels.

In 1984 Muhsin Mahdi published a definitive edition of *Alf layla wa-layla* in Arabic, from the Galland manuscript, with a volume of critical apparatus and a further volume of studies. Surprisingly, this was the first, and remains the only, critical edition of an Arabic *Nights* corpus. Because it uses the earliest surviving redaction of the stories, it contains only 282 nights and 34.5 of the tales (depending on how one counts the framing and embedded materials). Mahdi is a purist and argued that this "core" (it breaks off in the middle of "Qamar al-Zaman and Budur") constitutes the authentic surviving corpus of the *Nights*, and his prestige and learning have meant that the proliferating branches of stories in other Arabic manuscripts were relegated and, for a while, excluded from legitimate scrutiny. His edition was lucidly translated by Husain Haddawy (1990); but readers resisted this austerity, and by popular demand, Haddawy followed his translation of Mahdi's edition with a second volume, which includes "Sinbad" (a separate set of stories before Galland included them) and "Aladdin," one of the "orphan tales" with no known Arabic original antedating Galland and the most loved and best known of all the *Nights*. The disposition of Mahdi's work is to delineate and delimit an original (and authentic) Arabic text, while Irwin's *Companion* displays capaciously the cultural, social, and historical contexts that have given shape to the corpus both before and subsequent to Galland's remarkable achievement.

A pellucid new translation, *Les mille et une nuits*, based on the so-called Calcutta II edition (1839–42) appeared in 2005, rendered into modern French by André Miquel and Jamel Eddine Bencheikh, who, unlike Galland, include all the poetry. This was soon followed by Malcolm Lyons's translation (2009), the first full version in English which is not either expurgated or fancifully embellished but faithfully renders the Arabic of the same Calcutta II edition. These new versions have made the book available to readers in ways that most have not experienced before, since so very many of the tales have never been selected for publication, in children's or illustrated editions—for very obvious reasons in several cases. In 2004 Ulrich Marzolph and Richard van Leeuwen edited the indispensable *Arabian Nights Encyclopedia*, which guides readers through the complexities of the book and its history, with commentaries on every individual story and clear essays on general themes. It is no longer the case that contemporary readers need be confined to "Aladdin," "Ali Baba," "The Ebony Horse," and a scant handful of others, as so many of our forebears were. The stories need no longer be neglected but can now be read as works of literature, around which has effloresced multiple *Arabian Nights* fantasies, manifest in anything from the confectionery of a nightclub décor, enticing advertisements to travel, or a ballet such as Michel Fokine's's *Schéhérezade* (1910), itself adapted from Rimsky-Korsakov's symphonic suite of 1888.

The tricentenary of Galland's momentous publication in 2004 was marked by many celebrations and several more scholarly volumes. All variously informed by the work of predecessors in *Nights* scholarship, they share rather more the broad scope of Irwin in charting the contexts and influences on (and of) the *Nights* in its multilayered development. *Fabulous Orients: Fictions of the East in England, 1662–1785*, by Ros Ballaster, appeared in 2005 with a companion anthology, *Fables of the East:*

Selected Tales, 1662–1785. Both are exhilarating results of wide, deep reading in the genre. Three years later Aboubakr Chraïbi drew up the indispensable and authoritative *Les mille et une nuits: Histoire du texte et classification des contes.* A third remarkable meditation, on the radiating influence of the *Nights* in fin-de-siècle French literature, appeared in 2009 with Dominique Jullien's *Les amoureux de Schéhérazade: Variations modernes sur les Mille et une nuits.* And simultaneously, a surprising account of the cultural (and commercial) stock placed by nineteenth-century North Americans in remote imaginings, affiliations, and collectibles of Arabia and the East was given by Susan Nance in *How the Arabian Nights Inspired the American Dream, 1790–1935.* Most recently Marina Warner's *Stranger Magic* has explored the fascination the *Nights* wielded on Enlightenment and post-Enlightenment Europe on account of—not despite—the magical and irrational realms that the stories explore.

These monographs have been accompanied by a number of collected volumes containing discrete shorter studies on the reverberating echo chamber of the stories. In addition to the work of Makdisi and Nussbaum (mentioned earlier), these include a collection of fine essays edited by Chraïbi in 2004, with the title *Les mille et une nuits en partage*, and three comparable volumes that chart further the sprawling cartography of the *Nights* and its influences: *New Perspectives on Arabian Nights: Ideological Variations and Narrative Horizons*, edited by Wen-chin Ouyang and Geert Jan van Gelder (2005); *The Arabian Nights and Orientalism: Perspectives from East and West*, edited by Yuriko Yamanaka and Tetsuo Nishio (2006); and *The Arabian Nights in Transnational Perspective*, edited by Ulrich Marzolph (2007).

The majority of essays included in these compilations incline expansively to view the *Nights* corpus as a uniquely accretive cultural bundle that absorbs, and somehow comes to possess, the works on which it has exerted influence, in varying degrees. On this view, there are essentially both intrinsic and extrinsic properties to the *Nights*; it is a dynamic, living, and breathing cross-cultural phenomenon quite as much as a literary artifact with definable and original contours. The novelist A. S. Byatt has commented, "The great novels of Western culture, from *Don Quixote* to *War and Peace*, from *Moby Dick* to *Doctor Faustus* were constructed in the shadow of [Scheherazade's] story."[6] It is a challenge to scrutinize any intrinsic aspect of the *Nights* (the tales themselves in their earliest reconstructible forms) without being drawn to the influences that led variously to them and eventually issued from them as so much inspiration.

With the fastidious and revered empirical work of Mahdi imposing itself on the field (and sometimes working to constrain it), the act of discerning the influence the corpus has exerted can seem, at times, more fanciful than scholarly, more ingenious than truly tenable in any practical sense. Commentaries about the importance of the *Nights* in the development of world culture after 1704 may tend to the alluring sweeping statement; but undoubtedly at the granular level the need for study is colossal: three centuries hold up an abundance of material for scrutiny. The imperative now is to probe details of reception (of influence, variation, adaptation, interpretation); this is an important area of study in its own right, and it has always to a certain degree, in a circular and paradoxical turn, fed the importance of the original text.

All the volumes mentioned above rehearse different aspects of the historical development of the *Nights*; account is given of multiple layers and their significance: the pre-Islamic (and pre-Arab) origins in India and Persia of a core of stories and their translation into Arabic in the Umayyad and early Abbasid periods; their development in varying registers of middle Arabic until the beginning of the eighteenth century in three chief recensions (an early Syrian core, a later Egyptian collection that built accretions on the earlier core, and a relatively neglected North African recension titled the *Hundred and One Nights*); their momentous serialized translation into French by Galland in 1704 based adventitiously on the early Syrian core; their colossal impact ever since on European (and subsequently world) literature and cultures; Arabic manuscript developments after 1704; Arabic printed editions from the first half of the nineteenth century onward and their sometimes byzantine relationship with subsequent translations; and, lastly, adaptations and developments from the late nineteenth century to the present day across various creative media: drama, music, visual arts, dance, and film.

The compendious *Arabian Nights Encyclopedia* (mentioned earlier) gives erudite coverage in hundreds of entries on all seven areas of study outlined. One might aver, however, that this work has a dual tendency: to give the reader access to the scholarship that has established the core (or the various cores) of the *Nights* and to evince how the *Nights* has been received across cultural histories. Most known readings of individual tales, be they fundamental or tendentious, are recorded in the *Arabian Nights Encyclopedia* for reference where possible.[7] Aboubakr Chraïbi's 2008 monograph also has an encyclopedic quality; it is certainly now a basic scholarly reference tool, giving account of the layered history of the tales in all principal recensions. It establishes, in breathtaking scope for a single author, the various relationships between the stories and both their sources and analogues within the Arabic tradition and outside it, thus providing a sweeping and deep cross-cultural context for the tales of the corpus. Chraïbi works from empirical knowledge of the entire Arabic textual tradition; thus, what bears significantly on this volume is that the author adopts an indulgent attitude to (and takes a practical view of) the corpus's development and growth.[8]

> It is one of the rare collections of tales, to my knowledge, where the study of one work implies the need to cross several boundaries: first, that of authority and origins, since the *Nights* are a collective work and multiform even though one can discern this or that original touch and plan of composition; secondly, that of the unity of space and time, since their composition encompasses at least Persia, Iraq, Egypt, and Syria and lasted ten centuries (as the dynamic of the manuscripts testifies); and thirdly, that of language (middle and classical Arabic, French!), an obstacle when it comes to the distribution of disciplines, but not one that is insurmountable.[9]

Chraïbi proposes detectable affinities for most of the stories of the extended corpus he has studied. Thus, strikingly, his understanding of the frame story leads him to adduce tales from, among others, the Chinese *Tripitaka*, Ludovico Ariosto's *Orlando Furioso*, Somadeva's *Kathasaritsagara*, and the tenth-century Arabic histories of al-Dinawari and al-Tabari. Preserved in the last two sources, the story of Ardavan (a third-century Parthian king) and the vizier's daughter is a family romance that can be viewed, loosely, as a pseudohistorical protoversion of the *Nights*' frame story; it is a terse yet compelling paragon of the *Nights*' principal and engendering tale and adds further nuance to our historical knowledge of the corpus. Chraïbi in the main espies connections leading into, or existing in parallel to, the *Nights*; let us concentrate further on their cultural outgrowths represented in this collection.

Exfoliations

The Sanskrit scholar and narratologist Wendy Doniger, in "Engaging," part 2 of *Scheherazade's Children*, reads the romance of Qamar al-Zaman and Budur in the light of the cross-cultural affinities Chraïbi detects, and offers a profound reflection on the contradictory tensions between the traditional, near universal theme of women's wickedness and wiles and the thrust of the *Nights* toward the rehabilitation of Scheherazade and her sisters. The argument, implied throughout by the unfolding of Scheherazade's own ransom tale, is played out through the figure of Budur, resourceful and tricksterish in her resourcefulness, and follows the intricate mechanisms of recognition, the pivotal dynamic in this tale's compelling series of twists and reversals.

While Doniger brushes in the affiliations with more ancient and Easterly mythological storytelling, the other contributors listen in on resonances closer in time and space. Eliot Warburton offered a fertile image of the work's energy, which Robert Mack, editor of the first "Grub Street" English translation, has glossed:

> The collection was something wildly fertile and intrinsically organic—a forceful act of narration that would inevitably and paradoxically extend itself beyond the bounds of any possible human control. . . . The *Arabian Nights* seemed intrinsically to beg comparison with a plant of the rich and native narrative soil of "the sweet South"—a growth that "flourishes in all climates" with "luxuriance." Although an Eastern product not "indigenous to the soil" of Western Europe, it has "taken root" no less firmly than the works of Shakespeare, like an "ever-flourishing Banyan"; the Banyan or banian tree, of course, being the East Indian fig tree, the extended branches of which themselves drop shoots to the ground, which then take root and so support the parent branches in such a manner that a single tree can cover an astoundingly large expanse of ground.[10]

This is a highly suggestive metaphor, albeit not a precise model to calibrate the limits of a corpus, to measure its growths and its influences.

Only actual case studies can do this, such as Tim Fulford's essay on Coleridge in the same volume as Mack's essay. Fulford suggests that the *Arabian Nights* were sublimated into "The Rime of the Ancient Mariner," in which the influence of Oriental themes is far less obvious than it is in that other masterpiece "Kubla Khan": "The dislocation of conventional causality, the sudden appearance of supernatural beings, the absence of narratorial moralizing, the enclosure of the voyage with a framing story, were all features of 'The Merchant and the Genie' that give the poem its nightmarish fascination. By adapting the structure of the *Nights'* narrative to a traditionally English genre (the ballad) Coleridge was able to unsettle British expectations about moral order."[11] This account of Coleridge's enthrallment to the *Nights* offers a relatively benign view of essentially creative motivations: "Coleridge's late 1790s poems . . . are the best kind of Orientalist work—one that moves the East westwards, achieving an uncanny fusion which unsettles stereotypes about home and abroad."[12]

In Coleridge we have a noteworthy case of the way the *Nights* and loosely comparable Eastern stories provided both palpable and sublimated influence on the artist; we also have, on a separate tack, a good example of how narratives, not strictly part of the *Nights'* Arabic corpus, fascinated authors from the eighteenth century onward in discrete ways, according to quite varied aesthetic impulses. There is a marked contrast, for instance, between Coleridge's use of the pseudohistorical tragic romance of Abbasa (sister of Harun al-Rashid) and Jaafar al-Barmaki, on one hand,[13] and the way the translator Jean-Charles Mardrus, a century later, exploited a late Mamluk popular version of the story, inserting it capriciously into the *Nights* in order to adumbrate the closure of the frame story, on the other.[14]

Mardrus tends to get a bad press these days. Chraïbi, for one, does not accommodate him in his own pragmatically indulgent view of the corpus. Yet Mardrus's eccentrically fertile fashioning of the collection is significant since it may have given rise to a new predominantly visual aesthetic that came to be associated with the *Nights* in the West in the twentieth century. Jullien has written cogently about Mardrus: "Despite his infidelity, or perhaps in fact because of it, Mardrus's version contributed to a renewal of esthetic, which, while based on misunderstanding has nonetheless been prodigiously fertile."[15] Mardrus is crucial to the story of the *Nights* for several reasons. The illustrious circle for whom he produced his translation, whose fin-de-siècle taste he had in mind to please, gave him an enraptured reception, which was upheld by several more cultural luminaries of his epoch. His methods were also important to subsequent development, for he claimed textual fidelity when the truth was quite the contrary, and then, when he qualified this claim, explained that he had not relayed the *Nights* faithfully and literally but *in their spirit*, thus clearly reversing himself but suffering no detriment to his standing. Furthermore, though he was greatly approved for abandoning the antiquated features of Galland, which reflected the manners of another era, his own versions are profoundly colored by the milieu that produced them (Symbolism in the visual arts as well as literature). Critics of Mardrus, who found fault with his liberal approach, knew in rigorous terms the difference between the Arabic core and its accretions and recognized the accretions that owed more to European hands.

This understanding of the text's metamorphoses offers an essential backdrop to Rosie Thomas's study in this volume. Thomas's study is groundbreaking and explains the importance of this highly malleable, significantly visual register in influencing or setting off some of the earliest films inspired by the *Nights* in India. Little is known or has been written about the impact on early Indian cinema of the world of the *Arabian Nights*, its core and offshoots (especially those marked by Mardrus's lavish visual aesthetic). Thomas's essay adds a significant part to Robert Irwin's "*A Thousand and One Nights* at the Movies."[16] Irwin's list is characteristically exuberant. ("There is a Popeye version of Aladdin, a Fairbanks junior version of *Sinbad the Sailor*, Phil Silvers starred in *A Thousand and One Nights* (as a bespectacled Abdullah the Touched One). . . . So the first point is that *The Thousand and One Nights* genre includes hundreds of films. The second point is that most of them have been forgotten and deserve to be so.")[17] But there are some historical reference points (and, indeed, cultural masterpieces) that should be restored to our collective memory. Thomas examines the significance of some of the earliest Indian films, and possibly the oldest film inspired by the *Nights* of substantial length (to wit, Hiralal Sen's *Ali Baba and the Forty Thieves*); this should stand alongside Thomas Edison's 1902 *Ali Baba and the Forty Thieves*, directed by Ferdinand Zecca; George

Méliès's *Palais des mille et une nuits* (1905); and (again) Zecca's *Aladdin of the Marvelous Lamp* (1906). The divagations of cultural transmission which Thomas goes on to trace are quite unanticipated; she shows that the cultural milieu, formed by the reception of Mardrus's work in Europe, influenced the Ballets Russes (Diaghilev and his designer Leon Bakst) as well as the couturier Paul Poiret, impresario of themed Oriental balls. The popular Orientalism these figures and others alongside them promoted had far-reaching influence, impinging even on Indian vaudeville musical drama, dance, and conjuring, a fact that eventually led a disaffected Anna Pavlova, through her students, to encourage the renaissance of Indian classical dance in the 1920s and '30s. "Out of a fusion of European 'oriental dance,' Euro-American modernist free expression, and dutifully researched Indian vernacular and folk forms, the new Indian 'classical' dance was born."[18] This rediscovered classicism nourished a new Hindu-Indian nationalism which emerged as anathema to the "Islamicate" popular Orientalism of the *Nights* and its various artistic spinoffs; thus, "unlike Euro-American orientalism, which merged quasi-Hindu and Islamic elements without distinction, India's popular Orient from the 1930s onwards was effectively that which was outside or 'other' than—a putatively Hindu—India."[19] These important calibrations of home and elsewhere are essential background to the flurry of Indian *Arabian Nights* fantasies that appeared in the late '20s and early '30s, avatars of Hiralal Sen's *Ali Baba* of 1903.

There is a case for restoring to memory other works that have been ignored—forgotten and sometimes consciously excluded. Wen-chin Ouyang wrote in her foreword to *New Perspectives on Arabian Nights*, "The *Nights*' influence outside the Arabic-speaking world has been so pervasive in the arts throughout history that, according to Robert Irwin it is easier to name those who have not been influenced than those who have."[20] Irwin himself drew attention to this claim in his own subsequent preface to *The Arabian Nights and Orientalism* in order to qualify it.[21] Having once asserted, for the sake of example, that Vladimir Nabokov's work showed no traces of influence by the *Nights*, Irwin subsequently found reason to go back on his claim. His revision is fascinating and compelling. Writers often ignore the limits of their own prescriptions when they write, and the *Nights* is hard to encompass: as Ouyang herself remarks, Bruno Bettelheim once asserted "in his book on *The*

Uses of Enchantment, . . . 'one especially crucial limitation must be noted: The true meaning and impact of a fairy tale can be appreciated, its enchantment can be experienced, only from the story in its original form.' . . . Of course, he goes on to give a psychoanalytical reading of *Sindbad the Sailor* and the frame-tale based on a translation made for children."[22]

In *New Perspectives*, Peter Caracciolo contributed a compellingly innovatory essay on Henry Fielding, revealing how the novelist reworked elements of "The Barber's Tale" in *Tom Jones*; Caracciolo shows convincingly how the garrulous Barber Partridge, modeled on the Barber of Baghdad, resounds throughout Fielding's novel: "Far from just having local significance, these arabesque allusions turn out to be a crucial element in the novel. . . . Both barbers are intimately associated with the fate of a small creature whose apparently insignificant status belies what will turn out to be his importance in the community."[23] Most commentaries that point up the eighteenth- and nineteenth-century English novel's debt to the *Nights* underscore elements of the paranormal and romance (the eerie, the magical, the bizarre) in the original stories. The realism which the novel came increasingly to develop, or with which it is commonly associated in the classic Dickensian style, has been considered by and large anathema to the *Nights*. As Ros Ballaster notes in *Fabulous Orients* about Clara Reeve and James Beattie, "Both [authors] see the oriental fable as inclined to the amoral, the fantastic, and the supernatural: tendencies that the realist fiction of the second half of the eighteenth century, they argue, has succeeded in curbing."[24] Yet this is at best only half the story; in "The *Arabian Nights* and the Origins of the Western Novel" (chapter 7 in this volume), Irwin suggests guardedly that this commonly held assumption neglects what may strike many students as counterintuitive: that, at heart, it was the mesmerizing "Hunchback" cycle, more fabliau than fairy tale, that moved Fielding to weave realism into his own fiction; moreover, in this trait he may have begun to reflect one tendency of fictional writing in his and subsequent eras.

Fabulous Orients is a superb scholarly monograph, surveying an enormous geography (that is shared in scope with this book): from the Ottoman Arab world, through India, to the Far East. In the eighteenth century the distortions of cultural perception, some progressive and some hidebound, for which the *Nights* was held to be a touchstone, affected views about all three regions. They are still relevant today to detailed literary and cultural histories. That translations may also be interpretations and adaptations, as well as more passive vehicles, of their own era's reception of the corpus, informs many of the ensuing studies. The essential point to glean is that translations may be studied in the same purview as works that adapt the *Nights* creatively—what we commonly call rewritings. In Ballaster's contribution here, she builds on details of her own *Fabulous Orients* in showing how—and why—Byron distilled his heroine Gulnare into *The Corsair* with elements that are crucially distinct from the disposition of the original (story of) Jullanar. In this fascinating account of how Jullanar fares in English, first in Grub Street, then in Jonathan Scott, and thereafter displaced in the versified fiction of Byron, Ballaster begins by telling us that the early eighteenth-century English reader saw the *Arabian Nights' Entertainments* as offering "a better Account of Customs, Manners and Religion of the Eastern Nations, viz. Tartars, Persians and Indians than . . . is to be met in any Author hitherto published."[25] However, it becomes patently clear that the *Nights* and the adaptations the tales inspired are just as prone to reflect adaptors and their *Zeitgeist* as the cultures they were imagined to have stemmed from. The treatment of Jullanar traces across a century a kind of mitigated view of despotism. In the *Arabian Nights' Entertainments*, though a heroine, Jullanar was complicit with acquiescence in slavery and subordination; in *The Corsair* a century later her avatar in the figure of Gulnare strode—in the spirit of Byron's time—against such compliance. Thus the arc from the *Arabian Nights' Entertainments* to *The Corsair* traces for us the shifting terms in which Jullanar's "liberty" is presented—from Galland's *salonnière* to Jonathan Scott's sentimental heroine to Byron's revolutionary agent. (This is a variation on one of the fundamental drives of *Fabulous Orients* in which Ballaster wrote that "the framing devices of oriental fictional sequences . . . dramatize reading as an experience of abandoning rather than reinforcing sovereignty.")[26]

Fabulous Orients is amplified in this volume in both geographic breadth and thematic interest. Elizabeth Kuti's study of eighteenth-century drama reprises Ballaster's evocation of the figure of Roxolana/Roxelana/Roxana as "a place of dangerous excess"[27] Kuti picks up again the theme of women's frailty, here dominated by the vice of curiosity, and reveals the echoes back and forth between Charles Perrault's cautionary fairy tale *Barbe-Bleue* (Bluebeard) and the frame tale of the *Nights* about Shahriyar's vengeful rage. The fundamental idea that narrative can be made to resist the excesses of malevolent sovereignty is then developed further in Katie Trumpener's essay. The narratives examined in her study display no overt Orientalism: the *Nights* has no directly apparent presence, and certainly they offer no superficial Eastern flavor; rather they are distilled in a kind of structural hypostasis of story-framed-within-story as site (and voice) of resistance.

William Beckford, born in 1760 and a near contemporary of Byron, nevertheless has never quite taken his place in the insider circle of eighteenth-century fiction. Ballaster suggests that Beckford's Gothic vision, most palpable in his novel *Vathek* in the character of Nouronihar, honed a new psychology and aesthetic that transcended rather than simply translated the *Nights*. This all bears further scrutiny, and indeed in chapter 2 Laurent Châtel examines in cogent detail the implications of Beckford's having spent time "between 1780 and 1783 . . . working spasmodically on the translation from Arabic manuscripts of Arabian Nights stories collected by Edward Wortley Montagu, son of Lady Mary."[28] The evidence suggests that Beckford's own fiction was influenced in an organic way by his collaborative work translating from manuscripts of the *Nights*.

In "Staging," part 3 of this collection, the efflorescing manifestations of the *Nights* on stage and screen are explored, and exchanges between Japan and the *Nights* form the site of a circle of perceptions. In Irwin's preface to *The Arabian Nights and Orientalism*, we read that "when Japan opened its doors to the West there were many visitors who compared the country to something out of the *Arabian Nights*. Indeed that comparison became something of a cliché." The rigidity of such cultural appraisal was interestingly reversed by the Japanese: "Japanese study of Western culture was both more intense and more comprehensive than early Western studies of Japanese culture and it even embraced those aspects of Middle Eastern and Islamic culture that had become familiar to the Western reading public, including the *Arabian Nights*."[29] Japan absorbed from the West its fascination with the *Nights* and borrowed in some measure the predominantly demotic aesthetic that went with it. The end result takes us full circle: idiosyncrasies in the perceptions of a culture (Japan of Europe; Europe of Japan) issue from the gravity of fascination exerted by the originally Arabic corpus. And yet in Japan this borrowed and hybrid aesthetic has also been alloyed in the past 150 years with adaptations particular to sensibilities, at all levels, of Japanese literature and culture. How interesting that in Japan authors such as Kōnosuke Hinatsu (1890–1971), Yukio Mishima (1925–1970), and Hakushū Kithara (1885–1942) should have associated the *Nights* so strongly with their childhoods. This reminds one of Dickens and Tennyson and in particular of Coleridge, whose fearful enchantment with the tales in his boyhood evokes Hakushū, who "looked back upon his boyhood in his second collection of poems entitled *Omoide* (Recollections, 1911), in which Inoue's one-volume translation, called 'the red-covered *Arabian Nights*,' was regularly associated with a longing for, and fear of, the exotic world."[30] There is a universalism about the tie between the *Nights* and juvenilia; this is just one aspect of its universalism. Yet there are—of course—adaptations (and adaptations-in-translation) of the *Nights* that pay homage, in words and imagery, to some of the high water marks of Japanese letters: Tsutomu Inoue's 1880 translation "borrows a scene from Bakin's very popular novel, *Nansō Satomi hakkenden* (The Biographies of Eight Dogs, 1814–42), in which the author relates how the adulteress Tamazusa was put to death by the lord Satomi Yoshizane.... It is obvious that Inoue intended the effect of superposing these two texts, following the practice of traditional poets in taking the words of a classical work and incorporating them into his own composition without changing them."[31] This shows quite clearly how the Japanese adapted their translations to resonate with their own literature and also fashioned meaningful connections where they were perceived. This volume contains two studies, those by Yuriko Yamanaka and Tetsuo Nishio, that develop from the brief overview of "The *Arabian Nights* on the [Japanese] Stage" in *The Arabian Nights and Orientalism*.[32]

We have begun to sense (and suggest) that several of these studies include distinct genealogies of scholarly inquiry. The marvelously rich essay by Bridget Orr titled "Galland, Georgian Theatre, and the Creation of Popular Orientalism" in the Makdisi and Nussbaum volume is complemented now in diverse aspects across the essays here by Berta Joncus, Elizabeth Kuti, and Karl Sabbagh, all of which deal with aspects of the *Nights* on the British stage, in particular during the Georgian, Victorian, and Edwardian periods. Three of the subjects treated in *New Perspectives* are built on here: Robert Irwin on Caracciolo, as referred to already (on realism in the eighteenth-century English novel); Philip Kennedy on Evelyn Fishburn's "Traces of the *Thousand and One Nights* in Borges"; and Ferial Ghazoul on Ouyang's "Whose Story Is It? Sindbad the Sailor in Literature and Film." Let us signal further some of the kinds of connections that exist between earlier and later studies. For example, Caracciolo suggests in his study of Fielding that the cognitive structure of *Tom Jones*, resolved in the kind of untrammeled recognition scenes typical of romance, builds on the arc of disclosure that drives the "Hunchback" cycle. Similar structures, with paradoxes woven further into them, appear to have influenced Borges, as argued by Kennedy in chapter 10; secondly, Ouyang reminds us in her foreword that Sindbad is protean in his inspiration: "He may be a young boy, a dashing pirate, a majestic prince, a disgruntled old man or an Odysseus condemned to eternal wandering."[33] There appears to be no "kernel to these transformations," informed as they are by the epistemes of different eras—by shifting gender politics, for example, or the general spirit of the times: *Sinbad the Sailor* (the 1947 film) reflects the optimism of the postwar period; *Sinbad: The Legend of the Seven Seas* (2003) betrays a fearful post-9/11 world in which insidious parties lurk menacingly. Sindbad is always "shedding one identity for another"[34] In Ferial Ghazoul's study in this volume we find three further angles from which to view Sindbad: as a figure in a modern Arab political allegory by Radwa Ashour; as an image in a painting by Paul Klee; and as the inspiration for another historical reconstruction, the voyage of the Irish geographer and anthropologist Tim Severin. And Sindbad's shape-shiftings, any more than the jinn's apparitions, have not been exhausted.

Most of the studies in this volume treat influences on literature and art after 1704. But sometimes one has to reach back beyond 1704 to understand the eighteenth century properly. In Ballaster's *Fabulous Orients* we find account already of how the influence of Perrault's *contes* in France in the late seventeenth century affected to some degree the reception of the *Arabian Nights* in the next century. We know that part of its success was due to the adaptation of the Arabic tales to the tastes of Galland's readership—to the gallicization of the materials. Here the direction of influence according to which one culture imposed itself on another is quite clear. The trajectory of stimulus could be reversed, even come full circle, as Kuti shows in her discussion of Perrault's "Blue-beard" on the stage, where it was Orientalized and clearly influenced by the ambient cultural phenomenon of the *Nights*.

Malcolm Lyons's and Husain Haddawy's translations were referred to earlier. This is not to intimate that their predecessors have been exhaustively studied. There is a standard view of the characteristics of the principal eighteenth- and nineteenth-century translators: as Henry Reeve, writing for the *Edinburgh Review* in 1886, put it rather pungently, "Galland is for the nursery, [Edward] Lane is for the library, [John] Payne is for the study and Burton for the sewers."[35] Borges wrote about these translators in a famous essay. In this volume we sharpen our perspective on Borges, and on Lane and Burton, whose work on the *Nights* he greatly admired, by comparing the Argentine's treatment of the "Mirror of Ink"—an Oriental tale of divination—with its treatment in Lane and Burton. In chapter 3, Paulo Horta uses the "Mirror of Ink" as a precision gauge to appraise the distinct interests and temperaments of Burton and Lane (fig. 23). To be sure, there were similarities that the two men shared: In their own distinctive ways, both would fashion themselves as linguistic and cultural interpreters of the cultural universe of the *Nights*; and in their separate notes the evolution of the account of the "Mirror of Ink" speaks to the effacement of the role of the native Arab collaborator and the assertion of the translator himself as self-fashioned informant on the cultural universe of the *Nights*. But, and here is the crux of Horta's argument, Burton saw in the history of the mirror of ink, which Lane felt specific to [the practice of magic in] Cairo, evidence of how folktales such as the *Nights*' tales circulate. In the end what differentiates Burton from commentators like Lane, who stress the authenticity of their ethnographic experience, is his embrace of the privileged experience of the outsider, the cosmopolite, and the exile; his view, which is a window into many worlds, is superior to the specialization in one. Borges was philologically (and presumably deliberately) slapdash, falsely ascribing "The Mirror of Ink" to a collection in Burton from which it is in fact quite missing; nonetheless, he makes of it an exquisite narrative like no other extant version, crafting a window in the process from which to observe and assess his own engagement with the spirit of the *Nights*. It encapsulates the poetics of his invention, allowing us to explore the confluence in his short fiction of both influence and inspiration.

If one translator marked Borges more than any other it was Richard Burton (though he gave Gustav Weil's German rendering a key and concrete role in the plot of his tale *The South*). However, Edward W. Lane has pride of place (as chronology dictates) in the impact he had on George Eliot's *Daniel Deronda*, as shown in Horta's contribution in chapter 8; Horta's reading tells us something equally crucial about both Lane and *Daniel Deronda* and qualifies aspects of Edward Said's postcolonial reading of the novel in *The Question of Palestine*. The simple timeline of history can explain Lane's effect on Eliot, practically speaking; but there is something more essential to what the novelist gleaned from Lane. Eliot was a master of nineteenth-century realism but was also attracted by fairy-tale form, as evident in *Silas Marner*, and she produced in *Daniel Deronda* a composite work, one that interweaves the realist (English) novel of Gwendolen with the exotic romance of Deronda. The result is far from an awkward mismatch; Eliot of course knew what she was doing: from the earliest chapters of the novel the parallels drawn with the *Arabian Nights* tale of Qamar al-Zaman anticipate the shape of the novel's Jewish plotline and the development of Deronda as messianic figure, and attest to a structural and formal coherence Leavis famously found lacking. The elucidation of this enterprise comes itself in two parts, first, by identifying the underlying religious impetus for Lane's *Arabian Nights*; the limning of Deronda in the image of the princely Qamar al-Zaman, it is suggested, is partly related to the latter's role as geomancer. It was as an alternative to the dismissive stance of secular Orientalist scholarship that Lane's sympathetic portrayal of Islamic beliefs gained currency in the nineteenth century among figures such as Carlyle, Gérôme and Eliot.

Second, and relatedly, Horta posits links between images of Deronda as Qamar al-Zaman and the novel's program of "Orientalizing the Jews": the novel develops the explicit identification of Mirah as Budur and Mordecai as jinni. Mordecai and Budur are the instigators for Deronda to explore and test a more expansive notion of what constitutes rational, empirical, and verifiable knowledge. It is a striking paradox of literary and cultural history, sharpened further by hindsight and knowledge of subsequent political history, that the *Arabian Nights* should act in one of the great nineteenth-century novels as a vehicle of expression for the transformation of a young protagonist into a Jewish deliverer: "In *Daniel Deronda* the identification of Daniel with Qamar al-Zaman heightens the mythical quality of his transformation in the novel from English aristocrat into Jewish savior." The *Nights* and the novel as a whole acquire a mediating role; *Daniel Deronda* is not simply the mouthpiece of a Zionism that in 1876 had, in any event, not yet attracted the critique —and far less of the stigma—that attaches to it according any postcolonial view of (literary) history.

The volume closes with a reflection on Scheherazade by the Palestinian-Lebanese American novelist Alia Yunis; the story of the wanderings of the *Nights* and the odyssey of Scheherazade's many children continues to involve many contemporary writers and artists who, as Yunis does in her novel *The Night Counter*, are revisiting the tradition, on the page, screen, and stage. The filmmaker and *hakawati* (storyteller in Arabic) Nacer Khemir has made a trilogy of films (*Les Baliseurs du désert* [1984], *Le collier de la colombe* [1991], and *Bab 'Aziz* [2005]) that approach tales from the *Nights*, Sufi fables, and mystic beliefs in beautifully photographed urban settings and flowing desert landscapes. *Bab 'Aziz* does not retell a tale as such from the *Nights*, but it keeps to the spirit of the book and, like the first two films in Khemir's *Desert Trilogy*, weaves together uncanny and fairy-tale strands from many of the stories. Khemir has said, "*Bab 'Aziz* is a highly political film, and deliberately so. It is a duty nowadays to show to the world another aspect of Islam, otherwise each one of us will be stifled by his own ignorance of 'The Other.' It is fear that stifles people, not reality."[36] This desire is echoed in the watchword of the West-Eastern Divan orchestra, which Edward Said founded with Daniel Barenboim in 1999: "Knowledge is the beginning." These words capture the principles that this collection of essays aspires to observe.

NOTES

1. Saree Makdisi and Felicity Nussbaum, introduction to *The Arabian Nights in Historical Context: Between East and West*, ed. Saree Makdisi and Felicity Nussbaum (Oxford: Oxford University Press, 2008), 3.

2. Ibid.

3. Ibid., 9, 12.

4. Robert Irwin, *The Arabian Nights: A Companion* (1994; repr., London: I. B. Tauris, 2004).

5. Voltaire, "Sur la fable," in *Les œuvres complètes de Voltaire*, vol. 28B (Oxford, UK: Voltaire Foundation, 2008), 220.

6. A. S. Byatt, "The Greatest Story Ever Told," in *On Histories and Stories: Selected Essays* (London: Chatto and Windus, 2000), 170.

7. Ulrich Marzolph and Richard van Leeuwen's *Arabian Nights Encyclopedia* (Santa Barbara, CA: ABC-CLIO, 2004) appeared before the new English translation of the *Nights* by Malcolm Lyons (London: Penguin, 2010), and its editors decided to index according to Richard Burton's titles of the stories, which are often outlandish and unfortunately difficult to deduce from other versions; it would be desirable if this could be revised, but a helpful comparative table is available in an appendix to Nikita Elisséeff's *Thèmes et motifs des Mille et une nuits: Essai de classification* (Beirut: Institut Français de Damas, 1949).

8. At times he cautions against accepting as given facts assumptions that may be false. We assume, for example, that the *Thousand and One Nights* came after the *Thousand Nights*: the numerical sequence seems watertight and offers an easy clue to the stages of historical process; but we forget that in modern Arabic *Alf layla* stands often for the fuller title, *Alf layla wa-layla*.

9. Aboubakr Chraïbi, *Les mille et une nuits: Histoire du texte et classification des contes* (Paris: l'Harmattan, 2008), 71–72:

   > C'est l'un des rares [ensembles de contes], à ma connaissance, où l'étude d'une œuvre implique de franchir plusieurs barriers: 1—celle de l'autorité et des origines, puisque les *Nuits* sont une œuvre collective et multiforme, même si l'on peut y discerner telle touche originale ou tel projet de composition; 2—celle de l'unité de l'espace et du temps, puisque leur composition s'étale au moins sur la Perse, l'Irak, l'Egypte et la Syrie et a duré une dizaine de siècles (comme en témoigne la dynamique des manuscrits); 3—celle enfin de la langue (arabe moyen, classique, français!), obstacle gênant du point de vue de la répartition des spécialités, mais pas nécessairement infranchissable.

10. Robert Mack, "Cultivating the Garden: Antoine Galland's *Arabian Nights* in the Tradition of English Literature," in *The Arabian Nights in Historical Context: Between East and West*, ed. Saree Makdisi and Felicity Nussbaum (Oxford: Oxford University Press, 2008), 65.

11. Tim Fulford, "Coleridge and the Oriental Tale," in Makdisi and Nussbaum, *The Arabian Nights in Historical Context*, 220.

12. Ibid., 234.

13. See ibid., 222.

14. See E. Powys Mathers's English translation of Mardrus's original French version, vol. 4 in the 1990 Routledge edition: *The Book of the Thousand Nights and One Night* (London: Routledge, 1990).

15. Dominique Jullien, "Une lecture esthétique des *Nuits*," in *Les amoureux de Schéhérazade: Variations modernes sur les Mille et une nuits* (Geneva: Droz,

2009), 81 "Malgré son infidélité, ou peut-être justement grâce à elle, la version Mardrus va contribuer à un renouvellement esthétique, qui, pour être fondé sur un malentendu, n'en a pas moins été prodigieusement fécond."

16. Robert Irwin, "*A Thousand and One Nights* at the Movies," in *New Perspectives on Arabian Nights: Ideological Variations and Narrative Horizons*, ed. Wen-chin Ouyang and Geert Jan Van Gelder (New York: Routledge, 2005), 91–101.

17. Ibid., 92.

18. Rosie Thomas, "Thieves of the Orient," in this volume.

19. Ibid., 19.

20. Wen-chin Ouyang, "Foreword: Genres, Ideologies, Genre Ideologies and Narrative Transformations," in Ouyang and Van Gelder, *New Perspectives on Arabian Nights*, ix.

21. Robert Irwin, preface to *The Arabian Nights and Orientalism: Perspectives from East and West*, ed. Yuriko Yamanaka and Tetsuo Nishio, vii–xiii (London: I. B. Tauris, 2006).

22. Ouyang, "Foreword," x, quoting Bruno Bettelheim, *The Uses of Enchantment: The Meaning and Importance of Fairy Tales* (London: Penguin, 1991), 10.

23. Peter L. Caracciolo, in "The House of Fiction and *le jardin anglo-chinois*," in Ouyang and Van Gelder, *New Perspectives on Arabian Nights*, 71.

24. Ros Ballaster, *Fabulous Orients: Fictions of the East in England, 1662–1785* (Oxford: Oxford University Press, 2005), 19.

25. *The Arabian Nights' Entertainments* (London, 1705), quoted in notices appearing in the *Flying Post or the Post Master* 1635 (December 8–December 11, 1705).

26. Ballaster, *Fabulous Orients*, 14.

27. Ibid., 129.

28. Ibid., 368,

29. Irwin, preface to *Arabian Nights and Orientalism*, viii, ix.

30. Hideaki Sugita, "The *Arabian Nights* in Modern Japan: A Brief Historical Sketch," in Yamanaka and Nishio, *Arabian Nights and Orientalism*, 125.

31. Ibid., 124.

32. Ibid., 143–45.

33. Ouyang, "Foreword," 2.

34. Ibid., 7.

35. Henry Reeve, "*The Arabian Nights*," *Edinburgh Review* 164 (1886): 184.

36. Interview in *Nacer Khemir: Das Verlorene Halsband der Taube*, ed. Bruno Jaeggi and Walter Ruggle (Bade: Verlag Lars Muller / Trigon Films, 1992), 108, quoted in Roy Armes, "The Poetic Vision of Nacer Khemir," *Third Text* 24:1 (2010): 81.

PART I

Translating

1

The Sea-Born Tale

Eighteenth-Century English Translations of The Thousand and One Nights *and the Lure of Elemental Difference*

ROS BALLASTER

When British readers first encountered the tale sequence of the *Nights* in the early eighteenth century, what species of writing did they take it to be? And what kind of expectations and contexts for successful reading of the tales were promoted by its first English "translators"? The first two volumes of the *Arabian Nights' Entertainments* in English were published in London in December 1705, as we know from notices appearing in the *Flying Post or the Post Master* (December 8–December 11, 1705, issue 1635) and the *Post Man and the Historical Account* (December 4–December 6 1705, issue 1557). There are no copies extant of these first translations, but the text of the *Flying Post* advertisement reproduced the text found on the title page of the first volume:

Just published,
ARABIAN Nights' Entertainments, consisting of one thousand and one Stories, told by the Sultaness of the Indies to divert the Sultan from the

execution of a bloody Vow he had made, to marry a Lady every Day and have her cut off next Morning, to avenge himself for the Disloyalty of his first Sultaness, which contain a better Account of the Customs, Manners and Religion of the Eastern Nations, *viz.* Tartars, Persians and Indians, than is to be met in any Author hitherto published. Translated into French from the Arabian Manuscript by M. Galland, of the Royal Academy, and now done into English. In two Volumes. Printed for A. Bell, at the Cross-Keys and Bible in Cornhill, near Stocks Market.

We should not assume, however, that the only form in which British readers gained access to the *Nights* was that of the twelve small octavo volumes translated from Antoine Galland's French rendering by one or more anonymous "Grub Street" hacks between 1705 and 1717. That these volumes were popular there can be no doubt; by 1736 the complete twelve-volume sequence had gone into its eighth edition. The biweekly newspaper *Parker's Penny Post* serialized the tales in the mid-1720s (see fig. 19). The author of the *Universal Spectator and Weekly Journal* (November 1, 1729, issue 56) complains as follows:

It's true we every Day see Pamphlets with odd out-of-the-way Titles, which have a great Run, and then as trifling and insignificant as those Things are, they have something in them which amuses either by a Jingle of Words, or surprizes by monstrous Relations.

The Business of the Reader is to divert his Time, or, as the *French* more emphatically express it, *tuer le tems*, murder his Time; for which nothing can be more suited than the above Productions.

If then these Pieces alone have the Power of pleasure, and our Authors become as contemptible as the *Italians* of the last Century, let it not be imputed to them their Business is to please; and when the Writing with Judgment and Perspicuity becomes the only Method, to raise their Characters, when the preposterous Infants of a wreck'd Imagination are rejected, nothing shall meet a favourable Reception, but what at the same Time instructs and pleases; when Wit and Morality shall be allowed to go hand in hand, Judgment alone be esteem'd the Basis of the former, and nothing be receiv'd with Applause, but what is attended by a true Merit, either the present Writers will exert themselves, or others will appear, who are able to stretch an Eagle-Wing, and vindicate the *British* Genius.

The author presents the *Nights* as imported fodder for an expanding print market; his complaint particularly revolves around the vitiated taste for the foreign. He longs for a British Genius (rather than the Arabic jinn) who can successfully combine the power to promote judgment with that of giving pleasure.[1] Britishness will harness and contain the pleasure-giving luxury associated with the Eastern tale. Yet the "universal spectator" cannot apparently resist reusing elements of the very tales he or she sees as tiresomely recycled by modern periodicals. The pun on "retelling" and "retailing" reminds us that Scheherazade trades her tales for her life and that one of the best known sequences of the *Nights* concerns the mercantile achievements of the merchant-adventurer Sinbad, who profits from each successive adventure. The readers are paralleled mockingly with the auditor of Scheherazade's tales, the murderous Shahriyar, as they—like him—"kill time" indulging the tales. And finally the British writers are imagined as being lifted from the wreckage of these fanciful gruesome tales by the "eagle-wing" of genius, just as Sinbad in his second voyage escapes from a valley of diamonds and snakes, his coat pockets stuffed with gems, on an animal carcass lifted by a vast eagle.

For English readers of the translation of Galland's *Arabian Nights' Entertainments*, the sequence provided a window on cultures marked and marred by a despotism from which, they were repeatedly reminded, they were free. They were viewing not only the Tartars, Persians, and Indians (governed by Islamic sultanates) but also the French world of absolute monarchy, court favorites, and salon preciosity overseen by aristocratic women who exercised their sexual charms to political advantage. Parallels between the French court of Louis XIV and Islamic despotism were familiar from the hugely successful *Eight Volumes of Letters Writ by a Turkish Spy* (1687–1694) by Giovanni Paolo Marana, a fictional sequence of letters by an Arabian spy for the Ottoman court posing as a Moravian translator in the French city of Paris. Montesquieu was in turn to exploit the anagrammatic potential of "Paris" and "Persia" in the sustained critique of private and political despotism rehearsed in his *Lettres persanes* of 1721. Louis XIV had been explicitly paralleled with the Persian emperor, Abbas the Great (1588–1629), in a satirical tale by Peter Belon, *The Court Secret* of 1689, who in the second part encourages and supports the exiled Ottoman emperor, Murat III

(1574–1595), clearly a version of James II, who fled to France in the Glorious Revolution in 1688. Over fifteen years later, England could view its libertine courtly past as a culture *of* the past with the uxorious reigns of Mary II and Anne, Protestant-educated daughters of James II.

In what follows I take a closer look at the different English versions of the *Arabian Nights' Entertainments* through the consideration of a single tale not often addressed in the critical literature. The tale under discussion—"Jullanar the Sea-Born and Her Son King Badr Basim of Persia"—concerns not one but two protagonists, a mother and her son, who undergo a series of trials in order to achieve romantic happiness and political security. I summarize the changes of tone and lexical choices of successive eighteenth-century translators into English, often to make the story more accessible to Western readers and the story traditions familiar to them. I conclude with a consideration of Jullanar's reappearance in George Gordon, Lord Byron's *The Corsair* (1814), both a reiteration of the magical attractions of her watery element and a means to voice resistance to Jullanar's quietist politics of love won through submission to an absolute authority. Byron's treatment makes visible the continuing tendency on the part of English redactors of the *Arabian Nights*, their versions all derived from and in conversation with Galland's "translation," to deploy the *Arabian Nights* sequence as a means of differentiating English liberties from Oriental and Gallic despotism. Small but telling "liberties" were taken with the French source in English versions, I argue, to promote this comparative French/English, Catholic/Protestant, absolutist monarchy / limited contractual monarchy reading of the tales. However, the tale of Jullanar and Badr is also a tale (as are many in the *Nights*) about the appeal of difference itself, a tale of attraction between the creatures of different elements. The power of language to generate the allure of the strange is at the center of the tale and its telling. So, like all the versions of the *Nights* in different languages, these first English versions are creative transformations that make the tales "speak" in ways familiar to the cultures they enter but also voice their own attraction to the wild incommensurability of, and the inability to fully assimilate, elemental difference.

Jullanar and Badr

The "Jullanar and Badr" story appears in the seventh volume of the first English translation of the *Arabian Nights' Entertainments* under a title which significantly erases the maternal figure. "*The Story of* BEDER, *Prince of Persia, and* GIAHAURE, *Princess of* Samandal" couples the prince not with his mother but with the woman he pursues in marriage (see fig. 17). This may already be a hint that one way in which the stories of the *Arabian Nights* were mediated to a new audience unfamiliar with this story sequence was to associate it with an already familiar form, in this case the French fairy tale and stories of princes and princesses brought together through adversity, tales in which good mothers die and their children struggle against evil surrogate stepmothers; Charles Perrault's *Contes* were published in France 1691–95, including "Blue-beard" and "Cinderella."[2] The fairy tale, like its "sister genre," the Orien-tal tale, was received as a vehicle for the private critique of despotic rule exchanged between women. The old gossip instructs her young female aristocratic charge not only in moral absolutes but also in political diplomacy through fairy tales gathered from folk resources in the col-lections of Charles Perrault and Marie-Catherine d'Aulnoy;[3] the older sister Scheherazade tells her stories gathered from the folk tales of the East to her younger sibling, Dinarzade, as a covert means of correct-ing the murderous despotism of her husband. The Eastern genie, forged from the element of fire and able to govern the destinies of earthly mor-tals, is closely related to the fairy or the *fée* (creature of the air, whose name derives from the Latin term *fatum*, for a god of destiny)

The Jullanar tale is indeed a fairy tale, but probably one of Persian origin. It is found in the oldest preserved manuscript of the *Arabian Nights*, which contains only thirty-five and a half stories and belongs to the core corpus of the *Nights*. The story is told over the course of nights 230 to 271. It has been found in another medieval Arabic text, the four-teenth-century *Kitâb al-Hikâyât al-'ajîba*. Ulrich Marzolph and Richard van Leeuwen describe the two parts as follows: "a love story in which good behaviour is rewarded, and a love quest in which the hero falls in love by hearsay and sets out to conquer his beloved in magic worlds and dangerous lands."[4] The tales of mother and son, however, are not so simply summarized. The stories hinge on the pursuit of attractions across elemental divisions and in a context of an ambivalent attitude to the powers of verbal language as opposed to physical evidence.

Let us start with the "original" story insofar as such a thing exists in the context of the *Nights*. Husain Haddawy translates Muhsin Mahdi's critical edition based on the Syrian three-volume manuscript from which Galland worked and which is housed in Paris's Bibliothèque Nationale; this manuscript Mahdi dated to the fourteenth century, but it is now considered to date from the latter half of the fifteenth.[5] What is most striking in reading Haddawy's translation of Mahdi's edition is the careful disposition of the four elements in "Jullanar of the Sea": earth, water, air, and fire.[6] While the mother Jullanar is associated with the sea, her son is more often affiliated with air. Jullanar's name in Persian derives from *jul*, meaning "rose," and *anár*, "pomegranate," whereas in Arabic it forms the collocation *gul*/rose and *nár*/fire); she is the mysterious mute slave given to a powerful, generous, and benevolent king of Persia by a traveling merchant. He is so enamored that he gives up all his mistresses to live monogamously with his silent queen. A year later she responds to his pleas for her to speak in order to inform him that she is pregnant and hopes to give birth to the son he longs for; she also reveals, "I am an exile and a captive in a foreign land, with a broken heart aching for my people." She is the sister of a king of the sea named Sayih, whom she fled having in her temper declared an intention to throw herself into the "hands of a man of the land."[7] The king encourages her to invite her brother, mother, and their sea court to his castle, where, after his initial fear at their fire-breathing volatility, the king lives with them in good companionship. Jullanar gives birth to a son, who is named Badr (the full moon). The protective father is terrified to see his eleven-day-old son plunge into the sea in the arms of his uncle, but Badr is restored, now safe from any harm from water. Badr grows to be an accomplished and lovely young man, and the old king passes on the government of the kingdom to his son before he dies after contracting a chill in his bath (there must be irony in this detail that he dies by the touch of that element, water, which has so attracted him). A month after the king's funeral, when the sea people return to bring their condolences, Badr overhears (while he pretends to sleep) a conversation in which his uncle describes to Jullanar the loveliness of Jauhara, daughter of a vain sea king named al-Shamadal; Badr is instantly fired with love. When al-Shamadal, in a fit of vanity, rejects Sayih's proposals for the match, Sayih declares war, aided by troops sent from Gulnare. Badr, fleeing the conflict, finds Jauhara hiding up a tree on a nearby island. Jauhara pretends to be flattered by the young prince's advances, only to spit in his face and turn him into a pretty bird as an act of revenge. She tells her maid to dispose of the bird on the island of thirst, but the maid, out of pity, rather takes him to a green island, from which he is in turn seized by a bird catcher and presented to the latter's ruler as a gift. The queen of this kingdom is fortuitously also an enchantress and restores Badr to his rightful manly shape by sprinkling him with consecrated water. Badr takes ship and is the only one to survive in a storm, finding himself washed up on the shore by a floating "city as white as a fat dove."[8] Numerous beasts of burden attempt to prevent him from climbing the city walls, so he is forced to swim around to an alternative entrance. He befriends an elderly fava-bean seller who tells him that the city is governed by an enchantress queen named Lab (sun), who turns the men who love her into beasts.

The old man, Abu 'Abd-Allah, presents Badr to the sorcerer inhabitants of the city as his nephew but cannot prevent the queen from meeting and falling in love with him. She takes Badr to her castle swearing by her "Magian" (Zoroastrian) faith that she will not enchant him. Badr finds himself strongly attracted to the beautiful Lab and succumbs to her charms in forty days of drinking and revelry. However, he wakes on the forty-first morning to see in the garden a black bird mount a white she-bird on three occasions before the white bird resumes the shape of Lab and the black bird that of a mamluk. The fava-bean seller discloses that the black bird is a past lover who was unfaithful and has been enchanted as a punishment but for whom Lab retains strong feelings. Badr's adoptive uncle the fava-bean seller instructs him in the means to avoid falling victim to the same fate; when Lab tries to drug the young prince, he substitutes his own food, throws water in her face, and conjures her to take a form of his own choosing. Badr then departs from the city with Lab now in the shape of a bridled dappled she-mule. However, he is tricked by an old woman to whom he gives the bridle when she asks to purchase his mule; she is Lab's mother, and she swiftly restores her daughter to her womanly form. A huge demon flies all three back to Lab's palace, where the queen turns Badr into an ugly bird. Once again a maid takes pity on the bird-boy and feeds and waters him. She goes to seek help from the old man, who conjures his own demon and calls on Jullanar and her mother, Faratha, to come and counter Lab's magic with their own in order to save Badr. Jullanar, Faratha, and Sayih descend on the city from the air and kill its sorcerer-inhabitants. Jullanar restores her son once more to his natural shape, marries the old man to the obliging servant-girl, and finds al-Shamadal willing now to agree to the match between Jauhara and Badr. Jauhara obeys her father's commands, and the pair are united, finding that "they loved one another exceedingly."[9]

The story, like so many in the *Nights*, is a carefully patterned one with multiple repetitions and reworkings. Badr is, like his father, powerfully attracted to a princess of the sea. On two occasions an enchantress (Jauhara and Lab) turns him into a bird, and on two further occasions an enchantress (an unnamed queen and Jullanar) restores him to his proper shape. On two occasions a sympathetic serving-maid protects him from the wrath of a powerful aristocratic woman. On two occasions men with magic powers (his uncle Sayih and the old fava-bean seller) act to protect him (Sayih from the sea and the old man from Lab's enchanting). Powerful mothers with magical powers repeatedly take steps to save their imperiled offspring (Jullanar and Lab's mother). Lab is associated with fire, Jullanar and Jauhara with the sea, the king of Persia and the fava-bean seller with the earth, and Badr, son of the combined forces of earth and water, is associated with the air in his bird transformations. There are also significant references to the frame story, by parallels but also contrasts in plot. The vision of the black bird tupping the white bird in the garden recalls the traumatic scene of discovery which prompts the murderous reaction of Shahriyar. But Jullanar is silent and matched with a generous and loving king, whereas Scheherazade is necessarily loquacious in order to prevent the vengeful rage of a despotic ruler/husband. It is also a story concerning what in modern parlance might be seen as interspecies attractions: between creatures of the sea and the earth especially but also between jinns (the capacity of the sea creatures to breathe fire suggests their affinities with the jinn) and mortals. And it is a story about the capacity of language to prompt strong desire and to change the shapes of the things it addresses: Badr's quest is prompted by Sayih's description of Jauhara's charms;

magic words spoken by Jauhara, Lab, and Badr bring about physical transformations.

Let us turn next to consider the ways in which Galland, his English translators, and subsequent English translators of this story from different Arabic sources transformed the story through rendering it in their language and the terms of narrative and narration familiar to them, while retaining a strong attraction to the strangeness and wildness of this new species of story.

Antoine Galland

Galland's understanding of the conventions of prose narrative in Europe led him to numerous significant changes to his source text. Most relevant for our discussion of the Jullanar tale is Galland's stripping much of the eroticism and descriptive language found in the *Alf layla*, indicating aesthetic standards very different from those of Europe. Hence where the *Alf layla* describes Jullanar as "a tall girl, as slender as a spear, wrapped in a silk cloak embroidered with gold," and unveiled to have "hair hanging down to her anklets in seven tresses like horses' tails or the veil of the night, and with dark eyes, smooth cheeks, heavy hips and slender waist,"[10] Galland in English translation gives us only "a red Satin veil, strip'd with Gold, over her face" and "a Lady that surpass'd in beauty, not only his present Mistresses, but even all that he kept before."[11]

Galland's censoring of the eroticism of the original tale causes some difficulties for his reader's understanding of the tale. In Haddawy's translation, Sayih describes Jauhara to Gulnare in terms that might be expected to fire the interest of a hot-blooded young man, saying she has "jewel-like teeth, sweet lips, black eyes, a soft body, heavy hips, and a slender waist. When she turns, she shames the deer, and when she sways, she makes jealous the willow bough."[12] By contrast Galland's Saleh simply mentions the princess's name. In Galland's version Beder's (Badr's) suspicions of Queen Lab are reignited by his observation of her silent use of magic to produce a mysterious cake while she thinks he sleeps, and he has no vision of the black bird three times treading the white and no revelation that it is his mistress and her mamluk. Galland's conclusion suggests more passion in the reunion of mother and son than in the union of Beder with his longed-for bride. Thus, Galland describes the moment when Gulnare (Jullanar) has restored Beder to his proper form from his ugly owl enchantment: "She could not find in her Heart to let him go; and if he had not been in a manner torn from her by Queen *Farasche*, who had a Mind to embrace him in her turn, for ought I know, they might not have parted till now, so great Queen *Gulnare's* Affection was for him."[13]

Some other changes introduced by Galland are not vital for plot but certainly indicate a consistent attempt to tidy up the less respectable elements of his source. Galland has his king swiftly marry Gulnare and declare her queen once she has confided her pregnancy and her aristocratic birth; in his version Gulnare's mother, Farasche (Faratha), is swift to discover whether her daughter has been made an honest woman as soon as the family is reunited. In his account of the marriage that concludes the story Galland refers to the magnificence of the prince's nuptials, whereas the *Alf layla* concludes with a reference to the prince's joy to discover his new bride a virgin on their wedding night.[14] Galland's prince is twenty years of age when he first falls in love with the description of his future bride; in the *Alf layla* he is sixteen.

Galland does not only censor, however. He also adds and embellishes in ways that speak to the interests of his contemporary audience. An especially striking example is his expansion of Gulnare's description of the kingdom of the sea to the curious king of Persia, a description that he converts into a familiar (to seventeenth- and eighteenth-century readers) natural philosophical disquisition on the nature of other worlds. In *Alf layla*, Jullanar answers the king's query about how the people of the sea manage to live in that element without drowning by explaining that they can breathe in that element. In Galland, she goes on for several paragraphs describing the vastness and richness of the sea kingdoms and the special powers of the inhabitants. The sea, she tells the king, is divided into many provinces, and "an infinite Number of Nations differing in Manners and Customs."[15] The palaces of kings and princes "are very sumptuous and magnificent," and the lowest rank of citizens sport vast pearls:

As we have a marvellous, and almost incredible Agility, of transporting our selves whither we please, in the twinkling of an Eye; so we have no occasion for Coaches or Horses: Not but that every King has his Stables, and his Breed of Sea-Horses; but they seldom make use of them, but upon publick Feasts and rejoicing Days. After they have been well manag'd, they set Riders upon their Backs, who shew their Skill and Dexterity in the Art of Riding. Others are put to Chariots of Mother of Pearl, adorn'd with an infinite Number of Shells of all sorts, of the liveliest Colours in the World. . . . I pass over a Thousand other Particulars, relating to these Sea-Countries, full of Wonder and Curiosity, which would be very entertaining to your Majesty.[16]

While Gulnare may seem to echo Scheherazade here in her provision of things of wonder and curiosity to entertain her king-husband, she is also invoking a familiar mode of seventeenth-century European literature, the account of other worlds. Perhaps the best known and familiar to English readers was Bernard de la Bovier de Fontenelle's 1686 *Entretiens sur la pluralité des mondes* (translated into English by Aphra Behn in 1688). In this lively dialogue fiction an amorous young scientist-philosopher explains over a series of star-struck nights the heliocentric model of the world to a curious young marquise, imagining the strange worlds on other planets to attract her to his enlightened understanding. Galland here recalls this form of speculative science fiction and weaves it into the fabric of his version of the Persian fairy tale. The world of the sea is also recognizably the world of the salon and the romance. This was a world that English readers were accustomed to recognize but also inclined to treat with some mockery. Aphra Behn's "Essay on Translated Prose," prefixed to her 1688 translation of Fontenelle's work, is especially critical of his "design" in attempting to communicate science through the medium of gallant conversation:

> Endeavouring to render this part of Natural Philosophy familiar, he hath turned it into Ridicule; he hath pushed his wild Notion of the Plurality of Worlds to that heighth of Extravagancy, that he most certainly will confound those Readers, who have not Judgment and Wit to distinguish between what is truly solid (or, at least probably) and what is trifling and airy: and there is no less Skill and Understanding required in this, than in comprehending the whole Subject he treats of. And for his lady Marquiese, he makes her say a great many very silly things, tho' sometimes

she makes Observations so learned, that the greatest Philosophers in
Europe could make no better.[17]

Behn, like the "universal spectator," presents the French import as a
thing of airy fancy inclined to float away from the solid virtues that an
English reader pursues. The wonder tale imported from France turns
scientific discovery into fanciful puffs. Gulnare is an interesting figure,
however, in this regard since it is she who imparts the wonders to her
amazed male auditor. As so often with the *Arabian Nights*, readers may
have been attracted to the way in which the strange text (somewhere
between France and England) overturns the conventional and anticipated distribution of power in relation to both knowledge and narrative
(women listen to a male authority).

The "Grub Street" Translators and Jonathan Scott

The translation from French into English by what have been termed
the "Grub Street" translators is a faithful one. In defense of Galland's
text as the closest to the combination of colloquial energy and storytelling fluency found in the oral Arabic tradition from which the sequence
derived, C. Knipp comments, "as befits a piece of hack work far less
pretentious than Burton's, the Grub Street Galland departs little from
its source; one finds few actual cuts or alterations."[18] Perhaps the most
transformative decision in relation to the French source was to change
the title from *Les mille et une nuit: Contes arabes* to *Arabian Nights'
Entertainments*, associating the publication with the idea of a popular
amusement and foregrounding the difference of the text in terms of
a space (the "Arabian" regions) rather than a time (the time of story).
There are indications of haste either in translation or preparation of the
text for printing in minor errors which the next "translator" into English of the *Nights* was careful to correct.

Jonathan Scott, who had learned his Arabic and Persian in India,
where he had lived from 1766 to 1785 and served for a period as Warren Hastings's Persian secretary, worked from Galland's text in French
to complete his six-volume *Arabian Nights' Entertainments* in 1811.
Scott had compiled a table of contents, which he published in William
Ouseley's *Oriental Collections* in 1797, to a seven-volume manuscript

that came into his possession; it had been previously owned by Edward Wortley Montagu. Scott sold the manuscript to the Bodleian library in 1802, but he added extra stories, derived from the Montagu manuscript, to his new translation from Galland's French. Scott's text was the first literary translation of the *Nights* in English with a critical introduction and copious annotations concerning Muslim religion and customs. In the story under discussion here we see him silently correcting errors. Thus, in the courtship of Gulnare section of the story, when the king enters her apartments, we are told in the Grub Street translation that the mysterious mute slave turns from gazing at the sea to look at him "without an Air quite different from that of the Women-Slaves."[19] Scott corrects this to read "with an air quite different from that of the female slaves."[20]

Fatma Moussa Mahmoud observes that scrutiny of Scott's treatment of the manuscript reveals that his command of Arabic language and script was unimpressive and that, having disposed of the manuscript in Oxford, he changed his tune for the 1811 translation, conceding that Galland's work was better suited to European tastes and complaining in the introduction to his *Nights*,

> Vexatious indeed was [Scott's] disappointment as an orientalist, who had fancied that in seven volumes of Arabic copy of the 1001 Nights he possessed a treasure which would amply repay the labour of research, on discovering upon perusal that the greater part of them was unfit to appear in an English dress. Very many of the tales were both immoral and indecent in the construction; and of others the incidents are too meagre and puerile to interest a European reader of any taste, however they might have been, and still may be admired by the enshrined beauties of sacred harams, the auditors of an oriental coffee house.[21]

Nonetheless, Scott's minor changes to the Grub Street translation do indicate a response to a changed climate and expectations concerning the representation of the passions, particularly amorous ones, in prose fiction. Scott's is a slightly but discernibly more sentimental version of the tale of "Gulnare and Beder," one which quietly shifts the focus from dynastic struggle and the valide-sultana's, or French queen's, concern to ensure her precedence through securing her son's succession (Gulnare's passion for and government on behalf of her young son no doubt invoked parallels for French readers with the regency of Anne of Austria 1643–1651) to accounts of sentimental and romantic passion for the wild princesses of the sea on the part of father and son, the two kings of Persia.

Close attention to Scott's variants from his French source (he is translating from Galland's French but with reference to Arabic manuscripts) reveals a series of small but significant decisions which depart from the style of a *salonnière*'s romance narrative of high passion, demonstrating the familiar techniques of *bienséance* (propriety) and *vraisemblance* (truth to the ideal) associated with the French romance of authors such as Madeleine de Scudéry.[22] Thus, where the Grub Street translation has the king of Persia tell Gulnare of the "violence" of his passions,[23] Scott gives him the "ardour" of his passions.[24] At the end of Gulnare's year of silence the king complains to her that he has taken pains "to give her the most signal Proofs of his violent Passion," but in Scott's translation he refers to "the most signal proofs of sincere love."[25] Galland has the king tell his brother-in-law, "I love her with so tender and violent a Passion, that "tis plain, I never lov'd any Woman till I saw her. Oh! How I am bless'd and transported with her Charms," whereas Scott has, "I love her with so tender and ardent a passion, that I am satisfied I never loved any woman till I saw her."[26] The king's love in Scott's version is more often represented as tender and ardent than violent, and he is concerned to test his *own* feeling by contemplating it rather than to demonstrate it through public displays of devotion and service.

Gulnare's Submission

While we can measure the distance from the world of romance (long service, passionate love, formal and polite language) to that of the novel (sentimental pursuit, gentle and tender sociability, a more naturalistic language of feeling) in Scott's early nineteenth-century retranslation from the French of Galland's early eighteenth-century translation from the Arabic, it is striking that Scott hardly departs from Galland at all in one respect, and that is the terms in which Gulnare breaks her silence to declare the reasons for her eventual submission to her royal lover's pursuit. In the English translation from Galland there is a passage not found in the *Alf layla* source when Gulnare speaks to the king to explain her feelings of enslavement:

> The Love of your native Country is as natural to us as that of our Parents, and the Loss of Liberty is insupportable to every one who is not wholly destitute of Sense and Reason, and knows how to set a Value on it. The Body indeed may be enslaved, and under the Subjection of a Master, who has the Power and Authority in his Hands; but the Will can never be conquer'd or domineer'd over, but still remains free and unconfin'd, depending on it self alone, as your Majesty has found an Example of it in me: And 'tis a Wonder that I have not follow'd the Example of abundance of unfortunate Wretches, whom the Loss of Liberty has reduc'd to the mournful Resolution of procuring their own Deaths a thousand Ways, rather than survive it, and wear out a Wretched Life in a shameful Slavery.[27]

When Gulnare's relatives question the nature of her relationship with the king, her defense is much expanded and complicated from that given in *Alf layla* too. Haddawy's translation has, "O brother, you should know the man I am living with is a pious, generous, and honourable man who has never said one bad word to me, who has treated me kindly, and who has given me the best of lives."[28] In Galland, she explicitly refers to marital contract:

> I do not speak here of an Engagement between a Slave and her Master; if that were all, 'twould be easy to return the ten thousand Pieces of Gold that I cost him, but I speak now of a Contract between a Woman and her Husband, who has never given her the least Reason to complain, or be discontented: Besides, he is a King, wise, temperate, religious, and just, and has given me the most essential Demonstrations of his Love, that possibly he could.

And

> he has lately declar'd me Queen of *Persia*, and I am to sit with him in Council: Besides, I am breeding, and if Heaven will be pleas'd to favour

me with a Son, that will be another Motive to engage my Affections to him the more.[29]

In the early eighteenth century these passage could have been expected to resonate for English readers familiar with the popular and persuasive "contract" theory of Thomas Hobbes and John Locke, which identified kingly government as only secured and sustained through the willful submission of the people rather than "natural right." Subjects exchange individual liberties for collective security of property. However, as both Hobbes and Locke insist, the "will" remains the rightful property of the individual and cannot be contracted to another. Oriental empire was frequently invoked as the antithesis of contractual monarchy, subjecting an entire people to despotic rule. The Oriental harem and the subjection of many women to the sexual whimsy of a single male was frequently invoked as the sign of the luxurious decadence and despotism of Oriental empire, contrasted with the natural liberties enjoyed by European (especially Protestant) women in monogamous Christian marriages.[30] Sexual and marriage relations were especially fruitful sources in literature for the representation of an ideal "contractual" subject because they could convey the force of desire and feeling, the conscious "will" to submit, which best underpinned successful contractual structures. As Victoria Kahn puts it, "The seventeenth-century subject of contract was not the thin modern subject of formal equality but rather, at one and the same time, a richly imagined 'aesthetic' subject of passion and interest, and an artifact of the creative powers of language."[31] The passages referring to marital contract are given in Scott with little or no significant variation. By 1811 the context of a debate about the freedom of the will had, however, shifted radically, and Gulnare's speech about her slavery, her desire for liberty, and the attraction of suicide would have had especially powerful resonance in the context of the successful passage in 1807 by Grenville's newly elected Whig government of the Slave Trade Act, abolishing the slave trade between Africa, the West Indies, and England. In the early eighteenth century references to slavery were often to the forms of slavery practiced in Asian or Middle Eastern empires and a favorite image that of the Caucasian harem woman who chooses suicide over submission to the sexual demands of an Oriental despot. By the end of the same century it was the figure of the African slave, female or male, preferring to die in resistance to a plantation master's cruelty who would be more readily recalled in reading passages of passionate antislavery advocacy. And the narrative resolution, of genuine and ardent love resulting in reform of polygamous practice and a virtuous government based on tender submission to a woman (suggested in both Gulnare's story and the frame narrative of the *Arabian Nights*), looks neither plausible nor utopian but simply inappropriate in the context of debates over African slavery in the West.

Byron's Riposte

Three years after Scott's translation had brought the *Arabian Nights* and Galland's version of it to renewed attention in England, Byron, riding the wave of huge success with his first oriental poem, *The Giaour*, in 1813, composed *The Corsair*, a poem that has both explicit and implicit connections to the story of Jullanar. Byron took the name of his Turkish heroine, Gulnare, from the *Arabian Nights' Entertainments*. However, the poem has more pervasive debts to the story: like the Gulnare of the *Arabian Nights*, it consistently looks to the sea for a vision of liberty not afforded by a landlocked imagination. Byron's tale, which secured the extraordinary success of ten thousand sales on the first day of its publication on 1 February 1814, does not concern a mother and a daughter but the conflict between Turkish territorial rule and piratical Greek forces for control over the Aegean islands. It repeats, however, all the elements of the Gulnare and Beder story: earth, air, fire, and water. It opens with the pirate's song of liberty on water, describes the pirate-hero Conrad's farewell visit to his tearful wife, Medora, in her airy tower, transports us to a stony prison in which the Turkish Pasha Seyd confines his many slaves. Conrad infiltrates Seyd's stronghold in the disguise of a spy-dervish and saves the slave concubine Gulnare from the fire ignited in the ensuing battle between pirates and Turks, only to be imprisoned himself. The fiery Gulnare in turn liberates her liberator, Conrad, and herself by her secret nighttime stabbing of the pasha. The pair flee by boat, on which Gulnare steals a guilty kiss from Conrad; with their return to the Greek mainland and the discovery that Conrad's wife, Medora, has expired in despair at his absence, both Conrad and Gulnare disappear, and the poem concludes with mournful stanzas describing Medora laid out in death.

Byron returns to the language of liberty with which Gulnare breaks her silence in the *Arabian Nights*, but his Gulnare is swift to dismiss the notion that love can be the outcome of confinement, however luxurious. Gulnare tells Conrad that she could not love her captor, the Turkish pasha:

> Yet much this heart, that strives no more, once strove
> To meet his passion—but it would not be.
> I felt—I feel—Love dwells with—with the free.
> I am a slave, a favoured slave at best,
> To share his splendour, and seem very blest!
> Oft must my soul the question undergo,
> Of—"Dost thou love?" and burn to answer, "No!"[32]

Byron's Gulnare acts to protect another man who represents liberty for her against the violent constraint of her master. Unlike Scheherazade and Gulnare she cannot love where she is terrorized and oppressed, and unlike Gulnare she does not speak her consent; rather she imagines in her soul a resounding (and burning) negative, which she turns into violent action. Nigel Leask notes that the Turkish slave heroine acts decisively and self-consciously against masters and men in a way that the aristocratic republican Conrad, bound by a code of honor and ultimately driven by self-interest rather than altruism, and the revolutionary anarchist pirates he leads fail to do.[33] In this she bears traces of her namesake in her preference for action over speech and her willingness to take violent action to defend an ambiguous hero. (Gulnare's role in the story of her son is to lead her [supernatural] forces against his enemies, while Beder himself is driven by the desire to possess first the princess of the sea and next the enchantress of fire.)

Gulnare represents the resistance of enslaved nations: the poem mourns the suppression of Greek culture by what Byron saw as a violent Asiatic despotism in Ottoman Turkish rule. But Byron brings the analogy closer to home in the preface to *The Corsair* composed for his friend the Irishman Thomas Moore, a preface his conservative publisher, John

Murray, sought to suppress, considering it too incendiary and likely to mitigate the work's success. Byron refers to Moore's ongoing work on an Eastern tale, *Lalla Rookh* (not published until 1817), and parallels the Irish Catholics' struggle for liberty from England with that found in the East against a torpid and tyrannous despotism:

> The wrongs of your own country, the magnificent and fiery spirit of her *sons*, the beauty and feeling of her daughters, may there be found. . . . Your imagination will create a warmer sun, and less clouded sky; but wildness, tenderness, and originality are part of your national claim of oriental descent, to which you have already thus far proved your title more clearly than the most zealous of your country's antiquarians.[34]

Byron compounded the provocation to his enemies the Prince Regent and the Tories by appending an eight-line poem, "Lines to a Lady Weeping," to the main text of *The Corsair* with a pointed reference to Ireland (the tears of a "daughter of a royal line" in the poem are described as "auspicious to these suffering isles").[35] However, the tale of *The Corsair* warns its English readers that the response of an oppressed people embodied in female form may not be visible in the tears of an attractive and compliant woman: Medora's tears on Conrad's departure

> swim
> Through those long, dark, and glistening lashes dewed
> With drops of sadness oft to be renewed.[36]

Rather, that response is marked in the spot of blood on the forehead of the violent agent of revolutionary rebellion, "the slight but certain pledge of crime" Conrad sees on Gulnare's lovely brow, a streak of red which compromises the attractions of a guilty blush and "banished all the beauty from her cheek!"[37] Here, too, we can see traces of (one of) Byron's source texts, the Gulnare and Beder story, a story in which the lovely attractions of women conceal violent loyalties to their own creeds and nations (Jauhara pretends to accept Beder's advances only to spit on him to turn him into a bird and send him to his doom on the thirsty island; Queen Lab is swift to prepare to enslave Badr in animal form when he threatens her authority).

In a deeper sense, however, it is arguable that Byron returns to and restores elements of the *Nights* that were lost in its earlier English redactions: rather than *précieuse* princes with chivalric dedication to their mistresses, he gives us a compromised hero driven by conflicting impulses; rather than a woman who uses her verbal power to soothe and soften despotic tendencies, he gives us a woman who takes up a knife to liberate herself and her fellow slaves. But he also restores to the tales the element of poetry lost in Galland's prose translation. *The Corsair*'s dedication is as concerned with the choice of poetic form as it is with the analogy to Irish circumstances: "not the most difficult, but perhaps, the best adapted measure to our language, the good old and now neglected heroic couplet,"[38] Masculine rhymed couplets in iambic pentameter appear to be an appropriate formal correlative to the conflict between Turkish and Greek commanders, which is the motive of the tale. Early in the poem the flow of the verse is associated with the "boundless" freedoms of the sea; the pirates sing,

> Oh, who can tell, save he whose heart hath tried,
> And danced in triumph o'er the waters wide,
> The exulting sense—the pulse's maddening play,
> That thrills the wanderer of that trackless way?[39]

However, the women of the poem challenge this apparent "fit" of male hearts and the rhythm of the sea felt in the pulse of verse. In canto 1, the fair-haired Greek Medora interrupts the regularity of the heroic couplet with a song in four line alternate rhymes which demands that her grief and mourning be attended to and in canto 3, the dark-haired Eastern concubine Gulnare takes up the heroic couplet and makes it her own to express her desire for liberty, action, and freedom. Nigel Leask comments that Gulnare is an uncanny double not only of Medora but also of Conrad, but she exceeds him in her ability to take swift and decisive action, even while it desexes her in his eyes (and those of the Western readers who are reading the poem): "In the figure of Gulnare, the European self is mimicked and ultimately absorbed by its oriental Other."[40] The proximity of rhyming terms in the heroic couplet strengthens a power of "doubling" found everywhere in the Jullanar source story. Gulnare's closing words, her final couplet, reveal her ability to seize and

convert the terms of engagement in a tale otherwise haunted by a fear
that its Greek characters are trapped in a sterile cycle of directionless
action or sepulchral grief (Medora weeping or laid out for mourning in
her tower, Conrad apathetic and morose imprisoned in his cell):

> If I had never loved—though less my guilt,
> Thou hadst not lived to—hate me—if thou wilt.[41]

The power of the will ("if thou wilt"), which Gulnare in Galland's version of the tale has instructed her husband "can never be conquer'd
or domineer'd over,"[42] is restored by Byron's Gulnare to a culture that
appears to have lost sight of its primary purpose: to prompt subjects to
act to protect and secure their liberties.

Perhaps unsurprisingly, Byron became for many subsequent writers the poetic touchstone for that liberty. One of his most passionate
admirers is now most famous for his own translation of the *Alf layla*,
and it is with Richard Burton's treatment of the Jullanar story in his
1885–89 translation of the *Nights* that this tale of its shifting fortunes
will close. Burton was an admirer of Byron's Oriental tales. Indeed, one
of the first notes in his version of the Jullanar story, in which he explains
the etymology of her name, embarks on a defense of the authenticity
of Byron's "Orientalism," learned at an Armenian monastery in Venice. Burton complains that Byron's genius has gone uncelebrated in his
native country. Byron here is associated with Jullanar herself, a creature
of exile and genius (in the sense of the magical powers of the jinn as well
as the creativity of the Western poet) who is made mute in a strange
land. Burton does not include the digressive conversation on slavery
and contract between his Jullanar and the king of Persia. He simply has
Jullanar say that the king's passionate love has won her own.[43] Edward
Lane's translation of the tales from 1838–40 (a translation on which we
now know Burton relied heavily) also supplies the footnote concerning the etymology of the name Jullanár but makes no mention of the
(for Lane) clearly unrespectable Byron. His heroine simply tells her
king, "had not thy heart loved me, and hadst thou not preferred me
above all thy concubines, I had not remained with thee one hour; for
I should have cast myself into the sea from this window, and gone to
my mother and my people."[44] In keeping with Burton's far racier and

sexually curious version of the *Nights*, Burton restores the scene of bird congress between Queen Lab and her mamluk overseen by the prince-hero, whereas Lane has the prince simply imply it in the prince's observation of a black bird feeding a white one "with his bill like a pigeon."[45]

Conclusion

Shape-shifting and border crossings are vital elements in the narratives of *The Thousand and One Nights*. This essay has charted the ways in which one story changed its shape as it crossed seas to Britain in the eighteenth and nineteenth centuries. "Jullanar" is a "sea-born" story, a story carried across seas to be delivered anew to a fresh readership. It is reshaped by successive authors not only to be legible to their readers in terms and genres familiar to them but also to provide them with a frisson of the strange. Jullanar describes the kingdoms of the sea in just such terms to her besotted earth prince.

However, narratives that associate the siren attractions of women's voice with the sea all too often only seem to extend liberties to their female characters to imprison them once more. Hans Christian Andersen's "little mermaid" (*Den lille havfrue*, 1836) is the result of the author's enthusiasm for the Jullanar story.[46] Marina Warner's reading of Andersen's tale and its Disney "translation" alerts us to the ways in which women's speech is both imagined and curtailed in fairy-tale narratives.[47] In order for Andersen's heroine to make her transition from the element into which she is born to the element she must inhabit to win her prince's love, she must sacrifice her power of speech. Warner charts the ways in which the mermaid, the sea creature, is conflated in successive visual and verbal depictions from Homer onward with the siren (the bird), largely through their shared capacity for seductive song. But women must choose, these narratives reiterate, between their powers of verbal enchantment and their sexual maturity (Anderson's mermaid can have voice or legs, not both). The fairy-tale teller is a woman past child-bearing age, her chatter equated with that of birds (storks and geese), and her speech concerned with the secrets of gestation and childbirth.

We can, by contrast, read Jullanar's story as one of the triumph of a female "will"—Jullanar *chooses* to remain silent, and she *chooses* to speak, rather than having sacrificed her power of speech in exchange for an earth-bound love. However, Jullanar's choice (as all her translators make clear) is determined by her fertility. It is the fact that she is pregnant (and she hopes with a son) that leads her to speak and to decide to—indeed will herself to—love the child's father. And all her later actions are determined by her love for her son and her determination to protect him and advance his cause. Maternal investment in and worship of a son is the legitimating ground of women's public agency, as Julia Kristeva reminds us in her influential essay "Stabat Mater," in which she identifies submission to a son as the price of a patriarchal religion's worship of a female figure: that of the Virgin Mary in Christian religion.[48] That Byron's Gulnare is childless is significant here—her action is taken out of love, which, as she says in her final spoken words, lessens her guilt but still unsexes her because it is not the altruistic love of mother for son but the passionate sexual love of adult woman for adult man. And it is an act of liberation from slavery and death. The fact that Galland's conclusion to his *Nights* made no mention of the three children Scheherazade bears Shahriyar in *Alf layla* may also be significant here: her powers of verbal enchantment are exercised on behalf of herself and other women subject to Shahriyar's cruel edict as well as to maintain her powers of attraction for this powerful man. Storytelling (and its attendant liberties) is, for the European audience, not compatible with maternity. The *Arabian Nights' Entertainments* arrived in Britain, we should note, in the same decades that a liberal Cartesian protofeminism began to gain ideological purchase, grounded in the claim that women's equal capacity for reason entitled them to equal opportunities for education. In this context the frame tale of Scheherazade and Shahriyar presented women's capacities for reason, for retaining knowledge, and for human sympathy as ameliorating and necessary qualities in a state otherwise driven by male appetite and self-interest. The shifting terms in which Jullanar's "liberty" is presented and debated—from Galland's *salonnière* to Scott's sentimental heroine to Byron's revolutionary agent—can also be mapped onto the history of Enlightenment feminism and its troubled attempts to incorporate rather than simply negate the "wild," the "tender," and the "original" nature of women's love into its rationalist educational ideals.[49]

NOTES

1. In the eighteenth century the Latin term *genius*—referring to the tutelary god or attendant spirit allotted to individuals at birth to govern their fortunes, to determine their character, and finally to conduct them out of the world, or to the tutelary and controlling spirit of a place or institution—was extended to incorporate ideas derived from the Arabic *jinn*, the collective name of a class of spirits (some good, some evil) supposed to interfere powerfully in human affairs. Interestingly Samuel Johnson includes no entry for *genie* in his 1755 *Dictionary* and derives his definitions of the term solely from the Latin term *genius*. On these connections in the development of the early novel see my essay "Orienting the English Novel: The Shaping Genius of the Eastern Tale in Eighteenth-Century Britain," in *Remapping the Rise of the European Novel*, ed. Jenny Mander (Oxford, UK: Voltaire Foundation, 2007), 237–48.

2. See Marina Warner, *From the Beast to the Blonde: On Fairy-Tales and Their Tellers* (London: Chatto and Windus, 1994), esp. chaps. 13 ("Absent Mothers") and 14 ("Wicked Stepmothers"), 201–40.

3. Charles Perrault, *Histoires ou contes du temps passé* (*Contes de ma Mère l'Oye*) (Paris, 1697); and Marie-Catherine le Jumel de Barneville, Baronne d'Aulnoy, *Contes des fées* (Paris, 1699).

4. Ulrich Marzolph and Richard van Leeuwen, *The Arabian Nights Encyclopedia*, 2 vols. (Santa Barbara, CA: ABC-CLIO, 2004), 1:250.

5. Muhsin Mahdi, ed., *Alf layla wa-layla*, 3 vols. (Leiden: Brill, 1984). See Heinz Grotzfeld, "The Manuscript Tradition of the *Arabian Nights*," in Marzolph and van Leeuwen, *Arabian Nights Encyclopedia*, 1:18.

6. Husain Haddawy, trans., *The Arabian Nights*, 2 vols. (London: Everyman, 1992), 1:383–428.

7. Ibid., 1:389.

8. Ibid., 1:413

9. Ibid, 1:428.

10. Ibid., 1:385.

11. *Arabian Nights' Entertainments*, 7th ed. (1728), 7:63.

12. Haddawy, *Arabian Nights*, 1:400.

13. *Arabian Nights' Entertainments* (1728), 7:127–28.

14. Haddawy, *Arabian Nights*, 1:428.

15. *Arabian Nights' Entertainments* (1728), 7:75.

16. Ibid., 7:75–76.

17. Aphra Behn, "Essay on Translated Prose," preface to *A Discovery of New Worlds: From the French, Made English by Mrs. A. Behn*, by M. de Fontenelle, in *Seneca Unmasqued and Other Prose Translations: The Works of Aphra Behn*, ed. Janet Todd, 7 vols. (London: Pickering and Chatto, 1993), 4:77.

18. C. Knipp, "The 'Arabian Nights' in England: Galland's Translation and Its Successors," *Journal of Arabic Literature* 5 (1974): 52.

19. *Arabian Nights' Entertainments* (1728), 7:64.

20. Jonathan Scott, trans., *The Arabian Nights' Entertainments* (1811), Aldine Edition, 4 vols. (Teddington, UK: Echo Library, 2006), 3:6.

21. Quoted in Fatma Moussa Mahmoud, " A Manuscript Translation of the 'Arabian Nights' in the Beckford Papers," *Journal of Arabic Literature* 7 (1976): 9.

22. See "The French Romance," in chapter 2 of Ros Ballaster, *Seductive Forms: Women's Amatory Fiction from 1684–1740* (Oxford: Oxford University Press, 1992), 42–49.

23. *Arabian Nights' Entertainments* (1728), 7:65.

24. Scott, *Arabian Nights*, 3:6.

25. *Arabian Nights' Entertainments* (1728), 7:67; Scott, *Arabian Nights' Entertainments*, 3:7.

26. *Arabian Nights' Entertainments* (1728), 7:82; Scott, *Arabian Nights' Entertainments*, 3:17.

27. *Arabian Nights' Entertainments* (1728), 7:70.

28. Haddawy, *Arabian Nights*, 1:392.

29. *Arabian Nights' Entertainments* (1728), 1:79.

30. See Ros Ballaster, *Fabulous Orients: Fictions of the East in England, 1662–1785* (Oxford: Oxford University Press, 2005); Felicity Nussbaum, *Torrid Zones: Maternity, Sexuality, and Empire in Eighteenth-Century English Narratives* (Baltimore: Johns Hopkins University Press, 2003); Ruth Bernard Yeazell, *Harems of the Mind: Passages of Western Art and Literature* (New Haven: Yale University Press, 2000); and Reina Lewis, *Rethinking Orientalism: Women, Travel, and the Ottoman Harem* (New Brunswick: Rutgers University Press, 2004).

31. Victoria Kahn, *Wayward Contracts: The Crisis of Political Obligation in England, 1640–1783* (Princeton: Princeton University Press, 2004), 283.

32. Lord Byron, *The Corsair* (1814), in *The Complete Poetical Works*, ed. Jerome J. McGann, vol. 3 (Oxford: Oxford University Press, 1981), 148–213, canto 2, lines 1106–10.

33. Nigel Leask, *British Romantic Writers and the East: Anxieties of Empire* (Cambridge: Cambridge University Press, 1992), 51.

34. Byron, *Corsair*, 149.

35. Quoted and discussed in Jeffery W. Vail, *Lord Byron and Thomas Moore* (Baltimore: Johns Hopkins University Press, 2001), 60–64 (quote on 61).

36. Byron, *Corsair*, 167, canto 1, lines 496–98.

37. Ibid., 204, canto 3, lines 417, 427.

38. Ibid., 149.

39. Ibid., 151, canto 1, lines 13–16.

40. Leask, *British Romantic Writers*, 51.

41. Byron, *Corsair*, 296, canto 3, lines 474–75.

42. *Arabian Nights' Entertainments* (1728), 7:70.

43. Richard Burton, *A Plain and Literal Translation of the Arabian Nights' Entertainments*, 16 vols. (London, 1885–88), 7:267.

44. Edward William Lane, *The Thousand and One Nights, Commonly Called, in England, The Arabian Nights' Entertainments, . . . a New Edition, from a Copy Annotated by the Translator; edited by his Nephew, Edward Stanley Poole*, 3 vols. (London: John Murray, 1859), 3:238.

45. Ibid., 3:272.

46. Marzolph and van Leeuwen, *Arabian Nights Encyclopedia*, 1:250.

47. Warner, *From the Beast to the Blonde*, 396–404.

48. Julia Kristeva, "Stabat Mater" (1977), in *The Kristeva Reader*, ed. Toril Moi (Oxford, UK: Blackwell, 1986), 160–86.

49. For a helpful summary of these debates see Karen O'Brien, "From Savage to Scotswoman: The History of Femininity," chapter 2 of *Women and Enlightenment in Eighteenth-Century Britain* (Cambridge: Cambridge University Press, 2009), 68–109.

2

Re-Orienting William Beckford:
Transmission, Translation, and Continuation
of *The Thousand and One Nights*

LAURENT CHÂTEL

The name of William Beckford of Fonthill (1760–1844; fig. 4) is well
known to Orientalists, owing to the fame of *Vathek*, which is cited each
time a reference is made to Orientalism in eighteenth-century Britain,
the *Arabian Nights*, or Samuel Johnson's *Rasselas*. But the Orientalist
connection is undermined by the "gothic" label which has often been
tacked onto him: such a univocal gothicizing of Beckford does not do
justice to his Orientalism. Moreover, the troubled edition and publication both of *Vathek* and, posthumously, of *The Episodes of Vathek* has
puzzled generations of eighteenth-century scholars and damaged or
even annihilated his reputation as an Orientalist, since the project as
a whole never saw the light of day in his lifetime. The case of Beckford's Orientalism has therefore been poorly understood or simply
not been taken seriously, even if several studies have started to make
amends recently.[1]

Beckford is still presented as a figure belonging to what some call "pseudo-orientalism in transition,"[2] ranking him alongside other British contemporaries engaged in adapting Antoine Galland's *Arabian Nights* for the English market. I would argue that by now Beckford should have earned a different place in the history of Orientalist tale telling, on the basis of his direct exposure to and use of Arabic manuscripts. Indeed he was not just content with secondary sources but had a thirst for primary, original material. In the early 1780s, Lady Elizabeth Craven (1750–1828), later Margravine of Anspach (fig. 5), provided Beckford with a lifetime opportunity to have a firsthand access to Arabic manuscripts dated 1764—the Edward Wortley Montagu, or Bodleian, "Arabian Nights."[3] This was a great privilege at the time since apart from Galland, who had used a three- or four-volume set of medieval manuscripts of *Alf layla wa-layla* imported from Syria in 1701,[4] few "Orientalists" had had access to manuscripts. Beckford may not have had the early archetypal "mother" source that Galland had, but he came close to the Frenchman's scholarly perusal of genuine manuscripts, albeit eighteenth-century ones. A study of the Wortley Montagu "Arabian Nights" enlightens Beckford's Orientalism because the direct "encounter" with these manuscripts generated a complex and diversified creativity—a story which is still unrecorded in Anglo-American literary studies; it helps define his Orientalist taste as well as recontextualize his literary output. Here I document the corpus of Beckford's oeuvre and highlight his creative input in the light of his handling of the manuscripts.

One of the main reasons for focusing on the role of the Wortley Montagu manuscripts in Beckford's life is that on publishing *Vathek* in 1786, his tutor, Samuel Henley, insinuated that it was a translation, or as he put it in the title itself, "an Arabian tale," from an unpublished manuscript. Beckford added to the confusion in his preface to the Lausanne edition of *Vathek*, saying he would publish "other tales of this kind" and explicitly naming the Montagu manuscript as the source. An indication of the first reviewers' difficulty in pinning down the genetic cradle of *Vathek* can be gauged from the sense of loss felt by Henry Maty in *A New Review, with Literary Curiosities and Literary Intelligence for the Year* (June 1786): "In Consequence of the prevalence of this taste, many before unknown have been brought to Europe; and, but a few months since, several such MSS were offered for sale in a bookseller's common catalogue. The most valuable collection of this sort, however, is supposed to be the late Worthley Montague's [*sic*], which possibly is the same that the preface of Vathek refers to." In the first sentence of that preface is an ambiguity, which leaves it doubtful whether the history be an entire translation from an Arabic original or else only founded on one.

As late as 1802, Francis Douce could still remember Henley's insinuations about *Vathek*, as can be evidenced in his marginalia to a Bodleian copy of the tale:

> One of Wortley Montagu's Mss fell into M Beckford's hands. A Turk who was on a visit to him translated into very bad English the story of Vathek which was in this MSS. M Beckford translated the Turk's version into French with great alterations & additions. M (now Dr) H. procured M. Beckfords translation which he rendered into English with notes and illustrations, in which form, it was printed, as in the present copy. Dr H. thought that M. Beckford could have added but little, as the text afforded such genuine matter for the illustration of Oriental Manners; but he felt himself at liberty to make some slight alterations in M Beckford's translation.
> F. D. From Dr H's own information, Feb 14 1802[5]

Even though Henley's insinuation was undeniably an act of villainy and jealousy, I wish to show that *Vathek* and its *Episodes* are nonetheless a much more complex case than has been contemplated in the recent critical literature on eighteenth-century and Romantic fiction. One has to allow for the subtle ambivalence of Beckford's intimacy with the "Arabian Nights" manuscripts, which were a prompt for his creativity: while Beckford himself can be credited for "correctness of costume" and "power of imagination"—to quote Byron when he praised *Vathek* for ringing so true—the *Arabian Nights* manuscripts need to be foregrounded as genetic makeup for his work.[6] Admittedly, it would be tempting to portray Beckford as a mystifier, but this would be missing the point of Beckford's aesthetics of fusion/confusion. The terms used by Byron are not mutually exclusive and do not point to either faithfulness or invention; they are a balancing act and provide the adequate touchstone by which Beckford's output should be assessed. It is a plunge in and out of the matter of the *Nights*.

The Wortley Montagu *Arabian Nights* in the Bodleian Library, Oxford

The "Montagu" version of the "Thousand and One Nights" has always received short shrift in the literature on the *Arabian Nights*, even though it was recorded and discussed by nineteenth-century Orientalists[7] and twentieth-century scholars;[8] photographs of several pages of the seven bound volumes can be seen in Muhsin Mahdi's edition of *Alf layla wa-layla*. As Richard Burton remarked, "It is not the fault of English orientalists if the MS in question is not thoroughly well-known to the world of letters."[9] Henri Zotenberg ranked them in his third category: "III. MSS. mostly of Egyptian origin, differing as much among themselves in the arrangement of the tales as do those of the other groups."[10] The Montagu manuscript is dated 1764 (Hegira 1177–78), and the language is Nilotic, as was confirmed by Burton, Zotenberg, and Massa Mahmoud.[11] It is signed by "Umar al-Safti" in a colophon of black and red ink at the end (Orient.556, fol. 205). In 1802, Edward Forster, an early English translator of Galland, noted, "The copy also, which was formerly in the possession of Dr White, has the signature of the person, who transcribed it, and of the family, to which he belonged; namely, 'Omar al Siftee;' but it has not the name of the place, where he resided; it is now therefore impossible to ascertain the place, whence Mr Montague procured the manuscript."[12] Samuel Henley was the first to describe the manuscripts publicly as having been "collected in the East by a Man of Letters," in his preface to *Vathek*.[13] Montagu brought them back from Egypt; after his death, they were kept by his adopted son, "Fortunatus," and entrusted to Robert Palmer, the Duke of Bedford's executor, who kindly lent them to Lady Craven, who wrote to Beckford, "I have taken some steps towards the Arabian manuscripts and hope . . . to tell you all—all about it. . . . Ah! Ah! Voici—Mr Palmer has sent me a Catalogue—& there are so many Arabian Manuscripts that I and my friend and some Arabian Body must lay our three heads together in order not to have the wrong one translated."[14] Lady Craven passed on the bundles of manuscripts to Beckford, who made use of them between 1780 and 1787. In 1786 or '87, they went for sale: Beckford's agent bought one bundle or "volume," and Dr. Joseph White (bapt. 1746–1814), who had held the Laudian chair of Arabic at Oxford since 1774, acquired six volumes and later one other bundle. Was it at this point that Dr. White helped Lady Craven translate the "Story of Mazin"?[15] According to Burton, "Dr. White at one time intended to translate it literally, and thereby eclipse the Anglo-French version."[16] Subsequently, Dr. White disposed of the manuscripts to Jonathan Scott. However, Scott was at pains to define the exact number of Nights extant and had to apply to their owner for help. The 1787 *Sale Catalogue* stated that there were six volumes, but there were more in fact, as other related bundles were advertised separately. Having put the matter right, Scott still deplored yet another missing volume of 140 Nights, which, on inquiry, Dr. White deemed to be in Beckford's hands:

> One or two bundles of unbound Arabic Mss of the same size and hand writing of the second volume of the Arabian tales were purchased by an Agent, for Mr. Beckford of Fonthill and I have no doubt whatever, but that the deficient part of your tales is to be found in his possession.
>
> Not having the honour of being known to Mr Beckford, I could not take the liberty of requesting a sight of his purchase. Did he know the circumstance, he would, I imagine, readily permit a transcript to be made, which I should have great pleasure in doing for the use of the Bodleian if the curators could not procure a better Copyist than myself.[17]

On checking the archival records of the Bodleian Library minutes, I found no query between 1790 and 1850 related to Beckford. In Burton's words, "Thus the third of the original eight volumes is lost."[18] No one has located the whereabouts of the missing Beckford manuscript since. Curiously, Scott, who did not dare approach Beckford privately, did not attempt either to draw his attention by some public notice kindred to the aforementioned manuscript note, especially when he publicized the presence of the manuscript in Britain in his 1797 footnotes to "A Tale from an Original MS of the Arabian Nights Translated by Jonathan Scott, Esq. of Shrewsbury"[19]

Did Beckford ever find out Orientalists were after these missing manuscript bundles? In January 1798, Scott published a description of the "Contents of the Arabick Manuscript Volumes of the Arabian Nights or Thousand and One Nights, Now in the Collection of Jonathan Scott, Esq. of Netley in Shropshire" and confirmed his translation project of the tales.[20] No mention was made of either Henley or Beckford. As it turns out, the tales were never translated by Scott, on "account of his disappointment as an orientalist . . . on discovering upon perusal that the greater part of them was unfit to appear in an English dress."[21] In *Oriental Collections* (1798–99) appeared the bilingual edition of "Introductory Chapter of the Arabian Tales" and "Story Related to an Ameer of Egypt, by a Courtier of His Own Adventures—Nights 483–489."[22] In 1811 appeared *The Arabian Nights' Entertainments, Carefully Revised*, the longer title of which boasted for the sixth volume "tales selected from the Manuscript Copy of the 1001 Nights brought to Europe by Edward Wortley Montague, Esq." Therefore only a tiny portion of the whole manuscript saw the light of day, and since then it has never been translated as a whole, be it in French or in English. In the 1880s, Richard Burton used the manuscript for volume 5 of his *Supplemental Nights* (1888) and reproduced Scott's "Table of Contents." Finally, in the 1960s, Felix Tauer translated them into German.[23]

Beckford's Encounter with the Manuscripts: A Wide Gamut of Scriptural Activities

Such a direct contact with the manuscript had a diffuse influence on Beckford, and several conclusions about his overall aesthetics can be drawn from this. First of all, it has always been assumed that Beckford heavily relied for his expertise on Barthélémy d'Herbelot (1625–95), the greatest French Orientalist of his age, and his opus, *Bibliothèque orientale, ou dictionnaire universel contenant tout ce qui regarde la connoissance des peuples de l'Orient*, which was completed and published in 1697 by Antoine Galland. One may now argue that Beckford's knowledge of the *Nights* (and his Orientalist interests) was not just vicarious, via Galland or d'Herbelot, but that he saw, touched, and was confronted with the material itself. While Beckford undeniably relied on friends for translation since he was no Arabist, such a firsthand access to manuscripts constitutes a form of exposure to the *Nights* in terms of texture, form, typography, coloring of ink, which brought him even closer to the physical matter of the *Nights* than had ever been suspected. The pages of the manuscript even bear the mark of Beckford's handling since there is a reference to him, probably made by Scott: "This is the tale mentioned by Major Ouseley as given him by Mr. Henley and taken from the oral delivery of a Turk by Mr Beckford." In fact, the mediation of the oral delivery through Zemir (the "old Mahommedan" he hired) placed him on a par with Galland and Hanna Diab (a Christian Maronite monk from Aleppo) or Jacques Cazotte and Dom Chavis (an Arab priest employed in Paris), confronted as he was with the intricacies of collective "oral" work and cultural transfers. Cazotte was his exact French contemporary who published a *Suite des Mille et une nuits* (1788–89), but mischievously playing with the public's expectations of newly found *Nights*, he actually presented his tales as a genuine follow-up while it seems to have been part translation, part invention.[24] So, oddly enough, although Beckford is often accused of "composing" and "mystifying," in this case, his Orientalism bore a greater mark of authenticity than Cazotte's pretense.[25]

Second, I would like to argue that Beckford's encounter with the manuscript was essential to his literary aesthetics: it functioned both as a prompt (an incentive as well as a guiding voice) and as a framework for his creative output. It constituted the cradle within which Beckford initiated storytelling. The true range of Beckford's Orientalist creativity is a gamut of scriptural, or fictional, gestures—I would rather refer to it as fabling—the much-cherished Western concept of "Author" giving way to storyteller, performer, impersonator, and interpreter. Beckford availed himself of all the options that the elasticity of the manuscripts of the *Nights* offered to late eighteenth-century and later Orientalists, and his "children of the *Nights*" deserve a higher ranking in the tradition of migration of the Nights to Europe. Considering that none of Cazotte's, Scott's, or Burton's works had yet appeared, Beckford should in fact be seen as a pioneer cotransmitter of the *Nights* in England— provided one recognizes it was a private transmission for a happy few that never reached the public arena (since today his venture is still not common knowledge). Let us review the range of activities, some direct, some indirect, in which Beckford took part; his transmission and continuation falls into a typology of four categories: cotranslating, writing up, adding up, and extrapolating. One may number eight tales which were taken out of volumes 4, 5, and 6 and which were the first genuine translations of Oriental tales to come out privately in England in the eighteenth century; the tales can be listed thus:

Beckford's Encounters with the Montagu Bodleian Manuscripts: Translations, Grafts, and Outgrowths in the Beckford Papers

The tales emerging out of principally volumes 3, 4, and 5 (Orient.552–54) are

1. "Histoire d'Alraoui contée à l'Emir du grand Caire"
2. "Suite de l'Histoire d'Alraoui"
3. "Histoire d'Elouard Felkanam et d'Ansel Hougioud"
4. "Histoire de Mazin"
5. "Histoire d'Aladdin, Roi de l'Yemen"
6. "Histoire du Prince Mahmed"
7. "Histoire d'Abou Niah, Roi de Moussel"
8. "Histoire de la Princesse Fatimah, Fille du Roi Ben Amer"

Other tales cannot be traced back to the seven extant manuscript volumes and may have belonged to the missing bundles bought by Beckford's agent:

9. "Histoire du Prince Ahmed, fils du Roi de Khoten, et d'Ali Ben Hassan de Bagdad"
10. "Histoire de Kebal, Roi de Damas, contée par Mamalébé, Nourrice de la Princesse Hajaïa à la Chevelure blanche"
11. "Darianoc," "Histoire de Schahanazan, roi de Tartarie ou l'Année des Epreuves, Suite des Contes Arabes"
12. "Histoire de Zinan et des trois montagnes"
13. Vathek, conte arabe
14. "Les Episodes de Vathek"

Turning now to the first stage, translating, the evidence for Beckford's activities is as follows. In 1780, he mentioned Arabs and Gabel-al-Comar (mountain on the moon): "At night we will retire to the Cell and consult our Arabians penetrate into remote countries and fancy we discover the high mountains of Gabel al Comar."[26] On June 2, 1782, he already promised tales to Lady Catherine Hamilton: "I bring you an ample treasure of musick and many a strange Arabian tale which I sooth myself with the idea of reading to you under my favourite Cliffs of Pausillippo."[27] On June 13, he admitted, "[I] would give ten Arabian tales to stretch myself on the damp floor of some watery grotto"—all the more understandable as he had just received a bundle of manuscripts: "I am far advanced in a strange letter for the conclusion, nay it would have been finished had not the remainder of my Arabian M.S arrived from old Zemir."[28]This is the first occurrence of an Arabic speaker by the name of Zemir. In December 1781, Beckford organized revelries at Fonthill with Philip James de Loutherbourg's prototype experimentation with the Eidophusikon, a proto-cinematographic experience at Leicester Square, which provided a moving picture with colored glass, candles, and other contraptions to the amazement of painters, notably Thomas Gainsborough. He recalled, "Aunt Effingham blows up the flames. . . . She tells everybody that comes in her way, royal and unroyal that she, at least is completely scandalized and believes all that wild tales which were so charitably circulated of our orientalism last December at Fonthill."[29] In October 1782, he announced that the Christmas festivities would include "a right old Mussulman to serve up tales hot & hot."[30] In January 1783, he wrote from Fonthill, "We are very clean and quiet at Fonthill, ride out every Morn, and translate Arabic every Night."[31] In May 1783, on Beckford's wedding day, Marianne-Agnès de Fauques de Vaucluse (or "de la Cépédès" or yet again "de Starck"), who taught French to Lady Craven's daughters and Sir William Jones, told Beckford she had sent him a transcription of his "Darianoc" and asked him, "Are you taking Zemir along with you?"[32] While in Switzerland, Zemir thus shared the new married couple's life. In 1786, Beckford wrote to Henley and insisted with some vehemence, "butterflies of Cachemere are celebrated in a poem of Mesihi I slaved at with Zemir, the old Mahometan who assisted me in translating W. Montague's M.S, but they are hardly worth a note."[33] In 1788, from Spain, Beckford, pretending to be "Ansel Hougioud," referred to the Princess de Listenais as Elouard Felkanaman.[34] In 1791, William Jones was still writing to Madame de Starck and Beckford for news. Sometime after 1789 or 1799, Beckford prepared a preface to "Histoire d'Elouard Felkanaman," which he called "Introduction à la Suite des Contes arabes"[35] and which today may serve as a preface to his whole Orientalist opus. (The reference to Claude Savary's *Les amours d'Anas Eloujoud et de Ouardy*, which was published both in 1789 and 1799, helps date his preface.) These references therefore attest to Beckford's cotranslation of the "Arabian Nights"; they may appear limited in quantitative terms, considering the high degree of excitement and possibly pride one is entitled to expect from a body of men and women engaged in the resumption and continuation of a process started off by Antoine Galland. To me, this is a constant reminder of the private and secluded sphere of Beckford's ventures, which escape public notice and promotion.

The second stage was to make a transcript of the oral delivery, work it up, and write it down. This stage being unrecorded, it is not possible to attribute it wholly to Beckford himself, so that I like to think of the "texts" available in the archives as a collective work involving a motley crew: Zemir, Lady Craven, Dr. White, Madame de Starck, and Beckford. The language chosen was French, and it is important to see this as a strategy to translate the *Nights* away from "little England" and English letters. Beckford would have not have seen himself as ambassador of the *Nights* despite some degree of diplomatic pride always prevailing in his character. He was working in the wake of Galland and the Earl of Caylus, perhaps also knowingly competing with Cazotte and Dom Chavis, who themselves did publish their *Suite des mille et une nuits, contes arabes* in 1788. Note the title Beckford chose, "Suite des . . . ," which is literally a follow-up to Galland's work, subtitled "Contes arabes."[36] In order to appreciate the variations and adaptations from one single source, I turn to Beckford's "Histoire d'Elouard Felkanaman et d'Ansel Hougioud" (c. 1780–1800), which is a neat transcript and rendering of the "Story of Ins Al Wujjood and Ward fil—l Akmam daughter of Ibrahim, Vizier to Sultan Shamikh" from the Wortley Montagu manuscript.[37] This was a clearly exciting addition to the Galland corpus, and later translators included it in their "continuations," thus generating parallel French and English afterlives: Savary ("Les amours d'Anas Eloujoud et de Ouardy") in 1789, Joseph-Charles Mardrus (1868–1949) in the early twentieth century ("Histoire de Rose-dans-le-Calice et de Délice du Monde"), and in 2005 a new version by Andre Miquel and Jamel Eddine Bencheikh;[38] as for the English side, Jonathan Scott ("Story of Ins Al Wujjood and Wird Al Ikmaum") in 1811 and Richard

Burton in 1886–88. The concentric circles of Scheherazade's children from Beckford down to Burton are apt to spin one's mind dizzy.

The third stage of the encounter can be designated as adding up. It is the amplification process inherent in the *Nights*—once considered to be the Western prerogative and misuse of the original material but increasingly now also thought to be attuned with the incremental, oral, transnational storytelling process. Thus, Galland's adaptations were deemed to readjust his translated prose to his contemporary audience, while Scott, Lane, and Burton expurgated what they considered inappropriate or exaggerated. Beckford, so that his tales be better "received," himself explained his line of conduct in a preface as a way perhaps to avoid the mystification he had already suffered with *Vathek*:

> [Here is] yet more arabesque that I entrust to the indulgence of the public—to the original [*passage crossed out*] can be found in the same folio into which Jonathan Scott & several of the Orientalists have digged—Savary also paraphrased this small tale in his own way—I had started translating it literally—My arabic master, an old Muslim born in Mecca had recommended it to me as a language exercise—yet I found the narration so [*crossed out*] ordinary/pompously boring that I cast it aside—Zémir tried to bridle me, quite rightly, but having taken the bit between my teeth I galloped away into the regions of my own imagination. Here is the result—it is very little—it amused me in the past, but I do not guarantee that it will produce an equally pleasant effect on the readers/ the same effect on others:—[39]

Unlike Pétis de la Croix or his exact contemporary Cazotte, Beckford did not go for forgeries since his manuscripts were genuine. He acknowledged that the content of the tale could be found in the Montagu manuscript; he clearly discriminated between literal translations (which he made at one point for language training) and pleasant narrations "galloping out" of the translations. He was humorously outlining the nuances attendant on the handling of "Oriental" material, explaining the "Orientalist" process of transforming or "translating" the oral renderings of an Arabic speaker into a European language. Several types of "interpretations" can be identified.

First of all, Beckford often added spaces, settings, and landscapes as an extension of a topographical detail; such an "addition" ranged from one line to several lines: a long landscape description of a pond and pyramids ("bassin d'eau et pyramides"), the spatial evocations of the land of Camphre and Vac-Vac islands in "The Story of Mazin" or that of the Djinns' plain, Zouc-Zouc Valley, and the ruined tower in the "Story of Ahmed." The second type could be a psychological motivation absent from, or sometimes minimal, in the original. The third type is perhaps the most Beckfordian touch of all: a change of tone. Beckford's pervasive tonal strategy wavered between deflation and inflation, bathos and climax—as if he went up and down a spiral, now down in depths, now up in heights. Thus, by no means was his writing only a form of pastiche or parody, which is too strictly limited to humorous or satiric effect. Parody is only one side to his aesthetics of sublimity, which consisted in transcending radically the overall tone. His instrumentalization of the tales served a rhetoric of allurement and entrapment—in fact, just as much self-entrapment as entrapment of a prospective audience: opening the eyes and ears wider and wider, inoculating them radically to horror, the uncanny, the strange, and the great. The fourth type is the writing up of an episode over several pages, prompted by a reference in the original. In the "Histoire d'Elouard Felkanaman et d'Ansel Hougioud," one finds embedded in the tale a typically Beckfordian subterranean story (inside a pyramid). What appears as a tiny incidental tale in Jonathan Scott ("the mountainous island of Tukkalla, of which the vizier of sultan Shamikh gave to his companion the following account") is amplified by Beckford into a story within the story ("Story of the Ginn Fikelah and the Prince Chemnis"); in the economy of the whole tale it is justified, as it were, as it sheds light on the reasons for the terrible uproar of birds on the balustrade crying out "She has delivered! She has delivered!"[40] This principle of amplification leads me to the last stage in the typology: extrapolation. A number of tales cannot be traced back to the Montagu originals: "Darianoc," "Prince Ahmed," "Kebal," Vathek ("Wathiq"), and the "Episodes de Vathek." Although one is naturally left wondering whether the missing bundles of 140 Nights constituted starting points for some of Beckford's stories, it is more than likely that Vathek and The Episodes of Vathek was a creation ex nihilo. But the narrative about Beckford's Orientalism should be dual and ambivalent:

while there is no reason why one should suspect his writings to be lifted out of the *Nights*, yet one has every reason to suspect that they should somehow be connected with them.

Conclusion

A study of the Montagu "Arabian Nights" and Beckford's handling of them considerably complexifies Beckford's literary output. The isolation in which *Vathek* is often examined should give way to a contextualization within the bedrock of the *Nights*. While *Vathek* is inescapably, inevitably, and necessarily Beckfordian—and the hallmark of Western appropriation of the Oriental tale—I wish to contend that it should not be seen, read, or studied in isolation from Beckford's encounters with the *Nights*, since they are the proper framework or frame for which *Vathek* had been planned. Another reason why one should think of *Vathek* and *The Episodes of Vathek* as part of a whole is that this understanding sheds light on their genesis and making process. Instead of perceiving them as an ex nihilo creation (which would fit in neatly with the romantic and postromantic ideal of the demiurgic author), they ought to be conceived as a palimpsestual layering and an embedded crisscrossing of source materials. Beckford interpolated himself in the translated lace of *The Thousand and One Nights*, now varying the tone, now extrapolating to add a more oneiric or nightmarish episode; such interventions recall acts of impish and boyish playfulness typical of performers and impersonators. Admittedly, one could endlessly speculate as to what Beckford had envisaged as editorial project, perhaps a "Suite des contes arabes" followed up by *Vathek et les Episodes*, or the other way around. But there is no doubt that *Vathek* was *not* meant to stand on its own; Beckford's instructions were, for once, very clear in August 1786: "The anticipation of so principal a tale as that of the Caliph would be tearing the proudest feather from my turban," and "I would not have him on any account come forth without his companions."[41] In this light, *Vathek* and *The Episodes* appear to be a duplication of the cyclical process of storytelling of the *Nights*, a recycling of Scheherazade's voice. After all, the tales are motivated and actuated by an identical stratagem: to defer the death sentence which hangs over them, Scheherazade,

Vathek, and his companions alike perform a suspension of time. As Beckford's tale tellers put it, to "trace back our crimes to their source, though we are not permitted to repent, is the only employment suited to wretches like us!"[42]

NOTES

1. See Diego Saglia, "William Beckford's 'Sparks of Orientalism' and the Material-Discursive Orient of British Romanticism," *Textual Practice* 16:1 (2002): 75–92; and Donna Landry, "William Beckford's *Vathek* and the Uses of Oriental Re-enactment," in *The Arabian Nights in Historical Context: Between East and West*, ed. Saree Makdisi and Felicity Nussbaum, 167–94 (Oxford: Oxford University Press, 2008).

2. Mahmoud Manzalaoui, "Pseudo-Orientalism in Transition: The Age of Vathek," in *William Beckford of Fonthill, 1760–1844: Bicentenary Essays*, ed. Fatma Moussa Mahmoud, 123–50 (Port Washington, NY: Kennikot, 1964).

3. The Montagu manuscripts are housed in the Bodleian Library, Oxford, under the shelfmark Orient. 550–57. To add a sense of mystery, complexity, and confusion (not unlike all that concerns Beckford himself), it is to be noted that although there are eight volumes (550–57), there are in fact only seven volumes of *Nights* —the last one being Jonathan Scott's notes and table of contents. Since Beckford handed back the manuscript in 1787, one volume of 140 *Nights* has been missing and as yet never recovered.

4. Arabic MSS 3609–11, Bibliothèque Nationale de France, Paris.

5. This is written down on flyleaves in Francis Douce's copy of *Vathek*, Bodleian Library, Oxford.

6. George Gordon Byron, *The Giaour—A Fragment of a Turkish Tale* (London: John Murray, 1813), note 43, line 1334.

7. Jonathan Scott referred to them in the preface to his *Tales, Anecdotes, and Letters Translated from the Arabic and Persian* (London: Cadell and Davies, 1800) and published some of the tales in *The Arabian Nights' Entertainments, to Which Is Added a Selection of New Tales, Now First Translated from the Arabic Originals, Also with Introduction and Notes*, 6 vols. (London: Longman, Hurst, Rees, Orme, and Brown, 1811); Richard Burton published an explanatory note about the manuscripts in his *Supplemental Nights to the Book of The Thousand Nights and a Night: With Notes Anthropological and Explanatory*, 6 vols. (Benares: Kama-shastra Society, 1886–88), 5:ix–xvii; he also printed a "Catalogue of Wortley Montague Manuscript Contents," in *Supplemental Nights*, 5:497–505 (app. 1), and he translated a selection of tales which form the bulk of volume 5 of his *Supplemental Nights*. As for Henri Zotenberg, he referred to them in *Histoire d'Alâ Al-Dîn ou la lampe merveilleuse: Texte arabe publié avec une notice sur quelques manuscrits des Mille et une nuits* (Paris: Imprimerie Nationale, 1888), 50–51.

8. Victor Chauvin, *Bibliographie des ouvrages arabes ou relatifs aux arabes publiés dans l'Europe chrétienne de 1810 à 1885*, 12 vols. (Liège: Vaillant-Carmanne, 1892–1922); Nikita Elisséef, *Thèmes et motifs des Mille et une nuits* (Beirut: Institut Français de Damas, 1949); Mia I. Gerhardt, *The Art of Story-Telling: A Literary Study of the Thousand and One Nights* (Leiden: Brill, 1963); Muhsin Mahdi, *Alf layla wa-layla: From the Earliest Known Sources, Arabic Text Edited with Introduction and Notes*, 3 vols. (Leiden: Brill, 1984–94); Robert Irwin, *The Arabian Nights—A Companion* (London: Penguin Books, 1994).

9. Burton, "The Translator's Foreword," in *Supplemental Nights*, 5:x.

10. W. F. Kirby, "Additional Notes on the Bibliography of the *Thousand and One Nights*," in Burton, *Supplemental Nights*, 6:356–84 (app. 4; an updated version of his "Notes" previously published in Burton, *A Plain and Literal Translation of the Arabian Nights Entertainments*, 16 vols. [Benares: Kamashastra Society, 1885], 10:414 [app. 2]).

11. Burton, *Supplemental Nights*, 5:497–505; Zotenberg, *Histoire d'Alâ Al-Dîn*; Fatma Moussa Mahmoud, "A Manuscript Translation of the *Arabian Nights* in the Beckford Papers," *Journal of Arabic Literature* 7 (1976): 7–23.

12. Edward Forster, postscript to advertisement, in *The Arabian Nights in Five Volumes with Engravings by Robert Smirke*, 2nd ed. (London: William Miller, 1815), 5:lxi.

13. The first edition of *Vathek* was brought out not by Beckford himself but by Henley, who drafted a preface: *An Arabian Tale, from an Unpublished Manuscript: With Notes Critical and Explanatory* (London: Printed for J. Johnson, St. Paul's Church-Yard, and Entered at the Stationers' Hall, 1786), viii.

14. Lady Craven to Beckford, n.d. (c. 1780–82), MS Beckford c.29, Beckford Papers.

15. Jonathan Scott left an enlightening note in the margin of vol. 4 of the Montagu Papers: "The Story of Mazin, which Dr White says he translated for Lady Craven, now Margravine of Anspach" (Orient.553, fol. 179). This story is one of the translations in the Beckford Papers (MS Beckford d.25).

16. Burton, "Translator's Foreword," 5:ix.

17. Dr. Joseph White to Jonathan Scott, n.d., Orient.557, fols. 12–13, Montagu Papers.

18. Burton, *Supplemental Nights*, 5:499 (app. 1),

19. William Ouseley, *Oriental Collections: Consisting of Original Essays and Dissertations, Translations and Miscellaneous Papers; Illustrating the History and Antiquities, the Arts, Sciences, and Literature of Asia*, 3 vols. (London: Cadell and Davies, 1797–99), 1:245.

20. Ouseley, *Oriental Collections*, 2:25.

21. Scott, preface to *Arabian Nights' Entertainments*, 1:xv.

22. "Introductory Chapter of the Arabian Tales" (from Orient.550, Montagu Papers), in Ouseley, *Oriental Collections*, vol. 2, no. 2, 160–74; vol. 2, no. 3, 228–56; "Story Related to an Ameer of Egypt, by a Courtier of His Own Adventures—Nights 483–489" (from Orient.553, fols. 70–78, Montagu Papers), in Ouseley, *Oriental Collections*, vol. 2, no. 4, 349–67. The "Story . . . Egypt" corresponds to the "Story

of Al Raoui," which can be found both in French and in English in the Beckford Papers and in a printed form in *The Story of Al Raoui, a Tale from the Arabic*, almost certainly printed by Henley in 1799.

23. Felix Tauer, *Erzählungen aus den Tausendundein Nächten, zum ersten Male aus dem arabischen Urtext der Wortley-Montague-Handschrift der Oxforder Bodleian Library übertragen und hrsg. von Felix Tauer* (Frankfurt: Insel, 1966).

24. For recent light on the matter, see Joseph Sadan, "Jacques Cazotte, His Hero Xaïloun, and Hamîda the Kaslân: A Unique Feature of Cazotte's 'Continuation' of the *Arabian Nights* and a Newly Discovered Arabic Source That Inspired His Novel on Xaïloun," *Marvels & Tales* 18:2 (2004): 286–99.

25. Orient.553, fol. 78, Montagu Papers.

26. Beckford to unidentified correspondent (probably A. Cozens), dated "Naples, Nov 16th 1780," MS Beckford e.1, Red Copy Book no. 33, Beckford Papers; printed in Lewis Melville, *The Life and Letters of William Beckford of Fonthill, Author of "Vathek"* (London: W. Heinemann, 1910), 96.

27. Beckford to Lady C. Hamilton, June 2, 1782, MS Beckford e.1, Red Copy Book no. 37, Beckford Papers.

28. Beckford to S. Henley, June 13, 1782, MS Beckford e.1, Red Copy Book no. 48, Beckford Papers.

29. Beckford to Louisa Beckford, c. March 1782 but rewritten in the 1830s, MS Beckford d.1, Beckford Papers; printed in Guy Chapman, *Beckford* (London: J. Cape, 1937), 121.

30. Beckford to S. Henley, October 28, 1782, in Alfred Morrison, *Collection of Autograph Letters and Historical Documents*, 2nd ser. (privately printed, 1893), vol. 1, no. 18, 187..

31. Beckford to Sir William Hamilton, January 4, 1783, in Melville, *Life and Letters*, 165.

32. "Voilà votre Darianoc. C'est pour vous l'envoyer que je vous écris. N'est-ce pas aussi pour vous dire combien je vous souhaite de bonheur dans votre double voyage? Oh! cela n'est pas nécessaire; vous devez trop bien connaître le cœur de votre sincère amie. Vous emportez donc Zémir?" MS Beckford c.35, Beckford Papers.

33. Beckford to S. Henley, February 9, 1786, in Melville, *Life and Letters*, 135–36.

34. See correspondence with Prince de Carency (Paul-Maximilien-Casimir de Quelen de Stuer de Caussade), MS Beckford c.27, fols. 63–85, Beckford Papers.

35. MS Beckford d.23, Beckford Papers.

36. It is important to make this distinction, as the edition produced in France in the 1990s missed the point about the translation/adaptation makeup and got the title wrong; indeed "suite de," which means "a string of," does not convey the idea that Beckford was presenting himself as a direct follower of Galland; see *Suite de contes arabes*, ed. Didier Girard (Paris: José Corti, 1992).

37. Orient. 553 (vol. 4), "Night 520" (fols. 120 verso) up to "Night 540" (fol. 149), Montagu Papers.

38. Claude Savary, *Les amours d'Anas Eloujoud et de Ouardy* (Paris: Chez Onfroy, 1789); for Mardrus, see *Le livre des Mille et une nuit: Traduction littérale et complète du livre arabe*, 16 vols. (Paris: Editions de la Revue Blanche, 1899–1904). The latest French translation of the *Nights* is Andre Miquel and Jamel Eddine Bencheikh, *Les mille et une nuits*, 3 vols. (Paris: Gallimard, 2005–6).

39. "Preface," MS Beckford d.23, xix–xxi, Beckford Papers: "[Voici] encore de l'arabesque que je livre à l'indulgence publique—l'original [*crossed out*] se trouve dans le même recueil ou Jonathan Scott & plusieurs Orientalistes ont puizé —Savary aussi a paraphrasé ce petit conte à sa manière—J'avais commencé à le traduire litéralement—Mon maitre d'arabe, un vieux Musulman né natif de la Mecque, me l'avoit recommandé comme exercice de langue—J'ai trouvé pourtant la narration si si peu [*illegible*] si ordinaire ^{pompeusement ennuieuse} que je l'ai jetté de côté—Zémir voulut me brider, comme de raison, mais ayant pris le mors au dents je me suis emporté à grand galop dans les régions de ma propre imagination. Voici le résultat—c'est peu de chose—il m'a amusé dans le temps, mais je ne repond pas qu'il produira sur les lecteurs un effet également agréable:—WB ^{mais je ne repond pas qu'il produira le même effet sur les autres}." In Didier Girard's French edition of the tales, the spelling was changed, the variants left out, and "voyageuse imagination" (traveling imagination) substituted for "propre imagination" (my own imagination).

40. MS Beckford, d.23, Beckford Papers.

41. Beckford to S. Henley, February 1786 and August 1786, in Melville, *Life and Letters*, 135–36.

42. William Beckford, *Vathek*, ed. Roger Lonsdale (Oxford: Oxford University Press, 1970), 116.

3

The Collector of Worlds

Richard Burton, Cosmopolitan Translator of the Nights

PAULO LEMOS HORTA

In Iliya Troyanov's fictionalized life of Richard Burton, *The Collector of Worlds*, the author presents Burton's experience of exploration and travel as an unraveling of certainties and a journey from clarity into confusion. He imagines Burton in his 1853 pilgrimage to Mecca longing to gather his experiences in writing yet doubting his ability to convey the cognitive dissonance produced by travel and cultural immersion to a lay reader who has experienced neither:

> He will decipher his notes, stick the torn pieces of paper together, write up his observations. If there is something he is looking forward to, it is this recollection in writing. He won't write everything, confide every-thing. . . . He won't reveal his feelings, not all of them, especially because he hasn't always been sure of what they are. He doesn't want to bring more uncertainty into the world. That would be inappropriate, and he can't allow himself such openness. Who in England will be able to follow

him into that twilight; who will be able to understand that the answers are more heavily veiled than the questions?[1]

Collecting a foreign world signaled the undoing of, rather than the reinforcement of, an original worldview. In Burton's account he had found himself sharing in the spontaneous enthusiasm of the pilgrims when first sighting Medina, yet the enthusiasm that he felt seeing the Kaaba in Mecca was suffused with pride in having reached these sites of pilgrimage as an outsider. In his travelogues Burton wrote self-consciously from a third perspective, neither English nor local, which he alternatively termed that of the wanderer, the traveler, and the cosmopolite (fig. 22).

Troyanov, himself the author of travelogues, is finely attuned to the extent Burton in his travelogues tends to shield his innermost thoughts, evident in Burton's self-fashioning as a cosmopolite. Even as Burton laid claim to the word as a badge of honor, he appears to have deployed the term in his travelogues to emphasize his distance from other, more insular identities. The young Burton in South Asia had the habit of antagonistically addressing his voice, as if in a dramatic monologue, to an absent "John Bull," the prototypical Englishman with his ingrained opinions. Burton mocks John Bull for clinging to a maudlin sense of home inculcated through "rod-taught" lines that located English identity in the ruins of the countryside.[2] Burton was not the British Orientalist scholar abroad who arrived in South Asia with his prejudice in favor of Hindus and against Muslims, an equation Burton sought to reverse from the perspective of the "cosmopolite." And he was not the typical imperialist. As a critic of conventional British values and beliefs, Burton was deeply skeptical of the standard "improving" arguments for Empire, either through the missionary activity he disdained, the economic policy he felt to be misguided and of little benefit to colonial subjects, or the imposition of "civilizing" laws that would ban *sati* or polygamy. In his "Translator's Foreword" to the *Nights*, Burton argued that Britain, ever forgetful of being "the greatest Mohammedan Empire in the world," needed colonial administrators versed in Arabic rather than Greek and Latin and positively inclined to Muslim values.[3] His cosmopolitan theory of empire was predicated on the need to absorb foreign cultural influences, rather than to assert Britain abroad.

In the realm of literary translation, to which Burton's labor on the *Nights* pertains, he most clearly articulated the virtues of a cosmopolitan practice. "Let us not be behind our neighbours in the race for a truly cosmopolitan literature," he entreated his fellow readers of the *Athenaeum* in a letter in February 1872 titled "Translations."[4] He recalled being present at a dinner where Thackeray proclaimed French literature the "wisest" European literature because "the most cosmopolitan—cosmopolitan because most given to translating!" Translation gave French literature, Burton argues, "the enormous advantage of being capable of comparing native with foreign ideas and views of the world." Burton channels his traveler's experience to proclaim the virtues of a comparative perspective:

> [Through translation French literature] was a traveller who sees many men and their cities, instead of studying the circle, large or small, of his immediate neighbourhood. It was the novelist who seeks fresh impressions from life beyond his study, instead of . . . drawing solely upon one imagination, which is necessarily a limited liability affair, uncommonly likely some day not to honour his cheques.[5]

The cognitive dissonance made possible by the experience of a foreign culture was thus demonstrated via the impact of translations from foreign literature on the national culture. To enable English literature to become cosmopolitan in the manner of the French, Burton proposes the creation of a fund for translations from "all languages," England possessing "surely . . . a thousand men who are willing to subscribe a guinea per annum" to establish it.[6]

Contrary to the popular identification of Burton as an Orientalist, his letter to the *Athenaeum* on translations, with its privileging of Brazilian literature as a conspicuous absence from English letters, fairly reflected his preoccupations as a translator. His itinerant childhood on the Continent from the age of six months left him with a store of Latin languages (French, Spanish, Bernais, Italian, Neapolitan) that enabled him to quickly pick up Portuguese in Goa in his early twenties. Translating Camoes became a lifelong literary labor: from the first attempts published in the *Bombay Times* and the *Anglo-Brazilian Times* to the ten volumes completed in the 1880s. Burton's cosmopolitan practice calls for translation of unknown works rather than merely the retranslation of the already canonical, and in this respect Brazilian literature served his argument perfectly, as it was, in his view, a major body of work wrongly ignored in Britain. Burton himself translated José de Alencar's *Iracema*, J. M. Pereira da Silva's *Manuel de Morais*, and, in an intended demonstration of his argument, the colonial poem *O Uruguai* by Jose Basilio da Gama. The time he devoted to translating from the Portuguese rivaled that he devoted to Arabic, and his overall translation from Romance languages rivaled his output from "Oriental" languages. What appears to have determined the reception of Burton as an Orientalist was the greater demand for his translations from "Oriental" rather than Romance languages, which mirrored the greater interest in his "Oriental" travelogues.

In the 1872 letter Burton was appreciative of this gap in demand; for this reason he excepted Oriental literatures from his proposal for a fund for literary translation, reasoning that they were already well supported. This stance upends the assumptions of every scholar that has written on Burton after Said's *Orientalism*. Burton was quite aware that the political and economic interests of empire would guarantee a demand for Oriental literature; what he sought with his proposed fund was the translation precisely of what could not be so readily instrumentalized or commodified. While he made a claim for the potential enrichment of English letters by translation from Brazilian Portuguese, he expected other arguments to be made on behalf of translations from Russian, Dutch, Walloon, Bernais, Basque, and Scandinavian languages. This emphasis on what he believed to be relatively unappreciated traditions in England (Russian, Dutch, and Portuguese) and on "minor" languages hardly provides a guide to the imperial preoccupations of Britain in the late nineteenth century. A type of defensive imperialism is at play in Burton's call for London to become a more truly cosmopolitan (and presumably no less imperial) capital in the manner of Paris. But it does not amount to a simple one-to-one equivalency between the literatures he felt needed attention and the territories the British Empire needed to conquer, subdue, or trade with.

Burton's cosmopolitan case for translation reflects with characteristic extravagance his willingness to champion or reject specific national literary traditions. He thus argued that while English letters had under-appreciated the value of colonial Brazilian literature, it had greatly over-rated that of early colonial Anglo-American literature. Burton's Franco-philia, a product of his Continental upbringing, positively inclines him toward Brazilian improvisations on a French novelistic model, both original and derivative in nature. It also likely informs his dismissal of the aesthetics of early colonial American literature. That Burton argued for translations from all literatures did not mean that he believed that once available they should all be regarded as equal. He was not quite the cultural relativist and proto-postmodernist that some scholars—notably Dane Kennedy—would like to construe him to be.[7] Burton felt quite at ease from his perch as a cosmopolitan in dispensing judgments of relative cultural value. As a youth he had acquired and internalized tastes that famously alienated him from the conventions and fashions of England. As a literary commentator and translator he acknowledged his judgments of the relative aesthetic merit of different cultural products to be informed by his foreign cultural experiences and immersions. His judgment was informed by biases and preferences acquired abroad that inclined him in favor of and against particular cultures and national literary traditions, what one might term *cosmopolitan prejudices*.

Burton's gift for cultural shape-shifting and accumulating world-views, what Anthony Appiah terms his "freak" ability to go native "and so time and time again," served as the philosopher's point of departure in disentangling what he argues to be the two ethical imperatives of cosmopolitanism.[8] For Appiah Burton personifies the second cosmo-politan imperative, which he defines as "the recognition that human beings are different and that we can learn from each other's differ-ences."[9] Appiah inherits from Burton's biographers a sense of Burton's extreme malleability before cultural influences and his capacity to absorb foreign influences that "brought him to the point where he could see the world from perspectives different from the outlook in which he had been brought up."[10] Appiah also inherits from Burton scholars (Dane Kennedy in particular) the sense that Burton had remained in some respects rooted in a Victorian upbringing manifest in his writ-ing in the form of residual prejudices typical of Victorian Britain. For Appiah this ingrained bias explains why, when faced with the reality of slavery in East Africa, Burton failed to empathize or intervene.[11] While Burton was the consummate cosmopolitan according to Appiah's second cosmopolitan imperative, he fails to demonstrate the sense of ethical obligation toward all that Appiah claims as the first cosmopolitan imperative. Appiah thus declares Burton to be both cosmopolitan and countercosmopolitan. Yet on closer examination this demarcation between cosmopolitan and countercosmopolitan tendencies in Burton's writing appears artificial.

Appiah inherits from Kennedy the conviction that Burton was the most, as well as the least, Victorian of men. Kennedy contends that Burton was imbued with notions of English patriotism and superiority in expatriate British communities in his peripatetic childhood on the Continent. In Kennedy's stress, it was "the very precariousness of these expatriates' position on the continent that caused them to place so much emphasis on their English identity." No amount of travel and foreign residence could allow Burton to overcome "his society's ethnocentric conviction that Britain stood at the apex of civilization, serving as its avatar of progress."[12] In this hypothesis, Burton's childhood, however peripatetic, would not have been sufficiently cosmopolitan in Appiah's sense.

Appiah rightly draws attention to the presence of prejudice in Burton's cosmopolitan thinking, yet in the example that he gives (as so often the case with Burton) it is a prejudice acquired abroad, a cosmopolitan prejudice. Burton's "freak" talent for cultural immersion was nowhere more manifest than in his sympathy for an adopted culture's values and ability to internalize its prejudices. Sharing the prejudices of a foreign culture, for him, was a requisite step for acceptance and immersion. What is most distinctive about Burton's prejudice in the East African travels that Appiah refers to is Burton's indictment of certain tribes for failure to properly observe the rites of Islam. Local imams are chastised for failing to properly recite and interpret suras from the Qur'an.[13] Whatever the residual elements of prejudice in his thought, his proffered solution for the moral and economic development of East African tribes was hardly typically Victorian: not less but better adherence to Islam. As he ventured in the "Terminal Essay" to the *Nights*, Burton believed Islam more historically evolved and adaptable to modern circumstances than Christianity.[14]

Burton's case for translation as a cosmopolitan practice, inclusive of attendant prejudices, underscored the statement of his credentials to translate the *Nights* as a cosmopolite rather than as an Orientalist. Burton, self-styled collector of worlds, did not stake his authority as cultural interpreter of the *Nights* on knowledge of a single culture and country, as would previous and subsequent translators and editors of the *Nights*. His precursor Edward Lane's goal had been cultural authenticity. He translated and commented on the *Nights* (1838–1840) out of the conviction that the tales could be traced to Cairo.[15] He procured manuscripts and sought out cultural informants in Cairo during his sojourn in the 1830s that would illuminate this specifically Egyptian, Arab, and Muslim culture which he felt could still be glimpsed from under the successive impacts of Ottoman influence and French occupation. Modern scholarship on the *Nights*, as exemplified by the editorial practice of Muhsin Mahdi, is similarly motivated to identify a single genesis for the *Nights* and hence sculpt an ur-text. Lane and Mahdi would prune the corpus of tales that could not be traced to their preferred origin narratives for the story collection, notably the orphan tales added by Hanna Diyab and Antoine Galland but also numerous tales in Arabic added too late for their privileged time frames. Mahdi's ur-text, cleared of what Husain Haddawy would term the grime of European reception and translation,[16] became the basis for new versions of the *Nights* in English, Spanish, German, and Portuguese and established an editorial practice followed by editors of anthologies of world literature that determined that the later additions and the orphan tales did not warrant inclusion as they were not representative of the "actual" *Nights*.

For Burton the *Nights* offered a cosmopolitan education. For him the key, as in the letter to the *Athenaeum*, was the cognitive broadening of horizons that the reading of tales from differing cultures could provoke in the English and European reader. Magical tales with their "outraging probability" and "outstripping possibility" work "a strange fascination" on the European reader, who, surrendering to the spell, feels "almost inclined to enquire 'and why may it not be true?'"[17] The European reader is offered a disruptive education in the unknown and the unexplored. He or she encounters the *Nights'* tales of magic as the traveler does "the sudden prospect of magnificent mountains seen after a long desert-march: they arouse strange longings and indescribable desires; their marvelous imaginativeness produces an insensible brightening of the mind and an increase of fancy-power, making one dream that behind them lies the new and unseen, the strange and unexpected —in fact, all the glamour of the unknown."[18] The *Nights* tales afford a cognitive reorientation akin to that brought forth by geographical exploration.

For Burton only the traveler could translate the writing of the traveler, and only the cosmopolite could serve as guide to the cosmopolitan material of the *Nights*. The European reader of the *Nights* would be initiated into their cultural syncretism and into a religious and sexual cosmopolitanism. The *Nights* fable is a longer variation on the fable that allows for multiple morals and that speaks to the syncretism of its development: "Aegypto-Greco-Indian stories overran the civilized globe between Rome and China. Tales have wings and fly farther than the jade hatchets of proto-historic days."[19] Likewise the *Nights* fairy tale is not properly Arabian but Persian, the product of a culture that "repeated for Babylonian art and literature what Greece had done for Egyptian."[20] The *Nights* tales offer a kaleidoscopic unfolding of worldviews that only Burton as traveler feels qualified to explain. In the historical and legendary Baghdad of the caliph Haroun al-Rashid, Burton admires "the cosmopolitan views which suggest themselves in a meeting-place of nations."[21] Greek, Persian, and Sufi influences are key to what Burton finds to be the most timely cosmopolitan lesson the *Nights* tales have to teach his British contemporaries in 1885—tolerance of homosexuality.

To Burton's cosmopolitan practice of translation English literature owes its expansive and inclusive understanding of the corpus of the *Nights*. With regard to the "original" corpus of tales possessing Arabic originals Burton adopted the broadest criteria for inclusion, shoehorning very late additions to the story collection, such as the tales he grouped under the rubric of "*Ana*" that interested him for their frank discussion of sexual practices inclusive of homosexuality.[22] National literature specialists before and after him, from Lane to Mahdi, objected to this inclusiveness, insisting on the purity of an original text indebted to a particular urban culture at a specific moment in time. While the Grub Street edition from Antoine Galland's French translation had almost immediately established the popularity of the orphan tales contributed by Hanna Diyab, Lane had omitted them, and it was left for

Burton to reintroduce them under the rubric of a cosmopolitan rather than an Orientalist method and conception of the text.

Even John Payne, Burton's close collaborator, only introduced Aladdin under the impression that an Arabic original for the tale had been successfully procured. Burton tellingly included the tale despite misgivings about the Arabic manuscript, which he correctly judged to have been made from Galland's French, and brazenly proclaimed in an advertisement to subscribers that he was ready to produce Arabic originals for other orphan tales by translating first from French into Arabic and only then from Arabic into English. For scholars and translators who conceive of the *Nights* as transcending a single national tradition Burton's expansive sense of the corpus remains influential. All entries in Ulrich Marzolph and Richard van Leeuwen's *Arabian Nights Encyclopedia* refer to the tales by their titles in the Burton edition (because the most comprehensive),[23] and Malcolm Lyons likewise preferred the more complete Macnaghten text (Calcutta 1839–42 or Calcutta II) as the basis for his translation.[24] Yet Lyons includes only "Aladdin" and "Ali Baba" from the orphan tales of Diyab and Galland and excludes "Prince Achmed," which was so seminal in the early history of cinema.

The distinctiveness of Burton's cosmopolitan practice of translation vis-à-vis the national focus of Lane is evident in his treatment of the anecdote of the "Mirror of Ink," which both men combined to successfully affiliate with the literary universe of the *Nights* in English by alluding to it in notes to their versions of the tales. In the late 1830s the London press registered its astonishment at Edward Lane's account of "one of the most extraordinary feats of magic that have been recorded since the time of the Pharaohs."[25] In notes to his *Nights* translation and his travelogue *Modern Egyptians* Lane factually described the operation of a magic mirror of ink that with the mediation of the jinn show the visage of any man dead or alive. In Lane's drawing room in Cairo, Sheykh El Maghrabee had removed the veil from the invisible world through a magic diagram drawn on the palm of a young Egyptian boy (see fig. 23), who in response to Lane's challenge successfully described the distinctive features of Lord Horatio Nelson from the reflections in the ink pooled in his hand.[26] Lane's authority on the *Nights* was derived from his cultural immersion in Cairo in the 1830s and 1840s: Lane settled in a native quarter of the city, adopted the etiquette and dress of the Ottomanized elite, became fluent in Arabic, and took on the name al-Fackeer Mansoor. Sheykh El Maghrabee was one in a procession of locals who gifted him with the chance to witness forbidden knowledge of Cairo.

"The mirror of ink" proves uncannily prominent in Burton's self-fashioning as a cosmopolite, from his travelogues to his *Nights* translation. In an early travelogue of the Sindh, Burton intuited that the presence in India "of the Egyptian practice of seeing figures shifting over the ink poured into a boy's hand" must point to a pre-Islamic genesis for this mode of divination. He interprets the practice of clairvoyance with the mirror of ink in Sindh by Muslims and Hindus alike as evidence for his conjecture that "it probably originated in India, . . . thence it might have traveled westward to Egypt and the Maghrib."[27] In effect he rebukes Lane: you must collect many worldviews, not just one.

Likewise in Burton's account of his pilgrimage to Mecca, where he emerges in the guise of a dervish who himself has mastered the ink mirror, Burton stresses that the practice of clairvoyance with the aid of a magic mirror is not unique to Egypt or the Middle East but is universal and familiar to Western capitals. Burton observes with irony reports that Lane's account of the Egyptian magician "'excited considerable curiosity throughout the civilized world.' As usual in such matters, the civilized world was wholly ignorant of what was going on at home; otherwise in London, Paris, and New York, they might have found dozens studying the science."[28] To best Lane, Burton emphasizes the global history of the mirror of ink: "This invention dates from the most ancient times, and both in the East and West has been used by the weird brotherhood to produce the appearance of the absent and the dead, to discover treasure, to detect thieves, to cure disease, and to learn the secrets of the unknown world. The Greeks used oil poured into a boy's hand. . . . In Southern Persia, ink is rubbed upon the seer's thumb-nail. . . . Even the barbarous Finns look into a glass of brandy."[29] Here in the *Personal Narrative*, as in the *Nights*, the typical Burton note defers to Lane's authority as an Arabist by citing *Modern Egyptians* and then adds a cross-cultural observation, as a cosmopolitan flourish.

The contrast between authenticity and cosmopolitanism as governing principles of cross-cultural interpretation is evident in the manner in which both Lane and Burton integrate references to the mirror of ink in notes to their respective versions of the *Nights*. Both make reference to the "second-sight" afforded by the ink mirror to lend plausibility and verisimilitude to the use of magic in *Nights* tales that deal with the use of amulets and enchantments in intrigues of sexual jealousy and competition. Lane insists in his *Nights* commentary on the plausibility and historical authenticity of instances of natural magic such as the feats of magicians that might have been witnessed in the Cairo of his day and as recently as sixty years before his sojourn there. His recourse to the discourse of empiricism and experimentation is intended as a bridge to his Victorian reader, to whom he also appeals in referencing comparable instances of magic in the Old Testament. Burton, in contrast, even as he nonchalantly attests to the plausibility of the realm of the jinn invoked in a *Nights* tale, finds it necessary to intervene critically in debates concerning the most comparable cognate in English life, clairvoyance as practiced by spiritualists. Characteristically he boasts of knowledge but also a critical perspective acquired abroad, once more manifest in the form of a bias against a mainstream English view of a practice better understood elsewhere.

Lane's note to the *Nights* referencing the mirror of ink glosses a passage in the tale of the sheikh and the gazelle (an embedded tale in the tale of the merchant and the jinni) in which a jealous woman transforms her rival in love and her son into a cow and a calf. For enlightened Muslims, Lane stresses, "Darb el-Mendel" pertains to natural rather than spiritual magic, and the burning of perfumes in these performances might have had a hallucinogenic effect similar to that of opium. Perhaps because he is explaining a plot that includes an enchantment motivated by the sexual jealousy of a young slave, Lane includes in his commentary a comparable historical feat cited by al-Jabarti. A young slave woman who desires the love of her Mamluk owner seeks the assistance of Ahmad Sadoomeh, by this point a venerable figure who had attained fame for his feats in spiritual and natural magic and reported ability to converse with jinn and make them visible even to the blind. The magician writes a charm on her body, to attract the love of her owner, the Mamluk chief Yoosuf Bey. Yet when Yoosuf Bey sees the magic characters on her body, he is driven to distraction by jealousy and extracts from her via the threat of execution the name of the offending magician. At this point Lane switches from al-Jabarti to the report of a trusted "friend" for a description of the means by which the magician resisted arrest: "Several persons, one after another, endeavored to lay hold upon him; but every arm that was stretched forth for this purpose was instantly paralyzed, through a spell muttered by the magician; until a man behind him thrust a gag into his mouth, and so stopped his enchantment."[30]

Burton refers to the ink mirror in a note to "the history of Muhammad, Sultan of Cairo,"[31] and the context is the competition between a mischievous jinni and a trusting dervish to possess the sultan's daughter, who is protected against jinn by an amulet bracelet. The tale is distinctly preoccupied, as Ulrich Marzolph has observed, with "the rule of rational arguments that notably also apply to the application of magic and the way the jinn-king exercises his power."[32] The context for Burton's deployment of the account of the mirror of ink as evidence is extraordinary. When the misbehaving jinni is brought before the king of the Jann, Burton observes matter-of-factly that the description of the jinn king's retinue matches precisely that of accounts of clairvoyance with the ink mirror: "This Sultan of the Jann preceded by sweepers, flag-bearers and tent-pitchers always appears in the form of second-sight called by Egyptians 'Darb al-Mandal.'"[33] Within the context of the tale the footnote has the effect of lending its most fantastic of tableaux a semblance of verisimilitude.

Within the broader context of Burton's *Nights* commentary the note to the "Sultan of Cairo" is itself framed by two earlier notes that at once affiliate the ink mirror with "spiritualism" as a branch of high magic understood in Islam and other religious traditions and disentangle it from common English practices and perceptions of "spiritualism." In the first Burton defines *Al-Simiya*, or white magic, to which Darb al-Mandal would pertain "as a kind of natural and deceptive magic, in which drugs and perfumes exercise an important action" (in this echoing Lane). He clarifies that *Al-Simiya* is a subordinate branch of the *Ilm al-Ruhani* that he would translate as "Spiritualism."[34] In the second note Burton finds it necessary to complain of the inevitable distortion of the practice "amongst nervous and impressionable races like the Anglo-American": "the obtuse sensitiveness of a people bred on beef and beer has made the 'Religion of the Nineteenth Century' a manner of harmless magic, whose miracles are table-turning and ghost seeing whilst the prodigious rascality of its prophets (the so-called Mediums) has brought it into universal disrepute."[35] Burton's incorporation into the *Nights* of the anecdote of the mirror of ink exhibits the cosmopolitan knowledge that he has acquired abroad, but his comparative perspective on the practice of clairvoyance ends ultimately in a characteristic criticism of the English.

Translators and scholars have been puzzled by Jorge Luis Borges's use of a tale allegedly reported by Burton as the frame for his 1935 short story "The Mirror of Ink." The narrator of Borges's story states that Burton includes in *The Lake Regions of Equatorial Africa* an account of the sorcerer Abderramen al-Masmudi, rumored assassin of the "cruelest" governor of the Sudan, Yaqub the afflicted: "Captain Richard Francis Burton spoke with this sorcerer in 1853, and he reported that the sorcerer told him this story that I shall reproduce here."[36] The travelogue cited contains no such account of a magical mirror of ink, and certain elements of the account of clairvoyance in the story are evidently taken from Lane's *Modern Egyptians*. The tendency of scholarship has been to agree with Borges's translator Norman Thomas di Giovanni, who states categorically that Borges's "The Mirror of Ink" "has nothing whatever to do with Burton."[37] Yet if "The Mirror of Ink" is a story of elusive self-recognition, as Philip Kennedy observes,[38] the invocation of Burton provides in many respects a fitting frame given his genius for repeatedly "going native" and the limitations to his empathy and self-knowledge.

Borges demonstrated an intricate familiarity with the legend of Burton, the Arabian pilgrim who mastered the magic mirror, and drew attention in his essay "The Translators of *The 1001 Nights*" to Burton's first disguise en route to the hajj as a Persian dervish who practiced medicine, "alternating it with prestidigitation and magic so as to gain the trust of the sick."[39] Borges's story "The Mirror of Ink" retains the date, 1853, of Burton's pilgrimage, evoking Burton in these adopted personae of dervish and sorcerer. At the outset of the *Personal Narrative* Burton recalls arriving in 1853 at the port city of Alexandria and resuming his old character of a Persian dervish and wanderer, at once a vagrant, a merchant, and a philosopher, who emerges under the glare of the sun brightly decked out in the dervish's gown, large blue pantaloons, and short shirt, to present his credentials as a magician who heals with the aid of the magic mirror. Rather than dismiss the mythical personae of Burton (for "the Burton of the Burton legend is the translator of the

Nights"), Borges's essay identifies Burton as mythmaker in his travelogues of Africa: the survivor of a high fever on the quest for Lake
Tanganyika and a javelin wound to the jaw in Somalia, who "possibly
spread" and "certainly encouraged" rumors that he had "eaten strange
flesh" in Dahomey.[40]

In this context the misattribution in "The Mirror of Ink" of Burton's
exchange with the sorcerer to *Equatorial Africa* appears intentional: a
deliberate reference to Burton at his most fabulistic and prejudicial. It
removes the anecdote from the context of Lane's account, which Burton accurately termed "fair and dispassionate," and relocates it to the
legendary terrain of Burton's African travelogues, a realm of tyranny,
cruelty, and immanent violence more compatible with the subtext of
the story of Yakub the afflicted. To attribute the exchange to a travelogue of equatorial Africa rather than Arabia is to invoke Burton at his
least rather than at his most empathetic. Read in this light, the device
of the frame accentuates the callousness and stubborn curiosity of not
only the governor Yakub but, in a further act of doubling, the sorcerer's interlocutor, Richard Francis Burton. Borges's essayistic portrait of
Burton anticipated the paradox in Appiah's sketch, presenting Burton at
once as a cosmopolitan passionate for "the innumerable ways of being
a man that are known to mankind" and as a man of prejudices (against
"the Jews, democracy, the British Foreign Office, and Christianity").[41]
The frame in Borges's tale fittingly evokes the full range of the cosmopolitanism of Burton's cross-cultural commentary on the *Nights*, both
sympathetic to the supernatural processes of a wider world and riddled
with the biases of both European and non-European societies.

NOTES

1. Iliya Troyanov, *The Collector of Worlds: A Novel of Sir Richard Burton*, trans. William Hobson (New York: Ecco, 2009), 300.
2. Richard Francis Burton, *Scinde; or, The Unhappy Valley*, 2 vols. (London: Richard
   Bentley, 1851; repr., New Delhi: AES, 1998), 1:182. Citations refer to the reprint
   edition.
3. Richard Francis Burton, "The Translator's Foreword," in *The Book of the Thousand Nights and a Night, with Introduction, Explanatory Notes on the Manners
   and Customs of Moslem Men and a Terminal Essay upon the History of the
   Nights*, 10 vols. (Benares: Kamashastra Society, 1885–87), 1:xxiii.
4. Richard Francis Burton, "Translations," *Athenaeum* 2313 (February 1872): 242.

5. Ibid.

6. Ibid.

7. "His extended immersion in other cultures, especially those he entered by means of impersonation, gave him the experiential knowledge that made it possible for him to develop a relativist conception of difference. Once he understood that difference itself was a neutral epistemological device, a polarity that contained no inherent meaning, he began to wield it in ways that challenged the universalist claims of British society." Dane Kennedy, *The Highly Civilized Man: Richard Burton and the Victorian World* (Cambridge: Harvard University Press, 2005), 9.

8. Kwame Anthony Appiah, *Cosmopolitanism: Ethics in a World of Strangers* (New York: Norton, 2006), 11.

9. Ibid., 4.

10. Ibid., 5.

11. Ibid., 8. Appiah refers to Burton's account of a trip to East Africa in *Blackwood's Edinburgh Magazine*, February and March 1858.

12. Kennedy, *Highly Civilized Man*, 19, 25.

13. In this manner Burton positions himself as more Muslim than the Somali Muslims. See Burton, *First Footsteps in East Africa; or, An Exploration of Harar* (London: Longman, 1856), 61–63, 85–86, 348–49, 372–73.

14. "The true and simple explanation is that this grand Reformation of Christianity was urgently wanted when it appeared, that it suited people better than the creed which it superseded and that it has not ceased to be sufficient for their requirements, social, sexual and vital. As the practical Orientalist, Dr. Leitner, well observes from his own experience, 'The Mohammedan religion can adapt itself better than any other and has adapted itself to circumstances and to the needs of the various races which profess it, in accordance with the spirit of the age.'" Burton, *Nights*, 10:164.

15. "It is in Arabian countries, and especially in Egypt, that we see the people, the dresses, and the buildings, which it describes in almost every case, even when the scene is laid in Persia, in India or in China." Edward William Lane, preface to *The Thousand and One Nights* (London: Chatto and Windus, 1912), ix–x.

16. Muhsin Mahdi, introduction to *The Thousand and One Nights* (Leiden: Brill, 1995), 1–10. See also Husain Haddawy, introduction to *The Arabian Nights* (New York: Everyman, 1997), xix: "What emerges is a coherent and precise work of art that, unlike other versions, is like a restored icon or musical score, without the added layers of paint or distortions."

17. Burton, *Nights*, 10:113.

18. Ibid., 10:105.

19. Ibid., 10:109.

20. Ibid., 10:115.

21. Ibid., 10:156.

22. Ibid., 5:64–165.

23. Ulrich Marzolph, introduction to *The Arabian Nights Encyclopedia*, by Ulrich Marzolph and Richard van Leeuwen, 2 vols. (Santa Barbara, CA: ABC-CLIO, 2004), 1:xxv.

24. See Malcolm Lyons, "A Note on the Text," in *The Arabian Nights* (New York: Penguin, 2008), xxii.

25. "ART. VII. *An Account of the Manners and Customs of the Modern Egyptians, Written in Egypt during the Years 1833, 34, and 35, Partly from Notes Made during a Former Visit to That Country, in the Years 1825, 26, 27, and 28*, by Edward William Lane, 2 vols., London," *Quarterly Review* 59 (July 1837): 195.

26. Edward William Lane, "Domestic Life—Continued (The Lower Orders)," in *An Account of the Manners and Customs of the Modern Egyptians* (London: Society for the Diffusion of Useful Knowledge, 1836; repr., New York: Dover, 1973), 192–98. Citations refer to the reprint edition.

27. Richard Francis Burton, *Sindh and the Races That Inhabit the Valley of the Indus; with Notices of the Topography and History of the Province* (London: W. H. Allen, 1851; repr., Karachi: Oxford University Press, 1973), 181–82. Citations refer to the reprint edition.

28. Richard Francis Burton, *Personal Narrative of a Pilgrimage to El-Medinah and Meccah*, 3 vols. (London: Longman, 1855–56), 2:180.

29. Ibid., 2:178.

30. Edward William Lane, *The Thousand and One Nights, Commonly Called, in England, the Arabian Nights' Entertainments: A New Translation from the Arabic, with Copious Notes*, 3 vols. (London: Charles Knight, 1839–1841), 1:61.

31. Richard Francis Burton, *Supplemental Nights to the Book of the Thousand Nights and a Night*, 6 vols. (Benares: Kamashastra Society, 1886), 4:45.

32. Ulrich Marzolph, entry on "The History of Sultan Muhammad of Cairo," in Marzolph and van Leeuwen, *Arabian Nights Encyclopedia*, 1:307. See further Marzolph, "Narrative Strategies in Popular Literature. Ideology and Ethics in Tales from the *Arabian Nights* and Other Collections," *Middle Eastern Literatures* 7 (2004): 171–82.

33. Burton, *Supplemental Nights*, 4:45.

34. Burton, *Nights*, 1:306.

35. Ibid., 9:86.

36. Jorge Luis Borges, "The Mirror of Ink," in *Complete Fictions*, trans. Andrew Hurley (New York: Penguin, 1999), 60.

37. Norman Thomas di Giovanna, *The Lesson of the Master: Borges and His Work* (London: Continuum, 2003), 202.

38. Philip Kennedy, "Borges and the Missing Pages of the *Nights*," chapter 10 in this volume.

39. Borges, "The Mirror of Ink," 97.

40. Ibid., 97–98.

41. Ibid.

PART II

Engaging

4

The Porter and Portability

Figure and Narrative in the Nights

ELLIOTT COLLA

For good reason, *The Thousand and One Nights* conjures travel. Not only do many of the stories of the Arabic text tell of journeys across the territories of Islamdom and beyond, but the history of the text's reception and circulation is also one of extraordinary voyages between continents, languages, cultures, and historical periods. In this sense, the text invites us to consider portability as a problem of literature. But which elements of a literary text are most likely to travel?

The modern literary reception of the *Nights*—the many translations, adaptations, and rewritings of the text—provides some answers to this question. Of the many features of the oldest Arabic versions of the *Nights* that have traveled into other languages and literary traditions, the structures of the embedded-tale form seem to be those transported most intact.[1] While the frame tale has sometimes been removed from translations and adaptations of the *Nights*, this has not been the rule but rather an exception granted almost entirely to works intended for younger audiences.[2] Likewise, certain motifs and archetypes of the *Nights* have also traveled far and wide. It seems that no translation of the *Nights* fails to include jinn. Similarly, unfaithful wives and wily viziers seem to be essential citations in modern literary works inspired by the *Nights*. In this regard, those elements of the *Nights* cleared for travel would form a long list that would include sultans and garrulous barbers, eunuchs and automata, Rukhs and giant serpents, enchanted cities and flying carpets, desert isles and subterranean vaults.

The idea of the *Nights* as a global text is also a dominant theme of scholarship. In this literature, it is sometimes difficult to imagine that the *Nights* could ever belong, even for a moment, to any one culture, let alone that of the Arabo-Islamic world. This is in no small part because the *Nights*—even as an Arabic text—has so often been studied either through translation or as a problem of translation.[3] In recent decades, study has largely engaged with Galland's translation,[4] histories of the manuscripts, redactions and editions,[5] and considerations of the *Nights* as a motor for the production of modern European narrative and Orientalist knowledge.[6] Less often is the Arabic text—in any of its versions —studied in its own right and independent of its other lives in other languages.[7] With the recent rehabilitation of world literature as a critical field, the *Nights* is now perhaps approached not so much as a particular text (let alone *Arabic* text) but as a continually evolving—continually traveling—literary *project*, with multiple polyglot renditions and various unfinished itineraries.

Where does this leave the particularities of the versions of the Arabic text known as *Alf layla wa-layla*? The point of asking this is not to suggest that the text be considered as solely or primarily Arab(ic). Nor is it to suggest that recent accounts of the *Nights* have been misplaced. Rather, it is to highlight the challenges of seeking to read versions of the *Nights* closely as Arabic texts—that is, as single, discrete texts composed in a very particular and problematic Arabic that straddles the idioms and rhetorics of both formal and colloquial registers. Why, we might ask, are there so few close readings of the Arabic language in the *Nights*? Part of the answer is connected to longstanding biases against the language and themes of the text within scholarly institutions in the Arab world; part to the fact that the large holes in the manuscript history—and the gaps between the oral and written families of the text

—render particular historical claims about the text close to impossible; and part also to the fact that critical studies of the *Nights* in Arabic have long privileged colonial-era redactions of the text that were born in the shadow of Orientalist translation and adaptation and that strongly invite the reader to return to European horizons of reading.

Yet, even when the *Nights* has been read in the way I am suggesting, as an Arabic text, critics have still tended to focus on those aspects that are most global and generalizable—formal narrative structures,[8] genre conventions,[9] and recurring folkloric archetypes[10]—rather than those elements of the Arabic text most marked by cultural particularity and linguistic inalienability. Or, put differently, critical emphasis has been on questions of portability rather than of nonportability, travel rather than nontravel.

Though celebrated, the metaphor of travel raises more questions than it settles. The traveler, when she packs her bags, never takes everything, and no traveler ever arrives wholly intact. Travel suggests forms of movement that entail loss as much as gain. Addressing this issue with regard to the translation and circulation of critical theory, Edward Said wrote,

> Like people and schools of criticism, ideas and theories travel—from person to person, from situation to situation, from one period to another. Cultural and intellectual life are usually nourished and often sustained by this circulation of ideas, and whether it takes the form of acknowledged or unconscious influence, creative borrowing, or wholesale appropriation, the movement of ideas and theories from one place to another is both a fact of life and a usefully enabling condition of intellectual activity. Having said that, one should go on to specify the kinds of movement that are possible, in order to ask whether by virtue of having movement from one place and time to another an idea or theory gains or loses in strength, and whether a theory in one historical period and national culture becomes altogether different for another period or situation.[11]

Said's essay "Traveling Theory" describes histories of reception and dissemination, in which particular sets of ideas gain and lose meaning when resituated in new contexts and new languages. Said's emphasis context is key for our purposes here, because it reminds us that the travel of text is not merely an issue of language and ideas. The *situations of reception* include contexts of language and literature but also institutions, periods, and ideological investments. It is in the spirit of this that I want to consider those aspects of *The Thousand and One Nights* that have not traveled.

To ask which parts are less portable involves considering textual elements that are least likely to survive in translation or those that lose their source significance even in the most carefully translated target text. These are not minor issues when it comes to the travels of the *Nights*. Two examples will suffice to give an indication of how broad this problem is even in translations that cleave closely to the original. The first example has to do with how the particular literary topos of jinn appears when translated out of an Arabo-Islamic cosmology. The *Nights*, as is well known, is filled with references to jinn, afreet, and ghouls—supernatural beings that, for medieval Arab audiences (and for many even in the present day), would belong to a realist description of the world. In the Arabic text, the existence of such beings is taken as a given, as is the notion that the physical world has multiple planes of reality.[12] In this universe, encounters with jinn may be strange, startling, or unusual, but they do not connote magic or exoticness. This stands in stark contrast to the post-Enlightenment reception of the text in Europe. In that context, jinn connote a sense of elsewhere—both as an outdated time of folk superstition and as an outlandish realm of Oriental otherness. Even with elaborate footnotes and critical framing devices, the meaning of jinn in modern European translations of the *Nights* will share little with how the Arabic text has long been received in its Arabo-Islamic contexts.

The second example has to do with the status of particular usages of language whose cultural meanings are not purely semantic. The Arabic text of the *Nights* contains many pious phrases whose meanings, in Arabo-Islamic societies, are not solely linguistic. For instance, formulaic oaths and utterances regarding the will of God may express an interior set of pious beliefs, but not necessarily so. The meanings of such formulas are subtle and have to do with the articulation of status and place within a complex set of social signs and practices. Their meaning is often ambiguous, sometimes ironic, and always embedded within a fluid rhetorical context in which norms and values are asserted and negotiated, revised and undermined.[13] For good reason, translators have been unsure about how to render these particular aspects of the text. In some translations, they are rendered into a familiar archaic register (mimicking that of the other most popular work of translated Semitic literature in the English language, the King James Bible).[14] In this style of translation, piety is broadcast with a flatness and volume that does not square with the Arabic text of the *Nights*.[15]

This essay explores a particular feature of the Arabic text—the elaborate use of figurative language—that becomes largely illegible even when translated. While the narrative forms of the *Nights* have enjoyed multiple lives in other traditions, the same is not true of figure. Indeed, metaphor and pun in the *Nights* have proven not only to be quite resistant to translation and adaptation in other literatures, but they have been marginal as a subject of scholarly study.

This essay briefly addresses this issue within one particular story cycle, "The Tale of the Porter and the Three Ladies" (*al-Hammal wa-l-sabaya al-thalath*), within one particular rendition of the text, the Muhsin Mahdi edition, which is based on the oldest (and only premodern) manuscript of *Alf layla wa-layla*.[16] The figure of the eye plays a very central role within this story cycle and recurs in surprising ways through the text, through puns, metaphors, and allegories. The deliberate turns of these plays suggest that the figure of the eye is more than ornament in the text. The figure is, in fact, a deep part of the narrative structure itself.

To introduce this figure, we could start on night thirty-six, at the moment when "The Tale of the Porter and the Three Ladies" takes a dangerous turn. The caliph Harun al-Rashid and his vizier Ja'far are there, as is his imposing executioner and bodyguard, Masrur. Three one-eyed dervishes are also there, along with an unnamed porter. The hostesses of this gathering are three ladies of considerable beauty and means, known only as the shopper (*al-hawshkasha*), the doorkeeper (*al-bawwaba*), and the beauty (*al-maliha*). The men have just witnessed the strangest of spectacles: after enjoying much wine, poetry, and conversation, their hostesses interrupt the party to perform a series of cruel spectacles. In one act, the mistress of the house whips two black dogs with chains, then embraces the poor beasts, sobbing and kissing each in turn. In the second act, the shopper picks up a lute and three times sings a ballad about the pains of love. In one, she sings,

> Your brilliant *eyes* have wasted me
> Your jet-black hair has me in thrall
> Your rosy cheeks have vanquished me
> And told my tale to all. (81)

In another, she wails,

> You, who have long been absent from my *eyes*
> Will in my loving heart forever stay
> Was it you who have taught me how to love
> And from the pledge of love never to stray? (82)

At the end of each recital, the shopper's sister, the doorkeeper, tears off her dress and swoons—three times laying bare a body beaten black and blue. Each time, the caliph and his companions watch on in silence, even though they gradually decide they can stand it no longer. As a condition of their entrance into the home, they all have taken an oath not to speak or to ask questions about what they might see. The condition of their staying is that they "will be *eyes without tongues*." As the ladies put it, "you will not inquire about whatever you see. You speak not of what concerns you not, lest you hear what pleases you not" (79).[17]

Yet the men are overwhelmed by their curiosity and begin to ask questions among themselves—they want to know the story behind the spectacle. When their hostesses learn of this, they grow furious, and suddenly seven black slaves appear out of the wings. The slaves knock the men to the ground with their swords, then tie each one up. Their lives now in danger, the men are granted a reprieve only if each tells his story. If not, he will be decapitated. If before they had been asked to be eyes without tongues, now they are asked to be tongues telling the stories of eyes. And so one of the dervishes begins, "It was an amazing event and strange mischance that caused me to lose my *eye*. . . . Mine is a tale that, if it were engraved with needles at the corner of the *eye*, would be a lesson for those who would consider" (85). In this way erupts the first enframed tale of the cycle. And in this way we are introduced to one of the more memorable lines of the *Nights*, whose peculiarity survives even in translation.

Abdelfattah Kilito has argued that the figure of the eye and the needle in this phrase invites us to think about page and pen, reading and writing. For Kilito, the figure suggests the reading of lessons, or *'ibar*, contained in the story and the rewriting of these same lessons as *i'tibar*, not on pages but within one's contemplative mind.[18] Thus, in a sense, the image underscores the two different kinds of seeing that happen, or fail to happen, with the various characters in the story cycle: the first kind of seeing is tied to the act of being direct witness to events, and the second, a kind of seeing that involves the ability to see in one's imagination what one has heard second- or thirdhand in stories. Arguably, this then is what the figure of the needle and the eye teaches—that one might learn not just from what one directly sees but also from what one hears.

But this is only one of the many figures of eyes at play in this one scene: in addition to the eye and the needle, there are the eyes of lovers whose praises are sung in the poetry, and then there is the oath to be eyes without tongues. In short, we find eyes abounding throughout this scene alone—and throughout every page of the broader story cycle: there are the bewitching eyes of cloistered girls drawn straight from the classical poetic tradition; there is the language of eyes through which silenced lovers communicate; there is the eye of the calligrapher turning spoken language into silent image; there are the gluttonous eyes of party crashers and boors who impose on generous hosts; there is the eye of *fudul*, that is, the eye of curiosity, which causes trouble wherever it looks; and there is, most of all, the evil eye (*'ayn al-hasud*), the embodied-disembodied locus of an economy of envy that permeates the entire cycle.

But to appreciate the pregnancy of the figure, we need to consider the one-eyed dervishes themselves, whose figure very economically binds together two other key themes of the story cycle: retributive justice and sexual innuendo. The theme of justice is relatively straightforward, since each of the dervishes' tales tells the story of corporeal punishment—very literally, an eye for an eye. What is less obvious, perhaps, is how these characters extend the lusty sexual-linguistic romp that takes place earlier between the porter and the three ladies. According to 'Umar ibn Muhammad al-Nafzawi, author of the celebrated fourteenth-century work *The Perfumed Garden*, "the one-eyed man" was one of the many medieval euphemisms for the penis.[19] Burton translates Nafzawi's entry for this word, *al-a'war*, in this way: "the one-eyed, . . . it has but one eye [whose] eye is not like other eyes and does not see clearly," and "its one eye presents the peculiarity of being without pupil and [without] eyelashes."[20] Thus, some of the men in this story become, by way of this other set of eye motifs, phalloi with stories to tell. This pun grows more tumescent with each story. As each dervish narrates his tale, he cries copiously, which brings to mind other names from Nafzawi's list, such as *al-damma'* (the weeper) and *al-bakkay* (the crier), "so called on account of the many tears it sheds; as soon as it gets an erection, it weeps; when it sees a pretty face, it weeps; handling a woman, it weeps."[21] This certainly helps to explain how they are rewarded with the more than slightly lewd phrase, "Stroke your head and go." Once these ludic seeds are planted in our reading mind, we might return more suspiciously to the porter himself. The common translation of *al-hammal* is "the porter," which comes from the verb *h-m-l*, "to carry." Yet, since the same verb also connotes pregnancy and conception, his name suggests another slang term for the penis, "the impregnator."

Yet, because the play of pun is deeply rooted in the particular poly-semic possibilities of the Middle Arabic of the text, none of it has ever traveled in translation. This is not because of faults in the translation (here Husain Haddawy's excellent rendition) but because of limits to literary portability. It is not a question of determining semantic mean-ing and finding equivalents in the target language but rather of grasp-ing that the sort of indeterminacy allowed by the Arabic language of the text is part of its structure. The common translation of this story cycle provides some clues to how typically these aspects of the language are read. Almost universally, *al-hammal* is rendered as the title for the character, and it functions as his proper name: The Porter. The same is true of *al-a'war*. By reading these words as names rather than attributes, the figurative aspects of the text disappear from view. In a sense, the Arabic text provides a descriptive theory of sorts insofar as it contains a commentary on how idiomatic usage flattens the metaphors contained in common words by reactivating them through extended associations.

It also comments on the polysemic chaos of language. In the Arabic, the ludic connotations of these figures are not those necessarily most associated with their literal or conventional uses. Sometimes it is a secondary or tertiary connotation of a word that sets the play in motion. Which is to say, the text situates words in such a way that their conventional senses are disrupted by minor senses—and in this way, the order and seriousness of linguistic performance is replaced by chaos and play. Such play is obscure and, more importantly, deniable. And because it takes a dirty mind to recognize a dirty pun, there are incentives for silence around this aspect of the text. But ludic punning is only one part of the text's figurative play. The figure of the eye also serves to articulate the three dominant affective themes of the story cycle: courtly love, envy, and indiscreet curiosity.

First is the eye and the figuration of courtly desire. From the outset, the porter's encounter with the ladies takes place in the shadow cast by the classical poetic figure of the eye of the beloved. The story begins, "[Once] there lived in the city of Baghdad a bachelor who worked as a porter. One day he was standing in the market, leaning on his basket, when a woman approached him. . . . When she lifted her veil, she revealed a pair of beautiful dark eyes graced with long lashes and a tender expression, like those celebrated by the poets" (66–67). When this shopper takes him home, the porter sees "a full-bosomed girl, about five feet tall . . . [with] eyes like those of a deer or wild heifer, [and] eyebrows like the crescent in the month of Sha'ban" (68). The two girls admit the porter into a hall, where a girl emerges from behind a curtain: "She had an excellent figure, the scent of ambergris, sugared lips [and] Babylonian eyes with eyebrows as arched as a pair of bent bows" (69).

From the earliest of times, the eye has had a privileged place in the conventions of Arabic poetry.[22] As Richard Ettinghausen put it,

> In [Arabic courtly poetry] one reads that the ideal Arab woman must
> be so stout that she nearly falls asleep. . . . Her breasts should be full and
> rounded, her waist slender and graceful, her belly lean, her hips sloping,
> and her buttocks so fleshy as to impede her passage through a door. [Her
> neck is said to be] like that of a gazelle, while her arms are described as
> well rounded, with soft delicate elbows, full wrists, and long fingers. Her

face [has] white cheeks, . . . and her eyes are those of a gazelle with the white of the eye clearly marked.[23]

Far from expanding creatively on this set of classical formulas, the figures of feminine beauty in the *Nights* often repeat them mechanically. This story cycle is filled with over a dozen derivative poems that repeat, in cliché terms, this same image of the beloved's eye. At times, it even admits to the conventionality of the reference, as it does at the outset when it says the shopper "had eyes like those celebrated by the poets." In this story cycle, as in the poetic tradition, the eyes of the beloved hold a power over the lover who gazes on them. More exactly, the eye is pictured in a set of elements drawn from archery: in this image, the eyebrow of the beloved serves as the bow; the eyelashes, as a quiver of darts; and glances, as arrows that pierce and wound the lover.[24]

We might then consider lines from "The Third Dervish's Tale." Soon after arriving at a palace filled with forty beautiful women, the dervish chooses one to sleep with. He describes her by way of one of these poems:

> She bent and swayed like a ripe willow bough,
> O more lovely, sweet and delicious sight!
> She smiled and her glittering mouth revealed
> Flashing stars that answered light with light.
> . . . .
> How can such fledgling thing such beauties show,
> . . . .
> Such wide eyes that with the arrows of love
> The tortured victim pierce? (127)

The following evening, he chooses another girl, whom he describes the same way:

> I saw two caskets on her bosom fair,
> Shielded with musk seals from lovers' embrace.
> Against assault she guarded them with darts
> And arrowy glances from her lovely face. (128)

This convention of the beloved's eye does not discriminate along gender lines. During "The Tale of the First Lady," it applies also to a male beloved:

> By his enchanting eyelids and his slender waist,
> By his beguiling eyes so keen, so fair,
> By his sharp glances and his tender sides,
>
> . . . .
>
> By eyebrows that have robbed my eyes of sleep. (138)

At the same time, the eye serves as a figure of envy. Indeed, the centrality of the figure of the evil eye suggests that the moral economy of envy is the cycle's most pervasive, if disguised, theme. Like jinn and fate, the *Nights* assumes the existence of the evil eye and assumes some familiarity with its conventions. The tales are filled with both explicit and oblique references to such conventions. Strangers and disfigured men—and one-eyed men most especially—appear throughout this cycle, all of whom might be viewed with suspicion as conventional agents of the evil eye. Like the eye of courtly love, the covetous eye is also said to throw arrows and darts at its victims. The tales are also stuffed with many well-known examples of countermagical practices that protect from, offset, and undo the magic of the eye, such as symbolically gouging it out or piercing it with a horn or arrow.[25] And this in fact is what one man in "The Second Dervish's Tale" wishes he could do to the eyes that have afflicted him. Following the foretold death of his young son, the man recites a long poem—much of which describes the workings of the evil eye:

> we [once] lived together in one home
> A life of bliss that did no hindrance know
> Until with parting's arrow we were shot,
> And who can of such arrow bear the blow?
>
> . . . .
>
> On me and mine did envy fix his eye,
> O son, I'd have given my life for you.
>
> . . . .

> Some evil eyes on you have had their feast,
> Would they were pierced or black[ened] or blind did grow. (122)

There are less dramatic ways of combating the eye than poking it out. In this story cycle, characters are hidden away in underground chambers and distant palaces or disguised so as to hide them from envious eyes. Calligraphic talismans and charms are drawn up and worn to neutralize or deflect the envious eye.[26] Some scenes involve elaborate fumigations of burning wood and incense—rituals designed to hinder the sight of the evil eye or to purify people unfortunate enough to have been victims of its power.[27] It is well known that even just the representation of a hand or eye is, in itself, useful in this regard, since the likeness of the eye, or the fingers that might gouge it, are conventionally powerful counteragents. We might remember also that at the heart of "The Second Dervish's Tale," which is arguably the heart of the story cycle itself, is a strange exemplary tale titled "The Envious and the Envied."[28]

Finally, let us briefly consider the eye as a locus of curiosity. Importantly, the theme of curiosity, *fudul*, is always in this cycle, as elsewhere in the *Nights*, understood to be a form of heedlessness, or *jahl*. In that sense, it is always contrasted to discretion. As noted earlier, discretion features early in this cycle, as the ladies admit the dervishes into their home only on the condition of their absolute discretion. Earlier, they had posed this same rule to the porter, saying, "Whatever we do, and whatever happens to us, you shall refrain from asking for any explanation, for 'speak not of what concerns you not, lest you hear what pleases you not'" (76). The porter's reply, his pledge of discretion, brings us back to the eye. "Yes, yes, yes," he says. "Consider me eyeless and tongueless" (76; *ana bi-la ʿayn wa-la lisan*, 136).[29] Discretion is, in this model, a tongue that never tells what the eye sees. But inordinate curiosity poses a problem that is larger than mere indiscretion. The aspects of this are developed most fully in "The Third Dervish's Tale." After accidentally killing the young cloistered boy, this dervish walks and walks until he comes to a copper palace inhabited by ten one-eyed men. As the dervish demands to know the story behind the loss of their eyes, they tell him more than once, "We would be sitting pretty but for our curiosity" (125) (*Kunna bi-tulna ma-khallana fudulna*; 190). As it turns out, when the dervish asks these men about their story, he sets in motion a series of events that ends with the loss of his own eye. Returning to this palace after having his own eye gouged out, the men tell him, "because of our curious eyes, we lost our eyes" (132). We should not lose the irony: it is his obstinate curiosity about the consequences of their curiosity that brings about his misfortune. But this story, more than any other, seems to comment directly on the pleasure of consuming narrative—for what is the dervish's curiosity but the demand for a story that would explain the unusual and make sense of the amazing? In other words, what is this but the mirror of ourselves as readers of the *Nights*, seeking, demanding more and more stories to satisfy our own curious eyes?

The eye may serve as the privileged figure by which these three affects —love, envy, and curiosity—are developed. But are these the same eye? The brief answer is no. The differences between them are salient for understanding each affect: in the elaboration of envy, for instance, the evil eye figures as the lens that focuses a disembodied force on its objects; in the elaboration of courtly love, it is just the opposite—it is the very embodied eye of the beloved, the object of desire, that is said to wound the subject of that love, the lover; finally, with curiosity, it is never fully clear where the center of that affect lies—with either the subject of curiosity or with the object that draws people to look at it. Is something curious because of a quality within it, or is the curiosity of the dervishes a fault of their character? The figure of the eye asks but does not answer this question. To confuse matters even more, the eye is not just the figure for these affects; it is also as the privileged figure for an exploration of their consequences. Indeed, retribution—the taking of an eye for an eye—appears to be the same for envy as it is for curiosity and possibly also for love. In other words, by yoking together these affects in a single, shared figure, the story suggests that the similarities between love, envy, and curiosity might outweigh their differences.

In light of this reading, we might return to Kilito's reflections on the slogan of this cycle: "Mine is a tale that, if it were engraved with needles at the corner of the eye, would be a lesson for those who would consider." The language seems to suggest that this eye, of reading and writing, might be the most effective charm against the ills that attend these affects. But it would be naïve to say that the meaning of this figure is self-evident. A conventional reading of needles and eyes might lead us to dismiss the figure as mere hyperbole, expressing something like this:

it is as rare, and even marvelous, to write on eyes as it is for people to consider and take to heart the stories they hear. Yet the phrase makes some associations and puns that demand untangling. First, it needs pointing out that the tie between needles and eyes is not particularly odd. On the one hand, one can speak of "the eye of the needle" in Arabic as in English. On the other hand, needles, like hands and horns, are useful, everyday charms against the evil eye. But writing on the eye or, rather, on the corner of the eye—that is unusual. And what about the pun between needles and lessons—'*ibar* and *ibar* in the Arabic? The pun, possible in colloquials such as Egyptian, in which the letter *'ayn* is lightly pronounced, invites retranslation: "Mine is a tale that, if it were written in lessons at the corner of the eye, would be a needle for those who would consider"—or "for those who would be pricked."

And where does this writing take place anyway? What kind of eye are we speaking about—is this just another figure for yet another theme? *Miq al-'ayn* in the Middle Arabic of the *Nights* refers to the inner corner of the eye—neither inside nor outside the body but on the edge of one of its edges. Yet in this phrase, it is not *'ayn*, "eye," that appears but rather the word *basar*, which conventionally means "vision" or even "perception"—the mind's eye—and refers as much to the concept of discernment and judgment as it does to visual organs. So perhaps this writing is taking place not on an actual eye but rather in one's mental faculties. In this reading of the phrase, the process of consideration is not the consequence of writing but rather its condition: the learning of lessons is itself the needle, and it is the consideration of story that etches it in the imagination. Thus, the figure pulls us back into the argument for the serious consideration of narrative and the value of *adab* and story in the frame tale of the *Nights*. In this regard, we should not forget to recall how eyes and eyesight figure so importantly in Shahriyar's reckoning— a process which accords authority to narrative when grounded in eyewitness but which withholds it in the case of secondhand tales. The telling of stories is thus redeemed not through the tongue but through the association with eye. But that cannot be the whole of the story. The very figure by which the value of story is expressed here—the eye—suggests that narrative itself might share in the pleasures and punishments associated with envy and curiosity and the like.

The consideration of the eye as a shifting figure leads us into the smallest details of poems embedded within embedded stories and then pitches us back again into the broadest organizing polemic of *The Thousand and One Nights* as a whole—but now with questions. This story cycle builds and then binds itself to the frame tale of Scheherazade and Shahriyar not just through the repetition of fixed motifs but by developing organizing figures that ambiguate as much as they clarify.

To conclude, we should emphasize that figure in the *Nights* is not reducible to the kind of fixed and stable motif described by folklorists and that the movement of figure is as complex as its shifts of narrative frame. The slipperiness of figuration has been the topic of just a fraction of the scholarship on the *Nights*, almost exclusively in the work of Kilito, Sandra Naddaff, and Ferial Ghazoul. In an exemplary reading of "The Tale of the Porter and the Three Ladies," Ghazoul describes how the narrative redeploys motifs that had already appeared in two earlier cycles, "The Merchant and the Demon" and "The Fisherman and the Demon." Ghazoul shows how each cycle develops a different possibility of embedded narrative—what she calls subordination, coordination, and superordination. Yet, as she notes, these repetitions among enframed narratives borrow "motifs without hardly any elaboration. The relationship can be summed up as a figure which cannot be contained and keeps slipping from one narrative to another."[30]

Building on Ghazoul's insight, we might argue that while figures provide the thematic ligaments that hold the narrative boxes together, they are a stretchy kind of connective tissue. The figure of the eye serves to articulate the main themes, situations, and problems within the story cycle of "The Tale of the Porter and the Three Ladies" and thus suggests that our accounts of the *Nights* not only need to consider figure in the text but need to consider figure as an aspect of narrative structure. In the case of "The Tale of the Porter and the Three Ladies," the figure of the eye is what connects and develops the main themes of the story cycle—courtly love, sexual hint, indiscreet curiosity, inordinate appetite, retributive justice, and envy. But the kind of organization offered by this figure is one that is not free from ambiguity. The reason for this is simple: if each of these separate themes—love, desire, curiosity, justice, and envy—finds expression through this single figure of the eye, then what does that tell us about their differences? How are these themes distinct if they are produced by the same figure? In this sense, the figure of the eye provides us with an opportunity to explore the sense of articulation offered by Stuart Hall—that is, an instance of speech that joins together elements and themes generating from separate moral spheres, while also keeping them separate and distinct.[31]

NOTES

1. By this, I am referring to the experimentation with the frame tale as a narrative form in the works of writers as diverse as Mir Amman, Jorge Luis Borges, Isak Dinesen, Pier Paolo Pasolini, and Jan Potocki.

2. See, for example, *Tales from the Thousand and One Nights*, trans. N. J. Dawood (New York: Penguin, 1993).

3. See Muhsin Jassim Ali, *Scheherazade in England: A Study of Nineteenth-Century English Criticism of the Arabian Nights* (Boulder, CO: Three Continents, 1981); Ros Ballaster, *Fabulous Orients: Fictions of the East in England, 1662–1784* (Oxford: Oxford University Press, 2005); Jorge Luis Borges, "The Thousand and One Nights," in *Seven Nights: Lectures*, trans. Eliot Weinberger (New York: New Directions, 1984), 42–57; Peter L. Caracciolo, ed., *The Arabian Nights in English Literature: Studies in the Reception of the The Thousand and One Nights into British Culture* (New York: St. Martin's, 1988); Rana Kabbani, *Imperial Fictions: Europe's Myths of Orient* (London: Pandora, 1988); and Kamran Rastegar, "The Changing Value of *Alf Laylah Wa Laylah* for Nineteenth-Century Arabic, Persian, and English Readerships," *Journal of Arabic Literature* 36:3 (2005): 269–87.

4. See Mohamed Abdel-Halim, *Antoine Galland: Sa vie, son oeuvre* (Paris: A. G. Nizet, 1964); Claude Hagège, "Traitement du sens et fidélité dans l'adaptation classique: Sur la texte arabe des *Milles et une nuits* et las traduction de Galland," *Arabica* 27 (1980): 114–39; Rida Hawari, "Antoine Galland's Translation of the *Arabian Nights*," *Revue de la littérature comparée* 54 (1980): 150–64; C. Knipp, "*The Arabian Nights* in England: Galland's Translation and Its Successors," *Journal of Arabic Literature* 5 (1974): 44–54; and Muhsin Mahdi, "Antoine Galland and the *Nights*" and "Galland's Successors," in *The Thousand and One Nights* (Leiden: Brill, 1995), 11–86.

5. See Nabia Abbott, "A Ninth-Century Fragment of the 'Thousand Nights': New Light on the Early History of the *Arabian Nights*," *Journal of Near Eastern Studies* 8 (July 1949): 129–64; Heinz Grotzfeld, "Neglected Conclusions of the *Arabian Nights*: Gleanings in Forgotten and Overlooked Recensions," *Journal of Arabic Literature* 16 (1985): 73–87; D. B. MacDonald, "The Earlier History of the *Arabian Nights*," *Journal of the Royal Asiatic Society*, 1924, 353–97; Muhsin Mahdi, "Four Editions: 1814–1843," in *The Thousand and One Nights*, 87–126; David Pinault, "Bulaq, MacNaghten, and the New Leiden Edition Compared: Notes on

Storytelling Technique from the *Thousand and One Nights*," *Journal of Semitic Studies* 32:1 (1987): 125–57; Dwight F. Reynolds, "*A Thousand and One Nights*: A History of the Text and Its Reception," in *Arabic Literature in the Post-Classical Period*, ed. Roger Allen and D. S. Richards, 270–91 (Cambridge: Cambridge University Press, 2006).

6. See Michael Cooperson, "The Monstrous Births of Aladdin," *Harvard Review of Middle Eastern and Islamic Affairs* 1:1 (1994): 67–86; Muhsin Mahdi, "Retranslation: An Arabic Version of 'Ali Baba,'" in *The Thousand and One Nights*, 72–86.

7. Three notable exceptions to this are Ferial J. Ghazoul, *Nocturnal Poetics: The Arabian Nights in Comparative Contexts* (Cairo: American University Press, 1996); Abdelfattah Kilito, *L'œil et l'aiguille: Essais sur Les mille et une nuits* (Paris: La Découverte, 1992); and Sandra Naddaff, *Arabesque: Narrative Structure and the Aesthetics of Repetition in the 1001 Nights* (Evanston, IL: Northwestern University Press, 1991). Less often still has it been studied as an Arabic text marked by oral and literate structures of organization. Two exceptions to this are David Pinault, *Story-Telling Techniques in the Arabian Nights* (Leiden: Brill, 1992); and Suhayr Qalamawi, *Alf layla wa-layla* (Cairo: Dar al-Ma'arif, 1966).

8. See, for example, Mia Gerhardt, *The Art of Story-Telling: A Literary Study of the Thousand and One Nights* (Leiden: Brill, 1963); Tzvetan Todorov, "Narrative-Men" and "The Grammar of Narrative," in *The Poetics of Prose* (Ithaca: Cornell University Press, 1977), 66–79, 108–19; and Mark Turner, "Bedtime with Shahrazad," in *The Literary Mind* (Oxford: Oxford University Press, 1996), 3–11.

9. See Andras Hamori, *On the Art of Medieval Arabic Literature* (Princeton: Princeton University Press, 1974); Hamori, "Notes on Two Love Stories from the *Thousand and One Nights*," *Studia Islamica* 43 (1976); Hamori, "A Comic Romance from the *Thousand and One Nights*: The Tale of the Two Viziers," *Arabica* 30 (1983): 38–56; Hamori, "The Magian and the Whore: Readings of Qamar al-Zaman," in *The 1001 Nights: Critical Essays and Annotated Bibliography* (Cambridge, MA: Dar Mahjar, 1985), 25–40; Peter Heath, "Romance as Genre in *The Thousand and One Nights*" (in two parts), *Journal of Arabic Literature* 18 (1987) and 19 (1988); Malcolm Cameron Lyons, *The Arabian Epic: Heroic and Oral Story-Telling* (Cambridge: Cambridge University Press, 1995).

10. Examples of the motif study of the *Nights* include Ulrich Marzolph and Richard van Leeuwen, *The Arabian Nights Encyclopedia*, 2 vols. (Santa Barbara, CA: ABC-CLIO, 2004); Bruno Bettelheim, "The Frame Story of *Thousand and One Nights*," in *The Uses of Enchantment: The Meaning and Importance of Fairy Tales*, 86–90 (New York: Knopf, 1976); Stephanie Dalley, "Gilgamesh in the *Arabian Nights*," *Journal of the Royal Asiatic Society* (1991): 1–17; Hasan El-Shamy, *A Motif Index of The Thousand and One Nights* (Bloomington: Indiana University Press, 2006); James E. Montgomery, "Al-Sindibad and Polyphemus: Reflections on the Genesis of an Archetype," in *Myths, Historical Archetypes and Symbolic Figures in Arabic Literature: Towards a New Hermeneutic Approach*, ed. Angelika Neuwirth, Birgit Embaló, Sebastian Günther, and Maher Jarrar (Stuttgart:

Franz Steiner Verlag, 1999); Roy Mottahedeh, "'Aja'ib in *The Thousand and One Nights*," in *The Thousand and One Nights in Arabic Literature and Society*, ed. Richard C. Hovannisian and Georges Sabagh, 29–39 (Cambridge: Cambridge University Press, 1997); and Gustave E. von Grunebaum, "Creative Borrowing: Greece in the *Arabian Nights*," in *Medieval Islam: A Study in Cultural Orientation*, 294–319 (Chicago: University of Chicago Press, 1946).

11. Edward Said, "Traveling Theory," in *The World, the Text, and the Critic* (Cambridge: Harvard University Press, 1983), 226.

12. See Amira El-Zein, *Islam, Arabs, and the Intelligent World of the Jinn* (Syracuse: Syracuse University Press, 2009); and Robert Irwin, *The Arabian Nights: A Companion* (London: I. B. Tauris, 2004).

13. See Niloofar Haeri, *Sacred Language, Ordinary People: Dilemmas of Culture and Politics in Egypt* (New York: Palgrave Macmillan, 2003).

14. Richard Burton's translation is perhaps the best example of this style.

15. Rasheed El-Enany has made similar observations concerning the translation of religious discourse in Naguib Mahfouz's novels. See "Mahfouz: A Great Novel and a Wanting Translation," *Third World Quarterly* 13:1 (1992): 187–89.

16. Muhsin Mahdi, ed., *Kitab Alf layla wa-layla*, 3 vols. (Leiden: Brill, 1984) (hereafter cited parenthetically in the text). Unlike later, colonial-era redactions of the *Nights*, the Mahdi edition preserves the nonstandard, or Middle Arabic, register of the text in its oldest form. My transliterations reflect the spelling of the edition. English translations are taken from Hussein Haddawy's translation of the Mahdi edition, *The Arabian Nights* (New York: Norton, 1990) (hereafter cited parenthetically in the text).

17. Muhsin Musawi explores the place of writing in this story cycle and emphasizes the visual aspect of this phrase, which is inscribed above the door. See "Scheherazade's Nonverbal Narratives," *Journal of Arabic Literature* 36:3 (2005): 338–62.

18. Kilito, *L'œil et l'aiguille*, 105–7.

19. 'Umar ibn Muhammad al-Nafzawi, *al-Rawd al-'atir fi-nuzhat al-khatir*, ed. Jamal Jum'a (London: Riad al-Rayyes Books, 1993); Shaykh Nefzawi, *The Perfumed Garden of the Shaykh Nefzawi*, trans. Richard Burton (London: Granada, 1963).

20. Nefzawi, *Perfumed Garden*, 178.

21. Ibid., 179.

22. See J. C. Bürgel, "Love, Lust and Longing: Eroticism in Early Islam as Reflected in Literary Sources," in *Society and the Sexes in Medieval Islam*, ed. Afaf Lutfi Sayyid-Marsot, 81–118 (Malibu, CA: Undena, 1979), 81–118; Lois Griffen, *Theory of Profane Love among the Arabs* (London: Hodder and Stoughton, 1972).

23. As quoted in Irwin, *Arabian Nights: A Companion*, 166.

24. By way of comparison, we might think of the English saying "beauty is in the eye of the beholder." Nothing could be more different from the conventions of Arabic poetry, in which it is the eye of the beheld that captivates and wounds the beholder. These metaphors have apparent distant cousins in English, yet when

we speak of arching brows, sharp glances, and looking daggers at someone, we are speaking of enmity rather than desire.

25. See Edward Westermarck, "The Evil Eye," in *Ritual and Belief in Morocco*, 2 vols. (London: Macmillan, 1926), 1:414–78.

26. See ibid. James Trilling has pointed out how the origins of interlace, along with Arabesque ornament, might be in the desire to hide objects from the evil eye or to confuse its sight. See "Medieval Interlace Ornament: The Making of a Cross-Cultural Idiom," *Arte medievale* 9:2 (1995): 59–86.

27. See the relevant essays by Leonard W. Moss and Stephen Cappannari and Brian Spooner in *The Evil Eye*, ed. Clarence Maloney (New York: Columbia University Press, 1976).

28. In an article on the place of exemplary tales in the *Nights*, Mahdi comments on the ill fit of these stories and their failure to perform rhetorically. Mahdi suggests they were likely inserted by scribes who treated such stories as filler. While it is indeed true that this embedded story makes little sense according to the narrative logic of the cycle, thematically, it could not have been added in a more appropriate place—in terms of ring composition, right at the very heart of stories about envy. See Mahdi, *The Thousand and One Nights*, 156.

29. This is slightly different from the oath soon taken by the three dervishes, who agree to be "eyes without tongues," not inquiring about what concerns them not (79). These oaths share the connection between the eye and tongue.

30. Ghazoul, *Nocturnal Poetics*, 92.

31. Stuart Hall, "Race, Articulation and Societies Structured in Dominance," in *Sociological Theories: Race and Colonialism*, ed. UNESCO (Paris: UNESCO, 1980).

5

The Rings of Budur and Qamar al-Zaman

WENDY DONIGER

One of the best loved stories in the *Nights* is the tale usually referred to in terms of the men involved in it: Sir Richard Burton called it the "Tale of Kamar Al-Zaman,"[1] and Husain Haddawy expanded it to "The Story of Qamar al-Zaman and His Two Sons, Amjad and A'sad"[2] (three men, no women). But the true protagonist of the tale is, I think, not a man at all but a woman, who does make it into the title of the first translation into English: "The Story of the Amours of Camaralzaman, Prince of the Isles of the Children of Khaledan, and of Badoura, Princess of China"[3] (one man, one woman). Budur's centrality to the plot is best appreciated in the comparative context, and that is what I propose to explore in this essay. I begin with a brief summary of what is a long and complex tale, detour into the comparative material, and return to reconsider the Arabic tale in the light of that material. I would call the story "How Budur Became the Male Lover of Her Husband, Qamar."

King Shahraman had a handsome son named Qamar al-Zaman. When Qamar's father asked him to marry, he insisted, "Father, I have no wish to marry, nor am I inclined to women, for I have read tales of their guile and heard verses on their cunning." When he remained adamant, his father the king had him imprisoned in a tower. Meanwhile, the beautiful Princess Budur, the daughter of the king of the Interior Islands of China, had said, "I have no wish to marry, for I am a sovereign princess who rules over men, and I do not wish any man to rule over me." Her father had imprisoned her in a tower. Two djinns brought Budur to Qamar's tower in her sleep, to determine which was the more beautiful. They laid her beside the young man, and when they uncovered the faces of the two sleeping figures, they looked very much alike, as if they were twins or only brother and sister.

First the djinns awakened Qamar, who was stunned by Budur's beauty and desired to make love to her. He undressed her but could not awaken her, for the djinns kept her asleep; he wondered if this was the woman his father wanted him to marry or if his father had sent the woman to test the sincerity of his resolve not to marry. He therefore refrained from touching her, but in order to have a souvenir, he took from her little finger a ring worth a great deal of money, set with a precious gem, and placed it on his own little finger. The ring was inscribed with a verse that began, "Do not think that I have forgotten your vows, no matter how long your cruel disdain lasts." Then he turned his back to her and went to sleep.

The djinns then awakened Budur, who assumed that Qamar was the man her father had wanted her to marry. She, in turn, tried to awaken him to make love, but again the djinns kept him asleep. When she saw her ring on his little finger, she cried out, "I love you, and you love me, but you turn away from me out of coquetry; you came to me while I was asleep, and I do not know what you did to me, but I will not take off my ring from your finger." Then she searched for something to take from him but found nothing; she placed her hand under his shirt and felt his legs, and as his skin was very smooth, her hand slipped and touched his penis, and her heart ached and pounded with desire, for the lust of women is greater than the lust of men; she felt embarrassed. She took his ring from his finger and put it on her own and kissed his mouth and hands and every spot on his body. Then she took him in her arms, embraced him, and fell asleep.

The djinns returned Budur to China. At dawn, Budur and Qamar awoke; and each remembered the other and saw the ring, but each was told that no one had been there. After three years, Budur's stepbrother, Marzawan, entered the harem by dressing in women's clothes; he spoke to Budur and promised to help her find her prince. He brought Qamar to the kingdom of Budur; Qamar stained some of his clothes with the blood of a horse and left them behind, to make his father think that he had been killed. Qamar sent Budur a letter, enclosing her ring. They met and were married; they made love and slept in each other's arms until the morning.

But Qamar worried about his father, who must have thought him dead, and he persuaded Budur to come with him to his own country. On the journey, one day Qamar came upon Budur asleep; desiring her, he began to remove her pants, whereupon he discovered a blood-red jewel that she had kept tied to the ribbon of her pants and hidden in her most precious part, in order to guard it. He took it outside to look at it in the light, and a bird carried it off (fig. 6); when Qamar followed the bird, he fell among evil Magians. Budur awoke to find that he had gone and had taken the jewel, without knowing its secret power. Fearing that her servants would make bold with her if they knew her husband was gone, Budur put on some of Qamar's clothes and a turban like his and veiled the lower part of her face and departed, and no one discovered her identity, for she resembled Qamar so much that everyone took her for him.

She journeyed to the City of Ebony, where the king said to her, "I have not been blessed with a son, but I have one daughter, whose face and body resemble yours in beauty and grace. Will you be willing to live in my country? I will marry you to my daughter and give you the kingdom." Budur-as-Qamar agreed to this, but when she failed to consummate the marriage, the princess, Hayat al-Nufus, said, "Is every beautiful person so conceited? I am not saying this to make you desire me, but I am saying it out of fear for you from the king, for he has resolved that if you don't take my virginity and consummate the marriage tonight, he will depose you and banish you from his country; he may even become more enraged and kill you." When Budur-as-Qamar revealed that she was a woman, Hayat said, "I will not divulge your secret." She took a chicken, slaughtered it, and smeared herself with its blood. Then she took off her pants and cried out. The women of her family went in to her, and her waiting women let out trilling cries of joy.

After some time, Qamar found, in the craws of a dead bird, the jewel that was the cause of his separation from his wife. He hid it in a cask of gold on a ship that was to take him to the City of Ebony, but the ship sailed without him; and when it landed, Budur-as-Qamar, now king of the Ebony Islands, found the jewel. Through it she discovered Qamar's whereabouts and sent her men to capture him and bring him to her. When Qamar arrived, Budur-as-Qamar said to him, "I love you for your surpassing beauty and grace, and if you grant me my desire, I will grant you favors, make you prosperous, and appoint you vizier, just as the people made me king, in spite of my youth." When Qamar heard this, he felt embarrassed and blushed until his cheeks seemed on fire, and he said, "I have no need of favors that lead to sin."

Budur-as-Qamar kept arguing with him, reciting many obscene verses about men who prefer anal sex (with boys or with women) to full frontal sex with women. At last Qamar became convinced that there was no escape from compliance with the king's will. He said, "O King of the age, if you must do it, promise me that you will do it to me only once." He opened his trousers, feeling extremely embarrassed and shedding tears in fear. Budur-as-Qamar smiled, took him with her to bed, and said, "After tonight, you will experience nothing offensive again." Then she bent over him, kissing and embracing him and wrapping her leg around his. When Qamar discovered that she lacked male genitals, he said to himself, "Perhaps this king is a hermaphrodite, being neither male nor female." So he said to her, "O King, you don't seem to have a tool like other men. What then moved you to carry on like this?" When Budur-as-Qamar heard this, she laughed until she fell on her back, and she said, "O my darling, how quickly you have forgotten the nights we spent together!" Then she revealed herself to him, and he recognized her as his wife, Budur. So he embraced her and she embraced him, and he kissed her and she kissed him, and they made love.

Then he began to remonstrate with her, asking, "What made you treat me like this tonight?" She replied, "Do not reproach me, for I only did it in jest, to increase the pleasure and joy." Qamar married Hayat al-Nufus, and Budur, who was not jealous, willingly became her maidservant and co-wife. He conducted himself in a praiseworthy way toward his people and lived with his wives in happiness and delight and fidelity and cheerfulness, spending one night with each in turn.

But when the two women bore and raised sons, each woman fell in love with the other's son, propositioned him, was rejected, and accused the boy of rape. Qamar believed the women at first and ordered the boys killed, but they were spared and proved their innocence with the help of Budur's father and Qamar's father. Budur returned to her father's kingdom, and her son ruled there, while Hayat's son ruled on the throne of her father; and Qamar al-Zaman went back and ruled his father's kingdom.[4]

The Clever Wife

Scholars of Arabic have illuminated many aspects of this story that I, totally ignorant of Arabic, would not dare to venture on in this brief essay. But embedded within the story are a few somewhat atavistic traces of a plot structure that we can recognize from the outlines of a well-known folktale. This story, which has a very long shelf life indeed, is known to folklorists as "The Clever Wench" or "The Clever Wife"; Stith Thompson gives it the evocative title of "AT 891D," subtitled, "The Rejected Wife as Lover." In most variants of the story, a husband challenges his wife to get his ring (though he will never take it off) and have a child fathered by him (though he refuses to sleep with her); she succeeds by tricking him into bed when she masquerades as another woman and insists on having his ring before she will submit to him. She becomes pregnant, and when the legitimacy of her son is called into question, she produces the ring and the man acknowledges the child as his. Sometimes the wife disguises herself as a man, gains access to her husband, beats him at cards, and offers to provide him with a woman —that woman being, of course, herself in disguise.[5] Rarely does she remain in her male disguise when she seduces him. The tale of Budur also reflects another widely distributed, related plot: a man marries a woman from another world, begs leave to return home for a visit (in this case, to Qamar's father), forgets his wife, and fails to return to her.[6]

The best known example of the Clever Wife theme in English literature is Shakespeare's *All's Well That Ends Well*, which can be traced back, through French variants, to a story in Boccaccio's *Decameron*. (Some elements of the plot—not the challenge but the masquerade and the ring as identification—can also be traced back to the narrative of Tamar and Judah, in Genesis 38:12–26, c. eighth century BCE.) But Boccaccio did not make up the story; I think it can be traced back to Arabic variants carried to Europe and perhaps, behind those Arabic variants, to India, to the tale of Muladeva and the Brahmin's daughter. This is the final tale in Somadeva's *Ocean of the Rivers of Story* (*Kathasaritsagara*), a great compendium of stories, composed in Sanskrit in Kashmir in the tenth century CE, a massive text which may have fed its streams of story into that other great narrative ocean, the *Arabian Nights*. In the Indian text, on the wedding night, the husband fails to consummate the marriage and promises his bride that he will leave her and never return; then, as he tells the story, "She, too, made a promise: 'I swear that you will be bound and brought back to me by means of a son fathered by you.' When we had made these mutual vows, she turned her face from me and went to sleep, and I put my own ring on her finger while she slept." With the help of the ring (on which his name is engraved), and the usual masquerade, she keeps her promise. And the story concludes, "So you see, there really are in this world some women of good family who love their husbands; not all women misbehave always."[7] This is, of course, the moral of the frame story of Scheherazade in the *Nights*. The ring plays a far more important point in various Indian variants, folk variants, of this particular story[8] (for the story of Muladeva found its way into—more probably, back into—Indian folk literature), including another story in this same text, the *Ocean of the Rivers of Story*, that we will consider shortly.

Only a few elements of the story of Budur and Qamar can be mapped onto the outline of the Clever Wife theme, but these could be summarized as follows: Qamar vows never to marry. He encounters Budur, gives her his ring when she is asleep, takes her ring, and leaves her. Searching for her, he sends her a letter, enclosing her ring, and marries her, but again leaves her, again when she is asleep. Budur disguises herself as a king and seduces Qamar, who does not recognize her in her disguised form. At last she reveals herself to him, and he welcomes her. She bears him a son who becomes king of Budur's land.

The husband's refusal to sleep with his wife, in the folktale, appears here first in the form of Qamar's refusal to marry any woman at all and then in the episode in which he abandons Budur when he steals her jewel; it is also echoed in his violent resistance to sleeping with her (when he thinks she is a man). The riddles in the folktale appear here in the riddling verses that Budur-as-Qamar recites to Qamar, verses which are simultaneously obscene, misogynist, homophobic, and blasphemous.[9] And the ring that identifies the impregnator in other stories here appears as the ring with which the lovers are persuaded of the reality of their encounter as well as the ring with which Qamar identifies himself to Budur as her husband. The son is not, as he usually is, the pivot of the first part of the story, with its riddles and rings, but he appears at the end of this tale and then grows up to become one of the two protagonists of the second half of the story of what Haddawy calls "The Story of Qamar al-Zaman and His Two Sons, Amjad and A'sad."

The Arabian story can no more be reduced to this set of themes than Mozart's Twelve Variations on "Ah vous dirai-je, Maman" can be reduced to the jingle known as "Twinkle Twinkle Little Star." These narrative bones are grotesquely bare, but other details of the Arabian text flesh them out in interesting ways and tie up some loose ends that otherwise seem to play no significant role in the story as we have it. Let us begin with the most unusual feature of the tale of Budur, the gender reversal.

The Cross-Dressing

Unlike most cross-dressing wives, Budur does not bother to change back into a woman before she seduces her husband, which results in the strange case of the man who committed a homosexual act with his wife. Though Qamar longs for Budur, her longing is greater than his, and it is she who takes the active role in bringing them together on both occasions. Yet she never has to prove who she is. It is Qamar who must prove his identity; Budur, by contrast, remains disguised as she takes political power and forces Qamar into a bed that he loathes even more than the rejecting husband usually loathes his undisguised wife: for he thinks it is the bed of a man.[10] Budur looks so like her husband that she can take his place, not merely (like other Clever Wives) his mistress's place; her servants mistake Budur-as-Qamar for Qamar.

What does Qamar think when Budur-as-Qamar drags him into bed? That he is looking into a mirror? That every good-looking person looks like him? The fact that her natural resemblance to her husband allows Budur to play the role of a man, her man, lends this version of the story an unusual symmetry which is foreshadowed from the very start, when each desires the other at first sighting but fails to awaken the other and hence cannot satisfy his or her desire. They play similar tricks on other people, too; Qamar uses the blood of a horse to fake his own death for his father, and Budur uses the blood of a chicken to fake her deflowering of Hayat for Hayat's father.

The resemblance between the two lovers is particularly striking because they not only are not related by blood at all (so that family resemblance cannot explain the likeness) but are not even of the same ethnic background; he is presumably Persian and she Chinese. And Budur resembles not only Qamar but the daughter of the king who takes her to be a boy, presumably a dark-skinned woman (from the Ebony Isles). The hegemony of "beauty and grace" erases not only the difference between individuals but the difference between genders and transcends even the boundaries of ethnicity. They are both named after the moon; *Qamar* means "moon," and *Budur* means "full moon" or "circle of the moon"; significantly, the moon is a body that has no light but what is reflected from another body.

Budur, awakening from the couple's first magic encounter, feels that Qamar has rejected her ("You turn away from me out of coquetry"). He, on the other hand, feels no rejection but, rather, a kind of paranoia: he worries that his father is actually watching them to see if he was lying when he said he did not want to marry. When he runs off, she says that she is still confident of his love: "It must have been some extraordinary matter that drew him away, for he cannot bear to be without me even for an hour." And she curses not him but the jewel. It is therefore allegedly love, and the confidence of being loved, that drives Budur to play the active role in finding her partner in the second half of the story. Yet Qamar does not marry her first; he marries Hayat, while Budur takes up the role of the female servant (or lower-class woman) that the wife in other variants pretends to be when she sets the trap for her husband's intended adultery. Here, however, the other woman is not merely a mask that the wife assumes but a separate person, producing a sexual triangle with a difference: although we end up with the official, normal combination of a man (Qamar) who sleeps with two women (Hayat and Budur), the narrative brings us there through the far-from-normal detour of an apparent man (Budur-as-Qamar) who pretends to sleep first with a woman (Hayat) who thinks she is a man (same sex, different gender) and then with a man (Qamar) who thinks she is a man (same gender, different sex).

Does Budur feel that she has to become a man in order to win Qamar's love, since he does not really like women? Or does her masquerade as a man fulfill an impulse in her that is there from the very start, in her refusal to accept the subservient role of a wife, her desire to have the power and independence that men have?[11] On the other hand, are we to assume that Qamar is gay, because he does not like women and looks like one? I think not. This option seems to be ruled out by the horror and revulsion that he expresses when she proposes the homosexual act and his effuse relief and gratitude when he discovers that she has the right genitalia after all. Or is it (a suspicious Freudian hermeneut might ask) that he doth protest too much? The *Nights* often attributes homosexual desire to evil characters, but here it treats it as farce.[12] The misogyny expressed in the course of the bed trick is truly stunning, but it is coupled with a bitter, and obscene, mockery of male homosexuality. Budur-as-Qamar is a "man" who recites a series of poems about men who can only consummate a sexual act with their wives when they turn the women over and penetrate them like boys. Are we to read this as misogyny or as a kind of latent, repressed homosexuality, or both?

We may ask this same question of Qamar: how much homoeroticism are we justified in reading into or out of the behavior of Qamar?[13] Qamar at the very start of the story does not like women; he argues that he will not marry because he has "heard verses" about the cunning of women. His expectations are then more than met by the elaborate trick that his wife plays on him, while citing precisely the sort of "verses" that Qamar must have had in mind. His actions speak louder than his words: he keeps protesting that he loves her, but he does turn his back on her in bed on their first meeting, he does walk out on her after their marriage, and he has to be dragged kicking and screaming into bed with her at the end (thinking that she is a man, but still, he might have recognized her; even when he begins to recognize her genitalia, he still does not recognize *her*).

Budur may well blame Qamar for having left her (and robbed her: she comments, blandly, "It seems that he has taken the jewel and gone") as well as for turning his back to her in bed on their first encounter. This unexpressed (repressed?) resentment may best explain her quite evident sadistic pleasure in tormenting both Hayat and Qamar. Budur-as-Qamar is quite willing to humiliate the entirely innocent Hayat; when Budur-as-Qamar fails to consummate the marriage with Hayat, just as Qamar had failed to consummate his first assignation with Budur, Hayat wonders, "Is every beautiful person so conceited?" She is wrong about the primary reason for Budur's rejection of her but not entirely wrong: Budur's narcissism limits the field of her lovers not to herself but to someone who closely or exactly resembles her.

But it is Qamar whom Budur-as-Qamar truly humiliates when he thinks she is the king. Her own rather lame excuse ("Do not reproach me, for I only did it in jest, to increase the pleasure and joy") explains nothing but the pleasure that the trickster takes in manipulating others and keeping them in the power of the trickster's knowledge and the victim's ignorance.[14] The closeted sexual motives seem to me to make the best sense of this twisted story: she plays the trick on her husband in order to exert power over him as he had exerted power over her, to put him in danger of being raped just as his absence had put her in danger of being raped and his initial rejection of her had left her with the suspicion that he might have raped her in her sleep: "You came to me while I was asleep, and I do not know what you did to me." The rape of the husband by the wife in drag is actually carried out in another variant of the tale of the Clever Wife in which there is "a parodized sodomy which the woman carries out in the guise of a physician with a radish, and thus emasculates the man and dominates him."[15] Other men, too, in other stories (notably, Siegfried with Brünnhilde), exchange rings with sleeping women. Are these exchanges symbolic of rape?[16] What does it mean, then, to take the maidenhead/ring from a sleeping woman? The tale of Qamar and Budur conflates the two sexual extremes in two different ways: first a mock rape as a revenge for rejection (Budur-as-Qamar with Qamar) and then the accusation of rape in revenge for rejection (the two queens' calumny against the two sons). Jamel Eddine

Bencheikh sees Budur as an incarnation of the Greek mythic princess Kainis, who is raped and then obtains the boon of being transformed into a man, in order to be invulnerable.[17]

When Budur-as-Qamar teased Qamar about forgetting how she was in bed, she laughed "until she fell on her back," precisely the sexual position for a woman that the obscene poems explicitly rejected (advising the women to turn over on their stomachs) and that therefore may be an invitation for sex in the missionary position. The little touches of revenge in Budur's trick are bitter; in the couple's first encounter, she had touched Qamar's penis and felt ashamed of her own desire; now she gets him to touch what he thinks is her penis and enjoys his confusion when it is not there. Her revenge extends into the last part of the story, when she almost makes him destroy his son (by Hayat) when she claims that the boy had raped her.

One of the obscene verses that Budur-as-Qamar recites to Qamar implies that one of the reasons why Budur-as-Qamar does not sleep with women is that s/he does not want to have children[18] (though a legitimate son is the raison d'être of the typical Clever Wife). Budur does have a son, but he is a problem rather than a solution. The blithe statement that Qamar "lived with his wives in happiness and delight and fidelity and cheerfulness, spending one night with each in turn," evokes the Middle Eastern tradition that goes spectacularly awry in the Hebrew Bible story of Rachel and Leah and fares little better here, where the "fidelity and cheerfulness" is certainly short-lived. The women proposition one another's sons, are rejected, and cry rape. We know this as the "Potiphar's wife" scenario in the Hebrew Bible (Genesis 39), or the Greek myth of Phaedra, reprocessing rejection as rape, and it is one of the reasons for the frequent conflation of these two aspects of sex which appear to be polar opposites. The fact that the solution to all this transvestism and quasi-incest is to send the women home to live with their fathers might give a Freudian pause; but Qamar, too, ends up in his father's realm, and it was in order to return to his father that Qamar left Budur in the first place. Here I think the return to the fathers indicates little more than one more example of the virulent misogyny (and in this case the literal patriarchy) of the story.

But it is the narcissism, rather than the misogyny, that contributes most to our understanding of this permutation of the theme, for such excessive self-regard is surely one of the sources of self-imitation: if you cannot think of anyone you like better than yourself, why imitate anyone else? Daniel Beaumont has written eloquently on the narcissism in this tale, which he interprets in the light of the relevant insights of Freud and Lacan.[19] He remarks that "Qamar's inability to recognize Budur in the sexual masquerade further emphasizes the point in relation to him. While he loves her does he ever truly see her as she is? Or is he simply captured by his own image in the mirror of *Verliebtheit*?"[20] Bencheikh views the couple as an androgyne and explains, "From the moment when they perceive their mutual existence, they love one another because they recognize one another. . . . They actually constitute a double body that a single soul animates. . . . The world is nothing but a mirror that sends back to them a single image, their own."[21]

Moreover, since Qamar exactly resembles Budur, in imitating him she is imitating herself. The love of Budur and Qamar for partners who resemble them demonstrates the devastating self-reflexivity of narcissistic love. Budur is so beautiful "that everyone who sees her is jealous even of himself," a remark suggestive of the sexual transformation that allows a prince in a contemporary Kannada story to make love to his own left half.[22] They are alike, too, in the incestuous overtones of their narcissism. Before Budur and Qamar meet, neither wishes to marry; on the surface, they have very different reasons—he distrusts all women, while she does not want to give up her freedom[23]—but deeper down we encounter the same reason in both of them: he admires only his mother,[24] while she prefers her father to any other husband or lover: "Any one that did not know the king, or father of this incomparable princess, would be apt to imagine, from the great respect and kindness he shews her, that he was in love with his daughter. Never did lover do more for a mistress the most endearing, than he has been seen to do for her. In a word, never was jealousy more watchful over one than he is over her."[25] The narcissistic self replicates the self, projects the self onto all other love objects, resembles them, and, finally, becomes them.

The Rings

Budur and Qamar exchange two rings in a mock wedding ceremony, but neither ring is intentionally given: on the contrary, each of the lovers takes the ring from the hand of a partner who cannot give it freely because he or she is asleep. (In *The Arabian Nights' Entertainments*, but not in the Mahdi/Haddawy edition, Qamar puts one of his own rings on Budur's finger when he takes her ring, which has no inscription; she does not take his ring from him—nor does she touch or kiss any part of him but his hand.)[26] This episode was probably adapted from another tale in the *Ocean of the River of Stories*, the tale of the prince of Malava and the princess of Swan Island:[27]

A prince of Malava named Shridarshana married a princess named Padmishtha and enjoyed all pleasures with her. A merchant found, on the edge of a tank, an image of the god Ganesha, carved out of a jewel. He gave it to that prince, who, seeing that it was priceless, out of his devotion set it up in a very splendid manner in a temple. Ganesha, pleased, had his servants (Ganas) bring Shridarshana in his sleep to Anangamanjari, the princess of Hamsa-dvipa ("Swan Island"), who had begged him for a husband. The Ganas did as he told them to do.

The prince and princess woke up and fell in love and told one another their names and lineages and where they lived. Though they quickly shed their mistaken idea that they had dreamt of one another, they exchanged jewels in order to make certain. And though they were full of desire, and eager to consummate their union, the Ganas put them to sleep again.

As soon as Shridarshana fell asleep, his desire unsatisfied, they took him and carried him back to his own palace. He awoke and saw himself wearing a woman's ornaments and thought, "Oh, what is this? Where is the daughter of the king of Swan Island? And where is that heavenly room? And where am I here? It cannot be a dream, for here are those ornaments on me; so it must be some trick of fate." While he was engaged in these speculations, his loving wife Padmishtha woke up and questioned him and comforted him, and so he passed the night. On the next day, he appeared wearing the ornaments marked with the name of Anangamanjari. His people tried in vain to find out where Swan Island was, and the prince pined away.

Meanwhile the Princess Anangamanjari woke up and remembered what had taken place in the night, and saw her body adorned with Shridarshana's ornaments. And she thought, "These ornaments prove that I cannot have been deluded by a dream, and they fill me with love for an unattainable object." When her father saw her wearing the ornaments of a man, he sent an envoy, who went to Malava and brought Shridarshana to Swan Island. Shridarshana and Anangamanjari married and returned to Malava, where Shridarshana lived in happiness with his two wives.[28]

This version insists, again and again, on the role of exchanged jewelry—marked with the wearer's name—as proof of an experience that would otherwise be regarded as a dream. And as this jewelry is strongly gendered, the exchange of rings (and other things) amounts to a kind of muted cross-dressing, which may have inspired the more extensive cross-dressing later in the Arabic version.

Departing from the conventional roles of rings in tales of Clever Wives as proof that the lovers have slept together, the rings in the tale of Budur and Qamar, like the jewelry in the tale of Shridarshana and Anangamanjari, prove only that they have met and fallen in love, but that is enough. First, Qamar uses Budur's ring to persuade his father that he really did spend the night with Budur; he likens the ring's power of proof to that of a blood-stained sword as proof of a killing and says, "How could all this be a lie, when the matter of the ring is true? Were it not for the ring, I would have thought that it was a dream. This is her ring on my little finger at this moment. Look at the ring, O King, and see how valuable it is."[29] The fact that the ring is valuable is part of the proof: the dream woman was a princess. Later, Budur's ring, sent with a letter, is what makes Budur recognize Qamar after their first separation and before their marriage. (In *The Arabian Nights' Entertainments*, the letter says, "He presumes to present you with his ring, as a token of his passion; and, in exchange, would be proud to receive yours, which he encloses in this billet. If you will condescend to return it, as a reciprocal assurance of your love, he will reckon himself the happiest of all lovers.")[30]

Qamar's ring is equally useful to Budur. It convinces her that she did not dream their encounter, and it convinces her brother Marzawan, too; when Marzawan hears that Qamar had exchanged rings with his dream woman, he puts two and two together, and the sum is Qamar and Budur as a couple. But Budur never uses Qamar's ring to convince anyone else, and so they lock her up in the harem as a madwoman, until Marzawan rescues her. In the *Arabian Nights' Entertainments*, Budur does attempt to use the ring to persuade her father, but in vain: " 'But that your majesty may no longer doubt whether I have seen this cavalier, whether he has lain with me, whether I have caressed him, . . . see, if you please this ring.' She then reached forth her hand, and shewed the king a man's ring on her finger. The king did not know what to make of all this; but as he had confined her for mad, so now he began to think her more mad than ever."[31] And so he still locks her up as a madwoman. In both texts, the ring always works as hard evidence for the man, but not always for the woman.

As in several European medieval romances, the ring is inscribed with the foreknowledge that it will be given to someone who may abandon, betray, and/or forget the giver ("Do not think that I have forgotten your vows, no matter how long your cruel disdain lasts"). And this is precisely what happens, when the role of the ring(s) is taken up by the "blood-red jewel" that is hidden in Budur's genitals and acts as a metaphor for them.[32] Andras Hamori speaks of "the mysterious jewel . . . which, whatever else it is, is certainly a metonymy of sex."[33] But what of the writing on the jewel? *The Arabian Nights' Entertainments* tells us that this talisman was a kind of Chinese horoscope, a scheme of Budur's nativity, drawn from the constellations of heaven, which her mother had made for her as a charm that would keep her from any harm as long as she had it about her.[34] It was a carnelian engraved with unknown figures and characters, which would function to identify her. Hamori has this to say:

> The indecipherable jewel snatched from the hero by a predatory creature might be an image of anxiety about sexual possession, of a worry (justified by later events) much like Gratiano's about Nerissa's ring. Or, the failure to read the inscription on this intimate jewel might be seen as an encoding of fears of inadequacy. ("He does not know its secret," says Budur). Anxiety about the very nature of sexual passion would fit too: like magic, sexuality threatens to cut across the order of things, and sexual magic is like the magic of rings and lamps in being detachable from the rest of the personality.[35]

But in several Arabic texts, what is hidden in Budur's pants is not just a jewel but a ring set with a blood-red jewel.[36] The widely distributed theme of a ring of identity that is lost and then found in a fish (reuniting separated lovers)[37] is here conflated with the also common theme in which a bird mistakes a ruby for flesh and carries it off, causing the separation of lovers who are reunited when the ruby is found in the craw of the bird.[38] These myths convey the sense of the unbelievable, unlikely good luck of finding a jewel in an animal.

Two Viziers, Two Stories

The theme of the ring(s) found first in a dream and then in real life occurs elsewhere in the Indian,[39] Persian, and Arabic traditions. In a Jewish story from the Persian oral tradition, for instance, a woman who cross-dresses uses a ring to find the husband whose father has appeared to her in a dream and given her the ring.[40] The tale of Budur takes in new directions the theme of belief in a world that we encounter in dream and bring back into waking life, a world sometimes left hanging by the thread of a ring. But the tale of Budur and Qamar is *not*, in fact, about a dream meeting, though the characters in it think it is; they actually (magically) meet. The lovers also meet in "The Story of the Two Viziers" (within "The Story of the Three Apples"),[41] which is probably older than the tale of Budur.[42] In both stories, one male and one female djinn catch sight of a beautiful woman and a beautiful man who are asleep in far distant cities; the djinns think that (a) each is surpassingly beautiful (the male djinn admires the woman, and the female djinn, the man) and (b) they look alike. The theme of narcissism, and of a single, nongendered standard of beauty, is thus a basic underpinning of both plots. The djinns bring the lovers together for one night and then part them again, leaving them to find one another. But in "The Story of the Two Viziers," the lovers consummate their love on the first night, whereas Qamar and Budur do not. And in "The Story of the Two Viziers," there is no ring; instead there is an elaborate series of tests by which the hero proves that he was in bed with the woman (the taste of the pomegranate he cooks; the reconstruction of an entire room, with all his clothes, that he recognizes; a hunchback upside down in a privy; and so forth). This contrast is yet another indication that the ring in the tale of Budur, however muted, still bears a major proportion of the weight of the proof of identity in the plot of the tale of the Clever Wife.

And so the skeleton of the Clever Wife provides a framework that reveals Budur as the heroine of the story. For she is the one who breaks out of the initial conventional situation of amazing physical identity with her lover to become a most unconventional woman and someone quite different from him in every way—more active, more powerful, more deceptive. Yet she can only accomplish her goal of union with him by pretending to be him, using her cleverness to play on the convention of their identical beauty.

NOTES

1. Richard F. Burton, trans., *The Book of the Thousand Nights and a Night, with Introduction, Explanatory Notes on the Manners and Customs of Moslem Men and a Terminal Essay upon the History of the Nights*, 16 vols. (Benares: Kama-shastra Society, 1885–87), 3:212–309 (the 170th to 217th Nights, this being the end of the tale of Budur; the tale of her son goes on much longer).

2. Husain Haddawy, trans., *The Arabian Nights II: Sinbad and Other Popular Stories*, based on the text edited by Muhsin Mahdi (New York: Norton, 1996), 165–268.

3. Robert L. Mack, ed., *Arabian Nights' Entertainments* (Oxford: Oxford University Press, 1995), based on Antoine Galland's twelve-volume *Mille et une nuit* (1704–17, translated anonymously into English between 1706 and 1721), 357–440.

4. Haddawy, *Arabian Nights II*, 165–268.

5. Carol Thomas Neely, *Broken Nuptials in Shakespeare's Plays* (New Haven: Yale University Press, 1985), 78.

6. A frequent theme in Celtic literature in particular.

7. Somadeva, *Kathasaritsagara* (*The Ocean of the Rivers of Story*) (Bombay: Nirnaya Sagara Press, 1930), 124 (18.5).131–237. The story is translated as *The Ocean of Story*, 10 vols., ed. N. M. Penzer, trans. C. W. Tawney (London: Chas. J. Sawyer, 1924), 9:77 (chapter 124, or 171g).

8. S. M. Natesa Sastri, *Dravidian Nights: Being a Translation of Madanakamara-jankadai* (Madras: Excelsior, 1886), 246; James Hinton Knowles, *Folk-Tales of Kashmir* (London: Kegan Paul, Trench, Trübner, 1892), 104; Kamil Zvelebil, *Two Tamil Folktales: The Story of King Matanakama; The Story of Peacock Ravana* (Delhi: Motilal Banarsidass, 1987), 153–64.

9. The *Arabian Nights' Entertainments* omits the entire episode in which Budur-as-Qamar takes Qamar to bed in drag and therefore also omits all the obscene poetry; in this text, she brings him to her bedroom but then changes into women's clothing. Burton, of course, delights in the scene of cross-dressing and produces a number of stunningly obscene verses, of which one will have to suffice here:

    "The penis smooth and round was made with anus best to match it;
    Had it been made for cunnus' sake it had been formed like hatchet!"

Burton, *Book of the Thousand Nights and a Night*, 2:303.

10. The *Nights* as a whole condemns homosexuals. There are many stories in which the evil magician is imputed to be a pederast.

11. This idea is developed at some length by Jamel Eddine Bencheikh, in "Le conte de Qamar az-Zaman," chapter 3 of *Les mille et une nuits ou la parole prisonnière* (Paris: Gallimard, 1988), 97–135.

12. Daniel Beaumont, "The Mirror of Love," chapter 4 in *Slave of Desire: Sex, Love, and Death in The 1001 Nights* (Cranbury, NJ: Fairleigh Dickinson University Press, 2002), 66–88 (here 84).

13. And how much can we read into other stories of rejecting husbands? It is an argument that has been made about Bertram in Shakespeare's *All's Well That Ends Well*.

14. In the *Arabian Nights' Entertainments* the excuse is merely that "she put a constraint on herself, believing that it was for both their interests that she should act the part of a king a little longer before she made herself known" (406).

15. Galit Hasan-Rokem, *Proverbs in Israeli Folk Narratives: A Structural Semantic Analysis*, Folklore Fellows Communications 232 (Helsinki: Academia Scientiarum Fennica, 1982), 81, 94–95, citing IFA 7291, IFA 11911.

16. For an argument that certain Norse and German texts suppressed the rape of Brünnhilde by Siegfried, see Theodore Andersson, *The Legend of Brünnhilde* (Ithaca: Cornell University Press, 1980), 222–24. For the symbolic equation of taking a ring and taking a maidenhead, see A. T. Hatto, *The Nibelungenlied* (Harmondsworth, UK: Penguin, 1965), 298–99.

17. Bencheikh, "Le conte de Qamar az-Zaman," 106.

18. In Burton's translation, "My soul thy sacrifice! I chose thee out / Who art not menstruous nor oviparous. // Did I with woman mell, I should beget / Brats till the wide wide world grew strait for us" (*Book of the Thousand Nights and a Night*, 3:303).

19. Beaumont, "The Mirror of Love," 66–88.

20. Ibid., 85.

21. Bencheikh, "Le conte de Qamar az-Zaman," 105. My translation from the French.

22. A. K. Ramanujan, "The Prince Who Married His Own Left Side," in *A Flowering Tree, and Other Oral Tales from India* (Berkeley: University of California Press, 1997).

23. As the *Arabian Nights' Entertainments* translates this passage, she says, "Where shall I find such stately palaces and delicious gardens as I have with your majesty? Under your good pleasure I am unconstrained in all things, and have the same honours done me that are paid to your own person. These are advantages I cannot expect to find anywhere else; to whatsoever husband I should give myself, men love ever to be masters, and I do not care to be commanded" (365).

24. As the *Arabian Nights' Entertainments* translates this passage, "I know not whether I could ever prevail on myself to marry, not only on account of the troubles wives bring a man, and which I am very sensible of, though unmarried,

but also by reason of their many impostures, wickedness, and treacheries, which I have read of in authors. . . . [He tells his mother] I doubt not but there are a great number of wise, virtuous, good, affable, and generous women in the world; and would to God they all resembled you!" (359, 361).

25. Ibid., 365.
26. Ibid., 369–70.
27. Bencheikh, "Le conte de Qamar az-Zaman," 101, suggests this source.
28. Somadeva, *Kathasaritsagara* 12.6.(73), 325–97; Penzer, *Ocean of Story*, 6:124–26.
29. Haddawy, *Arabian Nights II*, 225.
30. *Arabian Nights' Entertainments*, 388.
31. Ibid., 377.
32. The jewels are similarly metaphorical in Denis Diderot's tale *Les bijoux indiscrets* (*The Indiscreet Jewels*), in *Œuvres complètes de Diderot, Philosophie IV, Belles-Lettres I* (*Romans, contes, critique littéraire*) (Paris: Garnier Frères, 1875), 130–378.
33. Andras Hamori, "The Magian and the Whore: Readings of Qamar al-Zaman," *Studia Islamica* 43 (1976), reprinted in *The 1001 Nights: Critical Essays and Annotated Bibliography*, ed. Kay Hardy Campbell, 25–40 (Cambridge, MA: Dar Mahjar, 1985), 26.
34. *Arabian Nights' Entertainments*, 391.
35. Hamori, "The Magian and the Whore," 34.
36. It is a ring with a blood-red stone in Robert Laffont's translation (Paris: Robert Laffont, collection "Bouquins," 1980) of Jean-Charles Mardrus's version, "Histoire de Kamaralzaman avec la princesse Boudour," cited in Bencheikh, "Le conte de Qamar az-Zaman," 98.
37. Wendy Doniger, "Magic Rings and the Return of the Repressed," in *Spirituality and Religion: Psychoanalytic Perspectives*, ed. Jerome A. Winer and James William Anderson (Catskill, NY: Mental Health Resources), 243–56.
38. In a further variant, in the *Kathasaritsagara*, a queen bathes in a tank filled with red dye and a bird mistakes her for raw flesh and carries her off. Somadeva, *Kathasaritsagara* 2.1(9.).40ff.; Penzer, *Ocean of Story*, 1:97–99.
39. Wendy Doniger O'Flaherty, *Dreams, Illusion, and Other Realities* (Chicago: University of Chicago Press, 1984), 61–64.
40. Howard Schwartz, "The Miracle of the Ring," in *Gabriel's Palace: Jewish Mystical Tales* (New York: Oxford University Press, 1993), 158–60 (source listed as "Persia: Oral Tradition").
41. "The Story of the Two Viziers" is elaborately developed in in Husain Haddawy, trans., *Arabian Nights* (New York: Norton, 1990), 157–206.
42. Scholars generally locate the tale of Qamar and Budur on the fringes of the oldest core of the *Arabian Nights* and "The Story of the Two Viziers" as a part of that core. We might therefore speculate that the author of the story of Budur knew the story of the two viziers. Robert Irwin, *The Arabian Nights: A Companion* (London: Allan Lane, 1994).

6

White Magic

Voltaire and Galland's Mille et une nuits

ROGER PEARSON

Si tu vas à l'orient, tu seras à l'occident.
—Voltaire, *Le blanc et le noir*

"Her stories are white magic," says Sultan Shahriyar delightedly of Shahrzad in the opening chapter of Naguib Mahfouz's 1982 novel *Arabian Nights and Days*: "Her stories are white magic. They open up worlds that invite reflection."[1] As we know, the "white magic" of *Alf layla wa-layla* first entered the bloodstream of European culture through Antoine Galland's translations-cum-adaptations published in French as *Les mille et une nuit* between 1704 and 1717.[2] Initially, as we also know, this bloodstream was aristocratically blue, from the marquise d'O . . .[3]—to whom the work is dedicated—to the various duchesses, marquises, and baronnes who borrowed and exchanged prepublication manuscripts of Galland's latest work.[4] Among these early enthusiasts was the duchesse du Maine, princess of the blood and granddaughter of the distinguished war hero le Grand Condé.

In 1692, when not quite sixteen, Louise-Bénédicte de Bourbon had
married the elder of Louis XIV's two illegitimate but subsequently
legitimized sons by Mme. de Montespan. In 1700 the duc and duchesse acquired the Château de Sceaux from the heirs of the king's finance
minister, Jean-Baptiste Colbert (1619–83), and the duchesse set about
creating a court of luxurious splendor that might lure allegiance away
from the dull pieties of Mme. de Maintenon at Versailles some ten miles
distant. The duchesse particularly loved the theater, and she arranged
and participated in lavish entertainments, for which she enlisted the
best literary and musical talents of the day, including Voltaire. These
entertainments culminated in the celebrated series of some fifteen or
sixteen "Grandes Nuits" held at Sceaux between July 1714 and May 1715:
fabulous, carefully scripted, all-night parties—so-called *nuits blanches*,[5]
or white nights like those of St. Petersburg—that might end with everyone assembling in the famous Pavillon de l'Aurore to witness the first
light of dawn. The Sun King, meanwhile, was dying and did so on 1
September 1715: the royally white magic of the duchesse was seemingly
in the ascendant.[6]

One of Voltaire's first surviving prose tales was most probably composed and orally delivered at Sceaux on the occasion of these "white
nights."[7] Entitled *Le crocheteur borgne* (The one-eyed porter), this brief
court entertainment wittily energizes the established tradition of the
conte libertin through the incorporation of newly fashionable Oriental motifs. In what turns out to be a drunkard's dream, the eponymous
Baghdad porter Mesrour (from the Arabic, meaning "happy"—for he
lacks, we are told, the eye "qui voit le mauvais côté des choses" [that sees
the bad side of things; 8])[8] saves the life of a princess during a carriage
accident and, as night falls, takes his sexual reward: without ceremony
but not without some cooperation. Following the arrival of the dawn—
"toujours trop diligente pour les amants" (ever too diligent for a lover's
liking; 6)—and in answer to Mesrour's prayer to the Prophet, the porter
and the princess enter a wonderful palace, and, after a splendid feast,
"tous les génies vinrent dans le plus grand ordre . . . prêter serment de
fidélité au maître de l'anneau, et baiser le doigt sacré auquel il le por-
tait" (all the djinns came in the most orderly fashion . . . to swear allegiance to the master of the ring, and to kiss the sacred finger on which
he wore it; 7). For Mesrour has unwittingly revealed himself possessor

of the magic ring of Solomon. This entry into the palace thus retells the incident of the almost-rape in fabulous terms that are at once sexually symbolic and an allegory of the bourgeois Voltaire's admission into the marvelous paradise of Sceaux. The story ends with the woken porter accepting without rancor that he must humbly return to his former state of unwashed unloveliness.[9]

Voltaire's sophisticated audience would have recognized several debts to Galland's *Mille et une nuits*, and in particular to the "The Sleeper Awakened" (in which the protagonist is transported to a magnificent palace where he feasts in the company of beautiful women and enjoys the powers of the most powerful caliph in Baghdad) and to "The Story of the Three Calenders" (in which Mesrour is Haroun Al Raschid's chief eunuch and a porter living in Baghdad, and the three calenders, all one-eyed, tell stories for a rich lady).[10] Mesrour's ring recalls that of Aladdin, while throughout the *Mille et une nuits* Solomon is credited with considerable powers, a feature that Galland in a footnote to the "Story of the Fisherman" attributes to Islamic belief.[11] As Voltaire and the duchesse stood together in the Pavilion of Aurora, awaiting light from the east, they must doubtless have savored the situation: a charismatic social inferior just turned twenty whiling the oh-so-brief night away in narrative flirtation with his forty-year-old hostess in a courtly setting that rather tended to confirm Sultan Shahriyar's dim view of conjugal behavior.[12]

In the event the duchesse's high ambitions came to naught, just as those of the young Voltaire met with several spectacular reverses. Both, indeed, spent time in prison.[13] They met again in late August 1746 when the duchesse, now seventy and widowed for the past ten years, invited Voltaire and Mme. Du Châtelet for a brief stay at the Château d'Anet, her summer residence near Dreux. They were invited back there one year later and stayed rather longer, performing in Voltaire's comedies for the pleasure of their theatrical hostess. Not long afterward, toward the end of 1747, Voltaire considered himself permitted on the basis of this renewed friendship to request refuge with the duchesse at Sceaux, following the celebrated occasion at Fontainebleau when he rather too audibly accused the queen of cheating at cards and he and Mme. Du Châtelet felt obliged to flee in the middle of the night.[14] According to Sébastien Longchamp,[15] Voltaire's secretary, Mme. Du Châtelet headed for Paris while Voltaire was smuggled under cover of darkness into a remote private apartment at Sceaux. And there, over a period of a fortnight or more,[16] he lay low, his shutters permanently closed. Each night, after the duchesse had retired and dismissed her servants, Voltaire was escorted to her bedroom by a valet-in-the-know and took supper by her bed. The arrangement preserved the secret of Voltaire's whereabouts—not to mention the lady's reputation—and the two victims of royal prerogative were able to exchange gossip and anecdotes into the wee small hours, often until shortly before dawn. According to Longchamp, it was during these days at Sceaux that Voltaire worked on a number of his prose tales: *Le monde comme il va* (The way of the world), *Zadig*, *Memnon*, and "others," which "others" most probably included *Micromégas* and the *Histoire des voyages de Scarmentado*.[17] And this, as Longchamp also notes, was the moment at which Voltaire's career as a published *conteur* or storyteller began.

All of these stories are indebted to the *Mille et une nuits* and represent an implicit tribute to the white nights of Sceaux.[18] Admittedly the voyages of Scarmentado bear only passing resemblance to those of Sindbad, and in *Micromégas* the debt is seemingly slight: just one "mufti" back on the hero's home star of Sirius who bans Micromégas's scientific study of fleas on grounds of heresy—an odd narrative detail, it seems, until one realizes that Micromégas, as an "inhabitant of Sirius," is also described as "le Sirien," as though he were a Syrian from the very land where Galland had procured his Oriental tales.[19] As to the three stories actually named, Longchamp does not explicitly mention that Voltaire read them to the duchesse; but it is almost inconceivable that he did not.[20] Fearing royal anger, like Scheherazade, Voltaire was buying time by illuminating the dark winter evenings of his duchesse-sultana with the white magic of the Oriental tale.

Thus in *Le monde comme il va* he presents an allegory of his own position as the man who has recently seen Louis XV's court at firsthand and is now reporting back to the duchesse. He is Babouc,[21] who is dispatched by the djinn Ituriel to study the ways of Persepolis and who gives his mixed report in the form of a statue composed of a combination of mud and precious stones. The story line of *Memnon* most probably derives from "The Sleeper Awakened," in which Abou Hassan's plans for ordering his life fail like Memnon's.[22] *Zadig* more explicitly commemorates the white nights of Sceaux by opening with the story of a one-eyed man (a familiar figure in the *Mille et une nuits*) and repeated tales of wifely infidelity. Like Mesrour in *Le crocheteur borgne* the temporarily one-eyed hero Zadig is a man of moderation and good sense, ready to take the rough with the smooth as he goes in search of happiness. Moreover he is the opposite of Sultan Shahriyar or is perhaps a Shahriyar who has learned his lesson from Scheherazade's tales: "Zadig surtout ne se vantait pas de mépriser les femmes et les subjuguer" (Above all, Zadig did not regard it as a matter of pride to despise and subjugate women; 56)—even though, in ironic counterpoint to the *Mille et une nuits*, this story constitutes a "female rogues' gallery"[23] in which Zadig's beloved, Astarté, is the only woman a man could possibly trust. And of course the remainder of the story plainly recalls the *Mille et une nuits*: the Middle Eastern setting, the journeys, the riddles, the references to griffins and basilisks, the story of the envier and the envied, and so on.[24] And here is Voltaire presenting himself in the Dedicatory Epistle at the beginning of *Zadig* as the Persian poet Sadi—Sadi/Zadig, for Voltaire is both writer and hero of his own story[25]—and dedicating his tale to Sultana Sheraa: *shera*, which Voltaire understood to mean "brightness" in Arabic, a name not quite that of Scheherazade but the name by which Voltaire also believed the Arab world to know the star Sirius.[26]

Here, too, is Voltaire pasticheing the style of the real Sadi and explaining the fictional provenance of *Zadig* in these terms:

> Il fut écrit d'abord en ancien chaldéen.[27] . . . On le traduisit en arabe, pour amuser le célèbre sultan Ouloug-beg. C'était du temps où les Arabes et les Persans commençaient à écrire des *Mille et Une Nuits*, des *Mille et Un Jours*, etc. Ouloug aimait mieux la lecture de *Zadig*; mais les sultanes aimaient mieux les *Mille et Un*. "Comment pouvez-vous préférer, leur disait le sage Ouloug, des contes qui sont sans raison et qui ne signifient rien?—C'est précisément pour cela que nous les aimons," répondaient les sultanes.—Je me flatte que vous ne leur ressemblerez pas, et que vous serez un vrai Ouloug. J'espère même que, quand vous serez lasse des conversations générales, qui ressemblent assez aux *Mille et Un*, à cela près qu'elles sont moins amusantes, je pourrai trouver une minute pour avoir l'honneur de vous parler raison. (*Romans et contes*, 56)

(It was originally written in the Ancient Chaldee. . . . It was translated into Arabic for the amusement of the celebrated Sultan Ouloug-Beg. This was about the time that the Arabs and the Persians were beginning to write the *Thousand and One Nights*, the *Thousand and One Days*, etc. Ouloug preferred *Zadig*; but the sultanas were fonder of the *Thousand and One Nights*. "How can thee possibly," wise Ouloug would say to them, "prefer stories that make no sense and have no point?"—"That is precisely why we do like them," would come the sultanas' reply.—I flatter myself that thou wilt not be as they, and that thou wilt be a real Ouloug. I venture even to hope that when thou tirest of general conversation, which is rather like the *Thousand and One Nights* except that it is less amusing, I shall find a minute in which to have the honour of a serious word with thee myself.)[28]

Voltaire, as Sadi, clearly hopes that the "brightness" of Sheraa will represent the "brightness" of enlightenment, but enlightenment comes in many forms. In describing *Zadig* as "a work which sayeth more than it may appear to say," Sadi-Voltaire may also be playfully sympathizing with the sultanas who have every reason to prefer Scheherazade's oblique didacticism.[29]

Was the duchesse responsible, then, for Voltaire's renewed involvement with the *Mille et une nuits* and thus responsible also for launching him on a path that would lead beyond the *conte oriental* to *Candide* and *L'Ingénu*?[30] Not exclusively. The 1740s in fact represented the high-water mark of the fashion for Oriental tales in France.[31] But nor was it fashion alone that spawned *Zadig*. Voltaire's attitude to storytelling was changing, from the disdain of a man who had sought fame in the classically respectable genres of tragedy, epic, and history to the delight of a deadpan polemicist and the wry satisfaction of a skeptic who increasingly regarded the notion of divine providence as the tallest of tall tales.[32] In 1745, for example, Voltaire had published a short essay on the fable in which he took issue with pious Jansenists who wished to proscribe all reference to Greek and Roman mythology on the grounds that such tales are but the puerile fictions of a pagan world not yet visited by Christ. Turning pious Jansenist moralizing against them, Voltaire argues that such myths often have a clear moral lesson to impart, while true stories from the past tend rather to display the success of the wicked: "L'histoire nous apprend ce que sont les humains, / La fable ce qu'ils doivent être" (History teaches us what human beings are, / Fable what human beings should be).[33] A desire to ban fiction, he concludes, is the hallmark of the fanatic.

The picture presented here of moralizing fiction is, of course, tactical, and Voltaire himself nowhere believes in such a simple view of the didactic function of literature. But increasingly from this point on we see him celebrating the humanizing effect of storytelling, how it breeds broad-mindedness and tolerance by presenting the perplexing details and contradictions of human experience. That indeed is the point of *Zadig*. And it is the point of the hero's famous response to the angel Jesrad's glib account of a well-regulated universe: "Mais . . ." (But . . .).[34] Rather than providing simple solutions, the story—as Mahfouz's Shahriyar says—"open[s] up worlds that invite reflection." Or as Voltaire himself says in his article on friendship in the *Dictionnaire philosophique* (1764), in which he praises Greek and Arab culture for the ability to evoke the warmth of friendship through story: "Les contes que ces peuples ont imaginé sur l'amitié sont admirables; nous n'en avons point de pareils, nous sommes un peu secs en tout" (The stories these peoples have imagined about friendship are admirable; we don't have any like them, we're a little cut-and-dried about everything).[35] This is the Voltaire also of the article titled "Arabes" in the *Questions sur l'Encyclopédie* (1770), in which he writes of the *Mille et une nuits* as exemplifying a tradition of imaginative genius that predates the Christian Bible and is with us still:

Leur génie n'a point changé, ils [les Arabes] font encore des *Mille et une nuits*, comme ils en faisaient du temps qu'ils imaginaient un Bach ou Bacchus, qui traversait la mer Rouge avec trois millions d'hommes, de femmes et d'enfants; qui arrêtait le soleil et la lune, qui faisait jaillir des fontaines de vin avec une baguette, laquelle il changeait en serpent, quand il voulait.

(Their genius has not changed, they [the Arabs] are still inventing *Thousand and One Nights*, the way they used to in the days when they imagined a Bach or Bacchus, who crossed the Red Sea with three million men, women and children; who stopped the sun and the moon in their course, who made fountains of wine spring up with a stick, which he could change into a snake as the fancy took him.)[36]

For a Voltaire whose deism has been shown to owe much to the example of Islam,[37] Moses is thus a recycled Bacchus, himself borrowed by the Greeks from the pre-Islamic Arabs.

It is conventional to argue that Voltaire, like others in the eighteenth century, used the Oriental tale for his own philosophical ends, cloaking his satirical barbs and his metaphysical quandaries in the quaint costumes of the East the better to impart the new gospel of reason. And it is certainly true that in Voltaire's response to the example of the *Mille et une nuits* up until *Zadig* and *Memnon* we see him carefully avoiding almost all elements of the supernatural. *Le crocheteur borgne* is the story of a dream; in *Le monde comme il va* only the initial premise of Babouc being dispatched by a djinn, Ituriel, bespeaks Oriental magic—though the story ends slyly with a reference (added in 1752) to Jonah spending three days in the belly of a whale, suggesting that the Old Testament is no more credible or historically true than the *Mille et une nuits*. In *Zadig* itself the laws of nature are broken only by the hermit who turns into the angel Jesrad, and this because his Leibnizian explanation of divine providence (like that delivered by the djinn in *Memnon, ou la sagesse* also) is the *one* unbelievable bit of nonsense in a story that has a quite different logic of its own. Admittedly, in chapter 6, a parrot says "yes," but we all know that parrots can speak.

But what about the talking phoenix in *La princesse de Babylone* (1768), not to mention his two friends from "l'Arabie heureuse" (today's Yemen), the griffins who will transport the princess eastward on a flying sofa complete with drawers containing her favorite biscuits? Or the marvelous menagerie of *Le taureau blanc* (1774), assembled on the banks of the Nile during those unfortunate seven years after Nebuchadnezzar had been magicked into the eponymous white bull? And what of *Le blanc et le noir* (1764), Voltaire's most evident pastiche of the *Mille et une nuits*,[38] in which, in a dream, the hero Rustan—a native of Kandahar—falls inconveniently for the princess of Kashmir at a fair in Kabul. His two servants, Topaze and Ébène, become, respectively, his good djinn and his bad djinn, exponents of white and black magic, as they mutate into all manner of creature or natural force in his service. When Rustan wonders on waking how he has managed to live six months of adventure in the space of one hour of sleep (a question broached in Galland's seventeenth night), Topaze offers to send him his parrot. The parrot is but one and a half years old and yet was with Noah on his ark. Perhaps he knows the answer? The story ends with the words, "On lui amena le perroquet, lequel parla ainsi" (They brought him the parrot, who spoke thus; *Romans et contes*, 267), followed by an editorial note to the effect that the rest of the manuscript of this story has never been found.

Voltaire's continued and indeed increasingly extensive recourse to the topoi of Oriental and biblical narrative in the last two decades of his life has generally been dismissed as enslavement to fashion, lack of narrative imagination, or even failing intellectual powers.[39] But the interest was genuine, and the reasons for it several. One motive, already apparent in his 1745 essay on fables, was to upset the Jansenists. *Le blanc et le noir* was first published in a collection of apparently miscellaneous tales and other documents titled the *Contes de Guillaume Vadé* that has the single, unifying agenda of disobeying every possible Jansenist stricture—hence the bawdy fairy tale in verse that opens it, *Ce qui plaît aux dames* (What pleases the ladies), and that laments the lost world of fireside stories telling of demons and sprites and will-o'-the wisps:

> On a banni les démons et les fées;
> Sous la raison les grâces étouffées
> Livrent nos cœurs à l'insipidité;
> Le raisonner tristement s'accrédite;
> On court, hélas! après la vérité;
> Ah! croyez-moi, l'erreur a son mérite.

> (And now they've banished spirits, fairies too;
> Reason rules, a story must be true.
> But the heart grows dull in a world of gray,
> Where sense and logic may not brook demur,
> And correctness is the order of the day.
> Believe me when I say: it can be right to err.)[40]

And for Jansenists, with their moral austerity and unwavering belief in predestination, read fanatics of every kind: people who like to think that all issues are nicely "cut-and-dried."

The errancy of fiction and what in 1774 Voltaire approvingly calls the "imagination" of the *Mille et une nuits*[41] are fundamental to human experience, a way of confronting the insoluble metaphysical conundrums of destiny and time, a way not of providing answers but rather of leaving the question open. For as he noted in the preface to the *Dictionnaire philosophique*, "Les livres les plus utiles sont ceux dont les lecteurs font eux-mêmes la moitié" (the most useful books are those where the readers themselves do half the work),[42] a lesson he could have learned—perhaps did learn—from the *Mille et une nuits*. Hence, like *Le blanc et le noir*, many of Voltaire's *contes* end with a blank space to be filled, sometimes metaphorically, sometimes literally. Thus Micromégas promises the earthlings "un beau livre de philosophie" (a fine book of philosophy) in which they would discover "le bout des choses" (what was what). Its white pages are empty, for such is the blank magic of story.[43] Like Scheherazade, Voltaire knows the art of the cliffhanger, leaving us poised on the brink of a resolution that can only come from us. Stories buy time, give pause.

In conclusion, I would suggest that the example of the *Mille et une nuits*, and of all the strange tales that it both recycled and spawned, gradually worked its magic on Voltaire's mind over the course of his life. He was a scrupulous and pioneering historian who fought to banish myth and hearsay from his histories, but he was also a dramatist who would, with poetic license, bend material from these histories in the service of pathos and instruction. He was an empiricist who loved facts and hated metaphysics, but he was also a skeptic who suspected firm conclusions, a polemicist who loathed all univocal and unilateral despotisms of system, governance, and book. He was the man who ridiculed literal, unswerving belief in the supernatural elements of religious doctrine, and he therefore warmed increasingly to the life-preserving and life-enhancing power of imagined stories for their very capacity to muddy the waters of the allegedly incontrovertible, "to open up worlds that invite reflection." Thus, it was not only by the light of reason but after rubbing Aladdin's lamp that Voltaire came to realize the full *compass* of story, not just its range and scope but also its capacity to measure and to guide, to orient. Ever since his first encounter with Galland's *Mille et une nuits*, the glow of an alternative enlightenment—a literary rather than a philosophical enlightenment—had been dawning on Voltaire from the East.

So we have the duchesse du Maine and her white nights (in the 1740s as well as the 1710s) to thank, at least in part, for the "white magic" of Voltaire's *contes*, and not least for *Candide*: *Candide*, whose inconclusive last chapter titled "Conclusion" is set just outside Constantinople, on the very threshold between Occident and Orient, and in which it is from the lips of "le bon musulman" (the good Muslim) that Candide learns the all-important final lesson: "il faut cultiver notre jardin" (we must cultivate our garden). So, too, it is time that we began to include Voltaire's "white magic" in the story, now increasingly told, of how Galland's *Mille et une nuits* transformed the European imagination and prompted both a remodeling of literary forms and a radical rethink of the very notion of *vraisemblance*.[44]

NOTES

1. Naguib Mahfouz, *Arabian Nights and Days*, trans. Denys Johnson-Davies (New York: Anchor Books, 1995), 2.
2. Voltaire's brief entry on Galland at the end of *Le siècle de Louis XIV* reads as follows: "Galland (Antoine), né en Picardie en 1646. Il apprit à Constantinople les langues orientales, et traduisit des contes arabes qu'on connaît sous le titre de *Mille et une nuits*; il y a mis beaucoup du sien. C'est un des livres les plus connus en Europe; il est amusant pour toutes les nations. Mort en 1715." [Galland (Antoine), born in Picardy in 1646. He studied Oriental languages in Constantinople and translated some Arab tales known as the *Thousand and One Nights*, into which he has put much of his own devising. This book is among the most widely known in Europe; all nations may find entertainment in it. Died in 1715.] Voltaire, *Œuvres historiques*, ed. René Pomeau (Paris: Gallimard [Bibliothèque de la Pléiade], 1957), 1164. Galland's original title, with *nuit* in the singular, reflected a contemporary usage that had the noun agree with the last preceding number: see Georges May, *Les mille et une nuits d'Antoine Galland, ou Le chef-d'œuvre invisible* (Paris: Presses Universitaires de France, 1986), 42n. 1.
3. Lady-in-waiting to the duchesse de Bourgogne, the wife of the king's grandson. The marquise was the daughter of the comte de Guilleragues (1628–85), author of the *Lettres portugaises* (1669) and from 1677 French ambassador to the Sublime Porte, where, on taking up his mission in 1679, he had employed Galland as his secretary.

4. May, *Les mille et une nuits d'Antoine Galland*, 44.

5. Voltaire refers them to as such in a letter to the marquise de Mimeure in the summer of 1716 (D40, in *Correspondance*, ed. Theodore Besterman, vols. 85–135 of *Les œuvres complètes de Voltaire* [*The Complete Works of Voltaire*], ed. Theodore Besterman et al. [Oxford, UK: Voltaire Foundation, 1968–] [henceforth cited as *OC*], 85:54; see also Jacqueline Hellegouarc'h, "Mélinade ou la duchesse du Maine: Deux contes de jeunesse de Voltaire: *Le crocheteur borgne* et *Cosi-Sancta*," *Revue d'histoire littéraire de la France* 78 [1978]: 728). So also does the duc de Saint-Simon in his *Mémoires*, ed. Gonzague Truc, 7 vols. (Paris: Gallimard [Bibliothèque de la Pléiade], 1947–61), 4:381, 722, 918.

6. Having hoped one day to be queen of France, the duchesse du Maine had marked time by founding in 1703 her own Order of the Honey Bee. She, of course, was Queen Bee: her chosen favorites swore an oath of allegiance on being inducted into the order and were each presented with a medal, on a yellow ribbon, that bore the image of her head and the elaborately coiffed mound of blond hair that was her honeycomb crown. One such favorite was Voltaire. For further information about her, see André Maurel, *La duchesse du Maine, reine de Sceaux* (Paris: Hachette, 1928); and Catherine Cessac, Manuel Couvreur, and Fabrice Peyrat, eds., *La duchesse du Maine (1676–1753): Une mécène à la croisée des arts et des siècles* (Brussels: Éditions de l'Université de Bruxelles, 2003).

7. See Hellegouarc'h, "Mélinade ou la duchesse du Maine"; Hellegouarc'h, "Genèse d'un conte de Voltaire," *Studies on Voltaire and the Eighteenth Century* (*SVEC*) 176 (1979): 7–36; and Christiane Mervaud's introduction in *OC*, 1B:51–81 (2002). The theme of the fifth "Grande Nuit," on 31 July 1714, was "le Sommeil chassé du château et retiré dans le pavillon de l'Aurore y est poursuivi par le lutin de S[c]eaux" (Sleep, banished from the château and now hiding in the Pavilion of the Dawn, is pursued there by the sprite of S[c]eaux) (see Maurel, *La duchesse du Maine*, 80), and it is tempting to imagine *Le crocheteur borgne* as fitting this particular bill.

8. Voltaire, *Romans et contes*, ed. Frédéric Deloffre and Jacques Van den Heuvel (Paris: Gallimard [Bibliothèque de la Pléiade], 1979). Further page references to this edition will be given parenthetically in the main text. All translations are mine.

9. For further discussion of this story see Roger Pearson, *The Fables of Reason: A Study of Voltaire's "contes philosophiques"* (Oxford, UK: Clarendon, 1993), 41–48.

10. See Hellegouarc'h, "Genèse d'un conte," 7–8.

11. Ibid., 8. She notes also an allusion to Ludovico Ariosto's *Orlando furioso* (9–10), a work often coupled with the *Mille et une nuits* in Voltaire's later correspondence (e.g., D8484, D19189, in *OC*, 104:359, 125:199).

12. The theme of wifely infidelity, on which the frame story of the *Mille et une nuits* turns, is treated comically in two *contes en vers* that Voltaire wrote at this time: "Le cocuage" and "Le cadenas." See *OC*, 1B:133–70.

13. Writing to the duchesse after these experiences (D89, in *OC*, 85:100) Voltaire

once again depicted their relationship in storybook terms, in this case (and doubtless in homage to Ariosto) with himself as lowly knight errant to her unhappy princess locked in an enchanted castle. See Manuel Couvreur, "Voltaire chez la duchesse ou Le Goût à l'épreuve," in Cessac, Couvreur, and Peyrat, *La duchesse du Maine*, 233.

14. For a fuller account see Roger Pearson, *Voltaire Almighty: A Life in Pursuit of Freedom* (London: Bloomsbury, 2005), 191–95.

15. The following information is derived from Longchamp's original manuscript and not from the embellished version produced by Jacques-Joseph-Marie Decroix (working editor of the Kehl edition of Voltaire's complete works) that appeared in 1826 in his and Adrien-Jean-Quentin Beuchot's two-volume edition of the *Mémoires sur Voltaire et ses ouvrages, par Longchamp et Wagnière ses secrétaires, suivis de divers écrits inédits* (Paris: André). See W. H. Barber, "Penny Plain, Twopence Coloured: Longchamp's Memoirs of Voltaire," in *Studies in the French Eighteenth Century Presented to John Lough*, ed. D. J. Mossop, G. E. Rodmell, and D. B. Wilson (Durham, UK: University of Durham, 1978), 9–21; and Sébastien Longchamp, *Anecdotes sur la vie privée de Monsieur de Voltaire*, ed. Raymond Trousson and Frédéric Eigeldinger (Paris: Honoré Champion, 2009), 55–64.

16. Longchamp says two months (*Anecdotes*, 58), but more recent biographers suggest a shorter period. See René Vaillot, *Avec Mme Du Châtelet*, in *Voltaire en son temps*, ed. René Pomeau, 2nd ed., 2 vols. (Oxford, UK: Fayard / Voltaire Foundation, 1995), 1:525–26.

17. Decroix's version of Longchamp names them: "Quelquefois après le repas il lisait un conte ou un petit roman qu'il avait écrit exprès dans la journée pour la divertir. C'est ainsi que furent composés *Babouc* [i.e., *Le monde comme il va*], *Memnon, Scarmentado, Micromégas, Zadig*, dont il faisait chaque jour quelques chapitres." (Sometimes after the meal he would read a tale or a short novel that he had worked on during the day expressly for the purpose of entertaining her. That is how *Babouc, Memnon, Scarmentado, Micromégas*, and *Zadig* were written, with a number of chapters being completed each day.) *Mémoires*, 2:140. But Decroix/Longchamp were wrong to say that Voltaire began only then to work on these stories: *Micromégas* dates back to the late 1730s, as does *Le monde comme il va* (to 1739). On the latter see Michael Cardy in *OC*, 30B:3–13 (2004). On the date of composition of *Memnon* see Katherine Astbury's introduction to her edition in *OC*, 30B:237–39. While she considers it "probable" that this tale was "written between the summer of 1748 and January 1749," we have no evidence to say that Voltaire did not already have a version on the stocks in 1747. At any rate the Oriental inspiration for the story springs from the same source as *Le monde comme il va* and the first *Memnon* (which became *Zadig* in its revised version). Note also that *Memnon* contains a possible allusion to the *Jeu de la reine* affair: see ibid., 30B:263n. 6.

18. The tribute is further signaled by occasional allusions to bees and honey (cf. note 6). The eponymous protagonist of *Micromégas*, a student of fleas (ch. 1), also

learns about bees (end of ch. 6). In *Le monde comme il va* freeloaders respond to Memnon's offer of hospitality as wasps attracted to honey (beginning of ch. 8). Compare also the *"rubans jaunes"* that Voltaire inserted in the 1756 edition of *Zadig* and that may have been part of his orally delivered version to the duchesse back in 1747. On this addition see Jacqueline Hellegouarc'h, "Encore sur la duchesse du Maine: Note sur les rubans jaunes de *Zadig*," *SVEC* 176 (1979): 37–40.

19. Cf. also the reference to the Sultan at war with Caesar (noted also by Marie-Louise Dufrenoy, *L'Orient romanesque en France, 1704–1789*, 3 vols. [Montreal: Beauchemin, 1946–1975], 3:217). The Syrian provenance of the original manuscripts underlying Galland's *Mille et une nuits* would have been widely known, as evidenced by these lines from the prefatory verses to Antoine Hamilton's *Les quatre Facardins*: "Ensuite vinrent de Syrie / Volumes de contes sans fin, / Où l'on avait mis à dessein / L'orientale allégorie, / Les énigmes, et le génie / Du Talmudiste, et du Rabbin, / Et ce bon goût de leur patrie, / Qui loin de se perdre en chemin, / Parut sortant de chez Barbin / Plus arabe qu'en Arabie." (Then came from Syria volumes of stories without end, in which had been purposely included the oriental allegory, riddles and genius [also, djinn] of the Talmudist, and of the Rabbi, and also the good taste of their country, which, far from being lost on the way, appeared from Barbin's presses more Arabic than in Arabia itself.) (*Les quatre Facardins*, ed. Georges May [Paris: Desjonquères, 2001], 35). Hamilton (1646–1720) was a regular at Sceaux, where he wrote his memoirs (published in 1713). *Les quatre Facardins*, one of his several spoofs of the *Mille et une nuits*, was written and privately circulated in the immediate aftermath of the publication of Galland's work (May suggests c. 1712: *Les mille et une nuits d'Antoine Galland*, 150n. 8) before being published by Jean-François Josse in 1730. On Hamilton as a forerunner of Voltaire see Marina Warner, *Stranger Magic: Charmed States and the Arabian Nights* (London: Chatto and Windus, 2011), 268–71.

20. While a first version of *Zadig* had appeared earlier in 1747 in Amsterdam under the title *Memnon*, this does not seem to have circulated widely in France, and it is quite plausible that since Voltaire was now quite extensively revising this version, he would have read chapters of the future *Zadig* to the duchesse.

21. The name Babouc figures in the Bible (see Deloffre and Van den Heuvel, eds., *Romans et contes*, 731n. 1) and Rabelais's *Pantagruel* as well as in the story told in the *Mille et une nuits* by the barber's eldest brother.

22. See Jacques Van den Heuvel, *Voltaire dans ses contes: De "Micromégas" à "L'Ingénu,"* 3rd ed. (Paris: Armand Colin, 1967), 213n. 4. Cf. Astbury, *OC*, 30B:247, where an alternative source—Chec Zadé's *Histoire de la sultane de Perse* (translated by Pétis de la Croix)—is suggested by Pietro Toldo.

23. Voltaire, *Zadig*, ed. Haydn T. Mason, in *OC*, 30B:86.

24. The story of Ogul and his cure by exercise recalls "The Story of the Grecian King and the Physician Douban" (part of "The Story of the Fisherman") in the *Mille et une nuits*: see Voltaire, *Zadig*, ed. Georges Ascoli, 2 vols. (Paris: Hachette, 1929),

2:125. The story of "L'Envieux (*Zadig*, ch. 6) recalls "The Story of the Envious Man, and of Him That He Envied," told by the second calender in "The Story of the Three Calenders": see *Zadig* (ed. Ascoli), 2:41.

25. Voltaire's manuscript transcription of Zadig into Sadi is discussed by Mason in *OC*, 30B:93.

26. Voltaire, *Zadig* (ed. Ascoli), 2:3.

27. That is, the language of ancient Babylon.

28. Cf. also the end of *L'homme aux quarante écus*: "De là vient que cent femmes lisent *Les Mille et Une Nuits* contre une qui lit Locke" (This is why there are a hundred women who read the *Thousand and One Nights* for every one who reads Locke) (Voltaire, *Romans et contes*, 475).

29. This point is made also by William H. Trapnell, "Destiny in Voltaire's *Zadig* and *The Arabian Nights*," *SVEC* 278 (1990): 147.

30. Not that these stories lack all "Oriental" motifs. In *Candide* la Vieille's destiny takes her to North Africa and the Middle East, while Candide and Cacambo's journey to El Dorado owes something to the voyages of Sindbad. See Dufrenoy, *L'Orient romanesque en France*, 3:218–20, where she also suggests further examples.

31. See Dufrenoy, *L'Orient romanesque en France*.

32. *Zadig*, true to its Oriental costume, bears the subtitle "ou la destinée," but Voltaire had Christian providence just as much as Islamic fatalism in mind. See Voltaire's letter to Bernis of 14 October 1748 (D3784, in *OC*, 94:337–38) and *Romans et contes*, 768.

33. Voltaire, "Sur la fable," in *OC*, 28B:220 (2008).

34. In the many different versions of this ancient story only Voltaire's Zadig answers back: see *Zadig* (ed. Ascoli), 2:159n. 178.

35. Voltaire, *Dictionnaire philosophique*, ed. Christiane Mervaud et al., in *OC*, 35:321–22 (1994).

36. Voltaire, "Arabes," in *Questions sur l'Encyclopédie*, in *OC*, 38:542 (2007).

37. See Moulay-Badreddine Jaouik, "La part de l'islam dans l'élaboration du théisme voltairien," *Cahiers Voltaire* 6 (2007): 59–78.

38. Together with the two additional chapters Voltaire wrote for *Zadig*—"La danse" and "Les yeux bleus"—in 1752–53.

39. Van den Heuvel, for example, ends his book *Voltaire dans ses contes* with *L'Ingénu* (1767) and dismisses later stories as stale repeats. For his account of Voltaire's debt to the *Mille et une nuits* see 183–200. Cf. also Voltaire, *Contes en vers et en prose*, ed. Sylvain Menant, 2 vols. (Paris: Bordas, 1992–93), 1:xxii–xxiii and 2:136.

40. Voltaire, *Contes en vers et en prose*, 1:346; and Voltaire, *Candide and Other Stories*, trans. and ed. Roger Pearson, 2nd ed. (Oxford: Oxford University Press, 2006), 189.

41. Voltaire to Chamfort, D19189, in *OC*, 125:199.

42. Voltaire, preface to *Dictionnaire philosophique*, in *OC*, 35:284.

43. Georges May has argued that this art of leaving room for readers to draw their own conclusions is illustrated by Galland's own, masterly narration of the Sindbad stories (see his "Sindbad le marin et les voyages à sens unique," in *Voltaire, the Enlightenment and the Comic Mode: Essays in Honor of Jean Sareil*, ed. Maxine G. Cutler, 143–58 [New York: Peter Lang, 1990]), but he is less persuasive in his contention that Voltaire did not see this also and in his acceptance at face value of the Dedicatory Epistle in *Zadig* in which the *Nights* is apparently disparaged for being frivolous and devoid of serious meaning (see May, *Les mille et une nuits d'Antoine Galland*, 122, 203).

44. See, for example, Richard van Leeuwen, "Orientalisme, genre et réception des *Mille et une nuits* en Europe," in *Les mille et une nuits en partage*, ed. Aboubakr Chraïbi, 121–41 (Paris: Actes Sud, 2004), esp. 140–41.

7

The *Arabian Nights* and the Origins of the Western Novel

ROBERT IRWIN

The embarrassments of fiction! It is after all a specialized form of lying. In the medieval Arab world, doubts about the value of fiction lay behind the frequent attempts in prefaces to justify the stories that followed. To take one of the most famous works of medieval Arabic prose fiction, *Kalila wa-Dimna*, Ibn al-Muqaffa''s eighth-century adaptation of what were originally Indian animal fables, this was presented by him as teaching wisdom and providing guidance for a virtuous life. Ibn al-Muqaffa' was explicit that the book was "not for entertainment only." (Interestingly, he was also explicit in stating that young people were among its target audience.)[1] On the other hand, in the case of al-Hariri's twelfth-century *Maqamat*, or "Assemblies," commentators on this no less famous work claimed that its wily and extraordinarily fluent protagonist, Abu Zayd, was a real person and so the work was not fiction.[2] *Alf layla wa-layla*, or *The Thousand and One Nights*, was not regarded by medieval literati as a classic work of literature at all, but even here the same sort of embarrassment can be detected in the preface to the fifteenth-century manuscript used by Antoine Galland:

I should like to inform the honourable gentlemen and noble readers that the purpose of writing this agreeable and entertaining book is the instruction of those who peruse it, for it abounds with highly edifying histories and excellent lessons for the people of distinction, and it provides them with the opportunity to learn the art of discourse, as well as what happened to kings from the beginnings of time. This book, which I have called *The Thousand and One Nights*, abounds also with splendid biographies that teach the reader to detect deception and to protect himself from it.[3]

In France and England in the eighteenth century, the century which saw the birth of the novel in the full sense of the word, a similar sort of embarrassment about fiction is easy to detect. For example, in the English translation of Galland's preface to *Les mille et une nuits*, it was argued that its stories "must also be pleasing, because of the Account they give of the Customs and Manners of the Eastern Nations, and the ceremonies of their Religion, as well Pagan as Mahometan, which are better describ'd here, than in any author that has wrote of 'em." Also "if those who read these stories, have but any Inclination to profit by the examples of Virtue and Vice, which they will here find exhibited, they may reap advantage by it, that is not to be reap'd in other Stories, which are more proper to corrupt than to reform our Manners."[4]

Aphra Behn's fiction *Oroonoko* (c. 1688) was published as nonfiction. When *Robinson Crusoe* was first published in 1719, it too was presented as nonfiction, as was *Journal of a Plague Year* a few years later. The English preface to Thomas-Simon Guellette's *Mogul Tales* (1736) claimed that such stories instill in young people "Address, Politeness, and a high sense of Virtue," as well as teaching them the geography and customs of foreign countries."[5] According to the title page of Samuel Richardson's *Pamela; or, Virtue Rewarded* (1740), it was published "in order to cultivate the virtue and religion in the minds of the youth of both sexes. A narrative which has its foundation in truth, and at the same time that it is agreeably entertaining."[6] Examples are easy to multiply.

When did the first novel appear? The *Satyricon* and *The Golden Ass* can be characterized as novels. So can Hellenistic romances (and this approach has formed the basis of Margaret Anne Doody's reinterpretation of the historical origins of the novel).[7] More modern examples might include the rambling farragoes of Madame de Scudéry, such as *Ibrahim ou l'Illustre Bassa* (1641–44) and François Fénelon's pedagogical romance *Télémaque* (c. 1695). And it would be hard to deny the picaresque *Don Quixote* (1605 seq.) the claim to be considered as a novel. Nevertheless, there is a strong tendency, especially among English literary critics such as Ian Watt, to site the birth of the novel in its fully fleshed sense in the early eighteenth century.[8] The landmarks include Daniel Defoe's *Robinson Crusoe* (1719), Richardson's *Pamela* (1740), and Henry Fielding's *Joseph Andrews* (1742) and *The History of Tom Jones* (1749). I here note that the publication of the first volume of the Grub Street translation of Galland, around 1706, fairly closely precedes these earliest specimens of the English novel.

There are all sorts of superficial ways in which the eighteenth-century novel in western Europe was influenced by *The Thousand and One Nights*: the *Nights* licensed fantasy and a breaking away from classical constraints; it provided a precedent for the eroticism of the libertine novels; contrariwise, it also spawned a lot of moral and didactic tales; its plots were borrowed; it stimulated a spate of mock Oriental romances by John Hawkesworth, Clara Reeve, James Ridley, and others; it was often alluded to and often approvingly. And so on.

According to Martha Pike Conant's *The Oriental Tale in England*, "the oriental tale was alien; and incident, atmosphere, fancies, understood and liked by Eastern listeners, seemed too grotesque and incredible to make more than a limited appeal to untravelled English readers. They welcomed, rather, with characteristic heartiness the homely, realistic background of Defoe's stories."[9] Conant received advance support of a kind from Henry Fielding, who, in *Joseph Andrews* disparaged the authors of *The Thousand and One Nights*, as well as various modern novelists "who without any assistance from nature or history, record persons who never were, or will be, and facts which never did, nor, possibly can happen."[10] But in what follows, I argue that the dichotomy between the homely realism of Defoe and other English novelists and the fantasies of the *Nights* is substantially false.

The argument presented here is not original. In an important article, that excellent academic critic Peter Caracciolo has shown how heavily indebted Fielding's picaresque novel *Tom Jones* was to the Hunchback cycle of stories in the *Nights*.[11] In part, it is a matter of allusion and structure. The garrulous and clinging barber Partridge, who delays the lover's meetings and the consummation of their love, is evidently and explicitly based on the barber in the Hunchback cycle of stories in the *Nights*, as he is referred to in one of the novel's subheadings as "one of the pleasantest barbers that was ever recorded in history, the Barber of Bagdad, or he in *Don Quixote* not excepted."[12]

But the "key parallel between *Tom Jones* and the Arabic story-cycle" is "the sense that the world is full of stories, and that the common and appropriate destiny of experience is to be rendered into tales."[13] Again according to Caracciolo,

> What the *Nights* uniquely offered to the author of *Tom Jones* and later generations of novelists for whom his masterpiece served as a prototype was a largely secular model of capacious, densely populated protean fictions employing an expressive amalgam of prose and verse, realism and fantasy, comedy and tragedy. Recycling old bits and pieces of ancient stories from different cultures to make new more intricate narratives, these tales within tales still have the capacity to respond to the needs of increasingly complex societies, both at home and abroad.

The Hunchback cycle provides "vivid details of urban life."[14]

In what follows, Caracciolo's brilliant but somewhat condensed insight (a matter of a couple of paragraphs) will be fleshed out. What is characteristic of the novel, at least in the eighteenth and nineteenth centuries, is firstly its density and circumstantial detail. When one thinks of *The Thousand and One Nights*, one's first thoughts are likely to be of flying horses, cannibalistic ghouls, and the jinn bursting out of bottles, and certainly all that is there. But what is characteristic of many of the early stories in the Arabic manuscript used by Galland, particularly those stories clustered together in the Hunchback cycle, is not so much magic and fantasy as documentary realism and a detailed evocation of everyday things. Pre-eighteenth-century romancers such as Ludovico Ariosto (1474–1533), Ginés Pérez de Hita (1544?–1619?), and de Scudéry (1608–1701) were strong on paratactic plot, on one thing after another—abductions, battles, assignations, and separations—but weak on concrete detail that could be visualized. What is new in the eighteenth-century novel is visual detail and density in plotting.

The Hunchback cycle of stories has been characterized by the authors of *The Arabian Nights Encyclopedia* as containing "a number of grotesque elements: the linking of food and death, physical deformation, violence and death, strange coincidences, drunkenness, sexual pranks, and stereotypical representations of characters, such as women, Jews, Christians and the barber."[15] But, given the context of these tales, what is above all striking is what is not there. There is a total absence of magic and monsters (fig. 24).

Instead, we have a naturalistic account of a hunchback buffoon who plays on the tabor and who chokes on a fish bone and the subsequent quandaries that arise from getting rid of his corpse. There is the Jew who invokes the prophet Esdras to save him from the police, the Muslim who "was one of the sultan's purveyors, for furnishing oil, butter, and all sorts of fat, tallow," and a heavy-drinking Christian merchant. The adventure of the latter begins when he is shown a handkerchief containing "a sample of sesame and Turkey corn." We then follow the financial details of his commodity transactions with their percentages in intense and realistic detail, and this account frames the story of the one-handed merchant and his no less realistic brokerage deals, followed by an ill-fated assignation with a lady. The story of the sultan's purveyor is of a financially embarrassed shopkeeper he encountered who became the victim of a painful assignation with a fastidious lady. The Jewish physician's tale, which includes a lengthy encomium of Cairo, is again about trade, erotic meetings, and mutilation. The tailor's story, about a failed erotic assignation and the consequent laming of its protagonist, frames the stories of the infernally garrulous barber and his unlucky malformed brothers.[16]

These stories gain density from little things: the lozenge taken for sweet breath; the books of sale; the mice that attack the Muslim merchant's butter; the crape that hung over a woman's muslin veil; the hiring of an ass and its attendant owner; the horseman's bag "half open, with a string of green silk hanging out of it";[17] the jelly broth of fowl offered to the merchant who has lost his hand; a ragout of garlic sauce; salt-wort soap; the gold chain necklace with ten very large and perfect pearls placed on it at certain distances; the barber's cupping glasses and astrolabe; the very well trimmed sofa; and so on. As it happens, the original Arabic version is yet richer in concretely realized visual detail than Galland and his Grub Street translator allow, but that is irrelevant in the present context.

In *Mimesis*, Erich Auerbach observed of the Abbé Prévost's *Manon Lescaut* (1731),

> When the occasion permits, clothes, utensils, furnishings are described or evoked with coquettish meticulousness and great delight in movement and colour. . . . Secondary characters from all classes, commercial transactions, and a variety of pictures of contemporary culture in general are woven into the action. . . . We hear a great deal about money; there are lackeys, inns, prisons. . . . There is realism everywhere.[18]

Yes, and the same sort of thing can be said about *Tom Jones* and about the Hunchback cycle of the *Nights*.

The *Nights* stories in question here are uniformly improbable, yet none are impossible. There is a general interest in the flow of money and how things are managed in the real world. The caliph Mustansir bi'llah, the sultan of Casgar, and, ultimately, King Shahriyar are told these stories, but the protagonists are all ordinary people—a tailor, a purveyor, a doctor, a broker, and the people they have dealings with—whereas the protagonists of Ariosto, Pérez de Hita, and de Scudéry were kings, knights, and princesses. Even in Aphra Behn's *Oroonoko*, the black slave was of royal origin, and he pursued the love of a princess. Aristocrats monopolized the action of the romances. So here again the Hunchback stories set a useful precedent for the more mundane English novel. The Hunchback cycle offered a precedent for having tradespeople as the protagonists of stories. So too did other *Nights* stories, such as the story of "Ali Khawaja and the Merchant of Bagdad" and the seven trading missions of Sinbad. (With respect to the Sinbad stories, readers tend to remember his encounters with the rukh and the man-eating ogre but tend to forget the amount of detail in the stories on normal trading transactions in things such as camphor and coconuts.) Sinbad and Robinson Crusoe were both alike capitalists.[19] This focus on the romance of trade may have appealed to the expanded reading public of the early eighteenth century. It is also noteworthy that for the most part, pre-eighteenth-century fictions have only perfunctory and brief dialogues (though *Don Quixote* is an exception). But the Hunchback cycle is rich in dialogue, and in its complex framing structure, the narrator narrates to narrator-framed conversations.

It might seem that the stories of the Christian merchant, the purveyor, and the Jewish merchant come under the medieval Arab category of *Faraj ba'd al-shidda*, or relief after grief, for after ordeal and mutilation, each man is reconciled with his lady and ends up wealthy; but this is not really so, for *Faraj ba'd al-shidda* is above all a pious genre, whereas in the stories there seems to be no patience in suffering and no trust in a God who will put things right.[20] The arbitrary turns of fortune mean that the protagonists end up just about all right, if a bit mutilated, but the narrator has produced a largely secular universe, in which God is mostly notable by his absence (and it would perhaps be inappropriate to show a Christian and a Jew as benefiting from the *faraj*, which comes from Allah).

A second characteristic of the Western novel is that it manages multiple narrative threads, and here again the *Nights*, with its complex *mise en abyme* employed by the anonymous narrator of the Hunchback cycle, provides a syntactic model that is in contrast to the paratactic narratives of earlier romances. It is important to realize that eighteenth-century readers of *The Thousand and One Nights* read a less exotic text than the one we read today. It is not simply a matter of Galland's translation, which presented a courtly and somewhat Westernized version of Oriental locutions and mores. It is also the case that in the eighteenth century there was very little sense of the otherness of the Arab world. Until the publication of first of the *Description de l'Egypte* and then of Edward William Lane's *Manners and Customs of the Modern Egyptians*, there were very few sources to fuel the Western visual imagination. If one looks at frontispieces and illustrations of early editions of the *Nights*, one sees that this is emphatically the case. It is true that the men in these images often wear turbans, but the rest of their apparel looks Western or ancient Roman (and besides, the turban tended to be worn by Turks rather than Arabs). Shahriyar and Scheherazade are waited on by Dunyazad in a sturdy four-poster bed. The interior of Shahriyar's palace looks like the interior of Versailles, and encounters with the jinn take place in a bosky countryside. The eighteenth-century *Nights* was to all intents and purposes imaginatively located in a Western and contemporary environment.[21] And one notes that Galland intended his translation to serve as a window not on the medieval Islamic world but on the Orient, including Persia, Tartary, and India, of his own day.[22] It is also the case that the craze in England for the *Nights* was not so much a craze for something truly Oriental but rather a determination to follow the latest fad out of Versailles and Paris—not so very different then from the English enthusiasm for Montesquieu's *Lettres persanes* a decade or two later. If this is correct, then there is a parallel somewhat later in the initial response to the *Nights* in Denmark and Japan, where it was treated as primarily a product of French or more broadly European culture.[23]

Of course, the development of the English novel, and here one thinks of such examples as *Moll Flanders*, *Tom Jones*, and *Roderick Random*, also owed something to the Spanish fictions in the picaresque genre. Yet it is interesting to note that the Spanish picaresque may have in turn had its precursor in the medieval Arabic *maqamat*s of al-Hamadhani and al-Hariri, concerning the exploits and travels of wily rogues. The preoccupations and narrative tricks of the authors of the *maqamat*s filtered through into Spanish, via the Jew al-Harizi's translation of al-Hariri's *Maqamat* into Hebrew, as well as al-Harizi's own original picaresque *maqamat*, the *Tahkemoni*. Early Spanish adaptations of the *maqamat* genre include the anonymous *Lazarillo de Tormes* (1554; English translation, 1576), which is clearly calqued on al-Harizi's fiction, and Francisco de Quevedo's *La historia de la vida del Buscón* (1626).[24]

Additionally, Ibn Tufayl's twelfth-century *Hayy ibn Yaqzan*, or "Alive, son of Awake," a philosophical and theological fantasy about a man fending for himself on a desert island, may have had a role in shaping *Robinson Crusoe* and its sequels. *Hayy ibn Yaqzan* had been translated into English twice in the seventeenth century and then again by Simon Ockley in 1708.[25] And 1708 happened to be the year that Alexander Selkirk, the real-life precursor of Robinson Crusoe, was rescued from the island of Juan Fernandes. Romances, featuring the adventures of improbable and aristocratic heroes, were customarily recounted in a distanced fashion. But *Hayy ibn Yaqzan* and *Robinson Crusoe* both invited the reader to identify with and internalize the predicament of the castaway.

It should also be noted in passing that perhaps the most important precursor of the eighteenth-century epistolary novel was a pseudo-

Oriental fiction, Giovanni Paolo Marana's *Espion Turc* (Paris, 1684). These supposed reports on France by Mahmut the Arabian back to the Turkish authorities appeared in English as *Letters Writ by a Turkish Spy Who Lived Five and Forty Years Undiscovered at Paris* (1691–94). Of its eight volumes, the first was from Marana's French, but the rest seem to be the inventions of various anonymous English hands.[26] Hayy ibn Yaqzan actually features as a character in the *Turkish Spy* speaking in favor of the natural state and freedom. Although the most obvious literary offspring of Marana's work is Montesquieu's *Lettres persanes* (1723), in England all sorts of collections of fictitious and satirical letters started appearing within a few years of the publication of the *Turkish Spy*.

The fantasy and the realism of the *Nights* and other works of Oriental literature were a source of inspiration to eighteenth-century novelists. But they were hardly the only source, and here I very briefly point to another type of fiction, the wholly or largely fictitious travel narrative. The travels of Sir John de Mandeville had been read as entertainment for centuries. But later examples include Denis Veiras's *Histoire des Severambes* (1677–79), set in a romantic, magic-infested Australia; George Psalmanazar's *An Historical and Geographical Description of Formosa* (1704), with its account of raw-meat-eating natives, floating villages, and vast carriages carried like sedan chairs by pairs of elephants; Aaron Hill's fantastical *A Full and Just Account of the Present State of the Ottoman Empire* (1709); and Thomas Killigrew's *Miscellenea Aurea* (1720), in which immigrants from ancient Greece are discovered to be sharing Australia with its native inhabitants. The fictitious travel narrative masquerading as nonfiction had become such a literary stock-in-trade in the eighteenth century that when James Bruce produced his largely veracious account of his travels in Ethiopia, most people, including Dr. Johnson, took it for granted that Bruce's book was another example of the fictional genre. The transition from the fraudulent or utopian travel fantasy to such novels as Defoe's *Adventures of Captain Singleton* (1720), his *A New Voyage around the World* (1724), and his *Robinson Crusoe*, as well as Jonathan Swift's *Gulliver's Travels*, is so easy as to be almost imperceptible.

But to conclude and to revert to the main point, which is the occasionally realistic quality of the *Nights* and its possible role in shaping the novel, it is appropriate to cite Auerbach's *Mimesis* once again:

The serious treatment of everyday reality, the rise of more extensive and socially inferior human groups to the position of subject matter for problematic-existential representation, on the one hand; on the other, the random persons and events in the general course of contemporary history, the fluid historical background—these, we believe are the foundations of modern realism, and it is natural that the broad and elastic form of the novel should increasingly impose itself for a rendering comprising so many elements.[27]

But of course, it is not possible to prove that Defoe, Fielding, and Tobias Smollett, having read *The Thousand and One Nights* (and they all did) were directly inspired by it to write the new type of fiction so lucidly described by Auerbach. It is merely plausible.

NOTES

1. Ibn al-Muqaffaʻ, *The Fables of Kalilah and Dimnah*, trans. Saleh Saʻadeh Jallad (London: Melisende, 2002), 29–36.
2. Abdelfattah Kilito, *Les séances: Récits et codes culturels chez Hamadhânî et Harîrî* (Paris: Sindbad, 1983), 257; cf. Devin Stewart, "Maqama," in *The Cambridge History of Arabic Literature: Arabic Literature in the Post-Classical Period* (Cambridge: Cambridge University Press, 2006), 149.
3. Husain Haddawy, trans., *The Arabian Nights* (New York: Norton, 1990), 1.
4. "From *The Arabian Nights' Entertainments*, 'Translated' by Antoine Galland," in *Fables of the East: Selected Tales, 1662–1785*, ed. Ros Ballaster (Oxford: Oxford University Press, 2005), 19.
5. Quoted in Martha Pike Conant, *The Oriental Tale in England in the Eighteenth Century* (New York: Columbia University Press, 1908), 85.
6. Samuel Richardson, *Pamela; or, Virtue Rewarded* (1740; repr., London: Penguin, 1980), 27, 31.
7. Margaret Anne Doody, *The True Story of the Novel* (New Brunswick: Rutgers University Press, 1994).
8. Ian Watt, *The Rise of the Novel: Studies in Defoe, Richardson and Fielding* (London: Chatto and Windus, 1957); cf. Lennard J. Davis, *Factual Fiction: The Origins of the English Novel* (New York: Columbia University Press, 1983); and Geoffrey Sill, *The Cure of Passions and the Origins of the English Novel* (Cambridge: Cambridge University Press, 2001).
9. Conant, *Oriental Tale in England*, 236–37.
10. Henry Fielding, *Joseph Andrews* (Dublin, 1742), vol. 2, book 3, ch. 1.
11. Peter L. Caracciolo, "The House of Fiction and *le jardin anglo-chinois*," *Middle Eastern Literatures* 7:2 (2004): 199–211, reprinted in *New Perspectives on Arabian*

Nights: *Ideological Variations and Narrative Horizons*, ed. Wen-chin Ouyang and Geert Jan van Gelder, 67–80 (London: Routledge, 2005). Page numbers refer to the *Middle Eastern Literatures* version.

12. Henry Fielding, *Tom Jones* (London, 1749), book 8, ch. 4.

13. Caracciolo, "House of Fiction," 201.

14. Ibid., 206.

15. Ulrich Marzolph and Richard van Leeuwen, *The Arabian Nights Encyclopedia*, 2 vols. (Santa Barbara, CA: ABC-CLIO, 2004), 1:225.

16. *Arabian Nights' Entertainments*, ed. Robert Mack (Oxford: Oxford University Press, 1995), 222–306. This is the anonymous Grub Street translation of the *Nights*. For a closer translation of the original Arabic, cf. Haddawy, *Arabian Nights*, 206–95.

17. *Arabian Nights' Entertainments*. 236.

18. Eric Auerbach, *Mimesis: The Representation of Reality in Western Literature*, trans. Willard R. Trask (Princeton: Princeton University Press, 1953), 399.

19. On Crusoe's capitalism, see Watt, *Rise of the Novel*, 61–73.

20. On the *Faraj ba'd al-shidda* genre, see A. Wiener, "Die Farağ ba'd aš-Šidda-Literatur," *Der Islam* 4 (1913): 290–98, 387–420; Robert Irwin, ed., *The Penguin Anthology of Classical Arabic Literature* (London: Penguin, 2006), 155–64.

21. Robert Irwin, *Visions of the Jinn: Illustrators of the Arabian Nights* (Oxford: Oxford University Press and the Arcadian Library, 2010), 15–29.

22. Antoine Galland, trans., *Les mille et une nuits*, ed. Jean-Paul Sermain and Abou-bakr Chraïbi, 3 vols. (Paris: Flammarion, 2004), 1:21.

23. Elisabeth Oxfeldt, *Nordic Orientalism: Paris and the Cosmopolitan Imagination, 1800–1900* (Copenhagen: Museum Tusculanum Press, 2005) 10, 24, 103; Tetsuo Nishio, "The *Arabian Nights* and Orientalism from a Japanese Perspective," in *The Arabian Nights and Orientalism: Perspectives from East and West*, ed. Yuriko Yamanaka and Tetsuo Nishio, 154–66 (London: I. B. Tauris, 2006), 158–60, 162–63.

24. Juan Vernet, *Ce que la culture doit aux Arabes d'Espagne* (Paris: Sindbad, 1985), 343–44; Philip Ward, *The Oxford Companion to Spanish Literature* (Oxford: Oxford University Press, 1978), 266.

25. Antonio Pastor, *The Idea of Robinson Crusoe* (Watford, UK: Gongora, 1980); Lawrence Conrad, ed., *The World of Ibn Tufayl: Interdisciplinary Perspectives on "Hayy ibn Yaqzan"* (Leiden: Brill, 1996).

26. Ros Ballaster, *Fabulous Orients: Fictions of the East in England, 1662–1785* (Oxford: Oxford University Press, 2005), 154–62.

27. Auerbach, *Mimesis*, 491.

8

"A Covenant for Reconciliation"

Lane's Thousand and One Nights *and Eliot's* Daniel Deronda

PAULO LEMOS HORTA

In *Daniel Deronda* (1876) the shift from realism to romance—an "Oriental Romance" with the title character's discovery of his Jewish identity in the novel's second half—has frustrated critics in George Eliot's time and since. Critics (notably F. R. Leavis)[1] would contend that Eliot never successfully integrated her two narratives and narrative modes: the realist English novel of Gwendolen Harleth and the Oriental romance of Deronda. Yet attention to the overlooked shaping intertext of the novel—the *Thousand and One Nights* tale of "Qamar al-Zaman" in Edward Lane's version—illuminates Eliot's foreshadowing in the English and realist half of the Jewish Oriental romance that follows with apparent implausibility. In formal terms, as Terence Cave has noted,[2] the deployment of intertextual references such as those to the *Nights* to bridge the narrative's two halves invites the reader to read the novel's romance through, rather than against, its realism. In political terms, the interweaving of the Jewish storyline with the universe of the *Nights* attests to Eliot's exploration of Zionism as part of what she imagined to be a possible covenant of reconciliation between Jewish and other Middle Eastern nationalist aspirations. Tracing Eliot's debt to Lane entails recuperating the neglected religious impetus and debt to traditions of biblical scholarship on Oriental peoples which animate both Lane's and Eliot's interest in the *Nights*. In Eliot's novel the parallels drawn with the *Nights* tale anticipate the development of Deronda as a messianic figure and attest to a structural coherence that Leavis famously felt lacking.

Eliot had a lifelong habit of reading and rereading *The Thousand and One Nights* in the 1838–40 translation of Edward William Lane. References to Lane's *Nights* crop up in her notebooks and in two novels that typify the genres of realism and romance, *Adam Bede* (1856) and *Daniel Deronda* (1876). From her youth a devotee and translator of the theology of David Friedrich Strauss, Eliot appears to have been captured by Lane's remarkable affirmation, in the preface to *Modern Egyptians* (1836), that he did not find it a contradiction to be a Christian and to believe, as his Cairene Muslim friends did, in the prophecy rather than the divinity of Christ. Eliot seems to have been struck by the resonance of this affirmation with David Friedrich Strauss's nearly contemporary articulation of a theology that was not predicated on the godhood of Christ in *The Life of Jesus Critically Examined*, the object of her first major literary labor (1846).

Lane had made no pretense of being an Egyptian, an Arab, or a Turk, though he dressed in the Ottoman style as other English travelers and expatriates did in 1830s Cairo (fig. 21). Rather he presented himself as an Englishman and a Christian who sought to be treated as a Muslim, as if almost a convert—or, more precisely, as an Englishman and a Christian who believed his views on Christ were compatible with those presented in the Qur'an. He did so by "freely acknowledging the hand of Providence in the introduction and diffusion of the religion of El-Islam, and, when interrogated, avowing [his] belief in the Messiah, in accordance with the words of the Ku-ran."[3] Lane paraphrased the Qur'anic verses on Christ in his first note to the *Nights*: "Jesus is held to be more excellent than any of those who preceded him; to have been born of a virgin, and to be the Messiah, and the word of God, and a Spirit proceeding from Him, but not partaking of his essence, and not to be called the Son of God."[4] The young Eliot would have been intrigued by Lane's emphasis that he found commonalities in conversations with Muslim friends in Cairo.

In the theological writings of David Friedrich Strauss, Eliot encountered a similarly controversial claim regarding the historical Jesus. Strauss did not find belief in the divinity of Christ to be a requisite for faith and instead stressed the divinity of all humanity. Each new believer ought to endeavor to become a "Messiah of Nature," and faith itself would fade unless new messiahs were able to inspire new generations of believers. Strauss stressed the mythmaking potential in religious communities and interpreted the Gospels as evangelical myths. For Strauss the risen Christ of the Gospels was the construct of the early community of Christian Jews who projected the Messianic ideal of the Old Testament onto the historical Jesus. Communal experience and expectations were responsible for imbuing Jesus with divine attributes in the language of supernaturalism and miracle. Miracles possessed a mythical truth. Jesus's multiplication of bread had been interpreted by rationalists as a parable of the need for sharing and by supernaturalists as a verifiable event. Strauss instead stressed the need of early Christian Jews to create a new myth of Christ that would accord with the Old Testament account of Jehovah feeding the Israelites in the desert with manna from heaven.[5]

Eliot's recourse to Lane in *Daniel Deronda*, a novel that deals with the competing claims on such a would-be modern messiah, constituted a case of reading Lane against himself. Lane believed the modern feats of magicians in Cairo corroborated accounts of sorcery in ancient Egypt at the time of Moses, and vice versa. The possibility of real magic, for him, ought to be considered by all who believed in the veracity of the Old Testament. Supernaturalism played a rather different role in the theology that interested Eliot and animated her Straussian novel of a contemporary Jewish messiah and his process of self-discovery. Her deployment of a frame of "Oriental" mythology in her novel of a modern-day messiah heightened the sense of self-conscious mythmaking and highlighted the process whereby communal belief could transmute man into messiah.

Lane's syncretic approximation of Islam and Christianity determined the distinctive traits of his version of the *Nights*: the adoption of the tone, diction, and style of the King James Bible; the sympathetic portrayal of Islamic beliefs and practices, notably belief in magic and the jinn; the omission of the crusades saga "Omar En-Noaman," which constituted one-eighth of the work and was characterized by antipathy between Christianity and Islam; and the commentary's emphasis on noting affinities between the Jews of the Old Testament and the Arabs of ancient and modern Egypt in order to invite sympathy for the practices of the latter. The distinction of Lane's *Nights* is to sympathetically present the enchantment of the tales as worthy of belief by their Christian readers and compatible with the empiricism of the Victorian era.

This imprint is evident in Lane's handling of a tale that trades on the interrelated appeal of magic and sex, "Qamar al-Zaman." The *Nights* tale is set in motion by the refusal of the prince—the most handsome man in the realm—to take a bride, an unwillingness which both the prince and the community interpret in the language of supernatural accusation. Orphaned by the death of his mother and prone to solitude and self-absorption, Qamar al-Zaman is particularly fearful of the "disturbances occasioned by women," with "their eyelids painted with kohl," attributing to them a supernatural ability to overcome the defenses of "a thousand castles encrusted with lead [a substance supposed to guard against evil jinn]."[6] Lane's commentary is uniquely attentive to the prince's fear of fascination, detailing that he recites the last two chapters of the Qur'an "because they serve as preventatives of, or antidotes against, the effects of the evil eye, or enchantment."[7] Conversely, the prince's beauty and self-absorption are themselves the object of the accusation of supernaturalism. Society holds that "his eye was more enchanting than Haroot; and the play of his glance, more seductive than Et-Taghoot"—that is, in Lane's gloss, more enchanting than the fallen angel sent to earth to tempt believers with knowledge of magic and more seductive than the devil.[8] In Lane's edition the prince's anxiety about the power of enchantment—both of women and his own—is well captured in William Harvey's illustration of the prince turning away from his family and community and averting his gaze (fig. 30).

A tale of the sexual transgression of humans and jinn that is resolved via a polygamous marriage, "Qamar al-Zaman" provided Lane with the most radical test of the imaginative sympathy toward Islam that he felt distinguished the method of his ethnographic commentary to the *Nights*. Qamar and Budur are first brought together from their far-flung kingdoms to settle a wager between the jinn Meymooneh and Dahnash as to which of the objects of their desire is the most beautiful. Qamar and Budur alike possess an androgynous beauty irresistible to both sexes, which allows them to take on a series of disguises—ranging from gardener to geomancer in the case of the prince and from a king to Qamar himself. Performing the part of a man, Budur first earns the hand of a king's daughter in marriage and in the tale's conclusion, after reciting seven poems in praise of sodomy, persuades her husband, the unaware Qamar, to consent to a homosexual act so as to increase the pleasure of their reunion. In the end Budur, Qamar, and the king's daughter, whose marriage contract is transferred to him, are invited to rule jointly over the kingdom. Lane's version of the tale is marked by the "scandalous decorum" that characterized Lane's retreat from sexual matters.[9] And it is animated by his belief that modern Arabs share affinities with the ancient Jews of Scripture, which he believed should lead to acceptance of the practice of polygamy and belief in magic in the Cairo of the *Nights* and of his present day.

Lane possessed the cultural experience to do justice to the androgyny of Qamar al-Zaman and the tale's suggestion of pockets of tolerance toward homosexuality. Lane's informants had immersed Lane in a sexual universe of such possibilities, but his treatment of "Qamar al-Zaman" reflected the unease he felt in this world. Lane had witnessed performances in which slaves theatrically enacted homosexual acts with wooden phalluses and in which androgynous men wiggled their hips in the manner of dancing girls. The evidence of his diary indicates that Lane was troubled by the ability of men to arouse desire by acting and looking like women. Might, he wondered, the audience's apparent lack of revulsion for the portrayal of these acts signal a wider tolerance for homosexuality than that of official discourse? His own observations seemed to indicate that homosexuality was common among the military officers of the Turkish elite.[10] The discomfort registered in his diary matches the edits he makes to "Qamar al-Zaman." Lane thus cuts the line that proclaims that Qamar's beauty ravished everyone, not merely women. He omits the androgynous traits accentuated in the original. He strikes the reference to the prince's hips, which "quiver" and are "fuller than two hills of sands, so that the heart was troubled with their softness," lines that might have echoed his own recorded discomfort at the wiggling of the hips of an androgynous man.[11] He skips over Budur's queer seduction of Qamar al-Zaman in the guise of a man. Instead of sex, Lane emphasizes magic. And in place of the prince's androgyny, he stresses his role as enchanter and geomancer (fig. 29).

Lane's commentary directs the reader's attention away from the predatory sexuality of the jinn and toward their role in divination, corroborating the depth of Lane's interest in the latter subject. His seminal note to the frame tale on the jinn had comparably circumvented the story's prompt (a jinni steals a young bride on her wedding night to keep her as his paramour) to offer a comprehensive cosmology. In "Qamar al-Zaman" Meymooneh ascends to the lowest heaven to eavesdrop on the conversation between angels when she is waylaid by a light shining from the uninhabited tower that leads her to the sleeping prince. Her desire to "listen by stealth to the conversation of the Angels," as Lane puts it in his commentary, represents his principal interest in the intrigue between the two jinn that first brings the two lovers together.[12] When Dahnash informs Meymooneh that the princess he desires has been committed as insane by her father for her failure to take a husband, Lane is puzzled by the female jinni's ability to reply that the prince she desires likewise has been committed to an abandoned tower for refusing a wife. Imagining that his reader will protest, "How did Meymooneh become acquainted with the youth's history?" Lane reasons, "probably, before she met Dahnash, she had reached the confines of the lowest heaven, and there heard the Angels conversing upon the subject."[13] Lane attributes a desexualized protectiveness to the female jinni's interest in Qamar (accentuated in the illustration provided by William Harvey, in which she stands attention over the sleeping prince with the maternal concern of a guardian angel).

Lane's emphasis is less on the threat of sexual violence posed by jinn to the prince than on the superstitions that sought to prevent it. Lane's commentary charts the possibility of their intervention in human affairs and the superstitious devices deployed to guard against it—talismans, amulets, and preventive prayers. Lane's tale is suffused with the fear of enchantment, and the superstition of the evil eye envelops the figure of Qamar throughout. Within this universe the pivotal roles played by geomancy in uniting the far-flung lovers and an amulet in separating them prove more plausible. Since the king is convinced that madness has descended on his daughter Budur like an enchantment or possession by a jinn, Qamar must proclaim himself a geomancer to approach her and sport a set of instruments with which he boasts he can make calculations, write geomantic characters, and write "sure charms."[14] The lovers' second separation is caused by Qamar's obsession with puzzling out the "secret property" of an amulet he discovers on the sleeping Budur.[15] As he holds up the red stone with talismanic markings for examination in the light of the desert, a bird swoops down and takes it from him, thus leading him away from the sleeping Budur in the tent. In Lane's telling, Qamar appears so inextricably linked to the language of enchantment—as the subject and object of fascination —that his obsession with divining the stone's power does not appear as implausible as it does in other renderings of the tale. In a note Lane invokes the authority of the Old Testament and the possible attribution of the invention of the science of geomancy to Ham, the son of Noah, to make belief in geomancy, and its role in the plot, more credible.[16]

Lane will defend the polygamous arrangement that ends the tale and resolves its sexual transgressions with a rationale reminiscent of the method of his friend and informant the Scottish convert to Islam Osman, who had sought to reconcile tenets of the Bible with those of the Qur'an. In condoning the practice of polygamy in Islam, Lane invokes the affinity between the ancient Jews and modern Arabs, citing the absence of censure in the Old Testament toward the polygamy practiced by the Patriarchs. In Budur's disguise as a man she has proven herself a wise politician and earned the favor of the king and the hand of his daughter, Hayat, in marriage. Yet after Qamar al-Zaman is reunited with her in this kingdom, Budur reveals to the king that she is his wife, and the king marvels at the turn of events. The king's solution is to propose that Qamar marry Hayat himself to solidify the alliance with Qamar and to retain the welcome counsel of Budur. Budur welcomes the arrangement and pledges to be a handmaiden to her husband's second wife, the princess Hayat.[17]

Lane deployed the Old Testament in his *Nights* commentary as a pivot to probe the affinities between the practices of the ancient Jews and the modern Arabs. In this manner Lane defends polygamy in "Qamar al-Zaman." "I think, too, that, as Moses allowed his people, for the hardness of their hearts, to put away their wives, and God denounced not polygamy when the patriarchs practiced it," Lane reasons in his commentary to the *Nights* to preempt a negative response from his English reader, "we should be more consistent as believers in the Scriptures if we admitted the permission of these practices to be more conducive to morality than their prohibition, *among a people similar to the ancient Jews* to whom Moses allowed such liberty."[18] Lane finds Christians "most unjust" when they condemn in particular those "Muslim laws and tenets" that "agree with the Mosaic code and the practices of holy men; such as polygamy (which Mohammad *limited*), divorce, war for the defence of religion, purification, and even minor matters."[19] Emboldened by the precedent in Scripture for polygamy, Lane rounds on its Christian critics. While Christians may reproach Islam for sanctioning the practice of polygamy, Muslims might counter that Christians practice unsanctioned polygamy that proves more degrading to the mind and to morality.[20]

Lane seeks, however, not merely to defend the general practice of polygamy within Islam as "necessary."[21] He insists on the plausibility of this polygamous arrangement as it appears within the story to evolve organically out of the genuine affection between Hayat and Budur. To this end he amasses historical evidence of "many instances of sincere affection existing in the hearts of fellow-wives."[22] Lane finds apropos an account from al-Jabarti of a first wife who became so enamored of a slave girl that she emancipated her, gave her to her husband in a marriage contract, and "could not bear to be separated from her even for an hour, although she had become her fellow-wife, and borne him children."[23] In his commentary the union of Qamar, Budur, and Hayat is not only morally justifiable and ethnographically correct but also historically credible.

In *Daniel Deronda* Eliot makes recourse to Lane in describing the process whereby Daniel must adjudicate the distinct claims of affinity made on him by Gwendolen and by Mirah and Mordecai, each defined in terms of a discourse of supernaturalism and parallels to the *Nights* tale of Qamar al-Zaman. In the plot of Gwendolen and Daniel, nods to Lane's version of "Qamar al-Zaman" serve well the novel's sublimation of the erotic possibilities between them via a game of superstition and talismans. The novel mythologizes Daniel and Mirah via parallels to Lane's "Qamar al-Zaman" that prefigure the role they are to play after Daniel discerns his Jewish roots and takes up Mordecai's mission of becoming a leader of his people. Eliot borrows from the cosmology of the jinn in Lane's *Nights* to inform the dynamic between Daniel and Mordecai for her "Jewish Oriental Romance," in which Daniel must decide whether to trust the visions of Mordecai. Throughout the novel references to Daniel as Qamar and a *Nights* figure weave together the projections of others onto him, prefiguring his discovery of his Semitic identity and his fulfillment of a community's prophecy.

In the novel's opening lines Daniel Deronda is apprehensive of the allure of a beautiful young stranger, Gwendolen Harleth, an allure that he likens to that of an evil genius, with a possible pun on *jinni*, and its power to coerce his stare.

> Was she beautiful or not beautiful? and what was the secret of form or expression which gave the *dynamic quality to her glance*? Was the good or the evil genius dominant in those beams? Probably the evil; else why was the effect that of unrest rather than of *undisturbed charm*? Why was the wish to look again felt as coercion and not as a longing in which the whole being consents?[24]

The circumstances of their meeting, at a casino under the aegis of gambling's "romantic superstition[s],"[25] echoes, in Daniel's musing on the dominance of the good or evil genius, the wager between the good and evil jinn which brings Qamar and Budur together at the start of the *Nights* tale. Daniel's opening words reflect the terms with which Qamar al-Zaman is himself described as subject and object of fascination in Lane's version, which Eliot had at her desk when penning the novel. Lane described Qamar's fear of the "*disturbances* occasioned by women" and also his own power of enchantment as a devilish seductiveness in the "*play of his glance*." Gwendolen, as she meets Daniel's eyes and finds herself unable to look away, "as she would have desired to do, [for] she was unpleasantly conscious that they were arrested," reciprocates the accusation of supernaturalism. "Deronda's gaze seemed to have acted as an evil eye," and Gwendolen's accusation is quickly confirmed by a sudden decline in her fortune at the wheel.[26]

The predicament of Daniel and Gwendolen recalls that of Qamar and Budur. The two beautiful narcissists are accused of madness or supernatural possession for their withdrawal from society; they negotiate the complex interplay of superstition and talismans that define them in their respective kingdoms and find a foreign land where they are able to indulge their obsessions with themselves and each other. Gwendolen and Daniel are likewise averse to marriage and accused of antisocial behavior, a charge that takes the form of the accusation of supernaturalism—fairies and furies in the case of Gwendolen, the evil eye and ancient charms in that of Daniel.

Lane's version, with its circumvention of the tale's erotic possibilities and attention to its implicit reliance on discourses of magic and superstition, serves well Eliot's purpose of investigating the process of mythmaking. Lane's commentary constantly draws the reader away from the sexual impetus that motivates jinn and protagonists alike in the tale, ascribing a primary rather than merely incidental role to the various manifestations of superstition in the tale (fear of the jinn and the evil eye, and the use of prayers and talismans to counteract these). His Qamar is defined more by his fear of jinn and trust in talismans than fear of women or initial preference for the company of men. Lane accentuates the significance of the prince's disguise as geomancer and proclaimed exorcist, less as a simple ruse to approach the princess Budur than as evidence of the tale's implicit debt to discourses of geomancy and clairvoyance.

In *Daniel Deronda* the identification of Daniel with Qamar al-Zaman heightens the mythical quality of his transformation in the novel from English aristocrat into Jewish savior. The projection of the traits associated with the *Nights* prince also draws attention to the potentially fabulist element in his mythologizing as a figure of salvation. In defining the dynamic between Daniel and Gwendolen in terms of superstition (and ascribing to Gwendolen's pawned and redeemed necklace a talismanic significance comparable to Budur's lost amulet in the *Nights* tale), Eliot accentuates the mythmaking effect. Daniel is identified with the *Nights* prince via the prism of the fairy-tale imagination of young girls—the sisters of Hans Meyrick, the painter and friend to whom Daniel acts as patron. When Daniel is introduced to the girls as an "ideal" and as Hans's "salvation," "the shy girls watched and registered every look of their brother's friend" and after his departure immediately began "to paint him as Prince Camaralzaman."[27] The children continue to attribute a talismanic power to their portrait of Daniel as he proceeds to rescue the Jewish singer Mirah, champion her singing career, and find her long-lost brother, Mordecai. As Mab explains to Mirah, in a virtual parody of Lane's commentary on the tale, "Kate burns a pastille before his portrait every day. . . . And I carry his signature in a little black-silk bag round my neck to keep off the cramp. And Amy says the multiplication table in his name."[28]

If the dynamic of superstition between Daniel and Gwendolen is patterned in part after that between Qamar and Budur, it is revealed increasingly to be founded on nothing more than a mutually reinforcing narcissism rather than imaginative sympathy, and it plays out in an almost parody of the discourses of supernaturalism that animate it. Eliot teases the reader with the possibility that, as in the *Nights* tale, the two beautiful and self-absorbed individuals will successfully negotiate their "superstitious dread" of each other,[29] partly with the help of objects that acquire a talismanic significance, such as the redeemed necklace which Gwendolen comes to wear (as if one of the Meyrick children) in honor of Daniel, and find happiness together in a foreign land more amenable to their self-possession and to the narcissistic basis of their mutual infatuation. Indeed such a resolution appears to be intimated in the discourse of supernaturalism which accompanies their unexpected reunion in Genoa, in the "strangely-mixed dream" which anticipates the meeting and her husband Grandcourt's own suspicion of a "miraculous foreknowledge" in Gwendolen, a "bird-like facility in flying about" in Daniel, and "a magical effect" in their close proximity.[30]

Eliot's novel deliberately subverts the pattern suggested by the polygamous resolution of the *Nights* tale, in which Budur allows the young princess whom she had taken as a bride to also marry Qamar, in explicitly identifying the frail singer Mirah as the Budur to Daniel's Qamar. In *Deronda* Mirah is identified as Budur through a direct quotation from Lane's translation: "two delicate feet, the work of the protecting and all-recomposing Creator, support her; and I wonder how they can sustain what is above them."[31] In mythologizing the story line of Daniel and Mirah that will lead them to her long-lost brother in London's East

End, the novel accentuates the supernaturalism of the prophetic claims Mordecai is to make on Daniel. In a manner reminiscent of Strauss's theology, the story line of Mirah and Daniel emphasizes the importance of community in the fashioning of the myth of a present-day messiah. Sounding a distinctly Straussian note, the terms of Mirah's gratitude to Daniel anticipate the role he is to play in the regeneration of her community: "For the first time in her life Mirah was among those whom she entirely trusted, and her original visionary impression that Deronda was a divinely-sent messenger hung about his image still, stirring always anew the disposition to reliance and openness."[32] The connection between sympathy, community, and the projection of the qualities of fable in the forging of a new messiah is likewise emphasized in the interplay of Mordecai and Daniel as prophet and messiah.

When Daniel meets Mordecai, it is unclear if the impression of Mordecai as a spirit is Daniel's or the narrator's. When Daniel denies the possibility that Mordecai is Jewish, Mordecai's grasp is "relaxed, the hand withdrawn, the eagerness of the face collapsed into uninterested melancholy, as if someone possessing spirit which had leaped into the eyes and gestures had sunk back again to the inmost recesses of the frame."[33] Indeed, even as the narrator plays on the identification of Mordecai as a *Nights* jinn and develops the parallel drawing on Lane's commentary to "Qamar al-Zaman," the element of projection and fabulation is emphasized: "the figure was probably familiar and unexciting enough to the inhabitants of this street; but to Deronda's mind it brought so strange a blending of the unwonted with the common."[34] The explicit identification of Mordecai with the figure of "an enslaved Djinn" is made by the bookstore owner Mr. Cohen, an incidence of Jewish self-Orientalism characteristic of a late nineteenth-century European moment.[35] Mordecai, empowered by his friendship with Daniel, feels as if he were a winged spirit freed from enslavement.[36]

Mordecai's foreknowledge of Daniel in turn is reminiscent of Lane's suggestion that the jinni infatuated with Qamar has eavesdropped on angels by reaching "the confines of the lowest heaven, . . . such being the usual way by which the Jinn arrive at the knowledge of things which otherwise remain hidden from them."[37] In Eliot's novel the identification of Mordecai as a jinni is directly preceded by his quest for "the influences of a large sky" from the vantage point of London's bridges. It is leaning on the parapet of the Blackfriars Bridge and listening to the distant traffic of boats and barges "as a fine symphony . . . that bears up our spiritual wings" that Mordecai apprehends the "visionary form" of Daniel.[38] When the rowing figure of Daniel confirms this vision and they meet on the bridge, Mordecai confides to Daniel that the bridge is "a meeting-place for the spiritual messengers" and that there he has "listened to the messages of earth and sky."[39]

The role of clairvoyance in Mordecai's prophecy, the repeated identification of him with the figure of a jinni or winged spirit, and his mood swings between mystical fervor and distance accentuate in the vocabulary of supernaturalism Daniel's dilemma of whether to accept the prophetic claims made on him by the bookseller. In borrowing images and patterns from Lane's "Qamar al-Zaman," Eliot would appear to share Lane's Victorian project of verifying instances of natural magic. Yet Eliot's purpose is different from Lane's: she is not aiming at a kind of Victorian magic realism that would ascribe to accounts of the supernatural the verisimilitude of realism, to reveal magic as fact. Her conscious departure from the realism of her previous fiction in the form of the Oriental romance signals a shift in subject and manner of representation. Unlike Lane, who seeks proof of the accounts of magic and sorcery in the Old Testament, Eliot wishes rather to draw attention to the mediation of community in the articulation of supernaturalism. She is interested in how communities create myth by investing history and people with mythological resonance and in the question of how a modern contemporary—a figure like Daniel—might be attracted to the continued appeal of myth understood as inextricable from the fabric of community.

The accent in Daniel's acceptance of Mordecai's claims on him is on the role of an imaginative sympathy that is open to the possibility of a cognitive expansion afforded by kinship and community. At the moment that Mordecai feels "that his inward prophecy was fulfilled," his "exultation was not widely different from that of the experimenter, bending over the first stirrings of change that correspond to what in the fervor of concentrated prevision his thought had foreshadowed."[40] Daniel draws a similar comparison in considering what his guardian would term the "fanaticism" of Mordecai "waiting on the bridge for the fulfillment of his visions,"[41] reasoning that "even strictly-measuring science could hardly have got on without that forecasting ardour which feels the agitations of discovery beforehand, and has a faith in its preconception that surmounts many failures of experiment."[42] For him sympathy affords a cognitive breakthrough unavailable to his guardian. Considered from the perspective of "*what is called* a rational way*," and discounting Mordecai's claims on Daniel's sympathy, Mordecai's visionary knowledge may be dismissed as "illusory."[43] Daniel operates from a richer understanding of the working of reason: "Our consciences are not all of the same pattern, an inner deliverance of fixed laws; they are the voice of sensibilities as various as our memories (which also have their kinship and likeness). And Deronda's conscience included sensibilities beyond the common, enlarged by his early habit of thinking himself imaginatively into the experience of others."[44] It is this imaginative sympathy, coinciding with the discovery of the Jewish identity that they share, that will enable Daniel to conceive of Mordecai's visionary project of a Jewish homeland in the Middle East as worth embarking on.

Engaging the genre of the romance, and self-consciously bringing its processes of mythmaking to the fore, Eliot in *Daniel Deronda* borrows from Lane's *Egyptians* and *Nights* for her own distinct purpose of exploring how communities weave mythologies out of history and individuals wrestle with the claims of community and myth on them. Influenced by the theology of David Friedrich Strauss that emphasizes the divinity of all rather than that of Christ, Eliot was intrigued by Lane's avowal, with his interlocutors in 1830s Cairo, of the prophecy rather than the divinity of Christ. Her novel engages the Straussian preoccupation with how communities of faith can achieve renewal via a contemporary figure of the Messiah. She borrows from Lane's *Nights* to dramatize the obstacles and possibilities Daniel Deronda faces in the exploration of the Jewish history and identity of Mirah and Mordecai. Throughout her novel of a modern-day Jewish Messiah, Eliot displays Straussian preoccupations with the way in which discourses of supernaturalism are projected on characters by others. Her use of the patterning of plot elements after characters and motifs from the *Nights* tale of Qamar al-Zaman serves to bind the realism and romance of her novel's two halves together. These parallels with the *Nights* also highlight communal mediation in the making of myth.

Interpreted as a proto-Zionist novel, *Daniel Deronda* proved controversial as it appeared to mythologize the self-renewal of one religious community at the expense of the claims of others. In this view, most notably articulated by Edward Said with respect to Eliot's novel, the romantic articulation of an early expedition to instill the seeds of Jewish nationhood in the Middle East (the novel's final image of Daniel and Mirah setting off for the Middle East) would implicitly deny the competing claims of other national movements (Arab, Persian) toward the turn of the century. Yet Eliot shared with Lane the larger strategy of using parallels or moments of historical overlap between the three monotheistic faiths (as in Daniel's Andalusian heritage) to interrogate Victorian prejudice (against Egyptian Islam in Lane's interest, against English Judaism in Eliot's). Eliot differed from Lane in that it was the Straussian process of mythmaking that interested her in all three faiths: her interest was not in affirming one particular religious or nationalist mythology over others but in interrogating the process whereby all religious and nationalist faith-based mythologies are created.

In Eliot's novel the movement from Mordecai to Daniel's Zionism entails a qualification and reconciliation of this Zionism in accordance with the Arabic elements associated with Deronda. Deronda's Orientalized and self-Orientalizing Zionism posits itself as mediating between Muslim and Jewish culture and between East and West, as if inheriting from the novel's epigrams from Goethe and Schiller the aspiration of German Orientalist discourse to itself reconcile Western and "Oriental" cultures.[45] Deronda envisions Jewish nationalism seeking inspiration in the success of a specifically Muslim national sentiment in Persia and joining in harmony with the nationalist aspirations of other Oriental peoples: "Let our wise and wealthy show themselves heroes. They have the memories of the East and West, and they have a full vision of a better. A new Persia with a purified religion magnified itself in art and wisdom. So will a new Judaea, poised between East and West—a covenant of reconciliation."[46] This sentiment speaks to a specific moment in the mid-nineteenth century when not only Gentiles such as Eliot but Jews such as Disraeli conceived of Jews and Arabs as "Orientals" and when some Jewish nationalists could find solace and inspiration in the success of other "Oriental" nationalist aspirations and causes. In the nineteenth century some Zionists may have believed not only in the possibility of fellowship and reconciliation between Jews and Arabs as Oriental people but in the possibility of the emergence of a shared Semitic consciousness.[47]

NOTES

1. F. R. Leavis, "Gwendolen Harleth," *London Review of Books* 4.1 (21 January 1982): 10–12.
2. See Terence Cave, introduction to *Daniel Deronda*, by George Eliot, ed. Terence Cave (London: Penguin, 1995), xxiv–xxxiii.
3. Edward William Lane, *An Account of the Manners and Customs of the Modern Egyptians: The Definitive 1860 Edition*, ed. Jason Thompson (Cairo: American University in Cairo Press, 2003), xv.
4. David Friedrich Strauss, *The Life of Jesus, Critically Examined*, trans. George Eliot, 3 vols. (London: Chapman, 1846). For the influence of Strauss on Victorian intellectual history, see W. David Shaw, *The Lucid Veil: Poetic Truth in the Victorian Age* (Madison: University of Wisconsin Press, 1987), 205–6.
5. Edward William Lane, *The Thousand and One Nights, Commonly Called, in England, the Arabian Nights' Entertainments: A New Translation from the Arabic, with Copious Notes*, 3 vols. (London: Chatto and Windus, 1912), 1:16n. 1.
6. Lane, *Nights*, 2:73.
7. Ibid., 2:202n. 18.
8. Ibid., 1:192–93n. 14, 2:74, 2:202n. 11.
9. Jorge Luis Borges, "The Translators of *The Thousand and One Nights*," in *Selected Non-Fictions* (New York: Penguin, 1999), 96.
10. See Jason Thompson, "Small Latin and Less Greek: Expurgated Passages from Edward William Lane's *An Account of the Manners and Customs of the Modern Egyptians*," *Quaderni di Studi Arabi* 1 (2006): 17.
11. Husain Haddawy, trans., *The Arabian Nights II: Sinbad and Other Popular Stories*, based on the text edited by Muhsin Mahdi (New York: Norton, 1996), 168.
12. Lane, *Nights*, 2:203n. 25.
13. Ibid., 2:205n. 36.
14. Ibid., 2:113.
15. Ibid., 2:119.
16. See Lane, "On Geomancy," in ibid., 2:207.
17. Ibid., 2:125.
18. Ibid., 2:211n. 84. Lane's emphasis.
19. Ibid.

20. Ibid., 2:212n. 84.

21. Ibid.

22. Ibid.

23. Ibid., 2:213n. 84.

24. George Eliot, *Daniel Deronda*, ed. Terence Cave (London: Penguin, 1995), 7.

25. Ibid., 19.

26. Ibid., 10.

27. Ibid., 184.

28. Ibid., 224–25.

29. Ibid., 329.

30. Ibid., 676–677, 679.

31. Ibid., 209. A recent scholar has mistakenly implied that the quotation is meant to serve in Eliot's text as metonym for a more extensive catalogue of Budur's sexually alluring features that readers would have known to have followed in Lane (Alicia Carroll, *Dark Smiles: Race and Desire in George Eliot* [Athens: Ohio University Press, 2003]). But Lane's translation in fact follows this line with a note that explains his rationale for omitting the original's sexually overt description of Budur, and only John Payne and Richard Burton made this description available in English a decade after *Deronda*. Lane muted the original manuscript's stress on the princess's voluptuous figure, and Eliot complements this rewriting of the tale by stressing her gift for empathy.

32. Eliot, *Daniel Deronda*, 465.

33. Ibid., 387.

34. Ibid., 386.

35. Mr. Cohen accepts Mordecai's "helpful cleverness" as "he might have taken the services of an enslaved Djinn," and throughout the novel he believes in Mordecai's learning "as something marvelous." Jacob in turn perceives the Hebrew verses learned from Mordecai as "a store of magical articulation." Ibid., 475, 504, and 477, respectively.

36. "The spirit of my youth has been stirred within me, and this body is not strong enough to bear the beatings of its wings. I am as a man bound and imprisoned through long years: behold him brought to speech of his fellow and his limbs set free: he weeps, he totters, the joy within him threatens to break and overthrow the tabernacle of flesh." Ibid., 521.

37. Lane, *Nights*, 2:204n. 36.

38. Eliot, *Daniel Deronda*, 474.

39. Ibid., 494.

40. Ibid., 493.

41. Ibid., 510.

42. Ibid., 513.

43. Ibid., 511. My emphasis.

44. Ibid. For a contemporary exploration of the implications of a postpositivist conception of reason and objectivity for identity, and in particular minority identity,

see Satya Mohanty, *Literary Theory and the Claims of History: Postmodernism, Objectivity, Multicultural Politics* (Ithaca: Cornell University Press, 1997); and Mohanty, "Can Our Values Be Objective? On Ethics, Aesthetics, and Progressive Politics," *New Literary History* 32:4 (Autumn 2001): 803–33.

45. See Todd Curtis Kontje, *German Orientalism* (Ann Arbor: University of Michigan Press, 2004).

46. Eliot, *Daniel Deronda*, 537.

47. Ivan Kalmar and Derek Penslar cite the example of an anonymous manuscript found in the papers of a leading Prague rabbi, in which the writer conceives of Zionism as part of the resurgence and "unification" of all Semitic nations: "The Orient as the old sight of spiritually infused Semitism (Semitentum) will, recognizing the spiritual emptiness and cowardice of the Aryan so-called culture, force back the Aryan where he belongs." "Aladar Deutsch File," MS, chap. 9, 144, Jewish Museum of Prague Archives, quoted in Ivan Davidson Kalmar and Derek J. Penslar, "Orientalism and the Jews: An Introduction," in *Orientalism and the Jews*, ed. Ivan Davidson Kalmar and Derek J. Penslar (Waltham, MA: Brandeis University Press, 2005), xxxvi.

9

Translating Destiny

Hugo von Hofmannsthal's "Tale of the 672nd Night"

DOMINIQUE JULLIEN

Many destinies with mine are woven;
Living plays them all through one another
—Hugo von Hofmannsthal, "Many Truly"[1]

Echoing Borges's laconic description of the *Arabian Nights* ("Chance has played at symmetries"),[2] Pasolini stresses the overwhelming presence of destiny in the tales: "the protagonist of the stories is in fact destiny itself."[3] What I propose here is a kind of cross-reading—intersecting, as it were, several texts that deal with destiny, primarily seen through the prism of the late nineteenth-century pseudo-*Arabian Nights* tale by Hugo von Hofmannsthal, "The Tale of the 672nd Night" (1895).[4] In this early story, a wealthy merchant's son lives in luxurious isolation in a mansion, from where he sets out one day to the city, only to meet a brutal and apparently meaningless death.

The story, we shall see, plays on different generic models—the romance or adventure tale, the fairy tale, the morality tale, the ascetic renunciation tale, but also the dream narrative—setting up competing reading protocols that complicate our understanding of the story (and the role of destiny within it), thus frustrating the reader's expectations and testing the limits of its readability.

Intertextual Connections

Because Hofmannsthal's title makes a direct, explicit reference to the *Arabian Nights*, we can go directly ourselves to the intertextual model thus invoked. The number "672" does not point to any story resembling Hofmannsthal's in the translations that Hofmannsthal would likely have had at his disposal at the time of his story (Maximilian Habicht's 1826 version, based largely on Antoine Galland's version, or Gustav Weil's 1837 translation, with a definitive edition in 1866). Nor do we find conclusive affinities in connection with the number 672 in any of the major translations: Galland quickly abandons the numbering device as tedious after the 27th night,[5] while in Richard Burton's version the 672nd night contains part of "Gharib and Ajib," and in Enno Littmann's version it contains "Asmai and the Three Maidens of Basra."[6] Therefore, we can assume, as most critics have done, that the number "672" is used simply to suggest an Oriental reference.

Hofmannsthal's interest in the *Nights* is well documented, and this story was written in the years of peak involvement with the book.[7] Other early texts also use the *Nights* as their intertextual background, notably a dramatic poem, *The Marriage of Zobeide*, as well as two unfinished texts, a variation on the *Arabian Nights* story of Amgiad and Assad, and the story "The Golden Apple."[8] In addition, Hofmannsthal wrote an essay on the *Nights* in 1907–8, when Felix Paul Greve published his German rendition of the Burton translation, and in 1925, following his journey to North Africa, Hofmannsthal published a travelogue, "Fez" (on which more later). Furthermore, his lifelong interest in the Orient extended to the Far East: we know that his Oriental library included Hermann Oldenberg's authoritative life of Buddha, Henry Clarke Warren and Karl Eugen Neumann's translations of the main canonical texts of Buddhism, and all the books by Lafcadio Hearn.[9] Like Jorge Luis Borges a little later, Hofmannsthal also encountered the key ideas of Buddhism through Schopenhauer.[10] His interest in Buddhism is noteworthy, since, as we shall see, both the destiny stories in the *Nights* and "The Tale of the 672nd Night" share motifs with the Great Renunciation story at the heart of Buddhism, the decisive episode when young prince Siddharta decides to venture out of the walled shelter of comfort and bliss that is his palace, to leave the gilded cage in which his father has raised him, and go out into the wider, cruel world. In Hofmannsthal's case, this interest in the Buddha story meets his lifelong fascination with a Western avatar of it, the story of prince Segismundo, the hero of Spanish Baroque playwright Pedro Calderón de la Barca in his famous play *La vida es sueño* (1635), a story Hofmannsthal rewrote in one of his last texts, the play *Der turm* (*The Tower*).[11] This highly syncretic understanding of Eastern cultures could be interpreted as typically fin-de-siècle "Orientalist," since Hofmannsthal's imagination appears to move effortlessly from Iraq to Japan, from India to Spain, blending cultural specificities into one vast Orient of the mind.

Quirks of Fate

My hypothesis in reading Hofmannsthal's story is, likewise, that it amalgamates various "destiny" motifs diverse in geographic origin and generic focus, dramatically complicating the readability of the story as a destiny story in the process. The first recognizable motif can be traced back to the *Nights* itself—the explicit intertext—in which the plot of numerous stories hinges on destiny. Of particular interest in the context of the present study are stories featuring the characters' vain attempts to thwart destiny.

Exemplary in this respect is the story of the third calender, which forms a part of the well-known cycle "The Tale of the Porter and the Three Ladies of Baghdad." Among the three mysterious mendicants who spend the evening as guests of the ladies, the third one tells one such story of fate inexorably fulfilled despite all possible precautions. A young merchant's son is hidden away in a secret underground location because of a prophecy that foretells he will be killed before manhood by a certain prince. This prince is the future calender, who happens on the secret hiding place, befriends the boy, and accidentally stabs him on the appointed day. (The story of how the prince later loses an eye and

becomes a mendicant forms the second part of the story and is uncon-
nected to the accidental death of the hidden boy.)[12]

From this story we derive the motif of a hidden shelter, which, however, fails to protect the designated victim, because fate will fulfill itself
regardless of efforts to prevent it. "However deep the beloved child is
hidden from the death that has been foretold, however far the doomed
victim runs, the appointment with fate will be kept":[13] destiny stories in
the *Nights* are an Arabic equivalent of the Greek Oedipus story.

Another variant of the destiny motif is that of the unsuccessful precaution. One exemplary illustration is found in the story of "Aladdin
Abu Shamat," also known as "Aladdin of the Beautiful Moles," which
is not in Galland or in the Dalziel brothers' illustrated anthology but
is featured in Burton and elsewhere (fig. 25).[14] There the destiny motif
is inserted in a long and meandering adventure tale featuring a long-
desired son whose birth to aging parents is something of a miracle.[15]
The child is so beautiful that, in fear of the evil eye, the father decides
to hide him in an underground room, where he spends the next fourteen years, emerging one day because a servant forgets to close the door
behind him when bringing his meal. The boy's intelligence and quick-
wittedness match his extraordinary beauty: he immediately requests to
be taken to the souk to learn the merchant's trade, then demands to be
allowed to travel and see the world. To his father's fear of misfortune,
the boy counters, convincingly, that no man may escape his fate: and
thus the second part of the tale is launched, as the young man sets out
with a caravan bound for Baghdad, where he plans to make a fortune
in trade. Of course, the young man is inexperienced and rather spoiled:
he refuses to heed the warnings about the Bedouin bandits, insists on
spending the night in the desert outside Baghdad to admire the moon,
and thus brings about the slaughter of his entire caravan at the hands
of the Bedouins. Interestingly, he himself survives by the miraculous
intervention of the saints he prayed to at the right moment: either his
time had not come or prayer is stronger than fate.[16] The rest of his
adventures show a characteristic succession of high and low, fortune
and misfortune—he is rescued by the same pedophile who had plagued
him during the journey; fleeing this unwanted attention, he enters into
an intermediary marriage in a divorce case, falls in love with the girl in

question, becomes fabulously wealthy and the caliph's favorite, is falsely accused of theft and almost hanged. . . . After a long and tangled series of breathless adventures and narrow escapes involving, among other devices, a flying sofa, Aladdin Abu Shamat ends up rich, respected, and blessed with children from three different wives.[17]

The motif of the unsuccessful precaution, in its varying forms, resonates with other similar motifs both within the circle of the *Nights* and outside it. The motif of the king, or prince, leaving the protective shelter of his palace and encountering danger as a result is also found in the Harun Al-Rashid cycle of the *Arabian Nights* stories. Every time the caliph exits his palace, he relinquishes the safety of his authority, guards, and palace walls, putting himself at risk for the excitement of seeking adventures in the streets of Baghdad. Several tales, including the "The Tale of the Porter and the Three Ladies of Baghdad," show the caliph in danger of his life because of his incognito (which entails a loss of social status) and curiosity (on which more later). In the two destiny stories just summarized, the threat coming from the outside world is severe, ending in death in the first case (the tale of the second calender), while the happy ending of the Abu Shamat tale is due primarily to the optimistic logic of the romance plot (which has Fate guiding and organizing life's events), and not necessarily to any intrinsic merit of the young hero, as Peter Heath has shown.[18]

In other cultural contexts, the motif lends itself to similarly dramatic variations: Segismundo, Calderón's hero, imprisoned in a tower until manhood, emerges raging and filled with bestial violence, which he will only learn to tame slowly (but we note that the imprisonment in his case is due, as in the Oedipus story, to a prophecy that he will kill his father, rather than to the father's desire to protect him from a threat).[19] In both *La vida es sueño* and the story of Abu Shamat, what is at stake is the young hero's education and his difficult but ultimately successful quest to find his proper place in society. Another variant is the Buddha story: beyond tragedy and comedy, Siddharta's momentous exit from the gilded cage leads to a series of life-changing encounters (the old man, the sick man, the dead man, and the ascetic) that will cause the young prince to leave behind the life of plenty of a king, henceforth dismissed as illusion, and embrace the more meaningful ascetic life of a hermit.

1. M. M. Samarkandi and M. Sharif, *A Reader in the World of Stories*, miniature, Iran, seventeenth century (© RMN-Grand Palais / Art Resource, NY)

2. *Top left*, François de Troy, *The duchesse du Maine*, circa 1700 (© Musée des Beaux-Arts d'Orléans); 3. *Top right*, Catherine Lusurier, after Nicolas de Largillière, portrait of Voltaire (François-Marie Arouet), at age thrity (© RMN-Grand Palais / Art Resource, NY); 4. *Bottom left*, Sir Joshua Reynolds, portrait of William Beckford, 1782 (© National Portrait Gallery, London); 5. *Bottom right*, Ozias Humphry, portrait of Elizabeth Berkeley, also known as Lady Craven, later Margravine of Anspach (© Tate 2013, on loan to the National Portrait Gallery, London)

6. Edmund Dulac, "Princess Badoura," from Laurence Housman's *Princess Badoura: A Tale of the Arabian Nights*, 1913 (© Arcadian Library 18401, London)

7. Hōsai, *Fūsennori uwasa no takadono* (The sensational balloonist), woodblock print, 1891
(© The Tsubouchi Memorial Theatre Museum)

8. Persian (*right*) and Turkish (*left*) depicted in *Bankoku jinbutsu emaki*, or "A Picture Scroll of People of the World," early nineteenth century (© National Museum of Ethnology, Osaka)

9. A scene from the revue of *Sabaku no kurobara*, or "A Black Rose in the Desert" (2000) (© Takarazuka)

10. *Left*, Film song booklet cover for *Gul Bakawali*, 1932; *Gul-e-Baka-vali* (The Bakavali flower), a *qissa-dastan* tale of Persian origin, was a popular subject for India's *Arabian Nights* fantasy films (© Virchand Dharamsey) 11. *Right*, Program cover for *Aladdin* at the Theatre Royal Drury Lane, 1885 (© City of Westminster Archives Centre)

12. Alfred Jacobsen, *Aladdin* Toy Theatre characters, 1889 (© Sven-Erik Olsen, Oldfux)

13. *Umanusubito* performed at the Nissay Theatre, July 2008 (© Shochiku)

14. Ian McKellen as Widow Twankey in British pantomime, 2006 (© Manuel Harlan)

15. Helen Stratton, "Next morning he followed the bird as it flew from tree to tree," illustration of Qamar al-Zaman for the 1899 edition of Edward W. Lane's *The Thousand and One Nights*, p. 254 (© Arcadian Library, London)

16. Paul Klee, *Sindbad the Sailor / The Seafarer*, 1923 (© Erich Lessing / Art Resource, NY. © 2013 Artists Rights Society, New York)

Leaving the Palace

Returning now to the "The Tale of the 672nd Night," we see how the story of the merchant's son weaves together destiny motifs from a variety of intertexts and contexts.[20] The unnamed young hero spends his life in luxurious isolation in his mansion, in the company of his precious collection of artistic objects and cared for by his four devoted servants:

> As his friends meant little to him, and no woman's beauty had captivated him enough to make him consider it desirable or even tolerable to have her permanently by him, he grew more and more accustomed to a life of virtual solitude. . . . The beauty of his carpets, silks and fabrics, his carved and paneled walls, his metal lamps and bowls, his glass and his earthenware collection came to mean more to him than he would ever have imagined. Gradually he came to appreciate how his beloved objects contained all the shapes and colors in the world. (47)

Like another merchant's son, Aladdin Abu Shamat, who has lived in gentle seclusion, knowing only his parents and servants, and also like prince Siddharta, who has been sheltered from all ugliness and all hardship by his overprotective father, Hofmannsthal's protagonist assumes, wrongly, that his small world of beautiful objects is the real world. Not surprisingly, the day the merchant's son wanders out of his "palace," he is in for a rude shock—in fact the encounter with the brutal reality of the outside world proves deadly, as he loses his way in a strange and hostile part of the city and eventually dies a slow and ignominious death after being kicked in the groin by a soldier's horse. In agreement with the generic constraints of romance, we have a young hero on the threshold of active, responsible manhood, whose emergence from the safety of his hidden childhood leads him into adventures and dangers that are a test by fate, the stakes being the hero's conquest of a place in society. Departing from the first destiny plot (the third calender story, in which the merchant's son is killed accidentally by virtue of a prophecy and despite protective seclusion), Hofmannsthal's recluse, it appears, dies for having wandered outside the shelter, in a variation on our second destiny plot, the story of Abu Shamat and his ill-fated caravan attacked by Bedouins. But contrary to Abu Shamat, who ultimately succeeds despite the accumulation of mishaps, Hofmannsthal's hapless hero never finds his way home, nor much less a place in society. The story is also a sinister variant of the Buddha plot, with the spiritual death experienced by prince Siddharta (who dies to the world after his three momentous encounters with age, illness, and death) replaced by literal death. In a wicked twist on the Buddha experience—in which the deeply shocking encounters ultimately work for the hero's greater good —the merchant's son in Hofmannsthal's story dies tormented by the thought of the straight causal line that fate appears to have traced from his earlier sheltered life to his untimely, gruesome death: "He looked back over his life with great bitterness and disavowed everything that he had cherished. He hated his untimely death so much that he hated his life for having led him to it" (63).

The Unhappy Prince

There is no redemption for Hofmannsthal's hero, who is a kind of reverse mirror image of his models. One key difference, perhaps, is that he is a voluntary recluse, unlike the sons in the other destiny stories (Abu Shamat, Siddharta), who are incarcerated on their fathers' wishes and who willfully go against their fathers' interdiction to exit the palace. Instead of pitting a father's heroic but failed attempt to stave off harm to his child against a son's forceful rebellion and choice of adventure and danger, Hofmannsthal's story presents us with an ineffective protector (a dead father) and a reclusive, inactive son. The passivity, even listlessness, of Hofmannsthal's hero is in stark contrast to so many merchants' sons in the real *Nights*, who exude confidence and energy, taking on the world as soon as they can escape from their confined circumstances, simply brimming over with lust of life. In the incipit of Hofmannsthal's story, the orphaned hero withdraws from the world because he feels no desire to take an active part in life outside his palace: "A very handsome young merchant's son, who had lost both father and mother, shortly after turning twenty-five grew weary of society and a life of entertaining" (47). Despite possessing the attributes that make him eligible for a typical tale of romance and adventure (youth, wealth, beauty), Hofmannsthal's merchant's son shows no desire for social or sexual pur-

suits. His pleasures are limited to contemplation of his precious collections—hardly a young man's occupation—and his erotic daydreaming
about his younger servant girl is halfhearted at best. Rather than explore
the world, he will only lose himself in it. Critics have by and large read
this as Hofmannsthal's condemnation of the sterility of the aesthete's
life, a refusal to engage with fellow humans and the life of the city, for
which he is punished terribly, first by the unexplained yet unanimous
hostility of the people he encounters, then by the gruesome attack by
the horse.[21] The anxiety over the aesthete's choice of life is a recurrent
theme in Hofmannsthal's early work (as well as in works by other writers of the Young Vienna movement, of course): it is also the theme of
his 1893 morality play *Death and the Fool,* in which the young protagonist is likewise punished for his estrangement from life by the untimely
appearance of Death itself:

> What do I know about human life?
> True, I appeared to stand inside it,
> But, at the most, I studied it,
> Never was caught, but held aloof,
> Never lost myself, but, alien, eyed it.
> Where others give and others take
> I stood aside, my inmost centre dumb.
> From all those charming lips I did not suck
> The true, essential potion, life by name.[22]

Isolation from his fellow human beings, lack of empathy for their
plight, in particular those less fortunate than himself—the protagonist's social inadequacy is stressed more forcefully in the story than
in the verse play, as the merchant's son meets his demise in the slums
of the town. This social dimension of Hofmannsthal's rewriting of the
Nights resonates with another palace story, by his contemporary Oscar
Wilde, the fairy tale titled "The Happy Prince," first published in 1888.
The happy prince lives out his life in blissful seclusion in the palace,
but after his death, his statue discovers the ugliness and misery of the
city around it. Not coincidentally, "The Tale of the 672nd Night," which
betrays a very somber view of the tales, was written at the time of the

Oscar Wilde scandal, a few months before the actual trial, which greatly depressed Hofmannsthal. The dark story of an aesthete's fall from grace is thus haunted by the tragic figure of Oscar Wilde.

Jorge Luis Borges, in his 1952 essay on Buddhism, "Forms of a Legend," refers to Oscar Wilde's children's story "The Happy Prince" as a variation on the Buddha motif: "At the end of the 19th century Oscar Wilde proposed a variation: The happy prince dies in the seclusion of the palace, without having discovered sorrow, but his posthumous effigy discerns it from atop his pedestal."[23] Curiously, Borges all but ignores the obvious social dimension of the Oscar Wilde story, which is set in the context of late Victorian England, obsessed with charitable works and social progress. The duty of being a good king, attentive to the plight of the people, generous toward his less fortunate subjects, falls to the statue. The statue gives away all the gold and the jewels that adorn it to the poor, including its sapphire eyes, feeling belatedly guilty that, during his lifetime, the prince never cared to look past the walls of his palace:

> "When I was alive and had a human heart," answered the statue, "I did not know what tears were, for I lived in the Palace of Sans-Souci, where sorrow is not allowed to enter. . . . Round the garden ran a very lofty wall, but I never cared to ask what lay beyond it, everything about me was so beautiful. My courtiers called me the Happy Prince, and happy indeed I was, if pleasure be happiness. So I lived, and so I died. And now that I am dead they have set me up here so high that I can see all the ugliness and all the misery of my city, and though my heart is made of lead yet I cannot choose but weep."[24]

While the young merchant's son in Hofmannsthal's "Tale of the 672nd Night" treasures his exotic collections and disdains human affection, in Wilde's story the statue of the happy prince (his good self—the reverse of the *Dorian Gray* plot, in which the picture is charged with evil) conversely dismisses exotic valuables, does not want to hear the swallow's tales about Egypt, and prizes only deeds of kindness: "'Dear little Swallow,' said the Prince, 'you tell me of marvellous things, but more marvellous than anything is the suffering of men and of women. There is no Mystery so great as Misery. Fly over my city, little Swallow, and tell me what you see there.'" In a final miracle, the statue atones posthumously for the prince's self-centered life by a radical displacement of values from the aesthetic to the ethical realms, with the statue's leaden heart and the dead bird being declared by God more valuable than all the riches of the palace.

Another contemporary children's story, Rudyard Kipling's "Miracle of Purun Baghat," the third story of *The Second Jungle Book* (1895), also features a "king" (the Brahmin Purun Dass, prime minister of an unnamed northern Indian state) turned hermit, like the Buddha, at the height of his powers. "Now he would let these things go, as a man drops a cloak he needs no longer."[25] The protagonist leaves his powerful and wealthy lifestyle, takes up the walking stick and begging bowl of a wandering mendicant, and disappears into the Himalayas, leading the life of an ascetic (under the name Purun Baghat) in an abandoned temple for years, fed by the people of the village below. One night in the rainy season, alerted by his animal companions, Purun Baghat goes down to warn the villagers of an impending landslide, sacrificing his life in the process. Both children's stories ("The Happy Prince" and "The Miracle of Purun Baghat"), in true Victorian fashion, are highly moralistic and didactic, focusing on duty to community and the best way to fulfill it.[26]

In Hofmannsthal's story, however, no such atonement seems to be available to the merchant's son, who dies rejecting everything he valued (including, presumably, his former aesthete's life) but without any sense of peace or wisdom, since he ends up taking on the grimacing features of his enemies, the sullen girls and the mad horses: "He looked back over his life with great bitterness and disavowed everything that he had cherished. He hated his untimely death so much that he hated his life for having led him to it. The wild inner frenzy consumed his last remaining strength." The merchant's son sleeps, wakes up, and finding himself alone, tries to scream. "Finally he vomited gall, then blood, and died, his features distorted, his lips so mangled that his teeth and gums were exposed, giving him an alien, evil expression" (63).

What then is the meaning of this tale? It imitates the major destiny tales in the *Arabian Nights* but departs from both their philosophical message (fate is inescapable, as both the story of the third calender and the story of Abu Shamat illustrate) and their moral message (a cautionary tale against the dangers of curiosity in the calender's case, a warning against stubbornness and vanity in the tale of Abu Shamat), while it also appears to stray from the spiritual message exemplified by renunciation stories of the Buddha type, as well as from modern morality tales such as Wilde's or Kipling's. In fact, the trajectory of the Hofmannsthal hero remains highly problematic—one cannot even compare it with the linear, processional sequence of high and low, success and failure characteristic of a romance plot such as we see in the tale of Aladdin Abu Shamat; it rather resembles a series of unfortunate events (to paraphrase a recent success of children's literature)[27] that lead to disaster through fortuitous paths. The merchant's son's exit from the palace is entirely serendipitous, motivated not by a lust for adventure but by the vague desire to investigate the unnamed Oriental servant's past after the hero receives an anonymous letter alluding to mysterious crimes committed by the man. The distress exhibited by the hero upon receiving the threatening letter seems quite disproportionate to the event, as he imagines being stripped of his possessions (his servants) and compares his anguish to that of a great king deprived of his empire: "And he understood why the very great king from the past would have been bound to die if he had been deprived of the lands he had traversed from coast to coast and conquered, the lands he had dreamed of ruling but which were so vast he neither had power over them nor received tribute from them beyond the satisfaction that he had conquered them and that nobody but he was their king" (54).[28] This anguish at the thought of losing his "empire" prompts his departure from the mansion; without notifying the servants, he goes off alone into the city to try to gather information about the accused butler. But this halfhearted attempt at detective work fails ludicrously—the Persian embassy is closed. Instead, he finds himself falling from one misfortune into another, at loggerheads with any kind of revelation narrative, Buddhist or otherwise, and at cross-purposes with the reader's expectations of closure, poetic justice, or reasonable comeuppance.[29]

Character and Fate

Ten years after "The Tale of the 672nd Night," Hofmannsthal published his essay on Wilde, "Sebastian Melmoth" (1905), which offers a hermeneutic clue for interpreting the earlier story. In the essay, he strove to reunite the two aspects of Oscar Wilde, the happy, success-ful, lighthearted aesthete of the early years, and the tragic, fallen, and broken convict of Reading Gaol, who lived out his final destitute years in Paris under the name Sebastian Melmoth, "the name of a ghost, a half-forgotten Balzacian character."[30] The point Hofmannsthal makes repeatedly in his essay is that it is wrong to separate character and des-tiny. Instead, he insists on an essential and profound continuity between the "Happy Prince" period of Oscar Wilde's life and the postscandal—or postmortem—darker years:

> Oscar Wilde's character and Oscar Wilde's fate are one and the same. He walked toward his catastrophe with the same steps as Oedipus, the seeing-blind one. The aesthete was tragic. The dandy was tragic. . . . Incessantly he felt the threat of life directed towards him. He kept chal-lenging life unceasingly. He insulted reality. And he sensed life lying in wait in order to spring upon him out of the darkness. (302–3)

The statue of the happy prince, we recall, asked the swallow to pluck out its sapphire eyes to give to the poor: in similar fashion, Oedipus and the one-eyed calender from the *Nights* were maimed and made wiser by misfortune. The moment of truth for Wilde came when, in his tragic folly, he decided to denounce Queensberry and provoke fate. This fate-ful decision fused his earlier laughing persona with his tragic mask: "for then the mask of Bacchus with its full, beautifully curved lips must have been transformed in an unforgettable manner into the mask of the seeing-blind Oedipus. . . . At that moment he must have worn round his magnificent brow the band of tragic fate, so rarely visible" (304). The encounter with Queensberry, a terrifying father figure who inflicted a ruthless punishment, echoes the fatal encounter with the horse that punishes the merchant's son so terribly.

"The Tale of the 672nd Night" also consists of two strikingly dispa-rate parts, a first part describing the beautiful and rather vain lifestyle of a Dorian Gray lookalike, and a second part that brings to pass the igno-minious fall of the handsome hero. "We must not degrade life," Hof-mannsthal urges, "by tearing character and fate asunder and separat-ing [Wilde's] misfortune from his fortune" ("Sebastian Melmoth," 304). Oscar Wilde's refined dandy's life is not separate from the ignominious prison bath that he was forced to use after ten other convicts and that, Hofmannsthal muses, was already somehow contained in the aesthete's love of luxury: "his limbs which toyed with orchids and lounged among cushions of ancient silks were in reality filled with an awful longing for the ghastly bath from which, however, at its first touch, they shrank in nauseated repugnance" (304). Likewise, we may infer, the squalid end of the merchant's son is not to be torn asunder from his beauteous beginning.

"It Was No Dream"

A different kind of reading protocol offers itself at this point.[31] We can make sense of "The Tale of the 672nd Night" if, as we would with a dream, we listen to echoes and repetitions between its two different parts. Reading it like a dream enables us to see continuities: the happy prince period is not so happy as it first seems and contains elements that are replicated in the second, darker part; the story can be interpreted, as Dorrit Cohn has done, as a punishment dream.[32]

The enigmatic feeling of the story is tied to its dreamlike quality. There is a logic to the hero's decisions that mimics the logic of dreams.[33] The unfamiliar city the hero wanders into, ultimately to meet his death, is at the same time a generic *Arabian Nights* city and Hofmannsthal's own Vienna, albeit its poorer neighborhoods rather than its well-known landmarks. As in a dream, places are multiple and contradictory entities, identities are condensed and displaced, people resemble each other or animals. The hero's anguished stumbling through the dark greenhouse (58–59) replicates his earlier creeping under the branches of an overgrown part of his garden (51–52). The four-year-old child who terrifies him in the greenhouse and precipitates his subsequent demise (57–58) is also the sullen servant girl in his own home (49). The contorted face of the thief caught in his father's shop (62) is also that of the horse (the Night Mare), with whom the girl shares the same angry look and which the hero will come to resemble himself when in his death agony he bares his teeth and glares angrily.[34]

The horse, obviously connected to the father in some essential way, is at the heart of the punishment dream since it delivers the fatal blow.

Perhaps even more important than the Oedipal plot favored by Dorrit Cohn (according to her, the hero is punished for a transgression connected to his desire for the mother, represented by the beryl necklace he drops under the horse's hoofs), what seems clear is that the horse in this context doubles as an image of destiny. The threat emanating from the horse is illuminated by Hofmannsthal's own personal difficulties in controlling his mare, Fuchs, which was given to him by his father when he left for his military service. Hofmannsthal's letters reveal ambivalent feelings for the horse: on the one hand, affection for the beautiful and spirited animal, as well as a sense of pride in his horsemanship, which he considered indispensable to a real gentleman; on the other hand, fear of his "wild, uncanny horse" and shame at his own deficiencies. On at least one occasion, he was nearly killed; thereafter the mare went lame, and Hofmannsthal was never able to cure her completely.[35] The feelings of helplessness, combined with a sense of incompetence, are a poisonous mix of physical and social anxieties. The protagonist revealingly refuses to look at the saddlebag ornaments in the jeweler's shop because, he claims, "as a merchant's son he had never much had to do with horses, indeed could not even ride" (56). Later, the malicious horse that will kill him reminds him of the thief whose "face was contorted with fear because people were threatening him, because he had a large gold coin and would not say where he had come by it" (62): not unlike the thief, it would seem that the merchant's son too has a guilty conscience concerning the source of his gold.

The young man who daydreams about the "great king" and his cavalry but cannot ride a horse[36] is killed by a horse that reminds him of a man guilty of possessing ill-gotten gold. Unlike the merchant's sons in the real *Nights*, who are legitimate and proud heirs to the paternal fortune, the Arabic equivalent of princes in European tales,[37] our modern merchant's son does not feel entitled to his fortune or his horse and thus cannot control this image of his destiny.

If the Night Mare serves as a vehicle for the expression of modern anxieties, in particular social anxieties, the hero's dreamlike wandering in the unknown city at nightfall also echoes another, later text, a description of Fez from Hofmannsthal's *Journey in North Africa* (1925). Here, however, the dream is euphoric rather than nightmarish, as the narrator describes an episode of leaving his palatial rented house and straying into the old labyrinthine streets, encountering characters that seem to come out of *The Thousand and One Nights*:

> And this relation of all things to all, this concatenation of dwellings and places of labor, of markets and mosques, this ornament of the intricately woven lettering that is everywhere repeated a thousandfold by the life-lines entangled one with the other, all this surrounds us with a sensation, a secret, a scent, wherein there is something primordial, a memory of preexistence—Greece and Rome, the Arabian fairytales, and the Bible; yet at the same time it has clinging to it a touch of something quietly threatening, the true secret of the exotic, and this scent, this secret, this being in the core of the tangle and the faint awareness of the Forbidden that is never entirely absent, this today is still and maybe still tomor-row—Fez. Fez, until twenty years ago the great untrodden, the auster-est, most forbidden of all Islamic towns, whose aroma has not yet com-pletely evaporated.[38]

The rational causality that would account for the sequence of events in a normal world is here substituted with an oneiric causality in which architecture, writing, and destiny ("the life-lines entangled one with the other") are continuous and in some way interchangeable, as they would be in a dream or a poem.[39]

Of course, wanderings into unknown cities or neighborhoods, along with strange encounters, are very common in the *Arabian Nights*, especially in tales with an urban backdrop such as the Harun al-Rashid stories or the Cairo stories. But the difference here is that the merchant's son is pursuing an aimless course that eventually takes him to a point-less death. The urban labyrinth into which he ventures never leads him either to an exit (he stumbles across the barracks while trying to find his way back to "the wealthy part of town, where he would be able to find lodging for the night"; 60) or to a center, contrary to the centripetal movement of labyrinthine quests that traditionally bring the hero to a locus of revelation. The very notion of destiny—as meaningful teleol-ogy—is threatened: with a character whose early life held no special distinction (he is an aesthete rather than an artist, enjoying passively the fruits of others' labors, an unmarried and childless son, and an unfulfilled dreamer whose favorite book, the story of a great king, is cruelly parodied by his absurd death by horse kick)—it is not possible to see in this absurd accidental death a fulfillment of any sort of destiny, nor is it possible to read the story as a morality tale.

Imperial Messages

"The Tale of the 672nd Night," then, retains its enigmatic character. Reading it as a dream helps us understand it, but it only takes us so far, since it is not a dream but only dreamlike. There is no awakening from the dream: so readers are thrown back as it were to the morality tale, only to find themselves mystified as to the moral. Rewriting, as the story purports to do, a well-established tradition of wisdom tales or destiny tales that claim to impart some lesson to the reader, it veers away from this traditional, or traditionary, form, leaving the reader perplexed. From the mention of a "tale" and the reference to the *Nights*, the reader naturally anticipates a more straightforward narrative. One expects, for example, a modern morality tale, something closer to Oscar Wilde's children's story "The Happy Prince" or Rudyard Kipling's "The Miracle of Purun Baghat," with a rather unambiguous moral—the importance of being charitable or the superiority of the hermit's sacrifice in the service of the people. Or one expects a romance. But if this is a tale—as the title claims, albeit ironically—where are the typical features of the genre? Where are the princess, the hazardous prowess, the kingdom won, the treasure? Where is the joyful urge to life that Hofmannsthal came later to celebrate in the *Arabian Nights*?[40] What, if this be a tale about destiny, is the character's destiny—to die of a kick in the groin, neglected by uncaring soldiers? What wisdom if any is taught or learned here? If this is a cautionary tale in the manner of the calender story, what is it cautioning against? Curiosity—the desire to investigate his manservant's past? But curiosity, for which the calender is punished by the loss of an eye, while the caliph is simply warned, here receives a gruesomely excessive punishment.[41] The punishment of the hero seems absurdly mismatched to his offenses (passivity? self-absorption? social disengagement?), and in any case, it is also most ironically mistimed, since he is struck precisely when he finally attempts to help others— reaching for money to give to the soldier, he drops his parcel and is kicked by the horse when he reaches down to retrieve it.[42] An evil twist indeed—he is, it would appear, punished for his good deed.

Despite appearances to the contrary, then, Hofmannsthal's "fairy tale" is no fairy tale. Hofmannsthal's fellow writer Arthur Schnitzler, who insisted that his friend had written not a fairy tale but a dream, was closer to the truth. The merchant's son, he recommended, should not be made to die but to wake up from his nightmare.[43] The protagonist of Hofmannsthal's earlier morality play *Death and the Fool* was allowed some such measure of consolatory self-reflection at the moment of his untimely death:

> Dying, at last I feel that I exist . . .
>
> . . . .
>
> So from the dream of life I now may wake,
> Cloyed with emotion, to death's wakefulness.[44]

No such death-awareness is granted to the merchant's son. Not only does he not wake up—chastened or otherwise—but furthermore, the dream sequence, in which the protagonist encounters reality in the outside world beyond his palace, becomes the reality which makes the first part of the tale seem all the more unreal. Like Gregor Samsa, who could not wake up from his nightmare because "it was no dream," the merchant's son is stranded in a dreamlike story from which there is no exit, and a parablelike tale in which there is no clear moral. "The Tale of the 672nd Night" confuses generic boundaries and reading protocols like, later, Kafka, of whose parables Walter Benjamin pointed out that neither a natural reading nor a supernatural one could be satisfying options, since they would both miss the point.[45]

Commenting on the dreamlike quality of modern parables, such as those found in Kafka and Borges, Gila Safran Naveh, taking her cue from Heinz Politzer's classic study *Franz Kafka: Parable and Paradox*, argues that they are impenetrable because their relation to a decodable wisdom derived from a divine Law has become problematic.[46] Like Kafka's dying emperor's last words, which are of such great importance yet will never reach their destination, these modern parabolic stories baffle interpretation. What is true of Kafka and Borges also applies to this Hofmannsthal story. The meaninglessness, the tongue-in-cheek despair exuded by the story, its perplexity, are strongly reminiscent of Kafka, in whose nightmarish universe this story belongs. While there is no evidence that Hofmannsthal ever read the stories of his contemporary Kafka, we know that Kafka was a great admirer of Hofmannsthal's work.[47] More importantly, what allows us to read this Hofmannsthal story of indecisive quest as "Kafkaesque" is the retroactive phenomenon described by Borges in his 1951 essay "Kafka and His Precursors." In this reverse conception of influence, the precursor becomes a notion born of an act of reading, not writing: "our reading of Kafka," Borges writes, "noticeably refines and diverts our reading" of, in this case, "The Tale of the 672nd Night." Today's reader now overlays Kafka—and Borges —over Hofmannsthal's rewriting of *The Thousand and One Nights*.[48]

In Borges's essay "The Translators of the *Thousand and One Nights*," he laments the inadequacy of German translations. "There are marvels in the *Nights* which I would like to see rethought in German." The greatly admired Enno Littmann, according to him, is solidly faithful but hopelessly tedious: "In Littmann, who like Washington cannot tell a lie, there is nothing but the probity of Germany. This is so little, so very little. The commerce between Germany and the *Nights* should have produced something more." Instead of this honest, unimaginative German translator, he dreams of a translation by Kafka, which could have yielded fantastic nightmares: "Chance has played at symmetries, contrasts, digressions. What might a man—a Kafka—do if he organized and intensified this play, remade it in line with the Germanic distortion, the *Unheimlichkeit* of Germany?"[49] Perhaps "The Tale of the 672nd Night," this story by Hofmannsthal—a Hofmannsthal who at least for a moment resembled Kafka[50]—is as close as we will ever get to realizing Borges's dream of a translation of the *Nights* by Franz Kafka.

NOTES

1. Hugo von Hofmannsthal, "Many Truly" (1895), translated by Vernon Watkins, in *Poems and Verse Plays*, bilingual edition, edited and introduced by Michael Hamburger, with a preface by T. S. Eliot, Bollingen Series 33, vol. 2 (New York: Pantheon Books, 1961), 35.

2. Jorge Luis Borges, "The Translators of the *Thousand and One Nights*," translated by Esther Allen, in *Selected Non-Fictions*, edited by Eliot Weinberger (New York: Penguin, 1999), 108.

3. Quoted in Marina Warner, *Stranger Magic: Charmed States and the Arabian Nights* (Cambridge: Belknap Press of Harvard University Press, 2012), 44.

4. Hugo von Hofmannsthal, "The Tale of the 672nd Night" (1895), in *Selected Tales*, translated by J. M. Q. Davies (London: Angel Classics, 2007) (hereafter cited parenthetically in the text).

5. *Arabian Nights' Entertainments*, edited with an introduction and notes by Robert L. Mack, based on Galland's translation (Oxford: Oxford University Press, 1995), 65.

6. See Mia Gerhardt's chronology of translations in *The Art of Story-Telling: A Literary Study of the Thousand and One Nights* (Leiden: Brill, 1963), 68. Margaret Jacobs proposes that "he was not re-writing any of the tales but making his own original contribution while adopting the role of the oriental story-teller" (introduction to *Four Stories*, by Hugo von Hofmannsthal, ed. Margaret Jacobs [Oxford: Oxford University Press, 1968], 22).

7. Hanna Lewis distinguishes three phases in Hofmannsthal's involvement with the *Nights*: first, unsurprisingly, Hofmannsthal's childhood (she mentions the Dalziel 1881 illustrated edition he read at the age of eight); then, the period of greatest influence, in the years 1895–97, when Hofmannsthal was in his twenties—this corresponds to our story, published in 1895; lastly, he returned to the book in 1907–8, when he wrote his essay. See Hanna B. Lewis, "The *Arabian Nights* and Young Hofmannsthal," *German Life and Letters* 3:3 (1984): 190. We note that the key periods of Hofmannsthal's involvement with the *Nights* coincide with new German translations: shortly after "The Tale of the 672nd Night," Max Henning published his version based mostly on the Bulaq edition (1895–99), and Felix Paul Greve's German rendition of the Burton translation appeared in 1908, prefaced by Hofmannsthal's essay. Enno Littmann's authoritative translation, according to Gerhardt "the first scholarly translation, with the necessary notes, and a valuable introduction" (*Art of Story-Telling*, 68), appeared in 1921–28, also during Hofmannsthal's lifetime. It is also possible, of course, that Hofmannsthal, who was fluent in English and French, read the translations by Galland, Joseph-Charles Mardrus, Edward Lane, and Burton in the original as well. On Hofmannsthal and the *Nights*, see also Ulrich Marzolph and Richard van Leeuwen, *The Arabian Nights Encyclopedia*, 2 vols. (Santa Barbara, CA: ABC-CLIO, 2004), 2:590; and Richard van Leeuwen, "The *Thousand and One Nights* and European Modernism: Hugo von Hofmannsthal," in *Les mille et une nuits et le récit oriental en Espagne et en Occident*, ed. Aboubakr Chraïbi and Carmen Ramírez (Paris: L'Harmattan, 2009), 175–88. On the robust reception of the *Arabian Nights* in turn-of-the-century German culture, see Donald Haase, "The *Arabian Nights*, Visual Culture, and Early German Cinema," in *The Arabian Nights in Transnational Perspective*, ed. Ulrich Marzolph (Detroit: Wayne State University Press, 2007), 245.

8. Hugo von Hofmannsthal, *The Marriage of Zobeide*, translated by Christopher Middleton, in *Poems and Verse Plays*, 366–525.

9. See Freny Mistry, "Hofmannsthal's Oriental Library," *Journal of English and Germanic Philology* 71 (1972): 177–97; and Mistry, "Towards Buddhahood: Some Remarks on the Sigismund Figure in Hofmannsthal's Turm Plays," *Modern Language Review* 69 (1974): 337–47.

10. On the affinities between Buddhism and Christianity as underlined in Schopenhauer's influential *Die Welt als Wille und Vorstellung*, see Mistry, "Hofmannsthal's Oriental Library," 178–79.

11. Hugo von Hofmannsthal, *The Tower*, translated by Alfred Schwartz, in *The Whole Difference: Selected Writings of Hugo von Hofmannsthal*, ed. J. D. McClatchy, 366–491 (Princeton: Princeton University Press, 2008). On the significance of the Calderón motif, see especially Mistry, "Towards Buddhahood."

12. As part of the original kernel of the tales, the story is to be found in all the different versions. It first appeared in Galland's translation: see "The Story of the Third Calender, a King's Son," in "The Story of the Three Calenders, Sons of Kings; and of the Five Ladies of Bagdad," in *Arabian Nights' Entertainments*, 106–23.

13. Warner, *Stranger Magic*, 11.

14. Richard Francis Burton, *The Book of the Thousand Nights and a Night, with Introduction, Explanatory Notes on the Manners and Customs of Moslem Men and a Terminal Essay upon the History of the Nights*, 16 vols. (Benares: Kamashastra Society, 1885–87), 4:29. Mardrus retells it as "Histoire de Grain-de-Beauté" (*Les mille nuits et une nuit* [Paris: Robert Laffont, collection "Bouquins," 1980], 1:625).

15. According to Marina Warner, the fertility potion the merchant is given is simply a placebo, whose efficiency relies entirely on faith (*Stranger Magic*, 403); this is especially significant in view of the fact that the story is an illustration of the power of fate to gratify or to thwart human volition.

16. According to Burton (4:45, 46).

17. On the motif of the flying bed (or sofa), see Marina Warner's analysis, which connects the device with the erotic sofa literature of the eighteenth century as well as with the psychoanalyst's couch (*Stranger Magic*, 405–24).

18. Peter Heath characterizes romance's basic attraction as a comforting plot meant to reassure its audience on the order and logic in the world despite its apparent chaos (see "Romance as Genre," in *The Arabian Nights Reader*, ed. Ulrich Marzolph [Detroit: Wayne State University Press, 2006], 210). On Hofmannsthal's identification with the figures of the erring prince and the merchant's son, see Richard van Leeuwen, "*Thousand and One Nights* and European Modernism," 181.

19. Pedro Calderón de la Barca, *La vida es sueño* (1635; repr., Paris: Aubier-Flammarion, 1976). Daniel Beaumont briefly discusses the play in the context of "The Sleeper Awakened" and the theme of the double: see *Slave of Desire: Sex, Love, and Death in The 1001 Nights* (Madison, NJ: Fairleigh Dickinson University Press, 2002), 102.

20. The recycling and recombination of various motifs and narrative units formally

connect Hofmannsthal's story with its primary intertext, since "the imaginative reuse of elements on all levels" is a key feature of the *Nights* themselves, as Daniel Beaumont points out (see his essay "Literary Style and Narrative Technique," in Marzolph and van Leeuwen, *Arabian Nights Encyclopedia*, 1:4).

21. On the condemnation of the aesthete's life, see Andrew W. Barker, "The Triumph of Life in Hofmannsthal's 'Das Märchen Der 672. Nacht,'" *Modern Language Review* 74 (1979): 341–48; Thomas Kovach, "Introduction: Hofmannsthal Today," in *A Companion to the Works of Hugo von Hofmannsthal*, edited by Thomas Kovach, 1–22 (Rochester, NY: Camden House, 2002), 6–8; as well as Richard Alewyn, *Über Hugo von Hofmannsthal* (Göttingen: Vandenhoeck and Ruprecht, 1963). More recently, Richard van Leeuwen, while acknowledging this critical tradition, connects the polar motifs of confinement and wandering rather to the modernist distortion of narrative time and space: see "The *Thousand and One Nights* and European Modernism," particularly 185–88.

22. Hugo von Hofmannsthal, *Death and the Fool*, translated by Michael Hamburger, in *Poems and Verse Plays*, 97.

23. Jorge Luis Borges, "Forms of a Legend," translated by Eliot Weinberger, in *Selected Non-Fictions*, 376.

24. Oscar Wilde, "The Happy Prince" (1888), in *The Happy Prince and Other Stories*, Project Gutenberg, http://www.gutenberg.org/dirs/etext97/hpao1oh.htm (further quotations from the story refer to this version).

25. Rudyard Kipling, "The Miracle of Purun Baghat" (1895), in *The Second Jungle Book*, readbookonline.net, http://www.readbookonline.net/read/8193/20419/.

26. Borges, whose essays so often mention Kipling, does not comment on "The Miracle of Purun Baghat" in particular, but his view of Kipling, whom he greatly admired, displays the same indifference to the social, political, or ideological dimensions of the stories. Instead, he focuses on Kipling's formal virtues, his craft, the complexity of his narrative technique, dismissing the ideology as simplistic or unimportant. For example: "Kipling's prose and poetic works are infinitely more complex than the theses they elucidate. . . . In his teeming life there was no passion like the passion for technique" (review of *Rudyard Kipling: A Study in Literature and Political Ideas*, by Edward Shanks, translated by Suzanne Jill Levine, in *Selected Non-Fictions*, 251).

27. Lemony Snicket, *A Series of Unfortunate Events*, 13 vols. (New York: HarperCollins, 2006).

28. Robert Lemon's postcolonial reading stresses the similarities between the four servants and the exotic, colonized peoples of Western empires: see *Imperial Messages: Orientalism as Self-Critique in the Habsburg Fin de Siècle* (Rochester, NY: Camden House, 2011), especially 20–26.

29. Not all stories in the *Nights* display straightforward moral closure, of course. Andras Hamori discusses the moral perplexity at the heart of "The Tale of the Porter and the Three Ladies of Baghdad" in his book *On the Art of Medieval Arabic Literature* (Princeton: Princeton University Press, 1974). The various and

morally capricious connections between actions and retributions, he claims, show "a structural coherence that ultimately speaks for a morally random universe" (164), one in which the final pairings in particular do not make satisfying moral sense for readers and frustrate our sense of justice, creating "a profound discomfort" (179). In the case of "The Tale of the 672nd Night," it could be argued that the ending frustrates *both* our desire for poetic closure and our desire for moral order.

30. Hugo von Hofmannsthal, "Sebastian Melmoth" (1905), in *Selected Prose*, translated by Mary Hottinger and Tania and James Stern, with an introduction by Hermann Broch, Bollingen Series 33, vol. 1, 302–3 (New York: Pantheon Books, 1952), 301 (hereafter cited parenthetically in the text).

31. The title of this section is from Franz Kafka, *The Metamorphosis*, translated by Willa and Edwin Muir, in *The Complete Stories* (New York: Schocken Books, 1971), 89.

32. Dorrit Cohn's Freudian reading of the story interprets it as "punishment dream," highlighting the Oedipal elements of the plot (" 'Als Traum erzählt': The Case for a Freudian Reading of Hofmannsthal's 'Märchen der 672. Nacht,' " *Deutsche Vierteljahresschrift* 54 [1980]: 284–305).

33. Dorrit Cohn points out the oneiric structure of the plot, which tends to progress "along the kinds of non-sequiturs we sometimes refer to as 'dream-logic' " ("Kafka and Hofmannsthal," *Modern Austrian Literature* 30:1 [1997]: 11).

34. For Dorrit Cohn, the quartet of servants should be understood as a replica of the family group, with the protagonist himself represented by the angry girl, "a replica of his own angry childhood self" ("Als Traum erzählt," 291).

35. On Hofmannsthal's conflicting feelings for his horse, see Helen Frink's analysis: *Animal Symbolism in Hofmannsthal's Works* (New York: Peter Lang, 1987), especially 12–34 (letter quoted on 20). "Expert horsemanship," she concludes, "develops in Hofmannsthal's writing into a symbol of absolute control over external circumstances by force of will" (32).

36. Robert Lemon reads the episode as an ironic reversal of the relation between Alexander the Great and his legendary horse, Bucephalus (*Imperial Messages*, 34–35).

37. "In the average '1001 Nights' story, wealthy merchants and merchants' sons are what kings and princes are in the average fairy-tale. They represent everything that is pleasant to hear about: opulence, refinement, a secured and honoured position. They are friends to caliph and sultan, connoisseurs in gentle living, the very pillars of society" (Gerhardt, *Art of Story-Telling*, 190). Conversely, Andrew Barker describes the conflicted feelings of the young Viennese artists: "Like the merchant's son, many of these young artists were able to lead their indulgently aesthetic lives thanks only to the despised business efforts of their ambitious, forceful, and practical fathers" ("Triumph of Life," 343).

38. Hugo von Hofmannsthal, "Fez," in *Journey in North Africa*, in *Selected Prose*, 197.

39. Nina Berman takes a harsh view of this text, criticizing Hofmannsthal's

Orientalist tendency to fictionalize his tourist experience in Morocco: see "K. u. K. Colonialism: Hofmannsthal in North Africa," *New German Critique* 75 (Autumn 1998): 3–27.

40. His 1907 preface to the German translation by Felix Paul Greve takes a far more optimistic view of the book: "Everything in us is revitalized and encouraged to enjoy" (quoted in Marzolph and van Leeuwen, *Arabian Nights Encyclopedia*, 2:590). It is perhaps not coincidental that this essay prefaced Greve's rendition of Burton's exuberant version and was published in the immediate aftermath of the Mardrus translation, by all accounts a joyful, even euphoric translation of the tales. Borges also praised Mardrus's "laughing paragraphs" ("Translators of the *Thousand and One Nights*," 108).

41. Daniel Beaumont discusses the "prohibition against knowing" at the heart of the stories that make up the cycle of "The Tale of the Porter and the Three Ladies of Baghdad" (*Slave of Desire*, 134). In the case of Hofmannsthal's young merchant, however, the cautionary mechanism appears to go awry, preventing any gain of wisdom from the punishment.

42. According to Andrew Barker, "it is also disturbingly ironic that death should overtake the merchant's son at this his first moment of genuine involvement in the plight of others less fortunate than himself" ("Triumph of Life," 344).

43. On Schnitzler's perceptive misreading, see Dorrit Cohn, "A Triad of Dream-Narratives: *Der Tod Georgs, Das Märchen der 672. Nacht, Traumnovelle*," in *Focus on Vienna 1900: Change and Continuity in Literature, Music, Art, and Intellectual History*, ed. Erika Nielsen, 58–71 (Munich: Fink, 1982), 60.

44. Hofmannsthal, *Death and the Fool*, 135.

45. Walter Benjamin, "Franz Kafka," in *Illuminations*, edited and with an introduction by Hannah Arendt, translated by Harry Zohn (New York: Schocken Books, 1968), 127.

46. Gila Safran Naveh, *Biblical Parables and Their Modern Re-Creations: From "Apples of Gold in Silver Settings" to "Imperial Messages"* (Albany: SUNY Press, 2000); Heinz Politzer, *Franz Kafka: Parable and Paradox* (Ithaca: Cornell University Press, 1966).

47. See Cohn, "Kafka and Hofmannsthal," 4–5.

48. Jorge Luis Borges, "Kafka and His Precursors," translated by Eliot Weinberger, in *Selected Non-Fictions*, 365.

49. Borges, "Translators of the *Thousand and One Nights*," 108–9.

50. It is perhaps no coincidence that Hofmannsthal's late work *Der Turm* (*The Tower*) is a rewriting of Calderón de la Barca's *La vida es sueño*, which, conversely, affirms the power of human agency and free will over destiny and foils the Oedipal prophecy.

10

Borges and the Missing Pages of the *Nights*

PHILIP F. KENNEDY

The biographer Edwin Williamson's grim account of a near fatal episode in the early adult life of Jorge Luis Borges will seem uncannily
familiar to amateurs of the latter's short fiction:

> By one of those strange ironies that seemed to manifest themselves peri-
> odically in Borges's life, [his] reflections on the death of the author were
> interrupted by a sudden brush with the reality of his own physical death
> in a strange accident that occurred on Christmas Eve, 1938. Borges had
> gone to fetch a girl at her apartment, some five blocks from where he
> lived . . . , in order to accompany her home for dinner with his mother.
> The elevator was out of order, so he decided to run up the stairs, but in
> the poor light he knocked his head against a newly painted casement
> window that had been left open to dry. Despite his receiving first aid, the
> wound became poisoned, and for a week he lay in bed with a high fever
> and suffering from insomnia and hallucinations. One evening he lost
> his power of speech and had to be rushed to hospital for an emergency
> operation in the middle of the night. He had developed septicemia, and

for a month he hovered between life and death. When he recovered, he feared he might have been left mentally impaired and might never write again. He decided to write something he had never done before so he would not feel so bad if he failed, and this led him to write "Pierre Menard, Author of *Don Quixote*," while convalescing.[1]

The incident is credited with importance in literary history insofar as it inspired the memorable conceit of "Pierre Menard," a creation of Borges and a personage who, as a latter-day author of a—not *the*—*Quixote*, represents, in the most tenuous sense, the death of Cervantes. That is Williamson's proposition; however, he does not at this point mention the incident's connection with "The South"—a haunting story which Borges published fourteen years later, giving the *Arabian Nights* a substantial (and uncanny) role in the process. Like Borges, I shall postpone treatment of "The South" (in my case, until the close of this essay), for arriving at that point we will understand better a related aspect of the Argentine genius's short fiction: to wit, the relationship between the *Nights* themselves and the shared epistemological construction of those Borgesian tales that borrow from them.

The profound relationship between Borges's creativity, his own life, and the *Arabian Nights* is encapsulated emblematically in "The Double"—which is one of the author's fanciful literary encounters with his own self. In this short story Borges imagined himself as an old man sitting by the banks of the River Charles in Cambridge, Massachusetts; he became aware of a young man sitting beside him:[2]

> I turned to the man and spoke.
> "Are you Uruguayan or Argentine?"
> "Argentine, but I've been living in Geneva since '14," came the reply.
> There was a long silence. Then I asked a second question.
> "[Do you live] at number 17 Malagnou, across the street from the Russian Orthodox Church?"
> He nodded.
> "In that case," I resolutely said to him, "your name is Jorge Luis Borges. I too am Jorge Luis Borges. We are in 1969, in the city of Cambridge."
> "No," he answered in my own, slightly distant, voice, "I am here in Geneva, on a bench, a few steps from the Rhone."

... "I can prove to you that I speak the truth," I answered. "I'll tell you things that a stranger couldn't know. In our house there's a silver *mate* cup with a base of serpents that our great-grandfather brought from Peru. . . . In the wardrobe closet in your room, there are two rows of books: the three volumes of Lane's translation of the *Thousand and One Nights*—which Lane called *The Arabian Nights Entertainment*[3] with steel engravings and notes in fine print between the chapters." (412)

Other works are listed but it is interesting to note that the *Nights* is offered too as a mark of Borges's own identity—a token, indeed, of how much he identified with the work. The recognition is mysterious and troubling, as most moments of discovery are in the author's work, but the point made here about warranted identity nevertheless holds true.

Shifting somewhat our perspective on the subject of recognition, we note that many such discoveries of both self and others feature in the way narratives unfold in Borges's oeuvre,[4] and this essay probes the extent to which these cognitive moments owe anything themselves to the *Nights*, noting that many literary works inspired by the corpus seem to borrow their epistemological shape from the original stories. (Salman Rushdie's *Haroun and the Sea of Stories* is just one latter-day case in point, for example's sake.) In the case of Borges, such structures certainly derive or borrow something from the *Nights* but by no means everything; the succinct literary reflection entitled "The Plot," which has nothing apparently to do with the Arabesque tales, makes this crystal clear:

To make his horror perfect, Caesar, hemmed about at the foot of a statue by his friends' impatient knives, discovers among the faces and the blades the face of Marcus Junius Brutus, his ward, perhaps his very son—and so Caesar stops defending himself, and cries out *Et tu, Brute?* Shakespeare and Quevedo record that pathetic cry.

Fate is partial to repetitions, variations, symmetries. Nineteen centuries later, in the southern part of the province of Buenos Aires, a gaucho is set upon by gauchos, and as he falls he recognizes a godson of his, and says to him in gentle remonstrance and slow surprise (these words must be heard, not read): *Pero, che!* He dies, but he does not know that he has died so that a scene can be played out again. (307)

Borges is inspired by the fact that one kind of recognition plot is a staple of literary shape (and meaning) in general, and he is aware of the way that such moments of revealed identity can both move and trouble the reader.

Reflections on East and West in Borges

Before returning to specific tales let us consider first more broadly Borges's creative, not to say imaginary, relationship with the East and begin with a quotation from him: "I think that the reader should enrich what he is reading. He should misunderstand the text; he should change it into something else."[5] The statement forms a challenging critical pronouncement about the interpretive act of reading. There is no doubt some degree of authorial affectation here (affectation is indeed married to extraordinary invention in Borges). But it also provides a useful hermeneutic lens through which to view his own relationship with—his reception and reading of—works for which he expressed fondness and engagement and by which he was often (sometimes clearly, sometimes just faintly) influenced.

To some extent Borges's imaginative reading of the Orient was, by his own tacit admission, an enthused process of artistic re-creation. The fluid impressions Borges had about the "East"—which he suggests was for him some indefinable imaginary construct—comes across in his essay "The Translators of *The Thousand and One Nights*," which appeared in the volume titled *Seven Nights*.[6] For Borges the Orient and the Occident cannot be defined, and yet they are *true*; in this regard they remind him "of what St. Augustine said about time: 'What is time? If you don't ask me, I know; but if you ask me, I don't know.'"[7] And so he settles ironically for "approximations."[8] There is a story about Alexander the Great (an invention by Robert Graves, in this instance) which Borges retells and which exemplifies within this loose scheme of rough-hewn cultural calculation a conjoining of East and West. Graves's story has a sharp structure familiar to students of narrative form, and it returns us to the cognitive scheme of narrative which this essay explores:

> Alexander does not die in Babylon at age thirty-three. . . . [Rather, he becomes a soldier of fortune in the East and forgets his former self; the

years pass, and on the day he is paid off, among the coins he receives]
one disturbs him. He has it in the palm of his hand, and he says: "You
are an old man; this is the medal that was struck for the victory of Arbela
when I was Alexander of Macedon." At that moment he remembers his
past.—but he returns as a mercenary to the Tartars and the Chinese or
whoever they were.[9]

It is this "diegetic" pattern of discovery that concerns us here, as well as
the effective welding of notions of East and West that the story—and
Alexander in general as a cultural, rather than a strictly historical, figure[10]—represents.

In this essay Borges states an essentialism that clearly fascinated him:
that the Persians, the Chinese, and the Indians lack an interest in linear literary history, as distinct from what is found in the Western tradition. "They believe that literature and poetry are eternal processes."[11]
This view carries over palpably into his interaction with the *Arabian
Nights*; in claiming this we are concerned with both the literary history
of the story collection, whose genesis or appearance Borges considered
mysterious,[12] and his own interaction with them. On the former, he
is quite forgiving of Antoine Galland's now well-known "inventions."
When discussing "Aladdin of the Lamp," one of the tales that has come
to define the *Nights* in most cultures (even in Arabic, one can argue),[13]
he states, "Some have suspected that Galland forged the tale. I think the
word *forged* is unjust and malign. Galland had as much right to invent
a story as did those *confabulatori nocturni*. Why shouldn't we suppose
that after having translated so many tales, he wanted to invent one himself, and did."[14] Of course, such permissive license, if it is not actual
encouragement to invention in cultural engagement with the corpus,
provides us at least with a sense that Borges in his own fiction may have
set down clues, perhaps even a restrained manifesto, about his views of
the aesthetics and poetics of the *Nights*.

There exist two excellent accounts of Borges's creative literary relationship with the Arabic collection in its manifold translated[15] forms:
(1) six limpid pages from Robert Irwin's chapter[16] titled "Children
of the *Nights*," in *The Arabian Nights: A Companion*; and (2) a more
recent article by Evelyn Fishburn titled "Traces of the *Thousand and
One Nights* in Borges," which appeared in 2004.[17] Irwin points up two

essential features. First, referring to Borges's translations and adaptations of the *Nights*, he remarks that "stories that have one meaning in the context of an anonymous medieval story collection acquire quite another when related by a twentieth-century modernist and Argentinian fabulist."[18] This is important to bear in mind always, for it salvages our sense of both the essential element of creativity and the distinct literary personality that characterize Borges's borrowings from the corpus of tales. Second, Irwin explores the author's attitude to literary antecedent; in *Other Imaginations* Borges himself remarked, "The word 'precursor' is indispensable in the vocabulary of criticism, but one should try to purify it from every connotation of polemic or rivalry. The fact is that each writer creates his precursors. His work modifies our conception of the past, as it will modify the future."[19]

Like Irwin, Evelyn Fishburn describes in varied detail the several tales by Borges that either refer to the *Nights* directly, allude to them in passing, or simply have an Eastern savor derivative of related interest and Arabesque inspiration. These are most importantly "Averroes's Quest," "The Approach to Al-Mu'tasim," "The Immortal" (inspired partially by the *Nights'* "The City of Brass"), "Tlön, Uqbar, Orbis Tertius," "The Garden of Forking Paths," "The Zahir," "The Man on the Threshold," and "The South" (which we return to later, at some length). The most strikingly conjectural part of Fishburn's study is her analysis of "Emma Zunz," a story that pays no overt lip service to the *Nights* and has neither Eastern setting nor Eastern detail or subject matter but that, Fishburn proposes, is structured and in a sense programmed on a recurring Arabesque template of narrative embedding that Borges was influenced by in fashioning the character of many fictions. The interpretation of Fishburn is challenging, and of particular significance is the implication that there exists a tacit poetics in Borges, across all subject matters, that may have been influenced by the *Nights*, determining the deep structure, aesthetics, and disposition of the materials.

Three related ideas about narrative generation and ontology in the *Nights* fascinated Borges and carried over into his own fashioning of fiction: the idea of infinity, the idea of the labyrinth, and the idea of embedding and *mise en abyme*. The idea of infinity—that stories can generate stories in an infinite process—can be seen to affect the texts extrinsically, according to the permissive view that the *Arabian Nights* as a collection can forever be supplemented in a sort of unabating cross-cultural process of inventive accretion. More concretely it affects them intrinsically, which is to say, in more specific internal ways; thus, for example, the manuscript in the tale titled "Brodie's Report" was found hidden inside a copy of the first volume of Lane's translation, with a suggestion that in time the story itself would become integrated into the Lane text. "The Book of Sand, so-called because 'neither sand nor this book has a beginning or an end . . .' most epitomizes the idea of the total and endless book. Its association with the Nights is suggested when the narrator chooses to hide it 'behind some imperfect volumes of the *Thousand and One Nights*.'"[20]

Let me stress the words of Fishburn, when she glosses her own point further: "I read the word 'imperfect' as a reference, precisely to the openendedness of the *Nights*, the fact that, . . . there is no canonical text."[21] This imperfection rears its head again distinctly and in a more developed form in the "The South," as we shall see—a story in which the conspicuous theme of textual imperfection in the German copy of the *Nights* hints at the fact that the collection was being creatively supplemented by Borges.

The idea of the labyrinth as a feature of the structure of stories (and their epistemological uncertainties), as perceived in the *Nights* and re-created with exquisite brevity by Borges, also characterizes the stories both internally and externally; Fishburn states as a general principle (evoking simultaneously the idea of infinitude), "The labyrinth is obviously related to the intricate pattern of self-proliferating stories within stories that are endlessly told by Scheherazade."[22] What I should like to stress is the cognitive element in the author's continuing analysis: "Scheherazade constructs her labyrinth of stories to prolong her life but when she reaches the symbolic centre she is saved: such a happy ending does not occur in Borges's fictions, where *there is often a moment of illumination*, or its delusion on reaching the symbolic centre of the labyrinth, but either madness, or death, inevitably awaits."[23]

Death certainly lurks expectantly in Borges's "Death and the Compass," as well as in "The South" and "The Mirror of Ink" (the complex origins of which are studied by Paulo Horta in chapter 3). But it would be wrong to imply, as Fishburn can seem to, that death is absent from the stories told by Scheherazade; for it is there disturbingly in the dark exemplary tale of "Duban and Yunan," which bears comparison with Borges's "The Mirror of Ink." Both stories are resolved in moments of striking self-recognition—end points from which lessons are gleaned by protagonists and readers alike.[24] Reading and recognition are often intricately linked in studies of narrative poetics: "the ancient Greek terms for 'recognition', 'reader', and 'reading' (respectively, *anagnôrisis*, *anagnôstês* and *anagnôsis*) are closely—phonetically and conceptually—related."[25] The observation has often been made in the context of the study of Western literature, yet it applies to all traditions. And the point is that Borges's first collection, with its many borrowings of Eastern Arab-Islamic themes, is full of this kind of anagnorisis that is both meaningful (hermeneutic) and structural—particularly, indeed, among those stories alluded to that have some Arabesque inspiration. One can conjecture, therefore, that the dynamic of recognition is part of an aesthetic of writing that was absorbed by Borges from either the real or his own imaginary East. This is perhaps overstated; but it is, in any case, only a question of degrees. That Borges was primed, to some extent that is hard to fix, consciously and unconsciously, to reproduce narratives of recognition from his immersion in the *Nights* is, to reiterate, the main proposition of this essay.

"Yunan and Duban"

In a cautionary tale contained within the *Nights*' "Fisherman and the Genie" (told by the fisherman to the genie), Duban is an itinerant physician who cures King Yunan of leprosy by secreting a medicine onto the sovereign's polo mallet. Duban becomes a stalwart of the king's entourage, to such an extent that malicious courtiers begin to speak badly of this foreign doctor. Though at first the king resists their calumnies, he eventually caves in to them and, in a horrifying show of ingratitude, orders Duban's summary execution. In David Pinault's excellent précis the denouement is recounted as follows:

> Seeing his death is inescapable, . . . Duban offers, he will present the king with a rare treasure: the choicest book from his library, one containing uncounted secrets. Furthermore, Duban continues, this book can effect great magic once he has been beheaded in Yunan's presence: . . . the

severed head will speak to Yunan and answer whatever question the king wishes. The unsuspecting king is delighted with this notion and allows Duban to bring the book from his room. . . .

Book in hand, Duban stands before the king, sprinkles a mysterious powder on a tray, and says simply that, once he is slain, his head is to be placed on the tray. Duban's beheading is narrated . . . in very cursory fashion:

"The executioner cast the head onto the middle of the tray and pressed it onto the powder. The blood stopped flowing. The physician Duban opened his eyes and said, 'Open the book, O King.' Then the king opened the book but found the pages stuck together. So he put his finger in his mouth and moistened it, and he opened the first page, and the second, and the third; and the pages could not be opened save with great effort.

"So the king opened six pages [in all] and looked in them, but found no writing therein. The king said, 'Physician, there's nothing written here!' The physician said, 'Open more pages.' So he opened three more; and at that moment the drug overwhelmed him; for the book had been poisoned."[26]

"The Mirror of Ink" is Borges's own version of this story.[27] It tells of a Sudanese magician's dealings with a once tyrannical ruler called "Yaqub the Ailing," who was about to have him executed:[28]

[I told Yaqub the Ailing that] if he spared my life I would show him shapes and appearances still more wonderful than those of the magic lantern. The tyrant demanded an immediate proof. . . . I cut up . . . paper into six strips, wrote charms and invocation on the first five, and on the remaining one wrote the following words, taken from the glorious Koran: "*And we have removed from thee thy veil; and thy sight today is piercing.*" Then I drew a magic square in the palm of Yaqub's right hand, told him to make a hollow of it, and into the center I poured a pool of ink. *I asked him if he saw himself clearly reflected in it*, and he answered that he did. . . . I next asked him to name the image he desired to see. . . . He asked me for a drove of horses . . . , and on the horizon he saw a cloud of dust, and then the drove. *It was at this point that I knew my life was spared.* . . . This man, whom I still hate, had in his palm everything seen by men now dead and everything seen by the living: the cities, the climates, the kingdoms into which the earth is divided; the treasure hidden in its bow-els; the ships that ply its seas. . . . Once, he ordered me to show him the city called Europe [*sic*]. I let him see its main thoroughfare, and it was there, I believe, in that great stream of men—all wearing black and using spectacles—*that he first set eyes on the Man with the Mask*. . . . He was never absent, and *we dared not divine who he was*. . . . We came to the dawn of the fourteenth day of the moon of Barmahat. . . . The two of us were alone. The Ailing ordered me to show him a punishment both law-ful and unappealable, for that day his heart hungered to view an execu-tion. . . . He asked me to have the doomed man brought forward. When this was done, seeing that the man to be executed was the mysterious man of the veil, the tyrant paled. *I was ordered to have the veil removed before justice was carried out*. . . . These things were done. At last, Yaqub's stricken eyes could see the face—*it was his own*. He was filled with fear and madness. I gripped his trembling hand in mine, which was steady, and I ordered him to go on witnessing the ceremony of his death. *He was possessed by the mirror*, so much so that he attempted neither to avert his eyes nor to spill the ink. When in the vision the sword fell on the guilty head, Yaqub moaned with a sound that left my pity untouched, and he tumbled to the floor, dead.[29]

It is noticeable, and perhaps significant, that one story ("Duban and Yunan") features blank pages without words, that is, no ink, and the other features ink, and the substance of images it can give life to, but no page. One can interpret this antithetical symmetry as one will; but there is surely some suggestive semantic connection beyond mere accidental contrast. In the first tale the absence of writing and words signals death on the same symbolic level that stories (which are made up of words) deliver life in the *Nights*; in the second the pool of ink signals a narrative store of infinite possibilities beyond human ken that ends inevitably in death—a symbolic token that what one sees is only a superficial fraction of the unseen (in Arabic, 'alam al-ghayb). The absence of blank pages is death; the infinite narrative possibility of ink must include death (and certainly must end in it inexorably). The Qur'anic verse quoted near the outset of the magic spectacle focalizes the human soul's ability to grasp what has been hidden and mocks the blind and spiritually ailing Yaqub. He grasps—recognizes—only his own face and then dies.

The king in "The Mirror of Ink" has the whole world literally (and physically) clasped in his hands, to discover and control, but he ignores the most rudimentary moral lesson about himself until it is too late. Thus in the tale's anagnorisis we find an alchemy that effects justice from injury: the king, rather than the condemned sorcerer, is killed. Seeing his own face unveiled on a face he presumed to be someone other— ironically, the same face he has seen more naturally in his own reflection on the ink's surface at the outset of the tale—Yaqub understands, in a macabre epiphany, his own inevitable and imminent demise. Recognition of self, which occurs evanescently with the falling of an executioner's blade, is coterminous with illumination in this version of the story; in "Yunan and Duban" the same powerful theme of enlightenment is conveyed without the explicit metonymy of facial recognition, though the cognitive structure of the two stories is quite identical.[30]

Recognition can be felt in a significant number of the tales in Borges's first collection of fiction, *A Universal History of Infamy*, many of which have Oriental themes. In the feature of anagnorisis we conjecture the presence of a nexus conjoining, in a structural and thematic dynamic, the Oriental tales with those that are not—the latter being fashioned by that same feature which, consciously or not, Borges was so fascinated by in the Eastern materials. This is to claim that many of the Argentinian's sculpted narratives share one of the fundamental features that he may have absorbed from the *Nights*. But we should add that there is a tension in Borges between the universalism of this epistemological tendency in narrative and the particular details disclosed that make each story so strikingly individual (and therefore typical of the author). Anagnorisis abets the coming-into-view of his characteristic paradoxes and conundrums—and this is certainly true in "The South." Paradoxes keep returning, for example, that of looking earnestly for someone but finding only oneself; and the reader is made aware of this at the points of self-recognition.

An excellent, albeit very understated, example of self-discovery in Borges comes in the final sentence of a reverie about Shakespeare ("England's verbal magic") that closes the afterword of his collection titled *The Maker* (1960): "A man sets out to draw the world. As the years go by, he peoples a space with images of provinces, kingdoms, mountains, bays, ships, islands, fishes, rooms, instruments, stars, horses, and individuals.

A short time before he dies, he discovers that that patient labyrinth of lines traces the lineaments of his own face" (*Collected Fictions*, 337).

Recognition of self is an archetype of some of the finest (or most gripping) literature.[31] Aristotle held great esteem for Sophocles's *Oedipus Rex*, in which tragic recognition unfolds simultaneously with reversal at the moment of the flawed hero's understanding of who he is and what this means about his actions; the Stagyrite considered this one of the paragons of the better kind of plot, in which recognition unfolds naturally from the events themselves, without the implausibly abrupt agency of *deus ex machina*.[32] Let us pause on Borges's "Averroes's Quest" for a moment since the towering figure of Aristotle casts its shadow on it. In this story Averroes (Ibn Rushd), the thirteenth-century Andalusian Arab commentator of Aristotle's works, struggles himself to understand the *Poetics*. He takes a break from his work at home and observes a group of children enacting the call of the Muezzin (one child plays the minaret, the other calls the faithful to prayer), but he fails to grasp that in this facile enactment the children have brushed with the essence of dramatic representation. That evening Averroes engages in debate with a group of scholars, among whom a seasoned traveler recounts his observation of Chinese plays in which the actions of people in stories are represented by individuals on makeshift stages. Still Averroes fails to perceive that in this account are displayed the rudiments of drama, ignoring the fact that an understanding of Aristotle's *Poetics* beckons at him (as it does also, frustratingly, to the reader). Instead, the subject of debate shifts to the relative merits of ancient Arabic poetry; the consensus of the discussion has it that within the images of pre-Islamic poetry inhere essential truths that each generation must discover for itself; and it is in the rediscovery of the truths of exquisite ancient imagery that the most profound value of literature is deemed effectively to lie. Thus, after the gathering of scholars disperses Averroes returns home to his work, having decided, as Ibn Sina and others had before him, that Aristotle's "tragedy" must be interpreted in Arabic as poetry of praise.[33] Averroes thus reinvents the poetics and the meaning of discovery.[34]

But there are other more classic examples of Aristotelian discovery and self-discovery in Borges; as he himself said, facetiously no doubt, "fiction has but a single plot, with every imaginable permutation."[35] Consider the following short stories: "The Approach to Al-Mu'tasim,"

"Death and the Compass," and "The Biography of Tadeo Isidoro Cruz (1829–1874)." The first two mix detective models of narrative: detective fiction in its most classic form and the metaphysical quest. The itinerant protagonist in "The Approach to Al-Mu'tasim" (which is framed as a fictive commentary on a fictive novel: the relativity generated by this *mise en abyme* is evident) begins his travels as a fugitive from a riot.

> The plot itself is this: A man (. . . the fleeing law student . . .) falls among people of the lowest, vilest sort and accommodates himself to them, in a kind of contest of iniquity. Suddenly—with the shock of Crusoe when he sees that human footprint in the sand—the law student perceives some mitigation of the evil: a moment of tenderness, of exaltation, of silence, in one of the abominable men. "It was as though a more complex interlocutor had spoken." He knows that the wretch with whom he is conversing is incapable of that momentary decency; thus the law student hypothesizes that the vile man before him has reflected a friend, or the friend of a friend. Rethinking the problem he comes to a mysterious solution: *Somewhere in the world there is a man from whom this clarity, this brightness, emanates; somewhere in the world there is a man who is equal to this brightness.* The law student resolves to devote his life to searching out that man. (*Collected Fictions*, 84)

This is the quest; but Borges's modernist take on the questing model (which is also postmodern *avant la lettre*) has it end in a final ellipse: when he finds the man identified as Al-Mu'tasim and is about to meet him in a secluded gallery, "he draws back the bead curtain and steps into the room. At that point the novel ends" (85). Borges goes on to make fun of the symbolic intensity and elliptical coyness typical of mystical allegories, for he continues by writing that to pull off such a plot the author "must not allow the hero prefigured by signs to become a mere phantasm or convention" (85). And even more caustically: "The unheard and unseen Al-Mu'tasim should impress us as being a real person, not some jumble of vapid superlatives" (85). Borges appears to mock the literary pitfall he alluded to as "the temptation to be a genius" (86). The account of the novel ends inconclusively and is followed by Borges's parodic framing device: the comments of a fictive critic about a fictive book: first, commentary and poetics about mixed models of writing and inspiration and, second, in a final understated paragraph, an indication that the seeker in this story is the same as the sought. In Islamic mystical literature the classic example of this kind of anagnorisis of self exists in Farid al-Din Attar's *Conference of the Birds* (*Mantiq al-Tayr*);[36] in the fictive novel of Borges "a few words attributed by a Persian bookseller to Al-Mu'tasim are perhaps an expansion of words spoken by the hero [of Attar's poem]; that and other ambiguous similarities may signal the identity of the seeker and the sought; they may also indicate that the sought has influenced the seeker" (*Collected Fictions*, 87). Borges in fact escapes the snare of narrative cliché—the overly familiar recognition of self in narrative quests of mundane or mystical detective work—by suspending the text at the critical point in the plot and turning aside to comment on it with the contrived objectivity of a student of poetics.[37]

"The Biography of Tadeo Isidoro Cruz (1829–1874)" is an apparently unadulterated Argentinian story and redresses the view that Borges was necessarily rewriting Eastern materials in his narratives of recognition. The account begins with the violent death of the eponymous hero's father, takes us through his life as a cutthroat and mercenary, and ends with his part in the hunting down of a fugitive criminal—an occasion on which he turns coat for reasons that take us back uncannily to the tale's point of departure when Cruz's father had been hunted down at the same outlying location:

> Cruz had the sense that he had lived the moment before. The outlaw stepped out from his hiding place to fight them. Cruz glimpsed the terrifying apparition—the long mane of hair and the gray beard seemed to consume his face. . . . As Cruz was fighting in the darkness (as his body was fighting in the darkness), he began to understand. . . . He realized his deep-rooted destiny as a wolf, not a gregarious dog; he realized that the other man was he himself. (*Collected Fictions*, 214)

This chimes unnervingly with the choice of epigraph from Yeats borrowed for this "biography":

> I'm looking for the face I had
> Before the world was made. (212)

The man Cruz turned coat to fight alongside turns out to be Martin Fierro, the great Argentinian folk hero. Nothing—and no one—could be more culturally emblematic of modern-day Argentina. We must acknowledge, therefore, that recognition is a common element in Borges; it is simply—we conjecture—highly present in the Arabesque materials he liked to toy with; and it is by these he may have been influenced while fashioning them in special ways both *as* Arabesque tales and otherwise. In the final two fictions we now consider, recognition is essential to both form and meaning.

"Hakim, the Masked Dyer of Merv"

Let us return gradually to the autobiographical theme with which we began our reflections: Borges had a horror of masks and mirrors; they disturbed him for masking the truth and for creating of reality a simulacrum. The distaste he wrote into "Hakim, the Masked Dyer of Merv," is distinctly personal.

"Hakim of Merv" is an elegantly balanced gothic sketch, combining in a well-wrought whole both structure (a movement toward recognition) and ironic symbolism (masks, blindness, and sight). It is an account of Al-Muqanna', the so-called "nativist" false prophet of Merv who rebelled against the Abbasids in the eighth century and is more dexterously rendered than those versions of his ill-starred calling that survive in the most significant Islamic sources.[38] Hakim was a dyer by trade but came to consider the act of coloring, that is, of masking reality, an abomination. He preached and touted a new mythology based in his numinous insights, for he claimed that his head had been decapitated by angels and set momentarily in heaven before God. His countenance took on such an overpowering aura that he was obliged ever after to mask himself from all human sight. The scene of his first appearance before expectant followers is told with exquisitely measured descriptive choreography. It brings the distant close to hand in a gradual movement, then unfolds in a vision of blindness and masks:

> From the other end of the shimmering desert (whose sun engenders fever, just as its moon engenders chills), the [followers] saw three approaching figures, which seemed to be of gigantic size. They were men,

and the middle one had the head of a bull. When they drew near, it was plain that this man was wearing a mask and that his companions were blind. Someone (as in the Arabian Nights) pressed him for the meaning of this wonder: "They are blind, . . . he said, because they have looked upon my face."[39]

Of course, this last detail is scheming and disingenuous. The opposite is true: the people around Hakim are blinded so as *not* to see him, for reasons that become apparent. The 114[40] women of his harem were all blind (the number suggests sanctity, the truth is a ghastly sham). The story crafts repeated reference to matters of sight and the deceptiveness of appearance: "mirrors, in [Hakim's] teaching, because they multiply and confirm the clumsy parody of the material world, are abominations."[41]

The tale comes to a close in a section titled "The Face." This denouement unmasks the dyer during a siege of his stronghold by the Abbasid caliph. At this time

an adulteress in the harem, as she was strangled by the eunuchs, had cried out that the ring finger of the Prophet's right hand was missing and that all his other fingers lacked nails. This rumour spread among the faithful. From the top of a terrace, in the midst of his people, Hakim was praying to the Lord for victory or for a special sign. Two captains, their heads bowed, slavish—as if beating into a driving rain—tore away the Veil. At first there was a shudder. The Apostle's promised face, the face that had been to the heavens, was indeed white—but with that whiteness peculiar to spotted leprosy. It was so bloated and unbelievable that to the mass of onlookers it seemed a mask.[42]

Borges revels in the paradoxes of masking and unveiling—the hideous nature of the physical truth that is exposed appears to be so unreal as to be like a mask. And with it all numinous promise vanishes. There is sardonic wit in the fact that Borges begins this powerful vignette about a prophetic peddler of charlatanry with the words "If I am not mistaken." He contrives doubt where he affects to dispel it; he delights in the descriptive ironies of concealment and disclosure, where truth and fiction coincide. Edwin Williamson has read this as reflecting Borges's disillusionment with the unfolding events in a failed courtship.[43]

"The South"

Recognition is less gothic and descriptively thick but decidedly more unnerving in "The South," in which the influence of the *Arabian Nights* is explicit and more palpable. It is set entirely in Buenos Aires and the countryside beyond its southern district, beyond the Avenida Rivadavia. Yet it features a German copy of the *Arabian Nights* in a role more tangible and meaningful than any role given to the collection in Borges's oeuvre. The protagonist, Juan Dahlmann (descendant of Johannes Dahlmann),[44] purchased a copy of Weil's translation of the *Arabian Nights* one day—*a copy, with some pages missing.* Eager to examine the volume, he climbed the stairs rather than wait for the elevator and brushed his head against the stairwell's casement window. His injury provoked septicemia and fever, and he was soon hospitalized. During this time he suffered nightmares animated by menacing illustrations from the *Arabian Nights*. He awoke eventually from delirium, feeling he had been on the outskirts of hell. "During these days, Dahlmann hated every inch of himself." Upon recovery he decided to go out to the country—to his house in the South—to convalesce. "By crossing the river Rivadavia one entered an older more stable world." When the train pulled out, "he opened his bag and after a slight hesitation took from it the first volume of *The Arabian Nights*. To travel with this book so closely linked to the history of his torment was an affirmation that the torment was past, and was a joyous, secret challenge to the frustrated forces of evil." (The sentiment is rash, and to Fate it is a provocation— especially in connection with a text so full of fateful ironies.) The truth is that Dahlmann only ever succeeds in reading very little: "happiness distracted Dahlmann from Scheherazade and her superfluous miracles; Dahlmann closed the book and allowed himself simply to live" (*Collected Fictions*, 176). The train drops him off at the railway station before his destination, but he accepts the walk as a small adventure. Resting at a local store,

> he thought he recognized the owner; then he realized that he'd been fooled by the man's resemblance to one of the employees at the sanatorium. . . . He decided to eat there in the country store. . . . Dahlmann suddenly felt something lightly brush his face. Next to the tumbler of

cloudy glass, on one of the stripes in the tablecloth, lay a little ball of wadded bread. That was all, but somebody had thrown it at him. . . . Dahlmann, puzzled, decided that nothing had happened, and he opened the volume of *The Arabian Nights, as though to block out reality.* The store owner tried to reassure him: "Sr. Dahlmann, ignore those boys over there—they're just feeling their oats." Dahlmann did not find it strange that the storekeeper—whom he didn't know—should know his name. (177–79, emphasis added)

In the end Dahlmann steps outside to the challenge of a knife duel—and, we presume, to his death.

That is the summary of the story inflected by the current argument. The references to the *Arabian Nights* are obviously not idle cultural fillers; they play an essential role. Why does Borges specify that pages are missing from the German copy? Might not the absent stories be filled out by the story of Dahlmann himself? This would explain why he never gets very far into the work every time he begins to read. He feels he has defeated the work; yet in a fateful irony the work has pulled him into its sphere of menacing determinism: of a narrative fulfillment—from being a mere reader he becomes protagonist, unwittingly. At one moment he opens the *Nights* "to block out reality," but the *Nights* has in fact become, or come to generate according to its narrative ilk, the reality he is living: a reality that can be read from the outside—from the true reader's vantage point—as a tale of inexorable destiny. Far from transcending the *Nights* that has caused his affliction, it continues to generate his demise.

The momentary recognition of the store owner by Dahlmann is a clue to how we tend to read the story, though the meaning of this detail is indeterminate. The reader reads it one way, and Dahlmann reads it quite another—he in fact misreads it altogether and so dismisses it. But the detail is undoubtedly, to Borges's audience at least, part of the epistemology of the story; it contains the moment of revealed identity that explains that there is an uncanny causal chain in the sequence of events. We often encounter such deterministic causality in the *Nights* (a good example existing in the tale of the lodestone mountain,[45] which is referred to during Dahlmann's train ride). Dahlmann was fated, according, one might say, to a nocturnal Arabesque determinism, to buy the incomplete *Nights*; and thus he began to fill the pages out with his own ill-starred misadventure: by bumping his head, by suffering delirium in a sanatorium, and by convalescing on a train, confident that he has escaped the fate it had provoked while riding, in tragic irony, blindly into the darker fate it has in fact designed for him.[46] The store owner's resemblance to one of the employees at the sanatorium, of course, throws up for the reader a meaning quite distinct from what it means to Dahlmann: his convalescence might be entirely delusional and the journey into the South (which is a netherworld of sorts) simply a heroic metaphor that supplants a prosaic death in a hospital bed. In the sanatorium, we remember, he had "hated every inch of himself"; by contrast, his death in the South in a vicious knife duel might reflect his acceptance of dying in a way that could afford him a greater degree of self-respect. In a tidy structure this detail takes one back to the first lines of the story, in which Dahlmann had hoped idly for a romantic death, marking himself as a Juan, not a Johannes. The "older more stable world" of the South might well be a metaphor for death's dominion.

Borges should have the suggestive last word on the general subject of this essay—on literary influence and reinvention, whether he was being facetious or not:

> It is generally understood that a modern-day book may honorably be based upon an older one. . . . No man likes owing anything to his contemporaries. ("The Approach to Al-Mu'tasim," in *Collected Fiction*, 86)

> It has been decided that all books are the work of a single author who is timeless and anonymous. Literary criticism often invents authors: It will take two dissimilar works—the *Tao Te Ching* and the *1001 Nights*, for instance—attribute them to a single author, and then in all good conscience determine the psychology of that most interesting *homme de lettres*. ("Tlön, Uqbar, Orbis Tertius," in *Collected Fiction*, 77)

NOTES

1. Edwin Williamson, *Borges: A Life* (New York: Penguin, 2004), 237.
2. Unless otherwise indicated, all quotations from Borges's stories are from Andrew Hurley's translations in *Collected Fictions* (New York: Penguin, 1998) (hereafter cited parenthetically in the text).
3. Lane did not coin this name: *The Arabian Nights' Entertainments* was the title

given to the first Grub Street English editions of the *Nights* translated anonymously from Galland's French; they first appeared as early as 1707.

4. And he was aware of such constructions in his reviews and criticism; see for
   example his review of *Citizen Kane* in *Selected Non-Fictions*, ed. Eliot Weinberger (New York: Penguin, 1999), 259.

5. Quoted in Robert Irwin, *The Arabian Nights: A Companion* (London: Allan
   Lane, 1994), 284.

6. See Jorge Luis Borges, "The Translators of *The Thousand and One Nights*," in
   Seven Nights: Lectures, trans. Eliot Weinberger (London: Faber and Faber, 1984),
   42–57. This essay may now be deemed superannuated in its cultural politics and
   scholastically shallow: famous and much cited simply because it is by Borges. Yet
   it is quite innocuous and quaintly charming as a textual curio, since it was written decades before the anxieties of cultural evaluation imposed on us by Edward
   Said's *Orientalism*, which has tended to inhibit the kind of personal reverie that
   Borges could allow himself, so blithely, to indulge in. Judgment is unfair when it
   is anachronistic and back-projects the values (and hang-ups) of the present onto
   the past.

7. Ibid., 42–43.

8. Ibid.

9. Ibid.

10. I refer to the importance of the Alexander romance in both Christian and
    Islamic popular literature; there are many stories in the latter that exaggerate the
    extent of "The Two-Horned One's" travels eastward, depicting his perambula-
    tions in China (see for example the anonymous Arabic collection of tales of
    trickery *Raqa'iq al-hilal fi daqa'iq al-hiyal* [London: al-Saqi, 1992], 141–42).

11. Borges, "The Thousand and One Nights," 51.

12. Ibid., 48.

13. Though Naguib Mahfouz may have tried to redress this effect by making the
    Aladdin he writes into his adaptation of the *Nights*, *Layali alf layla / Arabian
    Nights and Days*, "Aladdin of the Moles" rather than "Aladdin of the Lamp." See
    Naguib Mahfouz, *Arabian Nights and Days*, trans. Denys Johnson-Davies (New
    York: Anchor Books, 1995).

14. Borges, "The Thousand and One Nights," 55.

15. For the complex translation history of the *Arabian Nights* since the eighteenth
    century CE to the present see Irwin, "Beautiful Infidels," in *Arabian Nights: A
    Companion*, 9–41.

16. Irwin, *Arabian Nights: A Companion*, 282–87.

17. Evelyn Fishburn, "Traces of the *Thousand and One Nights* in Borges," *Middle
    Eastern Literatures* 7:2 (2004): 213–22.

18. Irwin, *Arabian Nights: A Companion*, 283.

19. Jorge Luis Borges, *Other Inquisitions, 1937–1952* (New York: Pocket Books /
    Simon and Schuster, 1966), 113, quoted in Irwin, *Arabian Nights: A Companion*,
    286.

20. Fishburn, "Traces," 216.

21. Ibid.

22. Ibid., 216. On this idea described in Borges's own nonfiction see "When Fiction Lives in Fiction," in *Selected Non-Fictions*, 160–62. It is in this essay that Borges writes his famous reflection on the *Nights* (and the source of much confusion): "The need to complete a thousand and one segments drove the work's copyists to all sorts of digressions. None of them as disturbing as that on night 602, a bit of magic among the nights. On that strange night, the king hears the beginning of the story, which includes all the others, and also—monstrously—itself" (161).

23. Fishburn, "Traces," 216.

24. These are stories in which at least one protagonist may be beckoned to become a reader of symbolic circumstance.

25. Philip F. Kennedy and Marilyn Lawrence, introduction to *Recognition: The Poetics of Narrative: Interdisciplinary Studies on Anagnorisis*, ed. Philip F. Kennedy and Marilyn Lawrence, 1–12 (New York: Peter Lang, 2009), 3, citing Terence Cave, *Recognition: A Study in Poetics* (Oxford, UK: Clarendon, 1988), 260; and Piero Boitani, *The Tragic and the Sublime in Medieval Literature* (Cambridge: Cambridge University Press, 1989), 161.

26. David Pinault, *Story-Telling Techniques in the Arabian Nights* (Leiden: Brill, 1992), 48–49. As Robert Irwin tells us in his companion, "Centuries later, the device of the poisoned book was to resurface again in Umberto Eco's *The Name of the Rose*" (*Arabian Nights: A Companion*, 178).

27. Borges tells us he found a version of the tale recounted by Richard F. Burton in his *The Lake Regions of Central Africa* (1860). But the tale is not there. On the relationship between this tale and both Lane and Burton see Paulo Horta's chapter 3 in this volume.

28. The story forms a full circle, as the *Nights* do when Scheherazade—in the version most appealing to Borges's literary sensibility—begins to tell Shahriyar's own story.

29. Abridged from Jorge Luis Borges, *A Universal History of Infamy*, trans. Norman Thomas di Giovanni (London: Penguin, 1975), 121–25 (emphasis added).

30. The Moroccan critic Abdelfattah Kilito's characteristically engaging commentary on the close of "Duban and Yunan" supports this perceived connection between it and "The Mirror of Ink": "En un instant fulgurant, le roi a dû comprendre le sens de l'avertissement que le sage, plus d'une fois, lui avait lancé. C'est comme si le livre révélait, au moment de la mort, un texte jusque-là dissimulé, comme si des caractères à la fois invisibles et évidents, inscrits au poison, couvraient sa surface. Certes, le livre ne contient aucune écriture, aucun texte, et n'offre aucun des innombrables secrets promis, mais le roi y lit en quelque sorte la sentence de mort qui frappe et dont l'exécution est déjà chose faite, il y lit l'accomplissement de son destin. . . . *Dans le miroir impitoyable des pages blanches, il aperçoit sa face épouvantée*; le sage a en effet réussi à lui faire prendre quelque chose dans la main, et le poison circule maintenant dans son corps, tout comme le remède

quelques jours plus tôt." *L'œil et l'aiguille: Essais sur Les milles et une nuits* (Paris: La Découverte, 1992), 48 (emphasis added).

31. *Shutter Island* (the novel, the film, the graphic novel) is just the latest prominent example—with a psychoanalytic twist.

32. For a detailed analysis of anagnorisis in Aristotle's *Poetics* and its influence in the Western tradition, both in poetics and in practice, see Cave, *Recognitions*. Aristotle discussed anagnorisis chiefly in chapters 6, 11, and 16 of the *Poetics*. Chapter 6 states tersely, "The most important devices by which tragedy sways emotion are parts of the plot, i.e. reversals and recognitions" (Aristotle, *Poetics*, trans. with an introduction and notes by Malcolm Heath [London: Penguin, 1996], 12). It is not until chapter 11 that Aristotle defines what he means: "As the term indicates, [anagnorisis] is a change from ignorance to knowledge, disclosing either a close relationship or enmity, on the part of the people marked out for good or bad fortune. Recognition is best when it occurs simultaneously with a reversal, like the one in the Oedipus." This part of the definition restricts anagnorisis largely to the recognition of persons; but the possibility of broadening the predicates of recognition is understood clearly from the added gloss that "it is also possible to recognize whether someone has or has not performed some action" (ibid., 14). This exiguous comment opens up immeasurably how anagnorisis can be understood, making it the key moment, both in the action itself and according to a hermeneutics of reading, when knowledge is revealed in narrative.

A typology of the mechanisms that trigger recognition is provided in chapter 16; it is said to occur (1) by means of tokens, congenital or acquired (e.g., scars or necklaces); (2) by contrivance, "for example, . . . in the *Iphigenia* . . . Orestes declares in person what the poet (instead of the plot) requires" (ibid., 26); (3) by means of memory, as when Odysseus listens to the tale told to Alcinous in the *Odyssey*, is reminded of his past, and weeps; (4) through inference: "someone similar has come; no one is similar except Orestes; so he has come" (26); (5) by false inference. The best recognition of all is (6) that which arises out of the actual events, so that the emotional impact is achieved through events that unfold plausibly, as in Sophocles's *Oedipus*. Only this kind does without contrived tokens and necklaces.

Aristotle makes further reference to recognition in chapter 17 in a brief synopsis of the *Odyssey*, which he observes is integrated as a story around the return of Odysseus, and in a significant remark that "recognition pervades" this particular epic (ibid., 39).

33. For a detailed commentary on the understanding of anagnorisis among the Islamic Aristotelian philosophers and commentator's see Philip F. Kennedy, "Anagnorisis," in the *Encyclopaedia of Islam* (Leiden: Brill, 2007–forthcoming); this includes a detailed section on Averroes / Ibn Rushd (d. 1198).

34. This kind of discovery lies only at the very peripheries of any definition of anagnorisis, where as a concept Aristotle's term can be infused with the sense

of grasping, at the point of narrative enlightenment, the profound meaning of human circumstance.

35. Borges, "Tlön, Uqbar and Orbis Tertius," in *Collected Fictions*, 77.

36. Borges wrote about the *Mantiq al-Tayr* with fascination and much comparative insight in his nonfiction also: see "The Simurgh and the Eagle," in *Selected Non-Fiction*, 294–97. See also in the same collection "The Enigma of Edward Fitzgerald," 367.

37. For mixed models of recognition in works of detective fiction (mundane and metaphysical) see Gina Welty Parkinson's "Looking for Patterns in Static: Recognition, Reading, and Detecting in G. K. Chesterton and Paul Auster's *City of Glass*," in Kennedy and Lawrence, *Recognition*, 163–77.

38. See especially Abu Bakr Muhammad ibn Ja'far al-Narkhashi, *Tarikh Bukhara* (Cairo: Dar al-Ma'arif, 1965), 94–102; translated by Richard N. Frye as *The History of Bukhara* (Cambridge, MA: Medieval Academy of America, 1954), 65–73.

39. Borges, "Hakim, the Masked Dyer of Merv," in *A Universal History of Infamy*, 79.

40. The number of Qur'anic suras is rendered blasphemously mundane.

41. Borges, "Hakim," 83.

42. Ibid., 85.

43. See Williamson, *Borges*, 212ff., for a discussion of the author's emotional state of mind during the composition of *A Universal History of Infamy*, the volume in which "Hakim, the Masked Dyer of Merv" appeared.

44. The translation of the name seems significant: the adaptation of one culture to another.

45. Told by the third dervish (or calendar) in "The Tale of the Porter and the Three Ladies of Baghdad" cycle.

46. Rather like the tale known as the "Appointment in Samarra."

11

The Politics of Conversation

Denis Diderot, Elio Vittorini, Manuel Puig,
Masaki Kobayashi, Vasily Grossman

KATIE TRUMPENER

The *Arabian Nights* implicitly counterpoises the power of the word against the power of the despot. Given its famous frame story—in which a resourceful narrator tames a dictator—the *Nights* offers an obvious point of departure for people writing (or filming) in the face of modern authoritarian, despotic, or dictatorial regimes. Indeed it has remained a shaping force for the modern political novel.

This essay analyses four widely influential political novels (while touching more briefly on two political films). Denis Diderot's *Jacques le fataliste et son maître* (*Jacques the Fatalist and His Master*), written around 1765–80 inside France's *ancien regime*, was published (and publishable) only posthumously, in 1796. Elio Vittorini's *Conversazione in Sicilia* (*Conversation in Sicily*), written in and about Mussolini's Italy, was published there in serialized installments in 1938, in book form in 1941. Manuel Puig's *El beso de la mujer araña* (*Kiss of the Spider Woman*) was written in self-imposed political exile from Perónist Argentina (and published in 1976, the year that the generals' coup began the Dirty War). Like *Jacques*, Vasily Grossman's *Vse techet* (*Everything Flows*) could be published only posthumously and abroad; begun in 1955 (and still undergoing revisions when Grossman died in 1964), it was published in West Germany in 1970 yet did not appear in the Soviet Union until the late 1980s, when Gorbachev's Perestroika had created a new climate of political discussion and retrospection. Masaki Kobayashi's remarkable *Seppuku* (a.k.a. *Harikiri*; Japan, 1962) and *Jôi-uchi: Hairyô tsuma shimats* (*Samurai Rebellion*; Japan, 1967) are antifeudalist samurai films whose plots of action and revenge remain inflected by *Nights*-style narration and gender politics and which meditate implicitly on Japan's recent past, as the culmination of a long tradition of authoritarian government.

These texts all engage in explicit dialogue with the *Nights*, yet they are not (indeed, given their wide divergences in historical, geopolitical, and linguistic contexts, could hardly be) in dialogue with one another. The political novel is itself an amorphous generic category, encompassing many different occasions, styles, and types of writing. Yet in their shared interest in (different facets of) the *Nights*, these particular novels provide at least some way of measuring the scope, possibilities, and recurrent narrative preoccupations of the political novel as a genre. In both novels and films, indeed, the implicit subject is the nature of dialogue, the possibilities and limitations of political speech, its relationship to ordinary language, conversation as a precondition for political life.

At the outset of Antoine Galland's source text, as Muhsin Mahdi's edition and Husain Haddawy's translation have shown us, Scheherazade's determination to save her fellow maidens is first challenged by her father, the vizier, who tells pointed, insulting stories to quash his daughter's plans. The rest of the narrative entails her long, gradual, implicit rebuttal of both her father and the enraged king Shahriyar. Initially, her stories offer tales of female infidelity as a character —and characteristically female—flaw. Yet over time, the stories begin to show us the complex background to women's—and men's—apparent moments of immorality: how women come to be imprisoned, how men come to be sexually maimed. What maddens Shahriyar initially is the discovery of his wife's adultery with a servant—a loss of innocence compounded and apparently universalized by the discovery that his brother's wife enjoys a similarly adulterous liaison with a black slave. Scheherazade, too, works as a narrator by accumulating a proliferation of cases but moves toward the opposite set of inferences. In retrospect, the wife's infidelity and the slave's sexual acting out appear as desperate attempts to find some narrow scope of action and freedom in a world that has enslaved or fettered them. Scheherazade's narratives give them back story and motivation. In the world of Scheherazade's stories, women are kidnapped and subjected, men are unmanned both physically and symbolically. Yet insofar as they retain their voices, they are able to narrate the story of their captivity—and find in the telling and the lament at least temporary release, a parallel to or substitute for the personal and sexual freedom they no longer enjoy.

The *Nights'* pedagogical structure (visible even in Galland's garbled form) redirects the energies and changes the course of the European novel. Novelists thus spend most of the eighteenth century experimenting with the new vistas it opens.[1] First and perhaps most fundamentally, the *Nights* gives writers a new awareness of their ability to stop and start narrative, to interrupt and shift tack, to create complex montage effects through interpolated stories. Eighteenth-century novels gain new temporal depth, new architectural complexity, and a renewed will to narrative experiment.

After Galland, epistolary novels such as Montesquieu's *Persian Letters* not only adopt Orientalist settings, characters, and accoutrements but meditate on the intersection between the exotic and the erotic, even as they stage the difficulty of representing different vantage points. Later political novelists, too, assimilate the *Nights'* persistent attention to sexual roles, persecution, and rapprochement. In this tradition, particular forms of textual innovation, political critique, and sexual politics remain tightly linked.

The *Nights*, moreover, accelerates the development of a new kind of novel guided and dominated by a single, seductive narrative voice. Hence obsessive, unreliable narrators/characters center Daniel Defoe's 1724 *Roxana*, Jonathan Swift's *Gulliver's Travels*, and eventually also the haunting first-person case studies of William Godwin's 1817 *Mandeville*, James Hogg's 1824 *Confessions of a Justified Sinner*, and John Galt's

1823 *Ringhan Gilhaize* and 1831 *Bogle Corbet*. In novels such as Laurence Sterne's *Tristram Shandy*, conversely, the narrator teasingly tightens and lengthens the narrative rope.

Yet conversationally based novels of ideas also use the novel form to stage narrative and ideological competition. The novels of Diderot (and later Thomas Love Peacock and much later yet Ivy Compton-Burnett) sometimes approach the status of drama in their alternation of voices and perspectives. Diderot, Vittorini, and Puig, moreover, use the *Nights* to question despotic authority, patriarchal gender norms, and, in a move that initially seems counterintuitive, the Socratic dialogue grounding Western philosophy and inextricably linked to it since antiquity. We are used to thinking about the *Nights'* famous narrative situation, like the Socratic dialogue, as rather one-sided. From one perspective, indeed, it appears literally monologic: a talking woman artfully ensnaring a wakeful, almost silent, inadvertently captivated listener. From another perspective, however, the *Nights* mobilizes a Babel of voices, one storyteller overlapping with and drowning out the next.[2] The cumulative effect is narrative overload. A very elaborate, nested puzzle is taken apart and fit back together, in a spiraling, shifting, metamorphic process, as one cluster of stories somehow dissolves into the next. And in the process, the listener, too, undergoes a slow but unmistakable metamorphosis.

As this essay describes, the novels of Diderot, Vittorini, and Puig assimilate the *Nights'* dialogical structure and formal innovations (its forking and relinking stories, its implicit yet unmarked narrative drift, its omnipresent yet increasingly attenuated frame narrator). The essay ends, however, with two implicit challenges to the *Nights'* viability as a narrative model. In different adaptations of the eunuchs' nested tales and Scheherazade's frame narrative, Kobayashi's *Seppuku* and *Samurai Rebellion* mobilize Scheherazadean narrative at once to expose the corruptions of feudal rule and to lament its inability to effect lasting political change.

Like Puig, Grossman focalizes his novel partly through a political prisoner. Puig's *Kiss* pivots on the dialogue between this prisoner and an apparently apolitical prisoner (serving a sentence for "morals" charges); their eventual rapprochement becomes a way of reconciling the political and the erotic, Marx and Freud. Grossman, too, uses the experience of an individual political prisoner as a way onto a vast terrain. Yet in his case, the terrain is not conceptual but historical—the Soviet 1930s, from the Stalinist purges to state-engineered famines.

Like *Tristram Shandy* and many other philosophical novels of its period, Diderot's *Jacques* evokes the Lisbon earthquake. Diderot and his contemporaries understood this as a catastrophe whose scale and apparent randomness of suffering calls into question the existence of God and of a divinely ordained order. Yet for Diderot, at least, that questioning is so intellectually liberating that it mitigates against any feelings of empathy or horror; instead, the reference is oddly lighthearted. Kobayashi's films and Grossman's novel measure a much greater scale of catastrophe. In Japan, militarist expansionism led to the occupation and often-brutal exploitation of surrounding countries, a Greater Asia Coprosperity Sphere buttressed by genocidal massacres, mass internments, and mass suicides. And in the Soviet Union, two overlapping, politically motivated and manmade catastrophes—the arrest, deportation, internment, and deaths of millions of putative political opponents; the orchestrated starvation of millions of men, women, and children —left Grossman struggling to find a scale appropriate to their political, human, and ethical consequences. For writers in other authoritarian contexts, the *Nights* held out the possibility simultaneously of narrative suspense, philosophical investigation of great intricacy, and a catalytic process of rapprochement between narrator and auditor. Grossman attempts to bear witness to suffering of such magnitude and scope that one thousand and one nights would not be long enough to narrate or encompass it. At the same time, the Soviet catastrophes have occurred on a scale that render them incommensurate with the *Nights'* narrative methods: its intricate intarsian inlays, its cumulative yet studiously indirect process of revelation.

Text as Tease, Conversation as Class Struggle

As befits a text repeatedly obsessed with the triangulation of desire, Diderot's *Jacques* places itself in complicated dialogue with the *Nights* by way of *Tristram Shandy*. In Sterne's famously digressive experimental novel, the narrator's inability to keep his story moving forward is mirrored by its characters' inability to sustain true conversation, since they too are continually pulled into their own obsessive monologues.

Sterne's characters continuously talk past each other. Only Uncle Toby and his personal attendant (and former army batman), Corporal Trim, manage to function as a cohesive narrative and emotional unit, as they reconstruct the interlocking stories of their own respective woundings at the Battle of Namur, where Toby's putative unmanning is offset by Trim's loss of virginity in the field hospital. Like the *Arabian Nights* itself, indeed, Sterne's novel alternates between salaciously interrupted detail and filling in the backstory of unwilling cripplings and castrations (with Toby and Tristram Shandy himself in the role of the mutilated or castrated men who populate or narrate the interpolated stories of "The Barber's Tale" and "The Porter's Tale").[3] And in the case of *Tristram Shandy*, at least, the eunuch or castrati narrator seems to take compensatory pleasure in a kind of narrative tickling or withholding.

In volume 8, *Tristram Shandy* moves into especially explicit borrowing from the *Arabian Nights*, with an almost interminable, staccato stopping, starting, stopping, and starting of "the story of the king of Bohemia and of his seven castles," intermingled with the teasing tale of the wounding of Uncle Toby's groin and Trim's reasoning that this misfortune (and his own) were preordained. Hence whereas Sterne's tale is closest to the *Nights* in terms of narrative format, it is also closest to the *Nights* in its mode of sexual teasing—and in its quasi-Eastern insistence on predestination and fatedness.

This section of Sterne's novel also becomes one point of departure for Diderot's subsequent novel, which closely paraphrases this stretch of *Tristram Shandy*. *Jacques* carries Sterne's nesting devices still further, since in the midst of its characters' opening meditations on predestination and fate, the narrator intervenes abruptly (for the first of many times throughout the novel) to announce his ability to shift narrative strands at will—as if Scheherazade had erupted into her own story to clear her throat. From beginning to end, Diderot piggybacks on, yet also pushes at the narrative conventions of, the *Nights* and of *Tristram Shandy*.

For *Jacques*'s Sternean paraphrases, its *Shandy*-esque tactics, quickly make clear that we are now in a different narrative—and political— universe. In lieu of the sentimentalized camaraderie between Toby and Trim, Jacques and his master prove locked into unspoken and sometimes open conflict. Here, moreover, conversation becomes a way not only of underscoring the separateness and existential isolation of varying perspectives but of airing and articulating underlying, apparently irresolvable social conflict. As the novel makes clear again and again, Jacques is "only" the servant yet is far more intelligent, resourceful, philosophically minded, and masterful than his master. And his ability to gain power over his master is rooted as much in his superior narrative abilities as in his wide philosophical purview. (The same seems to be true, at the next level up, about the invisible but sometimes obtrusive narrator, in a relationship of apparent superiority to both characters.)

Throughout *Jacques*, the conversations between Jacques and his master are covert duels. Yet they reach an unexpected, fragile rapprochement over Jacques's account of his loss of virginity. The story is an ugly one—the tale of a seduction under conditions of blackmail that bring it close to rape. The master alternately articulates his moral hesitation about this setup and pants to hear more. In a narrative and political world in which master and servant converse, almost always, with at least a subtext of antagonism, of opposing interests and will to power, they can meet only in a shared, prurient appreciation of female sexual abjection. At this moment, at least, homosocial bonding, and male complicity, trump even class struggle.

Males emasculated by social position are potentially remasculinized, made potent again, by sexual cruelty to women. All this echoes the opening scenario of the *Nights'* frame story. And it is relativized, in turn, by a long interpolated narrative, earlier in Diderot's novel and itself reminiscent of a different strand of Scheherazadean storytelling, in which the female innkeeper (with many interruptions and interpolations) tells the story of the vengeful Madame de la Pomeraye, who rewards her lover's desertion by luring him to fall in love with a putatively pure maiden who is actually a prostitute. In the frame story to the *Nights*, a woman held captive by a huge demon revenges herself by sleeping with a hundred men, including finally Shahriyar and his brother Shahzaman (themselves still reeling from their wives' infidelities and about to massacre many more slave girls in general revenge against the female sex). In Diderot's novel, as in the *Nights*, a tale of male sexual cruelty and predatory sexual contest thus coexists with a comparable tale of female sexual revenge.

17. Engraving illustrating "The Tale of Jullanar and the Sea," frontispiece of
the seventh volume of Antoine Galland's *Les mille et une nuit: Contes arabes*,
1706 (© Arcadian Library, London)

18. Pages from the Jewish Physician's tale in the fourteenth-century Galland manuscript (© Bibliothèque Nationale)

19. A 1668 illustration of a contemporary London coffeehouse (© Lordprice Collection)

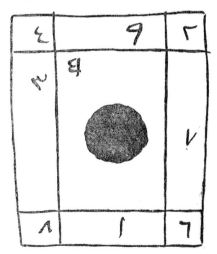

20. *Top left*, Title page of *History of Blue Beard* (© The Lilly Library); 21. *Top right*, Sculpture of Edward Lane, by his brother, Richard James Lane, 1829 (© National Portrait Gallery); 22. *Bottom left*, Captain Richard F. Burton wrapped in a blanket, c. 1853–55 (© Royal Geographical Society); 23. *Bottom right*, "Magic Diagram and Mirror of Ink," from Edward W. Lane's *Customs and Manners of the Modern Egyptians* (1835) (Travelers in the Middle East Archive [TIMEA], http://hdl.handle.net/1911/10095)

24. Thomas Stothard, scene from "The Tale of the Tailor" in
Arabian Nights' Entertainments, 1785 (© British Library)

25. Thomas Dalziel (1823–1906), "The Young Man Desiring to Depart,"
illustration to "The Story Told by the Tailor" in Dalziel's *Arabian Nights'
Entertainments*, 1865 (Scanned image and text by George P. Landow;
Victorian Web, http://www.victorianweb.org/)

26. Frontispiece of Charles-Simon Favart's *Soliman second* (1762): Soliman II bewitched by Roxelane, played by the playwright's wife, Justine Favart (© The Bodleian Library, University of Oxford, Taylorian Vet.Fr.II.B.321)

27. *Left*, F. Le Rousseau, "Türkish Dance Perform'd by Mr Desnoyer & Mrs Younger," c. 1725 (© The Bodleian Library, University of Oxford, G.Pamph, 1818); 28. *Right*, Joshua Reynolds's oil portrait of Frances Abington, later engraved, represents her in the character of Roxelana in Isaac Bickerstaff's *The Sultan* (© Trustees of the British Museum)

29. *Top left*, William Harvey, "Camaralzaman Disguised as an Astrologer," from Edward W. Lane's *The Thousand and One Nights*, 1835; 30. *Top right*, William Harvey, "Camaralzaman Standing before His Father," from Edward W. Lane's *The Thousand and One Nights*, 1835; 31. *Bottom left*, Dan Leno as Widow Twankey in *Aladdin* at the Drury Lane Theatre, London, 1896 (© Victoria and Albert Museum); 32. *Bottom right*, The frontispiece of Hideki Nagamine's *Kaikan Kyōki Arabiya Monogatari*, or "Strange and Marvelous Stories from Arabia" (1875)

33. The frontispiece of Ryukei Yano's *Perusia shinsetsu retsujo no homare*, or "A New Story from Persia: A Courageous Lady's Honor" (1887) (© National Diet Library)

34. A scene from Takarazuka revue of *Arabian naito*, or "The Arabian Nights" (1950) (© Takarazuka)

35. Scene from J. B. H. Wadia's *Arabian Nights* fantasy film *Lal-e-Yaman* (Jewel of Yemen; 1933) (© Wadia Movietone / Roy Wadia)

36. Wadia Movietone film song booklet for *Noor-e-Yaman* (Light of Yemen; 1935), the successful sequel to *Lal-e-Yaman* (© Wadia Movietone / Roy Wadia)

Yet while the *Nights* moves from tales of male revenge for female infidelity to tales justifying female infidelity as revenge, *Jacques* moves in the opposite direction, from the hostess's tale of female revenge to Jacques's lecherous, predatory tale of sexual conquest—and a mode of storytelling which exemplifies narrative conquest as well. The force of the hostess's tale is diffused by interruption (as she is repeatedly claimed by the daily business of running an inn and a household); Jacques's tale occasions shared male excitement over pornographic narration. At another moment in the book, a similar occasion forces the narrator to explain himself and to defend his own philosophical right to use obscene language. "How can a man of wisdom and morality, who fancies himself something of a philosopher, amuse himself by telling tales as obscene as this?" ("Comment un homme de sens, qui a des moeurs, qui se pique de philosophie, peut-il s'amuser à débiter des contes de cette obscénité?")[4] In answer, he evokes ancient belletristic and philosophical literature (from Catullus to Seneca), Rousseau, Voltaire, Montesquieu.

The Socratic dialogue is implicitly grounded in a notion of pedagogical eros, in which sexual initiation and philosophical enlightenment become intertwined. Yet Socratic dialogue also has a clear, asymmetrical power structure and a pedagogic inevitability. Everyday conversation and argument works differently—and their dynamics potentially suggest a different model of power. In lieu of the Socratic tradition, Diderot has used the *Nights* to develop an alternative form of (philosophical) dialogue, with a different kind of tension—political, narrative, and sometimes erotic—built into it. In Socrates's dialogues, Plato ends up victorious, deflating and sidelining rival positions. In Diderot's novel, in contrast, Jacques's narrative prowess remains unmatched by political power. Over the course of many nights, the *Nights* uses narrative rapprochement to develop a solution to despotic *droit de seigneur* and male sexual aggression. Diderot is interested rather in diagramming the conversational texture of domestic warfare, between the classes and between the sexes. Elsewhere—in the *Nights*-inspired *Les bijoux indiscrets* (*The Indiscreet Jewels*, 1748) and in the *Supplement au voyage du Bougainville* (*Supplement to the Voyage to Bougainville*, 1772)—Diderot elaborates alternative ethnographic or magical/Orientalist universes which circumvent such tensions.[5] Here he is interested not in utopian—or even narrative—resolutions but rather in the philosophical, ethical, and political questions that arise when people argue, talk past one another, snare listeners, or sleep with each other.

Sicilian Nights

In Elio Vittorini's antifascist novel *Conversation in Sicily*, the narrator, a factory worker in northern Italy, revisits his childhood home in Sicily after many years away. And over the course of this homeward journey, he remembers his deep childhood obsession with the *Arabian Nights*. On one level, like the narrator of James Joyce's "Araby" (or the protagonist of Umberto Saba's *Ernesto*), he apparently associated the *Nights* with an exotic and fabled Orient and hence also with inchoate romantic and sexual longings. Yet on another level, the *Nights* served him, already in childhood, as a guide to what was quite literally around him: "Terranova in Sicily, for me, embraced Baghdad and the Palace of Tears and the Hanging Gardens" ("Terranova la Sicilia significa anche Bagdad e Palazzo delle Lagrime e giardino di palmizi per me").[6]

This is partly a matter of projecting or interjecting described and imagined distant places onto an empirically known home base. Yet the child has also grasped, intuitively, the actual, empirical historical links between these places. For Terranova (present-day Gela) was once part of the Arab Empire, known to the Arabs as the "City of Columns."[7] Before that, it was part of the Greek, Roman, and Byzantine Empires; afterward, it was part of the Norman Empire and the post-Risorgimento Kingdom of Italy. Like many parts of the Mediterranean, Sicily has a long, complex, and layered history, visible, for those who know how to look for it, in its architecture, cuisine, and sensibility and in the physiognomies of its inhabitants. To read the *Nights* in Terranova is, for Vittorini's narrator, not only to shed light on Sicily's foundational layer of Arab heritage but also to grasp Sicily, suddenly, as an outpost of Baghdad, rather than as a distant, impoverished periphery of fascist Italy.

When we talk of the European reception of the *Arabian Nights*, we are usually thinking implicitly about western and northern Europe, and a reception which, despite Galland's muffling hand, still foregrounds the *Nights*' exotic, erotic, and narratological dimensions. We are less likely to consider its reception in southern Europe—including places which were once part of the Arab imperium and cosmos. For readers there,

Vittorini suggests, the text is not an opening onto an alien, unfamiliar, disorienting world so much as an occasion to see one's own terrain in a newly accurate light, now appearing not as a benighted place without culture but as deeply linked, historically, culturally, and narratively, to one of the wellsprings of World Literature.

Like Pier Paolo Pasolini's 1964 film *The Gospel According to Matthew* (shot in southern Italy and insistently envisioning Jesus as a Mediterranean peasant, the damned of the earth as the chosen people), Vittorini's novel makes clear the political stakes of such revision. For the narrator's journey is set at a very particular moment. The Italian air force has recently participated in the bombing of civilian populations in Republican Spain. And the Italian army has invaded and conquered Abyssinia; the narrator's brother served as a soldier and was killed during the course of this campaign. Mussolini is at the height of his powers. The narrator, by contrast and apparently in reaction, becomes increasingly depressed and shut down; the world around him becomes muffled and indistinct; he becomes incapable of talking to his wife, friends, or colleagues. Then, on an impulse, he sets off on his long pilgrimage to Sicily, triggered by news of a family crisis—but also by his growing sense of national crisis. During his journey south—and into his own past—he finds himself unexpectedly reviving, as he tastes the familiar food of his childhood; overhears and participates in a range of conversation (by turns casual, bitter, and combative); listens to his mother's familial reminiscences and confessions; engages her in surprisingly frank banter about her sexual history; accompanies her on her rounds as a kind of lay district nurse, inoculating—and flaunting the sexual charms of —female neighbors of a range of ages; spends an evening drinking with newfound free-thinking friends; and after a drunken vigil at the town's war memorial, engages both in visionary communion with his dead brother and a final, elliptical argument with his mother over the meaning of this brother's death. Then, abruptly, he begins the long journey back to the north, with the intention to return again soon.

In Vittorini's novel, as in the *Nights*, conversation often takes the form of extended monologues, which laid end to end mark not only a discernible narrative drift but a shifting discursive and hence political terrain. *Conversation in Sicily* implicitly charts a political transformation through conversational exchanges. Given the political climate within which *Conversations* was published, the novel's strategy, unsurprisingly, is indirect, using the apparently meandering form of the conversation (and the sustained conversational monologue) as a vehicle for implicit political analysis.

Passengers on the train grumble about the economic conditions that are pressing many into emigration and react angrily to the presence of police informers—first signs of their own nascent political resistance. One man complains to a fellow passenger about his starvation wages—and in this telling, activates a core of political bitterness within himself. The narrator's mother tells her son the story of her long-ago affair with an itinerant anarcho-syndicalist, to whom she gave herself as a kind of alms, only to find the object of her affectionate charity vanishing eventually in the wake of a police roundup. And this story, inconclusive as it seems, lingers throughout the novel, forcing her son to see her with new eyes, as a person with her own motivation and reasons, and forcing her, too, to remember a half-forgotten personal history linking the erotic and the political. Moreover, when she confesses this love affair, as when she remembers bygone workers' theater, outdoor Shakespeare performances attended by miners and railroad men, she parenthetically evokes long-ago labor agitation—and a worker's culture that saw literature as a means to enlightenment.

And at the novel's end, when mother and son argue about the legacy of the Gracchi, they are also implicitly arguing over what and whose history Italians are being told—and about Mussolini's claims to be rebuilding a new version of imperial Rome. In northern Italy, the narrator is silent in the face of the newspaper headlines, alone with his sense of malaise. As he moves southward, he moves back into a culture of conversation, storytelling, and dispute. In northern Italy, Mussolini's imperial model appeared a fait accompli. But Sicily tacitly resists enlistment into a neo-Roman empire—because it has already been occupied too many times before. Given Sicilians' own creolized culture, Vittorini suggests, they are innately skeptical when Mussolini mobilizes the rhetoric of racial superiority to promote Italian expansionism and to motivate the invasion of Abyssinia.

The *Arabian Nights* inoculated Vittorini's narrator permanently against the seductions of fascist nationalism by giving him an alternative, transnational vision of civilization. And in Sicily itself, Vittorini suggests, persistent narrative traditions—and local conversational rhythms and preoccupations—complicate not only the triumphalism of official nationalist/imperialist narratives but Gramscian notions of the organic intellectual. Who is to save or enlighten the rural working class save themselves? And what can save them except conversation and argument, talking to one another? In an area of longstanding, desperate poverty, talk is inexpensive. And complaint and argument have their own dialectic form.

Whereas Ignazio Silone's novel *Pane e vino* (*Bread and Wine*, 1936) depicts consciousness-raising partly by outside agitation, Vittorini envisions it arising out of the dynamic of conversation itself, pushing interlocutors into new questions about each other and about their own positions. The mother teaches her infant son to speak. Years later he returns to talk and argue with her, and their conversation—pointed questions, commonplaces, mutual revelations—potentially changes both. Like Diderot, Vittorini is interested in the dynamic and in the eros of conversation. Even more problematically than Scheherazade and King Shahriyar, Jacques and his listener found themselves aligned only over a scenario of erotic coercion. Vittorini's narrator and his mother, in contrast, use erotic confession not to titillate each other but to develop a new, multidimensional view of each other that pushes past their traditional gender and familial roles.

The Eunuch's Tale

In traditional Chinese literature, the eunuch typically appears as a conspirator seeking to dominate palace politics. In the *Arabian Nights*, in contrast—and hence also in Montesquieu's *Persian Letters*, in *Tristram Shandy*, and in *Kiss of the Spiderwoman*—the eunuch becomes the means of measuring the narrative's power to enlist audience sympathy.[8] In narrating the story of his own maiming, a figure who might seem only pitiable or risible instead becomes not only explicable and multifaceted but at moments charismatically charged. (Does this deployment of the eunuch, one might ask, intersect with the figure of the hermaphrodite in Plato's *Symposium*, a utopian embodiment of otherwise lost wholeness and unity? Do the sexual politics of the Western philosophical tradition here mesh, after all, with those of the *Nights*?)

In Puig's *Kiss of the Spiderwoman*, two very different kinds of men find themselves sharing the same small Argentine jail cell. The transvestite hairdresser, jailed on morals charges, is obsessed with gender markers, fashion, romantic suffering, and the memory of genre movies; the heterosexual revolutionary meditates on violence and a new world order, yearns for his girlfriend, and despises mass culture as an opiate of the people. Masochism meets machismo: the two represent entirely different life philosophies, and at first their interactions appear almost as conflict laden as those of Jacques and his master. Yet as a way of passing their long days in the cell, the transvestite begins retelling his favorite films. And his narratives generate various types of conversations and a gradual process of political convergence and personal rapprochement. Before the novel is over, the men have become friends, comrades, and even, unexpectedly, lovers.

During early film recountings, the revolutionary remains restive and repeatedly deploys the tools of Marxist critique to question, even attack, the ideology of the films being narrated. One, indeed, is a Nazi feature film, clearly designed to advance reactionary gender, racial, and national politics. Yet as the transvestite aficionado both insists and demonstrates, reception is complicated, diffuse, and unpredictable; sometimes the manifest content of the film is at odds with the emotions and autobiographical associations it induces in particular spectators. Nazi Germany persecuted and imprisoned homosexuals, yet for this gay postwar spectator, watching half a world away, a Nazi propaganda vehicle offers rich opportunities to meditate on his own experience and existence. The process of telling, moreover, often proves more important than narrative content itself; the transvestite's movie tales lead both into philosophical discussions and into autobiographical disclosures. Over days and nights of recounting, the revolutionary comes to understand the sufferings of his cellmate; both inmates begin to sense the implicitly political dimensions of homosexuals' attempt to live and love without persecution; and the transvestite gains a tentative new political consciousness.

The act of renarration, moreover, changes the framework—and hence the significance—of reception. Films are watched communally, by an audience whose pleasure is enhanced by a sense of simultaneous, shared enjoyment; the darkened auditorium, along with the film's luminous images, induces a sense of half-somnolent, collective dream life. Audience members, moreover, are both lulled and stimulated by the fact they already know many of the generic conventions being deployed; thanks to such tacit knowledge, it is often perfectly possible to arrive in the middle of a film yet still pick up the film's key relationships and plots.

Puig's novel, in fact, opens in the midst of the first of the film retellings—the narrative equivalent of walking into a cinema in midscreening. In the jail cell, however, the audience has shrunk to one, there are no images to lull, and the shared communal viewing experience has given way to analytic and emotional conversation about what the film might mean. Some retellings spark prolonged arguments which interrupt the narrative flow, halt it altogether, or generate (in the style of eighteenth-century antiquarian novels) extensive theoretical footnotes, an elaborate editorial apparatus which reveals, à la Diderot, the presence of a further, otherwise invisible narrator and the potential for further narrative layering. Scheherazade fascinated because her tales unexpectedly broke off, bifurcated, or opened a new narrative series. The transvestite's movie stories move their auditor in part because they are already profoundly familiar, expected—hence can exist comfortably in quotidian time and excite speculations about quotidian experience.

The *Nights* itself, and the political novels which follow it, proffer the possibility of a social world remade through communication. The deprived of the earth, the *Nights* shows us, can not only learn to tell their own story but, in so doing, change the attitudes and ideologies of those who listen. The deprived of the earth, Vittorini suggests, can find comfort in each other's company, comradeship in each other's conversation. And for Puig, as for Vittorini, narrative and conversation forge new bonds between those who are caught by similarly adverse political circumstances.

Diderot's focus is on narrative challenges to despotism—and this feeds his own commitment to open or unparsable narrative forms. Vittorini's and Puig's novels are more formally conventional, interested rather in honing conversationalists' ability to intuit their interlocutor's position. What they describe is the emergence of an inchoate political solidarity engendered by reciprocal listening and response.

The *Nights* implicitly teaches a mode of interchange and self-correction, one that Diderot, Vittorini, and Puig endorse and reenact. For Diderot, Scheherazadean narration becomes a means of anatomizing the underlying power dynamics of everyday life—and the narrative act itself. At key moments, the interests of storyteller and listener converge, preparing the way for *Jacques*'s (perfunctory) happy ending. Yet the novel's moments of putative narrative convergence or rapprochement consistently prove morally problematic—and Diderot just as consistently negates the possibility of reaching synthesis or closure. For Diderot, conversation—and communication—remain somewhat illusory, and he himself remains a skeptic.

Vittorini and Puig are much more sanguine about the possibilities both of communication and of a popular political front. Unlike Diderot, they underscore conversation's transformative power. And despite friction, interruption, and indirection, they demonstrate that narrative exchange can eventuate in emotional convergence and political conversion.

Samurai Rebellions: Questions of Scale

Masaki Kobayashi's *Seppuku* is set during a period in which many masterless samurai desperately traverse medieval Japan seeking employment. One samurai presents himself at the gate of a manor, asking either for sustenance or to be allowed to commit *seppuku* (ritual suicide through disemboweling) on the premises. He is warned that his request will not lead to financial rescue and that he will instead be forced to keep his word. As precedent, he is told, in flashbacks, the story of a previous petitioner, whose bluff was called: his urgent request to forestall his suicide by one day denied, he was instead forced to kill himself, agonizingly and slowly, with his own sword (which proved to be made of bamboo, evidence he had not really intended to kill himself). Now, in the outer frame, the latter-day petitioner insists that before he commits *seppuku*, he must tell his own story. This complex set of nested narratives not only forestalls his own self-execution but provides the backstory to both his own and his predecessor's deeds. His predecessor was his son-in-law and adoptive son, forced to sell his sword and risk his life in the attempt to buy medicine to save the life of his dying baby (and wife). Once the narrator has filled this all in, it is clear that his son's petition at the feudal manor was motivated not by greed or calculation but by love and honor—and that he himself has come to seek revenge on the callous lord and retainers who dared laugh at another man's plight and death throes. Before dying, he kills or humiliates his son's persecutors and denounces the entire feudal and samurai systems. Unfortunately, the historical chronicle deliberately suppresses this incident; had it not, the film suggests, the rest of Japanese history might have had another course, averting recent Japanese suffering.

Kobayashi's *Samurai Rebellion* features a similar plot of revenge and denunciation of the feudal system, as of samurai vows. Here, however, the pivot of plot is a droit de seigneur which enables the feudal lord to take women as concubines, removing them from their family, severing their engagements, and turning them into breeding animals to produce potential heirs. One girl initially accepts her fate, thinking that by sacrificing herself and giving the lord many children, she can save her fellow women from similar misuse. Yet even as she is recovering from the birth of her first child, he takes another concubine; in her anger, she physically attacks both the lord and her replacement and is sent from court in disgrace and married off to a vassal, only to be recalled by the lord once the heir to the throne dies. Now, as the mother of the new, replacement heir, she must be associated with court, not vassal circles. In the meantime, however, she has won the love of her new husband and father-in-law, and they refuse to surrender her. The standoff ends with her abduction by the court party, her husband and father-in-law's armed revenge on her persecutors, and the honor-filled, resistant death of the wife, the husband, and even the father-in-law, who had attempted to escape to Edo to publicize the injustices of feudal rule. Only the wife's second child, a baby girl, and the baby's wet nurse survive, along with the vague hope that they will somehow embody a principle of resistance, an inchoate memory of wrong.

Whereas *Seppuku* adapts the *Nights* by recasting the eunuch's vindication-through-narrative, *Samurai Rebellion* focuses on Scheherazadean courage and defiance. Yet those who are dishonored are still all killed by the system they denounce—and narrative virtuosity does not procure safety. In *Samurai Rebellion*, indeed, the heroine narrates her own story, binding her new family to her; but she is nonetheless unable to save her sisters from depredation, and the birth of the child conceived from her "lord" only makes her more vulnerable. As in the *Nights*, autobiographical backstory is transformative, giving persuasive force to those who have no other source of power. Yet the forces of despotism possess the more powerful and more lethal weapons; those who try to speak for justice wind up dead and unremembered. Only centuries later, after an age of even more lethal and more despotic neofeudalism which led to the deaths of millions, can these doomed earlier attempts to inaugurate a different political order be understood, tolerated, honored. In recounting life histories, Scheherazade's tales—and the interpolated tales of barbers or eunuchs—anchor the present in the recent past. The *Nights* imagines a political conversion which takes one thousand and one nights to complete, via the life histories of barbers and eunuchs; Kobayashi focuses on the tragedy of individual families yet imagines political conversion needing an entirely different time scale, working by millennium rather than by night or by year. The *Nights* conceives of despotism in terms of a king able to bed or behead individual subjects, and its explanatory, opinion-changing narratives too are conceived in multiples of the individual life span. Kobayashi returns to the medieval period in foreknowledge that Japanese authoritarianism was to cause the deaths of millions—and that a timescale of centuries will be needed to vindicate its victims.

A Thousand and One Arctic Nights

Grossman's *Everything Flows* tackles similar problems of scale. In the wake of Stalin's death, his protagonist, Ivan Grigoryevich, returns from Siberia to Moscow, amnestied after thirty years as a political prisoner in the gulag. Ivan spends his first evening back with his cousin, a biologist who owes his professional success to the purges which cumulatively swept away his more talented Jewish and nonconformist colleagues. In their youth, the biologist loved Ivan, yet for three decades after Ivan's arrest, he has avoided all contact with him. Now, reunited at last, the scientist feels the need to explain himself to Ivan, even fantasizes about making a long confession of his professional compromises. Instead, he expresses the polite wish that there were unlimited time, out of range of all bugging devices, to hear all about convict life in Siberia. Ivan in turn imagines himself narrating, at leisure, the "piercingly sad" fates of the many "people who had departed into eternal darkness." Yet

> even the tenderest, quietest, kindest word about these people would have been like the touch of a rough, heavy hand on a heart that had been torn open. No, there were things that could not be spoken.
>
> And, nodding his head, he said, "Yes, yes, yes. Tales of a Thousand and One Arctic Nights."[9]

Ivan's utterance makes a rhetorical gesture, proffers a literary model, apparently builds a conversational bridge. Yet shortly thereafter, Ivan abruptly leaves his cousin's apartment and Moscow, never to return, without having divulged anything.

In Leningrad, a few weeks later, Ivan begins sleeping with his land-lady, Anna Sergeyevna. It is his first sexual encounter with a woman in thirty years. Yet she spends their whole first night together uttering a long confession. Twenty years after the fact, she is tormented by her fail-ures of understanding, imagination, and compassion, as a government official in Ukraine in the early 1930s, and by what she sees as her own moral complicity in the "anti-kulak" campaigns and subsequent mass famine. Her narrative ends only with the night, as it is getting light. Even then, she closes by reiterating how haunted she is—particularly by the fact that such vast suffering—and millions of extinguished lives —seems to have left so few markers. "Where can that life have gone? And that suffering, that terrible suffering? Can there really be nothing left? Is it really true that no one will be held accountable for it all? That it all can be forgotten without a trace?" (138).

Later, after Anna is hospitalized for terminal cancer, Ivan mentally composes for her a counterposed narrative of his own sufferings, obser-vations, and thoughts. "He was trying to understand the truth of Rus-sian life, what it was that linked past and present. His hope was that Anna Sergeyevna would return from the hospital and he would tell her all he recalled, all he had thought, all he had understood. And she would share with him the burden, and the clarity, of understanding. This was the consolation for his grief. This was his love" (147).

But Anna dies before Ivan is able to tell her in person. Instead, he must utter his narrative in grieving soliloquy. Only Grossman's novel

itself—a patchwork of conversations in train compartments, bed, din-
ing rooms, flashbacks, case studies, memories, political analysis—can
serve as the place where different stories and strands of national catastrophe and tragedy are juxtaposed, in the effort to compass the scale of
human suffering unleashed by Stalin (and Lenin).

Grossman's protagonist initially imagines the *Arabian Nights* as a
possible model for reconstructing the epic narrative of gulag life. Yet
Ivan never recounts his "Tales of a Thousand and One Arctic Nights."
In fact, he never tells anything, at least not to a living soul. A century
earlier, tale collections such as Vladimir Fedorich Odoevsky's *Russian
Nights* (1844) had successfully adapted Scheherazade's—or Boccaccio's
—framed tale collection framework as a vehicle for Enlightenment
meditations on the condition of Russia, European politics, aesthetics, science, and religion. Yet by the mid-twentieth century, the scale
of depredation, the mutual annihilation of the Russian people, resists
the descriptive capacities of a single frame narrator. And those who
survived political catastrophe have often done so by long collusion and
internalized avoidance, both of which forestall easy self-revelation.
Mutual confession is sometimes possible, especially in the wake of sexual intimacy—coitus followed by harrowing eyewitness narrative—but
sustained narration is not.

In 1961, five years after Grossman began *Everything Flows*, the KGB
impounded the unpublished manuscript of Grossman's previous novel,
Life and Fate. A year later, the government-approved publication of
Alexander Solzhenitsyn's *A Day in the Life of Ivan Denisovich* inaugu-
rated a new public discussion of the gulag and its literary posterity. Yet
when Grossman died, in 1964, there was no guarantee that *Everything
Flows* or *Life and Fate* would ever be published.

If Grossman died unsure that either novel would ever reach readers, *Everything Flows* records a related uncertainty. Given the scale
of twentieth-century political cataclysm, and the nature of political
betrayal in the Soviet Union, Grossman registered uncertainty about
the further viability of the *Nights'* model of storytelling and political conversion. Theodor Adorno famously pondered the question of
whether there could be poetry after Auschwitz. Grossman wonders
whether the narrative contract of the *Nights* is still possible in the light
of engineered famine and the politically motivated decimation of one

generation, as well as a political culture which silenced the generation which followed.

Like Puig's *Kiss*, *Everything Flows* shows prisoners sharing their stories as well as their food, their beds, and their fate. It is when they leave the gulag and board the train to return to the "real world" that words begin to fail them—or perhaps, more precisely, that they begin to understand the political and conversational constraints of the "normal" world, of those who still have everything to lose. The ordinary passengers among whom Ivan rides back to Moscow joke, talk, and philosophize with one another. Yet unlike Vittorini's train passengers, en route back home to Sicily, who use covert codes to convey political trust or suspicion, these strangers avoid any real self-revelation and hence any real communication.

In Moscow and Leningrad, conditions prove far worse yet. En route to and in Sicily, Vittorini's returning prodigal had found himself drawn into a welter of conversations and, in the process, drawn out of his social and hence also his political isolation. Ivan, literally returning from political banishment, finds himself at once an invisible man and a figure whose visible history of suffering impels others to confess or at least to ruminate silently and anxiously on their own politically misspent lives.

For even after Stalin's death, even following a wave of political rehabilitations, habits of narrative caution and concealment predominate. At moments, characters feel the impulse to confess, especially to those whom they previously denounced, wronged, or abandoned. But they are afraid to tell each other anything, and they have forgotten how. They remain aware, moreover, that chance remarks may be overheard and recorded, that the telephones in their offices and apartments may be bugged, that any utterance may give their conversational partners long-term political leverage over their own fates. Only long-married couples are able to evoke, with a kind of narrative shorthand, their own long-standing compromises and sorrows. And only newly involved couples struggle to articulate the cumulative force of their own experiences.

Indeed, only at a single point in the novel (considerably predating the couple's sexual involvement) do the two main protagonists, Ivan and Anna, manage a political conversation, in the presence of Anna's young nephew. As in the *Nights*, the adults' telling of and listening to stories involves a virtually silent younger listener—in the *Nights*, Scheherazade's sister; here, Anna's nephew—whose narrative role might involve carrying such stories into a later future.

Even now, the couple's exchange takes the form of two consecutive manifestos. First, Anna soliloquizes about her growing sense of disparity as she measures what the government extracts economically from its workers and what it gives them in return. Ivan replies with a pithier and more abstract soliloquy about the nature of freedom.

> "Is it possible," she asked, "that this has put our whole lives out of kilter? . . . I do realize we're not meant to talk about these things. But I can see what kind of man you are. Otherwise I wouldn't ask such a question. But you haven't the least idea of what kind of person I am—so don't answer."
>
> "You don't need to say that," said Ivan Grigoryevich. "I certainly will answer. I used to think that freedom was freedom of speech, freedom of the press, freedom of conscience. But freedom needs to include all of the lives of all of the people. . . . It's the same whether you're a locksmith or a steelworker or an artist—freedom is the right to live and work as you wish and not as you're ordered to. But there's no freedom for anyone, whether you write books, whether you sow grain, or whether you make boots." (84)

What bridges these speeches, most crucially, is an exchange about the legal impermissibility and hence practical inadvisability of conversation itself, since "we're not meant to talk about these things." To expose their political doubts to each other is an act of trust—and a leap of faith —which seems historically unjustifiable, given a long period in which colleagues denounced each other, relatives pretended not to know one another, and husbands and wives were pressured by the authorities to confess each other's treasonous utterances. Yet Anna insists that she is able to articulate her long-held ideas, to expose her thoughts and hence herself, because she can see for herself that the person before her is upright and ethical. And he, in turn, having served thirty years for a long-ago insistence on speaking his own mind, now insists, even after decades of punishment, that he remains determined, unafraid, and that his ideas about the meaning of freedom have expanded from questions of conscience and speech to include the writing of books and the living of daily life.

For a brief moment, two dissidents open their mouths, their hearts, and their minds, feeling they have nothing left to lose. And with their mutually revelatory speeches, they begin to forge a new social, communicative (and erotic) contract. For what emerges, at least for a moment, at least in latent or nascent form, is the renewed possibility of conversation.

The political novel, in its modern form at least, builds on a fundamental Enlightenment notion of the epistemological possibility and political efficacy of probing, rational, investigative exchanges. Enlightenment science was based methodologically on empirical observation and institutionally on academies (or corresponding societies) of investigating intellectuals, including many who had trained themselves in scientific method. Enlightenment political culture, too, valued the free, uncensored, and robust exchange of ideas. Such exchange could take the transient oral form of the London coffeehouse culture (see fig. 19), the epistolary form of the radical correspondence society, or in the printed form of anonymous, sometimes scurrilous pamphlets.[10] In some contexts, such exchange styled itself in mercantilist terms, stressing the economic rather than the anthropological valences of "exchange," the competition between points of view as something resembling the capitalist marketplace. Yet in other contexts (from Paris to Edinburgh), such exchange understood itself rather as an instantiation of democracy, as a free mental meeting place of independent individuals, speaking not in the interests of or under the guidance of government, church, or other established institutions but out of their own idiosyncratic minds.

Diderot—and Jacques—epitomize such principles. Yet as Vittorini, Puig, and Grossman demonstrate, Enlightenment models of free thought and of political subversion are subsequently overlaid by others. Vittorini seems influenced by Marxist thought, whether the contemporaneous prison writings of Antonio Gramsci or nineteenth-century accounts of uneven development and agrarian unrest.[11] Grossman, in contrast, is interested in the emergence or reemergence of a confessional, ethically driven dissident strain of Russian intellectual culture, precisely in counterdistinction to official Soviet Marxist rhetoric, public proclamations, and orchestrated "self-criticism" sessions; in his novel's tone of moral concern as in its attempt to construct, from episodic experiences, an epic of carceral existence, *Everything Flows* self-consciously reanimates the protest tradition of nineteenth-century Russian prison fiction, from Fyodor Dostoevsky's 1861 *Memoirs from the House of the Dead* to Leo Tolstoy's 1899 *Resurrection*.[12] Puig, in contrast, filters his prison narrative through meditations on the imaginative freedom and constraints of the movie audience, theories of popular culture, and psychoanalysis, both as a body of theoretical work interested in psychic processing (and the psychic afterlife of aesthetic experience) and as a practice of structured, asymmetric confession, in which telling provides a sense of absolution—and the raw material for analytic conversation.

At first glance, post-Enlightenment literati—Marx, Dostoevsky, Tolstoy, Gramsci, or Freud—might seem peculiar bedfellows for Scheherazade. Yet as these novels show, an important strain within the political novel has pressed just such couplings. For these novels have represented the core of political life in ways that mesh the *Nights'* preoccupations with the cathartic effects of narration—and narration as power struggle —with the legacy of an Enlightenment belief in speech as politically leveling and transformative. Most interestingly and movingly, these novels take *everyday* conversation to constitute a crucial form of political speech. Any two people can create a shared experience of and through language. And in any exchange, something transformative can flare up, with the power to challenge despotism, unsettle the status quo, rewrite the social contract.

NOTES

1. Rebecca Johnson, Richard Maxwell and Katie Trumpener, "The *Arabian Nights*, Arab-European Literary Influence, and the Lineages of the Novel," in "Globalism on the Move," special issue, *Modern Language Quarterly* 68:2 (June 2007): 243–79, explored the *Nights'* impact on the eighteenth- and nineteenth-century novel. I remain grateful for Rebecca and Richard's comments on the present essay, as for Katerina Clark's editorial and John Mackay's bibliographic suggestions.

2. My emphasis on dialogue is of course influenced by the work of Mikhail Bakhtin ("The Dialogic Imagination," in *Four Essays*, ed. and trans. Michael Holquist and Caryl Emerson [Austin: University of Texas Press, 1982]), although my focus is literally on the structure of conversation in the novel, rather than the novel's

incorporation and juxtaposition of various sociolects. Bakhtin remains not only the most comprehensive and incisive guide to the history of the European novel but the theorist most interested in developing an account of the novel as a form built on the coexistence of different ideolects, linguistic registers, and narrative voices. His politics of the novelistic mode rests on the dialogic. Yet the *Nights* plays little role in his account of the novel's development (or indeed, it would seem, in his work as a whole).

3. In chapter 4 in this volume, Eliot Colla's "The Porter and Portability: Figure and Narrative in the *Nights*" explores the *Nights*' insistence in linking physical mutilation to sexual humiliation as to castration itself.

4. Denis Diderot, *Jacques the Fatalist and His Master*, trans. Michael Henry (Harmondsworth, UK: Penguin, 1986), 200; Diderot, *Jacques le fataliste et son maître* (Paris: Livre de poche, 1983), 247.

5. Yet *The Indiscreet Jewels*' polyglot erotic fantasies also stage the consolidation of male friendship over the shared body of a female prostitute. Diderot, *The Indiscreet Jewels*, trans. Sophie Hawkes (New York: Marsilio), 223–24. On *Jewels*' own rewriting of the *Nights*, see Johnson, Maxwell, and Trumpener, "The Arabian Nights."

6. Elio Vittorini, *Conversation in Sicily*, trans. Wilfred David (London: Quartet, 1988), 87; Vittorini, *Conversazione in Sicilia*, 8th ed. (Milan: Rizzoli, 2004), 268.

7. The *Nights* (and the Qur'an) reference a different, originary City of Columns, 'Iram in Arabia.

8. The *Nights* contains a series of castrated figures: the barber's sixth brother does not tell his own tale, but the three eunuchs whose tales of their castrations are embedded in the story of Ghanim do become narrators, as does Aziz in "Aziz and Azirah." For a more nuanced account of this range of eunuch narratives, see Daniel Beaumont, *Slaves of Desire: Sex, Love, and Death in The 1001 Nights* (Madison, NJ: Fairleigh Dickinson University Press, 2002).

9. Vasily Grossman, *Everything Flows*, trans. Robert and Elizabeth Chandler, with Anna Aslanyan (New York: New York Review of Books, 2009), 37 (hereafter cited parenthetically in the text).

10. On coffeehouse culture, see for instance Jürgen Habermas, *The Structural Transformation of the Public Sphere: An Inquiry into a Category of Bourgeois Society*, trans. Thomas Burger (Cambridge: MIT Press, 1989); on the radical correspondence societies, see E. P. Thompson, *The Making of the English Working Class* (London: Victor Gollanz, 1963); on free-thinking print culture, see for instance Robert Darnton, *Literary Underground in the Old Regime* (Cambridge: Harvard University Press, 1982); Jon Mee, *Dangerous Enthusiasm: William Blake and the Culture of Radicalism in the 1790s* (Oxford, UK: Clarendon, 1992); and Kevin Gilmartin, *Print Politics: The Press and Radical Opposition in Early Nineteenth-Century Britain* (New York: Cambridge University Press, 1996).

11. Antonio Gramsci, *Prison Notebooks*, ed. Joseph A. Buttigieg, trans. Joseph A. Buttigieg and Antonio Callari (New York: Columbia University Press, 1991);

Friedrich Engels, *The Condition of the Working Classes in England*, ed. W. O. Henderson and W. H. Chaloner (Stanford: Stanford University Press, 1968).

12. See Matthew Lenoe, *Closer to the Masses: Stalinist Culture, Social Revolution, and Soviet Newspapers* (Cambridge: Harvard University Press, 2004); and Nancy Ruttenburg, *Dostoevsky's Democracy* (Princeton: Princeton University Press, 2008).

12

Sindbad the Sailor: Textual, Visual, and
Performative Interpretations

FERIAL J. GHAZOUL

Sindbad, or Sinbad as often referred to in Western literatures, has become a synonym for the seafarer, the adventurous sailor who comes
across excruciating dangers.[1] The figure of Sindbad has inspired modern imagination in diverse ways—from James Joyce's *Ulysses* to Badr
Shakir al-Sayyab's poetry, from John Barth's *Last Voyage of Somebody
the Sailor* to Naguib Mahfouz's *Arabian Nights and Days*. This essay
deals with three works: the first, by the Egyptian novelist Radwa
Ashour, uses Sindbad's third voyage as a political allegory; the second,
by the Swiss German painter Paul Klee, translates Sindbad into another
medium, into an image and a painting that evokes the existential condition of life in a world full of threatening monsters; and the third is by
the Irish geographer and anthropologist Tim Severin, who undertakes a
voyage with a selected crew from Oman to China on a ship constructed
after the model of Sindbad's. Thus, Severin performs the Sindbad voyage, transforming fantasy into reality. The choice of these three works is
based on their relation to Sindbad of the *Arabian Nights* while rendering

him in different sign systems. Following the much quoted and anthologized article of Roman Jakobson, "On Linguistic Aspects of Translation" (1959), interpretations and adaptations of texts have come to be seen as translations.[2] Jakobson's article makes a distinction between three types of "translations." The first is *intralingual*, in which one text is rephrased within the same language, and this is the case for Ashour's novella, in which the voyage of Sindbad is retold in a summary fashion identifying it with the travel of the protagonist. The second type of translation that Jakobson identifies, *interlingual*, is what is commonly understood by translation, the transfer of a text from one language to another. This kind of translation is the way Ashour's novella was rendered in English and the way the *Arabian Nights* has been rendered in English and other languages. Jakobson's third type of translation, *intersemiotic*, is that of transfer from one medium to another medium, such as from text to film or from text to image. This applies to Klee's painting of Sindbad as an intersemiotic translation based on an interlinguistic translation of the *Arabian Nights*. Severin's reenacting of Sindbad's voyage can in some sense be considered an intersemiotic translation as it is a performance with a mise-en-scène and pretravel preparation, unfolding in an itinerary that resembles that of Sindbad and with an official ritual as finale. Severin ends up writing a book about his experience as well as producing a film, so there are many levels of translations and interpretations, including the presence in the film of paintings of Sindbad voyages as imagined by visual artists. In other words, these three works use extensively Jakobsonian modes of translation. In examining how Sindbad has been presented in these diverse modes, one can see how the figure of Sindbad has penetrated modern imagination, in the verbal, visual, and performative arts.

Radwa Ashour's novella *Siraaj: Hikaya 'Arabiyya*, published in 1992 and translated to English by Barbara Romaine in 2007 as *Siraaj: An Arab Tale*, mixes historical events with a fablelike narrative, using strands "from the popular heritage" to criticize both Western colonialism and Eastern authoritarianism.[3] Set in the late nineteenth century on an island that resembles geographically and historically Zanzibar with a touch of pre-Republican Yemeni court culture, the novella wavers cleverly between a political allegory and an elaborate folktale on resistance.[4]

The dominant theme is that of oppression and revolt. *Siraaj* revolves around Said, the son of a pearl diver who loses his life in a diving expedition. Said leaves on a ship to explore the world and ends up in rural Egypt, having been stranded there after his ship sailed without him. In Egypt, Said is "adopted" by the family of Umm Ibrahim, whose husband has left to fight with the Egyptian leader Orabi, just as Said was earlier welcomed in the family of his friend Mahmoud when he was in Alexandria. Said not only gets familial protection but engages in an exchange of stories and accounts of life styles with his Egyptian hosts. The Egyptian children in the village are shocked and puzzled to learn that Said does not know how to till the soil. He explains that this is a task for slaves in the plantations of his island. Using the technique of defamiliarization, as elaborated by the Russian critic Victor Shklovsky,[5] Ashour develops exchanges between Said and his hosts that illuminate the modes of exploitation of the simple folk on the island, named ironically Ghurrat al-'Arab (Arabs' Glory).

Siraaj opens with Said's mother, Amina, awaiting the return of her son from a sea voyage he has undertaken. Before she goes to the sultan's palace to bake, as well as on her return home, Amina stops by the port to check if there is any news of her son. Amina's waiting for him creates a mood full of expectation and anxiety, undercut by her memories of how she came to the sultan's island with her grandfather when she was only four years old. Thus, the social composition of the island is revealed—indigenous, freeborn, poor pearl divers and African slaves working on plantations, all in the service of the sultan and his court. The sea with its ambivalence looms darkly from the beginning: "Men go to sea, they go and they come back . . . they go and they don't come back, so the women go out to wait for them, their shoulders rigid with fear, furrows of anxiety etched in their faces."[6] Unlike Sindbad of the *Nights*, whose adventures concern him alone, the sea traveler in *Siraaj* is intimately linked with his family, and the agonies of absence are explored through the feelings of his mother.

The teenage protagonist, Said, leaves his island off the coast of Africa —run by a ludicrously authoritarian sultan—out of curiosity to know the rest of the world. He ends up stranded in Alexandria as his ship sails without him. This episode reminds us of Sindbad of the *Arabian Nights*, who is also left behind while his ship sails away. In Alexandria, Said

befriends another teenager, Mahmoud, who is a militant Egyptian peasant. Mahmoud fights with the Egyptian popular leader Ahmed Orabi
(1841–1911), who has said to the Khedive, the ruler of Egypt, "We are
not slaves and you are not our master" (Ashour 15). Orabi led a revolt
in the early 1880s against Khedive Ismail. It was during this period that
Britain invaded Egypt with its imperial fleet that shelled and bom-
barded Alexandria, putting an end to Orabi's uprising. Ashour's novella
itself reproduces the collaboration between foreign bases on the island
and the despotism of the sultan in order to refer to the Egypt of that
period while also alluding to present conditions in the Arab world. *Siraaj* embodies—stylistically and structurally—an *Arabian Nights* tale,
overdetermined by names of characters associated with *The Thousand
and One Nights*, such as Maarouf and Tawaddud, as well as direct reference to Sindbad.[7]

The parallelism between Said and Sindbad is indicated in the allitera-
tion of the two names. Furthermore, Mahmoud—who has never left his
country—refers to the Said-Sindbad parallelism, saying, "You are lucky,
man. . . . You travel by ship and roam the world, then come home like
Sindbad the Sailor and live in a palace, invite your friends, and hold parties and all-night bashes for them" (14). When Said asks, "Who is Sindbad the Sailor?" (14), Mahmoud is surprised that Said does not know
him, nor does he know the story of Hasan al-Shatir, Clever Hasan, or
for that matter that of the Egyptian leader Orabi. So Mahmoud begins
to tell Said the tales of Sindbad and Clever Hasan, adding to them how
Orabi confronted the ruler of Egypt and the British. What these narratives have in common—whether the tales of Hasan and Sindbad or
the historical accounts of Orabi—is the heroism of the protagonists
against overwhelming odds. Among all the stories associated with the
voyages of Sindbad, Mahmoud (or rather Ashour) selects the episode of
Sindbad's encounter with the Old Man of the Sea—and in Mahmoud's
abbreviated retelling, it is condensed: "Sindbad . . . carried an ailing
old man on his shoulders, then saw his hooves and realized that it was
the devil in disguise" (15). Sindbad's tale in Ashour's novella conjures
Sindbad the Porter of the *Nights* along with Sindbad the Sailor. In Mahmoud's family, the breadwinners—Mahmoud and his father—work as
porters in the railway station. This hints intertextually to Sinbad the
Porter, who listened day after day to Sindbad the Sailor recounting his

voyages. But there is a reversal here: the narrator in *Siraaj* is the porter Mahmoud, who is telling the story while the sailor Said is listening.

Mahmoud's father tries to explain to Said why his ship left before its expected departure time and left him behind: "They say that the English ships are drawing near to our shores, and that they have evil intentions toward us. It may be that the captain of your ship hastened his departure on hearing of this business" (16). The political dimension is present here, as the motivation for the early departure of the ship is added to the tale of Sindbad, as we know it in the *Nights*. This in turn contextualizes *Siraaj* in a colonial setting.

When Said eventually returns to his island and works clandestinely to overthrow the autocratic ruler, he dreams one night of being Sindbad: "Said felt as though he was choking, as the man who rode upon his shoulders wrapped his legs around his neck and exerted pressure, insulting him and beating him. The man, who had hooves like a horse or a donkey, began to urinate and defecate, and Said wished he might die. Then he woke up" (68). Even though this vision turns out to have been a nightmare, Said continues to feel ill at ease because of it. Ashour chooses to overdetermine the intertextual reference by pointing out that a few days later Said realizes that in the dream he had been remembering an episode from a story that his friend Mahmoud had told him when they were wandering in the streets of Alexandria: "The dream isn't strange, because Young Mahmoud told me the story of Sindbad the Sailor, who met a crippled old man and carried him, meaning to do a good deed. Then it became clear that the man was a devil with hooves, who kept tormenting him and beating him and forcing him to work, until Sindbad rid himself of it, threw it off his shoulders and beat it with a rock" (72).

Later on in this chapter, Said confides in the old African slave Ammar, whom he considers as a father, if not a grandfather, figure, about his dream, identifying the exploitive man on his back in the nightmare as the cruel captain of the fishing boat who punishes the crew severely for the slightest negligence and even for falling sick and not being able to work: "I go to the fishing boat in a bad mood, because I can no longer stand the sight of the captain. I dreamed about him. I dreamed he was riding on my shoulders, and he was about to choke me, wrapping his legs around my neck" (72). Ammar then asks how Sindbad got rid of the devil, and Said tells him how it was done: "He got a large fruit, removed its insides, and dried it. Then he filled it with grapes, and when fermented he got the devil to drink the juice, and when it got drunk its limbs loosened, and Sindbad knocked it off his back and killed it" (72). Then comes the interpretation of the dream by Ammar, who asks if the man in the dream had the face of the captain. Said answers in the negative but adds that it was an ugly oppressive face that was tormenting him, and thus he gathered it was the captain's. Ammar, however, asserts that the exploitive figure in the dream is "no other than the Sultan" (72) and insists that Said's dream was "a vision prophesying the downfall of the Sultan" (73).

Politicizing Sindbad's tale transforms it from being a sailor's yarn intended to make the audience wonder in amazement to an allegory of the unconscious anxiety of the subalterns. Ashour not only politicizes Sindbad's tale; she also modernizes it structurally through nonlinear unfolding of the narrative. In *The Thousand and One Nights*, Scheherazade tells the story of Sindbad, among other stories, to Shahriyar in a continuous flow, interrupted only by successive daybreaks; likewise, Sindbad the Sailor, who tells Sindbad the Porter his story in a continuous flow, is interrupted only by successive nightfalls. Ashour, on the other hand, being a contemporary writer, fragments the tale of Said in different parts of the overarching novella of *Siraaj*. It is for the reader to interweave together three motifs—departure, return, and dream of the wanderer—to extract the political significance of the narrative.

As in the *Arabian Nights*, we encounter in *Siraaj* several narratives, with some enveloping others in a *mise en abyme* or Chinese-boxes arrangement. In Ashour's novella, we encounter one fable within another: (A) the sultan's tale (and the revolt against him) and within it (B) the story of Said and of the Khedive (and Orabi's revolt against him) and lastly (C) the dream narrative of being oppressed as in Sindbad's third voyage and the revolt against the evil man on the shoulders of Said. It is through the dream interpretation of Ammar—the old African sage, oneiromancer, and slave—that the link between the nightmare and the sultan of the island is revealed. The political lesson of *Siraaj* is embodied in the borrowed tale of Sindbad and its transformation into a dream, interpreted by the characters in the novella—a lesson that was absent in the *Nights*' Sindbad. Here we have a case of staging the story of Sindbad in a narrative to shed light on the Arab world as victim of both external colonization and internal oppression. *Siraaj* is mimetic, using multiple codes of allegorical concealment. The novella tells the story of the uprising of the Arabs and their tragic failure due to collaboration between imperialism and dynastic autocracy. Said's exploitation by the captain and the sultan are presented through the Old Man of the Sea. Yet for the reader, the Old Man stands for misrule and abuses of patriarchy and oligarchy. Just as Ammar, the storyteller in the novella, explains the significance of Said's dream, so is Ashour inviting her readers to interpret her fiction in terms of the here and now. The story of Said's voyage and his dream in *Siraaj* are organically related to the unpacking of the complex plot and to the subaltern consciousness that develops on the island. In the *Nights*, Sindbad's story of the Old Man of the Sea is an autonomous segment juxtaposed to other voyages. Its narrative function in Scheherazade's discourse is time gaining; it is part of an episodic plot. In Ashour's narrative, on the other hand, it is a device contributing to the development of the plot and to a political semantic layer.

Paul Klee's painting known as *Sindbad the Sailor* ("Battle Scene" from the comic-operatic-fantasy *The Seafarer*)[8] is at times known simply as *The Seafarer* (see fig. 16). It presents a battle scene between a human figure and three scary fish surrounded by blue sea that verges on black. It is, in the words of one art critic, "an exercise in tonal gradations as basis for the confrontation of freely invented images representing man, boat and monsters";[9] and, in the words of another, "A scene from a fictitious opera is being enacted within a grid formed of different shades of blues and reds, which become darker towards the edges. The scene depicts the fight . . . between the anonymous hero and three grotesque sea-monsters."[10] The color scheme draws the attention of the viewer to the center of the painting, where the drama occurs, and a narrative component (whether from Sindbad's tale or Odysseus's epic) adds to its significance and complexity, while the lyrical tone envelopes it. In the painting, dramatic, poetic, and narrative elements associated with a wrecked mariner converge.

Paul Klee himself was attracted to more than one art genre. Besides being a painter, he was also a musician and a poet. His interest in drama came from his interest in opera and in making puppets for his only son, Felix. Klee's paintings often include scripts or letters and have been compared to hieroglyphs. The title he gives his works are also indicative of a literary background. Like many nineteenth- and twentieth-century writers and artists, Klee could not but be under the impact of the *Arabian Nights*. He went twice to the Arab world, once in spring 1914 to Tunisia and again in winter 1928–29 to Egypt.[11] His first voyage south was so influential on him that he took up coloring with passion, and it is said to have turned him from a draftsman to a painter. In his diaries during his trip to Tunisia, Klee referred to a wedding in "marvelous Kairouan," comparing it to the *Arabian Nights*: "At first, an overwhelming tumult, culminating that night with the *Mariage arabe*. No single thing, but the total effect. And what a totality it was! The essence of *A Thousand and One Nights*, with a ninety-nine percent reality content."[12]

When Klee was attacked by the Nazis for his "degenerate art," he was associated with the Semites and specifically Arabs: "Then that great fellow Klee comes onto the scene, already famed as Bauhaus teacher in Dassau. He tells everyone he's a thoroughbred Arab."[13] Klee's fascination with Arabesques, Arabic scripts, Arabic motifs, and the *Arabian Nights* is probably due to his interest in polyphony, counterpoint, and music in general. Rainer Maria Rilke commented once on Klee, saying, "Even if you hadn't told me he plays the violin, I would have guessed that on many occasions his drawings were transcriptions of music."[14] Sindbad's voyages, of course, offer a musical structure with repetitions that exhaust themselves at the finale. The very temperament and art of Klee, which combines sophistication with a childlike spirit, the elegant with the primitive, the philosophical with parody, make the *Nights* a suitable companion and a delightful frame of reference.

There are as many interpretations of Klee's art as there are critics. Even the angel in his painting *Angelus novus* is viewed as representative of progress in history, as Walter Benjamin interpreted it in his essay "Theses on the Philosophy of History," which is not surprising given the role of Klee in the leftist Munich Revolution in 1919.[15] O. K. Werckmeister sees in Klee's use of childlike images an expression of "a radical attitude of cultural critique, provocatively stated by means of simplistic images."[16] Others see affinities between his art and that of Tibetan cosmology (Julie Rauer), and also some find Heideggerian connections (Stephen Watson).[17]

If we look at Klee's painting of Sindbad, we see a fragile person confronting three monstrous fish. It is difficult to establish whether Klee is presenting a St. George fighting the dragon or a Don Quixote fighting windmills. Roger Lipsey comments on the painting, saying, "Klee reconceived the archaic theme of a hero combating monsters as a droll encounter between a stick-figure knight burdened by a voluminous, disabling helmet and quilted sea-creatures with confused flounder-like eyes. Klee set this vignette against a beautifully rendered gradation of blues and blacks, as abstract study that is as much the theme of the painting as the mock-heroic encounter itself."[18]

The painting is dated 1923, produced after the end of World War I, in which Klee was mobilized, though he was not sent to the frontlines. He lost many of his friends in the war, so I believe part of the horrors Sindbad is facing in the painting can be seen as those of war and destruction — the lonely soldier confronting the machinery of destruction. For me it is not so much the heroic or the mock-heroic in the seafarer, but it is the lonely man trying to struggle against all odds. The sailor in the painting is the existential hero doomed but still fighting. The landscape, or rather seascape, is cosmic and evokes the dangers of the fluid and unstable against the terra firma. The painting is, first and foremost, about vulnerability and resistance; and in this reading, it joins Ashour's novella. Mark Rosenthal considers the painting Klee's masterpiece, influencing Picasso's *Night Fishing*: "For Klee, the scene . . . concerns the implications of killing the fish, as well as the mythic symbolic suggestion of men alone on the sea at night."[19] William Melaney sees in it a search "to express certain emotional attributes—such as helplessness or human frailty."[20]

The spear in Klee's painting serves two purposes: it functions as a balance pole for the warrior and a deadly weapon.[21] Klee wrote about the dilemma of man caught between his ambitions and his impotence, and the statement seems relevant to the Sindbad painting.[22] He wrote in his *Pedagogical Sketchbook*, "The contrast between man's ideological capacity to move at random through material and metaphysical spaces and his physical limitations is the origin of all human tragedy. . . . Half winged—half imprisoned, this is man."[23]

Klee's painting associated with Sindbad in turn has inspired poets. In 1958, Sylvia Plath, in the spirit of Klee's painting, wrote a poem that both articulates the existential question of being and echoes a nursery rhyme: "Row, row, row your boat, / Gently down the stream. / Merrily, merrily, merrily, merrily, / Life is but a dream." The first of four stanzas sounds like a nursery song, and the second foregrounds human vulnerability in a dreadful world. Plath identifies the three fish as "the whale, the shark, the squid":

> *Battle-Scene*
> It beguiles—
> This little Odyssey
> In pink and lavender
> Over a surface of gently-
> Graded turquoise tiles
> That represent a sea
> With chequered waves and gaily
> Bear up the seafarer,
> Gaily, gaily,
> In his pink plume and armor.[24]

Plath condenses the fable of Sindbad while describing the painting:

> A lantern-frail
> Gondola of paper
> Ferries the fishpond Sindbad
> Who poises his pastel spear
> Toward three pinky-purple
> Monsters which uprear
> Off the ocean-floor
> With fanged and dreadful head.
> Beware, beware
> The whale, the shark, the squid.

Though Sylvia Plath was commissioned to write art poems by *Art News*, she did not do so simply as a way to gain a side income. She herself had been an experimental painter before she decided to focus her creativity on poetry. For her, modern art was an inspiration. In a BBC interview, she said, "I have a visual imagination. For instance, my inspiration is painting," and she wrote in her diaries,

> I had about seven or eight paintings and etchings I wanted to write on as poem-subjects and bang! After the first one, "A Virgin in a Tree," after an early etching by Paul Klee, I ripped into another etching by Klee titled "Perseus, or the Triumph of Wit over Suffering." . . . Friday went just as well: with a little lyric fantasy on a lovely painting by Klee on the comic opera The Seafarer, a long and big one on his painting "The Departure of the Ghost."[25]

What makes such ekphrastic texts successful is the interweaving of the personal in them.[26]

Jonathan Aldrich, on the other hand, uses Klee's painting in a poem he wrote in 1966 titled "To a Young Lady at the Museum," in which he depicts a young spectator seeing the painting and her reaction to it. The poem starts with the way art can represent life. Following the unacceptability in art of "possible improbability"—according to Aristotle—and the acceptability of "probable impossibility," the poet gives an example of a baby next door falling from the seventh floor without injury, which though it actually happened, will not work in a literary drama. The poet then moves in his third and fourth stanzas to Klee's painting and a young woman eyeing it and applying Aristotelian literary criticism to it:

> But take that curious painting by Paul Klee
> Of Sindbad battling a hostile water,
> How strange it seems, how wonderful it is,
> A spear too long for one his size to handle,
> A boat too small to keep a man afloat,
> Three variously decorated fishes,
> Open-jawed but ever held at bay,
> Flatly emerging from the shades of blue.
> No one questions the authenticity.
>
> And that young lady, barely out of school,
> And now passing to the outer gallery,

Having gazed awhile on Sinbad's critical danger
As if it couldn't apply: how could she feel,
In this current turn of nights and days,
The probable impossibility
That one day she will die?[27]

The poet here is using the painting and the viewer to examine the Aristotelian critical position on art: "It is also apparent . . . that the function of the poet is not to speak of incidents which have come to be, but rather of incidents which might come to be."[28] Sindbad as painted by Klee is the test for the theory. And while Aldrich opens the poem with life and art, "considering life, for once, in terms of art," he ends it with, "That one day she will die," thus also stirring issues related to life and death. In juxtaposition, Sylvia Plath presents the agony of Sindbad in the painting but then ends her poem by inserting it in dreams and in a bathtub in which children are playing. The anguish of mimesis and the relation of art to life—and specifically to life crowded with horrors —are at the core of the two poems.

Tim Severin follows the intellectual path taken by his Irish compatriot Oscar Wilde, who toppled the dictum of "art imitates nature," or "literature imitates life," by turning it on its head. In Severin's case, it is reality and life that imitates literature—and fantastic literature at that. He set himself the task of a Sindbadian voyage using the very kind of vessel that Sindbad would have had access to in the Middle Ages.

But before the dream of Severin came true in the early 1980s, adventurers from all over the world wanted to take journeys à la Sindbad using the available dhow sailing ships. Alan Villiers, an Australian journalist who was a commander in the royal navy, wrote about his experience on *Sheikh Mansour* and *Bayan*, sailing crafts commonly known as dhow, in the late 1940s. The title of his contribution to *National Geographic* magazine was "Sailing with Sindbad's Sons." In describing the goods the sailors kept in their chests on the ship, Villiers attaches a subtitle to that section: "Sindbads Gloat Over Their Treasures." He depicts how they examined their wares: "Each man was allowed to bring a chest of his own wares, as in ancient times, when each merchant carried his goods and helped sail the ship. . . . The sailors loved to crowd up on the poop to examine the treasures in their chests, one man turning out his wares, his friends admiringly pawing them, guessing their price in Mogadishu, Salale, or Lamu. I could visualize Sindbad and his companions doing the same."[29] While Villiers and his like visualized Sindbad in their seafaring with Arabs, Severin wanted to experience Sindbad's voyage by sailing from Oman to China.

If Villiers in his voyage was recalling Sindbad, Severin set out to perform the voyage itself to show that it is not mere fantasy of storytellers but corresponds to medieval Arabian travels, attributed in the *Nights* to a protagonist named Sindbad:

> So it is, in my view, with Sindbad the Sailor—or Sindbad of the Sea. His seven voyages . . . are based on real voyages by real sailors. . . . The exotic lands and peoples that Sindbad encountered have intriguing parallels with actual lands described by the early Arab geographers. The more I delved into the legend of Sindbad, the more I suspected that he was no mere fictional hero of children's tales. Rather, he was a composite figure, an amalgam of the Arab sea captains and merchants who ventured to the limits of the known world in the golden age of Arab sail between the 8th and 11th centuries.[30]

Severin describes the voyage of *Sohar*, which was named after the port in Oman from which it sailed but also because the inhabitants of Sohar considered Sindbad a native of the town.[31] Accordingly, Severin tries to locate episodes in the tale of Sindbad geographically. Sri Lanka, for example, is the place where in the second voyage Sindbad finds himself in the valley of diamonds and snakes:

> Although no diamonds are mined in Sri Lanka, the country is world famous for its other precious and semiprecious stones. . . . As in Sindbad's adventure, the gems are found on the valley floors and are dug from pit shafts sunk in the alluvial gravel. Snakes seek out the cool damp of the pit shafts, and it is perhaps significant that the gem trade is still in the hands of Muslims, whose oldest shrines are the graves of Arab sailors who brought their religion to Sri Lanka in the seventh century.[32]

Severin suggests Sumatra to be the location of the incident of the fourth voyage, in which Sindbad encounters cannibals: "Hashish, used in Northern Sumatra as a flavor in food, may have been one source for this gruesome yarn, as well as the existence of man-eating tribes in Sumatra."[33] As for the Old Man of the Sea who sat on the shoulders of Said in his dream—in Ashour's novella based on an episode in one of Sindbad's voyages—Severin believes it is "probably the great ape of Sumatra, the orangutan."[34]

The voyage itself had to be researched and a sailing craft reconstructed to resemble that of Sindbad's, including the stitching of parts rather than the use of nails, using hand-shaped timbers, filling holes with a mix of lime and gum, and mastering medieval technology that is mostly on the wane, if not altogether extinct. Severin wanted to build a classic merchant vessel which could have sailed straight from the pages of the *Arabian Nights*.[35] To capture this 1980 reenactment of a medieval voyage, a volunteer crew of Omani and European sailors was hired to reproduce the voyage of Sindbad crossing the Arabian Sea, the Indian Ocean, and the South China Sea. Cameramen and filmmakers David Bridges and Richard Greenhill were on the ship to keep visual records. Severin recorded the voyage textually in 1982 through an article and a book. Severin's *Sindbad Voyage* and a film with the same title (directed by David Bridges, scripted by Tim Severin, and narrated by Brian Hayes) reproduce the same wonder and amazement we experience when reading the Sindbad voyages in the *Nights*.

The book, besides having illustrations of the vessel and the crew on their voyage and sketches of animals and plants mentioned, also has illustrations from Edward Lane's translation of *The Arabian Nights' Entertainments* (1877). One example is sufficient to demonstrate the suspense readers experience, as if they were listening to the fictional Sindbad himself:

It happened at night. We were attempting to slant across the gut of the narrows, keeping a sharp lookout to avoid the heavy shipping, when the fickle wind swung around. "Captain! Captain! Course south-west!" called Khamees Police who was the watch leader and had the helm at the time. . . . My God! We were right on the edge of the Sands. The bank sloped up very steeply from the edge of the channel. If *Sohar* was caught there in the rising gale, we would be battered to bits. It was all happening quickly. There was not even time to wear ship. The wind was still changing direction. "Let go both anchors," I yelled.[36]

Tim Severin's astounding project is also about man's perseverance to accomplish and arrive at destinations against great odds. He combines reading of the Sindbad cycle with research in medieval geography and field work in Oman; he ends up fulfilling his ambitious dream of sailing in a medieval vessel from Muscat to Canton, following the footsteps of Sindbad and under the same precarious conditions. His experience, rendered in film and book, has inspired two graphic novellas, one by the Egyptian novelist Sonallah Ibrahim, *Rihlat al-Sindbad al-Thamina* (The eighth voyage of Sindbad), and the other by the Algerian artist 'Aidar Mahfouz, *Mughamarat al-Sindbad al-Bahri* (The adventures of Sindbad the Sailor). Ibrahim's graphic strip turns Severin into the hero; Severin's memoir is closely summarized and reproduced with its anthropological information and historical documentation for children and young readers. Combining images with dialogues in bubbles, Ibrahim tells the story of the twentieth-century adventurous voyage faithfully, if not fully. The Algerian author depends more on artistic representations with minimal words while reviving the stories of Sindbad the Sailor of the *Nights*.[37] In Ashour's work, the struggle ends in defeat of the rebellion, spearheaded by Said, the figure that corresponds to Sindbad, but it is nevertheless a heroic struggle. In Klee's work, the outcome of the struggle is not clear. One is left in suspense whether our seafarer is going to make it or succumb. With Tim Severin at last, we get a happy finale despite the dangers of the trip.

As for the film, the voice-over narrates the voyage from its inception as a research project to its departure from Oman and eventual arrival in China, including scenes of fishing aboard the ship, photographing the ship from cameras placed in the sea, meeting Vietnamese boat people seeking refuge, and fixing occasional breakdowns of the vessel. In this film based on live experience, the director inserts scenes based on three voyages of the *Nights'* Sindbad. They are narrated verbally and illustrated visually through a succession of miniature-like paintings. The film thus combines the lived experience, the text, and the image. Severin's astounding and yet factual voyage based on Sindbad's itinerary is also interwoven with John Barth's novel *The Last Voyage of Somebody the Sailor* (1991). Barth's semiautobiographical, magic-realist novel is the story of a certain Simon William Behler (the last name rhyming with "sailor" and the first name alliterating with "Sindbad"), who falls overboard from a ship and then is rescued: "I learned that I had been fished unconscious. . . . With great difficulty, owing to the dizzying coincidence of names, I got it eventually straight that the rescuing vessel was indeed not Captain Severin's *Sohar*, but a larger clone of it named incredibly, *Zahir*, bound from Basra for—incredibly!—the Omani port city of Sohar, the shipowner's birthplace."[38] No doubt Barth is winking to his readers by invoking yet another writer who was enamored by the *Arabian Nights*, Jorge Luis Borges—and in particular his "Partial Enchantment of the Quixote," in which there is a reference to a book called *Zohar*.[39]

The *Arabian Nights* has not only inspired other works in different mediums, but in turn the children of the *Nights* themselves begat other works, and in turn the children begat their own children. In Arabic, a fertile woman who bears many children is called *wallada*. *Alf layla wa-layla* is not only *wallada* or a mother of tales but also by now the grandmother of tales. If Scheherazade has come to be synonymous with the creative writer and narrator, Sindbad has equally become a universal metaphor for the traveler, the wanderer, and the adventurer—of human beings in their journey on earth.

The succession of stories of Sindbad and their transposition, enactment, or rendering in other genres—in paintings, miniatures, poetry, graphic strips, films, memoirs, and semifictional autobiographies—constitute a web of dizzying intertextual connections. What is significant in understanding what I call the syndrome of Sindbad, his presence in so many fields, is (1) how the relation of the real and the documentary, on the one hand, exists with the fantastic and magical, on the other hand, (2) how textual, artistic, and experiential interpretations of the tale are essentially exploration of and comments on mimesis and creativity, and (3) how the entire phenomenon of Sindbadian proliferation should not be confined to direct relations between the *Arabian Nights* as a source and the works inspired by it but should also take into consideration the role of mediations that impact new creations—innovations that build on earlier adaptations and interpretations of the source. Thus, the interpretation of works that recall Sindbad cannot be fully grasped by simply juxtaposing the Sindbad of the *Arabian Nights* to the text, image, or performance that relates to it. Such complex relations between the triggering source and the target outcome can only be understood if we take into consideration the cultural archive, with its intralingual, interlingual, and intersemiotic transfers that have framed the act of interpretation.

NOTES

1. Sindbad undertakes several voyages in the *Arabian Nights*. He recounts his adventures in front of a poor porter. The content of the voyages, including actions and details, change from one manuscript of the *Nights* to another, but all versions converge on the essential number of voyages (seven) and on most of the episodes. For more on Sindbad in the context of the *Arabian Nights*, see Ferial J. Ghazoul, *Nocturnal Poetics: The Arabian Nights in Comparative Contexts* (Cairo: American University Press, 1996), 68–81.

2. Roman Jakobson, "On Linguistic Aspects of Translation" (1959), in *Theories of Translation: An Anthology of Essays from Dryden to Derrida*, ed. Rainer Schulte and John Biguenet, 144–51 (Chicago: University of Chicago Press, 1992).

3. Nabil Haddad, "*Siraaj*: Radwa Ashour bayn al-mutakhayal wal-mawruth al-sha'abi," *Al-Ra'i* 12723 (July 22, 2005): 7.

4. In a review of Ashour's *Siraaj*, Rana Harouny sums up the thrust of the work: "The implacability of the historical forces against which the island's residents unknowingly pit themselves and against which they are ultimately powerless lends a low key menace to the unfolding narrative that is the author's dominant thematic preoccupation" (Rana Assem Harouny, "Review of *Siraaj: An Arab Tale*," *Arab Studies Journal* 15–16 [Fall–Spring 2007]: 169).

5. Victor Shklovsky, "Art as Technique," in *Russian Formalist Criticism: Four Essays*, trans. Lee T. Lemon and Marion J. Reis, 3–24 (Lincoln: University of Nebraska Press, 1965), 13–22.

6. Radwa Ashour, *Siraaj: An Arab Tale*, trans. Barbara Romaine (Austin: Center for Middle Eastern Studies at the University of Texas at Austin, 2007), 2 (hereafter cited parenthetically in the text).

7. Maarouf the cobbler is the protagonist of one of the better-known tales of the *Nights*, and so is Tawaddud, the highly learned slave girl. In *Siraaj*, Tawaddud is a freeborn, poor little girl who loves learning and knowledge, though she does not have access to it. Captivated by texts and literary narratives, she hides beneath a couch in order to eavesdrop on the private lessons of a rich pupil. She even takes away a book from the rich pupil's house, fascinated by its binding and calligraphy.

8. Painted in 1923, oil tracing, pencil, water color, and gouache on paper, bottom strip in water color and ink, framed with gouache and ink, mounted on cardboard. It is 34.5 × 50 cm, in the private collection of Frau T. Durst-Haas, Muttenz/Basel. There is also Klee's drawing of "Battle Scene" (1923) in Klee-Stiftung, Berne.

9. Norbert Lynton, *Klee* (London: Spring Books, 1964), 41.

10. Hajo Düchting, *Paul Klee: Painting and Music* (Munich: Prestel, 1997), 48.

11. Klee's fondness for Arab subjects, motifs, and styles has identified him as a Mediterranean Arab by some critics: "In photographs taken when he was a child, he has the secretive, sensual face of a little Arab. As an adult he was always to feel strongly the lure of the Mediterranean. The thin line of beard running straight from the corners of his mouth, his thick lips and dark, penetrating eyes are characteristically African. And because of this remote influence, which has never been accurately defined by his biographers, his family on his mother's side is suspected of North African connections" (Gualtieri Di San Lazzaro, *Klee: A Study of His Life and Work*, trans. Stuart Hood [New York: Praeger, 1957], 1–2). Apart from these far-fetched physical links, other critics have sought the connection of Klee's art with that of the Orient—China (Constance Naubert-Riser, "Paul Klee et la Chine." *Revue de l'art* 63 [1984]: 47–56) and India (Peg DeLamater, "Some Indian Sources in the Art of Paul Klee," *Art Bulletin* 66 [1984]: 657–72). It is surprising that there is no study I know of in which the Arabic connections with Klee's art have been analyzed.

12. Paul Klee, *The Diaries of Klee, 1898–1918*, ed. Felix Klee (Berkeley: University of California Press, 1964), 297. See also the film directed by Nacer Khemir and Bruno Moll, *Le voyage à Tunis* (Ennetbaden: Trigon-Film/Fama Film, 2007), in which the itinerary of Paul Klee in Tunisia in April 1914 (Tunis, Sidi Bou Said, Hammamat, and Kairouan) is retraced and contextualized. See also Jean Duvignaud, *Klee en Tunisie* (Tunis: Ceres, 1980).

13. *Die Rote Erde*, February 1, 1933, quoted in Susanna Partsch, *Paul Klee, 1879–1940* (Köln: Taschen, 1993), 55.

14. Quoted in Enric Jardi, *Paul Klee* (New York: Rizzoli, 1991), 8.

15. See Helmut Friedel and Justin Hoffmann, *Süddeutsche Freiheit: Kunst der Revolution in München 1919*, exhibition catalogue (Munich: Lenbachhaus, 1993), particularly 30–97. I am thankful to Nicholas S. Hopkins for drawing my attention to this catalogue and translating relevant passages from German for me.

16. O. K. Werckmeister, *The Making of Paul Klee's Career, 1914–1920* (Chicago: University of Chicago Press, 1989), 246–47.

17. Julie Rauer, "Klee's Mandalas: How a Swiss Orientalist Mapped His Tibetan Cosmos," *asianart.com*, April 19, 2006, http://www.asianart.com/articles/klee/index.html; Stephen Watson, *Crescent Moon over the Rational: Philosophical Interpretation of Paul Klee* (Stanford: Stanford University Press, 2009).

18. Roger Lipsey, *The Spiritual in Twentieth-Century Art* (Boston: Shambala, 1988), 186.

19. Mark Rosenthal, "Picasso's *Night Fishing at Antibes*: A Meditation on Death," *Art Bulletin* 65:4 (December 1983): 658.

20. William Melaney, "Paul Klee from Image to Text: A Phenomenological Study," *Constructions* 7 (1992): 32.

21. Rosenthal, "Picasso's *Night Fishing at Antibes*," 658.

22. Klee's "Battle Scene" / *Sindbad the Sailor* / *The Seafarer* has also suggested other seafaring protagonists: "The title of Klee's well-known 'Battle Scene' is not entirely a figment of his imagination for it evokes the water-borne heroes of Wagner's *Flying Dutchman*" (K. Porter Aichele, "Paul Klee's Operatic Themes and Variations," *Art Bulletin* 68:3 [September 1986]: 461).

23. Paul Klee, *Pedagogical Sketchbook*, quoted in ibid., 464.

24. Sylvia Plath, "Battle-Scene," in *The Collected Poems*, ed. Ted Hughes (New York: Harper and Row, 1981), 84–85.

25. Sylvia Plath, BBC interview and dairy entry of March 22, 1958, quoted in Kathleen Connors, "Living Color: The Interactive Arts of Sylvia Plath," in *Eye Rhymes: Sylvia Plath's Art of the Visual*, ed. Kathleen Connors and Sally Bayley (New York: Oxford University Press, 2007), 107.

26. Fan Jinghua, "Sylvia Plath's Visual Poetics," in Connors and Bayley, *Eye Rhymes*, 217. Sherry Lutz Zivley states that this poem of Plath "has no plot and no emotional resonance. If anything, she trivializes the painting's drama by describing the seafarer's 'Odyssey' with diction like 'little,' 'gently,' 'pink and lavender,' depicting the sea as a 'fish-pond' " ("Sylvia Plath's Transformation of Modernist Paintings," *College Literature* 29:3 [Summer 2002]: 37). In fact, Zivley misses on the childlike aspect of the poem, which embodies the very playfulness and childlike imagery that are typical of Klee.

27. Jonathan Aldrich, "To a Young Lady at the Museum," *Massachusetts Review* 7:1 (Winter 1966): 71–72.

28. Aristotle, *Poetics*, trans. Kenneth A. Telford (Chicago: Henry Regnery, 1961), 17.

29. Alan Villiers, "Sailing with Sindbad's Sons," *National Geographic* 94:5 (November 1948): 685.

30. Tim Severin, "In the Wake of Sindbad," *National Geographic* 162:1 (July 1982): 2–406.

31. Tim Severin, *The Sindbad Voyage* (London: Arena, 1983), 24.

32. Severin, "In the Wake of Sindbad," 20.

33. Ibid., 23.

34. Ibid., 29.

35. Severin, *Sindbad Voyage*, 14.

36. Ibid., 200–201.

37. Sa'id Allouch, "Alf Sindbad wa-la Sindbad," *Fusul* 13:2 (Summer 1994): 146–85.

38. Barth, *The Last Voyage of Somebody the Sailor* (Boston: Little, Brown, 1991), 400.

39. In this essay of Borges, in which he refers extensively to the *Arabian Nights'* convoluted structure, he uses the title of *Zohar* (echoing *Sohar*): "We are reminded of the Spanish Rabbi Moisés de Léon, who wrote *Zohar* or *Book of the Splendor*

and divulged it as the work of a Palestinian rabbi of the third century" (Jorge Luis Borges, "Partial Enchantment of the Quixote," in *Other Inquisitions, 1937–1952* [New York: Pocket Books / Simon and Schuster, 1966], 44). In his short story "The Zahir," Borges uses the term *Zahir* several times with different meanings (Jorge Luis Borges, "The Zahir," in *Labyrinths*, trans. Dudley Fitts [London: Penguin, 1962], 189–97).

PART III

Staging

13

The *Arabian Nights* in British Pantomime

KARL SABBAGH

The Christmas and New Year rituals of other countries can be a closed book to the rest of us. How many British (or American) people know that a short film called *Dinner for One* is mass viewing every New Year's Eve in Germany? This eleven-minute comic sketch, filmed in English, gets 20–30 percent of Germans sitting round their TV sets to watch an English comedian no one has heard of perform as an increasingly drunk butler serving his employer dinner with four imaginary guests.

Woody Allen it is not, and yet Germans watch it over and over again. The holiday season would not be the same for them without it. It is the familiarity that makes it important, the shared family experience watching something from those innocent far-off days in the 1960s when it was enough for a comedian to stagger a bit with a bottle in his hand and speak with a slur to get the audience convulsed with laughter.

America's shared family holiday experience is more sedate. I remember the surprise I felt, having been in the United States two or three times at Christmas, to see *The Nutcracker* advertised each time at a local theater. Surely once you have seen one *Nutcracker* you have seen them all? But this was to neglect the ritual nature of the experience, the way in which, for children at least, every viewing has different connotations, a mixture of the familiar overlaid with the new. The child watching *The Nutcracker* at the age of seven has lived through a significant period of her life since the last viewing, even if the parents can hardly believe that a year has passed so quickly.

For the British, a form of live theater called "pantomime" is our Christmas and New Year ritual, but I have found that most foreigners are entirely unaware of what the word has come to mean, let alone what a rich and bizarre variety of performances the word conceals. This is no sedate piece of Marcel Marceau performance art, as some people think. In fact, the word *mime* has nothing to do with the British pantomime these days, although, like the human appendix, it plays a vestigial role in the evolution of the modern performance. Pantomime in the United Kingdom is unique, although it has elements of American burlesque or musical theater. I suspect that if a typical British pantomime were to be mounted on Broadway for the first time, the audience would sit through it mute and uncomprehending while the assorted cast members went through what is for them a familiar and unquestioned series of tropes.

The British pantomime is not one single scripted performance. It is a manner of presenting for the stage one of perhaps twenty or more familiar stories in a stereotyped way. These stories emerged during the late eighteenth and nineteenth centuries from the wave of fantasy literature that included tales by Charles Perrault in France, the Grimm Brothers in Germany, and, of course, various translations of the *Arabian Nights* that reached the West as a result of Antoine Galland's famous version. Stories such as "Cinderella," "Jack and the Beanstalk," "Little Red Riding Hood," "Puss in Boots," "Dick Whittington," "Snow White," "Sleeping Beauty," and "Mother Goose" form the staple of modern Christmas pantomime shows, along with three familiar *Arabian Nights* stories— "Aladdin," "Ali Baba and the Forty Thieves," and "Sinbad the Sailor." In 2004, the latest year for which I have figures, there were fifteen *Aladdins*, fourteen *Snow Whites*, twelve *Cinderellas*, eleven *Dick Whittingtons*, and seven *Jack and the Beanstalks* produced by professional companies in theaters around the United Kingdom.

Each of the scripts of these shows rings the changes on characters, dialogue, and sets which have certain common factors whatever the core story is that is being dramatized. Every pantomime has the following:

- A beautiful young actress, playing a young man. She is known as the Principal Boy. The character of Aladdin would be cast in this way. She would often wear very short shorts, high boots, and flesh-colored tights. In the nineteenth century, at a time when excessive public exposure of female flesh was frowned on, this was seen as dramatic license, perhaps like the exception accorded to Victorian paintings of classical subjects including nude women. One commentator at the time was in no doubt what sort of license this really was:

    The chief object appears to be to put men in women's parts, and women into men's, and, at the same time, to make as great a display as possible of the feminine form. I do not say that this is a creditable object even in one who caters for the public generally; but I am quite sure that it is a vicious object on the part of one who ostensibly provides a holiday entertainment for "the children."[1]

- Another actress, who plays the Principal Boy's lover, or at least "his" sweetheart. Although these two characters are often found in scenes of chaste lovemaking, there is never any hint of lesbianism. It is played straight in both senses of the word.

- An elderly woman character who is played by a middle-aged male actor, usually a well-known comedian. "She" is known as the Pantomime Dame. In "Aladdin," the Pantomime Dame is Aladdin's mother, known as Widow Twankey. Leading tragic actors have also been attracted to the role: Sir Ian McKellen played this role to great acclaim (fig. 14). (I will deal with the Sinification of the Aladdin story later.)

- A Pantomime Villain, a character who becomes the focus of the audience's hostility when he or she appears at various points.

- A pair of characters involved in a lively physical activity such as baking or interior decorating whose main function is to perform slapstick activities with flour, whitewash, or the like.

- An animal character, played by one or two humans in a mock animal skin. The Pantomime Horse is the most frequent, with one actor in the front and one in the back.

- Guest artistes from the world of show business or sport, who play a significant character in the story. The boxer Frank Bruno played the Genie of the Lamp in a pantomime of "Aladdin."

One history of pantomime has summarized the essentials succinctly: "The plot is very simple: The girl dressed as a boy who is the son of a man dressed as a woman, will win the other girl (surprisingly dressed as a girl), with the assistance of a person(s) dressed in an animal skin."[2]

The evolution of the modern pantomime in Britain, and hence the application of an etymologically inappropriate term to the performance, started with a type of theatrical performance called the harlequinade, derived in turn from the commedia dell'arte, imported from Italy in the eighteenth century. This stylized type of theater included a set cast of characters—Harlequin, Columbine, Pierrot, Pantaloon (Pantalone), and Clown. This last character, also called Pulcinella, survives until today in another peculiar English institution, the Punch-and-Judy show.

There were elements of farce and slapstick in the original Harlequinade performance, which in its earliest form was mimed with music, hence panto-*mime*, but later acquired speech and a written script. In its English form, it became a hybrid of two stories, a play based on some folk story or fairy tale and the Harlequinade itself, which took over when characters in the play were transformed into the familiar Harlequinade characters.

The key function of the modern pantomime in British society is to provide a shared experience among a family audience, based on familiarity of story, characters, dialogue, and interactivity. It would be unusual for an individual theatergoer to decide on his or her own to go to a pantomime, whereas there is nothing strange about someone buying a single ticket for a Shakespeare play or a West End musical. Unlike most stage performances, pantomime encourages the audience to take part, in well-worn ways. When the villain comes on, whether an Ugly Sister in "Cinderella" or Abanazer (Abumazar) the evil sorcerer in "Aladdin," the audience is expected to boo. When one of the pair of slapstick comedians is looking for his or her partner, who is actually clearly visible to the audience, the audience is expected to shout out, "Behind you!" And there is then comic business while one actor pretends not to see the other, to paroxysms of giggles from the younger members of the audience. At a certain point in every pantomime, whatever the story, the scriptwriter must contrive a situation in which one character says to another that something is so, and the second character says, "Oh, no it isn't," at which point the first character turns to the audience, who all shout out, "Oh, yes, it is!"

From the earliest days, the repertoire of stories from which panto-mimes were drawn included a small subset of *Arabian Nights* stories. This was not because anyone looked up original Arabic manuscripts or versions but merely because in a wave of Orientalist popularity that followed Galland's translation of these rarely heard stories, they were printed, adapted, and reprinted as children's books and popular general fiction, until they became as familiar a part of the English storytelling repertoire as any of the classic European fairy tales, which share many elements—magic, villains and heroes, switches of fortune, and so on. As early as 1788 there was a production in London of *Aladdin*, inter-twined with the Harlequinade, and "Aladdin" has always been the most popular *Arabian Nights* story.[3]

By the late nineteenth century, the Harlequin elements had all but disappeared from all pantomimes, leaving different comic dramas, each with its own cast of characters, whose only connection with the Harlequinade was a series of comic dramatic elements such as a chase scene, lots of slapstick, and a transformation scene—originally trans-forming the frame story into the Harlequinade or vice versa—which became a theatrical moment in its own right, using the increasingly sophisticated machinery and gauzes that had become part of a large modern theater.

There are two points of interest in the way the *Arabian Nights* stories became part of the conventional popular drama repertoire. One is that only three stories seem to have become incorporated in this way; the other is that once they were part of the repertoire they were both angli-cized and popularized in the same way as every other fairy story or folk tale, grist to the mill whose end product was broad humor, outrageous costumes, magical sets, and typically English wordplay.

To take the first point, Robert Irwin has suggested that because at least two of the three—"Aladdin" and "Ali Baba"—are among the "orphan stories" of Galland's *Nights*, stories for which no original Arabic texts exist, they may have had more immediate appeal.[4] He suggests that Galland felt freer to provide more psychologically appropriate motivations for the characters and more Western-style humor. This would have led to these stories' slipping easily into the canon of Western fairy stories and then, by the same route as the other familiar themes, becoming the subject of pantomimes. "Sinbad," of course, did exist as an Arabic text which Galland translated, but here the material was so rich that you could extract almost any tale of marvels out of the many voyages and adventures he experienced. Perhaps, Irwin suggests, Britain's strong naval tradition made "The Voyages of Sinbad the Sailor" a particularly attractive story to dramatize for a patriotic British audience. There is a common factor in all three stories which may also explain their attraction to Victorian audiences: unlike many *Arabian Nights* stories, these three tales include no sexual content, no nasty erotic stories to be skirted around or bowdlerized.

If you look at the three *Arabian Nights* pantomimes in detail, they provide good examples of how British popular culture responds to ideas of the East. First, the settings as represented in stage sets and costumes are stereotypically "Orientalist": Eastern arches and towers, or desert landscapes and camels; "harem" pants and turbans, or *aqal* and *keffiyeh*; evil-looking moustaches and beards; beautiful dancing girls who perform parodies of belly dances. The picture is complicated by the fact that the story of "Aladdin" is set in China, even though culturally and in terms of the plot line it could be set in any Arab country. The tradition of lampooning China and the Chinese has a longer tradition in the United Kingdom than any caricaturing of Arabs and the Arab world, so a Chinese setting provides more scope for the type of broad humor and wordplay that the English like so much.

The typical pantomime is rooted in British culture, both as part of the professional theater and amateur theatricals. One script of a performance of "Aladdin" put on at a military camp in India in the late nineteenth century shows how rooted in English popular culture the typical pantomime is, and it requires some knowledge of British social history to decode many of the puns embedded in the pseudo-Oriental names. Some examples: Aladdin's mother is the Widow Twankey, named after a type of green China tea. The emperor of China is called Hang-Yu, a polite English curse. His vizier is called Ban-Ting, echoing a nineteenth-century dieting fad named after Dr. Banting, an overweight British undertaker. The vizier's son is Pekoe, another type of China tea. The genie of the ring is called Gin-Sling, a once fashionable cocktail drunk by English expatriates in the Far East. This production had a big cast, with a long list of mock Chinese names too tedious to mention, apart from the military flavor conveyed by the captain of the guard, Ten-Shun, and his lieutenant, Azu-Woz.

Although "Aladdin" is the only story with even a nominal Chinese setting, this Far Eastern tendency has spread occasionally to other *Arabian Nights* stories. In the 1930s musical and film *Chu Chin Chow*, the story of "Ali Baba" was transported to China.

In a recent pantomime of "Ali Baba and the Forty Thieves," a more restrained approach to naming the characters still produced the following: Heelam, a cobbler; Mustapha Dubbul, a fishmonger; and Mustapha Nutha, a greengrocer (English popular culture never tires of the variations that can be wrought on the Arab name Mustafa). "Ali" is another rich source, leading, for example, to Ali Whey and Back Ali, in a production of "Sinbad."

In addition to having funny names, foreigners speak English in very stereotypical ways, usually expressed in pantomime and other popular cultural products by seizing on some small feature in English which a particular foreign national might have difficulty with—pronouncing r as l for example, used interchangeably with both Chinese and Japanese characters, or French speakers' difficulty with *th*, replaced by *z*.

The relevant shibboleth in Arabic is the *p/b* duo—"Balestinian," for example—but this may be too subtle for pantomime scriptwriters, since I have not come across an instance of this particular linguistic foible. Comedy dialogue which stage Arabs speak focuses more on forms of speech than on pronunciation. Arabic uses typical oratorical flourishes such as the vocative *Ya fulan*—for example, *Ya abu shweirib*, "O father of moustaches," meaning a possessor of a distinctive moustache; and in pantomime, this can be exploited in various ways. Here is an interchange between two characters in a script of "Aladdin":

ABANAZAR: One of yours, O Piffling Pedlar of Paint Pots!
MUSTAPHA: (reacting) And who are you going to get to help you, O great and greasy Abanazar?

ABANAZAR: I don't want anyone to help me beat a spindle-shanked, bald-headed, broken-down artist like you, O Chewer of Cheap Chalk-sticks.

Just in case the audience has not yet become attuned to this alliterative trope, the dialogue continues with "O Pot-bellied Porpoise of Palookistan," "O Jerry-built Jiggler of Juvenile Juggling," "thou Dog-faced dauber of Distemper," and "thou Mumbling Muddler of Magic."[5]

"Aladdin," as a story which is set in a sort of Chino-Arabia, gives scope for making fun of citizens of both cultures. Later in the script with the pseudo-Arabic exchanges just quoted, there is this passage presenting all the hallmarks of how Chinese people speak in English pantomime, in the mouth of a laundry-boy called Hoo Sit: "Hoo: Oooo —me find all light. Ooo me find. Me no find—no good for Hoo Sit. Him gettum dirty clothes—soakum—dollyum—scrubum—no sleep —wringum—mangleum—hangum—dryum—ironum—foldum. Hoo Sit eat? No eat—put 'em in basket," and more of the same, ad nauseum, sorry nause*am*.[6]

This stuff is very crude stereotyping, of course, and I suspect that the writer would have put much the same words in the mouth of a character who was a Native American. What is going on here is not really based on the belief by the writer that this is how foreigners speak. Rather, it is part of the process of stimulating a shared recognition in the audience that this is how characters in comedies really speak, so that we are able easily to recognize their presumed nationality. We would be very puzzled, and a little disappointed, if a Chinese character in a pantomime spoke good English, although there are plenty of "real" Chinese who do.

So, as often happens when foreign ingredients are assimilated into British culture, the end product is a peculiarly British creation. Word-play, slapstick, *travesti*, even political and commercial slogans are woven into a performance in which the core story is often so overlaid with "business" that it is barely perceptible as part of the mix.

NOTES

1. W. Davenport Adams, "The Decline of Pantomime," *Theatre*, February 1882.
2. "The History of British Pantomime," *Limelight Scripts*, 2005, http://limelight scripts.co.uk/history.html.

3. John O'Keeffe, *Aladdin*, Theatre Royal, Covent Garden; see Marina Warner, *Fantastic Metamorphoses, Other Worlds: Ways of Telling the Self* (Oxford: Oxford University Press, 2002), 144–50.
4. Robert Irwin, *Arabian Nights: A Companion* (1994; repr., London: I. B. Tauris, 2004).
5. P. H. Adams and Conrad Carter, *Aladdin* (London: Samuel French, 1944), 4–5.
6. Ibid., 7.

14

The *Arabian Nights* in Traditional Japanese Performing Arts

YURIKO YAMANAKA

Ever since the tales of the *Arabian Nights* appeared on the intellectual horizon of the Japanese in the Meiji period (1868–1912), they have continued to be the source of inspiration for writers, poets, playwrights, artists, and cartoonists. Adaptations of the *Arabian Nights* can even be found in traditional and clearly indigenous Japanese performing arts, such as *kyōgen*, *kabuki*, *rakugo*, and *kōdan*. In these adaptations, the narrative structure of the *Nights'* tales has been adapted to suit the highly stylized forms of the traditional Japanese stage.

In order to provide context, let us first give a brief explanation of the genres of traditional performing arts, which might be unfamiliar to some readers. Names of persons are mentioned in the Japanese manner, that is, family name first, followed by the given name.

Kyōgen is a form of traditional Japanese theater that could be said to be an equivalent to a farce or comedy. It was performed along with *nō*, a highly stylized form of musical masked drama. Whereas the content of *nō* is symbolic, solemn, and often tragic, the lighter *kyōgen* pieces, played as an intermission between *nō* acts mainly without masks, provided comic relief with stories of roguery or satire.

Kabuki is a form of dance-drama originating in the seventeenth century. It is known for the elaborate makeup and costumes worn by some of the actors, and sometimes spectacular stage settings. In the very early stages of its development, only females performed. However, for fear of degrading public morals, women were soon banned from performing *kabuki* in 1629, and the all-male style came to be established. Although there are female *nō* and *kyōgen* performers these days, women are, to this day, strictly excluded from the *kabuki* stage (they can enjoy it as spectators, of course).

Kōdan is a style of oral storytelling which is said to have evolved out of lectures on historical or literary topics given by *otogishū* (storytellers) to the lords of the "Warring States" period (fifteenth to sixteenth centuries). It became a popular source of entertainment for the common people in the later Edo period (1603–1868) and Meiji period. *Kōdan* is performed by a single storyteller sitting behind a desk or lectern (*shakudai*) and using wooden clappers (*hyōshigi*) or a fan (*hariōgi*) to mark the rhythm of the recitation. The stories are often historical or historical fiction.

Rakugo is a genre of humorous narrative that is performed by a single storyteller sitting on a *zabuton*, or flat square cushion, on the stage, which is called *kōza*. Always ensconced within the spherical space of his seventy-by-seventy-centimeter-square cushion, the *rakugoka*, or *rakugo*-teller, entertains the audience with lively gestures and voice tones of various characters that he enacts. The differences between *kōdan* and *rakugo* are the following: *kōdan* is narrated usually in the third person, whereas in *rakugo*, the story is told mainly through conversation between the characters acted out by the *rakugoka*. Many *kōdan* tales belong to the "good versus evil" type of stories, with a didactic touch, advocating moral codes of loyalty, justice, and compassion. *Rakugo*, on the other hand, depict funny scenes of everyday life with which the audience can personally identify. A *kōdan* audience listens rather passively to the stories told to them, whereas a *rakugo* performance needs the reaction of the audience, in the form of laughter (or sometimes tears).

Although there have been several Japanese writers, such as Kinoshita Mokutarō or Mishima Yukio, who wrote plays based on the *Arabian Nights* for the "nontraditional" or Western-style theater, we will not be dealing with these in this essay.[1] Please also see my colleague Nishio's chapter 17 in this volume, about the *Arabian Nights* in the Takarazuka all-female musical revue.[2]

Modern Adaptations into Traditional Theatrical Forms

Adaptations of the *Arabian Nights* on the stage go hand in hand with the modernization of theater and importation of Western themes into traditional forms of Japanese theater after the fall of the Tokugawa Shogunate and the beginning of the Meiji period (1868–1912). The first *Arabian Nights* pieces performed onstage in Japan in the very early Meiji years were Christmas pantomimes for foreigners at the Yokohama Gaiety Theatre, which opened in 1870. Yokohama was the port town where many foreigners resided, and these performances were mainly for these foreign residents, acted by foreigners. But Japanese who traveled abroad soon became familiar with the *Arabian Nights* onstage in Europe, and they tried to import it. For example, Yano Ryūkei's translation of "Ali Baba," "Perusia shinsetsu retsujo no homare" (A new Persian story: The heroine's honor; 1887) seems to have been inspired by the pantomime he saw in London (see fig. 32).[3]

What was called the Improvement of Theater Movement (*Engeki-kairyō undō*) was initiated in 1886 in order to make traditional theater into something suitable for the upper- and middle-class public of a "civilized nation" that Japan was striving to be. Two advocates of this movement, a journalist and playwright named Fukuchi Gen'ichirō and an entrepreneur named Chiba Katsugorō, opened the *Kabukiza* (Kabuki theater) in Kobikichō in Tokyo in 1889. The theater had a Western-style façade, and it introduced a full electrical lighting system, keeping up with the most advanced technical trend of Western theaters.[4] Some of the pieces in the new genre called *Zangirimono* (literally "cropped-hair pieces") featured Japanese actors playing characters with cropped hair (as opposed to the traditional hairstyle with a topknot), such as the "Englishman Spencer" (see fig. 7).[5]

It was in this historical context that Enomoto Haryū (1866–1916), a playwright who was a disciple of the aforementioned Fukuchi, wrote "Kigeki Arabiya yobanashi" (A comedy from the *Arabian Nights*), based on Carl Maria von Weber's "Abu Hasan, or the Awakened Sleeper" (1811).

It was performed at the *Kabukiza* in 1906 (Meiji 39). What is interesting is that this comedy was set in modern Japan, and Harun al-Rashid and Zubayda were replaced with Japanese characters, Count and Countess Aoyama. The piece was then performed again in 1915, 1917, and 1919.[6]

Also in 1906, Iwaya Sazanami (1870–1933), a children's story writer, wrote "Uma nusubito" (The horse thief), a *kyōgen* version of "The Simpleton and the Rogue." The original story, night 388 of the *Nights*, is about two thieves who steal the donkey of a simpleton. One of the thieves remains with the donkey's rope around his neck and tricks the simpleton by making him believe that he had been turned into a donkey by the wrath of Allah but was turned back into human shape. Iwaya's adaptation of it, published in *Chūgaku Sekai* (Middle-school world), which was an educational literary journal for middle-school students, was meant to be an *otogikyōgen*, or fairy-tale *kyōgen*, to be performed by schoolchildren. With its limited number of characters, this story was suitable for *kyōgen*, since in most *kyōgen* plays only a few (normally two or three) actors appear. Also, foolishness and roguery are recurrent themes in *kyōgen*. The illustrations that accompanied Iwaya's reworking of the story attest to the fact that he most likely based it on C. F. Lauckhard's German version of the *Nights* for children, *Tausend und eine Nacht fürdie Jugend bearbeitet.*

Iwaya's son, Shin'ichi, later adapted this *kyōgen* script into a *kabuki* piece, and it was performed for the first time in 1956. This piece is played onstage even today (see fig. 13). For example, just recently, it was played at a summer family festival, "Kabuki for parents and children" (Oyako de tanoshimu Kabuki, July 27–29, 2008) at the Nissay theater in Tokyo. Humorous movements of the horse (enacted by two actors) make the piece enjoyable for the young and the old. The present author saw a television broadcasting of the performance of this piece at the Minamiza in Kyoto that was aired on NHK (Japan Broadcasting Company) in 2002. Most of the spectators do not realize at all that it is originally from the *Arabian Nights*. (Such explanations do not seem to appear in any of the theater pamphlets and *Kabuki* magazines.)

These examples of modern adaptations into traditional theatrical forms testify to the popularity of the *Arabian Nights* in Japan. But they also demonstrate how open traditional theater has been to experimentation. Playwrights recognized the entertainment factor in the *Arabian*

Nights stories that could be transferred into a setting and style that was more familiar to the Japanese public.

This sort of experimentation of transplanting foreign literary themes into Japanese theater had already started two decades before Enomoto or Iwaya. In 1884 (Meiji 17), Tsubouchi Shōyō, a famous writer known for introducing the notion of the "novel" into Japan, adapted Shakespeare's *Julius Caesar* into a *jōruri* puppet-play script titled "Shīzarukidan: Jiyū no tachi, nagorino kireaji" (Curious tale of Caesar: Sword of liberty, cutting edge of the aftershock).

As Sugita Hideaki and Nishio have discussed, the *Arabian Nights* in the Meiji period was considered to be part of the Western intellectual repertoire, and not something "Middle Eastern" or "Oriental."[7] This holds true for theatrical adaptations too. For playwrights, the *Arabian Nights* was regarded as one of the prevalent themes of "Western" theater, alongside Shakespeare.

Recent Storytelling Experimentations

We come now to more recent experimentations in the traditional Japanese stage adaptation of the *Arabian Nights*. In 2004, commemorating the tercentenary of the translation of the *Nights* by Galland, the National Museum of Ethnology (Kokuritsu Minzokugaku Hakubutsukan, also known as Minpaku) in Osaka held a special exhibition on the *Arabian Nights* (September 9–December 7, 2004), of which the present author was a curatorial staff member.[8] For the multimedia terminals of this special exhibition, the museum commissioned professional storytellers to perform *kōdan* and *rakugo* versions of the *Arabian Nights* stories. The choice of the tale and the scriptwriting was done in collaboration with the performers, the film team (Espa), and the curatorial staff of the special exhibition headed by Nishio Tetsuo. These films can still be viewed by visitors in the multimedia terminals in the permanent exhibition hall (multimedia program 6022, "Arabian Nights").

Kyokudō Nankai performed a *kōdan* version of the tale of "Ali Baba and the Forty Thieves." The story of the clever and loyal Marjiana protecting her master from the thieves fits the *kōdan* genre well, since loyalty and "good versus evil" are important themes in the didactically inclined *kōdan* tales. Kyokudō's well-timed beat of the clappers accentuates the rhythm of the narrative, and rich onomatopoeia ani-mates the scenes of suspense, for example, when Marjiana pours siz-zling hot oil into the pots where the thieves are hiding.

Next, Katsura Kujaku told the story of "The Hunchback" (nights 24–34) as *rakugo*. The interpolated episodes of the barber's brothers were cut out, of course, to keep the performance from being too lengthy. One can see in his performance how the *rakugoka* entertains the audience with lively gestures and voice tones to enact the various characters. For example, the scene in which the hunchback chokes on a big piece of fish that was served to him by his hosts is one of the high points of the narrative. Since "The Hunchback" is a story in which the humor is built around the reaction and interaction of the characters, it easily transforms into a *rakugo* performance. Moreover, there is a popular classic *rakugo* dating sometime from the later Edo period (first half of nineteenth century) titled *Rakuda* (Camel), which is about a corpse of a dead man, whose nickname was "Rakuda," that gets transported from place to place.[9] Thus, the motif of "what do we do with this dead body?" is actually familiar to *rakugo* fans.

In the filmed version for the multimedia program, the original Middle Eastern setting has not been changed so much: the Jewish doc-tor appears as a Jewish doctor, and a drunken Christian is a drunken Christian. However, for the gallery performance,[10] the scenario was completely readapted by a *rakugo* writer, Osada Sadao, who gave a completely Japanese setting to the story. The title was also changed to "Taheimochi" (Tahei's rice cake).

The new story line by Osada is as follows: A traveling comedian stops at an inn in the outskirts of Osaka, run by Tahei and his wife. Their specialty is a sweet called Taheimochi (*mochi* is a kind of sticky rice cake). In order to amuse the man and wife, the comedian makes a funny performance out of eating the *mochi* (throwing it in the air and catching it in his mouth), but he chokes on it and drops dead (or so they think). The fish fried whole in the hunchback story becomes a *mochi*, a Japanese sweet that actually is notorious for getting stuck in the throat if one does not chew on it well. Osada kept the main character types —the buffoon, the man and wife, the doctor, the servant, the drunkard, the judge—that are actually familiar figures that feature in many *rakugo* narratives. And instead the writer cleverly removed the religious factor

(Jew, Christian, Muslim) that stood out as exotic to the Japanese *rakugo* audience. Thus, the essence of the interaction is preserved and can be acted out by the skills of the *rakugoka*, without giving the audience the awkward feeling of seeing something "out of place." If one compares the film version and the gallery performance version (of which we unfortunately do not have a recording), one can see the different degrees of adaptation. Kujaku has performed this Japanized piece on several occasions to a general public, outside the context of the *Arabian Nights* exhibition, most recently on November 28, 2009, in Tokyo.

Conclusion

As we have seen, out of the great variety of tales in the *Arabian Nights*, the Japanese playwrights chose exactly the type of tale that would be congenial to the particular stage genre they were dealing with, and they did not always stick to the more familiar and well-known episodes of the *Nights*.[11] Iwaya chose for his *kyōgen* script the humorous tale of "The Simpleton and the Rogue." And when it was made into *kabuki* by his son, the entertainment factor was enhanced by the visual effects of funny costumes and makeup and flamboyant actions. "Ali Baba" conforms perfectly to the art of storytelling of *kōdan*. And looking at the *rakugo* performance of "The Hunchback," one can almost imagine the atmosphere of an oral performance of the hunchback story that might have taken place in a coffee shop in medieval Baghdad.

NOTES

1. See Sugita Hideaki, "The *Arabian Nights* in Modern Japan: A Brief Historical Sketch," in *The Arabian Nights and Orientalism: Perspectives from East and West*, ed. Yuriko Yamanaka and Tetsuo Nishio, 116–53 (London: I. B. Tauris, 2006).
2. For the general history of the reception of the *Arabian Nights* in Japan, see Yamanaka and Nishio, *Arabian Nights and Orientalism*.
3. Sugita, "*Arabian Nights* in Modern Japan," 143.
4. Edison invented the lightbulb in 1879, and the world's major grand theaters installed electric lighting systems soon after: Paris Opera in 1880, London Savoy in 1882, Boston Bijou in 1882, and Stuttgart Landes theater, Munich Residenz theater, and Vienna State Opera in 1883.
5. In 1891, an English balloonist named Spencer parachuted down into Ueno Park in Tokyo, causing such a sensation that the event was made into a *Kabuki* play.

6. Sugita, "*Arabian Nights* in Modern Japan," 144.

7. Ibid., 151; Nishio Tetsuo, "The *Arabian Nights* and Orientalism from a Japanese Perspective," in Yamanaka and Nishio, *Arabian Nights and Orientalism*, 162.

8. The catalogue of this exhibition is available in Japanese only: *Arabian naito hakubutsukan*, ed. Nishio Tetsuo (Osaka: Toho shuppan, 2004).

9. In 1821, two camels were brought to Japan for the first time by Dutch tradesmen and were paraded from Nagasaki to Edo (Tokyo) as a novel and curious attraction. The dead character in the *rakugo* is said to have been nicknamed after the camel because he was large and good-for-nothing like a camel. (The Japanese at the time did not know the practicality of the camel in its own habitat.)

10. Performed on September 12, October 10, October 29, November 3, and November 27, 2004, in the Special Exhibition Hall of the National Museum of Ethnology.

11. In Japan also, the most famous *Arabian Nights* tales are that of "Aladdin," "Ali Baba," and the frame story with Scheherazade.

15

"Nectar If You Taste and Go, Poison If You Stay"

Struggling with the Orient in Eighteenth-Century British Musical Theater

BERTA JONCUS

Music and dance were vital to eighteenth-century British theater and contributed strongly to how it staged the Orient. Compositions and choreographies coalesced with many other elements—dialogue, action, décor, and costume—in phantasmagoric conceits whose associations were typically made to dovetail with a production's generic demands. This Orient was a product, persistently reconfigured out of common biases toward the East and mapped onto existing practices of dance and music to attract audiences—and often to show a principal player to advantage. Early modern British writings had traditionally depicted the Orient as a theatricalized sphere where power was enacted, rather than possessed;[1] through the music and dance of mid-eighteenth-century London, this theatricalized Orient was plundered for its props.

"Eastness" was troped in instantly recognizable ways: sexual license —represented by the harem and its ruler—a surfeit of luxury, and excessive, corrupting passion. In typical late Baroque fashion, musical numbers were, dramatically, static: characters embodied, through song or dance, a series of affective states called for by the stage action. Because music and dance drew almost exclusively on standardized forms, these forms could seem to domesticate the East. Onstage figures were comfortably familiar, even in Oriental guise, in ways that adumbrated the appropriation of *Nights'* tales in pantomime a century later, as Karl Sabbagh describes in chapter 13 of this volume. An analysis of productions across a range of eighteenth-century genres—dance, masque, pantomime, and English opera—shows how London stage music and dance purged the Orient of otherness to gesture toward the East for its own pleasure.

Orientalism in Music and the Dynamics of Representation

The Oriental-themed musical productions reviewed for this essay share features and also imply certain practices of spectatorship. Unlike history-based serious drama, the action of Orientalist musical theater was either freely invented or lifted from earlier French theater. Invention in particular was used across genres: in the pantomime *The Genii* (1752) and in musical comedies such as *The Enchanter* (1760), *The Captive* (1769), and *The Seraglio* (1776). Nor did London musical theater productions aim for spectator identification with the onstage character. Unlike tragic actors, who might simultaneously impersonate and appear to be inhabited by the Orient,[2] players in Orientalist musical theater relied on virtuosity, either in song or dance, to engage their audiences. In this context, Oriental names, costumes, and settings were no more than a patina, lending exoticism to the players' representation of themselves. While serious drama might offer the potential for "interpenetration" between East and West,[3] musical theater conjured up an East whose appearance was foreign but whose sound and stage movements were bound to local tradition.

This was an Orient for Western consumers and theater habitués, designed, as in nineteenth-century pantomime, to be identifiable according to London's fashionable stage practices.[4] In eighteenth-century musical theater, Oriental figures of authority such as the sultan were either ridiculed or underwent a conversion to European manners thanks to a reforming female. This female (sometimes English, usually Oriental) enlightened the ruler through her faithfulness in love, a theme long popular in Enlightenment Italian opera. The reforming female's Oriental name and associations—Zayda, Selima—helped to spice up a dramatis persona that was otherwise wholly a product of the London stage. In this, British theater followed the pattern of earlier French Oriental romances in which, for instance, a fictional female figure, by improving manners, would articulate female agency within her own culture, whether Eastern or Western.[5] The characters of midcentury British Orientalist operas were also largely those of Italian opera, combined with British comic types in low-style or sentimental roles. The ruler facing conflict, the jealous queen, and the faithful maiden were reclothed as Oriental figures who expressed the affects traditionally linked to them. One finds, therefore, amorous and bellicose Eastern rulers expressing their fervor and/or rage, scheming sultanas singing about jealousy, and faithful young maids like Zayda voicing sentimental joy.

English opera composers, in setting either newly written or translated French librettos, drew on conventional Italianate, *galant*, and British vocal writing. The lexicon of "Turkish" stage choreographies was entirely French, with steps and gesture taken from court dance. In eighteenth-century pantomime, carnivalesque harlequinade filtered the Orient through discordant combinations of exhibitionist physical theater, riotous antinarrative, and *le danse noble*. The music in all these works was firmly rooted in London stage traditions. The curiosity about the East that inspired composers in Vienna and Paris was notably absent in London, even when British composers borrowed works from these urban centers. In France, ethnographic interest in Turkish music had been cultivated since the Renaissance; in central Europe, Jannisary bands had long influenced court music.[6] In British musical theater, by contrast, seeming "authenticity" was largely confined to stage décor.

Across London's musical stage genres, exotic Ottoman- or Arabic-style decoration suggested imperial and commercial ambitions, making far-flung domains seem at the command of a nation whose economic reach collapsed distance. Fantastic imaginings and fears of the Oriental Other were displayed, yet their power was denied through the conventionally sonic environment in which these works unfolded and the stock resolutions with which they ended. The principal vocalist or dancer typically emerged as the organizing force behind a production designed in the first instance to satisfy audience demand to see a celebrity in action. Stylized airs and choreographies heightened affective points featuring the player, while suspended action allowed the audience to appreciate visual spectacle.

In the sections which follow, individual studies show how the choreographies, compositional procedures, and stage designs of various musical theater genres refracted the Orient through London performance practices, creating an imagined East whose indigenous sounds and movements were left unvisited.

Dancing Turks and *The Sultan*

Among London theater genres, perhaps none showcased performers as much as did stage dance. From the Restoration onward, French dance masters had dazzled London's theatrical audiences with choreographies for themselves and their colleagues.[7] In masque, pantomime, and independent dance numbers, three types of stage dance were cultivated: serious dance based on *le danse noble*, such as the sarabande or the gavotte; scenic dance, relating a story in pantomimic movement; and grotesque dance, painting the humors of a character, such as a commedia dell'arte or stage stereotype such as the French peasant.[8] All choreographies combined standardized step units—for example, pirouettes, cabrioles, the *échappé, chassé, coupé, entrechat*, and *rond de jambe*—with carefully prescribed hand and head positions.[9]

Solo dances for the "Turk" were grotesque and as such representative of "character," that is to say, a reduction of perceived qualities shown in polite forms. One of the most celebrated such representations on the Baroque European stage was the final act ("La Turquie") of the opéra-ballet *L'Europe galante* (1697).[10] After this production in Paris, the vogue in London for such entertainments grew, and from 1720, dances by the "Turk" or the "Sultan" became the most frequent of new Ottoman-themed musical productions (see table 1).

Of the many advertised "Turkish" dance numbers in London, notation has survived for only one: the "Türkish Dance Perform'd by Mr Desnoyer & Mrs Younger" (fig. 27).[11] A three-part independent number performed by Philip Desnoyer and Elizabeth Young, its choreography by Anthony L'Abbé, concluded L'Abbé's *A New Collection of Dances*

Table 1. London Stage Orientalist Music and Dance, 1720–1778

Playwright/ composer	Title	Genre (as published)	First performed*	Music	Playbook/ song verses	Earlier source / notes from advertisement
	The Sultan and Sultaness	entertainment	LIF 24 Feb. 1720			*The Sultan and Sultaness* by de la Garde's Two Sons. Benefit de la Garde's Two Sons.
	Turkish Ceremony	dance	KT 29 Apr. 1720			*Le Bourgeois Gentilhomme* [with] *The Great Turkish Ceremony*. Dancing by Danjeville [visiting French Comedians, dir. Monsieur de Grimbergue; likely based on original scene by Molière, Lully, the tailor Baraillon, and the Chevalier D'Arvieux; first perf. Château of Chambord, 1670]
Anthony L'Abbé [choreog.] / André Campra	Turkish Dance	dance	DL Jan. 1721–22	*New Collection of Dances by Mr L'Abbé* (c. 1725)		Advertisement not found; edition states "Peform'd by Mr. Desnoyer & Mrs. Younger" [music by André Campra, *L'Europe Galante* (1697)]
	Dance after the Turkish Manner	dance	DL 6 Jun. 1723			After the Turkish Manner, as it was perform'd by the Kister Aga and the Eunuchs of the Seraglio, for the Diversion of the Grand Signior at the last Bairam Feast
	Turks' Dance	dance	DL 26 Mar. 1724			*Turks' Dance* by Thurmond and Mrs Younger
Anon. / J. C. Pepusch	The Sultan	masque	LIF 28 Nov. 1724			Vocal Parts all new Set to Musick. With proper Dances. With Alterations . . . all the Characters new dress'd [replaces Henry Purcell's original masque featuring Cupid, Silvanus, Bacchus, Flora; first perf. Dorset Gardens, 1690]

Micheal Poitiers [choreog.]	Diana's Madness; or, Fatime, a Favourite Slave in the Seraglio, Mad for Love, and Crown'd Empress by the Grand Signior: With Pantlon and Harlequin Eunuchs elected Kaimcan and Ciguir, the one impaled and the other sawed asunder, the Bashas Selim and Achmet ript [sic] open, Rabca strangled, and Chistar beheaded	dance	KT 5 Nov. 1726		The Carneval after the Venetian Manner. Dancing by Masqueraders in diverse Characters, by Madmen, and by Turks Men and Women being the Invention of Mr Poictiers [sic]. By His Majesty's Command
	Grand Turkish Dance	dance	DL 4 May 1726		A *Grand Turkish Dance* by Thurmond, Boval, Lally, Haughton, Duplessis
	The Sultana	dance	DL 5 Jan. 1728		By Miss Robinson, Jr, a Scholar of Mr Essex's, being the first Time of her performing in that Capacity, particularly *The Sultana*
	Turkish Dance	dance	GF 23 Feb. 1730	lost	A new *Turkish Dance* by Burny and Miss Sandham
Henry Carey / John F. Lampe	Amelia	opera	HAY 13 Mar. 1732	"Amelia wishes when she dies" British Library, G.316.q.(11.); "Farewel [sic] Amelia lovely Fair sweetest of thy sex," *British Musical Miscellany*, vol. 3 (1735)	A new English Opera (after the Italian Method)

(*continued*)

Table 1 (*continued*)

Playwright/ composer	Title	Genre (as published)	First performed*	Music	Playbook/ song verses	Earlier source / notes from advertisement
	Turkish Seraglio	dance	DL 25 Oct. 1742			The *Turkish Seraglio* by Brunoro, Boromeo, Mlle Bonneval, Sga Constanza, &c
	Turkish Dance	dance	DL 10 Mar. 1737			*Turkish Dance* by Muilment, Villeneuve, Livier
Giuseppe Salomon [choreog.]	Turkish Pirate; or, A Descent on the Grecian Coast	dance	DL 27 Dec. 1746			There is now in practice . . . the *Turkish Pirate* . . . compos'd by Giuseppe Salomon [adv. 25 Dec. 1746] A new Grand Dance call'd the *Turkish Pirate; or, A Descent on the Grecian Coast* by Salomon, Mlle Violetta, Sga Padouana, M. Mechel, Salomon's Son, etc. . . . New Scenes, Dresses and Decorations for the dances. The New Grand Ballet, call'd the *Turkish Pirate* [was] . . . perform'd last Monday at Drury Lane, with uncommon applause. The Scenery was well contriv'd, the habits very elegant, and the dance in a taste particularly agreeable. [*London Courant, or New Advertiser*, 31 Dec. 1746]
Henry Woodward / John E. Galliard	The Genii, An Arabian Night's Entertainment	pantomime	DL 26 Dec. 1752	*The comic Tunes in the Genii* (1753)	not pubd.	*Comic Tunes* only published
Anon. / Thomas Arne	The Sultan, or Solyman and Zaida	masque	CG 1 Feb. 1758, rev., 23 Nov. 1759	"Solyman and Zayda Sung by Mr Beard & Miss Brent," in T. Arne, *A Choice Collection of Songs*, xii (1761)	1759	Replaces 1724 music by Pepsuch; same characters
	A Grand Turk's Dance	dance	KT 24 Mar. 1760			*A Grand Turks Dance*

Author	Title	Genre	Theatre / Date	Music / Publication	Date	Notes
David Garrick / John C. Smith	The Enchanter	comic opera	DL 13 Dec. 1760	J. C. Smith, The Enchanter: A Musical Entertainment (1760)		
	Turkish Coffee House		KT 13 Dec. 176		1760	A Dance called The Turkish Coffee House
	New Turkish Dance	dance	CG 9 May 1765			A New Turkish Dance by Lariviere (his first appearance on [the] English Stage)
Isaac Bickerstaff / Charles Dibdin, et al.	The Captive	comic opera (pasticcio)	HAY 21 June 1769	The Songs in the Comic Opera of The Captive (1769)	1769	From John Dryden's Don Sebastian (preface to ed.); but see Lewis Theobald, Happy Captives (1741), after Book IV, Part 1, of Cervantes's Don Quixote ("The History of the Slave"). NB: Bickerstaff added harem; two rival females now inmates, rather than relatives
	Turkish Ballet	dance	KT 29 Apr. 1773			A Turkish Ballet in which Mlle Heinel will dance in the character of a Sultana, for the last time in this kingdom
Isaac Bickerstaff / Charles Dibdin, et al.	The Sultan; or, A Peep into the Seraglio	dramatic entertainment	DL 12 Dec. 1775	1775 music lost; four airs, two by Dibdin, settings of John C. Bach and Tommaso Giordani; "Blest Hero who in Peace and War," rev. John Hook, pubd. as songsheet (1783)	1778? 1780 Dublin	After Charles-Simon Favart, Soliman Second, airs by Paul César Gibert, first perf. Paris, Comédie-Italienne, 9 Apr. 1761 [based on Jean François Marmontel's Contes moraux, pubd. in Le Mercure]

(continued)

Table 1 (*continued*)

Playwright/composer	Title	Genre (as published)	First performed*	Music	Playbook/song verses	Earlier source / notes from advertisement
Charles Dibdin / Dibdin, et al.	The Seraglio	comic opera	CG 14 Nov. 1776	*The Overture, Songs, &c., in The Seraglio ... The Music chiefly compos'd by C. Dibdin* (1776)	1776	
George Collier / Thomas Linley, Sr.	Selima and Azor	Persian tale (comic opera)	DL 5 Dec. 1776	*Selima and Azor, A Persian Tale ... Composed by Tho. Linley, Senr* (1776)	1784 (songs pubd. 1776)	After *Zémire et Azor*, André-Ernest-Modeste Grétry, libretto Jean François Marmontel; Fontainebleau, 9 Nov. 1771; based on *La belle a la bête*; names and the setting from *Amour pour amour*, a verse play by Pierre-Claude Nivelle de la Chausée (1742)
Abraham Portal / Thomas Linley, Sr.	The Cady of Bagdad	comic opera	DL 19 Feb. 1778	Not pubd.; British Library, Add. MS 29297	1778, songs only	*Le cadi dupé*, Pierre-Alexandre Monsigny (Paris Foire St-Germain, 4 Feb. 1761) and Christoph Willibald Gluck (Vienna, Burgtheater, 8 Dec. 1761); libretto, Pierre René Lemonnier

* DL (Drury Lane); GF (Goodman's Fields); KT (King's Theatre); CG (Covent Garden)

(c. 1725).[12] Designed and performed by London's leading French dance masters—L'Abbé had been London's star dancer from 1698, and Desnoyer was in ascendance; both were dance masters to the royal family— it involved breathtaking displays of agility, virtuosity, and physical discipline. Desnoyer must have danced this number during his first London visit between January 1721 and May 1722, before L'Abbé documented this appearance in his collection.[13] The choreography of L'Abbé's "Türkish Dance" (fig. 27) is a veritable glossary of French dance steps. Yet, as Linda Tomko has shown, curious deviations from normative execution and ordering show how these steps could be used to aestheticize transgression and Otherness.[14]

L'Abbé set his dances to three accompaniments by André Campra from the finale of the epoch-making "La Turquie" in *L'Europe galante* referenced earlier. The three numbers were a march and two "airs" (dance tunes), all of which had alternated with vocal parts in the 1697 production.[15] Excerpted by L'Abbé in London twenty-five years later, the instrumental movements were strung together as three continuous dance sections: Desnoyer's solo, Young's solo ending in a duet with Desnoyer, and their final duet.

While relying on standardized steps, the choreography, as Tomko points out, abandons many conventions: asymmetries abound, standard individual steps are reconfigured, and combinations of steps push the boundaries of the physically possible.[16] Uniquely among independent dances for the London stage, both dancers remain onstage throughout and watch each other's solos. The solos themselves suggest a mood, personality, and story within a category of dance which was usually nonmimetic. The longest dance is Desnoyer's solo, set to the march. Watched by the female, the male dancer steps onto the flat of the foot—defying dance etiquette—then launches into a series of one-foot sustained holds, rapid one-foot hops, half-turn jumps, and *tour en l'air*, prowling about in front of the woman in an angular path that he finishes with his back to her. Changing speeds, turns in direction, and the asymmetry of recurrent triple-measure (rather than duple-measure) step units allude to an unruliness, otherness, and sexual license contained by courtly movement.[17] For Tomko, the second glissade in the music's last bar, which finishes by balancing on the left foot while lifting and suspending the right, resonates deeply with the cultural Othering in concurrent "Turkish" choreographies in Western European court culture, as well as with contemporary French illustrations of Turks.[18] L'Abbé seemingly exploited both Desnoyer's talents and London's tradition of pantomimic storytelling to leverage Orientalist biases into a spectacular, genre-bending display of le danse noble.

Campra's 1697 music, reused for this choreography, deployed more traditional signifiers to indulge appetites for the exotic. The metric structure and final cadence of the march draw on French versions of the moresca, a Renaissance dance whose identification with Moors was generic rather than ethnographic.[19] Cultivated in Germany, France, and England—where it was also known as the morris dance—it was traditionally performed by men with blackened face with bells attached to their legs; some Renaissance choreographies even showed a stylized battle between Moors and Christians.[20] In Campra's march/moresca for "La Turquie" (see ex. 1), he used this dance to signify primitivism, in part by thwarting contemporary conventions for a march. The first subject, played as a solo, outlines a simple tonic triad on the downbeat, signifying an impoverished musical vocabulary. The imitation, by being limited to the middle and lower voices instead of traveling throughout the texture, suggests ignorance of standard counterpoint. Imitation unfolds in square phrases without variation, conveying clumsiness.[21] Channeling the moresca's associations, Campra deformed the conventions of court music, as L'Abbé did those of dance, to depict an uncouth Other. For those who were educated in dance and music, this representation of "Turkish" ignorance and crudity would have been clear. Less erudite audience members could merely have reveled in Desnoyer's artistry.

Keying off L'Abbé's choreography was an important early Orientalist masque, The Sultan. Created in 1724, it replaced a masque by Henry Purcell that had traditionally concluded John Dryden's drama The Prophetess; or, The History of Dioclesian (1690).[22] The Sultan received two musical settings, first by John Pepusch in 1724 and then in 1758 by Thomas Arne; both are now lost, although a duet added by Arne in 1759 survives. John Rich, the manager of Lincoln's Inn Fields, revived Dryden's play as part of his strategy to rival Drury Lane's mainpieces.[23] Why the new masque? In Purcell's original, Cupid, Bacchus, and a shepherd each urge female characters to enjoy "the pleasures of love";[24]

Marche des Bostangis

In: André Campra, *L'Europe Galante*, "La Turquie" (1697)

Edited by Christopher Gould

André Campra

Original scoring: violin dessus, haute-contre de violon, taille de violon, quinte de violon and basso continuo

Ex. 1

the dramatis personae of *The Sultan* likewise advocate the pursuit of amorous delights. In *The Sultan's* seraglio, libidinous abandonment is sanctioned, even as it is in Purcell's scenes. Masques traditionally closed a play by representing scenes of revelry;[25] by switching Purcell's masque for *The Sultan*, Rich provided new diversion within a canonic main piece while still fulfilling generic expectations. The prominence of the Ottoman Sultan Ahmed III in London newspaper reports likely encouraged Rich to choose an Oriental theme when sprucing up *The Prophetess*. Throughout the spring of 1724, conflict threatened between Russian and Ottoman forces in rivalry for Persian territories, a stand-off culminating in the French-brokered Treaty of Constantinople on 12 June 1724.[26] News of these events appeared regularly in London news-papers, building in intensity from March 1724.[27]

Although public interest in far-off imperial disputes may have helped inspire Rich to mount *The Sultan*, its action was on a plane far removed from that of the geopolitical. Its playbook, formerly thought lost, reveals that this masque, like L'Abbé's "Türkish Dance," was based on "La Turquie" from *L'Europe galante*, which in June 1724 had been revived and republished in Paris.[28] Because Rich actively followed trends in French dance,[29] it is likely that this recent production, as well as the popularity of L'Abbé's choreography, also encouraged Rich to mount his own ver-sion the work. Yet *The Sultan* differed fundamentally from "La Turquie." While keeping the plot outline and *dramatis personae* of the source, the adaptors in London discarded its original music, verses, characteriza-tions, and (apparently) dances.

"La Turquie" of 1697 opens with Zayde celebrating her love for Zuli-man. Roxane enters, reproaching Zuliman for abandoning her for Zayde. Zuliman declares that he must follow his affections, against which Roxane protests. Zayde reenters to sing another air, accompanied by a female chorus ("les Sultanes"), rejoicing in Zuliman's love; Zuliman then joins her in a duet. Roxane reenters and tries to stab her rival, but Zuliman wrests the dagger from her hand and exiles her from court. The act concludes—in a manner standard to French court spectacle —with a six-section divertissement, titled "Fête Turque," from which L'Abbé had taken Campra's music for his "Türkish Dance."[30]

The action within each act of *L'Europe galante* represented the manner in which different nations—France, Spain, Italy, and Turkey—acted as lovers. In "La Turquie," representation of a "Turkish" *galant* involved a reversal of traditional accounts of Ottoman Soleyman I's enslavement to his concubine and later wife, the Slav Roxelane. According to early Oriental "histories," she convinced Soleyman to order the killing of his eldest son (by another woman) to clear the way for the accession of her son by Soleyman.[31] In "La Turquie," by contrast, the ruler proves his authority by disarming an opponent (Roxelane) and saving his own *amour propre*. Into this story was also inserted the "sensible" Zayde, whose name would have resonated with Madame de la Fayette's popular romance *Zaïde, une histoire espagnole* (1669; English translation 1678) and Molière's slave girl in *Le Sicilien* (1667; English translation 1714).[32]

The action of 1697 also capitalized on a longstanding fascination with the seraglio, which denoted, as was typical in Orientalist literature, the harem's apartments—rather than, as was correct, the Sultan's palace.[33] Depicted as a torrid zone forbidden to male visitors, the harem was a focal point of Orientalist fantasies, from fabricated accounts in travelogues through to letters and romances.[34] "La Turquie" and *The Sultan* were of a piece with earlier French and English works seeking to penetrate this forbidden sphere with pretended knowledge. Along with later British "seraglio" comic operas, *The Sultan* of 1724 teased, through title and setting, with the promise of a peepshow that never materialized. In London, titillation was paired with opprobrium, as generic plot types dictated that Oriental stage heroines reform their libidinous masters.

The Sultan of 1724, besides retaining its seraglio location, also kept the *dramatis personae* of "La Turquie." This choice highlights a function served by stage characters' names that was vital to London musical productions generally. Through apposite writings, fictional figures such as Soliman, Zayda, and Roxana invoked associations which could enrich an impoverished playbook. Not only did music necessarily reduce the dialogue, but theater personnel also proved willing to dumb down action and speech to appeal to London audiences, as they did when adapting *The Sultan*. Personae that were densely textured in earlier writings could in these circumstances restore dignity to the attenuated plot. Of the three figures in *The Sultan*, Roxana was the most celebrated. She had figured in early modern Oriental "descriptions" (histories), fictional writings, and stage productions. By the early eighteenth century, the name Roxane had come to denote a character who "no matter what the plot in which she appeared, embodied . . . womanhood itself; mysterious, sensual, resentful."[35]

The exigencies of the London stage demanded drastic revision, however, of all musical aspects of "La Turquie." The sung *récit* of the Paris original was replaced by spoken dialogue, as indicated by the playbook's typeface, sung sections being shown in italics. New material placed Roxana, played by the favorite soprano Jane Barbier, center stage; she received a revenge aria replete with similes, as was customary with the *dramma per musica*, roles in which she had often appeared.[36] Barbier's offstage reputation happily overlapped with the character of Roxelane: John Hughes, librettist of the English opera *Calypso and Telemachus* that Barbier had led in 1712, complained that the prima donna was an "Angel when pleas'd, when vex'd a shrew."[37] Her new aria articulated her volatile on- and offstage character. By contrast, her rival Zayde celebrated modern polite sentiments in a simple strophic air ("But, may a lasting Passion prove / Our Lives, one mutual Scene of Love"). This was performed by Isabella Chambers, a stage ingénue who had sung her first role the previous year.[38] Solyman, formerly a bass, was now a tenor—John Laguerre, another favorite singer—who praised Zaida's graces in song and rebuked Roxana in a short duet. The stage action was telescoped into just three sections: a solo scene for Zaida, a scene for Roxana, joined by Solyman, who rebukes her jealousy, and a finale in which Solyman defends Zaide by threatening to have servants remove Roxana, which prompts her to retire. The original's elaborate divertissement was collapsed into a "Grand Dance."[39]

The playbook's verses hint at the likely content of Pepusch's lost setting: the single-strophe sentimental airs of Zaida and Solyman suggests the *galant* style of his late cantatas, while the similes of Roxana's revenge aria would have invited the word-painting and vocal fireworks associated with the vengeance arias of antiheroines, such as Armida and her "Vo far' guerra" in Handel's ever-popular *Rinaldo*. The only surviving music to *The Sultan*, a *galant* duet for Solyman and Zayda added in 1759 by Arne to his 1758 version, stages a lovers' union between Solyman and Zayda. It was not included in the playbook and appears to have been added to showcase the tenor John Beard and the soprano Charlotte Brent. By the late 1750s, Arne had left his wife, a celebrated soprano, for his protégée Brent, who, through Arne's music, was soon to become London's new singing sensation.[40] In 1759, Brent appeared for the first time in *The Sultan*, and in the added duet Arne represented her as a tender lover.

The duet's music also played to Beard's strengths (see ex. 2). Its melody, key, scoring, verse sentiments, dance type, and harmonic treatment are typical not only of the English pastoral cantata generally but more specifically of Beard's repertory at Ranelagh Gardens, where he had led vocal concerts since the mid-1740s.[41] Vocal music at Ranelagh was generally amorous, facilitating a musical enactment of the pastoral pleasures promised in the Gardens' advertisements, and Beard was its celebrated exponent. Arne, appointed band leader and resident composer of Vauxhall in 1745,[42] was a master of this idiom, as is ably shown in his 1759 duet in *The Sultan*. Here, tenor and soprano voice chase each other, uniting at the close of phrases in blissful euphony. Voices move against paired obbligato flutes normally used to symbolize a shepherd and shepherdess. In the tradition of Baroque aria, the key of A major denotes love, and the minuet, the most refined of French court dances, signifies a sophistication that in performance would have been enhanced by appoggiaturas, trills, and ornaments improvised by the singers. The title of the volume in which the duet was preserved, *A Choice Collection of Songs Sung at Vaux-Hall Gardens* (1759), highlights the music's pastoral, rather than Oriental, musical content.[43]

That Arne's compositional procedures were so different from Campra's illuminates an important divide between English and French composers' approach to Orientalist productions generally. In Campra's march for "La Turquie," French music was assumed to be a universal language whose encoded critique of Oriental manners would be apprehended by audiences. This language could also mimic, adopting putative Oriental mannerisms to make its point. Arne's music, by contrast, served branding: music had to be instantly recognizable by genre and/or vocalist's specialization. Whereas the traditions of French court spectacle encouraged Campra to counterfeit and co-opt the Orient in his score, commerce obliterated the Orient from Arne's music altogether.

Solyman & Zayde Sung by Mr Beard & Miss Brent

In: Thomas Arne, *A Choice Collection of Songs sung at Vaux-Hall Gardens* ([1761])

Edited by Christopher Gould

Thomas Arne

Moderato e dolce

Original scoring: first traverse flute, second traverse flute, first violin, second violin and basso continuo

Ex. 2 (*above and facing page*)

ZAYDE

O the rapt - ure past__ ex -

gent - le beau - ty's end - less charms.

pres - sing circ - led in__ my Sult - an's arms.

O sweet re - ward for

The thorn is gone, the rose__ re - mains. O sweet re -

all__ my pains. O sweet re -

Pantomime: Not-So-Arabian Nights

Eighteenth-century pantomime was similar to masque in its fusion of dance, serious music, splendid designs, and sketchy narrative. It differed from masque by including harlequinade. Critics routinely castigated pantomime as a "depraved" and "prostituted" entertainment that "gratified" and "indulged" lowered taste.[44] The focus of this criticism was the carnivalesque nature of harlequinade. During carnival season in Italy, citizens masqueraded as commedia dell'arte figures whose stage escapades—Harlequin's trickery, Scaramouche's magical escapes, Puncinello's id-inspired excesses—offered enticing models. Carnival celebrations sanctioned vertiginous inversions of power, propriety, and identity between individuals. In London, the delights of carnival were commercialized, not only in pantomime but also from 1708 in public masquerades whose paying guests explored the dizzying pleasures of disguise.[45]

A favorite "habit" was that of the Turk, evidence for which was meticulously recorded by the longtime Constantinople resident Jean-Baptiste Van Mour in paintings commissioned by the French ambassador. These paintings were engraved in 1714 and drawn on by theater designers across Europe.[46] "Turkish" dress caught on in tragedy and opera seria[47] and by the mid-eighteenth century shared key components: a long gown or caftan with short or hanging sleeves kilted up with an elaborately jeweled girdle, baggy trousers, and a turban or asymmetrically placed aigrette of feathers or jewels, and, after 1760, semitransparent muslins.[48] In tragedy, Turkish "habit," when worn by a British actor, might aid the performance and blurring of ethnicities that potentially could take place in serious drama. Such dress could also carry an erotic charge, in part by displaying women's "breasts . . . at full liberty"—which likely furthered the popularity of Turkish disguise at masquerades and on the tragic stage.[49] By contrast, evidence from *The Sultan, or A Peep into the Seraglio*, discussed shortly, shows that Ottoman garb in comic opera was expendable, and I have found no iconography of Turkish dress for comic singer-actors.

Pantomime dancers did, however, don Turkish costumes. Presumed Ottoman identity and the license of carnival costume came together in the early eighteenth-century Orientalist pantomime *The Carneval after the Venetian Manner* [*with*] *Dancing by Masqueraders in Diverse Characters, by Madmen, and by Turks, Men and Women* (1726). The advertisement for this entertainment by Michael Poitier described it as "Diana's Madness; or, Fatime, a Favourite Slave in the Seraglio, Mad for Love, and Crown'd Empress by the Grand Signior: With Pantalon and Harlequin Eunuchs elected Kaimcan and Ciguir, the one impaled and the other sawed asunder, the Bashas Selim and Achmet ript [*sic*] open, Rabca strangled, and Chistar beheaded."[50] Here, a staged masquerade accommodated an anarchic display of Eastern barbarism—contained, however, through *la belle danse* and familiar harlequin figures burlesquing horrific tortures.

Ottoman-themed pantomime then seemingly disappeared until 1750, when commercial pressures forced newly appointed Drury Lane manager David Garrick to take up a genre he despised.[51] Having in 1747 opened his first season as manager by declaring his enmity to pantomime,[52] by 1750 Garrick faced competition not only for audiences—who flocked to pantomimes led by John Rich, manager of Covent Garden and London's most famous harlequin—but also for star players, who were leaving him to join Rich.[53] To retrench, Garrick engaged Henry Woodward, trained as harlequin by Rich, to write pantomimes and star in them. Garrick mounted five of Woodward's six pantomimes on Boxing Day, initiating thereby the British tradition of a Christmas pantomime season that, as Sabbagh outlines in chapter 13, still thrives today.[54]

The second of Woodward's six pantomimes, *The Genii, An Arabian Nights Entertainment* (26 December 1752), initiated another tradition: using the *Arabian Nights* for pantomimic entertainment. Woodward's *Genii* was an immediate hit and a repertory staple until 1764, with periodic revivals until 1780. Although hugely popular at the time, the pantomime has left practically no evidence—no playbook, no choreography, no iconography, and little commentary. What evidence does survive—one puff, some advertisements, a bound collection of its "Comic Tunes"—indicates a strange bifurcation between some brief flashes of Orientalism and the Britishness of everything else.

The puff for *The Genii* ran,

This new entertainment, I think, hath fully decided the controversy [between Rich and Garrick], and fix'd the superiority of pantomime to Drury-lane theatre, as it had before had of almost every thing else; and I must say that for beauty of scenery, elegance of dress, propriety of musick, and regularity of design, it exceeds all the boasted grandeur of *Harlequin Sorcerer*, or of any I have seen, either separate or collective.— The last scene beggars all description; the most romantic eastern account of sumptuous palaces are but faint to this display of beauty, this glow of light, this profusion of glittering gems, which adorn the whole, and much exceeds all expectation.[55]

How might this wondrous "last scene" have appeared? Because Baroque sets shared conventions across Europe, an engraving by Canaletto of the 1759 pantomime-ballet "Les Turcs généreux"—a direct dramatic descendant of "La Turquie"—suggests how, in *The Genii* or *The Sultan*, an Oriental palace might have been made to appear. The building is classical: two pairs of columns with Corinthian capitals frame a portico; they support a plain entablature and two pediments which likewise frame a balcony above. Some features are "Orientalized"—the portico arch's multifoils are reversed to outline an onion dome, the pediments sag, and a cornice at the top of the building curls upward, as on the roof of a Turkish kiosk.[56] Articulated decorations add Turkish flavor: the crescent moon centered above the arch, the banner flags, the sta-lactite ornaments circling the Corinthian columns, the onion-shaped orbs that replace terminal figures. In the game of representation/self-representation *à la turque*, this set's symbolic language flirted with Oth-erness but kept the West center stage.[57]

Woodward reportedly believed that a function of a pantomime's comic tunes was to "paint the several scenes & events of the piece."[58] Assuming this to be true for his *Genii*, the titles of its "Comic Tunes" can be used to reimagine the pantomime's action. Harlequin, entering a village, is visited by genies; an invisible genie grants him magic pow-ers. In a Brickyard, Harlequin spies and falls in love with Columbine, guarded by a matron whom Harlequin pretends to woo. He and Colum-bine escape into a fishmonger's shop, where Columbine is "discover'd" and taken from her lover. She mourns their separation. Harlequin arrives disguised as a postman and magically transforms the scene from that of a village into that of a rocky vale, where Columbine and Harlequin celebrate their love. The scene changes back into the village, where, discovered by Columbine's family, the lovers are again parted. Harlequin looks fruitlessly for Columbine—in the "Timberyard," in the "Wood," and at "The Bridge." Recalling his gift from the genii, he changes the scene to a marvelous Marble Hall, where he is united with Columbine. "Grand," that is, serious, dances celebrate their union. Villagers join the festivities, which culminate in a "Country Dance" and a "Ballad."

This extrapolated outline follows pantomime's characteristic story—Harlequin, after meeting obstacles, is united with Columbine—and the typically supernatural means through which normal cause-and-effect rules are suspended.[59] The "descent" of the genii apes Restoration music for gods' ascents and descents in stage machines—as, for instance, in the masque of *Neptune and Amphitrite*, which continued to hold the stage until 1760.[60] Ironically, the greatest musical novelty was the very un-Oriental fishmongers' street cries, whose intervals generated the melody for the ninth air. Serious dance numbers typically took place alongside the pantomimic dance, either interwoven into harlequinade's physical theater or featured in a finale. In *The Genii*, this tradition allowed Anne Auretti and Mr. Ferrer (Ferrère) to turn up in this "most romantic eastern account" to dance a musette and a bourrée, respectively. Apart from the "sumptuous" Marble Hall and two numbers for the genies—"The Descent of the Genii" and "The Invisible Genii"—the *Arabian Nights* evaporated in this production designed by and for Woodward. That Oriental accessories—"sumptuous palaces," "glittering gems," "glows of light"—alone were recollected in the puff suggests the reductive power of the consumer's gaze.

Oriental Comic Opera, or Polite Enchantment on the London Stage

Between 1760 and 1785 (see table 1), London's patent theaters mounted six Ottoman-themed operas and musical comedies, beginning with *The Enchanter*.[61] Only Garrick (for *The Enchanter*, 1760) and Charles Dibdin (for *The Seraglio*, 1776) wrote entirely new playbooks; the other productions were based on French comic operas, except for *The Captive* (1769, Bickerstaff/Dibdin), which claimed to be based on John Dryden's *Don Sebastian* (1690), although its action related little to this play. These works followed the English playhouse tradition of mixing spoken dialogue with musical numbers, which typically consisted of overtures, arias, ballads, interludes, duets, dances, ensembles, and choruses. Music culminated in the finale, for which band, soloists, and chorus alternated performing within the number. Dramatis personae invariably included a virtuous maiden whose fidelity in love is tested and a sultan, who usually threatens the maiden's virtue. Supplementing this core cast was always an amorous youth—who could be either the sultan himself or an opponent of the sultan—and a rustic or servant for comic relief.

Music could be diversely sourced. Isaac Bickerstaff's *The Captive* (1769) featured seven airs from fashionable Italian operas, arranged by Dibdin, who also contributed an overture, five airs, and a finale. Dibdin, having written the playbook to *The Seraglio*, composed its music together with Samuel Arnold, who contributed three airs; Dibdin also included an Irish and a Scottish ballad in the work. The airs of *The Sultan; or, A Peep into the Seraglio* (1775) recycled music by Johann Christian Bach and Tommaso Giordani, as well as including new songs by Dibdin;[62] ten years later, John Hook pumped up an incidental air ("Blest Hero") from this work into a lavish aria for the celebrated Margaret Martyr.[63] Despite the diversity of composers writing comic operas, vocal numbers fell into types: "jealousy" or "rage" arias, tender pastoral binary airs—frequently a siciliano—in triple time, square-phrased syllabic British strophic ballads or ballad-style airs, and "patter-songs" for male comic characters, first developed by Dibdin. There were also virtuosic showstoppers to show off the cast's prima donna, whether in bravura or pastoral idiom. One notable constant in the striking sameness of works was the "rage" or "jealousy" aria of the sultan (in *The Captive*, given to the sultana), whose boundless passions menace the happy ending. Its jagged lines, leaps, runs, and agitated accompaniment were taken from Italian opera. Counterbalancing Oriental villain's aria were the "rational" forms—the English ballad, the *galant* air, and a concluding chorus, summarizing the moral of the work.

London composers reshuffled these familiar forms to support a familiar didactic program: irrationality is the root of suffering, and sentimental union promises happiness. English vocal forms mediated rational action; Italianate rage arias signified excess to be avoided. Comic moments were set to English music, whose clarity of word setting facilitated actors' gags and audiences' comprehension of the verses.

That English opera's music served to moralize, and that this subservience constrained musical fantasy, is best illustrated by *The Enchanter*. Exceptionally, this work was all sung, as in Italian opera; John C. Smith set Garrick's libretto. In the plot, Moroc the Enchanter falls in love with his captive, Zaide, who stubbornly remains true to her husband, Zoreb. A servant summons female spirits, who, in dance and song, argue that love is "Nectar if you taste and go / Poison if you stay." Zaide inverts this argument: only constancy yields Love's rewards, which become "Poison if you taste and go / Nectar if you stay."[64] Enraged by Zaide's rejection, Moroc reveals to her her husband's slain body; she tries to stab herself, but a servant, seizing the sorcerer's fallen wand, kills Moroc, while the magic of Zaide's love restores her husband to life. The servant summons "purer spirits"—(British) shepherds and shepherdesses—to celebrate in music the triumph of "Love and Virtue."[65] The playbook's mix of finger-wagging and patriotism could not accommodate musical experimentation; Smith had to write in idioms—Italianate (excessive emotion), Restoration (magic), British (polite taste)—to fit and to articulate the playbook's agenda.

Beyond the need to moralize, composers labored under a second constraint: the principal vocalist. Audiences wanted to hear singers perform what they were celebrated for. Can these twinned pressures —to communicate the playbook's moral and to showcase the singer— account for the striking inferiority of English Oriental operas to their more sophisticated French models? Most strange is the gulf between the music of André-Ernest-Modeste Grétry's *Zémire and Azor* (1771) and Thomas Linley's setting of this piece. The libretto is based on *La belle et la bête*. This story of an unbridled id transformed through female virtue invited Orientalization, initially in a 1742 play.[66] To set the tale to music in 1771, Grétry simulated vivid colors *à l'Orient*, blending unusual combinations of instruments, particularly winds, in extended ensembles. In an act 3 *coup de théâtre*, Grétry deployed four clarinets —an instrument then practically unknown—and two bassoons to play mood music from behind the scenes while a magic "tableau" reveals to Zémire her family's suffering.[67] Close integration of music with narrative, extravagant diversity of forms—a richly scored overture mixed with offstage thunder, a duo *concertant* for the protagonists, a show-stopping aria for Azor, dancing genies—made not just an exotic but also an evocative aural tapestry into which an exploration of the characters' psyches was woven.[68] Indeed, *Zémire and Azor* proved to be a high point of Grétry's output.[69]

Thomas Linley's *Selima and Azor*, composed five years later, is old-fashioned and dull by comparison. Figured basses, strophic airs, English playhouse scoring, and an Italianate "rage aria" for Azor make up its conventional musical vocabulary. Structural parallels between Linley's and Grétry's finales—a duet interlaced with chorus accompanied by woodwind "commentary"—provokes the suspicion that Linley was familiar with Grétry's music. If so, Linley showed himself unable or unwilling to learn from Grétry. In contrast to Linley's barren score, however, the London production's décor was sumptuous: *Selima and Azor* was "splendidly got up . . . with Scenes, Dresses, and Decorations entirely New." Leading set designer Philip James De Loutherbourg, who created this production, was praised for his "skill . . . in raising a table with a supper, and whirling about stools for the guests."[70]

Affective highlights were the primary focus of London's Orientalist musical theater generally, and nowhere more than in operas; principal players helped to determine what form they would take. A comparison between Isaac Bickerstaff's *The Sultan; or, A Peep into the Seraglio* (1775) and its source, Charles-Simon Favart's *Soliman Second* (1761, after Jean François Marmontel's "Contes moraux") highlights how powerfully players could shape the production—in this case, by making music disappear. Modern scholars have maintained that Bickerstaff closely followed Favart.[71] In fact, the two versions differed substantially: for London, pivotal music was removed, new songs added, the story shortened, and the character of Solyman newly profiled. What remained largely untouched was the spoken dialogue of Roxelane, whom Bickerstaff had envisioned being played by star actress Frances Abington.

Abington was the prime mover behind mounting this work. She reported that her "stile of acting . . . first suggested to him [Bickerstaff] the idea of bringing Roxalina [*sic*] upon the English stage."[72] Between September 1771—when the work was first puffed—and June 1774, she urged Garrick to mount *A Peep into the Seraglio*, despite it being a *cause scandale*.[73] Charged with sodomy in 1772, Bickerstaff had been forced to flee to France; rumors that Garrick might produce *A Peep into the Seraglio* had provoked riots and charges against Garrick of "unnatural acts."[74] Garrick initially elected not to mount the work, notwithstanding his admiration for his friend Favart and his willingness to help the desperately poor Bickerstaff. By 18 June 1774, however, Garrick had capitulated to Abington's pestering.[75]

Favart's Roxelane—played by the celebrated singer-actress Justine Favart, his wife—is a *salonnière*, rather than the schemer invoked in "La Turquie" and in the 1724 *Sultan*. She invites Soliman to attend an assembly that she organizes among the household. She orders European entertainments—wine, polite conversation, diverse female company. Her wit, coquetry, and flouting of seraglio conventions entrance Soliman. Bickerstaff's version, by contrast, transforms Soliman from Favart's ardent yet inconstant lover—in the original, he pines first for the Spaniard Elmira, then for the Circassian Delia, then finally for the Frenchwoman Roxelane—into a battle-hardened leader. Weary of his military glories as well as of the seraglio's "varied charms," Bickerstaff's new Solyman finds that he is "untouched [by the] mere caressing machines" of his harem.[76] Enter Abington.

Critics praised Abington's "charmingly fascinating [manner]," her "melodious" speaking voice, her "strength" and "smartness" of figure that was "far beyond even the conception of modern fine ladies." She had "peculiar tricks in acting"; one was "turning her wrist, and seeming to stick a pin in the side of her waist; she was also very adroit in the use of her fan."[77] The irrepressible Roxelane was perfect for such "tricks." Abington, by her own admission, feared singing in *The Sultan*, because she thought herself "a bad stick in that line"[78]—possibly acknowledging tacitly that in Favart's original, music had been Roxelane's most powerful weapon.

In Favart's version, Roxelane plays a prelude on the harp, then sings, accompanying herself; she commands Turkish musicians to play and Elmira to dance while she and Delia sing a tender berceuse to accompany her. Stimulated beyond control, Soliman declares, "I can't hold out anymore, my heart is drunken" ("Je n'y tiens plus: mon cœur est dans l'ivresse") and signs to Roxelane, by dropping his silk handkerchief, that he chooses her to share his bed.[79] "Authentic" Turkish instruments —that is, reproductions of Ottoman artifacts documented by French authors and described in a footnote to Favart's play text—helped to fuse the erotic with the exotic.[80] The frontispiece to the playbook (fig. 26) highlights the moment of ensnarement, showing Justine Favart as Rox-elane in Turkish dress.[81] It also shows three Turkish instruments being played onstage—the *zil* (handheld cymbals), the *zurna* (an oboelike woodwind), and what seems to be a *tanbur* (a lutelike instrument) in the background.[82] Counterbalancing this climactic scene is Favart's grand finale, which brilliantly fuses airs with dancing dervishes, whose slow movements crescendo into wild spinning; the climax is crowned by the final chorus.[83]

In London, Garrick revised the work as Abington requested in letters to him, excising the only song she had been given.[84] Music, originally the chief mediator of the scene's eroticism, was cut down to one air for Ismena that Garrick, knowing that Abington was "uneasy" beside rival actresses, turned into a mere "gay Chansonette."[85] Three other inciden-tal numbers were tucked discreetly into the corners of the story where pastoral or nationalist sentiments *à l'anglais* would fit—a march to her-ald Solyman's entry, an air by Osmyn about gentle breezes, and another song for Ismena to praise Solyman ("Blest hero").[86] By the second night, only two musical numbers were performed.[87] As usual, however, no effort was spared on the décor. The scenes were "vastly well got up" to represent the Seraglio's rich interior: "curtained arch, low, deep Turkish sopha covered with long carpets and cushions, a gold table, rich gold sa[l]ver set with jewels, a spoon made of the beak of an Indian bird."[88] Drury Lane lavished three new sets on the production: the seraglio's "Outer Gate," its "Interior view," and a "Garden terminating in a pros-pect of the sea." The first set was reported to be only so-so ("but *la! la!*"), while the last two were thought "beautiful and picturesque."[89] Yet whereas Justine Favart's costume had been original, Abington, pictured as "Roxane" by Joshua Reynolds, wears an un-Turkish but highly flat-tering gown, to which an aigrette has been added (fig. 28). In Paris, the real or seeming authenticity of music and dress could lend frisson to climactic scenes; in this Abington vehicle, music and authenticity alike vanished to show off the actress as she wished to be seen.

Conclusion

Thanks to a growing corpus of studies, we are beginning to recognize the assumptions, agendas, and anxieties woven into many eighteenth-century London stage productions about the Orient. Scholars rightly emphasize reciprocity between West and East, and the East's agency within Western constructions of the Orient, where these obtain. I would argue, however, that a starting point for such reciprocity is the acknowledgment and mediation, however imperfect, of known Eastern practices and signifiers. In the stage dance and music of mid-eighteenth-century London, this starting point was never reached. The compositional procedures of London stage music and of French choreographies performed in London remained untouched by Eastern practices, leaving little but expression of common predilections and prejudices. Music and dance, responding to the commercial imperatives both to traffic in celebrities and to peddle self-improvement, precluded any genuine interaction with the Orient. Consumed by the spectator's gaze, the Orient was not so much domesticated as reduced to an ornament, designed to enhance its wearer.

NOTES

1. Richmond Barbour, *Before Orientalism: London's Theatre of the East, 1576–1626* (Cambridge: Cambridge University Press, 2003), 29. Barbour provides valuable insight on how, through literary and cultural texts (including Christopher Marlowe's *Tamburlaine the Great*), authors sought to allay their anxieties about the East's advances in politics and culture by presenting the Orient as a theater where Eastern rulers pretend to power that they allegedly do not possess. Focusing on seventeenth-century serious drama in London, Bridget Orr shows how staged versions of historical accounts about the Orient—for example, John Dryden's *Aurang-Zebe*, William Davenant's *Siege of Rhodes*, and Mary Pix's *Ibrahim*—could "refashion modern selves" among audiences. According to Orr, stage action deployed "emergent Orientalist discourses of despotism, irreligion and sexual license" to promulgate and problematize ambitions of Empire. Bridget Orr, *Empire on the English Stage, 1660–1714* (Cambridge: Cambridge University Press, 2001), 1–2. For Mita Choudhury, seventeenth- and eighteenth-century stage works, from adaptations of *Mustapha* to Orientalist comedies by female playwrights, facilitated a "cultural commingling" as well as "appropriation." Mita Choudhury, *Interculturalism and Resistance in the London Theater, 1660–1800: Identity, Performance, Empire* (Lewisburg, PA: Bucknell University Press, 2000), 15–34. On the "transmigration" between English heroic drama and the histories of Oriental rulers, see Ros Ballaster, *Fabulous Orients: Fictions of the East in England, 1662–1785* (Oxford: Oxford University Press, 2005), 52–57.
2. Ballaster, *Fabulous Orients*, 56–57.

3. In serious drama, the actor's embodiment of character could be underpinned by a familiarity with the Oriental character's source in literature and histories. Consequently, according to Choudhury, drama could generate an intercultural consciousness that not only constructed the East but also acknowledged an Orient capable of symbolizing Western dilemmas, including the burdens of empire. Choudhury, *Interculturalism and Resistance*, 20–23.

4. This same process took place in London stage productions featuring China, with the significant difference that these works sought to "capitalize on the moral and cultural fund of China's 'Eastern virtues.'" Chi-ming Yang, "Virtue's Vogues: Eastern Authenticity and the Commodification of Chinese-ness on the 18th-Century Stage," *Comparative Literature Studies* 39:4 (2002): 326.

5. Ballaster, *Fabulous Orients*, 129–30.

6. Thomas Betzwieser dates French musical representation of the Ottoman Empire from Jean-Baptiste Lully's compositions for the scenes featuring a Turkish envoy in Molière's *Le bourgeois gentilhomme* (1670). Early ethnographic writings stimulated an appetite for self-styled "Turkish" instruments, practices, and titles. Turkish exoticism found musical expression in seventeenth- and eighteenth-century harpsichord music, divertissements, fair stage entertainments, and exotic operas of the Académie Royale and the Opéra-Comique, as well as those by Christoph Willibald Gluck. Each repertory flirted with notions of Turkish music, from keyboard music's references to microtones in applied vibrato to the intervallic leaps, formulaic circling around the tonic, and rhythmic tensions of dances and opera airs. See Thomas Betzwieser, *Exotismus und "Türkenoper" in der französischen Musik des Ancien Régime: Studien zu einem ästhetischen Phänomen* (Laaber: Laaber-Verlag, 1993). Janissary music came to stand for both instrumentation and idioms of writing associated with the bands (*mehter*) of janissaries, the élite troops of the Ottoman Empire made up initially, in the fourteenth century, from converted Christian captives. The size, instruments (Turkish forms of trumpet, kettledrum, shawm, cymbals, and bass drums), and function of the *mehter* became known to central European courts, and *mehter* instruments began to be used in their military bands. After 1700, Turkish music became formalized not only through orchestral scoring—principally kettledrums, triangles, cymbals, tambourines, and high-pitched woodwinds—but also through compositional procedures. These are usefully summarized in Benjamin Perl, "Mozart in Turkey," *Cambridge Opera Journal* 12:3 (2001): 219–35. They include simple rhythms and harmony, frequent repetitions, accented downbeats, duple meter, a sharpened fourth scale degree, simple rhythmic patterns, a melodic line doubled at the octave, scoring for the *batterie turque* with percussion and piccolo, and the home tonic of C major.

7. Curtis A. Price, "'. . . To Make Amends for One Ill Dance': Conventions for Dancing in Restoration Plays," *Dance Research Journal* 10:1 (1977–78): 1–6.

8. Emmett L. Avery, "Dancing and Pantomime on the English Stage, 1700–1737," *Studies in Philology* 31:3 (1934): 417–52. See also Carol Marsh's introduction to *A*

New Collection of Dances, by Anthony L'Abbé (London: Stainer and Bell, 1991) (facsimile of the edition published in London in 1725 by Le Rousseau).

9. The notation for these choreographies was devised in the 1680s by Pierre Beauchamps and first published by Raoul-Auger Feuillet from 1700. It is commonly referred to as Beauchamps-Feuillet notation. Methods for its transcription are explained in Wendy Hilton, *Dance of Court and Theater: The French Noble Style, 1690–1725* (Princeton, NJ: Princeton Book Company, 1981).

10. Nathalie Lecomte, "L'orientalisme dans le ballet aux XVIIeme et XVIIIeme siècles," *La recherche en danse* 1:1 (1982): 54–60. Lecomte notes that due to the ephemeral nature of dance transmission, medieval and Renaissance dances representing Muslims—noted in *entremets de la cours, entrées triomphantes, carrousels*, and *mascarades*—cannot be precisely identified. She briefly describes the most evocative of 199 French spectacles mounted from 1626 to 1783 featuring Oriental figures. On "Turkish" ballets, their décor, their costume, and their notation, see Francoise Dartois-Lapeyre, "Turcs et Turqueries dans les représentations en musique," in *Turcs et turqueries (XVIe–XVIIIe siècle)*, ed. Gilles Veinstein, 164–215 (Paris: Presse de l'Université Paris-Sorbonne, 2009), esp. 183–94.

11. Although no other London stage choreographies survive, one can assume that the French practice of drawing exclusively on French traditions in "Turkish" dances was also followed in London. On the exclusion of Eastern practices from French choreographies, see Dartois-Lapeyre, "Turcs et Turqueries dans les représentations en musique," 183.

12. Anthony L'Abbé, *A New Collection of Dances* (London: Stainer and Bell, 1991) (facsimile of the edition published in London in 1725 by Le Rousseau).

13. No advertisement of his dance seems to have survived. See Marsh, introduction to *New Collection of Dances*.

14. Linda Tomko, "Framing Turkish Dances," *Music in Art: International Journal for Music Iconography* 36:1–2 (2011): 131–60.

15. André Campra, *L'Europe galante, ballet, représenté en l'an 1697* (Farnborough, UK: Gregg, 1967) (facsimile of the edition published in Paris in 1724 by Jean-Baptiste-Christophe Ballard), 240–56.

16.. See Tomko, "Framing Turkish Dances," esp. 132–40.

17. See Tomko, "Framing Turkish Dances," esp. 132–40.

18. Ibid., esp. 140–52.

19. Betzwieser, *Exotismus und "Türkenoper,"* 136.

20. Thoinot Arbeau, in his collection of dance compositions *Orchésographie* (1588), reported having seen "la dance des Morisques" by a young man. See Alan Brown and Donna G. Cardamone, "Moresca," in *Grove Music Online, Oxford Music Online*, http://www.oxfordmusiconline.com/subscriber/article/grove/music/19125?q=moresca.

21. Betzwieser reads this music similarly but without fully considering the denigration implicit in Campra's commingling of *moresca* and march. Betzwieser, *Exotismus und "Türkenoper,"* 136–37.

22. For a discussion of Purcell's masque in *The Prophetess*, see Curtis Price, *Henry Purcell and the London Stage* (Cambridge: Cambridge University Press, 1984), 282–88.

23. Robert D. Hume, "John Rich as Manager and Entrepreneur," in *"The Stage's Glory": John Rich (1692–1761)*, ed. Berta Joncus and Jeremy Barlow (Newark: University of Delaware Press, 2011), 46–47. Hume emphasizes that "the thirty performances of *The Prophetess* revival this season [1724] are in one sense extraordinary, but in another sense representative of the strengths and interests of Rich's company."

24. Henry Purcell, *Dioclesian*, ed. J. Frederick Bridge and John Pointer, rev. Margaret Laurie (London: Novello, 1979), xvii.

25. Typical seventeenth-century masques, which were used also to conclude semi-operas, are described in Curtis Price, *Music in the Restoration Theatre: With a Catalogue of Instrumental Music in the Plays, 1665–1713* (Ann Arbor, MI: UMI Research, 1979), 28–49; and Price, *Henry Purcell and the London Stage*, 3–16.

26. Newspaper coverage of deteriorating relations during 1724 was comprehensive. See for instance reports in the *British Journal*, the *Daily Post*, the *Daily Journal*, the *Weekly Journal or British Gazetteer*, and the *Daily Courant* (among others) March–June 1724. A particularly informative and lengthy report from Constantinople (dated 1 May), printed in the *Daily Post* on 10 June 1724, described how the "Bashaw Mehemet, who commands the Ottoman troops . . . [will] make proposals of accommodation."

27. Stanford Shaw, "Iranian Relations with the Ottoman Empire in the Eighteenth and Nineteenth Centuries," in *The Cambridge History of Iran*, vol. 7, *From Nadir Shah to the Islamic Republic*, ed. Peter Avery, Gavin Hambly, and Charles Melville, 297–313 (Cambridge: Cambridge University Press, 1991), esp. 297–300.

28. *The Sultan* was published in 1758 as "The Masque" in John Dryden's *The Prophetess*; this volume was reissued 1759. John Dryden, *The Prophetess; or, The History of Dioclesian: A Dramatic Opera: With All the New Songs, &c.* (London: J. and R. Tonson, 1758), 66–69. The 1724 *L'Europe galante* production in Paris was the fourth revival since 1697 ("Ballet representé pour la premier fois le 24 Octobre 1697. Remis ou Theatre pour la quatrieme fois le 20 Juin 1724"). Jacques Bernard Durey de Noinville and Louis Travenol, comp., *Histoire du théâtre de l'Opéra en France: Depuis l'établissement de l'Académie royale de musique, jusqu'à présent . . . deuxième partie* (Paris: Barbou, 1753), 115. The livret for *L'Europe galante* was by Houdard de la Motte. In later productions, Campra's music was adapted: the opening passacaglia fell away, and a Janissary march was added. Betzwieser, *Exotismus und "Türkenoper,"* 140.

29. Rich worked closely with principal dancers such as the Marie Sallé, facilitating their London performances. Sarah McCleave, "Dancing at the English Opera: Marie Sallé's Letter to the Duchess of Richmond," *Dance Research: The Journal of the Society for Dance Research* 17:1 (1999): 22–46. See also Moira Goff, "John

Rich, French Dancing, and English Pantomimes," in Joncus and Barlow, "*The Stage's Glory,*" 85–98.

30. Campra, *L'Europe galante,* 207–56.

31. "Roxane" stood for the Hürrem Sultana (1504–58), the courtesan and wife of Suleyman I (Suleyman the Magnificent), who ruled 1520–66. She became sultana in 1533, after the death of the mother of Suleyman I. Suleyman's first son, Mehmed, died of smallpox and not, as Ros Ballaster highlights, due to the intrigues of the Hürrem Sultana. The earliest reports about the "Russian" wife stem from Venetian ambassadors' reports beginning in 1526. Christine Pierce notes that the "Hurrem has always been a hated figure, . . . presented as a powerful schemer selfishly manipulating the sultan to secure the succession for one of her sons." According to Polish accounts, her original name was Alesandra Lisowska, and she was captured by Tartar raiders; "Roxelana" may have referred to her origin in the Ruthenian territories of the western Ukraine. Leslie P. Peirce, *The Imperial Harem: Women and Sovereignty in the Ottoman Empire* (New York: Oxford University Press, 1993), 58–65, 89; Ballaster, *Fabulous Orients,* 60n. 2.

32. Because this opéra-ballet embodies the submission of different identities to French polite taste, it can be read as a *galant* "makeover" of heroic glorifications of the king in *grand siècle* court spectacle. Formally, the work broke with the past: it replaced mythical figures with (putatively) flesh-and-blood characters, heroic deeds with *galant* scenes of amorous exchange, and imagined realms with (allegedly) contemporary settings. The production's action was linked to the reassertion of *galanterie* in French spectacle as the staging of pleasure, rather than power, which grew from around 1700 in response to a weakening of the king's hold on the nobility. This led to the opéra-ballets of Campra that "updated that older aesthetic for a new public." See Georgia Cowart, "Introduction: The Allure of Spectacle and the Prerogatives of Pleasure," in *The Triumph of Pleasure: Louis XIV and the Politics of Spectacle,* xv–xxiii (Chicago: University of Chicago Press, 2008).

33. "Thinking of women as literally locked up in the harem, Europeans mistakenly associated the Turco-Persian word for palace, *saray,* with the Italian *serrare,* to lock up or enclose—by which false etymology the English 'seraglio' and the French *sérial* came to signify not only an entire building (as in the 'Grand Seraglio' at Constantinople), but the apartments in which the women were confined and even the women themselves." Ruth Yeazell, *Harems of the Mind: Passages of Western Art and Literature* (New Haven: Yale University Press, 2000), 2.

34. Yeazell interprets several significant works from this seventeenth- and eighteenth-century corpus, including Rycaut's *The Present State of the Ottoman Empire* (1688), Aaron Hill's *A Full and Just Account of the Present State of the Ottoman Empire* (1709), Jean Chardin's *Voyages du Chevalier Charden, en Perse, et autres lieux de l'Orient* (1711), and *The Complete Letters of Lady Mary Montagu* (written from 1717). See Yeazell, "Some Traveler's Tales" and "Looking

for Liberty: Lady Mary Wortley Montagu and the Victorians," in *Harems of the Mind*, 13–21, 84–94.

35. Katie Trumpener, "Rewriting Roxane: Orientalism and Intertextuality in Montesquieu's *Lettres Persanes* and Defoe's *The Fortunate Mistress*," *Stanford French Review* 11:3 (1987): 178; cited also in Ballaster, *Fabulous Orients*, 63. Ballaster analyzes the many writings—including Knolles and Rycaut's *The Turkish History, from the Original of That Nation, to the Growth of the Ottoman Empire* (1687); William Davenant's Roxelana in the first English opera, *The Siege of Rhodes* (in the revised version of 1661); and Nathaniel Lee's *The Rival Queens* (1677)—in light of the Roxane myth. See Ballaster, "Roxolana: The Loquacious Courtesan," in *Fabulous Orients*, 59–69.

36. By 1724, Barbier was nearing the end of her successful career. She first appeared at the Queen's Theatre on 14 November 1711, singing Almanzor in *Almahida*. This was a demanding pasticcio based on Viennese operas by Giovanni Bononcini and Attilio Ariosti; the celebrated castrato Valentino Urbani had previously sung Almanzor. Barbier specialized in trouser roles, which included Rinaldo in a 1713 production of Handel's eponymous opera and Turnus in Bononcini's *Camilla* (Lincoln Inn's Fields, 1717). John Rich engaged her for £200 during the 1724–25 season. Philip H. Highfill, Jr., Kalman A. Burnim, and Edward A. Langhans, "Barbier, Jane," in *A Biographical Dictionary of Actors*, vol. 1, 281–84 (Carbondale: Southern Illinois University Press, 1973); and Winton Dean, "The English Background," in *Handel's Operas: 1704–1726*, by Winton Dean and John Merrill Knapp (Oxford, UK: Clarendon, 1987), 149–50.

37. John Hughes, "The Hue and Cry" (1717), quoted in Olive Baldwin and Thelma Wilson, "Barbier, Jane," *Oxford Dictionary of National Biography*, http://ezproxy .ouls.ox.ac.uk:2117/view/article/65863. By 1724, Barbier had acquired a reputation for unruliness as well as for first-rate vocal performances in Italian and English vocal repertory. In Hughes's poem summarizing her character—provoked seemingly by her unexpected elopement—he described her as mercurial, narcissistic, capricious, licentious and ungovernable—traits commonly ascribed to prima donnas: "Gay, scornful, sober, indiscreet, / In whom all contradictions meet / . . . Try if at church the [marriage] words she'll say, / Then teach her if you can,— t'obey. 1717" (italics original). "Hue and Cry" was, along with two other poems, "by some accident, omitted in the *Collection of His Poems* [Hughes's *Poems on Several Occasions* (1735)]," apparently first reaching print in 1773. See "Poetical Essays for April, 1773," *Gentleman's Magazine* 43 (1773): 195. I thank Olive Baldwin and Thelma Wilson for steering me to this source.

38. A student of the soprano Margherita de L'Epine, Chambers debuted on the stage as St. Cecilia in *The Union of Three Sisters Arts* on 22 November 1723, although she had appeared in concerts at the Hickford's music room, Haymarket Theatre, Drury Lane, and Lincoln's Inn Fields from March 1722. After her early appearances, she "established herself quickly as one of the finest singers in London." "Chambers, Isabella," in Highfill, Burnim, and Langhans, *A Biographical*

Dictionary of Actors, vol. 3 (Carbondale: Southern Illinois University Press, 1975), 145–46.

39. Advertisements in 1724 announced the celebrated baritone Richard Leveridge as the chief gardener, indicating that he likely sang a vocal number within the "Grand Dance." For Arne's 1758 and 1759 versions, the role was not billed, so presumably this air had fallen away.

40. Roger Fiske, *English Theatre Music in the Eighteenth Century* (New York: Oxford University Press, 1973), 622. Arne's biographer Todd Gilman objects to Fiske's claim that Brent caused Arne to leave his wife. Gilman admits, however, that Arne's return in 1756 from Ireland to London with Brent, and without his wife, who remained behind, indicates the Arnes' separation. Todd Gilman, *The Theatre Career of Thomas Arne* (Newark: University of Delaware Press, 2013), 301.

41. Berta Joncus, "'To Propagate Sound for Sense': Music for Diversion and Seduction at Ranelagh Gardens," *London Journal: A Review of Metropolitan Society Past and Present* 38:1 (2013): 34–66.

42. Gilman, *Theatre Career of Thomas Arne*, 225–27.

43. Thomas Arne, *A Choice Collection of Songs Sung at Vaux-Hall Gardens / by Miss Brent and Mr. Lowe Set to Musick . . . Book XII* (London: J. Walsh, [1761]), 10–11. Despite the collection's title, the Beard-Brent duet was issued in this volume.

44. Emmet Avery, "The Defense and Criticism of Pantomimic Entertainments in the Early Eighteenth Century," *English Literary History* 5:2 (1938): 127–45. John O'Brien explores how criticism about pantomime articulated and was embedded within debates over the Walpole government and the growing independence of apprentices. John O'Brien, *Harlequin Britain: Pantomime and Entertainment, 1690–1760* (Baltimore: Johns Hopkins University Press, 2004), 138–208.

45. Masquerade came to London at the beginning of the eighteenth century. From 1708, Count Heidegger organized masquerades as fashionable assemblies held at the opera house. With the reopening of the Vauxhall pleasure gardens in 1732, Vauxhall and later Ranelagh Gardens (opened 1742) become the locus for large-scale public masquerades. Terry Castle has sifted through a wealth of testimony to illuminate the imaginative play unleashed by masquerades in London. Terry Castle, *Masquerade and Civilisation: The Carnivalesque in Eighteenth-Century English Culture and Fiction* (London: Methuen, 1986). See especially chapter 1, "The Masquerade and Eighteenth-Century England," 1–51, and chapter 2, "Travesty and the Fate of the Carnivalesque," 52–109.

46. The French ambassador M. de Ferriol, arriving in Turkey in 1699, commissioned Van Mour to paint scenes and costumes of the Ottoman Empire. The paintings, now lost, were engraved and issued as *Recueil de cent estampes representant differentes nations de Levant* (1714). They became a vital source for dress and theater designers answering a demand for fashion, costumes, and theater *à la turque*. Aileen Ribeiro, *Dress in Eighteenth-Century Europe, 1715–1789* (London: Batsford, 1984), 175, and Tomko, "Framing Turkish Dances," 147–52. The prints also provided vital information about Turkish musical practices, particularly

about the construction of instruments, and nourished French ethnographic studies such as Charles-Henri de Blainville's chapter on Turkish music in *Histoire général, critique et philosophique de la musique* (1767) and Jean-Benjamin de la Borde's *Essai sure la musique ancienne et moderne* (1780). Albert P. de Mirimonde, "La musique orientale dans les œuvres de l'école Française du XVIIIe siècle," *Revue du Louvre et des Musées en France* 19:4–5 (1969): 231–46.

47. London's haberdashers, who supplied masquerade dress, lived near Covent Garden and probably supplied theatrical dress as well. Customers for masquerade dress could view a "Book" containing "Dresses from every Nation" at the haberdashers; this was likely Thomas Jefferys, *A Collection of the Dresses of Different Nations* (1757), which duplicated the Turkish dress engraved in the *Recueil de cent estampes* (1714). One of the most popular Oriental dresses was the "Sultana" illustrated by Jefferys, who relied on Jos Vien's drawings of a 1748 Turkish masquerade by students of the French academy in Rome, issued as *Caravane du Sultan à la Mecque*. These drawings in turn relied partly on *Recueil de cent estampes*. Aileen Ribeiro, *The Dress Worn at Masquerades in England, 1730 to 1790* (New York: Garland, 1984), 217–33.

48. Ribeiro, *Dress Worn at Masquerades*, 236–38.

49. Ribeiro, *Dress in Eighteenth-Century Europe*, 177. Two years after Vanmour's engravings, Lady Mary Wortley Montagu began recording, in her Turkish embassy letters, descriptions of the Turkish dress that she enjoyed adopting. She described also the attractions that dressing *à la turque* held for her. Her letters, which circulated in manuscript copies before their publication in 1763, helped to stimulate a vogue for Turkish dress in England, particularly at masquerades. Ribeiro, *Dress in Eighteenth-Century Europe*, 177. Elsewhere Ribeiro notes that the "indecency" of Turkish costume "resided more in its indolent and exotic associations than in any really revealing dress." Aileen Ribeiro, *Dress and Morality* (London: Batsford, 1986), 105. Montagu engaged in what modern critics call "ethnomasquerade," a practice in which Western travelers or diplomats to the East adopt indigenous costume, discussed in Nebahat Avcıoğlu, *Turquerie and the Politics of Representation, 1728–1876* (Aldershot, UK: Farnham, 2004), 45–54. Kader Konuk makes the important point that in Montagu's adopting and writing about her Turkish dress, she aimed principally "to strengthen her credibility as a travel writer" and thereby "demonstrate control over the perceived seductive allure of the Orient," rather than to understand or become the Other. Kader Konuk, "Ethnomasquerade in Ottoman-European Encounters: Reenacting Lady Mary Wortley Montagu," *Criticism* 46:3 (2004): 395

50. This was performed at the King's Theatre on 5 November 1726. This was Poitier's second season, and in this performance he choreographed a visiting commedia dell'arte troupe in which French players also performed. See Emmett L. Avery, ed., *The London Stage, 1660–1800: A Calendar of Plays*, part 2, vol. 2, *1717–1729* (Carbondale: Southern Illinois University Press, 1960), 889.

51. Garrick's antagonism toward, and complex relationship with, pantomime

culminated in 1759 in his "antipantomime" *Harlequin's Invasion*. This is the subject of John O'Brien's "David Garrick and the Institutionalization of English Pantomime," in *Harlequin Britain: Pantomime and Entertainment, 1690–1760* (Baltimore: Johns Hopkins University Press, 2004), 209–31.

52. "Forc'd, at length, her ancient reign to quit, / She saw great Faustus lay the ghost of wit; / Exulting Folly hail'd the joyous day, / And Pantomime and Song confirm'd her Sway . . . / Then prompt no more the Follies you decry, / As tyrants doom their tools of guilt to die; / Tis yours, this night, to bid the reign commence, / Of rescued Nature, and reviving Sense." Samuel Johnson, *Prologue and Epilogue, Spoken at the Opening of the Theatre in Drury-Lane 1747* (London: E. Cave and R. Dodsley, [1747]).

53. Toward the end of the summer break of 1750, Garrick learned "without warning" that his theater's two leading actors, Spranger Barry and Susannah Cibber, were joining forces at Covent Garden with John Quinn and Peg Woffington. Jean Benedetti, *David Garrick and the Birth of Modern Theatre* (London: Methuen, 2001), 158.

54. These pantomimes are listed and described in Roger Fiske, "Pantomime in the 1750s," in *English Theatre Music in the Eighteenth Century*, 229–39.

55. "Historical Chronicle—Plays Acted &c—Genii," *Gentleman's Magazine* 22 ([December]1752): 582.

56. The kiosk, or imperial pavilion, was typically a "light structure with pitched roof decorated with lattice work and round arches," such as that built by the deposed king of Poland Stanislas Leszczynski at Lunéville, Lorraine, in 1740. Frequent description in travelogues made the kiosk an "essential" feature in the representation of Turkish architecture. Avcioğlu, *Turquerie and the Politics of Representation*, 60.

57. This was not necessarily true of Ottoman-style architecture in Europe. Avcioğlu argues persuasively that in emulating and promoting Turkish architecture, British, French, and German rulers mined "otherness" in their attempts to establish autonomy within prescribed Western forms of state representation. Ibid., 8–41.

58. Charles Burney wrote that Woodward had "delivered to Oswald [the composer], in writing, subjects for the tunes that were to paint the several scenes & events of the piece." Roger Lonsdale, *Dr. Charles Burney: A Literary Biography* (Oxford, UK: Clarendon, 1965), 33; cited in Fiske, *English Theatre Music in the Eighteenth Century*, 231.

59. John O'Brien, "Pantomime," in *The Cambridge Companion to British Theatre, 1730–1830*, ed. Jane Moody and Daniel O'Quinn (Cambridge: Cambridge University Press, 2007), 103–14.

60. *Neptune and Amphitrite* was composed for Thomas Shadwell's 1674 adaptation of *The Tempest*. Its music is reconstructed in Matthew Locke, *Dramatic Music: With the Music by Humfrey, Banister, Reggio and Hart for "The Tempest,"* ed. Michael Tilmouth (London: Stainer and Bell, 1986).

61. I omit from this essay John F. Lampe's opera *Amelia* (1732) because, although it

features "Osmyn, Grand Visier of the Turks," it is not truly Ottoman themed. The action takes place in Hungary and revolves around members of the Hungarian court. See *Amelia: A New English Opera* (London: John Watts, [1732]); and Dennis R. Martin, *The Operas and Operatic Style of John Frederick Lampe* (Detroit: Information Coordinators, 1985), 21–23.

62. Peter Tasch, "Garrick's Revisions of Bickerstaff's 'The Sultan,'" *Philological Quarterly* 50:1 (1971): 145.

63. John Hook, *Blest Hero Who in Peace & War . . . Sung by Mrs. Martyr in the Sultan* (London: S. A. and P. Thompson, [1783]). Margaret Martyr's flamboyance of vocal technique matched that of her personal life. See "Martyr, Margaret née Thornton," in Highfill, Burnim, and Langhans, *A Biographical Dictionary of Actors*, vol. 10 (Carbondale: Southern Illinois University Press, 1984), 117–23.

64. David Garrick, *The Enchanter; or, Love and Magic* (London: J. and R. Tonson, 1760), 9. The music was published (without dances and chorus) as John C. Smith, *The Enchanter: A Musical Entertainment* (London: John Walsh, 1760).

65. Garrick, *The Enchanter*, 18.

66. Oriental names and a Persian setting were mapped onto the tale in *Amour pour amour*, a verse play by Pierre-Claude Nivelle de la Chauséee (1742). David Charlton, "*Zémire et Azor*," in *Grove Music Online, Oxford Music Online*, http://www.oxfordmusiconline.com/subscriber/article/grove/music/19125?q=zemireetazor. The narrative was first formulated in French not by Jeanne Marie Le Prince de Beaumont (as asserted by Charlton) but by Gabrielle-Susanne de Villeneuve, whose earlier, admittedly distinct, version was published in *La jeune Américaine et les contes marins* (1740). Her tale seemingly leaned on Apuleius's *The Golden Ass* (books 4 and 6), which in turn related to a vast repertory of folktales about a "monstrous spouse." Madame Gabrielle-Susanne de Villeneuve, *La jeune Américaine et les contes marins* (*La belle e la bête*), ed. Élisa Biancardi (1740; reprint, Paris: Honoré Champion, 2008), 9–10. On the psychic tensions manifested in this story, see Marina Warner, "Reluctant Brides: Beauty and the Beast I" and "Go! Be a Beast: Beauty and the Beast," chapters 17 and 18 in *From the Beast to the Blonde: On Fairy-Tales and Their Tellers* (London: Chatto and Windus, 1994), 273–318.

67. "Trio les instruments qui accompagnent sont derier [*sic*] le théâtre." André-Ernest-Modeste Grétry, *Zémire et Azor, Comédie ballet* (Paris: Montulay, 1771), 147–50.

68. On the penultimate page of the overture appear the directions, "The thunder and the wind should make themselves heard particularly during the forte [passages] ("Le tonerre [*sic*] et les vents se font entendre sur tout dans les Forte"). Ibid., 11. For the musical numbers mentioned in the text, see ibid., 210–12 (duo concertant), 135–46 (aria), 124–27 (dance).

69. David Charlton, "The Appeal of the Beast: A Note on Grétry and *Zémire et Azor*," *Musical Times* 121:1645 (1980): 169–72. Another illustrious forerunner for English Orientalist opera was Christoph Gluck's *Cade dupé*, whose Janissary

music created a sensation in Vienna through its novel use of the triangle, "biffero" (fife), Turkish drum, cymbals, and "salterio," or dulcimer. Premiered at the Burgtheater in Vienna on 8 December 1761, *Le cadi dupé* was the first of two "Turkish" *opéras comiques* by Gluck. Monsigny had earlier set the libretto of *Le cadi dupé* for a Paris production at the Foire St-Germain on 4 February 1761. The Orientalism of Gluck's opera lay almost entirely in the "Janissary" instruments added to standard vocal forms, as in "Entre ma femme e la table" (no. 8, with tambourines and cymbals). See Daniela Philippi, introduction to *Cadi dupé*, by Christoph W. Gluck, ed. Daniela Philippi (Kassel: Bärenreiter, 1999), xiii–xiv (Sämtliche Werke, Abt. IV, Bd. 6). Neither Monsigny's nor Gluck's score bears any resemblance to the pedestrian airs composed by Thomas Linley for his later version of this work, *The Cady of Bagdad*, which are preserved in the British Library, Add. MS 29297.

70. The playbill and the commentary (from *Westminster Magazine* of December 1776) is cited in Christopher Baugh, *Garrick and Loutherbourg* (Cambridge, UK: Chadwyck-Healey, 1990), 100. Grétry's opera was mounted at King's Theatre on 23 February 1779 but achieved only three performances.

71. René Guiet, "An English Imitator of Favart: Isaac Bickerstaffe," *Modern Language Notes* 38:1 (1923): 54–56. Daniel O'Quinn maintains also that "the Sultan is a very close adaptation of *Soliman II* by Charles Simon Favart." Daniel O'Quinn, *Staging Governance: Theatrical Imperialism in London, 1770–1800* (Baltimore: Johns Hopkins University Press, 2005), 17.

72. Frances Abington, letter of 14 June 1774, quoted in Tasch, "Garrick's Revisions," 142.

73. Tasch, "Garrick's Revisions," 142–43. The first puff for the play appeared in *Bingley's Journal*, 31 August–7 September 1771.

74. Invective against Garrick was led by William Kinreck, whose theatrical pieces Garrick refused to mount after two of Kinreck's plays flopped. See Peter A. Tasch, "The Deed without the Name," chapter 12 in *The Dramatic Cobbler: The Life and Works of Isaac Bickerstaff* (Lewisburg, PA: Bucknell University Press, 1971), 221–43; cited also in O'Quinn, *Staging Governance*, 18.

75. Garrick conceded but set conditions: Bickerstaff had to agree with the alterations; Garrick could mount the work at his convenience; and Abington would lead the cast. Tasch, "Garrick's Revisions," 143. In the preface, Abington was credited with bringing the work to the stage: "The following piece . . . made its first appearance . . . at the Request of that inimitable actress Mrs. Abington." [Isaac Bickerstaff], *The Sultan; or, A Peep into the Seraglio* (Cork, Ireland: J. Sullivan, 1781). This was the playbook's second edition; the first was issued in Dublin in 1780; the playbook was not published in London until 1787. One assumes that London booksellers were reluctant to issue the volume due to the scandal linked to Bickerstaff's name; the editions in Ireland appeared in response to Abington's visit to Dublin, as the preface makes clear.

76. Charles-Simon Favart, *Soliman second, en trois actes* (Paris: Duchesne, 1761), 8–9.

77. *The Life of Mrs. Abington (formerly Miss Barton), Celebrated Comic Actress* (London: Reader, 1888), 31.

78. "Thursday, two o'clock . . . I will endeavour, and I think it is possible to be ready by Tuesday, as I see 'The Sultan' is advertised for that day; but I shall want many little helps, particularly in the business of the dinner-scene, and about my song, as I am at best a bad stick in that line." Frances Abington to David Garrick, [between 7 March and 27 May] 1775, in *The Private Correspondence of David Garrick*, ed. James Boaden, vol. 2 (London: H. Colburn and R. Bentley, 1832), 27. This letter is cited also in Tasch, "Garrick's Revisions," 143.

79. Favart, *Soliman second*, 70.

80. Stage directions indicate that Delia should sing her song accompanied by the Turkish instruments on stage ("Delia, chante au son des Instruments Turcs"; ibid., 63). Roxelane then asks the musicians to play their flutes and cymbals ("Animez-vous, flutes cymbales"; 66). Here appears a footnote detailing the construction of the *zilli* : "Les Cymbales (ou Zilli comme les Turcs les nomment) sont de petits basins d'airain ou d'argent qui ont 8 a 10 pouces de diametre; leur concavité est d'environ 2 pouces de profondeur & leur plat-bord en a autant; une anse est soudée sure le coté convexe: on frappe des Cymbales l'une contre l'autre; ce qui rend un son éclatant, mais assez agréable." (The cymbals [or zilli as the Turks name them] are small bowls of bronze or silver that are eight to ten inches in diameter; their [concave] curvature is about two inches in depth, and the opposite side curves as much; a handle is welded onto the convex side: one strikes the cymbals against each other; which makes a sound loud but still pleasing.) Ibid., 63–66 (translation my own).

81. "Mme Favart wore a genuine Turkish costume in her role in *Soliman*." Ribeiro, *Dress in Eighteenth-Century Europe*, 178. During the run of Bickerstaff's Sultan, the *Westminster Magazine* ran a commentary, "A Comparison of Turkish and English Manners," which included a detailed discussion of Turkish dress. *The Westminster Magazine; or, The Pantheon of Taste: Containing a View of the Year 1782*, vol. 10 (London: T. Wright, 1776), 321–24.

82. Information about these instruments' construction had come to France largely through paintings and engravings. Albert P. de Mirimonde, "La musique orientale dans les œuvres de l'école Française du XVIIIᵉ siècle," *Revue du Louvre et des Musées en France* 19:4–5 (1969): 231–46.

83. Favart, *Soliman second*, 100–103. On page 103, the stage directions state, "Dance des Derviches. Ils commencent sur un air lent & mesuré au son de leurs tambours longs & de leurs flutes; ensuite ils tournent sur un air plus vif, jusqu'à ce qu'ils tombent comme en extase." (The Dance of the Dervishes. They begin with a slow tune measured in sound by the large drums [*tabbel*?] and flutes; thereafter they spin to a quick air until they fall as if in ecstasy.) (Translation my own.) The first playbook edition did not include all the notated music—it was initially published separately—but this scene with the music was printed in the 1763 playbook edition.

84. Garrick and Abington's correspondence about the revisions to Bickerstaff's *Sultan* is reprinted in Tasch, "Garrick's Revisions," 141–49.

85. David Garrick, letter no. 961, in *Letters of David Garrick*, vol. 2, ed. David M. Little and George M. Kahrl (Oxford: Oxford University Press, 1963), 1051–52; cited in Tasch, "Garrick's Revisions," 143.

86. Bickerstaff, *The Sultan*, as follows: "A grand March at Sultan's entry" (8); Osmyn's "Behold yonder zephyr how lightly it blows" (8); Ismena "Blest hero in Peace and War" (11); Ismena's song during the dinner is indicated by stage direction only, "Ismena, oblige us with a song" (22).

87. Tasch, "Garrick's Revisions," 145.

88. The prompter William Hopkins noted in his diary, "This farce was brought on the stage by Mrs Abington—it is very dull—It is vastly well got up and was received with great applause." William Hopkins, Manuscript Diary, 1769–76, Folger Shakespeare Library, Washington DC; cited in George W. Stone, ed., *The London Stage, 1660–1800: A Calendar of Plays*, part 4, vol. 3, *1767–76* (Carbondale: Southern Illinois University Press, 1962), 1937. The description of the set is contained in Larpent Manuscript Plays, MS 397, Henry E. Huntington Library, San Marino, California. The description is only partially reprinted in *The London Stage*; the editor notes that the Larpent manuscript for this work contains "one of the most elaborate stage directions of the period." Hopkins, *The London Stage*, 1908.

89. "The managers . . . bestowed three new scenes in it: The Outer Gate of the Seraglio—An Interior view of it—and a Garden terminating in a prospect of the sea. The first was but *la! la!* The last two were beautiful and picturesque." *Westminster Magazine*, December 1775, quoted in Stone, *The London Stage*, 1937. This report also states that "five airs were introduced into this piece," but the playbook indicates that only four numbers were used in the production.

16

Scheherazade, *Bluebeard*, and Theatrical Curiosity

ELIZABETH KUTI

Theatrical Orientalism was only one branch of a widespread cultural interest, even obsession, with representing "the East" which flourished in all branches of literature and the arts during the long eighteenth century. Onstage, these representations took the form of plays both serious and comic, as well as pantomimes, romances, innovative scenographic displays of the type developed by Philippe de Loutherbourg, melodramas, burlesques, and burlettas.[1] In *Orientalism* Edward Said famously proposed that "the idea of representation is a theatrical one. . . . The Orient is the stage on which the whole East is confined," and subsequent critics have echoed him, for example, Rana Kabbani in *Europe's Myths of Orient*: "The Orient is the malleable theatrical space in which can be played out the egocentric fantasies of Romanticism."[2] By invoking theatricality, Said and critics in his wake have emphasized the fakeness and inauthenticity of *all* Western representations of the East in their crude "theatrical" use of costumes, props, and sleight of hand.[3] It follows from this, therefore, that Orientalism *in the theater* must be doubly inauthentic, doubly fake.

However, perhaps another way of viewing this "double theatricality" might be to see it not as a double dose of fakery and inauthenticity but as metatheatricality: a performance which consciously represents or investigates its own theatricality, where not only is fantasy avowedly fantasy but the medium itself promotes an awareness, even an irony, about its own means of production and transmission. In the theater we know that the costumes and props are not real; we revel in artificiality; we are consciously and willingly engaging with an illusion. Theater provides a realm not of knowledge, in any secure or complacent sense, but of imagination. Furthermore, there may be levels of irony or consciousness of play and parody shared with the live audience in the moment of performance that are difficult to discern when looking at a printed text, decades or even centuries afterward.

To illustrate this point and to examine how Orientalism functioned in the theater in the past—and how it functions today—it seems helpful to turn to a specific example of a popular Orientalist play, one linked closely with the *Arabian Nights*, and to look in some detail at its origins, performance history, reception, and evolution. *Blue-beard, or Female Curiosity* (1798) by George Colman and Michael Kelly provides a rich example of theatrical Orientalism in its combination of two key, and very potent, threads of influence: first, the inherent power of the Bluebeard fairy tale (in which a tyrannical husband, with a terrifying blue beard, gives his new bride the keys to his castle and tells her she may look into any room, apart from the chamber to which the smallest key opens the door), and second, the frame story of the *Arabian Nights*, with which the Bluebeard tale resonates strongly when transposed by librettist Colman to an Eastern setting.

Colman and Kelly's *Blue-beard* potently combines many of the energies of the 1790s. It draws on late eighteenth-century experimentations in *Nights*-inspired Oriental drama (for example, John O'Keeffe's *Aladdin* of 1788) as well as a long native English stage tradition of "seraglio drama"—a tradition which existed before the translation of the *Nights* into English but which was then also reinvigorated by it. *Blue-beard* in 1798 furthermore combined Gothic spectacle with Romantic sensibility and (unsurprisingly given its theatrical origins in France in the early 1790s) revolutionary undertones (fig. 20). Like the *Nights*, *Blue-beard* is both a narrative and a metanarrative about the power of storytelling, with the provocation of curiosity at its core. It is also a compelling piece of metatheater, which foregrounds its own theatricality through presenting a stage-managing tyrant whose stage machinery is ultimately destroyed. And most significantly, perhaps, as both an Orientalist and a Romantic text, it foregrounds and examines the very notion of "curiosity," maintaining a provocative and inconsistent ambivalence about the value and significance of curiosity and the desire to know, to investigate taboo and forbidden terrain. The legend festooned across the moving, mechanical Skeleton inside Colman's Blue Chamber reads "The Punishment of Curiosity"; but in many ways the play dramatizes not the punishment but the rewards of curiosity, as the result of Fatima's curiosity is the destruction of Bluebeard and his tyrannical regime. Curiosity—encompassing lust for knowledge, sexual hunger, and voyeurism—are all explored in this resonant piece of theater, which, as Marjean D. Purinton has shown, drew on a Romantic "culture of curiosity" in which the discourses of science or pseudoscience, as manifested in the prevalence of the theatrically presented "curiosity cabinet" or scientific demonstration of wonder, merged with theater as a space for the visual pleasures of curiosity, horror, and wonder. Purinton argues that "just as curiosity cabinets put crime and sexuality on display, these plays [Colman's *Blue-beard* and *The Iron Chest*] use chests and closets, in which pathological impulses are secreted, to engineer a meta-performance of cultural curiosity."[4] Purinton thus sees the play merging scientific and theatrical discourses through its voyeuristic display of "the curious." Another discourse with which it engages is the "cultural curiosity" and "lust for knowing" associated with Orientalist discourse.[5] By linking this "lust for knowing" to theatricality, the play can be said perhaps to highlight the very "theatricality" of the Orientalist project to scrutinize and represent the East, as noted by Said. By looking closely at the origins, texture, and reception of *Bluebeard* in the theater, perhaps it may also be possible to suggest that many performances of *Bluebeard* were more complex cultural events than might at first appear, characterized by irony, metatheatrical awareness, and a self-conscious pleasure in fantasy and illusion.

Bluebeard's incarnation in the English theater began in 1797, when the Irish tenor and actor Michael Kelly persuaded the playwright George

Colman to collaborate with him in the creation of *Blue-beard, or Female Curiosity!*, a spectacular musical play based on Charles Perrault's fairy tale of Bluebeard.[6] Their "Dramatick Romance" was designed specifically, so Colman tells us in the preface, for the post-Christmas January slot at Drury Lane: "English Children, both old and young, are disappointed without a Pantomime at Christmas;—and, a Pantomime not being forthcoming in Drury Lane, I was prevail'd upon to make out the subsequent Sketch, expressly for that season, to supply the place of Harlequinade."[7] Perhaps because John O'Keeffe's *Aladdin and His Wonderful Lamp* had received its successful premiere at Covent Garden a decade before, Colman, as manager of Drury Lane, must have been looking for an opportunity to rival it, and he made the innovative decision to transpose the story and characters to an exotic Turkish setting.[8] From this decision sprang the most enduring characters of his libretto, the two seductively clad young heroines, Fatima and her sister Irene, and the murderous, blue-bearded Bashaw, Abomelique. These hybrid creatures, born seemingly equally of the *Arabian Nights*, Perrault's tale, and the Drury Lane wardrobe department, were to grip the public imagination for at least another hundred years. Within two years, Colman and Kelly's *Blue-beard*, according to Barry Sutcliffe, "stood unopposed as the most frequently performed afterpiece of the eighteenth century."[9] Revivals of the play were common throughout the nineteenth century, both in London and in provincial theaters across the country, and a host of imitations, pastiches, and parodies followed in its wake.

Because the Colman-Kelly *Blue-beard* became such a widespread phenomenon in theatrical and popular culture, it reveals a great deal about the texture of *Nights*-inspired Orientalism in the eighteenth and nineteenth centuries. It exemplifies the mixed parentage, the ability to transform and to travel, and the tireless absorption of the energies and cultural obsessions of the moment of so many of Scheherazade's children. In its many reincarnations, *Bluebeard* became a ubiquitous, self-parodying pastiche, referring metatheatrically to the comedic traditions of Punch and folk drama. The "Dramatick Romance" of 1798 had metamorphosed completely into a "Pantomime" by the close of the nineteenth century, but the *Nights* remained persistently at its core: sea serpents and elements of nautical drama, more fitting to Sinbad than Bluebeard, appeared in its ever more spectacular manifestations. While the radicalism of the 1798 text diminished, a flavor of subversiveness persisted in its pantomime incarnations; it remained a vehicle for topical jokes on the state of the nation and witty comment on technological innovations such as the advent of the "locomotive" and of electricity, as in, for example, *Blue-beard Repaired: A Worn-Out Subject Done Up Anew: An Operatic Extravaganza in One Act*, libretto by Henry Bellingham (1866), which featured a scene in which the dead wives are revived by electricity to form a kind of zombie harem.[10]

While Colman does not mention the *Arabian Nights* overtly (and in the preface dedicates the piece to Mother Goose as the originator of the story), nonetheless in choosing to set it in the Ottoman empire, he was undoubtedly drawing on the visual language of the *Nights* which the theater had enthusiastically embraced and developed over the century following the translation of Antoine Galland's *Nights* into English.[11] The folklorist Casie E. Hermansson has commented that Colman's choice to Orientalize the story meant that, "a century later, chapbook illustrations for *Bluebeard* and for the *Arabian Nights* were literally interchangeable."[12] The tyrannical Abomelique, the beautiful Fatima, and her lively younger sister Irene came to dominate not just theatrical but all representations of the tale of Bluebeard throughout the nineteenth century, reappearing in toy theaters, puppet shows, songbooks, chapbooks, pamphlets, and illustrated children's stories, long after their genesis in Colman and Kelly's "Syllabub" of a pantomime had been forgotten.[13] In a manner strangely appropriate to its fairy-tale origins, the Colman-Kelly *Blue-beard* acquired both anonymity and a chameleon-like ability to reinvent itself, over the decades, in rewritten and revised stage versions, both in Britain and in America. To this day Kelly's music still lingers piecemeal in the archives, unattributed scraps of it to be found as sheet music or in old songbooks, and there are references to its appearance on hurdy-gurdies and barrel organs.[14]

In particular, Colman's orientalizing libretto sets up a compelling and resonant connection to the frame story of the *Arabian Nights*. The murderous sultan of the *Nights*, whose bedchamber leads inevitably to death for a succession of sacrificial wives, is echoed in Abomelique, Colman's Turkish tyrant, the "three-tailed bashaw" whose "Blue Chamber" houses the decapitated remains of his former brides. The two sisters of the *Nights*, Scheherazade and Dinarzade, become Colman's sisters Fatima and Irene, who risk death and then ultimately defeat the despotic tyrant who has caused so much destruction among their countrywomen.[15] A more naïve version of Scheherazade, Fatima's role in the story is to evade the fate of all the previous unfortunate, murdered wives. In both plots, narrative curiosity motors the text; Scheherazade achieves a stay of execution on her wedding night, and then on each consecutive night, by provoking the sultan's curiosity to know the ending of the story, thus leading him along a labyrinthine narrative path that she stage-manages with the help of her sister. In a reversal of the Scheherazade/Shahriyar dynamic, however, in *Blue-beard* it is the male tyrant Abomelique who provokes the curiosity of his young wife and her sister by his elaborate stage-managing of the key and the Chamber.

While Colman's *Blue-beard* appealed generally to the widespread eighteenth-century taste for "Easternness" in myriad forms, both frivolous and highbrow, it has a particular affinity with those works in which curiosity about the harem or seraglio takes center stage. Penetrating into the "forbidden" space of the harem, a place normally shut off from the prying eyes of Westerners and outsiders, is a common topic of Orientalist art. Contrary to the normal model of a curious male gaze as the driving force of conquest and discovery, when it comes to the forbidden zone of the harem, female curiosity may be satisfied when male curiosity cannot be. Female artists and writers alone had the privilege of being able to look at and report back on the world of Eastern women, as Lady Mary Wortley Montagu unequivocally states in her famous account of a Turkish bagnio: "such a sight as you never saw in your life, and what no book of travels could inform you of, as 'tis no less than death for a man to be found in one of these places."[16] Wortley Montagu's account of the hammam in her *Turkish Embassy Letters* (1721) is notable for its acknowledgment, and enjoyment of, a mutual, intercultural female curiosity; the narrator herself is as much an object of curiosity to be explored and unveiled as she is a voyeuristic spectator. In one of the text's most memorable (and analyzed) moments, there is an unexpected, swooping reversal of viewpoint, in which the reader suddenly realizes, along with Lady Mary herself, that from the Turkish women's perspective, it is Lady Mary in her Western corsets who is "locked up" in a confined and inviolable space or "machine" to which they assume her husband must hold the key:

> The lady that seemed the most considerable amongst them entreated me to sit by her and would fain have undressed me for the bath. I excused myself with some difficulty, they being however all so earnest in persuading me, I was at last forced to open my shirt, and show them my stays, which satisfied them very well, for I saw they believed I was so locked up in that machine, that it was not in my own power to open it, which contrivance they attributed to my husband.[17]

Despite Lady Mary Wortley Montagu's covert acknowledgment of the constraints that she and all Western women lived within ("locked up in that machine"), the typical European view of the "Eastern" woman was that, in contrast to the liberty enjoyed by European women, she occupied forbidden and locked spaces: the "harem" or "seraglio" to which only a tyrannical male held the key. The difference between these two terms is instructive. Ruth Bernard Yeazell asserts that while the word *harem* derives from the Arabic word meaning "sacred" or "forbidden," the Western perception of Eastern women as "imprisoned" led to the coining of the word *seraglio*:

> Thinking of women as literally locked up in the harem, Europeans mistakenly associated the Turco-Persian word for palace, *saray*, with the Italian *serrare*, to lock up or enclose—by which false etymology the English "seraglio" and the French *serail* came to signify not only an entire building (as in the "Grand Seraglio" at Constantinople), but the apartments in which the women were confined.[18]

The connotations of the word *seraglio*, with its misconstrued etymological origins, therefore collapsed the notion of "palace" and "prison" into one, blending luxury and decadence with tyranny and oppression. It was a combination of meanings that in the 1790s had insistently radical overtones. If, as Yeazell suggests, the word *harem* meant a sacred or untouchable space which could as well be produced by the wearing of a veil when a woman went outside, the word *seraglio* connoted physical walls, locks, and keys: thus "identifying the harem as a seraglio could intensify its associations with slavery and imprisonment."[19] In post-1789 Europe, depicting the incarceration or liberation of female "slaves" from the seraglio could not help but raise the specter of the Bastille and acquire specific revolutionary associations that, for example, Montesquieu's *Persian Letters* in 1721, for all its satire of contemporary French society, had not.

The locked or forbidden room inspires curiosity; and Colman's *Blue-beard*, like many other Orientalist works of art, both explores and exploits the idea of curiosity provoked by the locked and "forbidden" space, in which women are housed or confined, such as the harem. The mingling of curiosity, sexuality, and terror, already a key feature of the Perrault fairy tale, transfers very easily to the *Nights*-inspired setting, reinforcing Western perceptions of the East as both more sensual and more cruel than Enlightenment Europe. The locked and forbidden room in this case is Abomelique's Blue Chamber, and it is both sepulcher and grisly harem, housing the tyrant's collection of corpse-brides. The much-quoted stage directions for the play's most famous spectacular scene read,

> The Door instantly sinks, with a tremendous crash: and the Blue Chamber appears streaked with vivid streams of Blood. The figures in the Picture over the Door change their position, and Abomelique is represented in the action of beheading the Beauty he was, before, supplicating.—The Pictures, and Devices, of Love, change to subjects of Horror and Death. The Interior apartment (which the sinking of the door discloses) exhibits various Tombs, in a sepulchral building;—in the midst of which ghastly and supernatural forms are seen; some in motion, some fix'd—In the centre is a large Skeleton seated on a tomb, (with a Dart in his hand) and, over his head, in characters of Blood, is written "THE PUNISHMENT OF CURIOSITY."[20]

The ghoulish "punishment" of curiosity is a significant departure here. European curiosity about the forbidden territory of the seraglio is the subject of a clutch of eighteenth-century plays, but while "reform" of the Eastern tyrant's polygamy is frequently a feature of the denouement, punishment of European prying curiosity usually is not. Instead European curiosity about Eastern sexual mores is frequently given a comic treatment: for example, Isaac Bickerstaff's comic opera *The Sultan; or A Peep behind the Seraglio* (1775) and Elizabeth Inchbald's later parodic response to Bickerstaff, *The Mogul Tale* (1784). Originally titled *A Peep into a Planet*, Inchbald's comedy has a hot-air balloon bring three Western visitors into the harem, among them "Fanny," a mocking representation of the character played by the actress Frances ("Fanny") Abington in Bickerstaff's earlier play.[21] Thus in *Mogul Tale*, the West's scientific curiosity, so typical of the Romantic era—in this case the obsession with flight and ballooning—is mingled with the curiosity of Orientalism and the desire to "peep" into hitherto inaccessible realms. Peeping and prying have sexual undertones in all these works and promise the audience the titillation of the harem being "unveiled" as a visual feast onstage.

In *Blue-beard*, the visual feast on offer is thrillingly horrible. Its blood-drenched "harem" is closely allied with the "bridal chamber" of the *Nights*, where the defloration of virgins has been swiftly followed by their execution. The link between sexual initiation and destruction is also played out in *Blue-beard*; Fatima's exploration on the eve of her wedding night is the drama of a young woman on the threshold of discovery (in Perrault's tale the wedding has taken place and a few weeks have passed since its consummation; in Colman's play eighteenth-century propriety demands that the ceremony has yet to take place, and so Fatima's virginity is preserved for her true love, the valiant Selim). The forbidden Blue Chamber is therefore the bridal chamber, a nightmarish version of the wedding night, where initiation into sexuality entails bloody consequences.[22] Irene's song earlier in the play, "Moving to the Melody of Music's Note," ends with "Cupid, Cupid, God of hearts, dancing sharpens all your darts," and Cupid's darts are grimly parodied when the Chamber transforms and scenes of courtship are replaced by "a large Skeleton seated on a Tomb (with a dart in his hand)." Betsy Bolton argues that Colman's "staging conflates sexuality and death: love turns to horror, supplication to severance. . . . The scene presents its specific threat to women's lives through an evocation of male sexual anxiety, in which women's bodies are figured as sepulchral and haunted spaces, running with blood."[23]

The "sepulchral and haunted space" is not only a figure for the female body but is the central imaginative site in Gothic dramas and narratives of the 1790s. Colman's Fatima is a Gothic heroine and Blue-beard's house the archetypal gloomy castle beckoning the young female heroine to discover its frightening secrets. Fatima's "disobedience" echoes Scheherazade's trickery of the sultan; and thus the *Nights* comes to resonate with the subversive and feminocentric undercurrents of Gothic fiction and drama of the 1790s. *Blue-beard* of course bears a familial resemblance to Gothic plays such as Matthew Gregory ("Monk") Lewis's *The Castle Spectre* (1797), which also dramatizes a trajectory from oppression to liberation, with the transgressive "curiosity" of its young heroine, Angela, resulting in the overthrow of a tyrant and the opening up of a sepulchral "prison." It seems appropriate that Michael Kelly, the composer of *Blue-beard*, had found his inspiration in Paris in August 1790, when he attended a performance of André Grétry's opera *Raoul Barbe-Bleue*.[24] Another reason for Colman to "Orientalize" the English Bluebeard and set it in Turkey (an element not present in Grétry's opera) may have been to distance it from its French source and the consequent political implications that a French setting might otherwise have made too direct.

However, as well as Perrault, the *Nights*, the French influence from Grétry, and the debt to Gothic, another influence on Colman's *Bluebeard* is the native English stage tradition of plays in which despotic Eastern tyrants are confronted and outwitted, tamed by romantic love or overthrown in some way by the young heroine. This family of plays, staging the conflict between an Eastern ruler and a defiant young female (whether his bride, captive, or object of courtship), is a feature of the British repertoire both from before the arrival of the *Arabian Nights* in English and after it throughout the eighteenth century. Playwrights and audiences clearly found in this story—both in comic and in tragic modes—a means to explore all sorts of power struggles, whether of politics, race, or gender; and it is of course a confrontation explored in many prose and verse narratives also.[25] Shakespeare's *Othello* is an early example of the prototype; another is William Davenant's *The Siege of Rhodes* (1656), in which the modest but desirable Christian Ianthe wins the heart of the sultan from his Eastern courtesan Roxolana.[26] Mary Pix's tragedy *Ibrahim, Thirteenth Emperor of the Turks* (1696) dramatizes Pix's Whig politics by portraying the morally justified overthrowing of a tyrannical and sexually corrupt "king"—here figured as the Emperor

Ibrahim—at the instigation of the young virtuous heroine, Morena.[27] Later rewritings in the mid-eighteenth century of the sultan-Roxolana story often, as we have noted, took a comic turn, as in the Bickerstaff and Inchbald comedies already discussed.[28]

However, there is one early eighteenth-century play with a particular relationship with *Blue-beard* as it too dramatizes the Scheherazade story. In December 1706, hot on the heels of the appearance of Galland's translation of *Arabian Nights' Entertainments*, Delariviere Manley wrote her "tragedy of state" *Almyna*, commenting in her preface, "The Fable is taken from the Life of that great Monarch, *Caliph Valid Almanzor*, who Conquer'd *Spain*, with something of a Hint from the *Arabian Nights Entertainments*." The piece is arguably the very first direct (literary or) theatrical response to the *Nights* in English.[29] Almyna's version of "female curiosity" is the thirst for knowledge which has led her, like Scheherazade, to become widely read and very learned—another kind of female transgression with which the playwright (who anagrammatically shares her name) clearly empathizes. A kind of Portia figure, Almyna attempts to break the sultan's tyrannical regime by drawing on historical examples and precedents to argue against his interpretation of the Qur'an (that women, like animals, have no souls and can therefore be killed with impunity).[30] Misogyny, and its fatal consequences for its female victims, is a serious concern in this play; the ill treatment of women by men is explored by Manley from several perspectives.[31] Almyna, like Scheherazade and Fatima in *Blue-beard*, is closely involved with her sister, Zoradia, and the fortunes of the two sisters are closely intertwined. In Manley's play, the Sultan Almanzor, anguished by his first wife's infidelity, has taken a vow to behead each new bride the morning after the wedding night. He is nonetheless a morally conscious being and is haunted by guilty dreams about his murdered brides:

> I dream'd that I was passing the deep Lake,
> The fatal Plank, laden with all my sins!
> Our Prophet, on the other side to Judgement,
> Encompast, with the ghost of those fair Queens,
> Whom in the fear of Jealousy, I'de Murther'd.
> To me they pointed, with Revengeful Rage,
> And cry'd, that was no landing place for me.

> Charg'd with the blood of Innocents I was,
> And must not hope to tread the blissful Plains;
> Unless I could Attonement make, for my rash Vow,
> And rather Deeds; but, oh!, 'twas now too late!
> Opprest with weight, the rotten Plank gave way,
> Deep in the horrid River I was plung'd,
> My Strugling Soul, already tasting Torments.
> Our Queen's aloud shouting revengful Joy! [*sic*][32]

It is not only the ghosts of the decapitated queens that cry for vengeance for crimes against women. Almyna has been promised in marriage to the sultan's nephew, Abdalla, but then finds out that Abdalla has previously made vows of love to her sister, before betraying and abandoning her in favor of Almyna herself. So to avoid a marriage that would break her sister's heart, as well as to attempt to end the murder of her countrywomen, Almyna offers herself as the next bride for the sultan—risking her own neck in an act of sisterhood both literal and metaphorical. Her plan is to argue him out of his vow, but in the climactic scene in act 4 in which she finally confronts him, the two fall mutually and passionately in love. Ultimately the "Arabian Vow" made by Almanzor, that he will execute each bride at daybreak and thereby wreak vengeance on all women because of his wife's infidelity, is broken by a theatrical performance staged-managed by Almanzor himself. After an ecstatic wedding night Almyna, wearing the Black Robe of Death, is about to be executed by the bowstring when Almanzor proclaims that her execution is merely a staged event—"it was ne'er designed but as a trial."[33] While Almyna had attempted to prove the case through eloquence and reasoned argument, ultimately it is the theatrical set piece of the Sultan Almanzor which clinches it, and thus Almyna and her countrywomen are saved from execution (the bowstring).[34]

The arrival of the *Arabian Nights' Entertainments* in the anonymous "Grub Street" English translation in 1706 thus clearly opened up new possibilities in "seraglio" drama: the conventional jealousy plot of sexually voracious, rival wives competing for favor (which Manley had explored in 1696 in an earlier Oriental tragedy, *The Royal Mischief*) could be replaced by a more sisterly, feminist narrative. This shift must have found favor in the more sentimental era of the eighteenth century, when even in the early decades the she-tragedy and the pathetic novel were celebrating suffering feminine virtue, while by the latter half of the century an early feminist movement was making its presence felt in the prominence of the Bluestocking Circle and of course in the landmark publication of Mary Wollstonecraft's *Vindication of the Rights of Woman* in 1792. With Scheherazade as a model, eloquence, wit, daring, and the outwitting of a despotic sultan could take place even in the context of a harem, and the saving of sisters, both literal and metaphorical, becomes the motivation. *Almyna* as a heroic verse tragedy is generically —and in most other ways—a world away from Colman's *Blue-beard*, yet the plays do share the key elements of the *Nights* frame tale: the two sisters, the murdered former wives, and a metatheatrical slant in their respective Eastern tyrants, who, like so many of their stage forbears and descendants, have something of the stage-manager or playwright about them (as we have seen, both Colman's Abomelique and Manley's Almanzor contrive elaborate theatrical scenarios in order to test their new wives.)[35]

Colman's *Blue-beard* furthermore imbues the *Nights'* frame story, of a male tyrant outwitted by female trickery, with the humanitarian, radical, and sentimental energies of the 1790s. Fatima prefers her true love, the valiant but impoverished young soldier Selim, to the wealthy "three-tailed bashaw" and piously declares, "I have no joy, now, Irene, in observing the idle glitter and luxury of wealth." She moralizes on the importance of obedience, even in the face of temptation: "Tempt me not to a breach of faith, Irene. When we betray the confidence reposed in us, to gratify our curiosity, a crime is coupled to a failing, and we employ a vice to feed a weakness."[36] These platitudes are discarded fairly quickly as they near the forbidden room. Hearing a groan from inside the Blue Chamber, Irene suggests there may be some "wretched soul" inside whom it would be "humanity" to rescue—Fatima seizes on this justification for defying Abomelique's command: "Humanity alone, my sister, could induce me to penetrate the mystery this Portal here incloses."[37] Curiosity can be closely allied with, or indeed dressed up as, humanitarianism; or it can be voyeuristic, rebellious, subversive, lascivious. The sisters' curiosity, despite the decorous humanitarian pretext they offer, proves to be an unruly force, the spur to defiance and disobedience. But despite the motto in the Chamber, the play enacts not the punishment of female curiosity but its triumph over injustice: Abomelique and his regime are overthrown, and a new egalitarian era is ushered in, headed by Selim, Fatima's true love. Outraged at Abomelique's abuse of power in abducting his beloved Fatima, Selim's words in act 1 are prophetic of the play's narrative shape: "When Power is respected its basis must be Justice. 'Tis then an edifice that gives the humble shelter and they reverence it:—But, 'tis a hated shallow fabric that rears itself upon oppression:—the breath of the discontented swells into a gale around it, till it totters."[38] Abomelique's edifice is indeed about to crumble; his "Power" in Colman's text is revealed to be intensely theatrical: a set of stage effects, a "shallow fabric" that can be torn away. And just as the Bluebeard tale, like the *Nights*, is a metanarrative about storytelling, *Bluebeard* the play is highly metatheatrical, dramatizing the notion that power behaves theatrically, securing its supremacy through spectacle and stage effects. Abomelique's mastery is of narrative and technological stage wizardry.

It seems some of the stage wizardry of the original 1798 production of *Blue-beard* at Drury Lane malfunctioned on opening night—which by all accounts only added to the entertainment value of the evening. The *St. James's Chronicle* reported on the scene in the Blue Chamber at the climax of the action thus, when the "Spectre of Death" did not collapse as it was supposed to:

> Kelly [playing Selim] attempted in vain to remove the Spectre of Death. In the height of his indignation he pummelled it several times thinking to force it to abscond from the public eye. The Spectre remained however incorrigible and shewed uncommon attention to the audience, by the most polite bows we ever witnessed from a Spectre! The spectators could not resist the temptation and laughed very heartily.[39]

The audience clearly enjoyed this reminder of the pitfalls of live theater. They also took the opportunity to enjoy any hint of political allusion or comment that they could wring from the evening's entertainment: the same newspaper reports on an incident occurring on the first night when one particular line of dialogue caused a protracted uproar, with the audience taking sides and cheering or booing accordingly: "A political allusion, 'that it was a fine thing to be a great man in office when no one could turn him out' was well received, although a long contention, in which the ayes had decidedly the advantage, arose in consequence of it."[40] This line was swiftly cut both from the production and from the published play text, as the *Whitehall Evening Post* makes clear: "We are happy to observe that a political allusion which created much discontent on the first night of representation, is omitted."[41]

However, though this one "political allusion" was omitted, the famous "March" scene in act 1 provided another excuse for political comment, this time from the reviewer in the *Morning Chronicle*. The stage directions in the script give a clear picture of the perspective effect, with Abomelique's camels and elephants appearing in miniature in the distance and then gradually following a winding path, reappearing bigger at each successive reappearance: "The Sun rises gradually.—A March is heard at a great distance.—Abomelique, and a magnificent train, appear, at the top of the Mountain—They descend through a winding path:—Sometimes they are lost to the sight, to mark the irregularities of the road. The Musick grows stronger as they approach.[42] To achieve this perspective effect, Abomelique's elephants, camels, and attendants were first played in the distance by small puppets; then, having disappeared offstage into the wings, they reappeared as though from around a bend in the road, this time played by children on scaled-down model animals; finally, having disappeared into the wings again, the procession arrived onstage, with adults appeared riding life-size models of elephants, camels, and horses. The reviewer in the *Morning Chronicle* makes this much-admired moment of spectacular scenography a pretext for a political witticism: "The Premier who is nearly as acute a Critic as he is a Politician, objects to that part of the machinery in *Blue-beard* which exhibits the progress from puppets to children, from children to men. Pantomimically this may be right, but politically the very reverse is found to answer best."[43]

The technological complexity and lavishness of *Blue-beard* might have ensured that it remained an entertainment reserved for the capital. Then, as now, very expensive spectacular entertainments were more the province of the West End than of smaller provincial theaters. However, *Blue-beard*'s popularity and commercial appeal meant that theater managers outside London made the extra investment to bring it to their lucky audiences: Salisbury, for example, saw an early revival of the play in 1799.[44] London audiences were treated to a famous revival at Covent Garden in February 1811, at the height of the Napoleonic wars—despite an angry article in the *Times* attacking Covent Garden's pandering to a low taste for "buffoonery and shew."[45] It seems the critics' hostility to Covent Garden's staging of spectacle could not stem the tide of revivals and productions of *Blue-beard* in London and across the country. Then in 1839 *Bluebeard* underwent a reincarnation at the hands of James Robertson Planché and Charles Dance, who created *Blue-beard: A Grand Musical, Comi-Tragical, Melo-Dramatic, Burlesque Burletta in One Act*, designed as a comeback vehicle for Madame Vestris at the Olympia and first performed on 1 January 1839. A review of the performance in the *Standard* is careful to stress the research and verisimilitude of the production, which prides itself on having "re-discovered" through "antiquarian" investigation the original French medieval setting of Perrault:

> The antiquarian researches of . . . [Planché] having discovered that Abomelique was no three-tailed bashaw, but a French knight in the middle of the thirteenth century, the costume of that period has been most carefully preserved . . . exhibiting a most artistical spirit, and a sedulous attention to antiquarian properties. . . . The interior of the terrible "Blue Chamber" was most whimsically conceived, and most ingeniously executed. The thirteen deceased wives of Abomelique were discovered with their heads under their arms, and sang a chorus to the tune of "Nid-nid-nodding," their hands nodding their heads to the music. As usual the dialogue contained smart hits to the present times, and some of them produced unanimous laughter. Madame Vestris's character corresponded to that known in the oriental version by the name of Fatima. Bland was a magnificently pompous Blue-beard and stormed, scowled, and brandished his sword in a way that would have filled the heart of Mother Goose with rapture; for, be it remembered, that that venerable old lady was the historian who in the tales that bear her name, handed down to posterity the fortunes of the cerulean-bearded hero.[46]

Planché refers to the original creators of the "oriental version," Kelly and Colman, but does not name them:

The melodramatists of the past century converted Blue-beard into an Eastern story but every child knows that the old nursery tale, by Mons. Charles Perrault, is nothing of the sort. . . . In accordance therefore with the laudable spirit of critical inquiry and antiquarian research, which distinguishes the present era, the scene of the drama has been restored to Brittany and the Costumes selected from authorities of the period mentioned above.[47]

Planché however justifies his continued use of the name Abomelique so as not "to wound the feelings of a noble family." Planché's 1839 text moves away from the "Grand Dramatick Romance" of Colman and deeper into pastiche and burletta. Abomelique is more ridiculous—and has a Punch-like ability to come back to life. After being slain he leaps up again—"They have but run me through my wedding clothes." Fleurette (the Fatima character, played by Vestris) comments, with metatheatrical irony, "Perhaps it's better so and for this reason / We humbly hope to run you through the season." The violence against women which is taken seriously to some extent in Colman's play has now, in Planché's reworking, become entirely humorous. Planché's play also features a Hibernianized version of the Turkish comic servant Shacabac, in the form of O'Shac O'Bac—described in the *Standard* review quoted earlier as the "Irish slave." His beloved, Margot, introduces him to the stage with the lines, "He comes! He heard me about whiskey talking; And to this spot the Irish dear is stalking." Shacabac's "Tink-a-tink" song in the original Kelly score, during which he plucked the strings of a guitar, is replaced in Planché by "Drink, drink, oh drink, oh, drink, I really cannot hear you! / 'Till, 'till for me you pour out whiskey, rum or gin!"[48] There are topical references to technological innovations, in particular the railroad: Selim arrives at the eleventh hour to save Fleurette, and when she reproaches him for his lateness, he replies, "No fault of mine; / The locomotive, love, got off the line! / And we were forced to post it as we might: / But here we are, you're safe and all is right!"[49] Topical references and jokes—a crucial ingredient, of course, of panto to this day—are a feature of subsequent *Bluebeards*, as it lent itself increasingly to parody throughout the nineteenth century.[50]

From an account of a production of *Bluebeard* at Drury Lane in 1880, it is clear that the Oriental setting and props are still there, but the piece has acquired all sorts of other machinery, stage props, and general story baggage from *Arabian Nights*—Sinbad in particular—mixed with elements of folk drama and Punch and Judy. The review in the *Era* reads,

> Blue-beard's domestic elephant has good support in Messrs Ridley and Ben Fielding, the fore and hind legs of the sagacious brute. . . . The properties, including a most wonderful sea-serpent (with a bright rolling eye, a restless tongue, a most ominous set of teeth, and a dangerously flexible body), a couple of elephants, a camel of magnificent proportions, all of the latter being capital imitations of nature, not to mention the swarm of spiders and the excellent masks and general get-up of the Giant Guards . . . are from the hands of Messrs Dykwynkin, Charles Halle and Powell; . . . the machinery . . . carried successfully the representation of Selim's ship, the advance of the Sea-Serpent and the ultimate rescue of the endangered sailor by the advent of a life-boat. . . . The lime-light effects etc and the gas are all under the control of Mr Randle and Mr Carter.[51]

The same review also describes how "Bluebeard's death à la Punch is also received with shouts of merriment, in spite of the intensity of people's serious interest a minute or two before." It is clear that the audience moves from "serious interest" to "shouts of merriment," laughter, and applause very quickly, in an emotional slalom recorded by the reviewer, who notes the "shouts of delight" greeting "each spectacular feature," followed quickly by "the intense vigilance of the spectators during the highly dramatic scene outside the Blue Chamber" and then "the enthusiasm with which is hailed a Transformation display which takes us back to the old days of Madame Vestris at the Lyceum."[52]

Each successive incarnation of *Bluebeard* seems to offer the pleasure of the old and the new: like a genetic trace, the *Nights* persists, not only in the Scheherazade/Shahriyar plot but with props and trappings from other stories: here, in particular, there are shades of Sinbad lurking in the sea serpents and rescue from a shipwreck by lifeboats. Previous much-loved performers of *Bluebeards* past haunt each new production ("the old days of Madame Vestris"), but new special effects and devices of horror crop up with each new revival (the swarm of spiders, for example, seems to be an innovation of Drury Lane's version of 1880). *Bluebeard* was a "gorgeous Christmas annual" which from its origins in

1798 was still entrancing audiences close to a hundred years later. And this is quite apart from its presence at regional theaters and its popularity as a "private theatrical" for home performance.[53]

In conclusion, Colman and Kelly's *Blue-beard* forged a connection between Perrault's tale of Barbe-bleue and the frame tale of the *Arabian Nights*, and in doing so, two powerful storytelling traditions were brought together in a collision that was to resonate for over a century through English theatrical and popular culture. With Scheherazade as an intertextual reference point, *Blue-beard* could profit, by association, from the subversive qualities of the *Nights*, bringing it into sympathy with the radical and feminist energies of the 1790s. Informed by late eighteenth-century experimentations in *Nights*-inspired Oriental drama, such as John O'Keeffe's *Aladdin*, as well as a native English stage tradition of "seraglio drama," *Blue-beard* is both metatheatrical and a metanarrative about the power of narrative, with the provocation of curiosity at its heart. And most significantly, perhaps, as an Orientalist text, it foregrounds and examines the notion of "curiosity," proclaiming to punish it while staging its reward.

What are we to make, then, of this piece of our theatrical history and tradition, which feeds in so clearly to our current, still widespread, Oriental pantomime culture? Just as *Blue-beard*'s critics did in its own time, we can see in its theatrical Orientalism all the flaws and failings pointed out by Said: inauthenticity, inaccuracy, and crude manipulation of stereotypes (such as O'Shac O'Back) to shore up national pride and assuage national guilt.[54] The Orientalism of *Blue-beard* is an act of masquerade from another age, a curio that we can only examine, chuckle, and exclaim over, as an evocative remnant of a disappeared time. But to recoil, quite properly, from certain elements of imperial Orientalism in the theater is perhaps also to ignore the complexity of the moment of a theatrical performance—to fail to acknowledge that the play happens in the space between the audience and the stage, at a particular historical juncture, with particular levels of shared irony, shared knowledge. To use an anecdotal example, I am reminded of my own experience as an actress, playing the Colleen Bawn in an Irish National Theatre Society production of Dion Boucicault's *The Colleen Bawn*. The production and its exuberant interpretation of Boucicault's crazed, cod "Oirish-ness" was met with joyous hilarity from Irish audiences at the Abbey Theatre in Dublin in 1998. This was at the height of Ireland's boom, with the Celtic tiger economy in full roar, *Riverdance* being packaged and sold all over the world, unfailing wins at Eurovision year after year, Irish pubs on every corner of every European city: Irish society had a new sense of confidence in and, indeed, irony about the brand of "Irish-ness" being packaged and sold globally. The amused indulgence, even rapturous enjoyment, demonstrated by Irish critics and audiences was replaced by a much colder response when the production transferred to the Lyttelton at the National Theatre in London. Theater critic Michael Billington accused the production of "perpetuating the myth of Killar-ney Blarney" (*Guardian*, 20 March 1999), and I remember being told by a friend in the audience that two American women sitting next to her stormed out midshow, appalled by this seemingly horrible parody of Irishness being perpetrated by (what they mistakenly assumed to be) a British National Theatre production with English actors. Context is everything. The shared knowledge between stage and auditorium in the moment of performance is all, and it is not necessarily captured by bare facts or by a surviving copy of a printed script.

The complex makeup of *Blue-beard* and its combination of many potent threads of influence perhaps suggest that it was more than simply being Colman's "Syllabub" of high commercial value to the-ater managers but of little nutritional value to its consumers. Perhaps it may also be possible to suggest that audiences had a more sophisti-cated awareness of the "performative" nature of "Orientalism" than has hitherto been assumed. Certainly the newspaper reviews of *Blue-beard* from 1798 onward suggest that audiences were quite able, and indeed were expected, to move swiftly from serious emotional engagement to uproarious laughter. From looking at the reviews and accounts of audi-ence responses to *Blue-beard* in the theater, we could hypothesize that there was perhaps a higher level than has previously been acknowl-edged of knowingness, a shared understanding, on both sides of the footlights, of the strings on which these Eastern puppets were dancing —and indeed, that the visibility of the strings was part of the pleasure of the spectacle.

NOTES

1. See John Mackenzie, *Orientalism: History, Theory and the Arts* (Manchester: Manchester University press, 1995), for a thorough survey of this topic; and Marina Warner, *Fantastic Metamorphoses, Other Worlds: Ways of Telling the Self* (Oxford: Oxford University Press, 2002), 141–50, on "Imperial Gothic" and other forms of Orientalism in the theater.

2. Edward Said, *Orientalism* (London: Penguin, 2003), 63; Rana Kabbani, *Europe's Myths of Orient: Devise and Rule* (Basingstoke, UK: Macmillan, 1986), 11.

3. See Jonas Barish, *The Antitheatrical Prejudice* (Berkeley: University of California Press, 1981), for a full-length treatment of the topic of theatricality as necessarily insincere, masked, superficial, and manipulating for effect.

4. Marjean D. Purinton, "George Colman's *The Iron Chest* and *Blue-beard* and the Pseudo-science of Curiosity Cabinets," *Victorian Studies* 49:2 (Winter 2007): 252.

5. Robert Irwin's 2006 study and defense of Orientalism was titled *For Lust of Knowing: The Orientalists and Their Enemies* (London: Allen Lane, 2006), the title being a quotation from the verse drama *Hassan: The story of Hassan of Baghdad and How He Came to Make the Golden Journey to Samarkand* (1922) by James Elroy Flecker: "For lust of knowing what should not be known / We take the golden road to Samarkand."

6. Michael Kelly, *Reminiscences* (London, 1826), 2:130–31; quoted in Barry Sutcliffe, introduction to *Plays by George Colman the Younger and Thomas Morton* (Cambridge: Cambridge University Press, 1983), 40.

7. George Colman, preface to *Blue-beard; or Female Curiosity! A Dramatick Romance* (London: Cadell and Davies, 1798), 3.

8. Ibid., 5.

9. Sutcliffe, introduction to *Plays by George Colman*, 40.

10. See Casie E. Hermansson, *Bluebeard: A Reader's Guide to the English Tradition* (Jackson: University Press of Mississippi, 2009), 103. Hermansson's monograph provides a very full account of the Bluebeard tale and its place in English culture.

11. See especially Bridget Orr's essay "Galland, Georgian Theatre, and the Creation of Popular Orientalism," in *The Arabian Nights in Historical Context*, ed. Saree Makdisi and Felicity Nussbaum, 103–29 (Oxford: Oxford University Press, 2008).

12. Hermansson, *Bluebeard*, 53.

13. "George Colman the Younger's . . . entertaining musical-play defined English perceptions of *Bluebeard* and inspired numerous *Bluebeard* burlesques, extravaganzas, and pantomimes in the nineteenth century." Michael Hiltbrunner, "The Grey Woman and Bluebeard's Bride," *Opticon1826* 7 (Autumn 2009): 5.

14. The entire score is still extant and a copy housed at the library of the Royal College of Music; my thanks to librarian and scholar Angela Escott for her help in locating it for me. See also Andrew Kuntz, "A Night at the Opera," *The Fiddler's Companion*, March 7, 2008, http://www.ibiblio.org/fiddlers/opera.htm, 9, for a

list of appearances of the march from *Blue-beard* in sheet music collections; also, "one of the oddest instances of the tune is on the barrel organ from the polar expedition of Admiral Parry of 1810. . . . Parry introduced a mechanical barrel organ on board ship to provide entertainment and a vehicle by which the men could exercise (i.e. by dancing). 'March in Blue-beard' was one of eight tunes on barrel no. 4" (ibid.).

15. Colman names the younger sister Irene, but her traditional fairy-tale name is Anne; this name does reappear in later nineteenth-century pastiches of *Blue-beard*, even when the names Abomelique and Fatima remain. In nineteenth-century "harlequin" or pantomime versions, "Sister Anne" was frequently played by a man. See Hermansson, *Bluebeard*, 94–97.

16. Lady Mary Wortley Montagu, letter 27, in *The Turkish Embassy Letters* (1721; repr., London: Virago, 1994), 60. Srinivas Aravamudan discusses this scene in his important article "Lady Mary Wortley Montagu in the Hammam: Masquerade, Womanliness and Levantinization," in *E.L.H.* 62:1 (Spring 1995): 69–104. See also Billie Melman, *Women's Orients: English Women and the Middle East, 1718–1918* (London: Macmillan, 1992); and Felicity A. Nussbaum, "British Women Write the East after 1750: Revisiting a 'Feminine' Orient," in *British Women's Writing in the Long Eighteenth Century*, ed. Jennie Batchelor and Cora Kaplan (London: Palgrave Macmillan, 2005).

17. Wortley Montagu, letter 27, 69–71.

18. Ruth Bernard Yeazell, *Harems of the Mind: Passages of Western Art and Literature* (New Haven: Yale University Press, 2000), 1–2.

19. Ibid., 2.

20. George Colman, *Blue-beard; or, Female Curiosity! A Dramatick Romance* (London: Cadell and Davies, 1798), 17.

21. See Daniel O'Quinn, *Staging Governance: Theatrical Imperialism in London, 1770–1800* (Baltimore: Johns Hopkins University Press, 2005), 18; and also Berta Joncus's discussion of Frances Abington and her role in *The Sultan* in chapter 15 in this volume (and fig. 28).

22. See Marina Warner's extensive discussion of the Bluebeard tale in *From the Beast to the Blonde: On Fairy-Tales and Their Tellers* (London: Chatto and Windus, 1994), especially 241–71; and on the interpretation of the "forbidden chamber" and its connection with childbirth and death, 263.

23. Betsy Bolton, *Women, Nationalism and the Romantic Stage: Theatre and Politics in Britain, 1780–1800* (Cambridge: Cambridge University Press, 2001), 69; also Warner, *From the Beast to the Blonde*, 263.

24. See Sutcliffe, introduction to *Plays by George Colman the Younger*, 39–40.

25. See also Yeazell, *Harems of the Mind*, for a full account of "harem" literature, especially chapter 14, "Taming Soliman and Other Great Ones," 149–60.

26. See Ros Ballaster's account of the "Roxolana" prototype in *Fabulous Orients: Fictions of the East in England, 1662–1785* (Oxford: Oxford University Press, 2005), 62: "The figure of Roxolana merges in the late seventeenth and early eighteenth

centuries with many other 'Roxolanas' and 'Roxanes'—some historical, some purely fictional—in dramatic, poetic and prose narrative."

27. The play draws on the drama of the Exclusion crisis and Glorious Revolution of 1688–90, with the Sultan Ibrahim a figure in which Charles II and James II are amalgamated. In Pix's play the virtuous Morena is raped by the Sultan Ibrahim; she invokes a military coup and revolution (before succumbing to madness and death), which results in Ibrahim's death and his regime brought to an end.

28. See the discussion previously of Bickerstaff, *The Sultan*, and Inchbald, *A Mogul's Tale*. Two years later Inchbald was to revisit the theme of Western curiosity about the East in more serious mode when she wrote her very popular "problem play" *Such Things Are* (1786), set in Sumatra, with the central character, Haswell, being modeled on the prison reformer John Howard. Here Orientalism and the Gothic were combined with a fashionable sentimental philanthropy as Inchbald's hero, Haswell, is taken on a tour on the gloomy, cavernous prison beneath the imperial palace. Haswell—a true eighteenth-century man of feeling —peers at and weeps for the prisoners who are incarcerated with little hope of reprieve from the merciless sultan; Haswell then mediates between the sultan and his abandoned lover, and the sultan's heart is melted and reformed. Another example of "seraglio comedy" from the 1790s with increasingly overt revolutionary undertones is Hannah Cowley's musical piece *A Day in Turkey; or, The Russian Slaves* (1791), in which much of the action takes place in the harem, and the captured Russian slave, Paulina, in typical Roxolana fashion, "educates" the sultan in the joys of freely given, monogamous love.

29. Delariviere Manley, *Almyna; or, The Arabian Vow* (London: William Turner, 1708), preface. See also Su Fang Ng, "Delariviere Manley's *Almyna* and Dating the First Edition of the English *Arabian Nights' Entertainments*," *English Language Notes* 40:3 (March 2003): 19–26.

30. Almyna points out to Almanzor the personal, psychological reasons behind his interpretation of the Qur'an: "thou securest thyself from thoughts of Sin: / For that our Prophet, in his Alcoran / As thou explain'st, says Women have no Souls, / But mighty Sultan, tell thy heart but this: / Had not thy beauteous, faulty Queen done ill? / Wouldst thou the Letter ere have expounded?" (Manley, *Almyna*, act 4, 45).

31. See Ballaster, *Fabulous Orients*, 84: "When he hears about her education at her father's hands and her intellectual brilliance, he [the sultan, Almanzor] dismisses her as 'A Contradiction, to her very nature.' Manley appears to be suggesting a symmetry between her own ambitions for political influence through witty writing and her heroine's verbal agency."

32. Manley, *Almyna*, act 4.

33. Ibid., act 5.

34. But though the sultan is reformed and united with Almyna in a loving and monogamous marriage, the generic demands of tragedy mean that the sultan's nephew, Abdalla, and Almyna's innocent sister, Zoradia, both die.

35. See also Voltaire's *Mahomet* (1742), adapted by James Miller and James Hoadly as *Mahomet the Imposter* (1742), in which the dramaturgical impulse of the Eastern tyrant is foregrounded. Ros Ballaster argues that the title of the Miller/Hoadly adaptation reinforces "the sense of Muhammad as consummate performer, an actor of a role he has invented to convey his authority, religious and secular" (Ballaster, *Fabulous Orients*, 53). Elizabeth Inchbald's Sumatran Sultan in *Such Things Are* (1783) is another such "performer," revealed to be an impersonator, a replacement for the "real" sultan, whom he physically resembles, performing the role of tyrant before his intimidated "people."

36. Colman and Kelly, *Blue-beard*, act 2, scene 2, 30–31.

37. Ibid., act 2, scene 4, 37.

38. Ibid., act 1, 8.

39. *The Oracle and Public Advertiser* 19,833 (January 17, 1798).

40. Perhaps this type of "long contention" among the audience, consisting of a group of "ayes" and "noes" in the audience, may be the origin of the British pantomime tradition in which audiences are encouraged to continue to chorus a dialogue of "Oh, yes it is" or "Oh, no it isn't" in response to action onstage, noted by Karl Sabbagh in chapter 13 in this volume.

41. *Whitehall Evening Post* 7986 (January 20, 1798).

42. Colman and Kelly, *Blue-beard*, act 1, 6.

43. *Morning Chronicle* 8944 (January 23, 1798). The same technology that created *Blue-beard*'s "March of Elephants" was in a few months put to a more directly ideological purpose, with the staging later the same year of James Cobb's *Ramah Droog; or, Wine Does Wonders* (1798), a play dramatizing and praising Britain's military victories in India. Daniel O'Quinn writes, "A great deal of attention is placed on the mechanical elephant as a figure not only for military might but also for technological rationality. . . . *Ramah Droog*'s procession acts as an allegory for acts of domination already achieved and yet to come." O'Quinn, *Staging Governance*, 333–34.

44. *Salisbury Journal*, February 1799 and January 1799: "Those who have seen this popular piece in London would scarce be persuaded it was practicable in a country theatre in so close a resemblance." Quoted in Arnold Hare, *The Georgian Theatre in Wessex* (London: Phoenix House, 1958), 156–57.

45. See Jane Moody, *Illegitimate Theatre in London, 1770–1840* (Cambridge: Cambridge University Press, 2000), 70–72.

46. *The Standard* (London) 4536 (January 3, 1839).

47. J. R. Planché and Charles Dance, *Blue-beard: A Grand Musical, Comi-Tragical, Melo-Dramatic, Burlesque Burletta in One Act*, in *The Extravaganzas of J. R. Planché, 1825–1871*, ed. T. F. Dillon Croker and Stephen Tucker, 5 vols. (London: Samuel French, 1879), 5:36.

48. Ibid., 5:43, 46.

49. Ibid., 5:62.

50. See Hermansson, "'You Outrageous Man!': Bluebeard on the Comic Stage," in

Blue-beard, 88–107. Karl Sabbagh's chapter 13 in this volume discusses the evolution and current state of British pantomime.

51. *Era* 2158 (February 1, 1880).

52. Ibid.

53. See, for example, Reginald Heber, *Blue-beard: A Serio-Comic Oriental Romance in One Act* (London and New York: Samuel French, 1874), first published in 1868. The foreword even promises, "with a view to obviate the great difficulty experienced by Amateurs (particularly in country houses) in obtaining Scenery etc, to fix in a Drawing room, and then only by considerable outlay for hire and great damage caused to walls, we have decided to keep a series of mounted Coloured Scenes which are ready for immediate use." A recent modern filmic evocation of *Bluebeard* as a Victorian home theatrical can be seen in Jane Campion's *The Piano* (which is itself a Bluebeard story).

54. See Moody, *Illegitimate Theatre*, 70, for an account of the criticism leveled at *Blue-beard* of inaccuracy and inappropriate pageantry: "critical reaction ranged from half-condescending rebukes about the play's alleged lack of oriental verisimilitude to downright fury."

17

The Takarazuka Revue and the Fantasy of "Arabia" in Japan

TETSUO NISHIO

Introducing the Arabian Nights into the Japanese Scene in the Meiji Era (1868–1912)

Figure 33 shows an illustration that appeared in a work of fiction that was translated into Japanese and published in 1887 (Meiji Era 20). At first glance, it seems to be an English novel, as might be expected from the figures dressed like Victorians. The illustration, however, shows a scene from a story of the *Arabian Nights*, with the Japanese title *Perusia shinsetsu retsujo no homare*, or "A New Story from Persia: A Courageous Lady's Honor," and the woman in the gorgeous dress is Marjana, the heroine of "Ali Baba and the Forty Thieves." From the last days of the Edo Era through the early Meiji Era (roughly in the eighteenth and nineteenth centuries), with the increase of information from overseas, many pictures representing foreign landscapes appeared. Most of them show Western cityscapes and figures, whereas pictures related to the Middle East are rare. Ryūkei Yano (1850–1931), who is thought to be the translator of "A Courageous Lady's Honor," wrote in the preface that "it is absolutely necessary to enlighten Japanese youth, and pass on to them information about the whole world."[1]

The *Arabian Nights* was first translated into Japanese in 1875 (Meiji Era 8), under the title *Kaikan kyōki Arabiya monogatari*, or "Strange and Marvelous Stories from Arabia" (fig. 32), by Hideki Nagamine (1848–1927), who was a teacher at the Naval Academy.[2] It was mainly based on Antoine Galland's edition through an English version of the *Arabian Nights* that was prepared by G. F. Townsend for young readers.[3] Nagamine's translation, however, was an abridged one.

Nagamine's intention in translating the *Arabian Nights* was not to introduce Japanese readers to Middle Eastern culture. He himself had learned about the world's situation through English books on history and was much concerned over the future of Japan. Consequently, he concluded that in order for Japan not to be colonized by European powers, the reinforcement of Japanese naval power was indispensable. In addition to the *Arabian Nights*, he translated many English works, including François Guizot's *The History of Civilization in Europe*.[4] According to his own explanation, his motivation for translating was to break down the island-nation mentality common among Japanese by spreading information about other countries of the world. That is to say, Nagamine considered the *Arabian Nights* to be a part of Western culture. In addition, Nagamine was much concerned with the education of women, so it seems curious in our modern eyes that Nagamine thought that the introduction of Western novels, especially the *Arabian Nights*, would form part of women's education suitable for the new era.

After Nagamine, the *Arabian Nights* was repeatedly translated. In 1883 (Meiji Era 16), Tsutomu Inoue (1850–1928) published *Zensekai ichidai kisho*, or "The Strangest Stories in the World," which became very popular for Japanese readers. Inoue was a governmental official but was also a prolific translator. His translations include William Shakespeare's *The Merchant of Venice*, Daniel Defoe's *Robinson Crusoe*, and Thomas More's *Utopia*. Inoue's translation of the *Arabian Nights* was widely read and went through several editions. Thanks to his translation, most of the stories included in the Galland edition were introduced to Japanese readers.

It seems that Inoue considered the *Arabian Nights* as entertainment and wrote in his preface, "The *Arabian Nights* is famous as a collection of curious stories, offering first-rate entertainment independently of period, nation, and country."[5] Inoue's *Arabian Nights* gained many readers and had a profound effect on the Japanese literary world. Not a few writers created their works under the influence of his translation of the *Arabian Nights*.

As I have indicated with respect to the early introduction of the *Arabian Nights* into the Japanese scene, its main stories were all translated into Japanese in the Meiji Era (1868–1912) and subsequently became popular stories for children in the next period, the Taishō Era (1912–1926).

The Historical Relationship between Japan and the Arab World

The historical relationship between Japan and the Arab world[6] was severely limited because of the great distance between the two areas, and consequently, it is obvious that the image that each had of the other was based on scarce information.[7] For instance, medieval Arab books on geography depicted a certain island named *Wāqwāq* where trees could be found bearing strange fruits like human faces. This island appears in "Sindbad the Sailor" in the *Arabian Nights*. It has been argued that this island, which was thought to be located beyond China, was actually Japan. Curiously enough, some Chinese and Japanese books also state, "in Tāji, which means Arabia in the Chinese language, there are strange trees that produce flowers like human faces."[8] It is probable that the same legend was used to describe the other people both in the Arab world and in Japan.

It should be noted here that although, until comparatively recent times, Japanese contacts with the Middle Eastern or Islamic cultures were indirect and limited, the source countries from which the information or artifacts pertaining to Middle Eastern or Arab-Islamic cultures were brought had rather great economic and political, sometimes military, interests in those areas. In this sense, Japan had a chance to obtain information of excellent quality, though very limited in quantity, about those areas throughout its history. First, China had a national border with the Abbasid dynasty; second, both the Portuguese and Spanish were hostile toward Islam after the so-called Reconquista; and third, the Dutch, who had a monopoly on trade with Japan during the

Edo Era, developed commercial interests with Islamic regions, especially South and Southeast Asia.

In the Edo Era (1603–1867), when contacts with foreign cultures
were very limited because of the policy of seclusion, the general public, however, had some chance to get information about the Middle
East, even though fragmentary. For instance, a Dutch ship which came
in Nagasaki, the only port open to foreign trade, brought two Arabian
camels in 1821 (the fourth year of Bunsei in the Edo Era).[9] These camels went on a tour around Japan and attracted great curiosity. The fliers
of that time listed the camels' positive value, claiming that they had an
effect on smallpox or skin disease. These two camels being a pair, it was
rumored that those who watched them would enjoy a happy married
life, and camel watchers scrambled to get commemorative goods.

The camels' boon (and boom) boosted the Japanese interest in getting knowledge about the geography of the Middle East. For instance,
Seizan Matsura (1760–1841), a Daimyo, or local lord, of Hirado and
renowned essayist of the Edo Era, correctly wrote in his famous essay
Kasshi yawa, or "Night-Stories in the Year of *Kasshi*" that "[these] camels are said to come from Mecca in Arabia."[10] The illustrators of that
period, however, usually presented figures standing by the camels as
Chinese, that is, as foreign or alien entitites.[11] The common people in
the Edo Era had few resources to imagine Arabia, the camels' home.

During the sixteenth and seventeenth centuries, in the Netherlands,
large and splendid maps were produced on the basis of geographical
information accumulated through the Age of Exploration. Many of
them illustrate symbolic figures representing different areas at the four
corners of the maps, and some maps of this kind were brought to Japan.
Being influenced by those imported maps, there appeared in the early
Edo Era gorgeous folding screens on which a Persian king and a Turkish king in turbans were painted. The Japanese intellectual elite, such as
Hakuseki Arai (1657–1725) and Joken Nishikawa (1628–1724), endeavored to get Western information through Chinese or Dutch documents
and published books depicting mummies, Mecca, and Muhammad.
Nishikawa wrote a treatise on the commercial goods of foreign countries, including in the Middle East, with detailed remarks about geographical and cultural traits. After having finished this work, he published a famous illustrated book, in which people in ethnic clothes from

forty-two countries were illustrated, including examples of Turkish and Persian people. His illustrated book was very popular and was reprinted many times (fig. 8).

On the other hand, common people also could access world maps based on Western information through popular encyclopedias. However, the Three Realms worldview based on Buddhist theory also had a strong influence.[12] The Three Realms worldview, which is a traditional interpretation of the world, specifies three areas, *Tenjiku* (India), *Kara* (China), and *Honchō* (Japan), forming the central area of the world. According to this worldview, so-called Western Asia, namely Persia, is located at a marginal region far beyond India. In due course, however, with the increasing influence of Western maps that were widely circulated among the general public, Europe took on larger significance,[13] whereas India lost its importance and Western Asia, or the Middle East, was fading, in turn, far beyond Europe and, in the same manner, was driven away into obscurity.

The Japanese view of the Middle East can be summed up as follows:

1. Until the Edo Era: A world far beyond China and India in terms of the Three Realms worldview.
2. After the Meiji Era: A world far beyond Europe in terms of a modernized or Westernized worldview.

As a consequence, the Middle East or the Arab world had come to be seen as a world of fantasy without any sense of reality. In this way, Japanese people considered the Middle East as an exotic locale, a suitable place for fantasies. The *Arabian Nights*, which was widely read after the Meiji Era, reinforced the imaginary Middle East as a fantastic world.

Stereotyped Ideas about the Middle East and *The Arabian Nights*

During the Edo Era, common people and children enjoyed reading *Kusa zōshi*, a kind of Japanese chapbook, which was written in simplified Chinese characters. Later, in the Taishō Era, a genre of juvenile literature was established under the influence of Western culture. In Europe, at this period, both Richard Burton's edition and Jean-Charles Mardrus's edition, each of which deliberately emphasized eroticism, were widely read, and, thanks to both of the translators, the readership of the *Arabian Nights* was divided between two genres, juvenile literature and pornography. In Japan, however, except for the intellectual elite, the complete version of the stories was not known; therefore, the *Arabian Nights* offered a perfect subject for juvenile literature.

In Europe, immediately after the appearance of the Galland edition, what is called "Oriental stories" in Japanese became popular. In Japan, however, with no link to the Middle East in terms of economics and history, the same kind of "Oriental stories" were not produced, but the fantastic stories found in the Galland edition fascinated young readers.

For this reason, the *Arabian Nights* as juvenile literature was transformed without any attention paid to its cultural or ethnographic background, especially pertaining to native life in the Middle East. Instead, it was adapted in such a way that Japanese children could accept those stories with no reference to the actual Middle East. It should be mentioned here that, immediately after the Great Kanto Earthquake (1923), there appeared a lot of magazines for children featuring the *Arabian Nights*, which included the popular characters such as Aladdin, Ali Baba, and Sindbad the Sailor. Within fifty years since the Galland edition's first translation into Japanese, it was firmly rooted in Japanese juvenile literature.

Accompanying this flourish of juvenile literature, talented illustrators made many romantic pieces. Kōji Fukiya (1898–1979), who is famous for a series of illustrations representing beautiful girls, painted many exotic pieces, but often they did not portray accurate costumes or commodities of the Middle East. Women's costumes illustrated by Fukiya, in particular, seem to be Indian. This imaginary vision of the Middle East, which had been fixed through the Three Realms worldview since the Edo Era, is still influential in Japan.

One of the most typical examples that reflect the vision of the *Arabian Nights* in Japan is a children's song titled *Tsuki no sabaku*, or "A Desert under the Moon." This song was published in 1923 (Taishō Era 12) in a children's magazine with an illustration.[14] The song still enjoys popularity today, with its melancholic melody. It is said that the author got inspiration from a sand dune on the Pacific Ocean, where statues stand representing a lonely pair of a prince and a princess riding camels over the desert. This scene became a favorite theme of artists, as found in a design that was adopted for a postal stamp (the first issue of the series representing favorite children's songs). Although the song renders an unrealistic scene in which a royal pair without company crosses a desert under moonlight, Japanese people have accepted it as a realization of the fantastic vision of the *Arabian Nights*.[15]

As in Europe, Japanese people have come to hold two extreme images of the *Arabian Nights*, one as juvenile literature for children and the other as pornographic literature for adults. But unlike the situation found in Europe,[16] the *Arabian Nights* has never played a role as a literary work containing ethnographic references to real life in the Middle East or the Arab world.

The Takarazuka Revue Company

Into this cultural background, the performance troupe Takarazuka Revue Company was founded in 1913. It must be mentioned first as a surprising fact that the troupe has never failed to promote the *Arabian Nights* as part of its repertoire of dreams and inspiration, even though the Burton edition, which was translated into Japanese in 1920s, gained much popularity and emphasized characteristics of the *Arabian Nights* as pornography.

The Takarazuka Revue Company was one of the first troupes to introduce a repertoire of *Nights*-inspired performances to Japan and indeed the only troupe to show its long-lasting interest in the *Arabian Nights* up to the present. The first performance was in 1914. The company is divided into five troupes called "Flower," "Moon," "Snow," "Star," and "Cosmos."[17] There is a very popular "top star" in each troupe playing a leading role. All performers are unmarried women and graduates of the Takarazuka Music and Opera School, which was established in 1919 in order to train Takarazuka performers. Presently, the number of students in the company is 430.[18] All of them are classified as either performers playing a male part dressed as men or those playing a female part dressed as women, in accordance with their height or voice quality. During their membership in Takarazuka, they cannot appear onstage other than in the Takarazuka Theater.

Takarazuka's motto is "Modesty, Fairness, and Grace," and its aim is to educate women through advanced music training. The competition among applicants for admission to the Takarazuka Music and Opera School is very intense. After being accepted into the school, students have special training in singing, Japanese traditional dance, ballet, acting, and so on. And it is well known that in the school they must adhere to a strict rule of courtesy, in particular toward their superiors. They are usually called "Takarasienne," which is named after "Parisienne." After leaving the company, they pursue various careers; some are active as singers or actresses, some marry and go into domestic life.[19]

Takarazuka's founder was Ichizō Kobayashi (1873–1957), a famous industrialist who founded a railway company (currently Hankyu Hanshin Holdings) in 1907. He contributed to the progress of railway management as a service industry. He promoted land development, department store operation, and so on. He believed that high-quality entertainment was absolutely necessary to improve Japanese pop culture. This is why he embarked on the establishment of an amusement center in the little spa town of Takarazuka near Osaka and founded the Takarazuka Revue Company. The company attracted spectators along the railway lines and still enjoys nationwide popularity.

The Takarazuka Revue Company presently has two grand theaters in Takarazuka and Tokyo. The first Takarazuka Grand Theater was built in 1924, and the company's first performance in 1927 was the revue *Mon Paris*. This was Japan's first revue in which a staging of the French revue was blended with traditional Japanese theater elements. The company has continued its many revues and has become one of the most popular revue companies in Japan. It also runs its own television channel. The Takarazuka Revue Company has provided many stars with a platform from which to embark on careers on the stage. In 1938, the Takarazuka Revue Company held its first overseas performance in Europe and then continued to win the admiration of audiences in the United States, Canada, China, and other countries.[20] And the troupe has introduced to Japan such Broadway musicals as *West Side Story*, has brought to the stage masterpieces such as *Gone with the Wind*, and in 1974 made a great hit of *The Rose of Versailles*.[21]

The Takarazuka Revue Company usually presents revues ten times a year, so each troupe by rotation performs on stage twice a year. Two types of stage performance are given: on the one hand, plays and musicals that present a story and, on the other, revues and shows composed mainly of music and dance. Its repertoire includes historical stories, literary genres, fantastic novels, and sometimes, Japanese Manga. For example, the company's great hit *The Rose of Versailles* was originally a best-selling Manga story.

The *Arabian Nights* in Takarazuka Revues

The typical plays in Takarazuka revues are dramatic stage performances whose cultural backgrounds are set in various periods and countries. The performances feature the stories of real and fictional heroes. The *Arabian Nights* is one of the favorite sources. Throughout the history of the Takarazuka Revue Company, it has produced many performances whose story lines were composed around themes found in the *Arabian Nights* or historical events relating to Middle Eastern affairs in one way or another. We find among them the revue *Tonde Arabian naito*, or "Flying with the *Arabian Nights*," which became so famous that some of the actresses became big stars in the history of Japanese stage performance. Most of the *Arabian Nights* revues became commercial successes, a good example being the revue titled *Sabaku no kurobara*, or "A Black Rose in the Desert" (2000) (fig. 9), which was a commemorative performance at the time when Asato Shizuki, a top star belonging to the "Cosmos" troupe, was about to leave the company. In such a commemorative revue, we always find many enthusiastic fans struggling to get tickets in order to see the last performance of their favorite actress.

Some of the earliest revues pertaining to the *Arabian Nights* drew, directly or indirectly, on juvenile storybooks which were popular at the time when the Takarazuka Revue Company was founded. In a few such cases, such as *Damasukusu no sannin musume*, or "Three Ladies in Damascus" (1916), whose script was written by Ichizō Kobayashi, the Takarazuka Revue Company's founder, some characters with Arabian-like names come onstage without any reference to real Arabian scenes.

Immediately after World War II ended, the Takarazuka Revue Company restarted its performances at the Grand Theater. In this period, the company staged frequent revues with direct reference to stories found in the *Arabian Nights* or, very often, arranged musical or cinema performances in Europe or America in Takarazuka style. This situation is very interesting when we compare it with the situation in which the *Arabian Nights* enjoyed a great vogue, especially for children's magazines, immediately after the Great Kanto Earthquake in 1923.

Among the many productions, that of the *Arabian naito*, or "The Arabian Nights" (fig. 34), which was presented first in 1950, had a very long run. Kobayashi congratulated himself on this success and wrote in his diary, "The revue of *Arabian Naito* is very amusing. . . . Most middle-aged or elderly people remarked that this was a masterpiece more wonderful than could be found anywhere recently." He also wrote in an essay, "I am very happy because the success of this revue will have a good effect on economic recovery."[22]

The opening scene of *Arabian naito* is a gathering place for people in the poor quarter in Paris on Bastille Day (July 14), and the hero, while sleeping there, dreams of Arabia. His dream is based on "Ma'ruf, the Cobbler" in the *Arabian Nights*. In his dream, he gets involved in a most strange accident with his friends, and he is nearly executed; but right at the very time of his execution, he wakes up from a nap.

Takarazuka's *Arabian Nights* repertoire distinctly shows the historical situation of the acceptance of the *Arabian Nights* in Japan. Through the translated version of the Galland edition, the *Arabian Nights* became familiar to Japanese children. Later in the Taishō Era, high-quality collected works for children were continuously being published. Furthermore, thanks to the work of talented illustrators, the *Arabian Nights* became recognized as a collection of marvelous stories set in an exotic locale.

Generally speaking, faithful adherence to the *Arabian Nights* is considered to be alien to the flavor of Takarazuka revues. When a story or theme from the *Arabian Nights* is chosen for a play, its content is skillfully arranged so as to be suitable for the style of Takarazuka revues. In terms of the degree of Takarazuka-styled arrangement, the revues pertaining to the *Arabian Nights* can be classified as follows:

1. Typical Takarazuka-styled revues as a love comedy: for example, Tonde *Arabian naito*, or "Flying with the Arabian Nights" (1983); Sabaku no kurobara, or "A Black Rose in the Desert" (2000)
2. Revues introducing the story line with some adaptationss:[23] for example, *Arabian naito*, or "The Arabian Nights" (1921); Aribaba monogatari, or

"The Story of Ali Baba" (1947); *Arabian naito*, or "The Arabian Nights" (1950)

3. Revues that directly accepted the presentations as performed in Europe: for example, Sheherazādo, or "Scheherazade" (1951); Kisumetto, or "Kismet" (1955)

4. Revues in which an Arab character acts as an alien presence: for example, Ivun Arajin (Ibn Aladdin) in Samarukando no akai bara, or "Red Rose in Samarkand" (1987); Arajin (Aladdin) in Janpu Oriento!, or "Jump Orient!" (1994)

On the Takarazuka stage, the cultural background of Arabia or the Middle East that is necessary to understand the *Arabian Nights* has tended to be omitted in order to focus on entertainment. On the other hand, in performances whose intent is to emphasize the fantastic quality of the program, Arabia or the Middle East has been chosen as a setting to increase the fantasy and stimulate the imagination. In a similar way, when an Arab character appears on a stage setting in Japan or Europe, his or her foreignness is highlighted. Or likewise, in some cases, Arab characters serve as go-betweens for the East and the West. The role of Arabs as dramatis personae in Takarazuka revues can be schematized as follows:

1. In order to strengthen the degree of fantasy, the relation with the real world may be radically diminished by making the setting some vague and alien Arabian region.

2. When an Arab appears in a performance whose locale is set in Japan or Europe, the character of the Arab as an alien may be emphasized.

3. In some cases, an Arab can play a positive role as the key person who connects the East or Japan to the West or Europe.

With the development of a relationship between Japan and the Middle East, such a one-sided vision for the Middle East has changed. It is consequently apparent that the Takarazuka Revue Company is also obliged to make an attempt in various ways to construct a new perspective for the stage performances, paying deliberate attention to the cultural background of the Arab or to current situations concerning the Middle East.

The New Movement: The *Arabian Nights* as a Window onto the
Middle East

As mentioned earlier, in the Taishō Era when the Takarazuka Revue
Company was founded, thanks to the publication of an excellent series
of juvenile literature, the *Arabian Nights* won a great many readers. But
these books were largely transformed in order to offer easy reading for
young people, and most of the information concerning Middle Eastern
culture, indispensable to understanding the original stories, was omitted. On the stage of Takarazuka revues, the *Arabian Nights* was a useful
vehicle to render fantastic or exotic effects.

In the revue of *Tonde Arabian naito*, well-known stock devices and
characters in the *Arabian Nights*, such as a flying carpet, evil magicians,
and beautiful slave girls appear one after another, and a chorus sings a
song: "Arabia, it's a distant place. Arabia, it's a fantastic place. And the
marvelous stories, their name is the *Arabian Nights!*"

The land of Arabia is a stage of dreamlike fantasy and, at the same
time, a place where an inexplicable fate rules. In order to increase the
degree of amusement, any explanation of the unfamiliar culture is
omitted. By intentionally excluding essential information concerning
Arabia, exoticism is vividly increased, and the visual aspect of Arabia
is emphasized.

Recently, however, when performing a revue concerning the Middle
East, the company has asked the advice of specialists in Middle Eastern culture. In 2008, when the company was to perform a revue titled
Ai to shi no Arabia, or "Love and Death in Arabia," whose setting is in
nineteenth-century Egypt, I was asked as a specialist of Arab culture
to supervise the production and to check its scenario. In viewing the
performance, I found that the costumes for Muhammad Ali, the nineteenth-century Egyptian ruler, or the Bedouins, nomadic people living
in the desert, were similar to real ones, such as the *kufiya* (a traditional
Arab headdress or scarf for men) or *gallabīya* (a full-length loose gown
for men), and the heroine followed the Islamic rules (*sharīʿa*) that a
maiden never show her face to men and never let men touch her body
unless they are her own family.

As mentioned earlier, in Japan, the distinction between the Middle
East and India has been obscure, but in the revue *Ai to shi no Arabia*,

such a conflated vision has begun to be transcended. This revue seems to be the first attempt to understand Arab culture and its uniqueness. It is almost a century since the Takarazuka Revue Company was founded. It may have finally succeeded in opening a window onto the Middle East through the *Arabian Nights*.

NOTES

1. Ryūkei Yano, *Perusia shinsetsu retsujo no homare* [A new story from Persia: A courageous lady's honor] (Tokyo: Bunseidō, 1887), 1. Ryūkei Yano was a famous journalist in Meiji Japan. His translation of "Ali Baba" first appeared in serial installments in his newspaper. Interestingly enough, the play was intended rather for stage performance. He had just returned from London and reported a Christmas pantomime that he had seen performed in London. See Hideaki Sugita, "The *Arabian Nights* in Modern Japan: A Brief Historical Sketch," in *The Arabian Nights and Orientalism: Perspectives from East and West*, ed. Yuriko Yamanaka and Tetsuo Nishio (London: I. B. Tauris, 2006), 143–44.

2. Hideki Nagamine, *Kaikan kyōki Arabiya monogatari* [Strange and marvelous stories from Arabia], 2 vols. (Tokyo: Keishōkaku, 1875). For general information about the introduction of the *Arabian Nights* into Japan, see Sugita, "The *Arabian Nights* in Modern Japan," 116–53; and Hideaki Sugita, "*Arabian naito* hon'yaku kotohajime: Meiji zenki nihon e no inyū to sono eikyō" [An early Japanese translation of the *Arabian Nights*], *Proceedings of the Foreign Language Sciences, Graduate School of Arts and Sciences, College of Arts and Sciences, University of Tokyo* 4 (1999): 1–57. Also see chapter 5 of Tetsuo Nishio, *Arabian Naito: Bunmei no hazama ni umareta monogatari* [The *Arabian Nights*: Stories generated among civilizations] (Tokyo: Iwanami-shoten, 2007), 135–68.

3. Nagamine stated in his preface that he translated from Townsend's edition, but actually he used, in addition, Edward Lane's English translation.

4. His other translations include Lord Chesterfield's *Letters to His Son* and E. F. Haskell's *The Housekeeper's Encyclopedia*. For his detailed biography, see Chūshin Hosaka, *Hyōden Nagamine Hideki* [The biography of Hideki Nagamine] (Tokyo: Liber, 1990).

5. Tsutomu Inoue's preface was printed in the later revised editions of his translation. For example, see *Kaitei Arabiyan naito monogatari* [The revised stories of the *Arabian Nights*] (Tokyo: Bunseidōshobō / Hattorishoten, 1908).

6. In the following discussion, I use the terms "Arab world," "Middle East," "West Asia," and even "Persia" rather loosely and interchangeably.

7. For a general history of Japanese encounters with the Middle East, see Hideaki Sugita, *Nihonjin no chūtou hakken* [The Japanese discovery of the Middle East] (Tokyo: University of Tokyo Press, 1995). See also Fujio Kobayashi, *Nihon Isrāmu-shi* [The history of Islam in Japan] (Tokyo: Nihon-Isrāmu-Yūkō-Renmei, 1988).

8. Quoted in Sugita, *Nihonjin no chūtou hakken*, 41–44. The original sources of the quoted passage are as follows: Ōki's *Sansaizue* (for Chinese version) and Ryōan Terajima's *Wakansansanzue* (for Japanese version).

9. These two camels are said to have come from the southeastern part of the Arabian Peninsula.

10. Seizan Matsura, *Kasshi yawa* [Night-stories in the year of *Kasshi*], 6 vols. (Tokyo: Heibonsha, 1977–78), 1:163.

11. The Japanese popular image of camels is a typical example of the historical formation of the image of the Middle East in Japan. Long before the Japanese people encountered Arabian camels, they had some knowledge about Bactrian camels through old Chinese literature. When the Japanese saw another type of camel, the dromedary, they understood the strange animals in connection with their old information, with the result that Arabian camels were illustrated like Bactrian ones, sometimes with the image of a Chinese person used as a symbol of foreignness.

12. For the formation of Japanese maps influenced by Buddhism, see Toshiaki Ōji, *Echizu no sekaizō* [The worldviews of illustrated maps] (Tokyo: Iwanami-shoten, 1996), especially 121–57.

13. We find many world maps depicted accurately as influenced by imported European maps. For example, *Chikyū bankoku sankai yochi zenzusetu*, or "Global Map Including Seas and Mountains in the World," made by Sekisui Nagakubo (1717–1801), in the late eighteenth century, is the first world map with latitude and longitude in Japan. Similar maps were circulated among elite people, although even just before the Meiji Era, popular world maps which were still influenced by Three Realms worldview were frequently printed and circulated. See *Sekai bankoku Nihon-yori kaijō-risū ōjō jinbutsu zu*, or "World Map in Which the Distance from Japan to the King's Capitals by Sea Is Indicated and People Are Depicted," cited in Tadayoshi Miyoshi, *Zusetsu sekai chizu korekushon* [Illustrated collection of old world maps] (Tokyo: Kawade-shobo-shinsha, 1999), 76. For the world map of Sekisui Nagakubo, see Hirotada Kawamura, *Kinsei Nihon no sekaizō* [The Japanese worldview in the early modern age] (Tokyo: Perikansha, 2003), 139–49.

14. This song was composed by Masawo Kato (1897–1977) in 1923. According to the writer of the song, he wrote it in association with the *Arabian Nights*. This association is shared with almost all Japanese people.

15. For a detailed discussion of the influence of the *Arabian Nights* on the formation of the Middle Eastern image in Japan, see Tetsuo Nishio, "*Les mille et une nuits* et la genèse littéraire de l'Orientalisme au Japon," in *Les mille et une nuits en partage*, ed. Aboubakr Chraïbi, 142–50 (Paris: Actes Sud, 2004); and Tetsuo Nishio, "The *Arabian Nights* and Orientalism from a Japanese Perspective," in Yamanaka and Nishio, *Arabian Nights and Orientalism*, 154–67.

16. For instance, Edward William Lane, with his scientific eyes as a linguist (or, more properly, lexicographer) and anthropologist, regarded the *Arabian Nights*

as an ethnographic text full of encyclopedic information concerning Middle Eastern popular culture. His evaluation seemed to be shared by Antoine Galland himself, who published the first academic encyclopedia of the Orient, *Bibliothèque Orientale*, almost a century and a half earlier. This holds no less true of the translation of Richard Francis Burton.

17. In addition to these five troupes, there also are actresses belonging to the *Senka*, or "Special Course." They perform as special guests at each troupe's show.

18. The number reported as of 2009. The company is composed of over five hundred people, of which some four hundred are actresses and one hundred are specialists including producers, writers, directors, musicians, costumers, and scenery experts.

19. It is well known that the Japanese former first lady Miyuki Hatoyama is a graduate of the Takarazuka Music and Opera School.

20. The Takarazuka Revue Company has visited more than eighteen countries and 120 cities.

21. This revue became a huge hit, being performed 1,446 times, including in its rerun, attracting a total audience of 3.6 million. It is regarded as one of the leading plays performed in Japan.

22. *Kobayashi Ichizō nikki* [Diary of Ichizō Kobayashi], 3 vols. (Osaka: Hankyū-Dentetsu, 1991), 3:215 (entry for 12 August 1950). For his essay titled "*Omohitsuki*," see *Kageki* (monthly magazine for the Takarazuka Revue) 301 (October 1950): 46.

23. To this category belong almost all the revues pertaining to the *Arabian Nights* that were performed before 1950.

18

Thieves of the Orient

The Arabian Nights *in Early Indian Cinema*

ROSIE THOMAS

In 1917 a fire broke out in a Calcutta warehouse, destroying a priceless haul of film history riches. Inside was the life's work of Hiralal Sen, India's unsung film pioneer. It is claimed the treasures included footage of a dance from *Flower of Persia*, an 1898 "Arabian Nights opera" of the Calcutta stage, as well as a one-hour compilation of dance scenes from another big theater hit, K. P. Vidyavinode's *Ali Baba*, that had been screened alongside the play from Classic Theatres in 1901. But, even more astonishing if true, the warehouse is said to have contained a "full-length" film version of the same *Ali Baba* stage play, which included closeups, pans, and tilts and was edited to a length of over two hours and screened at the theater in 1903 or 1904.[1]

While lists of cinema "firsts" are always contentious and ultimately irrelevant, revelations that hint at stolen glories are irresistibly intriguing. If the tales of Hiralal Sen's filmmaking are correct, it would mean not only that India's own first feature film was an *Arabian Nights* tale with a loosely Islamicate[2] setting but that India produced both the world's first *Arabian Nights* film footage and its first full-length *Arabian Nights* film. These claims are controversial: Edison's catalogue included a European *Ali Baba* made in 1902, but this was a short, as was the French *Aladdin and the Wonderful Lamp* "in 45 tableaux," which played in Madras in 1902.[3] Moreover, the Indian film industry has long celebrated as its founding moment a 1913 film version of a story from Hindu mythology, Dadasaheb Phalke's *Raja Harishchandra*. Hiralal Sen's *Ali Baba and the Forty Thieves* has, for the past hundred years, been mostly either quietly ignored or dismissed as "just" a film record of a Bengali stage hit, and without any hard evidence to go on, skeptical historians have been free to dispute its length and significance.

Whatever the truth about Sen's films, there is no doubt that the *Arabian Nights* was present at the birth of cinema in India, just as it was in America, France, and Germany. Moreover, Indian filmmakers' enthusiasm for the *Nights* owed little to film pioneers elsewhere in the world. At least one Indian film in the oriental[4] fantasy genre was a box-office hit well before Douglas Fairbanks's *Thief of Bagdad* (Raoul Walsh, 1924) took India by storm from mid-1925.[5] In these early years Indian filmmakers were borrowing less from Hollywood than from their own local traditions of "oriental" tales, albeit refracted through an Urdu Parsi theater as steeped in European theater and literature as in the Indian vernacular forms that circulated orally and through the popular printing presses. Tales and tropes from the *Arabian Nights* fed Indian cinema's fantasy and costume genres throughout the late 1920s and early 1930s and remained a mainstay of the subaltern cinema audience circuits until the 1960s and beyond.

This essay explores what Ira Bhaskar and Richard Allen refer to as the "oriental genre" in early Indian cinema.[6] Given the centrality of the *Arabian Nights* to these predominantly fantasy films, I focus on how that body of stories and motifs—with its complex transcultural history—circulated within India and was drawn on by Indian filmmakers in the preindependence years.[7] I argue that while films referencing the *Arabian Nights* had much in common with others with a Muslim ethos (such as Muslim socials, historicals, and courtesan films)—offering a strong cultural appeal to Muslim and subaltern audiences as well as scope for spectacle, poetry, romance, stunts, and anticommunalist politics—their appeal was broader and their construction of an "Islamicate" world somewhat looser than those other genres. Key to India's oriental fantasy film was its setting within an imaginary world outside India. Although sometimes coded as quasi-Arabian / ancient Iranian, this was in fact a hybrid never-never land, as we shall see. This fantastical Orient—its magical qualities invariably conjured up through inventive special effects—also drew heavily, both directly and indirectly, on the fashionable orientalism that infused Euro-American art, literature, cinema, and performing arts of the eighteenth to early twentieth centuries, in the construction of which the *Arabian Nights* had played a major role. This transnational orientalism penetrated both high- and low-culture performance forms of 1920s and 1930s India, rendering them spaces of multiple and curious appropriations—a veritable hall of mirrors. Cross-fertilization with the ubiquitous traces of Mughal or Rajput courtly culture and a Hinduizing nationalism complicated things further. Through all these processes, India constructed its own imaginary, quasi-Islamicate, Orient. Although marked by both similarities to and differences from the European Orient, this was equally a site of essentialist "othering" and cultural thievery.

I argue that within India the *Arabian Nights* fantasy film operated on two levels, perceived not only as local and "traditional" but also, apparently paradoxically, as international and "modern." Focusing on *Lal-e-Yaman* (Jewel of Yemen; J. B. H. Wadia, 1933), Bombay cinema's earliest surviving *Arabian Nights* fantasy film and one of the most successful of its day, and drawing comparisons with *Gul-e-Bakavali* (The Bakavali flower; Kanjibhai Rathod, 1924), this essay begins to tease out this conundrum. The first part examines the processes of adaption and circulation of the *Nights* in early Indian cinema; the second part explores India's Islamicate Orient in the context of Euro-American orientalism; the conclusion discusses the appeal of Indian cinema's fantasy genre and its complex series of appropriations.

The *Arabian Nights* in India: Circulation and Adaptation

In the Bombay film industry context, an *Arabian Nights* film was not just a film that reworked recognizable tales such as "Ali Baba" and "Aladdin." Echoing the Hollywood producers of *Thief of Bagdad*, the term "Arabian Nights fantasy film" was used by Indian filmmakers to describe film hybrids created from a number of different *Nights* stories and motifs. These included fantasy films based on Persian *qissa-dastan* literature and legend, notably the so-called *pari*/fairy films.[8] Although not strictly *Arabian Nights* tales, many of their story lines and motifs overlap with the *Nights* as *pari* stories evolved from similar original sources.[9] Thus, in India, the term's colloquial usage referred to all films with an *Arabian Nights* ethos, which meant, broadly, films of magical and wondrous happenings set in a quasi-Persian/Arabic, and usually loosely Islamicate, culture. Older cinema workers I have met referred to such films as *jadoo* (magic) films, and a 1930s source suggests they were also known as "Mahomedan pictures."[10] As we will see, what they all drew on, alongside their common indigenous roots, was a transnational imaginary Orient. Indeed, the Indian film industry trade press of the early 1930s advertised distributors' lists of imported "Oriental" and "Semi-Oriental" films.[11] Moreover, the hybridity of such fantasy films was in keeping with the spirit of the *Nights'* own evolution through oral traditions over many centuries. As Robert Irwin explains, "Plot motifs within the *Nights* combine and recombine. . . . The stories are full of echoes and half echoes of one another, like recurrent dreams in which the landscape is thoroughly familiar, though what is to come is utterly unpredictable."[12]

Scholars agree that the "sea of stories" that constitute the *Arabian Nights* originated—and evolved—within ancient Indian, Persian, and Arabic low-culture oral traditions. Although Emmanuel Cosquin persuasively demonstrated that three elements of the frame story had their origins in Indian tales, little more is known about the *Nights'* early history and development within India.[13] However, there is no doubt that by Victorian times the stories were circulating widely across the subcontinent—alongside the *qissa-dastan* from which they were mostly indistinguishable in the popular imagination. This was in part a continuation of local and vernacular performance traditions, notably theater and oral storytelling cultures, but it was also inspired by the popularity of the *Nights'* various European translations around the world. Although the publication of two Arabic manuscripts in Calcutta in 1814–18 and 1839–42, originally as textbooks for British civil servants to learn Arabic, did not immediately filter through to Indian readers, with the rise of vernacular commercial presses from the mid-nineteenth century, Indian language translations began to proliferate. Thus, for example, while an (abridged) Urdu translation of the *Nights* was published in Lahore in 1844, it was largely after 1867, with the more ornate Urdu prose and poetry versions (considered more "authentic") from Naval Kishore's Lucknow press, that the *Nights* "became popular reading for all."[14] Meanwhile in late nineteenth-century Calcutta the cheap, popular *bat-tala* presses hawked *Arabian Nights* stories in Bengali.[15]

It is impossible to unravel how much of the *Nights'* presence in Victorian India evolved from the earliest Indian tales, how much derived directly from Persian legend and the bazaars of the Arab world, what came through local printing presses and their *munshis*,[16] and what arrived back in India through the detour of eighteenth-century European high culture or, indeed, nineteenth-century low culture. Suffice it to say that Indian filmmakers and their audiences in the 1920s and 1930s would have encountered the *Nights* through a number of overlapping routes, foremost among these being urban theater.

Nineteenth-century Urdu Parsi theater did much to popularize the *Nights* across India's cities. *Arabian Nights* plays were staples of the commercial theater repertoire from at least the 1870s: *Ali Baba, Aladdin,* and *Hatim Tai* all figure in the records, presumably reflecting not only popular reading tastes but also the *Nights'* prevalence in eighteenth- and nineteenth-century British theater and pantomime. But the Indian playwrights were reworking these stories on their own terms. Empress Victoria Theatrical Company, for example, was touring an Urdu *Ali Baba aur Chalis Chor* across north India in the 1870s, playing it in Chinese costumes and Chinese-style sets as part of its repertory over a five-month stay in Lahore in 1878.[17] Meanwhile, on India's east coast, as we have seen, Vidyavinode's Bengali adaptation of the "Ali Baba" story, advertised as a "magnificent Comic Opera" and a "genuine Fountain of Mirth and Merriment," dominated the turn-of-century Calcutta theater.[18]

In Indian theater, as in cinema, straightforward adaptations of well-known *Arabian Nights* tales existed alongside more hybrid fantasies. The Urdu Parsi theater was a notoriously eclectic form: elements of the *Arabian Nights* coexisted with Shakespeare, Victorian literature, and a range of Persian, Indian, and Arabic literature and legend, from the eleventh-century Persian *shahnama* to the tales-within-tales of Sufi *masnawi* or the *pari*/fairy romances of the *qissa-dastan* oral repertoire such as *Gul Sanobar* and *Gul-e-Bakavali*, not to mention the ever popular tales from Hindu mythology. Thus, a vernacular tradition of integrating the *Arabian Nights* within other local and foreign forms was well established by the time the cinema arrived in India and was an obvious port of call for film writers and directors.

The first *Arabian Nights* films were effectively filmed stage plays, like Hiralal Sen's *Ali Baba*. Dance shorts were common: J. F. Madan & Sons' Elphinstone Bioscope Company was showing "the tableaux dance of *Kamr-al-Zaman-Badoora*" on "bioscope worked by electricity" at the Corinthian Theatre, Calcutta, alongside a Parsi theater version of *Hamlet*, in 1905.[19] This same Madan family, whose vast cinema distribution and exhibition empire of the 1920s evolved out of its Urdu Parsi Theatre business ventures, produced India's first (recognized) *Arabian Nights* fantasy film, *Princess Budur* (*The Story of Qamar-e-Zaman*; J. J. Madan), in 1922. The Madans went on to make a string of such films throughout the silent era, notably *Hoor-e-Arab* (1928), *Aladdin* (1931), and (the talkie) *Ali Baba* (1932), all starring their top actress, the "Anglo-Indian" Patience Cooper.

A sudden surge in fantasy film production in India from 1925 onward undoubtedly, in part, reflected the extraordinary box-office success of the *pari*/fairy fantasy film *Gul-e-Bakavali*, Bombay's first all-India superhit.[20] Based on a Persian legend about the fairy princess Bakavali, the handsome prince Taj-al-Mulk, and his quest for Gul-e-Bakavali, the magic flower that will cure his father's blindness, the *qissa* had circulated orally in poetry and prose for centuries. Fort William College published the first Urdu translation in 1803 (in press alongside an Urdu *Alif Laila*) as part of its language curriculum. By the mid- to late nineteenth century *Gul-e-Bakavali*, like the *Nights*, was a staple of the vernacular commercial presses.[21]

Gul-e-Bakavali became an Urdu Parsi theater favorite, capitalizing on the scope it offered for staging spectacular magical transformations, and it is no surprise that early filmmakers also saw its potential. A shooting script of Kohinoor's 1924 film has recently come to light, courtesy of Virchand Dharamsey, revealing conclusively that tropes we associate with *Arabian Nights* films were already well established in cinema before *Thief of Bagdad* arrived in India: the hero receives "magical gifts" from a fakir[22] to assist in his fights against evil beings; he finds his entrancing fairy princess asleep on a couch and exchanges a magic ring with her; with a "trick shot" she emerges "slowly slowly" from a giant flower painted on a curtain; an elixir poured on another ring opens the door to her secret garden; horses gallop "at the speed of wind," and several characters fly through the clouds, including fairies who scatter flowers on the earth below.[23] Such fantastical material, with strong echoes of the *Nights'* magical worlds, would have offered many opportunities for the "trick shots" that had been such a favorite of the earlier mythological films of the 1910s and early 1920s. A cameraman working for Krishna Film Company described the ingenious, if low-tech, special effects he used in another contemporary fantasy, *Jalkumari/Hoor-al-Bahar* (H. Mehta, 1925), in which he filmed fairies in flight dodging oncoming clouds by suspending the "celestial creatures" on wires against a black curtain, filming them waving their arms, and then double exposing this footage with a live panning shot of the sky.[24]

By 1927, when the Indian Cinematograph Committee (ICC) was taking its evidence, three fantasy films, including *Gul-e-Bakavali* and *Aladdin and His Wonderful Lamp* (B. P. Mishra, 1927), turn up repeatedly on witnesses' lists of the top eight or nine Indian box-office successes.[25] Films from the *Arabian Nights* were cited approvingly as "films of general appeal" that could bridge provincial—and even religious—differences of taste.[26] The proprietors of Imperial Film Company reported that *Aladdin* was their most popular film ever—"wherever it is sent it is popular"—and some exhibitors confirmed that Indian films such as *Aladdin* could be more profitable than Western films.[27] However, the final ICC report categorically concluded, "The most popular film ever shown in India was the *Thief of Baghdad* [sic] with Douglas Fairbanks in an Oriental setting."[28] Billed in its opening titles as "An Arabian Nights Fantasy," the *Thief of Bagdad*, which hit Calcutta in March 1925, was a hybrid spun—with considerable latitude—from the tales of "Aladdin," "The Magic Horse," and "Prince Achmed." Witness after witness testified to the success of this Hollywood extravaganza, which would have made its distributors/exhibitors, Madan Theatres, far more money than all their own *Arabian Nights* films put together. Resonating with indigenous fantasy traditions, this was, almost certainly, the most important catalyst for the surge of "Arabian Nights fantasy films" in the late 1920s and early 1930s.

We can no longer properly assess the scale of the *Nights'* influence on Indian silent cinema. Only two dozen of India's thirteen hundred or so silent films have survived, none of them fantasy films.[29] Apart from the Indian Cinematograph Committee evidence—and now the *Gul-e-Bakavali* script—our only resources are film titles, newspaper advertisements, censorship records, a few film stills, and earlier historians' genre classifications. Somewhat confusingly, while some historians distinguish between "fantasy" and "costume" films, others subsume under "costume film" everything from Ruritanian swashbuckling adventures and Rajput, Mughal, and Sultanate courtly dramas to the more overtly Islamicate fantasy films that interest us here.[30] We can, nevertheless, draw a few tentative conclusions. Between 1925 and 1934 (when silent film production ceased) more than 40 percent of all productions can be classified as "costume film" in its widest sense. Less than 20 percent of these costume films can be confidently said to be "fantasy," "*pari,*" or "*jadoo*" films.[31] In other words, direct *Arabian Nights* (including *qissa-dastan*) influence accounted for a steady trickle of films throughout the silent cinema of the late 1920s and early 1930s—half a dozen to a dozen films each year. However, a number of so-called costume films would have been hybrids that incorporated *Nights* and *qissa* motifs, and many others would have been influenced by Fairbanks's swashbuckling persona and thus, less directly, the *Arabian Nights.*[32]

Such statistics say nothing about the scale, popularity, and influence of individual films or how the landscape appeared to people at the time. One or two "straight" *Nights* tales were made each year between 1927 and 1931—in the Indian context the favorites were the universally popular "orphan stories" *Aladdin* and *Ali Baba,* together with *Hatimtai, Qamar-al-Zaman* (a.k.a. *Princess Budur*), and, to a lesser extent, *Sinbad.* As these films were produced by wealthy, high-profile companies such as Madan and Imperial—predominantly but not exclusively companies run by Parsis—they would have had disproportionate impact and status. Thus, for example, Krishna Film Company's *Hatimtai* (Prafulla Ghosh, 1929), which drew on a crossover tale more familiar from *qissa-dastan* than the *Nights* (the seven adventures of Hatim, the exemplarily generous traveler, and the fairy Gulnar), made waves as a big-budget, spectacular, four-part serial with extravagant sets. Other films appear to have been more opportunistically hybrid: Madan's *Hoor-e-Arab* was, according to Firoze Rangoonwalla, another reworking of *Aladdin*, while Ranjit Movietone's *Siren of Bagdad* (*Bagdad ka Bulbul*; Nanubhai Vakil, 1931) traded shamelessly not only on the *Thief of Bagdad* brand but also on the audience's prurient interest in erotic display, according to hints in a not untypical *Bombay Chronicle* advertisement of the day. "Do you know the fascination of Arabian atmosphere! Bagdad, where moon-beams light the blue sky, where pure love is the religion, where nature dances in a nude form. If you want to be thrilled by such a romance then you must see: SIREN OF BAGDAD."[33]

In 1931, 55 percent of the silent films released were costume films, many in the Rajput idiom but a significant number of others in the quasi-Islamicate hybrid idiom that brought *Nights-qissa* "marvels" and "enchantments" together with stunt action. These were all part of what Kaushik Bhaumik describes as the "adventure romance" genre that dominated the era.[34]

With the arrival of sound in 1931 and an influx of talented writers, directors, and actors from Parsi theater, the trend for fantasy and costume films accelerated. India's first talkie, Imperial's *Alam Ara* (Light of the world; Ardeshir Irani, 1931), written by the Urdu Parsi theater writer/director Joseph David, boasted seven songs, extravagant spectacle, a loosely Persianate setting, and a story of romance between a gypsy girl and a prince and of harem rivalry between two queens after a Sufi fakir predicts that the younger will produce the king's heir. Its success, and that of other similar films, including Wadia Movietone's first sound venture, *Lal-e-Yaman* (Jewel of Yemen; J. B. H. Wadia, 1933), produced a rash of *Arabian Nights* hybrids up until the midthirties.[35] The trend petered out by the end of the decade, as the "realist" social melodramas became increasingly fashionable, although a trickle of cheaply made fantasy films fed the subaltern audiences of the 1940s. With the success of Basant's *Aladdin and the Wonderful Lamp* (Homi Wadia, 1952), a new vogue for fantasy films on the B- and C-grade cinema circuits began in the 1950s, with films such as K. Amarnath's *Alif Laila* (A thousand nights, 1953) and a string of cult classics from the Wadia brothers. These include *Gul Sanobar* (Aspi, 1953), *Ali Baba and the Forty Thieves* (Homi Wadia, 1954), *Hatimtai* (Homi Wadia, 1956), and *Baghdad ka Jadu*

(Magic of Baghdad; John Cawas, 1956), a comedy spoof starring Fearless Nadia, after which the studio returned to producing mostly stunt and mythological films. By the midfifties fantasy and costume films together accounted for around a third of all productions.[36] *Arabian Nights* fantasy films only died away as a genre in the 1970s, although occasional revivals have continued even to 2009.[37] Moreover, Ramanand Sagar's 260-episode *Alif Laila* was one of Indian television's most popular series of the early 1990s.[38]

Lal-e-Yaman (1933) and *Noor-e-Yaman* (1935)

J. B. H. Wadia always referred to *Lal-e-Yaman* and its sequel, *Noor-e-Yaman* (Light of Yemen; J. B. H. Wadia, 1935), as "Arabian Nights fantasies," although he explained in his memoirs that he chose *Lal-e-Yaman*'s story precisely because of its generic mix. "At last my choice fell upon an Arabian Nights story. . . . I was impressed with its dramatic potential. Behind the veneer of fantasy, it had all the elements of a social film —rich in human values."[39]

Lal-e-Yaman is of interest today as the earliest Indian *Arabian Nights* film to have survived and one of the biggest cinema hits of its day. But unlike other films of the era that were straight adaptations of theater productions of favorite *Nights* stories such as "Ali Baba" and "Aladdin," *Lal-e-Yaman* was an *Arabian Nights–qissa* hybrid. Based on no individual known tale, the story was dreamed up for the film by the Urdu Parsi theater impresario Joseph David (*Alam Ara*'s writer), in collaboration with J. B. H. Wadia, whose family had long enjoyed David's Islamicate plays, such as *Hoor-e-Arab*, *Khaki Putla*, *Noor-e-Watan*, and *Baagh-e-Iran*, performed by the Parsi Imperial Theatre Company at Bombay's Coronation Theatre.

Wadia's memoirs give a vivid insight into the process of constructing this *Arabian Nights* hybrid—as well as the intellectual and cultural backgrounds of the people involved. While Wadia was an upper-class Parsi, with an LLB and postgraduate degrees in English literature and Avesta Pehlavi, David was a self-taught man of Indian Jewish (Bene Israeli) origin, who had left school young and began working in his local theater in rural Maharashtra as a child. However, by the time David was in his sixties, when Wadia met him, his modest flat at Dongri, Central

Bombay, housed a vast library that ranged across European and Indian literature, arts, and drama. He not only read voraciously in English but also wrote and read in Urdu, Hindi, Marathi, Gujarati, and Hebrew. Wadia was thrilled to be able to discuss world theater with this erudite and cultured man, whom he admiringly referred to as "Dada."[40]

> [His flat] contained more books and manuscripts in his favourite languages than household furniture. His study of the World drama was remarkable and his memory phenomenal. It was a real pleasure for me to discuss with Joseph David not only Shakespeare, Marlowe and B Johnson but even lesser Elizabethan dramatists like Beaumont and Fletcher, Massingham and Greene, the eighteenth-century English dramatists and early moderns like Ibsen and Shaw.

Not only was David steeped in a European literature replete with *Arabian Nights* references, but he was also *au fait* with Asian and Middle Eastern literary traditions. Moreover, he was himself a prolific storyteller, constantly creating new plots out of this rich sea of stories from around the world. "Joseph David, respected Dada to us all, had only to pull out the papers from his fabulous collection of stories and plays written out in Gujarati script in his own hand for future use. . . . They consist of story kernels and an endless stream of quotations in Hindi and Urdu (couplets, quatrains, etc.)."[41]

In a process of creative dialogue and bricolage among these "story kernels," the two men narrowed down the options for Wadia's first talkie. When the team finally got to work, "Dada" was centrally involved in all decisions: writing the script and dialogues, devising the music and songs strictly in accordance with classical raga theory, and helping to cast and eventually coach the actors.

Lal-e-Yaman is set in a mythical time past, advertised in the *Bombay Chronicle* as "a golden chapter from the legendary history of humanity, when angels stalked the earth and men believed in miracles."[42] The film tells of a Yemeni royal family torn apart by a woman's jealousy and human greed; the family eventually finds truth and happiness through a fakir's[43] wisdom and supernatural powers. The opening scene shows the wedding celebrations of the king of Yemen and his new second wife. A female dancer and musicians are entertaining the assembled court when the mournful singing of a fakir passing by outside catches the king's attention. The blind fakir is invited in but proceeds to warn the king that his new wife's poisonous nature will ruin him. When the queen protests her innocence, the fakir is whipped for his insolence. The rest of the film unfolds ten years later. The ruthless queen tries to kill the king's first son, Parviz, so that Nadir, her own son, can become king. However, the fakir helps Parviz escape from the palace dungeon, giving him a magic knife that can make him invisible. After melodramatic twists and turns and adventures in an enchanted land ruled by a wicked djinn, Parviz rescues the Egyptian Princess Parizad, killing the djinn by means of a magic rose. The prince returns home to find his father in exile in the fakir's forest retreat. The king is now a widower, ranting and confused, his only consolation the beautiful singing of his younger son, Prince Nadir. With the fakir's help—and the magic knife —Parviz reclaims the family's kingdom and marries Parizad. But just as Parviz is about to be crowned king, the fakir intervenes and announces God's will: Nadir must be king, while Parviz and Parizad must go to her land, Misr (Egypt), to spread the word of Islam and sing the praises of Allah there. They depart, blessed by the old king, while the new king, Nadir, sings against the background of a flag embroidered with the Islamic crescent moon and star.[44]

Although the film does not derive from an existing *Arabian Nights* or *qissa* tale, we recognize these tales both thematically and structurally. Like many *Nights* stories, *Lal-e-Yaman* moves between three realms: the djinn's magic land, the Yemeni royal court, and an (implicit) celestial realm that controls human destinies. Moreover, the film alludes directly to existing *Nights* tales: for example, Princess Parizad is guarded by a capricious parrot, echoing not only the *Nights* story of the jealous merchant who leaves a talking parrot to keep watch over his beautiful but deceitful wife but also a *qissa* along similar lines.[45] Familiar generic motifs abound: the prince on his quest is lured into the djinn's land by a seminaked nymph frolicking in a lake; he becomes entranced by the sight of a bejeweled princess asleep on a gilded couch who can only be woken by rubbing two sticks together; and he must use his magic dagger's cloak of invisibility to vanquish the monstrously ugly being who has kept her captive. In fact, the fakir's magic powers center primarily on visibility and invisibility: crude optical effects create his miracles

—weeping trees, illusory beings, snakes, and prison chains that turn into garlands. This visual magic draws on conventions of Parsi theater and of the costume, fantasy, and action genres of India's later silent cinema, as seen in *Gul-e-Bakavali*, but also, somewhat eclectically, the film cites both Shakespeare and Hollywood: the king is a King Lear figure, while the djinn's bodyguard is an apelike monster that swings through the jungle just like Johnny Weissmuller's Tarzan.[46] *Lal-e-Yaman* is an improvisation around *Arabian Nights* themes and story lines, combining these with contemporary popular culture references, much in the spirit of the *Arabian Nights'* own evolution.

Wadia Movietone worked closely with Joseph David on five Islamicate films between 1933 and 1935, including two "historicals," *Bagh-e-Misr* (Tiger of Egypt; J. B. Wadia, 1934), set in ancient Egypt, and *Josh-e-Watan / Desh Deepak* (Light of the homeland, 1935), set in ancient Iran, as well as *Kala Gulab / Black Rose* (1934), based on an Urdu stage play set in a Muslim milieu. But the studio's two *Arabian Nights* fantasies were by far the most successful at the box office.[47] *Noor-e-Yaman* (Light of Yemen, 1935) appears to have pushed the fantasy elements much further than *Lal-e-Yaman*. Its convoluted plot again stars the wise fakir and the prince (now king) with the golden voice but adds bevies of bathing nymphs, a flying carpet, messenger parrots and doves, a skull and a ring for distance seeing, a magic pebble to make its owners invisible, mystic incense that makes a man fall in love, a magic spell that transforms a wicked man's lower body into a tree trunk, which can only be undone by sprinkling djinn's blood onto him, and much besides.[48] Judging by images in *Noor-e-Yaman*'s song booklet, the film was also considerably more spectacular than its predecessor, with chorus lines of fairies and nymphs, dungeons of skeletons, and ornate Islamicate court settings. Most intriguingly, the seductress Princess Parizad, who spent much of the film imprisoned and tortured for refusing to forsake Islam, was played by an exotic, blue-eyed blonde in her first proper screen role: the former cabaret dancer then known as Miss Nadia.[49] This was the Islamicate never-never land at its most excessive, drawing deliriously from a cosmopolitan repertoire of orientalist signifiers.

So what can these films tell us about India's homegrown Orient—this imaginary (magical) space that is "other than" India? We must return to the question of where the fantasy genre sits within the spectrum of

India's so-called Islamicate cinematic forms and examine the relationship between orientalism and the Islamicate.

Orientalism and the Islamicate

The question of orientalism within Indian performing arts has been surprisingly little explored, although Gregory Booth's groundbreaking essay on musical orientalism in Hindi cinema usefully sets out its complexities.[50] His discussion includes the conventionalized use of the oboe and the "gapped scale" for "Arab spice"—a conscious borrowing from Hollywood—as well as Hindi cinema's more idiosyncratic tendency to exoticize background (nondiegetic) rather than diegetic music and songs. However, Booth's central focus on postindependence cinema oversimplifies matters. While he correctly notes that "orientalist baggage" was imported into Hindi cinema through the traditions of Euro-American film and theater on which it drew so closely—and, as he puts it, "Orientals can indeed be Orientalist"—it is misleading to contend that this was primarily a postindependence development. As we have just seen, an orientalist sensibility was rife in early Indian cinema, especially in *Arabian Nights* fantasy films, and this included a tendency to "other" its Muslims. But as the term *orientalism* nowadays subsumes a variety of differing practices and forms, it would be useful to unravel its complex histories within both Euro-American and Indian contexts.

It has been well documented that throughout the eighteenth and nineteenth centuries European arts and literature were fascinated by representations of an Orient that was largely a projection of Western political fears and erotic fantasies—as Edward Said and many others have described.[51] Antoine Galland's French translation of the *Arabian Nights* in 1704–17 undoubtedly helped to fuel this obsession. This European popular Orient was a confused imaginary space in which the harem and the despot primarily defined the Arab world, while South Asia became the domain of magic, mysticism, and sensual dancing girls, the latter pruriently fantasized as "a symbol for oriental opulence . . . and uncurbed sensuousness."[52] Aspects of this orientalist imagination were embraced, with some enthusiasm, within India itself, finding expression, as discussed earlier, in nineteenth-century Urdu Parsi theater as well as in other fields, including painting and architecture.

From an Indian perspective, although Chinoiserie made its mark here, the gaze was in fact mostly directed *westward* toward an "Orient" broadly associated with Persia, the Arab world, and central Asia and marked loosely, but not exclusively, by an Islamicate ethos. Although India's Orient was not identical with that of the Europeans, it was similarly hazy.

In the context of early Indian cinema, however, it was the second wave of European orientalist fantasy in the early decades of the twentieth century that was most significant. This arrived from several directions simultaneously—France, England, America—with the *Arabian Nights* recurring yet again as a catalyst. In France the new orientalism had been importantly inspired by the publication of Joseph Mardrus's translation of the *Nights* between 1899 and 1904. This was a decidedly loose and flamboyantly eroticized adaptation that epitomized fin-de-siècle decadence. Nevertheless, it was wildly popular and directly inspired Serge Diaghilev's *Schéhérazade*, the "oriental ballet" with which the Ballets Russes conquered Paris in 1910, before making waves around the world. Starring Vaslav Nijinsky as the Golden Slave, whose "frenzied voluptuousness" both scandalized and titillated its audiences, *Schéhérazade* was even more of a travesty of the *Arabian Nights* than Mardrus's work. Shamelessly dispensing with the clever woman storyteller—Scheherazade herself—the ballet was confected around one scene of the introductory frame story, which reveled in the despot, slave, harem, and orgy motifs that so excited the European imagination. But, as Peter Wollen describes, with its sensationalist spectacle and Leon Bakst's jewel-colored sets and costumes, this twenty-minute extravaganza set the agenda for an explosion of orientalist modernism across the European decorative arts. Paul Poiret's influential "oriental look" fashions helped to popularize this sensibility: by the time the Exhibition of Decorative Arts opened in Paris in 1925 French department stores were awash with art deco orientalist clothing accessories, and turbans and harem pants had become de rigueur for the fashionable of both sexes.[53] The new orientalism, now a consumer movement, had extraordinary global reach—with art deco coming to connote modernity around the world, including India.[54]

Cinema in Europe and America was deeply influenced by the Ballets Russes' modernist orientalism (and Poiret's fashions), especially after the dance company's 1916 American tour, on which it performed its full oriental cycle. According to Matthew Bernstein, building on Wollen and Gaylyn Studlar, "Serge Diaghilev's Ballets Russes with its staging of *Cleopatra*, *Thamar* and *Schéhérazade* . . . contributed decisively to the mise-en-scène of Orientalist cinema."[55] In Hollywood, admirers of "the Diaghilev ballet" included Douglas Fairbanks and the creative team of *Thief of Bagdad*.[56] But *Schéhérazade*'s influence on this film touched far more than its mise-en-scène. As Studlar argues, "*Thief of Bagdad* . . . is driven by dance aesthetics at every level in spite of not containing one conventional dance scene"—a telling observation in the context of the film's popularity across India.[57]

Considerable as Diaghilev's influence was on twentieth-century orientalism, it should not be overstated. Orientalist performance was already well established in European and American popular entertainment. Joan Erdman reminds us that "the 1909 season of Diaghilev's Russian dancers, with their elaborate costumes, exquisite sets, and extraordinary themes, brought to ballet what had already been viewed on the stages of music hall and in the Folies Bergère: the exotic Orient."[58] Salome's Dance of the Seven Veils—veils removed with wild abandon in the course of the dance, as immortalized by Maud Allen —was a vaudeville craze in Paris, London, Vienna, New York, and elsewhere in America at the turn of the century, as were Loie Fuller and her diaphanous "Hindu skirt" and Mata Hari as Shiva's temptress, all familiar to early Indian filmgoers.[59] There were strange crosscurrents and multiple appropriations. As Wollen points out, while in earlier years fashionable St. Petersburg had eagerly imported Parisian orientalism, after Diaghilev's arrival in 1909 Paris started to import a Russian orientalism marked by central Asian cultural forms—arguably one of the Ballets Russes' key contributions to the international orientalist imaginary and one that resonated with India's experience of central Asian cultures.[60]

However, other currents influenced Indian film, dance, and arts more directly and bizarrely. In the turn-of-the-century United States an "aesthetic dance" movement was evolving out of vaudeville. This new breed of dancers, among them Isadora Duncan and Ruth St. Denis, was even more committed to orientalist masquerade than their music hall predecessors. Ruth St. Denis, who became particularly influential both in

Hollywood and within India's new dance movement of the 1930s, began her solo career touring with her "Radha," "Cobra," and "Incense" dances in the 1900s, in which little distinction was made between Hindu, Jain, Buddhist, and Islamic influences.[61] According to Adrienne McLean, St. Denis's "Indian dances" and exotic props and costumes were mostly inspired by imaginative encounters with found imagery, just as her "Egyptian dance" was allegedly based on an advertisement she had seen for Turkish cigarettes. Like all her peers, she had never seen any Indian dance. In 1915 she and her husband, Ted Shawn, set up a dance school in Hollywood, which trained many future leading choreographers, dancers, and Hollywood stars, including Martha Graham, Louise Brooks, and Jack Cole. By this point Ruth and Ted, calling themselves "Denishawn" and openly influenced by the Ballets Russes, advertised as the school's specialty its "Oriental Suite" routines—in which fuzzy notions of ancient Egypt, Persia, Siam, Greece, and India were pilfered interchangeably. Denishawn's stage-show tours repeated this popular—and much imitated—formula with relentless enthusiasm. One disillusioned former Denishawn protégé, the dancer and choreographer Doris Humphrey, later grumbled, "I just got tired of being Siamese, Burmese, Japanese, all the other 'eses.' I came from Oak Park Illinois and I wanted to find out as a dancer who I was."[62]

England's answers to *Schéhérazade*—the stage shows *Kismet* (1911) and *Chu Chin Chow* (1916)—were just as hazy about their Orient, which was similarly derived from popular theater and music-hall traditions. Once again the *Arabian Nights* has much to answer for, and "Ali Baba" turns up again here. Oscar Ashe's musical comedy *Chu Chin Chow*, a version of the "Ali Baba" story, broke all London theater box-office records between 1916 and 1921, toured North America in the 1920s, and was made into a successful film by Gainsborough Studios in 1934, spreading its racist stereotypes and quasi-oriental styles around the globe, including India.[63] An illustration in the *Tatler* to mark the first anniversary of the show's "reconstruction of the days of Haroun al Raschid" depicts six "new dresses for *Chu Chin Chow*, very suitable to the sultry climate of old Bagdad." The caption continues, "Mr Oscar Ashe is one of the greatest manufacturers of Eastern atmosphere that the stage has ever seen, and fanciful as some of his colour schemes may perhaps sometimes appear they are not very far wide of things that can be seen to-day in almost any of the big native cities of Ajmere and Rajputana."⁶⁴ The influence of Euro-American popular culture—and its higher-culture variants via Diaghilev and Poiret—is clear: China, India, and "old Bagdad" were interchangeable; the "Islamic" was barely marked; and ultimately no one cared too much about authenticity. This was a fashionable, fantastical Orient that existed only in its consumers' imaginations. It no longer referenced any putatively real geographical space "over there." As David Bate puts it, orientalism had become "a type of cultural practice internalized, paradoxically, as modern forms for pleasure, eroticism and leisure."⁶⁵

Within urban India, the new orientalism was enthusiastically received, especially in film and performance circles. The pervasive orientalist motifs and masquerade that had become a mainstay of Euro-American theatrical dance and vaudeville were exported directly onto India's own variety entertainment circuit, where they fused with new forms of *nautch* dance in the public domain. Bombay, Madras, and Calcutta were major stopover destinations on the tours that followed the steamship routes between England and Australia. European artistes on the Indian circuits rubbed shoulders with entertainers of Anglo-Indian, eastern European, Central Asian, and South and Southeast Asian backgrounds, all touting the "oriental dance" that so conveniently legitimized the display of eroticized female bodies. By the 1920s and early 1930s the form had trickled down to the lowest levels, and its lure was inescapable. Again and again the Indian newspapers of the day advertised exotic "oriental dance": Turkish, Russian, Armenian, Japanese, Burmese—where these dancers were originally from is anyone's guess. A number of these women soon found careers in India's emerging film industry, including the Madans' Patience Cooper, a former variety show dancer with impresario Maurice Bandmann's company, as well as the Wadias' Mary Evans, a.k.a. Fearless Nadia, an Anglo-Greek soldier's daughter of Australian origin. Advertisements for Miss Nadia, making her cabaret debut at the Regal Cinema Lahore in 1934, describe her "Gypsy" and "Persian" dances, while a series of images from her photo album of the same year shows the range of her exotic stage costumes, which include the bare midriff, harem pants, and veil of an *Arabian Nights* temptress whose distant roots stretch visibly back to the imaginings of Bakst and Poiret.⁶⁶

However, Indian filmmakers were also enthralled by other imported —and confused—orientalist forms, notably in the dance field. Alongside vaudeville the Indian entertainment circuits hosted the higher-culture variants of "oriental dance" that boasted allegiances with—and even direct links to—the prestigious Ballets Russes and the new Euro-American modernist dance arts. Both Anna Pavlova and Denishawn came to India on their world tours in the 1920s, not only to perform for enraptured Indian audiences but also to see the "real" Indian dance for themselves at last. Both were sadly disappointed. Pavlova had been performing as a "devadasi" temple dancer in *La bayadere* since 1909, her routines based on an India imagined on the basis of books, paintings, and vague notions of Central Asian culture from her Russian youth. The Madans, her Parsi hosts in both Bombay and Calcutta in 1922, obliged her with displays of local *nautch* dancers, but she was not impressed. "But where is your dance?" she is rumored to have exclaimed.[67] When Denishawn visited India in 1925, their entourage was similarly feted by high society, including a glittering soiree at the Nizam of Hyderabad's "palace" on Malabar Hill in Bombay. But they were even more disparaging about the dancers they were shown. Comparing the dances they found in India with a vaudeville act, "The Dancing Girl of Delhi," by their own American protégé Vanda Hoff, Ted Shawn later claimed, "In loveliness, charm and real ability, what infinite worlds above the real dancing girls of Delhi was our Vanda."[68]

Pavlova's disappointment fired a determination to change things: on returning to London she developed and choreographed her own *Oriental Impressions* suite—a series of dances that included "Krishna and Radha" and "A Hindu Wedding," for which she enlisted the help of Uday Shankar, a wealthy young Bengali art student she met on London's fashionable Hampstead social scene. The results, once again, had more to do with European dance and fantasy than with any authentic Indian traditions. However, this did not deter the ecstatic Indian elites who thronged to see her around the world, including in Calcutta and Bombay in 1928–29. Thereafter, Uday Shankar and Rukmini Devi, Pavlova's two young, cosmopolitan, upper-class, Indian associates, were tasked by her with reviving and (re)inventing Indian classical dance. Throughout the 1930s, while Rukmini energetically championed the emergent Bharat Natyam, Uday Shankar introduced the modernist movement into Indian dance.[69] Thus, out of a fusion of European "oriental dance," Euro-American modernist free expression, and dutifully researched Indian vernacular and folk forms, the new Indian "classical" dance was born. It was ineffably "modern" and unquestionably nationalistic.

We have strayed into curious territory—a universe of shifting sands. As Joan Erdman points out, "In India . . . oriental dance meant dance from Europe."[70] Ultimately, of course, oriental dance (everywhere) meant modernity. India's creative practitioners and audiences borrowed an already incoherent Euro-American fantasy Orient, took from it what they wanted—just as Europe had pilfered for its own Orient—and used this to reinvent their own modern forms (and India's own modern self). It was an orgy of cultural theft, but, in the spirit of the "Ali Baba" story, stealing from robbers was questioned no more than living comfortably on the proceeds of stolen property. Broadly speaking, by the 1930s the purportedly Hindu Orient was appropriated and reworked within India's nationalist high culture, while the quasi-Islamic elements of this Orient were relegated to lower cultural forms, where, cross-fertilized with local vestiges of Mughal and Persian cultural forms, they fed into a more cosmopolitan Indian modernity. So how did this doubly phantasmagoric Orient play out in early Indian cinema?

Many Indian filmmakers and their audiences—both highbrow and lowbrow—enthusiastically embraced the fashionable international orientalism, as can be seen both by films celebrating the new "classical" dance forms (for example Madhu Bose's films *Alibaba* [1937] and *Court Dancer* [1942], starring his dancer wife Sadhana Bose) and by the popularity of the lower-brow oriental fantasy genre.[71] In so doing these filmmakers took their place at the high table of global modernity. As this Orient was an imaginary space—without precise geographical or historical referent—it could be more or less unproblematically accepted: the Orient of India's early twentieth-century performing arts was a space of magic and wondrous happenings, of spirituality and sensuality. Clichés often projected onto India by the West could in turn be deflected onto a predominantly Islamicate never-never land. This was an imaginary Middle Eastern, Central and Western Asian world, comprising a fuzzy mix of Afghan, Persian, "Arab," and even, loosely, eastern European subaltern "others," which recycled international orientalist tropes. As we have seen, not only was "oriental dance" understood to mean European dance (and hence nothing to do with India), but also a blond European cabaret dancer was considered sufficiently exotic to play the Egyptian Princess Parizad, who proselytizes for Islam in *Noor-e-Yaman*. Insofar as we can generalize from the few surviving films, it appears that, unlike Euro-American orientalism, which merged quasi-Hindu and Islamic elements without distinction, India's popular Orient from the 1930s onward was effectively that which was outside or "other" than—a putatively Hindu—India.

Lal-e-Yaman provides a useful example of this process, situated within Indo-Persian storytelling forms but referencing on its own terms the Orient of international subaltern popular culture and Hollywood's "lower genres."[72] The film's opening scene, shot on a set of the king of Yemen's palace as he celebrates his second wedding, begins with a mid-shot of the back of a young woman, clad in diaphanous "harem pants" and a skimpy *choli*, dancing seductively—with bare midriff—to a slow, rhythmic musical accompaniment of violin, sarangi, and tabla. The scene pulls out to reveal the full court *durbah*, including the king, his new queen, and his older son, arranged in a semicircle across a palatial set, extravagantly painted with ornate, quasi-Islamicate motifs. Wadia in later years admitted that he drew inspiration for all his Islamicate sets primarily from "profusely illustrated books on art, architecture, costumes and furniture designs," including "beautifully bound German volumes" that he and his art director, formerly a Parsi theater set designer, owned. "How many times must Homi and I have gone through them for modelling sets in our umpteen films?"[73] Moreover, *Lal-e-Yaman*'s court dancer was neither Arab nor Indian but a European cabaret dancer, Miss Lola, married to the German Agfa representative in Bombay and paid by the hour to perform the mimic oriental dance of the Indian variety circuit.

On the other hand, Wadia and David paid great attention to composing music based on classical Indian ragas. J. B. H. Wadia was a passionate devotee of Indian music, and his decision to promote the classical singing abilities of the young Firoz Dastur, the prince with the golden voice, was a bold one. "Suddenly a thought came to me that if I was to assign the pivotal role of the boy prince to Firoz why should I not make him sing in the classical music vein? I took Dada into my confidence and he too fell in line with my idea which was rather crazy from a box-office angle."[74] They modified their script and increased Dastur's role from two to six classical songs. The risk paid off: by *Lal-e-Yaman*'s seventh week "its melodious music and sweetest songs ha[d] become so popular that they [we]re heard being sung and repeated at many street-corners in the city."[75]

However, *Lal-e-Yaman*'s most marked difference from the Euro-American Orient lies in its depiction—and celebration—of a recognizable Islamic religion and philosophy. In this it differs from the earlier film *Gul-e-Bakavali*, which had, in Dharamsey's words, "secularised" its source story.[76] *Gul-e-Bakavali*, as published by Naval Kishore, was set in an unambiguously Islamic context, with direct references to God and the Prophet Muhammed.[77] The 1924 film blithely changed the king's name from Zeen-ul-Mulk to Raja Jalad Sang/Singh (albeit with a son called Taj-ul-Mulk)[78] and introduced Yakshas, Indra, *sati*, views of Bombay, and Rajputana skirts alongside *paris*, fakirs, and burquas. While box-office and nationalist pressures undoubtedly drove this syncretism, which was already a feature of the Parsi stage, it also reflected the ubiquitous, transnational, hybrid Orient, traces of which pepper the *Gul-e-Bakavali* film script.

With *Lal-e-Yaman*, on the other hand, Sufi mystical philosophy sits at the heart of the film: truth is reached by hearing the voice of God and avoiding distraction by the illusory spectacle of the material world. The film's ending celebrates Islam visually (the Caliphate flag), aurally (a song praising God and enjoining Parviz to devote his life to spreading the word of Allah), and as narrative resolution (Nadir becomes king through divine will). Its sequel, *Noor-e-Yaman*, similarly stars the wise fakir and even introduces a second heroine who refuses to renounce Islam. For Wadia this undoubtedly involved a political dimension: he was a committed nationalist, with what he later referred to as a "passion" for Hindu-Muslim unity and anticommunalist politics. I have argued elsewhere that Wadia's use of the Islamicate idiom may also be seen as a counter to the already incipient hegemony of a Hinduizing *bhakti* movement, as reflected in some films of rival studios such as Prabhat.[79] But while Wadia was undoubtedly unusual in his political aspirations for his films, the Indian *Arabian Nights* fantasy films' greater respect for—and knowledge of—Islam (than their Euro-American counterparts), especially after 1933, reflected their very real engagement with India's Muslim audiences.

Perhaps more surprisingly, given the influence that the Douglas Fairbanks persona had on Wadia's earlier stunt films, *Lal-e-Yaman* makes limited reference to *Thief of Bagdad*. On the surface there are generic echoes—for example the sword fights, invisible swashbucklers, and the hero's discovery of his beautiful princess asleep on a couch—but the film's visual and aural references are closer to Urdu theater and *qissa* traditions than to Hollywood, building on motifs already present in *Gul-e-Bakavali*. *Lal-e-Yaman* is not, as Studlar observed (earlier) of *Thief of Bagdad*, "driven by dance aesthetics at every level": neither the costume nor the balletic movements and androgynous eroticism of Fairbanks's thief are emulated, nor is the scale of the sets and the all-encompassing dreamlike quality of the *Thief of Bagdad* world.[80] *Lal-e-Yaman* moves, like most *Arabian Nights* and *qissa* stories and unlike *Thief of Bagdad*, between different domains of reality. Moreover, whereas *Thief of Bagdad* is a quasi-morality tale about theft, the dignity of labor, and the irresistible lure of unearned wealth, *Lal-e-Yaman* is about the power of spirituality, music, and divine destiny.

The early sound era appears to mark a turning point in screen depictions of India's Orient. Certainly by the 1950s the fantasy films were consistently set within recognizably Muslim milieux but were, at the same time (and apparently paradoxically), more closely derivative of British and Hollywood orientalist films than in the 1930s, as comparison between the Wadias' 1930s and 1950s *Arabian Nights* films shows.[81] *Lal-e-Yaman* illustrates that 1930s transitional moment and also highlights the complexity—and futility—of essentialist attempts to disentangle influences: the "Islamicate" and the orientalist are not easily distinguished. But, I argue, the *Arabian Nights* film as a genre puts the notion of the Islamicate under particular strain. As we have seen, India's fantasy films drew, like the Muslim socials, historicals, and courtesan films, on an imagined Mughal past and Indo-Persian culture as expressed in theater, visual arts, and performing arts. However, unlike those other genres, fantasy films simultaneously referenced fashionable international orientalism. Consequently, their "Islamicate" world was a double—even triple—mirage, reflecting a transnational Orient

that had evolved through a complex series of borrowings and projections. Moreover, the *Arabian Nights* itself had, by the twentieth century, become a curiously hybrid transnational form, albeit within India
popularly—and uniquely—conflated with Indo-Persian stories little
known in Europe. But precisely these factors ensured the genre's wide
appeal. Just as "oriental dance" was understood within India to be European dance, so, I suggest, by the early 1930s "oriental film"—the "*Arabian Nights* fantasy film"—was importantly understood to be film that
engaged with international cosmopolitan modernity.

The Appeal

Finally, we must ask why the *Arabian Nights* was so key to India's fantasy genre. What work did the *Arabian Nights* do or allow to be done?
On the one hand the *Nights* provided recognizable motifs from a familiar body of stories that had cultural resonance within the Indian subcontinent and beyond. As we saw, these offered unparalleled license for
spectacular excess and surprising twists and turns in the story lines:
the films could boast splendid sets and gorgeous costumes, memorable song and dance, as well as Urduized poetic and theatrical dialogue.
Moreover the *Nights'* tales are full of magical transformations and masquerade, with all the potential for drama and special effects that these
open up. These films—like the *Nights'* stories that inspired them—offer
the extravagant pleasures of utopian worlds.

On the other hand the Islamicate world of such films may well have
been a deliberate bid to reach out to the Muslim audience: as the Indian
Cinematograph Committee evidence cited earlier suggests, there was a
need to find films that appealed across the board. It should be stressed
that, despite the disparaging tag of "Mahomedan pictures," fantasy films
were popular not just with Muslims. Nevertheless, box-office figures
show that *Lal-e-Yaman* and *Noor-e-Yaman* played particularly well in
Bombay and the north Indian territories, where large Muslim audiences
existed, as well as in the overseas territories that included Baghdad and
the Arab world.[82]

I suggest that the *Arabian Nights* fantasy film worked well with
Indian audiences because of its inherent ambiguity. It was on the one
hand modern and Western—carrying the prestige and branding of the

genre's Hollywood successes and a fashionable Europeanism—but it also carried an apparent cultural authenticity as a refusal of all things Western. While the films' settings were outside—and "other than"—contemporary India, motifs from the stories reverberated with audiences' broader cultural knowledge and histories. The *Arabian Nights* was, above all, a shared set of fantasies of the culture, a set of exciting reference points, celebrating the nonrationality that was the integral flipside of cosmopolitan modernity around the world. But such films played on a knife edge between glorifying India's Islamic heritage and dismissing its Muslims as exotic and "other." This was a complex hybrid space, used to different effect by different producers at different periods.

In contrast to Wadia Movietone's contemporary films in other genres, its fantasy and stunt films opened up spaces for a nationalist modernity that differed from both the Hinduized and the Westernized forms found within, for example, the mythologicals and socials.[83] *Lal-e-Yaman* effortlessly combines motifs from Indo-Persian story traditions with the modernity of Hollywood, as the fleeting appearance of Tarzan within the land of the djinn suggests. But this eclecticism is brought to the service of an alternative nationalist sensibility, which in Wadia's case included a call for "Hindu-Muslim unity" or, more specifically, for a cosmopolitan modernity that recognized the heterogeneity of India and its porous borders within a transnational world. Of course this opened Wadia up to criticism. *Varieties Weekly*, for example, smugly asserted that films such as *Lal-e-Yaman* were for "the Muslim class," and while "welcome entertainment," they "should not become the order of the day."[84] While oriental fantasy films were undeniably mostly lowbrow, even the best would be routinely disparaged as "Muslim" films by a Hindu supremacist tendency that wished to exorcize—or exoticize —Islamic influences. Wadia suffered for this throughout his career.

Revealingly, while films of magical and wondrous happenings within an Islamicate world were known—and invariably dismissed—as "fantasies," those of wondrous happenings within a Hindu cosmology were celebrated as "mythologicals." It may be no accident that claims that Hiralal Sen's *Ali Baba and the Forty Thieves* was India's first film have been largely forgotten in favor of a conveniently Hindu mythological, *Raja Harischandra*. "Ali Baba" is a story about thieving that has been a perennial hit, but perhaps the tragic irony of Hiralal Sen's film is to have had its glory, as probably the world's first *Arabian Nights* film, stolen from it by histories written, on the one hand, by a complacent West that has remained for the most part blithely ignorant of Indian cinema history and, on the other, by an Indian nationalism that has preferred to champion a Hindu mythological as Indian cinema's moment of origin.

NOTES

1. This account draws on several (somewhat contradictory) secondary sources, primarily Sajal Chattopadhyay, *Aar Rekho Na Andhare* (Calcutta: Jogomaya Prakashani, 1998); B. Jha, "Profiles of Pioneers," *Cinema Vision India* 1:1 (January 1980): 54–55; Prabhat Mukherjee, "Hiralal Sen," in *70 Years of Indian Cinema, 1913–1983*, ed. T. M. Ramachandran (Bombay: CINEMA India-International, 1985), 49–53; Firoze Rangoonwalla, *Indian Cinema: Past and Present* (New Delhi: Clarion Books, 1983), 12–14. I thank Ranita Chatterjee for finding and translating Bengali sources for me throughout this essay.

2. Although the term *Islamicate* is controversial, it has gained currency among Indian film scholars since Mukul Kesavan first used it in connection with Hindi cinema in "Urdu, Awadh, and the Tawaif: The Islamicate Roots of Hindi Cinema," in *Forging Identities: Gender, Communities, and the State in India*, ed. Zoya Hasan (Boulder, CO: Westview, 1994), 244–57. He draws on Marshall G. S. Hodgson, who coined *Islamicate* to refer not directly to the Islamic religion per se "but to the social and cultural complex historically associated with Islam and the Muslims, both among Muslims themselves and even when found among non-Muslims." Marshall G. S. Hodgson, *The Venture of Islam: Conscience and History in a World Civilization*, 3 vols. (Chicago: University of Chicago Press, 1974), 1:57. See also Rachel Dwyer, *Filming the Gods: Religion and Indian Cinema* (London: Routledge, 2006), 97–131. My own use of the term in this essay refers to stereotyped conventions that construct an exotic fantasy of a historical cultural complex associated with Islam. This bears no necessary relationship to "real" Islamic cultures—nor can one disentangle essentially "Muslim," "Hindu," or any other elements within this.

3. Advertised in the *Madras Mail*, 24 January 1902. I thank Steve Hughes for this reference.

4. For consistency, I use upper-case *O* for the proper noun *Orient*, to refer to a fantastical imaginary space, and the lower case *o* for all its derivatives, including adjectives and nouns that describe a critical position, as in *orientalist* and *orientalism*.

5. *Gul-e-Bakavali* (The Bakavali flower; Kanjibhai Rathod, 1924) released in Bombay in March 1924. *Thief of Bagdad* opened in Calcutta in March 1925 and in Bombay in May 1925 (and in the United States in May 1924).

6. Ira Bhaskar and Richard Allen, *Islamicate Cultures of Bombay Cinema* (New Delhi: Tulika, 2009), xiii

7. The scope of this essay is limited to northern India, including Bombay and Calcutta. While evidence exists of the *Nights'* popularity in southern India—and *Nights* films certainly played there—more research is needed.

8. *Qissa-dastan* (two Persian/Urdu words for "story") refers to a traditional Persian —and subsequently Urdu/Hindi—narrative genre that evolved out of medieval Persian-Arabic folk forms, usually involving adventurous quests, romantic love, and magic "enchantments" across human and fairy/spirit worlds. Famous *qissa-dastan* include *Hatimtai, Char Darvesh, Gul-e-Bakavali, Gul Sanobar,* and *Amir Hamza.* First published from 1803 at Calcutta's Fort William College, *qissa-dastan* storytelling survived as an oral tradition in north India until the late 1920s. See Frances Pritchett, *Marvelous Encounters: Folk Romances in Urdu and Hindi* (Delhi: Manohar, 1985), 1–19; and Francesca Orsini, *Print and Pleasure: Popular Literature and Entertaining Fictions in Colonial North India* (New Delhi: Permanent Black, 2009), 106–16.

9. For example the full-length story *Hatimtai* was both a well-known *qissa-dastan* and also a cycle of Arabic folktales, to which just one episode in the *Nights* alludes.

10. Jatindra Nath Mitra, "A Review of Indian Pictures," *Filmland*, Puja issue, 1934, reprinted in *Indian Cinema: Contemporary Perceptions from the Thirties*, ed. Samik Bandyopadhyay (Jamshedpur: Celluloid Chapter, 1993), 31.

11. See a series of advertisements for Variety Film Services (distributors/exhibitors) in the trade journal *Cinema* in 1931–32.

12. Robert Irwin, introduction to *The Arabian Nights: Tales of 1001 Nights*, trans. from the Arabic by Malcolm Lyons, with Ursula Lyons, vol. 1 (London: Penguin, 2008), ix–x.

13. Cosquin demonstrated similarities between three elements of the *Arabian Nights* frame story and numerous ancient Indian tales including the Buddhist *Tripitaka*, the Sanskrit *Sukasaptati*, the Buddhist *Jatakas* and the eleventh-century Sanskrit *Kathasaritsagara*. Emmanuel Cosquin, "Le prologue-cadre des *Mille et une Nuits*," *Revue Biblique* 6:7 (1909): 7–49. Moreover, the talking animals of the *Tales of Bidpai* (a Pehlavi translation of the *Panchatantra*) also suggest Indian precursors. However, as the *Arabian Nights Encyclopedia* points out, "There is no evidence to suggest a direct relationship between the mentioned texts and the *Arabian Nights*. All that one can say with certainty is that the compiler of the frame story of the *Arabian Nights* relied on various components from Sanskrit texts to compose a new story." Ulrich Marzolph and Richard van Leeuwen, *Arabian Nights Encyclopedia*, vol. 1 (Santa Barbara, CA: ABC-CLIO, 2004), 372.

14. See Ulrike Stark, *An Empire of Books: The Naval Kishore Press and the Diffusion of the Printed Word in Colonial India* (Ranikhet: Permanent Black, 2007), 308–10. Regarding Urdu translations, see Shaista Akhtar Banu Suhrawardy, *A*

Critical Survey of the Development of the Urdu Novel and Short Story (London: Longmans, Green, 1945), 26.

15. Nikhil Sarkar, "Printing and the Spirit of Calcutta," in *Calcutta Living City*, ed. Sukanta Chaudhuri, vol. 1 (1990; Calcutta: Oxford University Press, 1995), 133–34.

16. *Munshi*: scribe, secretary, clerk. Although often credited as the stories' authors, they did not invent the stories, only the mode of telling them: they were primarily editors/translators/transcribers. See Sisir Kumar Das, *Sahibs and Munshis: An Account of the College of Fort William* (Calcutta: Orion, 1978). Interestingly, Wadia writes of a *munshi* involved in script writing for *Lal-e-Yaman*. J. B. H. Wadia, "The Story behind the Making of *Lal-e-Yaman*," from unpublished memoirs, 1980, in Wadia Movietone Archives, Bombay. Accessed with kind permission of Vinci Wadia.

17. It is not clear whether this was the play written originally by Vinayak Prasad Talib for the Victoria Company and published in 1900 or a different adaptation by star actor Kavasji Khatau, who played Ali Baba in 1878, with the female impersonator Naslu Sarkari as Marjana (or if these are the same). See Somnath Gupt, *The Parsi Theatre: Its Origins and Development* (1981), trans. from the Hindi and edited by Kathryn Hansen (New Delhi: Seagull Books, 2005), 70–71, 126.

18. See Sushil Kumar Mukherjee, *The Story of the Calcutta Theatres: 1753–1980* (Calcutta: K. P. Bagchi, 1982), 99, 594, 797.

19. Ranabir Ray Choudhury, *Early Calcutta Advertisements, 1875–1925* (Bombay: Nichiketa, 1992), 108.

20. "*Gul-e-Bakavali*," in *Encyclopaedia of Indian Cinema*, ed. Ashish Rajadhyaksha and Paul Willemen, new rev. ed. (London: BFI and Oxford University Press, 1999), 245–46.

21. Nihal Chand's Urdu *Gul-e-Bakavali* was published in 1803–4 according to Pritchett, *Marvelous Encounters*, 21 (1803), 197 (1804). Pritchett's subsequent (1991) catalogue of Fort William publications (http://www.columbia.edu/itc/mealac/pritchett/00urdu/baghobahar/BBFORTWM.pdf) mentions an Urdu *Alif Laila* as "preparing for press" in 1803—a decade before its famous Arabic translation, *Calcutta 1*.

22. *Fakir*: Muslim Sufi holy man.

23. Indian film scholarship is deeply indebted to Virchand Dharamsey for bringing this extraordinary manuscript to light: "The Script of *Gul-e-Bakavali* (Kohinoor, 1924)," *BioScope* 3:2 (2012): 175–207.

24. He added, "Most of the films in those years . . . were either mythologicals or fantasies that abounded in trick scenes." See Ram Mohan, "The Closely Guarded Secrets of the Special Effects Men," *Cinema Vision India* 1:1 (January 1980): 89.

25. The third was *Magician of Bengal* (*Gaud Bangal*, a.k.a. *Kamroo Deshni Kamini*; K. P. Bhave, 1925).

26. Indian Cinematograph Committee, *Report of the Indian Cinematograph Committee, 1927–8* (Calcutta: Government of India Central Publication Branch, 1928), 40 (hereafter *ICCR*).

27. Indian Cinematograph Committee, *Indian Cinematograph Committee 1927–8, Evidence*, vol. 1 (Calcutta: Government of India Central Publication Branch, 1928), 24, 172, 288 (hereafter *ICCE*).

28. *ICCR*, 21. Witness testimonies include, for example, *ICCE*, 1:70, 442, 457, 505, 594.

29. Suresh Chabria and Paolo Cherchi Usai, eds., *Light of Asia: Indian Silent Cinema, 1912–1935* (New Delhi: Wiley Eastern, 1994).

30. Although Virchand Dharamsey uses these categories, we have insufficient evidence to assess how distinguishable these actually were, especially when settings were hybrid or fantastical. See Virchand Dharamsey, "The Advent of Sound in Indian Cinema: Theatre, Orientalism, Action, Magic," *Journal of the Moving Image* 9 (2010), http://www.jmionline.org/film_journal/jmi_09/article_02.php (accessed 15 July 2012).

31. Out of 1,051 silent films between 1925 and 1934, 425 were classified by Virchand Dharamsey (in his filmography in Chabria and Usai, *Light of Asia*) as "costume" films. As Dharamsey eschews the "fantasy" category, I cross-reference his more reliable filmography with Firoze Rangoonwalla, *Indian Filmography* (Bombay: J. Udeshi, 1970), and Rajendra Ojha, *75 Glorious Years of Indian Cinema* (Bombay: Screen World, 1988), despite some inconsistencies between the three. As with all attributions of genre, definitive classifications are neither possible nor useful: approximations are all we need in the present context.

32. As we will see, although *Lal-e-Yaman* was classified as a costume film by Rangoonwalla (*Indian Filmography*) and Ojha (*75 Glorious Years of Indian Cinema*), it was explicitly seen as an *Arabian Nights* fantasy film by its makers.

33. *Bombay Chronicle*, 14 February 1931.

34. Kaushik Bhaumik, "Querying the 'Traditional' Roots of Silent Cinema in Asia," *Journal of the Moving Image* 7 (December 2008), http://www.jmionline.org/jmi7.htm (accessed 6 January 2011).

35. Jamshed (J. B. H.) and Homi Wadia were Parsi brothers who made successful stunt films in the silent era, set up Wadia Movietone in 1933, and from 1942 onward made many films together at Homi's company, Basant Pictures. See Rosie Thomas, "Not Quite (Pearl) White: Fearless Nadia Queen of the Stunts," in *Bollyworld*, ed. Raminder Kaur and Ajay Sinha, 35–69 (New Delhi: Sage, 2005).

36. According to my own calculations based on Rangoonwalla (*Indian Filmography*), in 1950 there were no fantasy films and just 3 "costume" films released; by 1955 out of 125 releases there were 8 fantasy and 32 costume films.

37. For example *Aladin* (Sujoy Ghosh, 2009) with Amitabh Bachchan and Sanjay Dutt playing, respectively, good and bad genies/djinni.

38. *Alif Laila*, directed by Ramanand Sagar, was broadcast on Doordarshan and SAB TV between 1993 and 1996.

39. J. B. H. Wadia, "JBH in Talkieland," *Cinema Vision India* 1:2 (January 1980): 82.

40. *Dada*: respected elder male, literally grandfather or older brother.

41. Material on Joseph David and all quotes are from J. B. H. Wadia's essay "Joseph David: Tribute to a Forgotten Pioneer," from unpublished memoirs, 1980, in Wadia Movietone Archives, Bombay. Accessed with kind permission of Vinci Wadia.

42. *Bombay Chronicle*, 24 September 1933.

43. The terms *pir mard*, *darvesh*, and *fakir* are used interchangeably within the film to refer to this Sufi holy man.

44. For more details and analysis of this complex narrative see Rosie Thomas, "Distant Voices, Magic Knives," in *Beyond the Boundaries of Bollywood*, ed. Rachel Dwyer and Jerry Pinto, 53–76 (New Delhi: Oxford University Press, 2010).

45. In the *Nights* the wife ingeniously fools the parrot with sounds of thunder, lightning, and rain so that when the merchant returns, knowing there was no storm, he kills what he thinks is an untrustworthy parrot, only to repent when he realizes it is his wayward wife who is untrustworthy. The *qissa-dastan Tota Kahani* (Parrot's tale), narrated by the parrot, also involves a parrot guarding a potentially unfaithful wife, as does the Sanskrit *Sukasaptati*.

46. Hollywood's silent Tarzan films had done well in India. However, this visual reference was probably to Johnny Weissmuller's famous *Tarzan the Ape Man* (dir. W. S. Van Dyke, 1932) which by 1933, according to Wadia, had "made Tarzan a household name even in remote small towns in India." For more on Tarzan in India see Rosie Thomas, "Zimbo and Son Meet the Girl with the Gun," in *Living Pictures: Indian Film Poster Art*, ed. David Blamey and Robert D'Souza, 27–44 (London: Open Editions, 2005).

47. According to figures in a 1941 document in the Wadia Movietone archive, *Lal-e-Yaman* was Wadia Movietone's tenth most profitable film, making a respectable Rs 1,52,000 in its first eight years. Although *Noor-e-Yaman* did not do quite so well (1,21K compared with 1,52K), it earned more than *Lal-e-Yaman* in every territory apart from Bombay and Delhi, and especially overseas.

48. Story line and visuals are deduced from the song booklet—all that survives of this film.

49. Just one year later, as Fearless Nadia, a.k.a. *Hunterwali*, she transformed Wadia Movietone's fortunes and changed its production priorities from Islamicate melodrama to stunt films.

50. Gregory D. Booth, "Musicking the Other: Orientalism in the Hindi Cinema," in *Music and Orientalism in the British Empire, 1780s–1940s: Portrayal of the East*, ed. Martin Clayton and Bennett Zon, 315–38 (Aldershot, UK: Ashgate, 2007).

51. The key text is Edward W. Said, *Orientalism* (New York: Vintage, 1979). See also Linda Nochlin "The Imaginary Orient," *Art in America* 71 (May 1983), among very many others.

52. Otto Rothfeld, *Women of India* (London: Simpkin, Marshall, Hamilton, Kent, 1920), 154.

53. Peter Wollen, *Raiding the Icebox: Reflections on Twentieth-Century Culture* (London: Verso, 1993), 1–34.

54. The term *art deco* was used only from the 1960s. For more on art deco in India see Rachel Dwyer and Divia Patel, *Cinema India: The Visual Culture of Hindi Film* (London: Reaktion Books, 2002), 124–35.

55. Matthew Bernstein, introduction to *Visions of the East: Orientalism in Film*, ed. Matthew Bernstein and Gaylyn Studlar (London: I. B. Tauris, 1997), 4.

56. As Douglas Fairbanks's son recounts in an interview released on the VHS of *Thief of Bagdad* (Thames Television for Channel Four, 1985).

57. Gaylyn Studlar, "Douglas Fairbanks: Thief of the Ballets Russes," in *Bodies of the Text: Dance as Theory, Literature as Dance*, ed. Ellen W. Goellner and Jacqueline Shea Murphy (New Brunswick: Rutgers University Press, 1995), 109.

58. Joan L. Erdman, "Dance Discourses: Rethinking the History of the 'Oriental Dance,'" in *Moving Words: Rewriting Dance*, ed. Gay Morris (London: Routledge, 1996), 289.

59. Gaylyn Studlar, "Out-Salomeing Salome: Dance, the New Woman, and Fan Magazine Orientalism," in Bernstein and Studlar, *Visions of the East*, 106–7.

60. Wollen, *Raiding the Icebox*, 10.

61. Material on Ruth St. Denis/Denishawn draws on numerous sources, notably Elizabeth Kendall, *Where She Danced* (New York: Kopf, 1979); Ted Shawn, *Gods Who Dance* (New York: Dutton, 1929); Adrienne L. McLean, "The Thousand Ways There Are to Move," in Bernstein and Studlar, *Visions of the East*, 130–157; and Studlar, "Out-Salomeing Salome."

62. Quoted in McLean, "The Thousand Ways There Are to Move," 155.

63. William A. Everett, "*Chu Chin Chow* and Orientalist Musical Theatre in Britain during the First World War," in Clayton and Zon, *Music and Orientalism in the British Empire*, 277–96. The film's influence is visible in Homi Wadia's 1954 *Alibaba*.

64. *Tatler*, 12 September 1917.

65. David Bate, *Photography and Surrealism: Sexuality, Colonialism and Social Dissent* (London: I. B. Tauris, 2004), 127.

66. Photo album filmed by author during an interview with Mary Wadia in January 1986.

67. Pushpa Sunder, *Patrons and Philistines: Arts and the State in British India, 1773–1947* (Delhi: Oxford University Press, 1995), 249.

68. Shawn, *Gods Who Dance*, 99.

69. I thank Ann David for useful discussion of ideas in this section.

70. Erdman, "Dance Discourses," 289.

71. Madhu Bose's 1937 Bengali *Alibaba*, based on the same Calcutta stage play as Hiralal Sen's 1903–4 film, was widely celebrated and seen as more "respectable" than the Wadias' Islamicate films, despite being more obviously derivative of Hollywood (and Western theater) and less directly related to indigenous traditions.

72. My use of the terms "low" and "lower" genre follows Miriam Hansen and others to denote the "sensational, attractionist genres" of early cinema or, following Yuri Tsivian, the "adventure serials, detective thrillers and slap-stick comedies" so beloved of the Soviet modernists. See Miriam Hansen, "The Mass Production of the Senses," in *Reinventing Film Studies*, ed. Christine Gledhill and Linda Williams (London: Arnold, 2000), 332–50.

73. J. B. H. Wadia, "How *Bagh-e-Misr* Came to Be Produced," from unpublished memoirs, 1980, in Wadia Movietone Archives, Bombay. Accessed with kind permission of Vinci Wadia.

74. Wadia, "Story behind the Making of *Lal-e-Yaman*."

75. *Bombay Chronicle*, 11 November 1933.

76. "The Script of *Gul-e-Bakavali*," 180.

77. *Gool-i Bukawulee*, trans. from Urdu by Thomas Philip Manuel (Lucknow: Naval Kishore Press, 1882).

78. Zeen-ul-Mulk and Taj-ul-Mulk would be recognized by Indian audiences as Muslim names, Raja Jalad Sang/Singh as Hindu (Rajput or Sikh).

79. Thomas, "Distant Voices, Magic Knives."

80. As Wadia's first talkie, *Lal-e-Yaman* was a much more cheaply and crudely made film, as Wadia himself admits.

81. Homi Wadia's *Aladdin* (1952) and *Ali Baba* (1954) both copy visual and plot motifs from British and Hollywood versions of the stories—albeit integrated within distinctively "Indianized" tellings of the tales. See Rosie Thomas, "Still Magic: An Aladdin's Cave of 1950s B Movie Fantasy," a visual essay at *Tasveer Ghar*, n.d., http://tasveerghar.net/cmsdesk/essay/103/ (accessed 7 June 2011).

82. By 1941 *Lal-e-Yaman*'s total profits across the seven distribution territories were Rs 1,52,793, i.e., Bombay: Rs 68,131 (c. 45%); Lahore: Rs 14,072 (c. 9%); Delhi: Rs 34,396 (c. 25%); Central Provinces: Rs 4,223 (c. 3%); Calcutta: Rs 13,899 (c. 9%); Madrid: Rs 9,000 (c. 6%); and Overseas: Rs 7,654: (c. 5%) (figures from documents in the Wadia Movietone Archive).

83. Thomas, "Not Quite (Pearl) White," 45–50.

84. *Varieties Weekly*, 23 February 1934, 9–10, quoted in Kaushik Bhaumik, "The Emergence of the Bombay Film Industry, 1913–36" (D.Phil. thesis, University of Oxford, 2001), 174.

Afterword

My Arabian Superheroine

ALIA YUNIS

When I was a child in White Bear Lake, the small town in Minnesota where we lived, I used to dress up like Scheherazade for Halloween. I didn't feel American enough to think the neighbors would let me get away with dressing up as the Bionic Woman or a Charlie's Angel. But I wanted to be glamorous and gutsy like those glorious women of TV and tabloids. And so I would put on a long dress some relative I had never met had sent me from Lebanon or Jordan or Palestine and wrap my head in a colorful scarf with fake coins on it, have the mom next door put some heavy-duty makeup on me, and top it off with gargantuan hoop earrings. Most people thought I was dressed as a fortune-teller, but I wasn't a mere soothsayer. I was Scheherazade, the Wonder Woman of the Middle East, the prettiest and most powerful person I knew.

Of course, I didn't know Scheherazade at all. I certainly didn't know that she seduced a king with sexually provocative and perverse tales, that she was at the center of a body of work that has kept scholars and historians busy for centuries, and that her collection of tales has become one of the most recognized frameworks in literature. All I knew about her was based on the story I was told by my mother when I asked her why my cousin in Chicago was named Scheherazade or, in her Americanized form, Sherry. My mother's answer was the kind of answer a pan-Arab nationalist gives to girl who cries, like her daughter, at beauty pageants on TV: Scheherazade was the most beautiful woman in the Arab world, which therefore meant the whole world. And she went around being beautiful by swirling around in lots of diaphanous veils and telling stories of magical people, stories my mother explained to me Disney had stolen for its movies, like the tales of Aladdin and Ali Baba and his forty thieves. Soon I also figured out that Scheherazade must have gotten everywhere on a self-chauffeuring magic carpet. This last part I didn't learn from my mother but rather extrapolated from TV reruns of *I Dream of Jeannie, Bewitched,* and Saturday-morning cartoons.

Television and my mother, even before books, were the first of the many Scheherazades in my life who would entrance me with their stories, but unlike television, my mother didn't know about the magic carpet because she didn't really know anything more about the *Arabian Nights* than Walt Disney did. In fact, in her day, girls were educated in fancy French- and British-based schools, or they were barely educated at all, and in neither case was Arab literature a prime part of the curriculum. What little she did know was from the private school she attended, which came with the British-based Orientalist stories, not the original work (keeping in mind that the original is hard to define clearly).

But my mother was never one for magic carpets and fairy tales, Orientalist or otherwise. Her stories were always about reality, perhaps embellished reality, but rarely with forever-after happy endings. For her, Scheherazade was a woman who told stories to stay alive to protect her own life but more importantly the lives of her beloved sister and other family members. And that's what made her worthy, how my mother hoped I saw her and my ancestors, and how she hoped I would be one day. The resilience and quick thinking of a woman was essentially at the heart of every story my mother told me about "back home," as were the other stories told to me by the other Scheherazades I met when we moved "back home." Aunts, teachers, cousins, neighbors—all their stories were allegedly true tales of women who defied

Mother Nature, the men in their lives, and invading armies to rescue their families, neighbors, and true loves from fate or from cognitive skills inferior to hers.

Indeed, Scheherazade is what Middle Eastern women have been in my life, not the harem sexpots of old Hollywood or the black-enrobed, faceless blobs of today's mainstream literature and cinema, but rather women with strength that isn't dependent on a formal position in government or at a Fortune 500 company. They claimed control in their own ways without asking for it. Arab women traditionally have, like Scheherazade, held power when they have used their imagination to take charge of their domestic world, and not necessarily when they conquered business, be it Souq Al Hamadieh or Wall Street.

Holding a big title at a big company is how we define female empowerment in the West. But for Arab women, power is something better defined by Scheherazade. The influence Arab women had over the people they loved and/or married to wasn't earned through bra-burning demonstrations but through generations of tradition, a tradition so old that I suspect Scheherazade was born out of it, rather than being the trendsetter. Either way, Scheherazade understood, unlike the women sent to King Shahriyar before her, that her sexuality, her wit, and her intellect were a combination that when used properly served as a brilliant weapon.

Scheherazade's qualities of survival were very manifest in the Arab women around me in my childhood and teen years—ingenious women in a way all their own, and fierce in spirit, in a discreet, subtle way or in a backhanded way, depending on how you viewed the situation. They were smartly seductive, quick on their feet when it came to figuring out how to survive, the weight bearers of their homes and troubled nations. And always raconteurs. They didn't—still don't—do silence well and can fill any void with a story whether it is to save a life, give advice, or pass the time. They lure their children into doing right and wrong through their stories, and they caution their men with tales that carry warnings of what will happen to them if they don't take their advice. Today's postcolonial subjugation of many Arab women in a patriarchal society in which Western feminism has somewhat negated Arab feminism is not something Scheherazade would have put up with—she would tell today's women to embrace their womanhood with humor and foresight and create stories around it that will give them the life they want.

Scheherazade was a feminist centuries before the word became part of Western society. While she was hanging out in the Middle East and East, Cinderella, Sleeping Beauty, and Rapunzel were self-absorbedly waiting around to be rescued. Unlike Scheherazade, they were not smart, wise, brave, imaginative, and sexy. Mythical females of the West could not be smart, wise, caring, sexy, and beautiful all at once. If they were caring and smart, they were sexless, like Mary Poppins. If they were beautiful, they were simpering. If they were wise, they were shriveled.

Without possessing the powers of Greek goddesses but with only her human skills, Scheherazade was the first Arab Superheroine. She's better than a superhero because her immense power comes from her head, not from gadgets, a seemingly steroid-enhanced body, and fanciful killing instruments. The jinn, afreet, and others in her stories had mysterious, otherworldly ways, but she really didn't.

We are empowered by the stories we are told, and eventually many of us discover a way of making the world more defined for ourselves through creating our own stories for others—whether through music, art, poetry, film, dance, or most obviously literature.

Indeed, while Scheherazade is a mythical character herself, her storytelling powers embody all that writing students have been taught from the time of Aristotle to today. First and foremost, she knew how to enclose her audience into her story circle, where he could not escape easily with a finite "happily ever after." Rather, she left him every night asking, "what happens next, even after ever after?" She knew how to pace a story so that she could build tension; she wove together multidimensional characters, each who could eventually become a major character in his own tale. She built tension and sprinkled it with universal themes, sexual innuendo, and humor, the first an essential, the latter two often-colorful additions.

And sometimes one storyteller's tales can rescue another storyteller. While I can never compare myself to Scheherazade—after all, I'm human, not a superhero—*The Night Counter* taught me there was a bit of her in me, too, as I believe there is in all of us, male or female. I had spent years struggling in Hollywood, the cliché story of coming this close to the big break more than once, only to have it disappear and another carrot dangled in front of me, just so I wouldn't move out of town. Hollywood, like publishing, music, and all other art businesses, like Scheherazade, is not just a mythmaker for the world at large but within itself as well, egging an artist to do yet another project if you want to survive, that is, to get that break. Still, I was very active with my small writer's group, and they all decided to apply for the Squaw Valley Writer's Conference. I refused to spend another dime on screenwriting, but I loved the idea of going to Squaw Valley; so I applied for the fiction section and started up a story just to have something to workshop. Someone there mentioned the PEN Emerging Voices Fellowship, which I had not heard of before. I applied and then forgot all about it, as I was told it was a very brutal competition and favored writers with a darker, more literary style—and who had actually attempted novels already. However, PEN did call me in as a final candidate, and I found myself in a small, cramped room being interrogated by six people lined up on the opposite wall. I got increasingly claustrophobic, especially when they started asking me questions about my "novel-in-progress," which wasn't in progress at all. They glared at me in expressionless anticipation, waiting for an excuse to cast me aside. The room was stark and bare, but there was a little orange paper hanging on the wall. This was October, Halloween weekend, and the orange paper was some invitation to some costume party. It had been years since I dressed up as Scheherazade, but as the six people continued to stare at me, Scheherazade came to my mind then. I began to spin a tale in my head, not to save my life but to spare my pride and dignity, such as they were. I had my first "What would Scheherazade do?" moment. Scheherazade I knew would concoct a tale as quickly as she could toss a veil across her hair. I wondered where she would find a story in Los Angeles, and that was when I realized it would be with an older woman who shared the Middle East with her but had the struggles of America as the framework for her stories. And so I began to tell a story about Fatima and how she survived her first years in the United States. The interviewers' stone faces began to crack a bit. I wouldn't say they smiled, but close enough. When they asked me what happens to the main character in the end, I shrugged and said, "We'll have to wait and see."

The next week, I received a call telling me I had been given the fellowship, and I went on to write a novel with Fatima and Scheherazade as the main characters and found myself using the premise of the *Arabian Nights*, one story folding into another and then interconnecting again, to develop their friendship and reveal the copious layers of Fatima's family.

Every Halloween I still think of Scheherazade when I see little girls dressed up as the Catwoman, Lara Croft, or Spider Woman. There is a much more powerful superheroine out there, I want to tell them, one who doesn't need to kill anyone to reveal her strength. But perhaps they are getting to know a version of her through the stories their mothers and the other Scheherazades in their lives tell them, and I hope that they have a lot of them.

LIST OF STORIES

1. THE STORY OF KING SHAHRIYAR AND QUEEN SCHEHERAZADE

Translations

Antoine Galland, trans., *Les mille et une nuit* (12 vols. [Paris, 1704–17], vol. 1)

Arabian Nights' Entertainments (hereafter *ANE*), "Frame Story of Scheherazade" ("Grub Street" translation, 12 vols. [London, 1705], vol. 1)

Richard Burton, trans., "Story of King Shahryar and His Brother" (*The Book of the Thousand Nights and a Night, with Introduction, Explanatory Notes on the Manners and Customs of Moslem Men and a Terminal Essay upon the History of the Nights*, 16 vols. [Benares: Kamashastra Society, 1885–87], vol. 1)

E. Powys Mathers, trans., "The Tale of King Shahryar and His Brother King Shahzaman" (*The Book of the Thousand Nights and One Night* [London: Routledge, 1990], based on the French edition by Jean-Charles Mardrus)

Husain Haddawy, trans., "The Story of King Shahrayar and Shahrazad, His Vizier's Daughter" (*Arabian Nights* [New York: Norton, 1990], based on the manuscript edited by Muhsin Mahdi)

Malcolm Lyons, trans., "King Shahryar and Shahrazad" (*The Arabian Nights: Tales of 1001 Nights*, 3 vols. [London: Penguin, 2010], vol. 1)

2. PRINCESS BUDUR (THE STORY OF QAMAR AL-ZAMAN)

Translations

Galland, "Histoire des amours de Camaralzaman Prince de l'Isle des enfants de Khalendan, et de Badoure Princesse de la Chine" (vol. 2)

ANE, "The Story of the Amours of Camaralzaman, Prince of the Isles of the Children of Khaledan, and of Badoura, Princess of China" (vol. 6)

Edward Lane, trans., "Story of the Prince Camaralzaman and the Princess Badoura" (*The Thousand and One Nights, Commonly Called, in England, the Arabian Nights' Entertainments: A New Translation from the Arabic, with Copious Notes*, 3 vols. [London: Charles Knight, 1838–40], vol. 2)

Burton, "Tale of Kamar Al-Zaman" (vol. 3)

Jean-Charles Mardrus, trans., "Histoire du Kamaralzanam avec la princesse Boudour, la plus belle lune d'entre toutes les lunes" (*Les mille nuits et une nuit*, 16 vols. [Paris: Robert Laffont, collection "Bouquins," 1980], vol. 5)

Haddawy, "The Story of Qamar al-Zaman and His Two Sons, Amjad and A'sad"

Lyons, "The Story of King Shahriman and His Son, Qamar al-Zaman" (vol. 1)

Adaptations

J. F. Madan, *Kamr-al-Zaman-Badoora* (1905), drama

J. J. Madan, *Princess Budur* (*The Story of Qamar-e-Zaman*) (1922), film

3. ALADDIN'S WONDROUS LAMP

Translations

Galland, "Histoire d'Aladdin ou la lampe merveilleuse" (vol. 1)

ANE, "The Story of Aladdin; or, The Wonderful Lamp" (vol. 9)

Lane, "Story of Aladdin Abushamat" (vol. 2)

Burton, "Ala al-Din Abu al-Shamat" (vol. 4)

Mathers, "The Tale of Aladdin and the Wonderful Lamp"

John Payne, trans., "Alaeddin Abou Esh Shamat," in *The Book of the Thousand Nights and One Night* (1882–84), translation in nine volumes.

Haddawy, "Aladdin and the Magic Lamp"

Lyons, "Ala al-Din Abu al-Shamat" (vol. 1)

Adaptations

William Beckford, *Histoire d'Aladdin, Roi de l'Yemen*

John O'Keeffe, *Aladdin and His Wonderful Lamp* (1788), drama

Ferdinand Zecca, *Aladdin of the Marvelous Lamp* (1906), film

B. P. Mishra, *Aladdin and His Wonderful Lamp* (1927), film

J. J. Madan, *Aladdin* (1931), film

Basant Pictures, *Aladdin Aur Jadiu Chirag* (Aladdin and the wonderful lamp) (1952), film

Naguib Mahfouz, "Aladdin with the Moles on His Cheeks" (*Layali alf layla / Arabian Nights and Days*) (1995), literature

4. THE SEVEN VOYAGES OF SINBAD THE SAILOR

Translations

Galland, "Histoire de Sindbad le marin" (vol. 3)

ANE, "The Story of Sindbad the Sailor" (vol. 3)

Lane, "Story of Sindbad the Sailor and Sindbad the Porter" (vol. 2)

Burton, "Sindbad the Seaman and Sindbad the Landsman" (vol. 6)

Mardrus, "Histoire de Sindbad le marin" (vol. 6)

Payne, "Sindbad the Sailor and Sindbad the Porter"

Haddawy, "The Story of Sindbad the Sailor"

Lyons, "Sindbad the Sailor" (vol. 2)

Adaptations

Paul Klee, *Sindbad the Sailor* (*Battle Scene from the Comic-Operatic-Fantasy "The Seafarer"*) (1928), painting

Richard Wallace, *Sinbad, the Sailor* (1947), film

Tim Severin, *The Sindbad Voyage* (1982), literature

Radwa Ashour, *Siraaj* (1992), literature

David Bridges, *The Sindbad Voyage* (1992) film
Patrick Gilmore, *Sinbad: The Legend of the Seven Seas* (2003), film

5. ALI BABA AND THE FORTY THIEVES

Translations
Galland, "Histoire d'Ali Baba (et de quarante voleurs exterminés par une esclave)" (vol. 11)
ANE, "The Story of Ali Baba, and the Forty Thieves Destroy'd by a Slave" (vol. 11)
Burton, "Story of Ali Baba and the Forty Thieves" (supp. vol. 3)
Mathers, "The Tale of Ali Baba and the Forty Thieves"
Haddawy, "The Story of 'Ali Baba and the Forty Thieves"
Lyons, "The Story of Ali Baba and the Forty Thieves Killed by a Slave Girl" (vol. 1)

Adaptations
Ferdinand Zecca, *Ali Baba and the Forty Thieves* (1902), film
Hiralal Sen, *Ali Baba and the Forty Thieves* (1906), film
Chu Chin Chow (1916), drama
Madan, *Ali Baba* (1932), film
Homi Wadia, *Ali Baba and the Forty Thieves* (1954), film
Kyokudō Nankai, *Ali Baba and the Forty Thieves* (*kōdan*) (2004), drama

6. THE EBONY HORSE

Translations
Galland, "Histoire du cheval enchanté" (vol. 3)
ANE, "The Story of the Enchanted Horse"
Lane, "Story of the Magic Horse" (vol. 2)
Burton, "The Ebony Horse" (vol. 1)
Mathers, "The Magic Tale of the Ebony Horse" (vol. 3)
Payne, "The Enchanted Horse"
Haddawy, "The Ebony Horse"
Lyons, "The Ebony Horse" (vol. 2)

7. THE MERCHANT AND THE GENIE

Translations
Galland, "Le marchand et le génie" (vol. 1)
ANE, "The First Night: The Merchant and the Genie" (vol. 1)
Lane, "Story of the Merchant and the Jinn" (vol. 1)
Burton, "Tale of the Trader and the Jinni" (vol. 1)
Mardrus, "Histoire du marchand" (vol. 1)
Payne, "The Merchant and the Genie"
Haddawy, "The Story of the Merchant and the Demon"
Lyons, "The Merchant and the Jinni" (vol. 1)

8. STORY OF THE HUNCHBACK

Translations
Galland, "Histoire du petit bossu" (vol. 4)
ANE, "The Story of the Little Hunch-Back" (vol. 4)
Lane, "Story of the Humpback" (chap. 5)
Burton, "The Hunchback's Tale" (vol. 1)
Mathers, "The Tale of the Hunchback with the Tailor, the Christian Broker, the
    Steward and the Jewish Doctor; What Followed After; and the Tales Which Each
    of Them Told"
Payne, "Story of the Hunchback"
Haddawy, "The Story of the Hunchback"
Lyons, "The Hunchback"

Adaptations
Katsura Kujaku, *The Hunch Back* (*rakugo*) (2004), drama

9. THE STORY OF JULLANAR OF THE SEA

Translations
Lane, "Story of Gulnare of the Sea" (vol. 3)
Burton, "Julnar the Sea-Born and Her Son King Badr Basim of Persia" (vol. 7)
Payne, "Julnar of the Sea and Her Son King Bedr Basim of Persia"
Haddawy, "The Story of Jullanar of the Sea"
Lyons, "Julnar of the Sea and Her Son, Badr Basim" (vol. 3)

10. STORY OF AL-RAOUI

Adaptations
William Beckford, *Histoire d'Alraoui contée à l'Emir du grand Caire* (c. 1790) (MS
    Beckford d.20)

11. STORY OF FELKANAMAN

Adaptations
William Beckford, *Histoire d'Elouard Felkanaman et d'Ansel Hougioud* (MS Beckford
    d.23)

12. STORY OF MAZIN

Adaptations
William Beckford, *Histoire de Mazin* (MS Beckford d.25)

13. STORY OF PRINCE MAHMED

Adaptations
William Beckford, *Histoire du Prince Mahmed* (MS Beckford d.26)

14. STORY OF ABUNIAH KING OF MOUSSEL

Adaptations
William Beckford, *Histoire d'Abou Niah Roi de Moussel* (MS Beckford d.26)

15. STORY OF PRINCESS FATIMA, DAUGHTER OF KING BEN AMER

Adaptations
William Beckford, *Histoire de la Princesse Fatimah fille du Roi Ben Amer* (MS Beckford
    d.26)

16. PRINCE ACHMED

Translations
Galland, "Histoire du prince Ahmed et de la fee Pari-Banou" (vol. 12)
ANE, "The Story of Prince Ahmed and the Fairy Pari Banon" (vol. 12)
Burton, "Adventures of Prince Ahmad and the Fairy Peribanu" (supp. vol. 3)

Adaptations
Raoul Walsh, *The Thief of Baghdad* (1924–25), film
William Beckford, *Histoire du Prince Ahmed, fils du Roi de Khoten, et d'Ali Ben Hassan
    de Bagdad* (1780), literature

17. STORY OF KEBAL KING OF DAMAS

Adaptations
William Beckford, *Histoire de Kebal Roi de Damas contée par Mamalebé nourrice de la
    Princesse Hasaia à la chevelure blanche* (MS Beckford d.26)

18. STORY OF DARIANOC

Adaptations
William Beckford, *Histoire de Darianoc* (MS Beckford d.12)

19. STORY OF SCHAHANAZAN

Adaptations
William Beckford, *Histoire de Schahanazan, Roi de Tartarie ou l'année des epreuves,
    suite des Contes Arabes* (MS Beckford d.23)

20. STORY OF ZINAN

Adaptations
William Beckford, *Histoire de Zinan* (MS Beckford d.21)

21. STORY OF VATHEK

Adaptations
William Beckford, *Les episodes de Vathek* (MS Beckford d.13–19)

22. STORY OF THE PORTER AND THE LADIES OF BAGHDAD

Translations
Galland, "Histoire des trois calenders, fils de roi, et de cinq dames de Bagdad"
ANE, "Story of the Three Calenders, Sons of Kings, and of Five Ladies of Bagdad"
Lane, "Story of the Porter and the Ladies of Bagdad, and of the Three Royal
    Mendicants" (vol. 1)
Burton, "The Porter and the Three-Ladies of Baghdad" (vol. 1)
Mathers, "The Tale of the Porter and the Young Girls"
Payne, "The Porter and the Three Ladies of Baghdad"
Haddawy, *The Story of the Porter and the Three Ladies*
Lyons, "The Porter and the Three Ladies"

23. STORY OF THE ENVIOUS MAN AND OF HIM THAT HE ENVIED

Translations
Galland, "Histoire de l'envieux et de l'envie"
ANE, "The Story of the Envious Man, and of Him That He Envied" (vol. 2)
Lane, "Story of the Envier and the Envied" (vol. 1)
Burton, "Tale of the Envier and the Envied" (vol. 1)
Payne, "Story of the Envier and the Envied"
Haddawy, "The Tale of the Envious and the Envied"
Lyons, "The Story of the Envious and the Envied" (vol. 1)

24. STORY OF THE FISHERMAN

Translations
Galland, "Histoire du pêcheur" (vol. 1)
Lane, "Story of the Fisherman" (vol. 1)
Burton, "The Fisherman and the Jinni" (vol. 1)
Mardrus, "Histoire du pêcheur" (vol. 1)
Payne, "The Fisherman and the Genie"
Haddawy, "The Story of the Fisherman and the Demon"

25. THE SLEEPER AWAKENED OR STORY OF THE AWAKENED SLEEPER

Translations
Galland, "Histoire du dormeur éveillé" (vol. 9)
ANE, "The Story of the Sleeper Awaken'd" (vol. 9)
Lane, "Story of Abon-Hassan the Wag, or the Sleeper Awakened" (vol. 2)
Burton, "The Sleeper and the Waker" (supp. vol. 1)
Mardrus, "Histoire du dormeur éveillé" (vol. 10)
Payne, "Asleep and Awake"

Adaptations
Carl Maria von Weber, *Abu Hasan, or the Awakened Sleeper* (1811), drama
Enomoto Haryū, *Kigeki Arabiya yobanashi* (A comedy from the *Arabian Nights*)
   (1906), drama

26. STORY OF ALI KHAWAJA AND THE MERCHANT OF BAGDAD

Translations
Galland, "Histoire d'Ali Cogia, marchand de Bagdad" (vol. 11)
ANE, "The Story of Ali Cogia, a Merchant of Bagdad" (vol. 11)
Burton, "Story of Ali Khwajah and the Merchant of Baghdad" (supp. vol. 3)

27. HATIM OF THE TRIBE OF TAYY

Translations
Burton, "Hatim of the Tribe of Tayy" (vol. 4)
Payne, "Hatim et Yai: His Generosity after Death"
Lyons, "Hatim of Tayy"

Adaptations
Hatim Tai (c. 1870s), drama
Homi Wadia, *Hatimtai* (1956), film.
Krishna Film, *Hatimtai* (1929), film

28. THE STORY OF THE GRECIAN KING AND THE PHYSICIAN DOUBAN

Translations
Galland, "Histoire du roi grec et du médecin Douban" (vol. 1)
ANE, "The Story of the Grecian King and the Physician Douban"
Lane, "Story of the Grecian King and the Sage Douban "(vol. 1)
Burton, "The Story of the King Yûnân and the Sage Dûbân" (vol. 1)
Mathers, "The Tale of the Wazīr of Yūnān and Rayyān the Doctor" (vol. 1)
Haddawy, "The Tale of King Yunan and the Sage Duban"
Lyons, "The Story of King Yunan and Duban the Sage" (vol. 1)

SELECTED BIBLIOGRAPHY

Adams, W. Davenport. "The Decline of Pantomime." *Theatre*, February 1882.

Aichele, K. Porter. "Paul Klee's Operatic Themes and Variations." *Art Bulletin* 68:3 (September 1986): 450–66.

Aldrich, Jonathan. "To a Young Lady at the Museum." *Massachusetts Review* 7:1 (Winter 1966): 71–72.

Alewyn, Richard. *Über Hugo von Hofmannsthal*. Göttingen: Vandenhoeck and Ruprecht, 1963.

Allouch, Sa'id. "Alf Sindbad wa-la Sindbad." *Fusul* 13:2 (Summer 1994): 146–85.

Andersson, Theodore. *The Legend of Brünnhilde*. Ithaca: Cornell University Press, 1980.

Appiah, Kwame Anthony. *Cosmopolitanism: Ethics in a World of Strangers*. New York: Norton, 2006.

Aravamudan, Srinivas. *Enlightenment Orientalism: Resisting the Rise of the Novel*. Chicago: University of Chicago Press, 2012.

Aristotle. *Poetics*. Translated and with an introduction and notes by Malcolm Heath. London: Penguin, 1996.

———. *Poetics*. Translated by Kenneth A. Telford. Chicago: Henry Regnery, 1961.

Armes, Roy. "The Poetic Vision of Nacer Khemir." *Third Text* 24:1 (2010): 69–82.

Arne, Thomas. *A Choice Collection of Songs Sung at Vaux-Hall Gardens, by Miss Brent and Mr. Lowe Set to Musick . . . Book XII*. London: J. Walsh, [1761].

Ashour, Radwa. *Siraaj: An Arab Tale*. Translated by Barbara Romaine. Austin: Center for Middle Eastern Studies at the University of Texas at Austin, 2007.

Auerbach, Eric. *Mimesis: The Representation of Reality in Western Literature*. Translated by Willard R. Trask. Princeton: Princeton University Press, 1953.

d'Aulnoy, Baronne (Marie-Catherine le Jumel de Barneville). *Contes des fées*. Paris, 1699.

Avcioğlu, Nebahat. *Turquerie and the Politics of Representation, 1728–1876*. Aldershot, UK: Farnham, 2004.

Avery, Emmett L. "Dancing and Pantomime on the English Stage, 1700–1737." *Studies in Philology* 31:3 (1934): 417–52.

———. "The Defense and Criticism of Pantomimic Entertainments in the Early Eighteenth Century." *English Literary History* 5:2 (1938): 127–45.

———. *The London Stage, 1660–1800: A Calendar of Plays*, part 2, vol. 2, *1717–1729*. Carbondale: Southern Illinois University Press, 1960.

Ballaster, Ros, ed. *Fables of the East: Selected Tales, 1662–1785*. Oxford: Oxford University Press, 2005.

Ballaster, Ros. *Fabulous Orients: Fictions of the East in England, 1662–1785.* Oxford: Oxford University Press, 2005.

———. "Orienting the English Novel: The Shaping Genius of the Eastern Tale in Eighteenth-Century Britain." In *Remapping the Rise of the European Novel*, edited by Jenny Mander, 237–48. Oxford, UK: Voltaire Foundation, 2007.

———. *Seductive Forms: Women's Amatory Fiction from 1684–1740.* Oxford: Oxford University Press, 1992.

Bandyopadhyay, Samik, ed. *Indian Cinema: Contemporary Perceptions from the Thirties.* Jamshedpur: Celluloid Chapter, 1993.

Barber, W. H. "Penny Plain, Twopence Coloured: Longchamp's Memoirs of Voltaire." In *Studies in the French Eighteenth Century: Presented to John Lough*, edited by D. J. Mossop, G. E. Rodmell, and D. B. Wilson, 9–21. Durham, UK: University of Durham, 1978.

Barbour, Richmond. *Before Orientalism: London's Theatre of the East, 1576–1626.* Cambridge: Cambridge University Press, 2003.

Barker, Andrew W. "The Triumph of Life in Hofmannsthal's 'Das Märchen Der 672. Nacht.'" *Modern Language Review* 74 (1979): 341–48.

Barth, John. *The Last Voyage of Somebody the Sailor.* Boston: Little, Brown, 1991.

Bate, David. *Photography and Surrealism: Sexuality, Colonialism and Social Dissent.* London: I. B. Tauris, 2004.

Baugh, Christopher. *Garrick and Loutherbourg.* Cambridge, UK: Chadwyck-Healey, 1990.

Beaumont, Daniel. *Slave of Desire: Sex, Love, and Death in The 1001 Nights.* Madison, NJ: Fairleigh Dickinson University Press, 2002.

Beckford, William. *An Arabian Tale, from an Unpublished Manuscript: With Notes Critical and Explanatory.* Edited by Samuel Henley. London: Printed for J. Johnson, St Paul's Church-Yard, and Entered at the Stationers' Hall, 1786.

———. *An Arabian Tale, from an un Unpublished Manuscript: With Notes Critical and Explanatory.* London: Printed for W. Clarke, 1809.

———. *Life at Fonthill, with Interludes in London and Paris.* Edited and translated by Boyd Alexander. London: Hart-Davis, 1957.

———. *Vathek.* Lausanne: Chez Isaac Hignou, 1787.

———. *Vathek, Conte arabe.* Paris: Chez Poinçot, Libraire, 1787.

———. *Vathek.* London: New Bond Street, 1815.

———. *Vathek: Translated from the Original French.* 3rd ed., revised and corrected. London: Printed for W. Clarke, 1816.

———. *Vathek: Translated from the Original French.* 4th ed., revised and corrected. London: Printed for W. Clarke, 1823. (Different frontispiece from the 1816 edition.)

———. *Le Vathek de Beckford, réimprimé sur l'édition française originale.* Paris: Adolphe Labitte; Geneva: Fick, 1876.

———. *Vathek.* Edited by Roger Lonsdale. Oxford: Oxford University Press, 1970.

Behn, Aphra. "Essay on Translated Prose." In *Seneca Unmasqued and Other Prose*

Translations: The Works of Aphra Behn, edited by Janet Todd. London: Pickering and Chatto, 1993.

Benedetti, Jean. *David Garrick and the Birth of Modern Theatre*. London: Methuen, 2001.

Benjamin, Walter. "Franz Kafka." In *Illuminations*, edited by Hannah Arendt, translated by Harry Zohn. New York: Schocken Books, 1968.

Berman, Nina. "K. u. K. Colonialism: Hofmannsthal in North Africa." *New German Critique* 75 (Autumn 1998): 3–27.

Bernstein, Matthew, and Gaylyn Studlar, eds. *Visions of the East: Orientalism in Film*. London: I. B. Tauris, 1997.

Betzwieser, Thomas. *Exotismus und "Türkenoper" in der französischen Musik des Ancien Régime: Studien zu einem ästhetischen Phänomen*. Laaber: Laaber-Verlag, 1993.

Bhaskar, Ira, and Richard Allen. *Islamicate Cultures of Bombay Cinema*. New Delhi: Tulika, 2009.

Bhaumik, Kaushik. "The Emergence of the Bombay Film Industry, 1913–36." D.Phil. thesis, University of Oxford, 2001.

———. "Querying the 'Traditional' Roots of Silent Cinema in Asia." *Journal of the Moving Image* 7 (December 2008). http://www.jmionline.org/jmi7.htm (accessed January 6, 2011).

Bolton, Betsy. *Women, Nationalism and the Romantic Stage: Theatre and Politics in Britain, 1780–1800*. Cambridge: Cambridge University Press, 2001.

Booth, Gregory D. "Musicking the Other: Orientalism in the Hindi Cinema." In *Music and Orientalism in the British Empire, 1780s–1940s: Portrayal of the East*, edited by Martin Clayton and Bennett Zon. Aldershot, UK: Ashgate, 2007.

Bridges, David, dir. *The Sindbad Voyage*. Princeton: Films for the Humanities and Sciences, 1993. Video.

Borges, Jorge Luis. *Collected Fictions*. Translated by Andrew Hurley. New York: Penguin, 1998.

———. *Labyrinths*. Translated by Dudley Fitts. London: Penguin, 1962.

———. *Other Inquisitions, 1937–1952*. New York: Pocket Books / Simon and Schuster, 1966.

———. Review of *Rudyard Kipling: A Study in Literature and Political Ideas*, by Edward Shanks. Translated by Suzanne Jill Levine. In *Selected Non-Fictions*, edited by Eliot Weinberger, 250–51. New York: Penguin, 1999.

———. *Selected Non-Fictions*. Edited by Eliot Weinberger. New York: Penguin, 1999.

———. "The Translators of *The Thousand and One Nights*." In *Seven Nights: Lectures*, translated by Eliot Weinberger. New York: New Directions, 1984; London: Faber and Faber, 1984.

———. *A Universal History of Infamy*. Translated by Norman Thomas di Giovanni. London: Penguin, 1975.

Brown, Alan, and Donna G. Cardamone. "Moresca." *Grove Music Online. Oxford Music Online*. http://www.oxfordmusiconline.com/subscriber/article/grove/music/19125?q=moresca.

Burton, Richard Francis. *The Book of the Thousand Nights and a Night, with Introduction, Explanatory Notes on the Manners and Customs of Moslem Men and a Terminal Essay upon the History of the Nights.* 16 vols. Benares: Kamashastra Society, 1885–87.

———. *First Footsteps in East Africa; or, An Exploration of Harar.* London: Longman, 1856.

———. *Personal Narrative of a Pilgrimage to El-Medinah and Meccah.* 3 vols. London: Longman, 1855–56.

———. *A Plain and Literal Translation of the Arabian Nights' Entertainments.* 16 vols. London, 1885–88.

———. *Scinde; or, The Unhappy Valley.* 2 vols. London: Richard Bentley, 1851. Reprint, New Delhi: AES, 1998.

———. *Sindh and the Races That Inhabit the Valley of the Indus; with Notices of the Topography and History of the Province.* London: W. H. Allen, 1851. Reprint, Karachi: Oxford University Press, 1973.

———. *Supplemental Nights to the Book of the Thousand Nights and a Night: With Notes Anthropological and Explanatory.* Vol 5. Benares: Kamashastra Society, 1886–88.

———. "Translations." *Athenaeum* 2313 (February 1872): 241–43.

Byron, George Gordon, Lord. *The Corsair* (1814). In *The Complete Poetical Works*, edited by Jerome J. McGann, 7 vols. Oxford: Oxford University Press, 1981.

Calderón de la Barca, Pedro. *La vida es sueño.* 1635–36. Reprint, Paris: Aubier-Flammarion, 1976.

Campra, André. *L'Europe galante, ballet, représenté en l'an 1697.* Farnborough, UK: Gregg, 1967.

Caracciolo, Peter L., ed. *The Arabian Nights in English Literature: Studies in the Reception of The Thousand and One Nights into British Culture.* New York: St. Martin's, 1988.

———. "The House of Fiction and *le jardin anglo-chinois.*" *Middle Eastern Literatures* 7:2 (2004): 199–211. Reprinted in *New Perspectives on Arabian Nights: Ideological Variations and Narrative Horizons*, edited by Wen-chin Ouyang and Geert Jan van Gelder, 67–80. London: Routledge, 2005.

Carroll, Alicia. *Dark Smiles: Race and Desire in George Eliot.* Athens: Ohio University Press, 2003.

Carter, John. "The Lausanne Edition of Beckford's *Vathek.*" *The Library* 17 (1937): 369–94.

Castle, Terry. *Masquerade and Civilisation: The Carnivalesque in Eighteenth-Century English Culture and Fiction.* London: Methuen, 1986.

Cave, Terence. *Recognitions: A Study in Poetics.* Oxford, UK: Clarendon, 1988.

Cazotte, Jacques. *Suite des Mille et une nuits.* In *Bibliothèque des Génies et des Fées* (1788–89). Edited by Pierre Brunel. Reprint, Paris: Champion, 2005.

Chabria, Suresh, and Paolo Cherchi Usai, eds. *Light of Asia: Indian Silent Cinema, 1912–1935.* New Delhi: Wiley Eastern, 1994.

Chapman, Guy, and John Hodgkin. *A Bibliography of Wiliam Beckford of Fonthill:*

Bibliographia; Studies in Book History and Book Structure, 1750–1900. London: Constable, 1930.

Charlton, David. "The Appeal of the Beast: A Note on Grétry and *Zémire et Azor*." *Musical Times* 121:1645 (1980): 169–72.

———. "*Zémire et Azor*." *Grove Music Online. Oxford Music Online*. http://www.oxford musiconline.com/subscriber/article/grove/music/19125?q=zemireetazor.

Châtel, Laurent. "Landscaping Utopias: Beckford's Gardens and the Politics of the Sublime." In *William Beckford and the New Millenium*, edited by Kenneth Graham and Kevin Berland, 222–50. New York: AMS, 2004.

———. "Les Sources des contes orientaux de William Beckford (Vathek et la "Suite des contes arabes"): Bilan de recherches sur les écrits et l'esthétique de Beckford." *Etudes epistémé* 7 (2005): 93–106. Available online at http://revue.etudes-episteme .org/?les-sources-des-contes-orientaux.

———. "The Lures of Eastern Lore: William Beckford's Oriental 'Dangerous Supplements.'" *RSEAA* 17–18 (2010): 127–44.

———. "One Must Become Half-Catholic: William Beckford as Impolite and Uncommercial Aesthete." In *Marketing Art in the British Isles, 1700 to the Present—A Cultural History*, edited by Charlotte Gould and Sophie Mesplède, 195–211. Aldershot, UK: Ashgate, 2012.

———. "Recycling Orientalia: William Beckford's Aesthetics of Appropriation." In *The Afterlife of Used Things: Recycling in the Long Eighteenth Century*, edited by Ariane Fenneteaux, Amélie Junqua and Sophie Vasset. New York: Taylor & Francis / Routledge, forthcoming.

———. "Utopies paysagères: Vues et visions dans les écrits et dans les jardins de William Beckford." Ph.D. diss., 2 vols., Paris: University Sorbonne-Nouvelle, 2000.

———. "William Beckford et *Les mille et une nuits*: Suite des contes arabes, *Vathek* et les *Episodes*." In *Les mille et une nuits*, 127–29. Paris: Hazan, 2012.

Chattopadhyay, Sajal. *Aar Rekho Na Andhare*. Calcutta: Jogomaya Prakashani, 1998.

Chauvin, Victor. *Bibliographie des ouvrages arabes ou relatifs aux Arabes publiés dans l'Europe chrétienne de 1810 à 1885*. 12 vols. Liège: H. Vaillant-Carmanne, 1892–1922.

Choudhury, Mita. *Interculturalism and Resistance in the London Theater, 1660–1800: Identity, Performance, Empire*. Lewisburg, PA: Bucknell University Press, 2000.

Choudhury, Ranabir Ray. *Early Calcutta Advertisements, 1875–1925*. Bombay: Nichiketa, 1992.

Chraïbi, Aboubakr, ed. *Les mille et une nuits en partage*. Arles: Actes Sud, 2004.

———. *Les mille et une nuits: Histoire du texte et classification des contes*. Paris: l'Harmattan, 2008.

Cibber, Theophilus. *The Harlot's Progress; or, The Ridotto al Fresco: A Grotesque Pantomime Entertainment*. London: Printed and Sold at the Theatre, 1733.

Codrescu, Andrei. *Whatever Gets You through the Night: A Story of Sheherezade and the Arabian Entertainments*. Princeton: Princeton University Press, 2011.

Cohn, Dorrit. "'Als Traum erzählt': The Case for a Freudian Reading of Hofmannsthal's 'Märchen der 672. Nacht.'" *Deutsche Vierteljahresschrift* 54 (1980): 284–305.

Cohn, Dorrit. "Kafka and Hofmannsthal." *Modern Austrian Literature* 30:1 (1997): 1–19.

Colman, George. *Blue-beard; or, Female Curiosity! A Dramatick Romance.* London: Cadell and Davies, 1798.

Conant, Martha Pike. *The Oriental Tale in England in the Eighteenth Century.* New York: Columbia University Press, 1908.

Connors, Kathleen. "Living Color: The Interactive Arts of Sylvia Plath." In *Eye Rhymes: Sylvia Plath's Art of the Visual,* edited by Kathleen Connors and Sally Bayley. New York: Oxford University Press, 2007.

Conrad, Lawrence, ed. *The World of Ibn Tufayl: Interdisciplinary Perspectives on "Hayy ibn Yaqzan."* Leiden: Brill, 1996.

Couvreur, Manuel. "Voltaire chez la duchesse ou Le Goût à l'épreuve." In *La duchesse du Maine (1676–1753),* edited by Catherine Cessac, Manuel Couvreur, and Fabrice Preyat, 231–48 (Brussels: Éditions de l'Université de Bruxelles, 2003).

Cowart, Georgia. *The Triumph of Pleasure: Louis XIV and the Politics of Spectacle.* Chicago: University of Chicago Press, 2008.

Craven, Lady Elizabeth. *Memoirs of the Margravines of Anspach, Formerly Lady Craven.* 2 vols. Paris: A. & W. Galignani, 1826.

Das, Sisir Kumar. *Sahibs and Munshis: An Account of the College of Fort William.* Calcutta: Orion, 1978.

Davis, Lennard J. *Factual Fiction: The Origins of the English Novel.* New York: Columbia University Press, 1983.

Dean, Winton. "The English Background." In *Handel's Operas: 1704–1726,* by Winton Dean and John Merrill Knapp. Oxford, UK: Clarendon, 1987.

DeLamater, Peg. "Some Indian Sources in the Art of Paul Klee." *Art Bulletin* 66 (1984): 657–72.

Deneys-Tunney, Anne. "*Les bijoux indiscrets*: Transition or Translation?" In *New Essays on Diderot,* edited by James Fowler. Cambridge: Cambridge University Press, 2011.

Dharamsey, Virchand. "The Advent of Sound in Indian Cinema: Theatre, Orientalism, Action, Magic." *Journal of the Moving Image* 9 (2010). http://www.jmionline.org/film_journal/jmi_09/article_02.php (accessed July 15, 2012).

Diderot, Denis. *Jacques the Fatalist and His Master.* Translated by Michael Henry. Harmondsworth, UK: Penguin, 1986.

———. *Les bijoux indiscrets* (*The Indiscreet Jewels*). In *Œuvres complètes de Diderot, Philosophie IV, Belles-Lettres I (Romans, contes, critique littéraire).* Paris: Garnier Frères, 1875.

Di San Lazzaro, Gualtieri. *Klee: A Study of His Life and Work.* Translated by Stuart Hood. New York: Praeger, 1957.

Doniger O'Flaherty, Wendy. *Dreams, Illusion, and Other Realities.* Chicago: University of Chicago Press, 1984.

———. "Magic Rings and the Return of the Repressed." In *Spirituality and Religion: Psychoanalytic Perspectives,* edited by Jerome A. Winer and James William Anderson. Catskill, NY: Mental Health Resources, 2012.

Doody, Margaret Anne. *The True Story of the Novel*. New Brunswick: Rutgers University Press, 1994.

Dryden, John. *The Prophetess; or, The History of Dioclesian: A Dramatic Opera: With All the New Songs, &c.* London: J. and R. Tonson, 1758.

Düchting, Hajo. *Paul Klee: Painting and Music*. Munich: Prestel, 1997.

Dufrenoy, Marie-Louise. *L'Orient romanesque en France 1704–1789*. 3 vols. Montreal: Beauchemin, 1946–1975.

Duvignaud, Jean. *Klee en Tunisie*. Tunis: Ceres, 1980.

Dwyer, Rachel. *Filming the Gods: Religion and Indian Cinema*. London: Routledge, 2006.

Eliot, George. *Daniel Deronda*. Edited by Terence Cave. London: Penguin, 1995.

Engels, Friedrich. *The Condition of the Working Classes in England*. Edited by W. O. Henderson and W. H. Chaloner. Stanford: Stanford University Press, 1968.

Erdman, Joan L. "Dance Discourses: Rethinking the History of the 'Oriental Dance.' " In *Moving Words: Rewriting Dance*, edited by Gay Morris. London: Routledge, 1996.

Everett, William A. "*Chu Chin Chow* and Orientalist Musical Theatre in Britain during the First World War." In *Music and Orientalism in the British Empire, 1780s–1940s: Portrayal of the East*, edited by Martin Clayton and Bennett Zon, 277–96. Aldershot, UK: Ashgate, 2007.

Favart, Charles-Simon. *Soliman second, en trois actes*. Paris: Duchesne, 1761.

Felman, Shoshana. "Rereading Femininity." *Yale French Studies* 62 (1981): 19.

Fielding, Henry. *Joseph Andrews*. Dublin, 1742.

Fiske, Roger. *English Theatre Music in the Eighteenth Century*. New York: Oxford University Press, 1973.

Friedel, Helmut, and Justin Hoffman. *Süddeutsche Freiheit: Kunst der Revolution in München 1919*. Exhibition catalogue. Munich: Lenbachhaus, 1993.

Frink, Helen. *Animal Symbolism in Hofmannsthal's Works*. New York: Peter Lang, 1987.

Fulford, Tim. "Coleridge and the Oriental Tale." In *The Arabian Nights in Historical Context*, edited by Saree Makdisi and Felicity Nussbaum. Oxford: Oxford University Press, 2008.

Galland, Antoine, trans. *Les mille et une nuits*. Edited by Jean-Paul Sermain and Aboubakr Chraïbi. 3 vols. Paris: Flammarion, 2004.

———. *Paroles remarquables et Maximes des orientaux recueillies par Mr Antoine Galand [sic], Membre de l'Académie des Inscriptions et Médailles, et Professeur en Arabe au College Royal à Paris* (1694). In *Bibliothèque orientale*, by Barthélémy d'Herbelot. The Hague: J. Neaulme et N. Van Daalen, 1777–79.

Garrick, David. *The Enchanter; or, Love and Magic*. London: J. and R. Tonson, 1760.

———. *The Letters of David Garrick*. Vol. 2. Edited by David M. Little and George M. Kahrl. Oxford: Oxford University Press, 1963.

———. *The Private Correspondence of David Garrick*. Edited by James Boaden. 2 vols. London: H. Colburn and R. Bentley, 1832.

Gerhardt, Mia. *The Art of Story-Telling: A Literary Study of the Thousand and One Nights*. Leiden: Brill, 1963.

Ghazoul, Ferial J. *Nocturnal Poetics: The Arabian Nights in Comparative Contexts.* Cairo: American University Press, 1996.

di Giovanni, Norman Thomas. *The Lesson of the Master: Borges and His Work.* London: Continuum, 2003.

Gluck, Christoph W. *Cadi dupe.* Edited by Daniela Philippi. Kassel: Bärenreiter, 1999.

Goff, Moira. "John Rich, French Dancing, and English Pantomimes." In *"The Stage's Glory": John Rich (1692–1761),* edited by Berta Joncus and Jeremy Barlow, 85–98. Newark: University of Delaware Press, 2011.

Gramsci, Antonio. *Prison Notebooks.* Edited by Joseph A. Buttigieg. Translated by Joseph A. Buttigieg and Antonio Callari. New York: Columbia University Press, 1991.

Grétry, André-Ernest-Modeste. *Zémire et Azor: Comédie ballet.* Paris: Montulay, 1771.

Grossman, Vasily. *Everything Flows.* Translated by Robert and Elizabeth Chandler, with Anna Aslanyan. New York: New York Review of Books, 2009.

Guiet, René. "An English Imitator of Favart: Isaac Bickerstaffe." *Modern Language Notes* 38:1 (1923): 54–56.

Gupt, Somnath. *The Parsi Theatre: Its Origins and Development.* 1981. Translated from the Hindi and edited by Kathryn Hansen. New Delhi: Seagull Books, 2005.

Haddad, Nabil. "*Siraaj*: Radwa Ashour bayn al-mutakhayal wal-mawruth al-sha'abi." *Al-Ra'i* 12723 (July 22, 2005): 7.

Haddawy, Husain, trans. *Arabian Nights.* New York: Norton, 1990; London: Everyman, 1992. Reprint, New York: Norton, 2008.

———, trans. *The Arabian Nights II: Sinbad and Other Popular Stories.* New York: Norton, 1996.

Hamilton, Antoine. *Les quatre Facardins.* Edited by Georges May. Paris: Éditions Desjonquères, 2001.

Hare, Arnold. *The Georgian Theatre in Wessex.* London: Phoenix House, 1958.

Hariharan, Githa. *When Dreams Travel.* New York: Penguin, 2011.

Harouny, Rana Assem. "Review of *Siraaj: An Arab Tale.*" *Arab Studies Journal* 15–16 (Fall–Spring 2007): 169–72.

Hasan-Rokem, Galit. *Proverbs in Israeli Folk Narratives: A Structural Semantic Analysis.* Folklore Fellows Communications 232. Helsinki: Academia Scientiarum Fennica, 1982.

Hatto, A. T. *The Nibelungenlied.* Harmondsworth, UK: Penguin, 1965.

Hauptman, William. "Beckford, Brandoin, and the 'Rajah.'" *Apollo* 142 (May 1996): 30–39.

Heber, Reginald. *Blue-beard: A Serio-Comic Oriental Romance in One Act.* London and New York: Samuel French, 1874.

Hellegouarc'h, Jacqueline. "Genèse d'un conte de Voltaire." *Studies on Voltaire and the Eighteenth Century* 176 (1979): 7–36.

———. "Mélinade ou la duchesse du Maine: Deux contes de jeunesse de Voltaire: *Le crocheteur borgne* et *Cosi-Sancta.*" *Revue d'histoire littéraire de la France* 78 (1978): 722–35.

Henley, Samuel. "Notes to *Vathek*." In *Vathek*. London: Printed for J. Johnson, St Paul's Church-Yard, and Entered at the Stationers' Hall, 1786.

———. *The Story of Al Raoui, a Tale from the Arabic*. London: Printed by C. Whittingham for C. Geisweiller, 1797.

Heraclitus. *Fragments: The Collected Wisdom of Heraclitus*. Translated by Brooks Haxton. New York: Viking, 2001.

d'Herbelot, Barthélémy. *Bibliothèque orientale, ou dictionnaire universel contenant généralement tout ce qui regarde la connoissance des Peuples de l'Orient*. Paris: Par la Compagnie des Libraires, 1697.

———. *Supplément à la Bibliothèque Orientale de d'Herbelot, de Messieurs A Visdelou et C. Galand* [sic], *contenant les observations sur ce que les Historiens Arabes et Persiens rapportent de la Chine et de la Tartarie, dans la Bibliothèque orientale de M. d'Herbelot*. The Hague: J. Neaulme et N. Van Daalen, 1777–79.

Hermansson, Casie E. *Bluebeard: A Reader's Guide to the English Tradition*. Jackson: University Press of Mississippi, 2009.

Highfill, Philip H., Jr., Kalman A. Burnim, and Edward A. Langhans. "Barbier, Jane." In *A Biographical Dictionary of Actors*, vol. 1, 281–84. Carbondale: Southern Illinois University Press, 1973.

Hiltbrunner, Michael. "The Grey Woman and Bluebeard's Bride." *Opticon1826* 7 (Autumn 2009): 5.

Hilton, Wendy. *Dance of Court and Theater: The French Noble Style, 1690–1725*. Princeton, NJ: Princeton Book Company, 1981.

Hirsch, Edward. *The Demon and the Angel: Searching for the Source of Artistic Inspiration*. New York: Harcourt, 2002.

Hodgson, Marshall G. S. *The Venture of Islam: Conscience and History in a World Civilization*. 3 vols. Chicago: University of Chicago Press, 1974.

Hofmannsthal, Hugo von. *Death and the Fool*. Translated by Michael Hamburger. In *Poems and Verse Plays*, vol. 2. New York: Pantheon Books, 1961.

———. *Four Stories*. Edited by Margaret Jacobs. Oxford: Oxford University Press, 1968.

———. "Many Truly" (1895). Translated by Vernon Watkins. In *Poems and Verse Plays*, bilingual edition, edited and introduced by Michael Hamburger, with a preface by T. S. Eliot, Bollingen Series 33, vol. 2. New York: Pantheon Books, 1961.

———. *The Marriage of Zobeide*. Translated by Christopher Middleton. In *Poems and Verse Plays*, vol. 2, 366–525. New York: Pantheon Books, 1961.

———. *Selected Prose*. Translated by Mary Hottinger and Tania and James Stern. Bollingen Series 33, vol. 1, 302–3. New York: Pantheon Books, 1952.

———. *Selected Tales*. Translated by J. M. Q. Davies. London: Angel Classics, 2007.

Hook, John. *Blest Hero Who in Peace & War . . . Sung by Mrs. Martyr in the Sultan*. London: S. A. and P. Thompson, [1783].

Hume, Robert D. "John Rich as Manager and Entrepreneur." In *"The Stage's Glory": John Rich (1692–1761)*, edited by Berta Joncus and Jeremy Barlow, 46–47. Newark: University of Delaware Press, 2011.

Ibn al-Muqaffaʿ. *The Fables of Kalilah and Dimnah*. Translated by Saleh Saʿadeh Jallad. London: Melisende, 2002.

Ibn Tufayl. *Hayy ibn Yaqzan: A Philosophical Tale*. Translated by Lenn Evan Goodman. Chicago: University of Chicago Press, 2009.

Irwin, Robert. *The Arabian Nights: A Companion*. London: Allan Lane, 1994. Reprint, London: I. B. Tauris, 2004.

———. *Visions of the Jinn: Illustrators of the Arabian Nights*. Oxford: Oxford University Press and the Arcadian Library, 2010.

Jaeggi, Bruno, and Walter Ruggle, eds. *Nacer Khemir: Das Verlorene Halsband der Taube*. Bade: Verlag Lars Muller / Trigon Films, 1992.

Jakobson, Roman. "On Linguistic Aspects of Translation." In *Theories of Translation: An Anthology of Essays from Dryden to Derrida*, edited by Rainer Schulte and John Biguenet, 144–51. Chicago: University of Chicago Press, 1992.

Jaouik, Moulay-Badreddine. "La part de l'islam dans l'élaboration du théisme voltairien. " *Cahiers Voltaire* 6 (2007): 59–78.

Jardi, Enric. *Paul Klee*. New York: Rizzoli, 1991.

Jha, B. "Profiles of Pioneers." *Cinema Vision India* 1:1 (January 1980): 54–59

Jinghua, Fan. "Sylvia Plath's Visual Poetics." In *Eye Rhymes: Sylvia Plath's Art of the Visual*, edited by Kathleen Connors and Sally Bayley, 205–22. Oxford: Oxford University Press, 2007.

Johnson, Rebecca, Richard Maxwell, and Katie Trumpener. "The *Arabian Nights*, Arab-European Literary Influence, and the Lineages of the Novel." In "Globalism on the Move," special issue, *Modern Language Quarterly* 68:2 (June 2007): 243–79.

Johnson, Samuel. *Prologue and Epilogue, Spoken at the Opening of the Theatre in Drury-Lane 1747*. London: E. Cave and R. Dodsley, [1747].

Joncus, Berta. "'To Propagate Sound for Sense': Music for Diversion and Seduction at Ranelagh Gardens." *London Journal: A Review of Metropolitan Society Past and Present* 38:1 (2013).

Jullien, Dominique. *Les amoureux de Schéhérazade: Variations modernes sur les Mille et une nuits*. Geneva: Droz, 2009.

Kabbani, Rana. *Europe's Myths of Orient: Devise and Rule*. Basingstoke, UK: Macmillan, 1986.

Kafka, Franz. *The Complete Stories*. Translated by Willa and Edwin Muir. New York: Schocken Books, 1971.

Kahn, Victoria. *Wayward Contracts: The Crisis of Political Obligation in England, 1640–1783*. Princeton: Princeton University Press, 2004.

Kalmar, Ivan Davidson. "Moorish Style: Orientalism, the Jews, and Synagogue Architecture." *Jewish Social Studies: History, Culture, and Society* 7:3 (2001): 68–100.

Kalmar, Ivan Davidson, and Derek J. Penslar. "Orientalism and the Jews: An Introduction." In *Orientalism and the Jews*, edited by Ivan Davidson Kalmar and Derek J. Penslar. Waltham, MA: Brandeis University Press, 2005.

Kelly, Michael. *Reminiscences*. London, 1826.

Kendall, Elizabeth. *Where She Danced*. New York: Kopf, 1979.

Kennedy, Dane. *The Highly Civilized Man: Richard Burton and the Victorian World.* Cambridge: Harvard University Press, 2005.

Kennedy, Philip F., and Marilyn Lawrence, eds. *Recognition: The Poetics of Narrative: Interdisciplinary Studies on Anagnorisis.* New York: Peter Lang, 2009.

Kesavan, Mukul. "Urdu, Awadh, and the Tawaif: The Islamicate Roots of Hindi Cinema." In *Forging Identities: Gender, Communities, and the State in India,* edited by Zoya Hasan, 244–57. Boulder, CO: Westview, 1994.

Khemir, Nacer, and Bruno Moll, dir. *Le Voyage à Tunis.* Ennetbaden: Trigon-Film / Fama Film, 2007. Video.

Kilito, Abdelfattah. *Les séances: Récits et codes culturels chez Hamadhânî et Harîrî.* Paris: Sindbad, 1983.

———. *L'Œil et l'aiguille: Essais sur Les milles et une nuits.* Paris: La Découverte, 1992.

Kipling, Rudyard. "The Miracle of Purun Baghat" (1895). In *The Second Jungle Book,* readbookonline.net, http://www.readbookonline.net/read/8193/20419/.

Kirby, W. F. "Additional Notes on the Bibliography of the *Thousand and One Nights* in Burton." In *Supplemental Nights to the Book of the Thousand Nights and a Night: With Notes Anthropological and Explanatory,* vol. 10, app. 2, 414. Benares: Kamashastra Society, 1888.

Klee, Paul. *The Diaries of Klee, 1898–1918.* Edited by Felix Klee. Berkeley: University of California Press, 1964.

Knipp, C. "*The Arabian Nights* in England: Galland's Translation and Its Successors." *Journal of Arabic Literature* 5 (1974): 44–54.

Kobayashi, Fujio. *Nihon Isrāmu-shi* [The history of Islam in Japan]. Tokyo: Nihon-Isrāmu-Yūkō-Renmei, 1988.

Kontje, Todd Curtis. *German Orientalism.* Ann Arbor: University of Michigan Press, 2004.

Konuk, Kader. "Ethnomasquerade in Ottoman-European Encounters: Reenacting Lady Mary Wortley Montagu." *Criticism* 46:3 (2004): 393–416.

Kovach, Thomas. "Introduction: Hofmannsthal Today." In *A Companion to the Works of Hugo von Hofmannsthal,* edited by Thomas Kovach, 1–22. Rochester, NY: Camden House, 2002.

Kristeva, Julia. "Stabat Mater." 1977. In *The Kristeva Reader,* edited by Toril Moi. Oxford, UK: Blackwell, 1986.

L'Abbé, Anthony. *A New Collection of Dances.* London: Stainer and Bell, 1991.

Landry, Donna. "William Beckford's Vathek and the Uses of Oriental Re-enactment." In *The Arabian Nights in Historical Context: Between East and West,* edited by Saree Makdisi and Felicity Nussbaum, 167–94. Oxford University Press, 2008.

Lane, E. W. (Edward William). *An Account of the Manners and Customs of the Modern Egyptians.* London: Society for the Diffusion of Useful Knowledge, 1836. Reprint, New York: Dover, 1973. Electronic version available at Travelers in the Middle East Archive (TIMEA), http://hdl.handle.net/1911/9174.

———. "ART. VII. *An Account of the Manners and Customs of the Modern Egyptians, Written in Egypt during the Years 1833, 34, and 35, Partly from Notes Made during a*

Former Visit to That Country, in the Years 1825, 26, 27, and 28, by Edward William Lane, 2 vols., London." *Quarterly Review* 59 (July 1837): 165–208.

Lane, E. W. (Edward William). *The Thousand and One Nights, Commonly Called, in England, the Arabian Nights' Entertainments: A New Translation from the Arabic, with Copious Notes*. 3 vols. London: Charles Knight, 1838–40.

Lauckhard, C. F. *Tausend und eine Nacht für die Jugend bearbeitet*. 17th ed. Leipzig: Abel & Müller, 1900.

Leask, Nigel. *British Romantic Writers and the East: Anxieties of Empire*. Cambridge: Cambridge University Press, 1992.

Lecomte, Nathalie. "L'orientalisme dans le ballet aux XVIIème et XVIIIème siècles." *La recherche en danse* 1:1 (1982): 54–60.

van Leeuwen, Richard. "Orientalisme, genre et réception des *Mille et une nuits* en Europe." In *Les mille et une nuits en partage*, edited by Aboubakr Chraïbi, 121–41. Paris: Actes Sud, 2004.

Lemon, Robert. *Imperial Messages: Orientalism as Self-Critique in the Habsburg Fin de Siècle*. Rochester, NY: Camden House, 2011.

Lenoe, Matthew. *Closer to the Masses: Stalinist Culture, Social Revolution, and Soviet Newspapers*. Cambridge: Harvard University Press, 2004.

Les mille nuits et une nuit. Paris: Robert Laffont, collection "Bouquins," 1980.

Lewis, Hanna B. "The *Arabian Nights* and Young Hofmannsthal." *German Life and Letters* 37:3 (1984): 186–96.

Lewis, Reina. *Rethinking Orientalism: Women, Travel, and the Ottoman Harem*. New Brunswick: Rutgers University Press, 2004.

Life of Mrs. Abington (formerly Miss Barton), celebrated Comic Actress, The. London: Reader, 1888.

Lipsey, Roger. *The Spiritual in Twentieth-Century Art*. Boston: Shambala, 1988.

Locke, Matthew. *Dramatic Music: With the Music by Humfrey, Banister, Reggio and Hart for "The Tempest."* Edited by Michael Tilmouth. London: Stainer and Bell, 1986.

Longchamp, Sébastien. *Anecdotes sur la vie privée de Monsieur de Voltaire*. Edited by Raymond Trousson and Frédéric Eigeldinger. Paris: Honoré Champion, 2009.

Lonsdale, Roger. *Dr. Charles Burney: A Literary Biography*. Oxford, UK: Clarendon, 1965.

Lynton, Norbert. *Klee*. London: Spring Books, 1964.

Lyons, Malcolm, trans. *The Arabian Nights: Tales of 1001 Nights*. 3 vols. London: Penguin, 2010.

Macdonald, Duncan B. "On Translating the *Arabian Nights*." *Nation* 71:6 (September 1900): 167–68.

Mack, Robert L., ed. *Arabian Nights' Entertainments*. Oxford: Oxford University Press, 1995.

———. "Cultivating the Garden: Antoine Galland's *Arabian Nights* in the Tradition of English Literature." In *The Arabian Nights in Historical Context: Between East and West*, edited by Saree Makdisi and Felicity Nussbaum, 51–82. Oxford: Oxford University Press, 2008.

Mahdi, Muhsin, ed. *Kitab Alf layla wa-layla.* 3 vols. Leiden: Brill, 1984.

Mahfouz, Naguib. *Arabian Nights and Days.* Translated by Denys Johnson-Davies. New York: Anchor Books, 1995.

Manley, Delariviere. *Almyna; or, The Arabian Vow.* London: William Turner, 1708.

Manuel, Thomas Philip, trans. *Gool-i Bukawulee.* Lucknow: Naval Kishore Press, 1882.

Manzalaoui, Mahmoud. "Pseudo-Orientalism in Transition: The Age of *Vathek*." In *William Beckford of Fonthill, 1760–1844: Bicentenary Essays,* edited by Fatma Moussa Mahmoud, 123–50. Port Washington, NY: Kennikot, 1964.

Marana, Giovanni Paolo. *The Eight Volumes of Letters Writ by a Turkish Spy.* Translated by William Bradshaw. 5th ed. London: H. Rhodes and S. Sare, 1702.

Marzolph, Ulrich, ed. *The Arabian Nights in Transnational Perspective.* Detroit: Wayne State University Press, 2007.

———, ed. *The Arabian Nights Reader.* Detroit: Wayne State University Press, 2006.

Marzolph, Ulrich, and Richard van Leeuwen. *The Arabian Nights Encyclopedia.* 2 vols. Santa Barbara, CA: ABC-CLIO, 2004.

Mathers, E. Powys, trans. *The Book of the Thousand Nights and One Night.* 4 vols. London: Routledge, 1990.

May, Georges. *Les mille et une nuits d'Antoine Galland, ou le chef-d'œuvre invisible.* Paris: Presse Universitaires de France, 1986.

———. "Sindbad le marin et les voyages à sens unique." In *Voltaire, the Enlightenment and the Comic Mode: Essays in Honor of Jean Sareil,* edited by Maxine G. Cutler, 143–58. New York: Peter Lang, 1990.

McCleave, Sarah. "Dancing at the English Opera: Marie Sallé's Letter to the Duchess of Richmond." *Dance Research: The Journal of the Society for Dance Research* 17:1 (1999): 22–46.

Melaney, William. "Paul Klee from Image to Text: A Phenomenological Study." *Constructions* 7 (1992): 23–35.

Melville, Lewis. *The Life and Letters of William Beckford of Fonthill* (*Author of Vathek*). London: Heinemann, 1910.

Miquel, André, and Jamel Eddine Bencheikh, trans. *Les milles et une nuit.* Paris: Gallimard, 2005.

Miquel-Ravenel, J. "À la rencontre d'Antoine Galland, premier traducteur des *Mille et une nuits.*" *Arabica* 41:2 (1994): 147–61.

de Mirimonde, Albert P. "La musique orientale dans les œuvres de l'école Française du XVIIIᵉ siècle." *Revue du Louvre et des Musées en France* 19:4–5 (1969): 231–46.

Mistry, Freny. "Hofmannsthal's Oriental Library." *Journal of English and Germanic Philology* 71 (1972): 177–97.

———. "Towards Buddhahood: Some Remarks on the Sigismund Figure in Hofmannsthal's Turm Plays." *Modern Language Review* 69 (1974): 337–47.

Miyoshi, Tadayoshi. *Zusetsu sekai chizu korekushon* [Illustrated collection of old world maps]. Tokyo: Kawade-shobo-shinsha, 1999.

Mohan, Ram. "The Closely Guarded Secrets of the Special Effects Men." *Cinema Vision India* 1:1 (January 1980): 89.

Mohanty, Satya. "Can Our Values Be Objective? On Ethics, Aesthetics, and Progressive Politics." *New Literary History* 32:4 (Autumn 2001): 803–33.

——. *Literary Theory and the Claims of History: Postmodernism, Objectivity, Multicultural Politics.* Ithaca: Cornell University Press, 1997.

Montagu, Lady Mary Wortley. *The Turkish Embassy Letters.* 1721. Reprint, London: Virago, 1994.

Moody, Jane. *Illegitimate Theatre in London, 1770–1840.* Cambridge: Cambridge University Press, 2000.

Morrison, Alfred. *Collection of Autograph Letters and Historical Documents.* 2nd series. Privately printed, 1893.

Moussa Mahmoud, Fatma. "A Manuscript Translation of the 'Arabian Nights' in the Beckford Papers." *Journal of Arabic Literature* 7 (1976): 7–23.

——, ed. *William Beckford of Fonthill, 1760–1844: Bicentenary Essays.* Port Washington, NY: Kennikot, 1964.

Mukherjee, Prabhat. "Hiralal Sen." In *70 Years of Indian Cinema, 1913–1983*, edited by T. M. Ramachandran. Bombay: CINEMA India-International, 1985.

Mukherjee, Sushil Kumar. *The Story of the Calcutta Theatres: 1753–1980.* Calcutta: K. P. Bagchi, 1982.

Naddaf, Sandra. *Arabesque: Narrative Structure and the Aesthetics of Repetition in 1001 Nights.* Evanston, IL: Northwestern University Press, 1991.

Nance, Susan. *How the Arabian Nights Inspired the American Dream, 1790–1935.* Chapel Hill: University of North Carolina Press, 2009.

Naubert-Riser, Constance. "Paul Klee et la Chine." *Revue de l'art* 63 (1984): 47–56.

Naveh, Gila Safran. *Biblical Parables and Their Modern Re-Creations: From "Apples of Gold in Silver Settings" to "Imperial Messages."* Albany: SUNY Press, 2000.

Neely, Carol Thomas. *Broken Nuptials in Shakespeare's Plays.* New Haven: Yale University Press, 1985.

Ng, Su Fang. "Delariviere Manley's *Almyna* and Dating the First Edition of the English *Arabian Nights' Entertainments.*" *English Language Notes* 40:3 (March 2003): 19–26.

Nishio, Tetsuo. *"Arabian Naito": Bunmei no hazama ni umareta monogatari* [The *Arabian Nights*: Stories generated among civilizations]. Tokyo: Iwanami-shoten, 2007.

——. "The *Arabian Nights* and Orientalism from a Japanese Perspective." In *The Arabian Nights and Orientalism: Perspectives from East and West*, edited by Yuriko Yamanaka and Tetsuo Nishio, 154–66. London: I. B. Tauris, 2006.

Nochlin, Linda. "The Imaginary Orient." *Art in America* 71 (May 1983).

Nussbaum, Felicity. *Torrid Zones: Maternity, Sexuality, and Empire in Eighteenth-Century English Narratives.* Baltimore: Johns Hopkins University Press, 2003.

O'Brien, John. *Harlequin Britain: Pantomime and Entertainment, 1690–1760.* Baltimore: Johns Hopkins University Press, 2004.

——. "Pantomime." In *The Cambridge Companion to British Theatre, 1730–1830*, edited by Jane Moody and Daniel O'Quinn, 103–14. Cambridge: Cambridge University Press, 2007.

O'Brien, Karen. "From Savage to Scotswoman: The History of Femininity." In *Women and Enlightenment in Eighteenth-Century Britain,* 68–109. Cambridge: Cambridge University Press, 2009.

Oliver, John W. *The Life of William Beckford.* Oxford : Oxford University Press, 1932.

O'Quinn, Daniel. *Staging Governance: Theatrical Imperialism in London, 1770–1800.* Baltimore: Johns Hopkins University Press, 2005.

Orr, Bridget. *Empire on the English Stage, 1660–1714.* Cambridge: Cambridge University Press, 2001.

———. "Galland, Georgian Theatre, and the Creation of Popular Orientalism." In *The Arabian Nights in Historical Context,* edited by Saree Makdisi and Felicity Nussbaum, 103–29. Oxford: Oxford University Press, 2008.

Orsini, Francesca. *Print and Pleasure: Popular Literature and Entertaining Fictions in Colonial North India.* New Delhi: Permanent Black, 2009.

Ouseley, William. *Oriental Collections: Consisting of Original Essays and Dissertations, Translations and Miscellaneous Papers; Illustrating the History and Antiquities, the Arts, Sciences, and Literature of Asia.* 3 vols. London, 1797–99.

Ouyang, Wen-chin, and Geert Jan van Gelder, eds. *New Perspectives on Arabian Nights: Ideological Variations and Narrative Horizons.* London: Routledge, 2005.

Oxfeldt, Elisabeth. *Nordic Orientalism: Paris and the Cosmopolitan Imagination, 1800–1900.* Copenhagen: Museum Tusculanum Press, 2005.

Parreaux, André. *William Beckford Auteur de "Vathek" (1760–1844): Etude de la Création Littéraire.* Paris: Nizet, 1960.

Partsch, Susanna. *Paul Klee, 1879–1940.* Köln: Taschen, 1993.

Pasto, James. "Islam's 'Strange Secret Sharer': Orientalism, Judaism, and the Jewish Question." *Comparative Studies of Society and History* 40 (1998): 437–74.

Pastor, Antonio. *The Idea of Robinson Crusoe.* Watford, UK: Gongora, 1980.

Peirce, Leslie P. *The Imperial Harem: Women and Sovereignty in the Ottoman Empire.* Oxford: Oxford University Press, 1993.

Perl, Benjamin. "Mozart in Turkey." *Cambridge Opera Journal* 12:3 (2001): 219–35.

Perrault, Charles. *Histoires ou contes du temps passé (Contes de ma Mère l'Oye).* Paris, 1697.

Pinault, David. *Story-Telling Techniques in the Arabian Nights.* Leiden: Brill, 1992.

Planché, J. R., and Charles Dance. *Blue-beard: A Grand Musical, Comi-Tragical, Melo-Dramatic, Burlesque Burletta in One Act.* In *The Extravaganzas of J. R. Planché, 1825–1871,* edited by T. F. Dillon Croker and Stephen Tucker. London: Samuel French, 1879.

Plath, Sylvia. *The Collected Poems.* Edited by Ted Hughes. New York: Harper and Row, 1981.

Price, Curtis A. *Henry Purcell and the London Stage.* Cambridge: Cambridge University Press, 1984.

———. *Music in the Restoration Theatre: With a Catalogue of Instrumental Music in the Plays, 1665–1713.* Ann Arbor, MI: UMI Research, 1979.

———. "'. . . To Make Amends for One Ill Dance': Conventions for Dancing in Restoration Plays." *Dance Research Journal* 10:1 (1977–78): 1–6.

Pritchett, Frances. *Marvelous Encounters: Folk Romances in Urdu and Hindi*. Delhi: Manohar, 1985.

Purcell, Henry. *Dioclesian*. Edited by J. Frederick Bridge and John Pointer. Revised by Margaret Laurie. London: Novello, 1979.

Purinton, Marjorie. "George Colman's *The Iron Chest* and *Blue-beard* and the Pseudo-Science of Curiosity Cabinets." *Victorian Studies* 49:2 (Winter 2007): 250–57.

Raine, Kathleen. "The Underlying Unity: Nature and the Imagination." In *The Spirit of Science: From Experiment to Experience*, edited by David Lorimer. New York: Continuum, 1999.

Ramanujan, A. K. "The Prince Who Married His Own Left Side." In *A Flowering Tree, and Other Oral Tales from India*. Berkeley: University of California Press, 1997.

———. "Towards a Counter-System: Women's Tales." In *Gender, Discourse, and Power in South Asian Expressive Traditions*, edited by Arjun Appadurai, Frank J. Korom, and Margaret A. Mills, 33–55 Philadelphia: University of Pennsylvania Press, 1991.

Rangoonwalla, Firoze. *Indian Cinema: Past and Present*. New Delhi: Clarion Books, 1983.

Rauer, Julie. "Klee's Mandalas: How a Swiss Orientalist Mapped His Tibetan Cosmos." *asianart.com*, April 19, 2006. http://www.asianart.com/articles/klee/index.html.

Ribeiro, Aileen. *Dress and Morality*. London: Batsford, 1986.

———. *Dress in Eighteenth-Century Europe, 1715–1789*. London: Batsford, 1984.

———. *The Dress Worn at Masquerades in England, 1730 to 1790*. New York: Garland, 1984.

Richardson, Samuel. *Pamela; or, Virtue Rewarded*. 1740. Reprint, London: Penguin, 1980.

Rosenthal, Mark. "Picasso's *Night Fishing at Antibes*: A Meditation on Death." *Art Bulletin* 65:4 (December 1983): 649–58.

Rothfeld, Otto. *Women of India*. London: Simpkin, Marshall, Hamilton, Kent, 1920.

Ruttenburg, Nancy. *Dostoevsky's Democracy*. Princeton: Princeton University Press, 2008.

Sabbagh, Karl. *Palestine: A Personal History*. New York: Atlantic Books, 2006.

Saglia, Diego. "William Beckford's 'Sparks of Orientalism' and the Material-Discursive Orient of British Romanticism." *Textual Practice* 16:1 (2002): 75–92.

Said, Edward. *Orientalism*. New York: Vintage, 1979; London: Penguin, 2003.

———. *The Question of Palestine*. New York: Vintage Books, 1980.

Saint-Simon, Louis de Rouvroy, duc de. *Mémoires*. Edited by Gonzague Truc. 7 vols. Paris: Gallimard (Bibliothèque de la Pléiade), 1947–61.

Sazanami, Iwaya. "Uma nusubito" [The horse thief]. *Chūgaku Sekai* (Middle-school world) 9:1 (1906): 2–12.

Schacker-Mill, Jennifer. "Otherness and Otherworldliness: Edward W. Lane's Ethnographic Treatment of *The Arabian Nights*." *Journal of American Folklore* 113 (448): 170–71.

Schwartz, Howard. *Gabriel's Palace: Jewish Mystical Tales*. New York: Oxford University Press, 1993.

Scott, Jonathan, trans. *The Arabian Nights' Entertainments*. 1811. Aldine Edition. 4 vols. Teddington, UK: Echo Library, 2006.

"Script of *Gul-e-Bakavali* (Kohinoor, 1924), The." *BioScope* 3:2 (2012): 175–207.

Seagal, Robert A. *The Gnostic Jung*. Princeton: Princeton University Press, 1992.

Severin, Tim. "In the Wake of Sindbad." *National Geographic* 162:1 (July 1982): 2–40.

———. *The Sindbad Voyage*. London: Arena, 1983.

Shaffer, E. S. *Kubla Khan and the Fall of Jerusalem: The Mythological School in Biblical Criticism and Secular Literature, 1770–1880*. Cambridge: Cambridge University Press, 1980.

Shaw, Stanford. "Iranian Relations with the Ottoman Empire in the Eighteenth and Nineteenth Centuries." In *The Cambridge History of Iran*, vol. 7, *From Nadir Shah to the Islamic Republic*, edited by Peter Avery, Gavin Hambly, and Charles Melville, 297–313. Cambridge: Cambridge University Press, 1991.

Shawn, Ted. *Gods Who Dance*. New York: Dutton, 1929.

al-Shaykh, Hanan. *One Thousand and One Nights (Modern Plays)*. London: Methuen Drama, 2011.

Shklovsky, Victor. "Art as Technique." In *Russian Formalist Criticism: Four Essays*, translated by Lee T. Lemon and Marion J. Reis, 3–24. Lincoln: University of Nebraska Press, 1965.

Sill, Geoffrey. *The Cure of Passions and the Origins of the English Novel*. Cambridge: Cambridge University Press, 2001.

Snicket, Lemony. *A Series of Unfortunate Events*. 13 vols. New York: HarperCollins, 2006.

Somadeva. *Kathasaritsagara (The Ocean of the Rivers of Story)*. Bombay: Nirnara Sagara Press, 1930. Translated by C. W. Tawney as *The Ocean of Story*, 10 vols., edited by N. M. Penzer. London: Chas. J. Sawyer, 1924.

Stark, Ulrike. *An Empire of Books: The Naval Kishore Press and the Diffusion of the Printed Word in Colonial India*. Ranikhet: Permanent Black, 2007.

Stewart, Devin. "Maqama." In *The Cambridge History of Arabic Literature: Arabic Literature in the Post-Classical Period*. Cambridge: Cambridge University Press, 2006.

Stone, George W., ed. *The London Stage, 1660–1800: A Calendar of Plays*, part 4, vol. 3, *1767–76*. Carbondale: Southern Illinois University Press, 1962.

Studlar, Gaylyn. "Douglas Fairbanks: Thief of the Ballets Russes." In *Bodies of the Text: Dance as Theory, Literature as Dance*, edited by Ellen W. Goellner and Jacqueline Shea Murphy. New Brunswick: Rutgers University Press, 1995.

Sugita, Hideaki. "*Arabian naito* hon'yaku kotohajime: Meiji zenki nihon e no inyū to sono eikyō" [An early Japanese translation of the *Arabian Nights*]. *Proceedings of the Foreign Language Sciences, Graduate School of Arts and Sciences, College of Arts and Sciences, University of Tokyo* 4 (1999): 1–57.

———. "The *Arabian Nights* in Modern Japan: A Brief Historical Sketch." In *The Arabian Nights and Orientalism: Perspectives from East and West*, edited by Yuriko Yamanaka and Tetsuo Nishio. London: I. B. Tauris, 2006.

Sugita, Hideaki. *Nihonjin no chūtou hakken* [The Japanese discovery of the Middle East]. Tokyo: University of Tokyo Press, 1995.

Sutcliffe, Barry. Introduction to *Plays by George Colman the Younger and Thomas Morton*. Cambridge: Cambridge University Press, 1983.

Tasch, Peter A. *The Dramatic Cobbler: The Life and Works of Isaac Bickerstaff*. Lewisburg, PA: Bucknell University Press, 1971.

———. "Garrick's Revisions of Bickerstaff's 'The Sultan.'" *Philological Quarterly* 50:1 (1971): 141–49.

Thomas, Rosie. "Not Quite (Pearl) White: Fearless Nadia Queen of the Stunts." In *Bollyworld*, edited by Raminder Kaur and Ajay Sinha, 35–69. New Delhi: Sage, 2005.

———. "Still Magic: An Aladdin's Cave of 1950s B Movie Fantasy." *Tasveer Ghar*, n.d. http://tasveerghar.net/cmsdesk/essay/103/ (accessed June 7, 2011).

Thompson, Jason. "Small Latin and Less Greek: Expurgated Passages from Edward William Lane's *An Account of the Manners and Customs of the Modern Egyptians*." *Quaderni di Studi Arabi* 1 (2006): 7–28.

Tomko, Linda. "Framing Turkish Dances." *Music in Art: International Journal for Music Iconography* 36:1–2 (2011): 131–60.

Troyanov, Iliya. *The Collector of Worlds: A Novel of Sir Richard Burton*. Translated by William Hobson. New York: Ecco, 2009.

Trumpener, Katie. "Rewriting Roxane: Orientalism and Intertextuality in Montesquieu's *Lettres Persanes* and Defoe's *The Fortunate Mistress*." *Stanford French Review* 11:3 (1987): 178.

Vail, Jeffery W. *Lord Byron and Thomas Moore*. Baltimore: Johns Hopkins University Press, 2001.

Vaillot, René. *Avec Mme du Châtelet*. In *Voltaire en son temps*, edited by René Pomeau, 2nd ed., vol. 1, 525–26. Oxford, UK: Fayard / Voltaire Foundation, 1995.

Van den Heuvel, Jacques. *Voltaire dans ses contes: De "Micromégas" à "L'Ingénu."* 3rd ed. Paris: Armand Colin, 1967.

Vernet, Juan. *Ce que la culture doit aux Arabes d'Espagne*. Paris: Sindbad, 1985.

Villeneuve, Madame Gabrielle-Susanne de. *La jeune Américaine et les contes marins* (*La belle e la bête*). 1740. Edited by Élisa Biancardi. Paris: Honoré Champion, 2008.

Villiers, Alan. "Sailing with Sindbad's Sons." *National Geographic* 94:5 (November 1948): 675–88.

Vittorini, Elio. *Conversation in Sicily*. Translated by Wilfred David. London: Quartet, 1988.

Voltaire. *Candide and Other Stories*. Translated and edited by Roger Pearson. 2nd ed. Oxford: Oxford University Press, 2006.

———. *Contes en vers et en prose*. Edited by Sylvain Menant. 2 vols. Paris: Bordas, 1992–93.

———. *Les œuvres complètes de Voltaire*. Edited by Theodore Besterman et al. Oxford, UK: Voltaire Foundation, 1968–.

———. *Œuvres historiques*. Edited by René Pomeau. Paris: Gallimard (Bibliothèque de la Pléiade), 1957.

———. *Romans et contes*. Edited by Frédéric Deloffre and Jacques Van den Heuvel. Paris: Gallimard (Bibliothèque de la Pléiade), 1979.

———. *Zadig*. Edited by Georges Ascoli. 2 vols. Paris: Hachette, 1929.

Wadia, J. B. H. "How *Bagh-e-Misr* Came to Be Produced." Unpublished memoirs. Wadia Movietone Archives, Bombay, 1980.

———. "Joseph David—Tribute to a Forgotten Pioneer." Unpublished memoirs. Wadia Movietone Archives, Bombay, 1980.

———. "The Story behind the Making of *Lal-e-Yaman*." Unpublished memoirs. Wadia Movietone Archives, Bombay, 1980.

Ward, Philip. *The Oxford Companion to Spanish Literature*. Oxford: Oxford University Press, 1978.

Warner, Marina. *Fantastic Metamorphoses, Other Worlds: Ways of Telling the Self*. Oxford: Oxford University Press, 2002.

———. *From the Beast to the Blonde: On Fairy-Tales and Their Tellers*. London: Chatto and Windus, 1994.

———. *Stranger Magic: Charmed States and the Arabian Nights*. London: Chatto and Windus, 2011; Cambridge: Belknap Press of Harvard University Press, 2012.

Watson, Stephen. *Crescent Moon over the Rational: Philosophical Interpretation of Paul Klee*. Stanford: Stanford University Press, 2009.

Watt, Ian. *The Rise of the Novel: Studies in Defoe, Richardson and Fielding*. London: Chatto and Windus, 1957.

Werckmeister, O. K. *The Making of Paul Klee's Career, 1914–1920*. Chicago: University of Chicago Press, 1989.

Wilde, Oscar. "The Happy Prince" (1988). In *The Happy Prince and Other Stories*, Project Gutenberg, http://www.gutenberg.org/dirs/etext97/hpao1oh.htm.

Williamson, Edwin. *Borges: A Life*. New York: Penguin, 2004.

Wollen, Peter. *Raiding the Icebox: Reflections on Twentieth-Century Culture*. London: Verso, 1993.

Yamanaka, Yuriko, and Tetsuo Nishio, eds. *The Arabian Nights and Orientalism: Perspectives from East and West*. London: I. B. Tauris, 2006.

Yang, Chi-ming. "Virtue's Vogues: Eastern Authenticity and the Commodification of Chinese-ness on the 18th-Century Stage." *Comparative Literature Studies* 39:4 (2002): 326–46.

Yared, Aida. "Joyce's Sources: Sir Richard Burton's *Terminal Essay* in *Finnegans Wake*." *Joyce Studies Annual* 11 (Summer 2000): 124.

Yeats, W. B. *The Collected Poems of W. B. Yeats*. New York: Macmillan, 1956.

———. *Interviews and Recollections*. New York: Barnes and Noble Books, 1977.

Yeazell, Ruth Bernard. *Harems of the Mind: Passages of Western Art and Literature*. New Haven: Yale University Press, 2000.

Yunis, Alia. *The Night Counter*. New York: Broadway, 2010.

El-Zein, Amira. *Islam, Arabs, and the Intelligent World of the Jinn*. Syracuse: Syracuse University Press, 2009.

———. *The Jinn and Other Poems*. Boston: Arrowsmith, 2006.

Zivley, Sherry Lutz. "Sylvia Plath's Transformation of Modernist Paintings." *College Literature* 29:3 (Summer 2002): 35–56.

Zotenberg, Henri. *Histoire d'Alâ Al-Dîn ou la Lampe Merveilleuse: Texte Arabe publié avec une notice sur quelques manuscrits des Mille et une Nuits*. 8 vols. Paris: Imprimerie Nationale, 1888.

Ros Ballaster is Professor of Eighteenth-Century Studies in the Faculty of English, Mansfield College, Oxford University. Her book *Fabulous Orients: Fictions of the East in England, 1662–1785* was published in 2005 with an accompanying edited anthology, *Fables of the East: Selected Tales, 1662–1785*. She has published widely on eighteenth-century literature, especially women's writing and the oriental tale.

Laurent Châtel is Senior Lecturer at Paris-Sorbonne University and a Research Fellow at the University of Oxford (CNRS, Maison Française, USR 3129). His main areas are eighteenth-century British visual culture (landscape gardening and painting) and the reception of the *Arabian Nights*. He is the author of numerous studies on Enlightenment gardens in Britain, considering them to be a field of study through which one might examine questions of national rhetoric, utopia, and cultural transfers between France and Britain. He has written many articles on the aesthetics of William Beckford (1760–1844) and recently contributed to the "Arabian Nights" exhibition catalogue of the Institut du Monde Arabe in Paris (2013).

Elliott Colla is Associate Professor of Arabic and Islamic Studies at Georgetown University. He is author of *Conflicted Antiquities: Egyptology, Egyptomania, Egyptian Modernity* (2007). He has translated many works of contemporary Arabic literature, including Ibrahim Aslan's novel *The Heron*, Idris Ali's *Poor*, Ibrahim al-Koni's *Gold Dust*, and Rabai al-Madhoun's *The Lady from Tel Aviv*, as well as works by Kamel Riahi, Yahya al-Tahir 'Abdallah, Ghada Abdel Meniem, and others.

Wendy Doniger is the Mircea Eliade Distinguished Service Professor of the History of Religions at the University Chicago Divinity School. Among her thirty published books are sixteen interpretative works, including *Śiva: The Erotic Ascetic, The Origins of Evil in Hindu Mythology, The Bedtrick: Tales of Sex and Masquerade, The Hindus: An Alternative History*, and a new translation of the *Kamasutra* (with Sudhir Kakar).

Ferial J. Ghazoul is Chair and Professor of English and Comparative Literature at the American University in Cairo. She is the editor of *Alif: Journal of Comparative Poetics* and is on the advisory board of several journals and foundations, including Thaqafat, Fusul, Kitab-fi-jarida, and the Arab Fund for Arts and Culture. Her research interests include medieval literature (European and Middle Eastern); gender studies; Arabic, African, and French literatures; and postcolonial theory. She holds a Ph.D. in comparative literature from Columbia University, 1978.

Paulo Lemos Horta is a scholar of world literature. He is currently interested in the cross-cultural collaborations that influenced *The Thousand and One Nights*, and the reception of the works of sixteenth-century Portuguese author Luís de Camões, who lived in the Middle East and South Asia. He is coediting a volume with Philip Kennedy, *Inventing World Literature*. Horta holds a Ph.D. in English from the University of Toronto, an M.A. in English from Queen's University, and a B.A. and an M.A. in political science from the University of British Columbia.

Robert Irwin is currently Research Associate at the School of Oriental and African Studies and the Middle East editor of the *Times Literary Supplement*. His study *The Arabian Nights: A Companion* (1994) helped to jump-start the recent upsurge in academic interest in the history and reception of the *Nights*. More recently, he is the author of *For Lust of Knowing: The Orientalists and Their Enemies* (2006) and *Visions of the Jinn: Illustrators of the Arabian Nights* (2010).

Berta Joncus is Head of Department and Senior Lecturer in Music at Goldsmiths (University of London) and Research Associate of the Faculty of Music, University of Oxford. At Oxford, she completed a British Academy Post-Doctoral Fellowship (2004–7) and her D.Phil. degree (1999–2004). Before studying at Oxford, she was an editor at the *New*

Grove Dictionary of Music. She took her M.A. at the University of Bonn, Germany, and worked earlier as professional singer after finishing a performance degree at the Franz Schubert Conservatory of Vienna.

Dominique Jullien is Professor of French and Comparative Literature at UC Santa Barbara. She holds a Doctorat de Lettres Modernes from the Université de Paris III–Sorbonne Nouvelle and is the author of several books, including *Proust et ses modèles: Les mille et une nuits et les "Mémoires" de Saint-Simon* (1989) and *Les amoureux de Schéhérazade: Variations modernes sur Les mille et une nuits* (Scheherazade's lovers: Modern variations on *The Thousand and One Nights*; 2009).

Philip F. Kennedy is Associate Professor of Middle Eastern and Islamic Studies and Comparative Literature at New York University, General Editor of *The Library of Arabic Literature*, and Vice Provost for Public Programming for the NYU Abu Dhabi Institute. As author or editor, Kennedy has published several writings on Arabic literature, including *The Wine Song in Classical Arabic Poetry: Abu Nuwas and the Literary Tradition* (1997); *Abu Nuwas: A Genius of Poetry* (2005; in the series Makers of the Muslim World); *On Fiction and Adab in Medieval Arabic Literature* (2004; in the series Studies in Arabic Language and Literature); *Recognition: The Poetics of Narrative* (2008); and *Islamic Reflections, Arabic Musings* (coeditor with Robert Hoyland; 2004). As a student, he studied in Oxford, Cairo, Madrid, Aix-en-Provence, and the UAE. He has just finished writing a monograph on the use of anagnorisis in the Arabic narrative tradition.

Elizabeth Kuti is a playwright and Senior Lecturer in Drama at the University of Essex. Her plays for theater include *Treehouses* (2000); *The Sugar Wife* (2005); *The Six-Days World* (2007); and, in collaboration with Frances Sheridan, *The Whisperers* (1999). Her plays for radio include *May Child* (BBC Radio 4, 2004); *Mr Fielding's Scandalshop* (BBC Radio 3, 2005); and *Dear Mr Spectator* (a radio adaptation of Addison and Steele's *Spectator* for BBC Radio 4, 2010–11). She is currently writing a new play commissioned by the National Theatre, London, and also a history of the strolling players of East Anglia.

Tetsuo Nishio (Ph.D., Kyoto University, Linguistics) is Professor at the National Museum of Ethnology and the Graduate University of Advanced Studies in Osaka. His major concern is the linguistic and cultural anthropological study of Arab Bedouin society. Recent publications include *The Arabian Nights: Stories Generated among Civilizations* (2007; in Japanese).

Roger Pearson is Professor of French at the University of Oxford and Fellow and Tutor in French at The Queen's College, Oxford. His publications on Voltaire include *The Fables of Reason: A Study of Voltaire's "Contes philosophiques"* (1993), a translation of selected prose and verse tales (2nd ed., 2006), and *Voltaire Almighty: A Life in Pursuit of Freedom* (2005), which was short-listed for the James Tait Black Memorial Prize for Biography (2006) and the Marsh Biography Award (2007). As well as translations of novels by Zola and Maupassant, he has also published books on Stendhal (1988) and Mallarmé (1996, 2004, 2010). His monograph *Mallarmé and Circumstance: The Translation of Silence* (2004) was awarded the 2005 R. H. Gapper Prize by the UK Society for French Studies. He is a Fellow of the British Academy and Officier dans l'Ordre des Palmes Académiques. He is currently completing the first volume of a three-volume study of the poet as lawgiver in nineteenth-century France, a project for which he was awarded a Leverhulme Major Research Fellowship (2009–11).

Karl Sabbagh is a writer and television producer with thirty-five years of experience describing complex events and subjects for a nonspecialist audience. His programs for the BBC and PBS have encompassed physics, medicine, psychology, philosophy, technology, and anthropology. Three of his television projects have been accompanied by best-selling books: *The Living Body, Skyscraper*, and *21st Century Jet*. Sabbagh has written numerous articles for newspapers and magazines, including the *Sunday Times, New Scientist*, the *Listener*, and *Punch*. His other books include *A Rum Affair: A True Story of Botanical Fraud, Palestine: A Personal History, The Riemann Hypothesis: The Greatest Unsolved Problem in Mathematics*, and *Remembering Our Childhood*.

Rosie Thomas is Professor of Film and Director for the Center for Research and Education in Arts and Media at the University of Westminster. She is a pioneer of the academic study of popular Indian cinema and has written widely on Indian cinema, contributing to numerous books and journals. She is cofounder and coeditor of the international Sage journal *BioScope: South Asian Screen Studies*, a forum for new research on the history and theory of South Asian film, screen-based arts, and new media screen cultures. Originally trained as a social anthropologist at the London School of Economics, she did her first fieldwork in the Bombay film industry in the early 1980s. She has also worked as an independent documentary television producer, running her own company, Hindi Picture, in the 1980s and 1990s.

Katie Trumpener is Professor of English and Comparative Literature at Yale University. She holds a Ph.D. in comparative literature from Stanford. Her work covers the modern period (late eighteenth century to the present), with particular interests in the history of the British and European novel; Anglophone fiction; European film history; literature's relationship to social and cultural history, visual culture, and music; the literature/culture of World War I, World War II, and the Cold War; and the history of children's literature from the eighteenth century onward. Her books include *Bardic Nationalism: The Romantic Novel and the British Empire* (1997) and *Cambridge Companion to Fiction of the Romantic Period* (coedited with Richard Maxwell; 2008).

Marina Warner is a writer of cultural history, criticism, and fiction. Her award-winning books include *Alone of All Her Sex: The Myth and the Cult of the Virgin Mary* (1976), *Joan of Arc: The Image of Female Heroism* (1982), *From the Beast to the Blonde* (1994), and *No Go the Bogeyman* (1998). In 1994 she gave the BBC Reith Lectures on the theme of *Six Myths of Our Time*. Recent works include *Phantasmagoria: Spirit Visions, Metaphors, and Media* (2006) and *Stranger Magic: Charmed States and the Arabian Nights*. She also writes fiction: *The Lost Father* (1998) was short-listed and *The Leto Bundle* (2000) long-listed for the Booker Prize. A collection of essays on art and artists, *The Symbol Gives Rise to Thought*, is coming out in 2014. She has curated exhibitions, including *The Inner Eye* (1996), *Metamorphing* (2002–3), and *Only*

Make-Believe: Ways of Playing (2005). She has been a Getty Scholar; a Fellow Commoner at Trinity College, London; and a Fellow of the Remarque Institute. She is Professor of Literature, Film, and Theatre Studies at the University of Essex, Visiting Professor at NYUAD, a Fellow of All Souls College, Oxford, and Fellow of the British Academy. She is now working on a memoir-cum-novel set in Cairo in the fifties.

Yuriko Yamanaka is Associate Professor at the National Museum of Ethnology, Osaka, and, with Tetsuo Nishio, is the editor of *Arabian Nights and Orientalism: Perspectives from East and West* (2006). Her book *Allegoresis of Alexander: From Antiquity to Mediaeval Islam* (2009 [in Japanese]) has been awarded the Japan Academy Medal, the Japan Society for the Promotion of Sciences Prize, the Japan Comparative Literature Association Award, and the Shimada Kinji Memorial Prize.

Alia Yunis is the author of the critically acclaimed novel *The Night Counter* (2009). She was born in Chicago and grew up in the United States, Greece, and the Middle East, particularly Beirut during its civil war. She has worked as a filmmaker and journalist in several cities, especially Los Angeles. Her fiction has appeared in several anthologies, including the Robert Olen Butler *Best Short Stories* collection, and her nonfiction work includes articles for the *Los Angeles Times*, *Saveur*, *Sports+Travel*, and *Aramco World*. She currently teaches film and television at Zayed University in Abu Dhabi.

Page numbers in italics refer to figures and tables.

ABOUT THE NYU ABU DHABI INSTITUTE

This publication is supported by a grant from the NYU Abu Dhabi Institute, a major hub of intellectual and creative activity, and advanced research. The Institute hosts academic conferences, workshops, lectures, film series, performances, and other public programs directed both to audiences within the UAE and to the worldwide academic and research community. It is a center of the scholarly community for Abu Dhabi, bringing together faculty and researchers from institutions of higher learning throughout the region.

NYU Abu Dhabi, through the NYU Abu Dhabi Institute, is a world-class center of cutting-edge research, scholarship, and cultural activity. The Institute creates singular opportunities for leading researchers from across the arts, humanities, social sciences, sciences, engineering, and the professions to carry out creative scholarship and conduct research on issues of major disciplinary, multidisciplinary, and global significance.